AMERICAN SAMPLERS

LOARA STANDISH'S SAMPLER. Plymouth, Mass. Cir. 1640
Pilgrim Hall, Plymouth
Plate presented by Mrs. William L. McKee

AMERICAN SAMPLERS

BY

ETHEL STANWOOD BOLTON
and EVA JOHNSTON COE

WEATHERVANE BOOKS · NEW YORK

Needlework picture on cover, 1836,
by Ann Elizabeth Brokaw, aged eight,
of Bound Brook, from the collection of
Mr. and Mrs. David McGrail.
Photo by Robert Froehlich,
courtesy the New Jersey State Museum.

PREFATORY NOTE

IN preserving the memory of our ancestors, their domestic virtues have been scantily recorded, a neglect which demands attention. Unable to answer many inquiries for publications on early American needlework, the Massachusetts Society of the Colonial Dames took upon itself the task of remedying in part this neglect. Considering samplers to be the primary basis and training school of American needlework in the early days of the Nation, our associates have collected materials and discussed needlework in this volume.

With the wish to make this work national and not local, an appeal for aid was made to our sister societies, which brought prompt and generous response. Through their coöperation, this volume contains contributions from many of the societies of the Colonial Dames in the United States and from many interested friends. The New Jersey Society, through its chairman, Mrs. Trueman Clayton, has furnished the largest number of descriptions outside of Massachusetts. Mrs. Clayton worked untiringly, and her descriptions were so clear, not only in matter but in chirography, that they were a delight to all who used them.

The late Mrs. T. Harrison Garrett, of Baltimore, had gathered for the Maryland Dames more than a hundred records of samplers from that state, which were most welcome, as our collection of Southern samplers was somewhat meager. The Connecticut and Kansas Societies, and many others, have responded to the best of their ability. Mrs. Cyrus Walker, of California, spent one of her summers in northern Maine, collecting and photographing the samplers she found there.

In March, 1920, the Rhode Island Historical Society arranged an exhibit of samplers, partly from a local interest in such things and partly to aid in the preparation of this book. It was under the direction of the librarian, Howard M. Chapin, Esq., of Providence, assisted by a committee of the Society. It was a most successful affair, and brought together nearly three hundred samplers which would not otherwise have come to our notice. Mrs. Powel, the acting president of the Colonial Dames of Rhode Island, contributed to the book descriptions of all the samplers in the exhibition.

In our own Society, Mrs. Edwin A. Daniels, of Boston, collected a very large number of descriptions.

Mrs. Henry E. Coe, of New York, who has a wonderful collection of her own, has added a very large number of descriptions, enhanced by pictures taken with her kodak. Many friends have contributed pictures, and to them our thanks are due. The Committee wishes that it could reproduce in the book many more pictures of very real interest which it has in its archives; but it has felt, in choosing the illustrations, that the pictures must be either typical or necessary to bring out some point under discussion. Therefore, those only have been chosen which exhibit American types or are interesting historically.

It is believed that there are here reproduced examples of most of the various stitches and model patterns used in such needlework. While many American samplers contain only the alphabet and numerals, with added moral mottoes, yet others display such sense of artistic feeling and tasteful ornamentation as merit attention.

The book is based upon some twenty-five hundred descriptions of samplers which have been collected by the Committee and its friends during the last five years. We have also got together nearly four hundred pictures of samplers that we felt might be especially interesting. In addition, many other samplers have been seen. The Committee believes that every book on needlework, ancient and modern, has been searched in the hope of finding material. Of course, there are many samplers that are not recorded here, for until one begins the search, it is impossible to realize how busy the fingers of our young ancestresses were. We do feel, however, that we have collected enough to have a good basis for our assertions.

In order to increase the value of this monograph, it seemed wise to focus attention on that period in which sampler work was at its best, and no samplers have been included of later date than 1830.

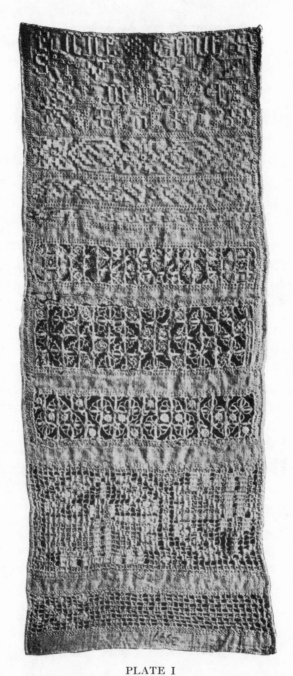

PLATE I

ANNE GOWER'S SAMPLER. Salem, Mass. About 1610
Owned by the Essex Institute

PLATE II

MARY HOLLINGSWORTH'S SAMPLER. Salem, Mass. Cir. 1665
Owned by the Essex Institute

Although this volume comprises the work of many, the successful consummation of the plan is due to the administrative ability, enthusiasm, and ready sympathy of Mrs. Barrett Wendell, President of the Massachusetts Society of Colonial Dames.

MARGARET WOODBRIDGE CUSHING,
For the Committee.

Newburyport, Massachusetts,
December, 1920.

MARGARET WOODBRIDGE CUSHING
ETHEL STANWOOD BOLTON
GEORGIANNA WEST PERRY

"He errs who thinks those hands were set
    All spinster-like and cold
Who spelt a scarlet alphabet,
    And birds of blue and gold,
And made immortal garden plots
Of daisies and forget-me-nots.

"The bodkins wove an even pace,
    Yet these are lyrics too,
Breathing of spectral lawn and lace,
    Old ardors to renew;
For in the corners love would keep
His fold among the little sheep."

John Drinkwater, "Samplers."

CONTENTS

PLATE III

SARAH LORD'S SAMPLER. 1668
Owned by Mrs. Thomas Sinnickson, Jr.

PLATE IV

ISABELLA ERCY'S SAMPLER. 1675
Owned by Daniel Penton Hitchner, Esq.

LIST OF ILLUSTRATIONS

AMERICAN SAMPLERS

SEVENTEENTH CENTURY SAMPLERS

THOSE who go fishing for whales in the ocean of the past, sometimes catch only sprats. Unfortunately, this is the result of fishing in the past for the origin of the sampler. Not only are sprats the only fish, but they are thin and very few. Just when samplers began to be worked no one now knows, for aside from a few rather casual remarks in literature, we have nothing to tell us.

The earliest mention of a sampler so far found is in 1502, when Elizabeth of York paid 8d. for an ell of linen cloth for one. Her account book shows the entry on July 10, 1502: "an for an elne of lynnyn cloth for a sampler for the Queen viii d. To Thomas Fische." John Skelton, the poet, at about this same time in Norfolk, wrote, "The Sampler to sowe on, the lacis to embroid."

In 1546, Margaret Thompson, of Freston-in-Holland, Lincolnshire, left a will, in which she says, "I gyve to Alys Pynchebeck my syster's doughter my sawmpler with semes." This last item would seem to indicate that probably the Tudor sampler, of which we have no survival, was the same long and very narrow affair that the seventeenth century shows. The loom of the day was quite narrow, and this accounts for the width of the sampler. Thus the "semes" may mean that several pieces were joined together, or perhaps, as one writer suggests, the word is used in an obsolete and transferred meaning, and shows that it was made in ordered rows, like the seventeenth century sampler. Much fine work was done to make beautiful the "open seam," which the narrow loom rendered necessary.

Certainly toward the middle of the sixteenth century the sampler was growing in popularity, for an inventory taken in the fourth year of Edward VI's reign shows:

"Item......xii samplers

"Item......one sampler of Normandie Canvas wrought with green and black silk."*

* Harleian Manuscript No. 1419.

1

The *raison d'être* of the sampler is most practical. Needlework and embroidery were practically the only relaxation of most women, and almost everything was embroidered. In the seventeenth century a book called "Needles Excellency"* gives a list of things for which a sampler was required. They include "handkerchiefs, table cloathes for parlours or for halls, sheets, towels, napkins, pillow-beares." A long period of peace had brought luxury to the household in the sixteenth century. Napery and drapery increased, and along with them the craze for embroidery. In fact, so great was the craze, that clothing, household linen, and everything of the sort fell a victim. France had the same tendency, and in 1586 Catherine de Medici was petitioned to put a stop to it, on the plea that "mills, pastures, woods and all the revenues are wasted on embroideries, insertions, trimmings, tassells, fringes, hangings, gimps, needleworks, small chain stitchings, quiltings, back stitchings, etc., new diversities of which are invented daily." The need for the sampler lay in the fact that there were few, if any, books of patterns. Thus the sampler was the pattern-book, and long or short, contained the designs which appealed to each girl's taste. So we can imagine that each girl, as she gathered together her linen for filling one of those lovely old oak dower-chests, added a sampler to take with her on her new adventure in life.

There have been many surmises as to just how these patterns grew up in England, and many experts favor the idea that most of them came from Italy and from other foreign sources. Certainly one did, for an Italian towel shows the same design as that on Mary Hudson's sampler. (See Plate ix.)

One book tells us of "a tradition that Catherine of Aragon taught the Bedfordshire women cut-work or reticella made of linen, an art which we know to have been practised in Italy and Spain at the time, and which the early evidences of old English samplers prove to have been made, though with less taste, in England."†

---

*"The Needles Excellency. A New Booke wherein are Divers admirable workes wrought with the needle, newly invented and cut in Copper for the pleasure and profit of the industrious. Printed for James Boler and are to be sold at the Syne of the Marigold in Paules Churchyard. 1632." There were twelve editions before 1640, but the book is extremely rare.

† "Buckinghamshire and Bedfordshire Lace in Point and Pillow Lace," by A. M. S. 1899.

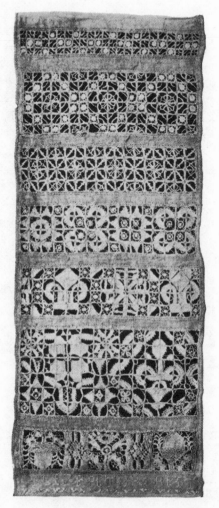

PLATE V

ELIZABETH ROBERT'S SAMPLER. Cir. 1665
Owned by Miss Georgianna Welles Sargent

PLATE VI

Elizabeth Robert's Sampler. Cir. 1665
Owned by Miss Georgianna Welles Sargent

Perhaps our ancestors did have "less taste," but I think there is no question that needlework on the older English samplers is most exquisite. The earliest samplers which we know were, as has been said, very long and narrow. The upper portion was nearly always given to elaborate running designs in color of conventionalized roses, tulips, strawberries, trefoil, "Indian pink," the "tree of life," and geometric designs, either alone or in combination. Sometimes human figures were inserted, but not often, the famous "boxers" being the most frequent. The lower half was often filled with lovely drawn- or cut-work designs in white. Occasionally an alphabet appeared, but in so subordinate a position that it is quite negligible, and was evidently included merely as a pattern for marking linen. So the sampler was really an "Examplar," as some of our modern American specimens still call it. Some early English references call them "samp-cloths" or "samplettes."

A great deal of stress has of late been laid upon the affiliation of the sampler and the horn-book, but it seems as if the horn-book, if it had any influence upon the sampler at all, was distinctly toward its degeneration. Certainly the seventeenth century sampler shows not the slightest influence of the horn-book, for it was not until the early eighteenth century that the dismal sampler, containing merely rows of alphabet, appeared at all.

But to return to the Tudor sampler, which lives only in our imagination, it is interesting to know that Sir Philip Sydney, in his "Arcadia," wrote:

"O love, why dost thou in thy beautiful sampler set such a work for my desire, to set out which is impossible?"

and that Shakespeare, in the "Midsummer Night's Dream," makes Helena exclaim:

"We, Hermia, like two artificial Gods,
Have with our needles created both one flower,
Both on one sampler, sitting on one cushion."

Shakespeare certainly reflected the state of mind of the children of a later date, who were doomed by stern schoolmistresses to sew on samplers, when he says:

"Fair Philomela, she but lost her tongue,
And in a tedious sampler sew'd her mind." *
(*Titus Andronicus*)

These first samplers had no names or dates upon them, for probably they were a continuous performance, and so could never be dated. The early ones were kept on a roll as a convenience, for one English sampler done in 1664, while but seven inches wide, was three feet long. The old samplers were always on linen, and were not done by children, but by girls and women, for very practical use. The earliest appear to be entirely of lace or drawn-work. Of seventeenth century samplers, it may also be said that the needlework in itself was more beautiful and the design more intricate and definite. One English writer goes so far as to say that the oldest were the best and the youngest the worst. That would not be entirely true of American samplers.

As the sampler grew out of the lack of books on embroidery, it is interesting to know that there was a progressive soul, one Peter Quentel, who printed a book of patterns as early as 1527. No copy exists, so far as is known; but in 1701 a similar book "gives borders and corner pieces, some few of which, at least, are derived from those included in the book of patterns for various kinds of needlework published by Peter Quentel." The ubiquitous Germans also printed a book in Nuremberg, in 1748.

There has been an amusing controversy between English and American collectors as to which nation owned the oldest dated sampler. These many years we have held the palm, for Anne Gower's sampler is in the Essex Institute in Salem, Massachusetts. Now Anne Gower became the wife of Governor Endecott before 1628; and while it was embroidered, of course, in England, the sampler itself was here, and we claimed it as American. The English connoisseurs date it at about 1610. There is one other American claimant earlier than the earliest English one of 1643; this is Loara Standish's, now in Pilgrim Hall at Plymouth. Loara Standish, the daughter of Captain Myles Standish, was born in 1623 and died before 1656. It is probable that the sampler was made before she was twenty, so that it was

* This verse is on the sampler of Anne Hathaway, 1797.

done before or at nearly the same time as the *punto in aria* sampler of Elizabeth Hinde, in 1643. This latter sampler would be more convincing if the name and date were not on finer linen sewed to the bottom.

Anne Gower's sampler was, of course, done in England, and is a good specimen of drawn-work, filet, and the flat white-stitch used on damask. So it is to Loara Standish's sampler that we must turn for our earliest American-made example. It is in the regular English style, done in blues and browns, soft now with time. The designs are intricate and beautifully done. Our Loara, besides making the first American sampler, worked upon it the first aphorism which appears upon any sampler. She began, poor Pilgrim maid, that long line of pious verse that decorates, even unto the end, both English and American samplers.

> "Lord Guide my Heart that I may do Thy Will
> And fill my heart with such convenient skill
> As will conduce to Virtue void of Shame
> And I will give the Glory to Thy Name."

She worked upon her sampler, also, "Loara Standish is my name," and so was the forerunner of that long series of girls who so indicated the work of their hands. Evidently she did not know the whole verse as it later came into use.

New England was the home of all but one of the seventeenth century samplers that have so far been reported. The next oldest after Loara Standish's was made by Mary Hollingsworth, of Salem. She was born in 1650 and married, in 1675, Phillip English, a Salem merchant. Her sampler, probably made about 1665, is typical of the time, but bears an alphabet and her name. Mary Hollingsworth English was accused of witchcraft in 1692, but escaped with her life to New York. She was so overcome by the shock of the accusation that she died soon after her escape.

At about the same time another New England maid, Sarah Lord, made a lovely sampler in 1668. It is of extremely fine needlework, and shows a tendency, which was apparently developing in America, toward shorter and broader samplers. The workmanship had not degenerated as yet, nor had the patterns, but there are fewer of them. Sarah Lord made one pattern upon her sampler in which the petals of the roses are raised and free from the groundwork, done in button-hole-stitch. Some English samplers of the same time show this form of work, in the raised draperies of ladies' dresses and men's coats.

Only two other American seventeenth century samplers have been reported, and both, perhaps, may be questioned. The first, done in 1675 by Isabella Ercy, is very attractive, though it shows the tendency toward less interesting and less elaborate design. It bears the inscription:

> "WORKE. ANd. LETTERd. 1675
> WOULD. HAVE. MENDED. BOTH.
> MY. SKILL. HAD. BEN. BETTER. I.
> ROUGHT. THE. SAME. BUT. IF.
> WITH. NEDEL. AND. SCILK. I. W.
> ISABELLA ERCY IS MY NAME."

The owner of this sampler frankly acknowledges that he does not know who Isabella Ercy was, and so we cannot be sure that it is really American after all.

The other sampler bears no name, but has the date 1698. It is long and narrow and is done in crewel in brilliant hues, which is not an especially common medium for either English or American samplers of the period.

It is impossible to call this chapter complete without mentioning three samplers which were, of course, made in England, but which have been in this country for over two hundred years. About 1650, Elizabeth, daughter of Nicholas Roberts, of London, was born in England. As a young girl, about to be married to a Mr. Breeden, she embroidered two samplers; one contains designs in color, and one is of *punto tagliato*. The lace one is signed "Elizabeth Robert," and the other has her initials "E R" many times repeated. She was a widow in 1672, when she married Colonel Samuel Shrimpton, a wealthy merchant, and owner of Noddle's Island in Boston Harbor. When she came to Boston she brought her samplers with her, as all thrifty housewives should. Later, a wealthy widow, she married Simeon Stoddard, another Boston merchant, and she lived in Boston until her death in 1713. The chief interest that these two samplers have is this: that they are the earliest samplers, either in England or America, which were worked by some one whose portrait we also have. The portrait hangs in the rooms of the Massachusetts Historical Society, and for the benefit of the curious we will say that the eyes and hair are light brown, and the dress black and white.

The third sampler, which was brought by the Quincys to New England before 1700, is signed:

"Miles Fletwood, Abigail Fletwood 1654.
In prosperity friends will be plenty, but
In adversity not one in twenty."

Mrs. Henry Quincy, who was Mary Salter and herself an expert needlewoman, gave this sampler to her daughter, with the remark that it was "an old family thing." Tradition says that a General Charles Fleetwood, of Cromwell's army, had a brother Miles who retained his allegiance to the King. His experience in those troublous times perhaps inspired the verse, if these two Miles's are the same man. The connection with the Quincys is not clear, but it is true that at this time the Quincys lived in Thorpe-Achurch and the Fleetwoods in Aldwinckle, in Northamptonshire, not thirteen miles apart. The sampler has the figures of three ladies in flowing skirts at the top. Over the central one are the initials "S. Q." The others are labeled, respectively, "A" and "E." The former owner thinks that these letters, added in steel beads, are a later addition when the sampler passed into the hands of the Quincys. The ladies themselves, as you see them depicted in the sampler, are Quincy ladies. The heads are stuffed and the dresses sewed on. Underneath the heads and the dresses are the heads of the Fleetwood ladies, and their much more archaic dresses. The back of the sampler discloses the substitution. Below the three ladies are a man and a woman on either side of an unrestful lion seated beneath a tree. The rest of the sampler is taken up with repeating designs of more or less elaborateness, and is unusual and lovely.

So the seventeenth century ended, showing several distinct tendencies in sampler art.

Samplers in America were broadening and shortening, they were becoming distinctly less interesting, and the elaborate embroidery of household linen had vanished from the land. Folk were too busy taming the wilderness to attach much importance to the frills and furbelows, and one can feel this distinctly as one realizes how very few samplers our American girls did in the seventeenth century. One may say that the sampler of that type became extinct, for while there were echoes of a design here and there in the next century, such as that of Grace Tay, it was a very feeble echo, and is more like the haunting of a ghost than anything else. The reason for the sampler had gone, and the revival was on different lines and for a different purpose. As one caustic writer says, "When meaning is gone, art and beauty vanish too." While they did vanish for a time, a purpose later crept in which gave our American samplers some art and much quaintness.

ETHEL STANWOOD BOLTON.

MARY LEAVITT. 1718
Owned by Miss A. B. Willson

SAMPLERS—1600–1700

ERCY, ISABELLA. 1675. 8″ x 16″. Line, satin, and cross-stitch. Cross-borders of conventional-ized roses, carnations, urns, birds, animals, etc. Verse 128 (var.). Illustrated.
Daniel Penton Hitchner, Esq.

GOWER, ANNE. [Cir. 1610.] 6″ x 16″. Alphabet. Eyelet, satin, and various kinds of lace stitches. Worked in bands across sampler. Illustrated. *Essex Institute, Salem*

HOLLINGSWORTH, MARY. [Cir. 1665.] 7″ x 25″. 1 alphabet. Cross-stitch. The patterns in the cross-borders are those used for shawl borders and the squares at the top those used for the corners. Illustrated. *Essex Institute*

HUDSON, MARY. 1700. 8 yrs. 7″ x 29″. Eyelet, outline, stem, satin, and cross-stitch. Cross-borders of conventional leaves and rosebuds, also Italian designs. Illustrated.
Miss Sarah Rebecca Nicholson

LORD, SARAH. 1668. 9¾″ x 17¾″. Eyelet, satin, buttonhole, chain, outline, and cross-stitch. Wide bands of elaborate needlework and embroidery, with geometrical and floral designs. In band across center the flowers and figures are raised from linen and attached only at center of figure. Illustrated. *Mrs. Thomas Sinnickson, Jr.*

STANDISH, LOARA. [Cir. 1636.] Cross-borders like the others of this period. Verses 128 (1st line), 338. Illustrated in color. *Pilgrim Hall, Plymouth*

UNKNOWN. 1698. 8¼″ x 33″. 1 alphabet. Buttonhole, eyelet, flat, and cross-stitch, also hem-stitching. Long series of conventional flowers in brilliant crewel. *Mrs. Thomas A. Lawton*

EIGHTEENTH CENTURY SAMPLERS

HISTORY would be so much more comfortable for those who indulge in writing it if its terminations were more abrupt, and if its characters had a less ghost-like manner of melting into space—and lo! the place that knew them knows them no more. So it would be much more comfortable, in considering samplers, to say that when we meet a new century we meet a new style of sampler; but the truth is that it took about twenty years after the new century came in before the English sampler types became sufficiently ghostly to ignore in favor of the new and truly American development.

The maiden to be married, on her outlying farm, in her frontier town, now happily freed from Indian terror, had no use for embroidery as an accessory for either her clothes or her linen; she was thankful for either unadorned. Life in the towns, too, was hard and poor after the Indian wars had taken their toll of the Colonies' wealth. Even so, we have one beautiful specimen of the old English style which was done by Grace Tay, or Toy as she calls herself. She was born in Woburn, Massachusetts, May 18, 1704; married, in 1724, Benjamin Walker, and went with him to Andover to live. It is a beautiful example of colored and white work, a yard long; the looms were capable of making quite wide linen before this sampler was made, for the selvage is at the top and bottom. (See Plate x.)

Having laid this last ghost, we can turn to other samplers made during the same years that Grace Toy wrought, and we see the beginnings of the essentially American sampler. Let us look first at the English sampler, which also changed at this same period, but in a different way. The English sampler clung much longer than did the American to the form of the seventeenth century. By the middle of the eighteenth century, by gradual stages, it had become square and had acquired a border. It soon had verses, alphabets, and numerals; and then, toward the end of the century, more and more tended toward

PLATE VII

ELIZABETH ROBERT
Owned by the Massachusetts Historical Society

PLATE VIII

MILES FLETWOD   ABIGAL FLETWOOD.   1654
Owned by Mrs. Michael Foster

a mass of unrelated designs; so that in the end it looked more like a sale-sheet of a modern vender of cross-stitch designs than anything else.

We may consider that we in America were more fortunate, for while many of the samplers contain little but alphabets, numbers, and verses, separated by rows of extremely debased patterns, yet as a rule they had form and coherence of design, which the English sampler lacks.

In the first half of the eighteenth century, as in the entire seventeenth, New England furnishes by far the largest number of samplers, followed by Long Island, New Jersey, and Pennsylvania. It is, perhaps, inevitable that, as the material has been collected from Boston as a center, New England should have been more easily reached and more prolifically represented than are other parts of the coast.

The girls of most of the great nations of Europe worked samplers, quite characteristic and differing in their basic essentials. The Spaniards brought the art to Mexico, but neither the early Dutch nor the early Germans seem to have brought their particular form to this country. In the late eighteenth and early nineteenth centuries in certain localities—such as parts of Pennsylvania—a certain Dutch or German influence can be seen, but it is quite rare; so we are really left with a very clear-cut result. We have first a century of imitation of the old English model, good but gradually degenerating, followed by a very distinct type of American sampler. It is the development of this second type with which we now have to do. It is inevitable, as one considers the schools of this century, to feel that the samplers, like the schools, fall into two classes. First came the Dame School, where the very young were taught, and where the samplers done by these small hands were very simple things indeed. And so we have the commonest form of sampler, that which contains merely alphabets and numbers. Not much from an artistic point of view, we shall all agree, but very much as an indication that our ancestresses got a little learning, meager though it was. This sampler must have been a wonderful assistance in driving home to the weary, childish brain the letter learned from her horn-book primer. And so we have poor little Mary Smith, in her sixth year, in 1714, working a simple form of the long sampler, with one large and one small alphabet. It was done on fine linen, and contained that most frequent of all verses, "Mary Smith is my name and with my nedel I wroght the same." She is not, by any manner of means, the only child of five who worked a sampler at this time.

The other form, done by the older girl at her finishing school, was, as a rule, a more elaborate object. Quite early in the century, originality began to be shown. Take, for instance, Mary Leavitt's sampler, done in 1718. Having accomplished the stupid task of embroidering four sets of alphabets separated by the simplest of cross-borders, she then, at the bottom, made a nice green hill, with one fair plant upon it, and "Ashur" and "Elisha" in long-tailed coats, white stockings, and black shoes, dancing and playing pipes thereon. (See tailpiece, page 8.) Mary Leavitt was a Salem, Massachusetts, girl; and that same year Eunice Bowditch, another Salem girl, embroidered a sampler, but she did not have Mary's originality.

By 1721 we may feel that the real American sampler is with us, for in that year Mary Daintery, aged eight, embroidered a sampler broader than it was long, and put a border all around it. This is the first example of a border as a frame which has come to our notice on an authentic American sampler, though of course there may be earlier cases. In the upper center stands the figure of Christ, and all around and beneath is "PUBLIUS LENTULUS his Letter to the Senate OF Rome Concerning JeSUS ChrIST (&c.)." (See Plate xi.) This fascinating sampler is owned on Long Island, but came from a farmhouse near New Haven, Connecticut. Until 1730, with this one exception, the samplers are, as a rule, alphabets separated by very simple cross-borders, with little or no design. A few had framing borders. The childish hands were not able to make the lovely, complicated "Indian pink," the rose, and "Tree of life" that the older girls of a previous century had done so beautifully. So we have simple strawberry, acorn, and Greek frets, varied occasionally with a vine made free-hand. One small girl, in 1724, Mary Frye, made a cross-border of hearts, and her biographer tells of her that "she was an orphan from infancy, but an heiress and a belle, if a devout Quaker maiden can be called a belle. When young Samuel Willis fell in love with her, he found he must win her from many competitors. But he had this in his favor, she was his father's ward and was dwelling under his father's roof."

In 1730, Pennsylvania contributes a wonderful sampler; it is only saved from ostracism as a needlework picture by the fact that Mary or Martha Bulyn signed and dated it. Thus early in the century does the decision as to what a sampler is and what is a needlework picture have to be made. The needlework picture of the period, like many that preceded it, was done all over the linen canvas in either petit-point, cross-stitch, or, occasionally, tent-stitch. This form of needlework had been done in England since the days of the Conqueror. Our ancestors, lacking pictures and feeling the need for some form of wall decoration, used the needlework pictures and samplers in that way. The story has come down to us of one little girl who left out her middle name when she worked her sampler. She put the initial in up above, but her parents were so annoyed at the omission that as a punishment they refused to frame her sampler. Poor mite! she may have hated that middle name as many of us hate ours to this day.

To return to our muttons, an arbitrary ruling was felt to be necessary to distinguish between these two forms, and so all needlework signed and dated by the maker has been accepted as a sampler. Thus we have had to eliminate much that was lovely and interesting. Mary Bulyn's sampler is of a shepherdess beneath a tree, surrounded by her flocks and dogs. The perspective is what one expects on a sampler of any age; the flowers are much bigger than the sheep, and the birds that roost upon the tree inevitably, in any other world, would tear it limb from limb, so large and fat are they. But it is most charming. (See Plate xii.) Just at this same time, Pennsylvania gave us another form of sampler. Two lines of verse and then a rather elaborate cross-border, in some cases returning to seventeenth century design; then two more lines and another border, and so on, the whole framed in a simple border or not, as the case might be.   (See Plate xiii, Sarah Howell, Plate cxi, and Abigail Pinniger, Plate cxii.)   This precise form appears but once after 1735, though the alternation of verse and cross-borders in other mixtures does appear spasmodically.   The exception is Ann Tatnal's sampler, done in Delaware in 1785; and it is so like the Pennsylvania ones, both in form and detail, as to make us suspect that she copied an early one.   Even from the beginning, when Loara Standish put her short verse upon her sampler, pious verse was always an adjunct.   Verse was not inevitable; sometimes there were prose quotations of a religious nature, often the Lord's Prayer, the Creed, or a metrical version of the Ten Commandments. The Lord's Prayer and the Creed were most frequently done in a form to reproduce the tablets to be seen, during the eighteenth century, in the east end of English and American Episcopal churches.   Hannah Trecothick, of Boston, did one such in 1738, and she had many followers.   (See Plate xiv.)

About this time some school, evidently near Boston, conceived the idea of using Adam and Eve and the apple as a subject for the religious enlightenment of its pupils.   Two samplers, done in 1741, and one in 1753, are practically identical, design for design.   The apple trees are laden with fruit of such a size as to make the modern farmer green with envy.   Adam is accompanied by a goose and Eve by a rabbit.   Let us hope that there was no irony in the tender minds of those whose fingers wrought so well.   And each of the six figures presses one hand upon man's dearest spot, as if already each felt the result of the coming indigestible meal.   The serpent—he looks much more like a fat angle worm—embraces the tree with one or more coils, tempting our universal mother.   The fig leaves are large and very modest.   In 1745, we find another version of the story, for Adam and Eve face us; and Adam has one of those lovely beards, now so little seen, running under the chin and up in front of the ears, which most Irish laborers of our early childhood fancied.   Eve has an enormous quantity of hair, and the serpent has his eye on all comers.   He is just as short and fat as his predecessors. Thereafter, Adam and Eve appear quite often, but later times were far more modest and less true to history than were our mid-eighteenth century grandmothers. (See Plates xv and xvi.)

One other sampler of the forties is unique. Mary Ellis, of Milton, Massachusetts, inside a border made a hundred diamonds, and on the diamonds embroidered the multiplication table. Only a few of the figures are still visible. Of course she made such a sampler at school, for no one but a schoolmarm would condemn any small girl to such a task as making a hundred diamonds all alike for such a prosaic result. Perhaps Mary wasn't good at arithmetic and needed severe discipline. (See Plate xvii.) At this time, too, we first find the two spies returning from Palestine, bearing between them the grapes of Eschol. Needless to say that none of our sampler artists in any way scamped the bunch, which was usually carried between the two staggering men upon a pole.

About 1750, the sampler becomes a much freer and more original piece of work than was true of the first half of the century. The "period of gloom," as so many writers designate the first fifty years, was over. The wilderness, so far as our original thirteen states were concerned, was pretty well conquered, and prosperous towns had taken the place of struggling and toiling settlements. Once again the amenities of life could be considered, and once again the children had some leisure to cultivate them. The result is an increasing variety of design. In fact, if we look at Elizabeth Pecker's sampler, made at the age of fifteen in 1750, we may realize that the sampler artist at this time went back to nature for her models—more or less. Two trees stand on hillocks on either side, with birds both roosting and flying. Between stands a mammoth basket of flowers. Deer, dogs, and enormous fowl disport themselves on the greensward for the edification of a damsel in the lower left-hand corner. She is dressed, not in embroidery, but in a lovely brocaded skirt, appliquéd upon the canvas, and she has a lock of real red-gray hair upon her head. (See Plate xviii.) The truth is that we had so few models that we were forced to try to depict the scenes around us. We began with animals and trees, and later progressed to more complicated scenes. Western Pennsylvania,* in 1755, contributes a sampler with verses and a tapestry design in diamond shapes; while the next year conservative Massachusetts, under cross-borders of the older style, gives us an orchard scene† with an apple tree, two deer, two rabbits, two bumblebees, and two eagles. "The animals walked in two by two" upon her sampler. The chief interest, however, lies in the fact that this is the first time that eagles, later symbolic of the country, appear. The same year Sarah Afflick, whom we suspect of Pennsylvania lineage, put three open baskets at the bottom of her sampler, and therein vines of an infinite variety of leaves upon the same parent stems; while tulips, pinks, roses, peonies, and flowers only conceived by the imaginative mind of seven adorn the vines also. And while we laugh, we know that it is very lovely as a piece of design, harmonious in color, and covering the space most interestingly. Really it is a sampler of Oriental design tinged with American feeling, and is unique in its appeal.

It would be unfair to leave this period without mentioning Dorothy Lynde's sampler, now forever on exhibition at the Old South Church on Washington Street, Boston. Most of it is beautifully worked petit-point, with just enough embroidery in other stitches to give it the needed variety. Overhead is a very startled-looking sun, flanked on either side by a cherub. Below, on either side of the square containing the lettering and verse, stand two figures upon pedestals. The left-hand one carries a book, and some one has carefully cut out the head. Below is a rural scene; a shepherdess and crook, a bounding, spotted black dog, and two meek sheep with huge black eyes. The coloring is lovely, and the illustration gives but a poor idea of its beauty. (See Plate xix.)

When once you have let originality run riot, you cease to have conventionality, and it becomes increasingly hard to say that any sampler belongs to any period, because it may be a survival of an older period, copied by a girl in an isolated town where new models were

* Margaret Simpson.
† Sarah Toppan.

hard to come at. Perhaps that is the secret of the charm of samplers, that they were distinctly the expression of the mind of the girl or of her mother or her teacher, and so they are pretty nearly as varied as the mind of man. Even among those which have alphabets alone, there are seldom two alike, because the form varies and so does the color. Probably it is lucky for us that many years separate us from the new and freshly done sampler. Home-dyed colors were, as a rule, quite soft and lovely, and the combinations were almost always felicitous and according to our taste—if it is still uncorrupted by futurist art. It is, perhaps, cruel to say it of the Shakers, but it seems as if they alone had held over from an earlier century their delight in crude and clashing colors, such as our ancestresses used in their youth and inexperience. These distressing mixtures time and the sun have softened and blended into an harmonious whole.

And so, having turned to nature as a model, these dear girls saw it through the distorted glasses of their imagination. And the result? A wonderful mixture of animals, birds, trees, houses, urns, baskets of flowers and fruit. Vines bearing six kinds of flowers are the ordinary sort on samplers. Perspective there was none, and comparative size matters not at all. Usually our beruffled shepherdess is at least three times the size of her house, and once in a while her sheep are so large that they might swallow her whole without inconvenience. But all this was a fairy story, taking form under the child's needle, and all such things happen naturally in fairy tales. Sometimes the children painted in the faces of their people; sometimes they gave them the real hair of the person whose portrait they were attempting.

About 1760 began the period when no sampler was quite complete without its pious verse, and it makes our untheological modern minds ache to think what these children must have been like, if their verses and sayings were anything more than conventional usage. Yet when one reads the records of almost any town, it is to have the realization thrust upon one that at that time theological discussion gave the most abounding joy to our forefathers. So why should not the children, too, have put forth their religious or pious convictions upon the sampler which was to hang upon the wall? They wished to show that they were not one whit behind their elders in taking up cudgels for their pet dogma, to show that death and the tomb had no terrors for their well-prepared souls.

Mary Webb, a nice little Pennsylvania girl, in 1760 made a clever sampler. She encircled it with a carnation border, and turned the corners with a tulip. Inside she divided the space into nine squares. The middle and the corners she decorated with delightful flowers, and in the four remaining squares embroidered her pious sentiments. She also gives a hint here of the genealogical sampler soon to come, for she put her parents' names upon it. This type, which is quite unusual in America, was more common in England. Perhaps she copied some English model brought overseas. (See Plate xx.)

The genealogical sampler, in all its glory, did not come into ripe fruition until late in the eighteenth century, but as early as 1730 Ann Robins put her father's, mother's, and grandparents' names upon her sampler. Sarah van Forhies, in 1742, embroidered the initials of her family, and the habit was quite common until the real genealogy came to displace them. Margaret Swain, in 1754, embroidered the initials, but she went a step farther and added the dates of births and deaths. Catherine Van Maater, in 1765, records that her "Father" was Daniel Van Maater, her mother, Mary Covenhaven, and that her brothers and sisters were Sarah, Gilbert, Micah, and Milly.

The first real genealogy seems to be of the Olmsteads, of Connecticut, made in 1774, but it has not half the charm of one done by an unknown girl, recording an unknown family, which probably resided in or near Springfield, Massachusetts:

"Phoebe   Born April 7, 1751
"Lew"   bor feb 23, 1753
"Zebbo"   Au 29, 1755
"Cal"   bor Jun 29, 1758

and then only initials up to the last child's birth in 1771.

From 1780, on to the end of the century, the real genealogy and the one containing initials only, flourished side by side, but were never

PLATE IX

MARY HUDSON'S SAMPLER. 1700
Owned by Miss Sarah Rebecca Robinson

PLATE X

GRACE TOY'S SAMPLER. Woburn, Mass. Cir. 1717
Owned by Mrs. N. A. Prentiss

nearly as common as they were after 1800. These samplers are just as useful to the student as the Family Bible, and should be cherished for their information with equal care.

It is just at this time that the little Dutch sampler of Catherine van Schaick was done in Albany. The border is difficult to place; two birds stand on two unnameable objects, one of which may be a house. She signed it "C V S–OUT 10–JAER 1763". (See Plate xxi.)

By 1766, the South had taken up Adam and Eve, and Sally Rea gives us a very interesting example. Adam and Eve, encircled in ballet skirts of fig leaves, stand in the attitude of the minuet, holding the apple together. The serpent coiled around the tree leans out and whispers in Eve's ear, while her accompanying rabbit stands in a scared attitude, ready to run at need. Adam, who looks a most courtly and smiling gentleman, is in this instance accompanied by two very interested dogs, one white with black decorations, the other "counterchanged." The whole thing is adorable, and envy surges in your breast. (See Plate xxii.)

The same year a child in Dighton, Massachusetts, Bath-sheba Searing her name, began that noble series of samplers which grew from picturing one's own house and yard to putting public buildings on the "carpet" of the sampler, and finally led to the delineation of whole towns. (See tailpiece, p. 254, the town of Crawford, New Hampshire.) Bath-sheba made a picture of her nice, hip-roofed brick house, and she pictured her mother in one window and her father in the other. Sarah van Forhies, of New Jersey, mentioned above, had made a house in 1742, but it seems to have been an isolated experiment and had no copiers until this later time.

About this time, too, the girls in the Southern states began to make samplers. South Carolina has one as early as 1752, and Georgia in 1763. Sarah Jones, of Savannah, did the Ten Commandments in verse, the Lord's Prayer, and the Creed, surrounded it with a flowered vine, and added a basket and flowers. It was not only Puritan New England, but the South also, which mixed religion and samplers inextricably. Philadelphia, in the person of Elizabeth Coleman, offers

Pope's "Universal Prayer"; and so it is with relief that we turn to Margaret Calef and her wonderful scene, undisturbed by pious sentiments. This Middletown, Connecticut, girl shows us the fruit of her imagination in most beautiful petit-point. There is a brick castle with high tower and many windows, with five straight poplar trees looking over the roof; on either side an apple tree, and on the lawn in front a lamb and a mottled dog. To the left, a wasp-waisted lady sits on a chair, with one dog behind and one with three white spots leaping up in front. She holds an enormous rose to her painted face. Before her stands her husband, long, buttoned coat, silk stockings, and shoes, all of the latest cut, his queue correctly tied, holding a parrot in his hand. And as a background, high hills, with poplar trees and deer, and a huge tulip plant, that dwarfs the trees. The sky is cloudy and contains one star. Each time you look you find some new delight. And if you love this sampler, doubly will you love Hannah Johnson's, made in 1768 in "Newbury Newton" (Newburyport). Never before and never again will the mind of child conceive such a flirtatious and lovely cow as Hannah Johnson did. The deer with which she's flirting is almost as charming. (Plates xxiii and xxiv.)

The next decade seems to have been given over to country scenes, to shepherds and shepherdesses, flocks and herds, houses and farm buildings. It also introduced a new stitch which was developed in two ways. At this period appears the crinkled silk, which looks as if it were unwound from larger and tight-twisted hanks. This silk is most commonly applied in long stitches as a background for vines or animals in a closer satin-stitch. Occasionally it is appliquéd, when the embroidery represents the bricks of a house or something else appropriate. At one school in Essex County, Massachusetts, taught by Sarah Stivour, the children used long stitches in this crinkly silk to represent the grass and sky. The particular use is limited to that school, and to the years between 1778 and 1786. Work from her school can be identified at a glance. (See Plates xc and xci.)

The scenes depicted become more elaborate during this ten years, and are saved from being classed as needlework pictures by a very narrow margin. This is true as far south as Georgia. But even in their elaboration, the feeling persists that if one could only really know their history, many samplers that are now far separated over the country were made under the same school-mistress's eye. These samplers are not always identical, but the whole action and design savor of the same controlling mind. Grace Welsh, Sukey Makepeace, Abigail Mears, and perhaps Elizabeth Pecker, who used a form of hunting scene, illustrate very well the probable common origin of a group. (See Plates xxv, cvi, xxvi, and xviii.)

Now the stiff cross-stitch trees of a former decade give place to those with gracefully bending trunks, and tops that look like dejected and lop-sided feather dusters. This is well exemplified on Betsey Adams's sampler. She lived in Quincy, Massachusetts, as all the great Adamses did, but I'm sure that she never saw the prototype of those trees in Quincy. (See Plate xxvii.)

The children of this decade abandoned cross-stitch and its kindred stitches more than their predecessors, and used satin-stitch increasingly. They also added queen-stitch, with very pleasing results, and often included punch-work fruit.

It would be unfair to leave the time of the Revolution without mentioning the unknown child who embroidered Christ at the foot of a huge tree, with arms outstretched. From the branches hang fruit labeled "Peace," "Sanctification," "Election," "Refuge," "Repent," "Buffeting," "Temptation," "Reproach," "Everlasting Love," "Death," and many more. This and Mary Daintery's, earlier in the century, are the only representations of Christ on samplers so far known. (See Plate xxviii.)

A form of sampler very common in England was little used in this country, though a few have been recorded—the map sampler. The earliest example which has come to light in the Colonies was a map of France done on an oval of satin by Frances Brenton, of Newport, Rhode Island, in 1775. Perhaps the education of the girls began at this period to include a knowledge of the world outside their own narrow horizon. Ann Smith made a map of Europe in 1787. Later, in 1793, Betty Scott, whose mother became John Hancock's second wife, made a beautiful map of England, very accurate, and beautifully worked. It was, perhaps, one of those stamped in England and brought to this country. At one time they were very popular with English damsels. Five years later, Leonora Louisa Spechet also made a map of England, and Frances Wade made a map of North and South America, which was of her own drawing, one might surmise. Her geography was almost as frenzied as that during the war, and even Mercator's projection looks far less queer. (See Plate xxix.)

During the last years of the Revolution, the sampler began to increase in the land. Originality ran riot, and everything that the children saw was pictured with more or less fidelity to nature. Perhaps the most interesting pair of samplers done in the 1780's are two which come from Tuckerton, New Jersey. They are painted samplers done by John Mason, in 1780, and by Sarah Platt, about 1784. (See Plate xxx.) Sarah painted a picture of herself in an oval at the bottom, and we should guess that John tried to portray his father and mother. The pair of samplers is most interesting, and calls to mind that later, by some fifty years, pen and ink samplers were accomplished by some pupils in the schools. They are quite rare now, as, of course, paper is much more perishable than linen.

There is a unique little sampler in Essex County, Massachusetts, which was cut in the form of a Liberty Bell, with a little ring at the top. It was done by "Rocksalana Willes," in 1783. What she put on the sampler was neither very artistic nor interesting, but it certainly was of the era. (See Plate xxxi.)

Two years later, Hannah Janney made a sampler, and worked upon it a verse "On Education." One might almost feel that this was truly prophetic on her part, for later she became the mother of Johns Hopkins, who founded the University which bears his name. Just at this time began that most interesting series of pictures of Brown University which is discussed in the chapter on Schools. They are so lovely that it is impossible to refrain from mentioning them again here. From the college on the hill at Providence to Pennsylvania is not so very far, so at the same time that our New England maidens were learning to embroider what they saw, little Ann Buller made her unique contribution in Philadelphia. She pictured scenes which never were on sea or land.   One can almost see the child sitting in wrapt silence, drinking in the strange tales of some sailor-man who had been overseas and in far Eastern lands.   He had told her of the Arab in his tent, of camels, and flocks, and herds.   Perhaps she remembered Abraham sitting in his tent door, with all his flocks around him.   And then she constructed her amazing country. In the middle, at the right, sits her hero in the door of a large, white tent, while before him graze six of the leanest sheep that sampler-land has ever produced. Next a lean cow stands, wondering, with mournful eyes; and then a woman and two men, in modern dress, one of whom holds a camel by its bridle. Below two camels, with protuberant necks, eat fruit from two trees, and a man and woman stand near a well-house.   Desert camels and a typical New World well!   (See Plates xxxii and xxxiii.)

Then we come to the very modest era when Adam and Eve went clothed to their doom, and fig leaves were insufficient. In Salem, Massachusetts, there was a Quaker maid who pictured Adam and Eve in plain Quaker dress, with Cain and Abel standing beside them in knee breeches. The "tree of knowledge" is there and many animals, but Rebekah Hacker's childish heart was too tender toward the sinful pair to put in the serpent as a reminder of their fall. Margaret Ramsay (see Plate xxxiv) helped out our first parents in a different way, for she planted her tree of knowledge just outside the garden fence, and back of its flower-borders she put a comfortable cottage, with nice lace windows. From this time on, Adam and Eve again become a favorite theme, clothed or unclothed, fat or lean. Meanwhile, all through the period, we have lovely pictures of workless shepherds courting with pipes the equally workless shepherdesses; beside them bloom flowers as large as cabbages. Their houses are flanked with trees, or, as Lucy Cushing embroidered her home, set between two enormous sunflowers reaching the second-story windows. Newport and Sally Munro give us a wonderful doctor's gig with a horribly knock-kneed horse. (See Plate xxxv.)

By 1790, the variety of sampler work was infinite. Two Philadelphians, Jane Humphreys and Elizabeth Lehman, and one Delaware girl, Mary Clark, each made on fine linen a basket filled with flowers in the finest "hollie-point." These three samplers are exquisite things, and most beautifully wrought. By this time, sampler making seems to have become an art and many new stitches came in fashion, so Zebiah Gore made her lambs in bullion-stitch. One often wonders just how the child carried out the design which she or her teacher had conceived. Sally Baldwin, of Providence, never finished her sampler, and so our question is answered. A house and a cow stand stark in their nakedness of pen and ink. In one case, the needle and thread are left to this day in a child's unfinished work. (See Plates xxxvi-xxxix.)

At the end of the century, we are on the verge of several new methods of work. Again, alas! the magic of a new century does not create the beginning of a new era sharply, though one may feel that the increasing prosperity of the country and the awakening interest in the education of girls elaborates and develops what has gone before. Pious verse is not always a *sine qua non,* and at times neither verse nor alphabet appear. The borders, done now as fancy wills, are not the old repeating designs which have held sway since first the sampler formed part of the maiden's outfit.

The genealogical sampler had had no great vogue, and the new century was to develop that form most interestingly. Houses at this period begin to sit on terraces, each step of which displays a tree, and on many samplers the house is broader than this pyramid of green lawns. True to this pastoral era, sheep and a shepherd invariably disport upon the lawns. Beulah Hollinshead was the first girl, apparently, who started this fashion, which the new century adopted most enthusiastically.

PLATE XI

Mary Daintery's Sampler.   New Haven, Conn.?   1721
Owned by Mrs. G. H. Buek

PLATE XII

MARY OR MARTHA BULYN. Kensington, Pa. 1730
Owned by Mrs. Frederick F. Thompson

Ann Macomber, in the last year of the century, revived a fashion originally set by Miss Polly Balch, of Providence, Rhode Island, at her school. No one, apparently, had followed her idea of depicting public buildings, until Ann Macomber put Liberty Hall, Philadelphia, upon her work. She set the building in more rural surroundings than we are used to associating with it, for a horse and two dogs run merrily about in the grass on either side. (See Plates xl and xli.)

During the study of the records and pictures which make up the material from which these facts are drawn, certain small things obtrude themselves and give a human interest to all this needlework. We are struck, at first, by the number of surnames which have died out in the course of years. Perhaps some of them have only gone West, leaving no one in the East to carry on the family. Certain it is that many names are strangers to their east-coast homes now. Again, the names left by the Roundheads impress us, and we meet Constant Brayton, Content Silsbee, Content Wing, Faithy Trumbull, Desire Williams, Temperance Matthews, and Charity Peters. Our forefathers were greatly daring in their choice of names, as witness: Rosefair Brooks, Welthe Barker, Lucretia Creaton, Sarah Doubt, Perese Hopton, Leafea Ide, Maieson Howard, Rocksalana Willes, Robe A. Ormsbee, Lendamine Draper, Increase Githernon, Sibilah Moore, and Petheny Geer. The most amazing family as to names, however, was the Jones family, duly recorded with births and deaths in 1797. Perhaps the name Jones seemed too feeble in its appeal, and so "Pappa" and "Mamma" Jones named their children Thetis, Thisbe, Sabra, Atlas, the twins Mithra and Luna, and Andes. No one could ever brand that Jones family as commonplace.

Another interest is in noticing just what each girl says about her work. They "wrought" it in many ways, according to their own testimony. One was "written by Tabitha Smith Feb 18th 1713 being then aged 9 years." Sometimes they tell when they began, as did Sarah Troup, in 1738; and some are cryptic, like the child who says, "I made it in the year of January 1st 1751." Most children tell you when they finished their work, and you can almost feel the pride with which they worked the date. There are, however, some rather odd ways of conveying their meaning:

"In the year of our Lord, 1793".
"Hannah Sanderson Her Exampler", 1789.
"Drusilla Tomlin Her Sampler and Work", 1793.

But of them all, none gives the hustling American view of life so succinctly as did one child in the strained year of the outbreak of the Revolution:

"Sarah Ann Souder worked this in great speed
And left it here for you to read."

Of the children who embroidered samplers, there were some who deserve mention because they themselves or their near relatives became well-known. We have recorded the sampler of Abigail Williams, granddaughter of the "Redeemed Captive" of Deerfield, Massachusetts, the Rev. John Williams. Abigail Wadsworth, of Hartford, whose sampler is dated 1730, was the daughter of Jonathan Wadsworth, the great Indian fighter, and granddaughter of Joseph, who hid the Charter in the "Charter Oak." Dorcas Gatcomb, who made a sampler two years later, became the wife of John Welch, who carved the original "Codfish" weathervane, now in the Old State House; and a sampler having a date somewhat later, 1751, bears the name of Dorcas Welch, daughter of the carver. Abigail Janney, as we have mentioned before, was the mother of Johns Hopkins. Mary Sterrett, of Baltimore, made a sampler when she was eleven; at sixteen, a famous beauty and belle, she had married Richard Gittings, of Long Green, Maryland. The Massachusetts Historical Society owns a pair, one done by the sister and one by the niece of Governor Thomas Hutchinson, of Massachusetts. Doubtless there were other famous people in this long list of girls, but their fame has not come down to us.

Various other strange things may be noted in passing. Mary Studley, of Portsmouth, made two samplers in 1753, and so far as we know broke all known records by each one. The habit of sampler makers, as a rule, was to make the numerals from 1 to 9 and then to add a 0. Sometimes they go to 12, and once in a while to 20; but

Mary Studley made one sampler with the numerals from 1 to 49, and another one marked from 1 to 50. One sampler bears two dates and two names, that of "Mary Wheatley, 1760," and "Isabella Thompson, 1797." Apparently, Mary Wheatley never finished her work, and Isabella Thompson used the unfinished linen to try her skill. Margaret Starr, in 1795, worked the name of William Cox with her design, and so helps us all to suspect a romance.

Roman numerals were only occasionally used on samplers. Elizabeth Holyoke said that her age was xiii in 1784, and Susanna Holyoke confessed to x in 1790.

The average age of the sampler makers after the seventeenth century was about thirteen, but we have a record of one made by a woman of sixty. At the other end of the scale we find Mary Smith, who was six years old in the year "17014." In her fifth year, Agnes Rust made one which was only three and a half inches wide, but sixteen inches long. Polly Fuller, in 1790, was only four years old; and Catherine Bispham, in 1755, was five. Phebe Cash, a Negro child belonging to the widow of Dudley Atkins, Esq., of Newbury, Massachusetts, worked her sampler in 1789. We might add that there are at least three in the collection done by boys. Lemuel Vose, of Milton, Massachusetts, worked one in 1773; and two years earlier, Gideon Freeborn, of Rhode Island, embroidered one. He covered the canvas with diagonal lines in black, with diamonds of yellow, purple, pink, green, blue, and red between. It would seem to be a rather garish sampler. Nicholas Bleecker, of Albany, worked one in 1790.

And so the century ended which had seen the growth of a truly American handicraft, crude in many cases, but a real and sincere effort to develop artistically. Best of all, it was a growth along original lines, and no slavish copying of English models; for the American sampler, bound by no conventional type, is more varied and more interesting from 1740 on than its English cousin. Being a freer art, the result is generally pleasing and often quite beautiful.

ETHEL STANWOOD BOLTON.

THE EARLIEST SAMPLER KNOWN IN THE VARIOUS STATES

Massachusetts	1630	New Jersey (1675?)	1740
New York	1720	Delaware	1747
Long Island	1713	Maine	1750
New Hampshire	1719	Georgia	1763
Connecticut	1721	Virginia	1765
Pennsylvania	1724	Maryland	1766
Rhode Island	1725	North Carolina	1786
Vermont	1728	Kentucky	1800
South Carolina	1734	Ohio	1807

EARLIEST APPEARANCE OF VARIOUS DESIGNS

Cir. 1610	Alphabet (part). *Anne Gower.*
Cir. 1610	Name of maker. *Anne Gower.*
Cir. 1610	Alphabet in eyelet-stitch. *Anne Gower.*
1630–40	Verse. *Loara Standish.*
1708	House and tree (doubtful).
1714	Church (doubtful).
1718	Pot of flowers.
1718	Use of "carpet." "Ashur" and "Elisha." *Mary Leavitt.*
1720	Numerals.
1721	First border used as a frame. *Mary Daintery.*
1730	Shepherdess. *Mary or Martha Bulyn.*
1738	Lord's Prayer and Creed in Tablets. *Hannah Trecothick.*
1738	Queen-stitch.
1741	Adam and Eve.
1742	House. Does not appear often until 1766.
1743	Multiplication Table. *Mary Ellis.*
1747	Grapes of Eschol.
1750	Appliqué dress and real hair.
1752	Abraham and Isaac. South Carolina.
1754	Heart.
1756	Eagle.
1763	Revival of lace-work, "hollie-point," "darned lace," and drawn-work.
1766	House.
1774	Genealogical sampler.
1775	Map. France. *Frances Brenton.*
1778	First Public Building. Brown University and the Old State House, Providence, Rhode Island.
1780	Painted Sampler. *John Mason.*
1791	Anchor.
1799	Public Buildings. Liberty Hall. *Ann Macomber.*

REGISTER OF SAMPLERS, 1700-1799

ADAMS, BETSEY. [1773.] Quincy [Mass.]. 8 yrs. Born in 1764. 17″ x 22″. 1 alphabet. Cross, satin, French knot, and stem-stitch. Borders of carnation, strawberry, Greek fret, vine, tree of life. House and trees. Verse 603. Illustrated. *Mrs. Henry Eugene Coe*

ADAMS, ELIZABETH. 1776. 3 alphabets. Cross and eyelet-stitch. Strawberry cross-border. *Mrs. Emma B. Hodge*

ADAMS, ELIZABETH. [1791.] Red Hook [N. Y.]. 12 yrs. Born March 20, 1779. 8″ x 10½″. 2 alphabets. Cross-stitch. Border of cross-stitch blocks. *Mrs. Hubert G. Rose*

ADAMS, POLLY. 1779. 7½″ x 8¼″. 2 alphabets. Cross-stitch. Cross-stitch border. Conventional design, punch-work corners. *Herbert N. Hixon, Esq.*

ADAMS, SARAH. 1786. Medway [Mass.]. 13 yrs. Born September 26, 1773. 6½″ x 8″. 1 alphabet. Cross-stitch. Plain border. *Herbert N. Hixon, Esq.*

AFFLICK, SARAH. 1756. 6 yrs. Three vases containing vines which cover the whole sampler. Illustrated. *Mrs. Henry E. Coe*

AKERLY, SUSAN. 1797. 8″ x 22″. 3 alphabets. Cross-stitch. 2 small dogs, 2 small trees, large basket of flowers. *Mrs. Henry E. Coe*

AKIN, MARY. 1715. Born near Providence [R. I.]. 8¼″ x 18½″. 1 alphabet. Cross, satin, and eyelet-stitch. Strawberry border. Flower and conventional cross-borders. Verse 491. *Miss Alice Henderson*

ALGER, SALLY. 1782. [Providence, R. I.] 14½″ x 12″. Stem, satin, cross-stitch, and chain. House with figures above it. [Miss Polly Balch's School.] Verse 611. *Mrs. Alfred H. Wilkinson*

ALLEN, ABBY. [Cir. 1793.] Born September 6, 1782. 9″ x 5½″. 1 alphabet. Cross and chain-stitch. Unfinished. *Miss Marie L. Hawkins*

ALLEN, AME. 1791. Medfield [Mass.]. 12 yrs. 8″ x 9″. 2 alphabets. Cross-stitch. *Mrs. Myra B. Whittemore*

ALLEN, ELIZABETH. 1774. 19 yrs. 6″ x 5″. Cross-stitch. *Mrs. William H. Gilbane*

ALLEN, ELIZABETH. 1793. Smithfield. 7 yrs. 12″ x 5″. 1 alphabet. Cross-stitch. Verse 377. *The Misses Austin*

ALLEN, LYDIA. 1796. 11½″ x 16½″. 1 alphabet. Carnation border. Hill surmounted with vase of flowers, also 2 trees with a bird on the top of each. Verse 343 (1, 7). *Memorial Hall, Fairmount Park, Philadelphia*

ALLEN, MARGARET. [1728. Vermont.] 7 yrs. Born January 20, 1721. 9″ x 12″. 3 alphabets. Cross, satin, stem, chain, and eyelet-stitch. Plain hemstitched border. Conventional vine, leaves, and blossoms. *Mrs. James H. Bailey*

ALMY, ANN. 1783. 11 yrs. 8″ x 19″. 3 alphabets. Eyelet and cross-stitch. Various cross-borders in rose, carnation, and strawberry designs. Verses 488, 489 (2, 3). Illustrated. *Mrs. John H. Morison*

ALMY, KATHARINE. [Cir. 1728.] 6″ x 9½″. 1 alphabet. French knot, chain, and cross-stitch. Cross-borders in various designs. Initials "H T" [Hannah Townsend] in lower corner. Verse 128.
The Misses Kenyon

ALSOP, MARY. 1772. 9 yrs. 2 alphabets. Cross-stitch and eyelet-stitch. Greek fret. Butterflies, birds, flowers, animals. Verse 602.
Mrs. A. E. Alsop

ANDREW, ELIZABETH ANN HERETH. 1755. [Woodbury, Conn.?] 6 yrs. and 10 dys. 8½″ x 13½″. 3 alphabets; 1 alone, 3 grouped. Cross-stitch. Trefoil border. Conventional flowers and cross-borders.
Mrs. Henry Eugene Coe

ANTHONY, RUTH. 1797. 12 yrs. 6″ x 5″. 2 alphabets. Cross-stitch.
Mrs. Walter Slade Gardner

ANTHONY, SARAH. Verses 129 (var.), 182 (1, 2), 488, 490.

ARNOLD, ELIZABETH. 1737. 12 yrs. 9″ x 9″. 2 alphabets. Chain and cross-stitch. Verse 184.
Arthur H. Smith, Esq.

ATKINS, HANNAH. 1758. Boston [Mass.]. 20 yrs. 7½″ x 14¾″. 3 alphabets. Cross, satin, and eyelet-stitch. Cross-borders.
Miss Helen L. Wells

ATKINS, MARY RUSSELL. 1762. Newbury [Mass.]. 9 yrs. Born August 30, 1753. 7″ x 11″. 2 alphabets. Cross, satin, and eyelet-stitch. Greek fret. *The Misses Marquand*

ATKINSON, ABIGAIL. 12 yrs. 8″ x 12″. Cross-stitch. Carnation border. *Miss Sarah C. Currier*

ATKINSON, JUDITH. [Cir. 1735.] Newbury [Mass.]. 6½″ x 11″. 1 alphabet. Cross-stitch. Cross-border.
Miss Sarah Jackson Leigh

AYER, PATTY. 1792. Haverhill [Mass.]. 10 yrs. 13″ x 7″. 2 alphabets and parts of 3 others. Cross, satin, stem, and eyelet-stitch. Strawberry and conventional border. Baskets of flowers. Verse 223.
Mrs. Thomas A. Lawton

BACKLER, SARAH. 1788. 17½″ x 14″. Cross and satin-stitch. Border of strawberry, rose, carnation, and other flowers. Trees, birds, butterfly, and rabbit. Verse 210.
Mrs. Thomas A. Lawton

BAIN, ELIZA M. 1795. East Nottingham [Md.]. 8 yrs. 15″ x 17″. 3 alphabets. Cross and flat-stitch. Greek fret border. Verse 648.
Mrs. A. G. Brandace

BAKER, BETSY. [Cir. 1789.] Ipswich [Mass.]. 12″ x 13″. Verses 371, 490. *Mrs. H. C. Bunner*

BAKER, ELIZABETH. 1786. [Milton or Dorchester?] 11 yrs. 8½″ x 18½″. 2 alphabets. Cross-stitch. Verse 40 (var.).
Mrs. Lydia Bowman Taft

BAKER, LYDIA. [Cir. 1790.] Born January 1, 1777. 8″ x 11″. 2 alphabets. Cross, stem, chain, French knot, cat, hem, queen, buttonhole, and satin-stitch. Vine border and queen-stitch border.
Mrs. Lydia Bowman Taft

BALCH, BETTY. 1786. Bradford [Mass.]. 12 yrs. 8½″ x 10¾″. 1 alphabet. Satin-stitch. Verse 364. [Grandmother of General Greeley.] *Mrs. Adolphus W. Greeley*

BALCH, POLLY. [Cir. 1788.] Born December 3, 1776. 8½″ x 11¾″. 3 alphabets. Cross-stitch. Border of wild roses, thistles, clover. Name of Clarissa Wallingsford at bottom.
Miss Lucasta J. Boynton

BALDWIN, ELIZA. 1780. 10½″ x 12″. 2½ alphabets. Cross-stitch. Vine border. Baskets of fruit and conventional clover.
Mrs. Frederick F. Thompson

PLATE XIII

KATHERINE HOLDEN'S SAMPLER.   Providence, R. I.?   **1733**
Owned by Miss M. Frances Babcock and Mrs. Winslow Upton

PLATE XIV

HANNAH TRECOTHICK'S SAMPLER. Boston, Mass. 1738
Owned by Miss Jane E. C. Chapman

BALDWIN, RUTHE. 1794. 11 yrs. Satin, stem, cat, chain, and cross-stitch. Elaborate floral border. In upper section large bush with two birds and lamb on mound. In lower section two large birds on tree stumps and sheep on mound in center. Verse 92 (2).

Edward R. Trowbridge, Esq.

BALDWIN, SALLY. [Cir. 1794.] Satin, stem, cat, chain, and cross-stitch. Floral border. House sketched in at bottom and unfinished. Two birds on branch growing from tree stump at right and bird on stump at left. Sheep at either side of house climbing up steep bank, house and one sheep sketched in but unfinished. Verse 72. Illustrated.

Edward R. Trowbridge, Esq.

BALEY, SARAH. 1738. 10 yrs. 8" x 16". 3 alphabets. Cross and queen-stitch. Conventional border. Rose and carnation, queen-stitch strawberries. Verse 184.

Newport Historical Society

BALL, JANE. 1762. Charleston [S. C.]. 8¼" x 8½". Cross-stitch. Hemstitched edge with Greek key design on sides. 4 hearts forming an oval at top and bottom. Verses 92 (2, var.), 185 (var.), 345.

Mrs. William Ball

BANCROFT, MARY STANCLIFFE. 1792. 7 yrs. 16" x 16". Cross and satin-stitch. Carnation border. Cross-borders of animals, trees, dishes, carnations, and acorns. Verse 636.

Robert P. Jordan, Esq.

BANCROFT, RACHEL. 1793. Barnard [Vt.]. 11 yrs. 17½" x 17½". 3 alphabets. Cross, chain, eyelet, and loop-stitch. Outside border, openwork; inside border, vine and flowers. Greek fret cross-borders. Verse 617.

Mrs. W. P. Brooks

BANCROFT, SARAH. 1795. [12 yrs.] 8½" x 8½". Cross, stem, and tent-stitch. Vine border with roses. Scene with church, house, and man fishing. "Do justly, love mercy, walk humbly with thy God." See Cover.

Estate of Samuel Bancroft, Jr.

BARCLAY, ANNE. 1797. 8 yrs. 12" x 15". 2 alphabets. Cross and eyelet-stitch. 2 large vases containing carnations, 1 small vase. Verse 655.

Barclay Ward, Esq.

BARKER, WELTHE. 1781. 9 yrs. 7¾" x 9¾". 2 alphabets. Cross and satin-stitch. Strawberry border. Verse 506.

Miss Ruth B. Franklin

BARNEY, SARAH. 1741. 11 yrs. 8" x 15". 3 alphabets. Petit-point and very fine cross-stitch. Tulip border with cross-borders of rose, Greek fret, wide conventionalized tulip, rose, and fuchsia, and wide conventionalized passion flower and bird, and trefoil designs. Verse 489.

Brooks-Reed Gallery

BARTLETT, ELIZABETH. 1762. Plymouth [Mass.]. 7 yrs. 12¼" x 15". 1 alphabet. Cross and satin-stitch. Strawberry border. Cross-borders of flowers and scrolls. "Remember your Creator," etc. Verse 595.

Mrs. Cora L. Pike

BATCHELDER, MARY. [1773.] Born June 13, 1757. 10½" x 16". 3 alphabets. Eyelet, stem, satin, and cross-stitch. Trefoil border on three sides. Cross-borders of conventionalized carnations. Large vase filled with carnations, two birds, two butterflies, and flowers growing in the grass. Verse 211.

Mrs. Henry E. Coe

BEAL, SUSANNA. 1784. 10 yrs. 8½" x 9¼". 1 alphabet. Cross-stitch. Hemstitched with Greek border at top. Sheep, lambs, and trees.

Mrs. Lillian M. Highley

BECK, ELIZABETH. 1791. Philadelphia [Pa.]. 21 yrs. 4½" x 7¾". 1 alphabet. Cross, cat, and eyelet-stitch. Conventional cross-border, pine trees.

Mrs. Henry I. Budd

BECKET, SALLY. 1782. Salem [Mass.]. 14 yrs. 15" x 18½". 1 alphabet. Stem, eyelet, satin, and tent-stitch. Solid stem-stitch border. Flowers, trees, house, building at bottom; flowers, birds, vines, plant in tub at top. Verse 490 (var.).

Louis D. Millett, Esq.

BERRY, MARY. 1799. 11 yrs. 11" x 18". 2 alphabets. Cross, satin, and eyelet-stitch. Border, baskets of flowers, strawberries, etc. House, 2 women, bird, conventional tree.

Mrs. Richard H. Hunt

BEVIS, HANNAH. 1769. 11 yrs. 7½" x 9½". 1 alphabet. Cross-stitch. Conventional cross-borders. Verse 9. *Miss Susan W. Osgood*

BICKNALL, MARY. [1798. Barrington, R. I. Born in 1783.] 8" x 7". 1 alphabet. Cross-stitch.

Howard M. Chapin, Esq.

BICKNELL, ELIZA [or Elizabeth]. 1793. Abington [Mass.]. 17 yrs. 9" x 8". Alphabet. Cross-stitch. Verse 490 (var.). *Mrs. James M. Hunnewell*

BIGBI, ELIZABETH. 1796. 8 yrs. and 8 mos. 12" x 15". 1 alphabet. Cross-stitch. Carnation and vine cross-borders. Animals and plants. Verses 230, 522. *Robert P. Jordan, Esq.*

BILLINGS, HANNAH R. 1784. 15 yrs. 16½" x 16½". 3 alphabets. Border of flowers and vines. Verse 136. *Estate of James L. Little, Esq.*

BISPHAM, CATHERINE. 1755. 5 yrs. 7½" x 10". Parts of 3 alphabets. Plain, broad border.

Mrs. R. S. Southard

BLÜCKER, NICHOLAS. 1790. Albany [N. Y.]. 9 yrs., 7 mos., 11 dys. 20½" x 24". 2 alphabets. Cross-stitch. Rose border. Conventional cross-border. Verse 215.
Sons and daughters of John N. and Margaret Blücker
Perry Blücker, Mary Blücker, Anatla Blücker, Letty
Blücker, Elizabeth Blücker, Hannah Blücker, Nicholas Blücker

Mrs. George Walton Green

BLUNT, MARY ANN. 1799. 10 yrs. Alphabet. Verse 601 (1, 2). *Miss Frances Goodwin*

BOARDMAN, SARAH. 1799. Newburyport [Mass. 12 yrs.]. Born April 2, 1787. 8½" x 11". 3 alphabets. Cross, satin, and eyelet-stitch. Hemstitched at sides. Greek fret cross-border at bottom, also birds, tree, and strawberries. *Offin Boardman Marshall, Esq.*

BOLLARD, SUSANNAH. 1787. 11½" x 19¼". Cross and satin-stitch. Strawberry border. Trees, antelope, birds, and basket of flowers. "If thou scorn the Rod, Believe and tremble, thou art judged of God." Verse 208. *Miss Isabella Hagner*

BOND, CATHERINE. 1797. 12 yrs. 13" x 14½". Alphabet. Cross and eyelet-stitch. Conventional border. Hearts, pedestals, baskets, animals, etc. Verses 99, 232, 345.

Mrs. Bradbury Bedell

BOND, LYDIA. 1794. Leicester [Mass.]. 12" x 7". 2 alphabets. Cross-stitch. *Mrs. Brouwer*

BOSWORTH, OLIVE. 1795. 10 yrs. 9½" x 14". 2 alphabets. Cross and satin-stitch. Border of flowers. Panel with verse and flowers. Verse 140. *Mrs. Robert Mercur*

BOUTIN, ANNE. 1769. 11 yrs. 9" x 11". 1 alphabet. Very fine cross and satin-stitch. Border of upright trees. House and tree, etc. Verses 129, 358. *Estate of James L. Little, Esq.*

BOWDITCH, EUNICE. 1718. Salem [Mass.]. 11 yrs. Born March 22, 1707. 4 alphabets. Cross-stitch. Narrow conventional cross-borders. *Essex Institute*

BOWERS, MARTHA. [1790.] 11 yrs. Born May 21, 1779. 8" x 11". 1 alphabet. Cross-stitch. Cross-border of irregular figures at top. *Horace Cecil Fisher, Esq.*

BOWMAN, ANNE. 1779. Brownsville [Pa.]. 8 yrs. 18" x 21". Cross and stem-stitch. Rose border. Trees, flower-pots, and bees. Verse 504. *Mrs. William G. Park*

BOWMAN, LYDIA. 1757. 15 yrs. 6¼" x 7½". 2 alphabets. Cross-stitch. Greek fret border.

Mrs. Lydia Bowman Taft

BOYLSTON, MARY. 1763. [Boston?]. 11 yrs. 8″ x 12″. 3 alphabets. Eyelet, stem, and cross-stitch. Strawberry cross-border. Verse 596. *Mrs. Charles E. Cotting*

BRADBURY, HARRIET. 1786. 15″ x 17¼″. Cross and stem-stitch. Rose border. Vase of flowers. Verse 625. *Mrs. Henry E. Coe*

BRADFORD, SYLVIA. 1788. 2½″ x 11″. 1 alphabet. Cross-stitch. *Pamelia Washburn Cram*

BRADLEE, RACHEL. 1792. Milton [Mass.]. 13 yrs. Cross-stitch. Verse 637. *Mrs. E. D. Wadsworth*

BRADLEY, ELIZABETH. 1792. Dracut [Mass.]. 10 yrs. 3 alphabets. Cross-stitch. Vine border. Verse 513. *Mrs. Edward Steese*

BRADWAY, SARAH. 1792. [Lower Alloway Creek Township, N. J. 17 yrs.] Born June 12, 1775. 8¾″ x 12″. 3 alphabets. Eyelet, cross, and flat-stitch. Flat-stitch border. Cross-borders, Greek cross and strawberry. Verse 586 (1, 2). S. B. [Sarah Bradway], A. B. [Anna Bradway], E. B. [Ezra Bradway], J. B. [John Bradway], R. B. [Rachel Bradway]. William Bradway, Sarah Bradway [née Hancock], [parents]. *Miss Kate S. Harris*

BRAY, NANCY. 1799. 10¾″ x 17¼″. 3 alphabets. Eyelet and cross-stitch. Plain cross-stitch border. Trees, diamonds, hearts, etc. "John Bray Susan Bray." *Mrs. William H. Chew*

BRAYTON, CONSTANT. 1770. Somerset [Mass.]. 12 yrs. 15″ x 20″. [Born 1758.] 1 alphabet. Cross-stitch. Vine border. Conventional cross-borders of flowers and birds. Verses 127, 488 (var.). *Miss Nancy Winslow Mitchell*

BRAYTON, REBECCA. [1788.] 9″ x 9″. 2 alphabets. Chain and cross-stitch. *Mrs. James N. Bourne*

BRECK, MARGARET. 1741. Dorchester [Mass.]. 12 yrs. 7½″ x 16″. 1 alphabet. Cross and satin-stitch. Conventional cross-borders. Verses 128 (1, var.), 188. *Miss Helen M. Shaw*

BRECK, MELIA. 1781. Boston [Mass.]. 10 yrs. 17″ x 18″. 3 alphabets. Cross, satin, flat, and cat-stitch. Vine border. Verse 507. *Mrs. Bradbury Bedell*

BREED, HANNAH. 1760. Charlestown[?]. [13 yrs.] Born December 28, 1747. 11½″ x 7¾″. 4 alphabets. Eyelet, cross, and stem-stitch. Hemstitched edge. Conventional border in cross and stem-stitch. Conventional cross-borders. Verse 132 (1, var.). *Mrs. Mary H. Hayes*

BRENTON, FRANCES. 1775. Newport [R. I.]. Oval shape. Outline-stitch. Border of flowers. Design, map of France. Illustrated. *Mrs. Thomas A. Lawton*

BREWSTER, SARAH. 1777. Unfinished. Preston [Conn.?]. 8 yrs. 8½″ x 11½″. 1 alphabet. Cross-stitch. Two rows of stars connected by cross-lines. Verses 128 (1), 188. *W. G. Bowdoin, Esq.*

BRIGGS, ANNA. 1799. Salem [Mass.]. 17″ x 17″. 3 alphabets. Stem and chain-stitch. Border of vine and flowers. Flower baskets in corners and small arbor in center. *Mrs. Lucy Lyman*

BRIGHAM, SUKEY LORINDA. 1786. Boston [Mass.]. 10 yrs. 12¾″ x 16¾″. 2 alphabets. Flat, cross, and stem-stitch. Vine border. Wild rose vine around panel. *Thomas Munroe Shepherd, Esq.*

BRITTON, CATHARINE. 1786. Near Wilmington [Del.]. 7″ x 7½″. 1 alphabet. Eyelet, flat, chain, and cross-stitch. Cross-stitch border. Family initials. *Mrs. Richard T. Cann*

BROMFEILD, ABIGAIL. 1737. 11 yrs. 8½″ x 16½″. 3 alphabets. French knot, stem, eyelet, and cross-stitch. Cross-borders in rose and vine designs. Verse 185. *Mrs. M. A. DeWolfe Howe*

BROOKS, ROSEFAIR. 1786. Barre [Mass.]. 15 yrs. 11″ x 14″. 2 alphabets. Eyelet, cross, and satin-stitch. Berry and vine border. Ephraim Brooks her father, Eunice Brooks her mother.   *Miss Fanny Young*

BROWN, ABIGAIL ("Nabby"). 1774. Tiverton [R. I.]. 15 yrs. 10″ x 12″. 3 alphabets. Cross-stitch. Symmetrical floral design.   *Adoniram B. Judson, M.D.*

BROWN, ANNA. 1797. 13 yrs. 18″ x 22″. 1 alphabet. Tapestry, eyelet, stem, satin, and cross-stitch. Border of vivid and elaborate conventional flowers. Conventional cross-borders of flowers. House, trees, and birds in center. Verse 100.   *Mrs. Thomas A. Lawton*

BROWN, BETTY. 1793. Lexington [Mass.]. 10 yrs. 8″ x 9½″. 1 alphabet. Eyelet and cross-stitch. Border of scrolls. Birds and strawberries.   *Miss Emily A. Peirce*

B[ROWN], E[LIZA]. 1793. Salem [N. J.]. 7 yrs. 8″ x 7¾″. 1 alphabet. Eyelet, buttonhole, and cross-stitch. Border across top and sides of modified Greek fret with strawberries. F. B. E. B. F. A. E. A. F. B. A. B. E. B. A. B. M. A. B. (Supposed to be initials of members of family of E. B.) Verse 343 (1).   *Miss Lucy Dennis Holme*

BROWN, ELIZABETH. August 16, 1770. 12½″ x 13″. Eyelet and cross-stitch. Saw-tooth and carnation border. Hill, sheep, trees, conventional urns with flowers, etc. Verses 500, 501.   *Mrs. Bradbury Bedell*

BROWN, EUNICE. 12 yrs. 7½″ x 21½″. 3 alphabets. Cross-stitch.   *Mrs. Flower*

BROWN, FANNY. 1773. 9 yrs. 7½″ x 9½″. Cross-stitch. Adam and Eve and Tree of Knowledge; sun and moon in upper corners.   *Mrs. Renwick C. Hurry*

BROWN, JOANNA. 1794. 9 yrs. 8″ x 5″. 1 alphabet. Cross-stitch.   *Mrs. Willis H. White*

BROWN, MARY. 1761. 9″ x 11″. 1 alphabet. Satin, stem, and cross-stitch. Border of vines and rosebuds. Trees and baskets of flowers. Verse 594 (1).   *Mrs. Winthrop H. Wade*

BROWN, MARY. [1785.] 9 yrs. Born January 19, 1776. 17″ x 23″. 4 alphabets. Petit-point, eyelet, and cross-stitch. Border of vines, strawberries, and saw-teeth. Cross-borders. Trees, birds, animals, baskets, etc. Verse 202 (1).   *Mrs. Bradbury Bedell*

BROWN, MARY. 1787. [Salem, Mass.?] 11 yrs. 17″ x 22″. 1 alphabet. Cross and overhand stitch. Shepherd and shepherdess at bottom with lambs; trees and vines at sides; roses at top. Verse 40 (var.).   *Francis H. Bigelow, Esq.*

BROWN, MARY. 1792. 8 yrs. 13″ x 17″. Cross-stitch. Carnation border. Adam and Eve, apple tree, serpent, and bay trees, at bottom. In center, two men, stag, crowns, etc. Verse 71.   *Mrs. Willard Saulsbury*

BROWN, MARY. 1793. New Haven [Conn.]. 15 yrs. 10″ x 12″. [Born 1777.] 2 alphabets. Eyelet, stem, satin, and cross-stitch. Hemstitched border. Cross-borders, trees, and fancy stitches. Verse 377.   *Edward M. Bradley, Esq.*

BROWN, MARY. 1799. Newburyport [Mass.]. 16″ x 18″. Alphabets. Chain, eyelet, stem, feather, cross, and other stitches. "How ridiculous is the girl who wilfully swallows the poison of flattery. For any personal charms, and, in the height of her intoxication can be insolent or conceited! What woman of spirit should not aspire to qualities that are less accidental and less subject to change! What woman of reflexion should not resolve to adorn and cultivate a mind whose treasure may be inexhaustible and whose attractions never die." "Each pleasing art lends highness to our minds, and with our studies are our lives refin'd?" Verse 102.   *Newburyport Historical Society*

BROWN, POLLY. 1785. [Boston?] 15 yrs. Born May 19, 1770. 8½" x 12½". 2 alphabets. Cross and stem-stitch. Flowers and vines around panel with name; also flanked by Continental soldier. Verse 599. *Thomas Munroe Shepherd, Esq.*

BROWN, SARAH. [Cir. 1750.] Salem [Mass.]. 12 yrs. 11½" x 15½". 4 alphabets. Cross and satin-stitch. Strawberry borders. *Mrs. Elizabeth Babbidge Heald*

BRUCE, OLIVE. 13 yrs. 8" x 8". 3 alphabets. Cross, satin, and cat-stitch. Cross-borders. Verse 668. *Fitchburg Antique Shop, 1917*

BUCK, PHEBE. 1798. [Fairfield Township, N. J.] 10 yrs. Born November 4, 1787. 13¾" x 17¾". 5 alphabets. Cross, satin, stem, eyelet, chain, queen, tent, and outline stitch. Cross-borders of rosebuds and strawberries; urns of flowers on sides; detached geometrical designs at bottom. Verse 662. *Mrs. J. Ogden Burt*

BUCKLIN, BETSY. 1781. Providence [R. I.]. 12" x 16". Great variety of stitches. Strawberry border. House, trees, a man and two women, sheep, and angels. Verses 2, 366. *Miss Elizabeth L. Betton*

BUCKMINSTER, MARY. [Cir. 1740.] Framingham [Mass.]. Born November 5, 1726. 7¼" x 9". 2 alphabets. Cross-stitch. Hemstitched border. Greek fret cross-borders. *Miss Frances M. Lincoln*

BUFFUM, LUCY. 1786. 14 yrs. 6" x 4". 1 alphabet. Chain and cross-stitch. *The Misses Collins*

BULIOD, MERCY. [Cir. 1770.] Born July 30, 1757. 7" x 13". 2 alphabets. Petit-point, queen, and cross-stitch. Queen-stitch border. Cross-stitch designs of strawberries, birds, roses, house, trees, man, and woman. Verse undecipherable. *Miss Deborah Stoddard*

BULL, MARTHA H. 1795. 8" x 8". 2 alphabets. Eight lines and a serpentine border at bottom. *Walpole Galleries, 1917*

BULLARD, MAR[Y]. 1781. Oakham [Mass.]. 12 yrs. Cross and stem-stitch. Flowers. Verse 490 (var.). *Miss Editha Keefe*

BULLER, ANN. 1786. [Philadelphia?] 21" x 20". Fine cross-stitch, satin, eyelet, stem-stitch, buttonholing in scallops, chain-stitch. Strawberry border, trefoil and saw-tooth cross-borders. Man sitting in a tent, orange trees, camels, six lean sheep, a cow, and men and women. Also a well-house. Verses, top and middle, too indistinct to read. Illustrated. *Mrs. Charles M. Greene*

BULYN, MARY or MARTHA[?]. 1730. Kensington [Pa.]. 9½" x 9½". Petit-point and background stitch. Tree, birds, shepherdess, sheep, and other animals. Illustrated. *Mrs. Frederick F. Thompson*

BURGESS, MARY. August 23, 1725. 10 yrs. 17" x 17½". 1 alphabet. Flat, satin, and cross-stitch. Cross-borders of carnation. Greek fret. Rose, vine, trefoil, trees, birds, and small designs. Verse 127. *The Misses Kenyon*

BURRAGE, MEHITABEL. 1747. 6" x 7¼". 1 alphabet. Eyelet and cross-stitch. *Miss H. E. Cummings*

BURRILL, HANNAH. June 2, 1770. 11 yrs. "Born September 10, 1758." 14" x 18". 2 alphabets. Cross, satin, stem, flat-stitch. Floral border. At top, two couples sitting under a tree. In center, a lady and gentleman, each with a large bird on the hand, on either side of an urn. *George L. Shepley, Esq.*

BUTCHER, MARY. 1740. [New Jersey.] 12" x 18". 1 alphabet. Satin, eyelet, and cross-stitch. Greek fret border. Father and mother, John and Mary Butcher. Grandfathers and grandmothers, John and Damaris Butcher, Peter and Sarah Harvey. Brothers and sisters, Sarah, John, Jonathan, Kathtura, Thomas. Chinese designs, trees, and birds. Verse 488 (var.).   *Miss Jessie Nicholson*

C——, B——. 179–. 4 yrs. Born February 17, [?]. 8½″ x 11½″. 2 alphabets. Cross-stitch. Saw-tooth border. Strawberry and carnation border at bottom. *Mrs. Thomas A. Lawton*

C——, E——. 1796. 4″ x 2¾″. 1 alphabet. Cross-stitch. Parrots and baskets of flowers.
Mrs. Miles White, Jr.

CALDWELL, LYDIA. 1796. [11 yrs.] Born March 27, 1785. Eyelet, satin, and cross-stitch. Verse 386.   *Mrs. George F. Choate*

CALDWELL, RUTH. [Cir. 1780.] Hartford [Conn.]. Born August 12, 1767. 8″ x 9½″. 1 alphabet. Cross-stitch. Trees, birds, fruit, flowers, and lambs. Fancy design below name.
Mrs. Henry P. Briggs

CALDWELL, SUSANNA. 1797. Ipswich [Mass.]. 9 yrs. 8″ x 9″. 1 alphabet. Chain and cross-stitch. Scroll border. Verses 10 (1), 128 (1, var.).   *Miss Martha A. Palmer*

CALEF, MARGARET. 1767. Middletown [Conn.]. 13″ x 16″. Cross-stitch. House, hill, trees, man, woman, birds, sheep, and flowers. Illustrated.   *Mrs. W. S. Fulton*

CAPEN, MARY. 1784. 11 yrs. 12″ x 14½″. 2 alphabets. Tapestry, eyelet, satin, and cross-stitch. Strawberry border. Elaborate pastoral scene. Unfinished verse 43.
Estate of James L. Little, Esq.

CARBUTT, MARY. 1761. 13 yrs. 8″ x 4″. 2 alphabets. Satin, bird's-eye, and cross-stitch. Plain cross-borders. Birds and conventional designs.   *Mrs. Thomas A. Lawton*

CARLETON, SARAH. 1789. Methuen [Mass.]. 10 yrs. 15″ in length. 2 alphabets. Tent, stem, satin, and cross-stitch. Vine and strawberry border. Trees, rose-bush, and bird.
Miss Lucy W. Davis

CARPENTER, ABBY. 1795. 11¾″ x 8¼″. 5 alphabets. Chain and cross-stitch. Cross-stitch border. Verse 520 (2). (Unfinished.)   *Edward I. Mulchahey, Esq.*

CARPENTER, ELIZA. 1797. 16½″ x 16½″. 1 alphabet. Eyelet and cross-stitch. Vine and strawberry border. Houses, trees, man, woman, children, deer, birds, and flowers.
W. R. Lawshe, Esq.

CARR, WAIT. 1737. 10 yrs. 20¼″ x 10¼″. 3 alphabets. Verses 186 (1), 343 (1, 2), 346.

CARRELL, MEHETABLE. 1773. [Near Salem, Mass.] 10 yrs. 10½″ x 16¾″. 2 alphabets. Eyelet, flat, stem, and cross-stitch. Vine and flower border. Bunches of strawberries. Verse 128.
Miss Elizabeth R. Colles

CARROLL, MARY CLARE. 1738. 12″ x 24″. 10 alphabets. Cross-stitch. Large vases of flowers, roses on each side, flower border below. Verses 130, 345 (1).
Exhibited in National Museum, Washington, D. C., by National Society of Colonial Dames

CARROLL, MARY CLARE. 1739. 18″ x 9″. Alphabets. French knot, chain, eyelet, stem, cat, tent, satin, and cross-stitch. Flowers and cross-borders.
Maryland Society of the Colonial Dames

CARVEL, PATIENCE. 1785. Middleborough [Plymouth County, Mass.]. 3 alphabets. Unfinished.
Old Dartmouth Historical Society

CASH, PHEBE. 1789. Newbury [Mass.]. 14 yrs. 9¼″ x 11½″. 2 alphabets. Eyelet, cross, and quadruple cross-stitch. House, trees, and shed. Below, second design of birds and trees. Made by Negro child belonging to Mrs. Sarah (Kent) Atkins, widow of Dudley Atkins, Esq., of Newbury.   *The Misses Marquand*

CHACE, ELIZABETH D. 1743. 3 alphabets. Cross-stitch. Verses 189, 342 (var.), 390. "Value your time. The foundations of virtue and knowledge are laid in youth."
Old Dartmouth Historical Society

CHACE, MARY. 1788. [North Paxton, Mass.] 11 yrs. 16" x 16". 3 alphabets. Stem-stitch. Rose border. Shield, eagle, and horn of plenty. "In God we Hope." Verse 2a.
Mrs. George H. Davenport

CHADWICK, CHARLOT. 1798. [Huntington or Greenport, L. I.] 12" x 14". Cross-stitch. Acorn border. Verse at top; scattered designs of trees, flowers, houses, etc., in center; row of conventional flowers at bottom. Verse 26. *Mrs. Henry Eugene Coe*

CHALMERSS, KATHRINE. 1796. 12⅜" x 17¾". Cross-stitch, long and short. Strawberry border. Lady and gentleman in Colonial dress, also dogs, birds, trees, etc. *Mrs. George C. Fraser*

CHAMBERLAIN, HETTY S. 1774. 9" x 8". 3 alphabets. Cross-stitch. Hemstitched border, plain cross-borders. *Miss Eleanor S. Hall*

CHANDLER, ANNA and ELIZABETH. [Cir. 1774.] Gloucester [Mass.]. "A. Chandler born in York March 8th 1743 E. Chandler born in Gloucester May 2nd 1763". 16½" x 15⅞". 3 alphabets. Eyelet, cross, and satin-stitch. Small triangular pattern cross-borders. Verses 128, 187, 490 (var.). *Dedham Historical Society*

CHASE, SALLY. [Cir. 1790.] Newbury [Mass.]. Born September 5, 1779. 7" x 7". 1 alphabet. Cross-stitch. Cross-stitch border. *The Misses Tenney*

CHAVER, ELIZABETH. 1758. 8" x 11". *Mrs. H. E. Gillingham*

CHELTON, JOANNA. 1796. 10" x 17½". 3 alphabets. Tent, eyelet, and cross-stitch. Rose border. Trees and scattered blossoms on a grassy slope. "J C. A C. T E C. W C. J C. E C." *W. R. Lawshe*

CHEQUIRE, ANN LOUISE. 1799. Baltimore [Md.]. 9 yrs. 15" x 18". 4 alphabets. Cross, eyelet, and chain-stitch. Hemstitched edge with strawberry border. Verse 665.
National Museum, Washington, D. C.

CHESTER, ELIZABETH. 1784. 11 yrs. 9" x 12". 2 alphabets. Cross-stitch. Elaborate cross-stitch border. Rising sun in center. *Elsie Schuyler Cram*

CHILD, ELIZABETH. 1764. 12 yrs. 13½" x 11½". 2 alphabets. Satin, bird's-eye, and cross-stitch. Zigzag border. Basket of carnations. *Mrs. Thomas A. Lawton*

CHURCH, HANNAH. 1747. 14 yrs. 10½" x 26½". 2 alphabets. Cross and satin-stitch. Conventional borders. Figures of persons and trees in pots. Verse 40 (var.) and Collect for the Fourth Sunday after Trinity. *Edward R. Andrews, Esq.*

CHURCH, LYDIA. 1791. New Haven [Conn.]. "Mrs. Mansfield's School." 4 alphabets. Petit-point, stem, satin, chain, queen, eyelet, couching, and cross-stitch, also spangles sewed on. Vine and flower border rising out of vases at lower corners. Large flowers in upper corners. At bottom, scene with house, trees, fence, two men and a woman, and several small animals. Verse 217. Illustrated. *Hartford Historical Society*

CHUTE, JUDITH. 1762. [Rowley, Mass.] 18 yrs. 8" x 13". 3 alphabets. Satin and cross-stitch. Cross-borders in various stitches. *Howard M. Chapin, Esq.*

CLAP, HANNAH. 1770. Dorchester [Mass.]. 11 yrs. 13½" x 16½". Stem, cross, and other stitches. Strawberry border. Conventional cross-borders. Fruit tree, birds, animals, etc. Verse 129 (var.). *Miss Marion S. Abbot*

CLAPP, CATHERINE. 1793. Dorchester [Mass.]. 12 yrs. 16" x 16". Cross-stitch. Strawberry border and cross-borders. Flowers, lions, etc. Verse 516. *Miss Anna Humphreys*

CLARK, MARY. 1716. 13 yrs. 7½" x 18". Alphabet. Cross-stitch, very little satin-stitch. Part of sampler worked upside down.   *Mrs. Charles H. Atkinson*

CLARK, MARY. 1789. 19" x 16¾". Floral and vine border in outline, chain, French knot, satin, stem, and cat-stitch. Center of sampler done in great variety of hollie-point lace. Illustrated.   *Mrs. Caroline R. Patterson*

CLARK, PHŒBE. 1798. Stony Brook [N. J.]. 14½" x 20". Cross, satin, and stem-stitch. Carnation and tulip border. House on terrace, trees, flowers, cows, and sheep. Verse 236 (var.).   *Charles Clark Black, Esq.*

CLARK, RUTH. [Cir. 1798. Vermont.] 11" x 14". 3 alphabets. Cross-stitch. Greek fret border across center. Initials of 13 persons with date of birth, and initials of 4 persons with date of death, probably the Clark family.   *Mrs. George G. Barnes*

CLASSEN, MARY. 1725. [Newport, R. I.] 7 yrs. 10" x 17". 2 alphabets. Cross, satin, and cat-stitch. Carnation, trefoil, and Greek fret borders. Birds and flowers at the bottom. Verse 342.   *Mrs. Charles K. Bolton*

CLAYTON, MARY. 1787. 18" x 25". Cross-stitch. Morning-glory border. Strawberry and other conventional designs across top. Verse 370.
Sale of Ross H. Maynard, Esq., March, 1916

COALE, MARY ABBY. 1797. ["Morven" in Anne Arundel County, Md.] 8 yrs. [Born February 4, 1789.] 7" x 10½". 4 alphabets. Cross-stitch. Cross-borders of different stitches.
Mrs. Francis T. Redwood

COALE, MARY ABBY. [1799 or 1800. "Morven," Anne Arundel County, Md. 10 or 11 yrs.] 7½" x 8½". 1 alphabet. Cross-borders.   *Mrs. Francis T. Redwood*

COFFIN, DOROTHY F. [Cir. 1785.] Born May 8, 1774, at Newburyport [Mass.]. 17" x 22". 4 alphabets. Cross, satin, and eyelet-stitch. Strawberry border. Hill, trees, flowers, birds, animals, etc. Verse 368.   *Miss Helen Pike*

COFFIN, MARY JOHNSON. 1799. Newbury [Mass.]. 8 yrs. 11" x 14¼". 2 alphabets. French knot, stem, satin, outline, and cross-stitch. Hemstitched and rose borders. Cherry tree, bird, lamb, vase of roses, etc.   *Mrs. Edward O. Shepard*

COGGESHALL, ELIZA. 1784. 10 yrs. 16½" x 12". 1 alphabet. Stem, satin, and cross-stitch. Rose border. House, people, birds, and dogs. "Duty to God Fear and Love we owe above."
Miss Eliza A. Kaighn

COGGESHALL, MARY. 1774. Newport. 15" x 10½". 2 alphabets. Eyelet and cross-stitch. Verse 502 (var.).   *Miss Eliza A. Kaighn*

COGGESHALL, PATTY. [Cir. 1790.] "Bristol New E." Born February 15, 1780. 15" x 20". 1 alphabet. Cross, split, satin, and queen-stitch. Border of various flowers at sides, and at top figures of men, women, animals, etc. In center, two scenes with men, women, children, trees, birds, animals, etc. Verse 594 (1, var.). Illustrated in color.
Metropolitan Museum, New York

COGILL, MARTHA. 1763. Philadelphia. 18 yrs. 18" x 12". Eyelet, satin, petit-point, drawn-work, and hemstitch. Drawn-work and buttonhole-stitch in border. Flower-pot with sprays of flowers. Flowers in drawn-work in 14th century embroidery. Name and date on pot.   *Mrs. Clarence North*

COGSWELL, ABIGAIL. 1792. Ipswich [Mass.]. 11 yrs. Born January 7, 1781. 8" x 9½". 3 alphabets. Eyelet and cross-stitch. Plain hemstitched border. Conventional design in eyelet-stitch.   *Mrs. William C. West*

PLATE XV

MARIAH DEAVENPORT'S SAMPLER. 1741
Owned by the Windham Library

MARY PARKER'S SAMPLER. 1741
Owned by Mrs. Henry H. Edes

PLATE XVI

Ruth Haskell's Sampler.   Cir. 1760
Owned by the Society for the Preservation of New England Antiquities

COGSWELL, BETSY. [Cir. 1775.] Born August 25, 1764. 13″ x 17″. 2 alphabets. Cross and satin-stitch. Space left unfinished. *Mrs. Henry Lowell Hiscock*

COGSWELL, HANNAH. [Cir. 1778.] Born November 6, 1767. 9½″ x 10″. 1 alphabet. Cross and satin-stitch. Cross-borders. Trees. *Mrs. Henry Lowell Hiscock*

COGSWELL, SARAH. 1773. Born June 8, 1763. 8″ x 8½″. 2 alphabets. Cross and satin-stitch. Cross-borders. *Mrs. Henry Lowell Hiscock*

COLCOTT, DORCAS. 1796. Romsey. 16″ x 24″. 2 alphabets. Stem, petit-point, eyelet, cross, satin, and 2-sided line-stitch. Strawberry border. Darky stealing a chicken, bushes, birds, parrot on a tree, pillars of flowers, etc., in center; at bottom, parrot on a tree, house, fence, barn, deer, etc. Verse 531a. *Mr. Colket*

COLEMAN, ANN. Verse 341.

COLEMAN, ELIZABETH. 1766. Philadelphia [Pa.]. 9 yrs. 12½″ x 12½″. Cross, satin, stem, and tent-stitch. Floral border. Verse, "The Universal Prayer," by Pope. *Horace Wells Sellers, Esq.*

COLLINS, RUTH. [Cir. 1795.] Hopkinton, R. I. [Born May 2, 1784.] 7½″ x 11″. 2 alphabets. Eyelet, satin, and cross-stitch. Floral borders. Fruit trees topped by large birds. Verse 649. *Miss F. R. Kenyon*

[COLLINS, TRYPHENIA. Cir. 1790.] 21″ x 22″. Cross-stitch. Rosebud border. Strawberry and conventional cross-borders. Large sprays of flowers and two butterflies in center. Verses 23, 34. Illustrated. *Mrs. B. Osgood Peirce*

CONANT, CHARLOTTE. 1790. 4″ x 6½″. "Her Examplar." 1 alphabet. *A. Stainforth, Dealer, 1917*

CONANT, SARAH. 1790. 6″ x 4″. "Her Exampler." 1 alphabet. Cross-stitch. *M. B. Lemon, Dealer*

COOCHE, FRANCIS ELIZABETH. 1735. 11″ x 14″. Large vase with handles, holding carnations, tulips, and rosebuds. Flowers scattered on grass. *Mrs. E. A. Whelan and Miss Mary Zellar*

COOK, MORILLA. 1714. [Date questionable.] 10 yrs. 9″ x 7″. Satin and cross-stitch. House, trees, and shrubs, also large detached rose in upper corner. *Mrs. Thomas A. Lawton*

COOPER, ELIZABETH. 1763. Woodbury [N. J.]. 11 yrs. 9″ x 11½″. 2 alphabets. Eyelet and cross-stitch. Cross-borders. Initials: J.C. A.C. T.M. M.M. D.C. S.C. A.C. A.C. P.C. A.C. W.C. Verse 597. *Miss Sibyl T. Jones*

COOPER, SUSANNA. 1798. 12 yrs. 12½″ x 13½″. Stem, satin, chain, and cross-stitch. Vine and flower border. In center, large basket filled with fruit. *Mrs. G. H. Buek*

COPP, ESTER. 1755. 11 yrs. 12″ x 15″. 3 alphabets. Cross-stitch. Tree and tulips. "Better it is to be of an humble spirit with the lowly, than to divide the spoil with the proud." *Gift of John B. Copp to the National Museum, Washington, D. C.*

COWAN, ELEANOR. 1797. Salem [Mass.]. 8 yrs. 12½″ x 17″. 2 alphabets. Stem and cross-stitch. Strawberry. Verse 601 (1, 2, 3). *Miss Susan W. Osgood*

COWDREY, ELIZA. 1787. 12 yrs. 13″ x 17½″. Satin, stem, and cross-stitch. Border at top and bottom of carnations and vine; at sides of vine and triangular leaves. House, peacocks at each side of door, birds, children, men, and animals in upper half. Large tree, men, children, birds, flowers, and shrubs in lower half. Verse 41. *Alice W. Belcher*

COWING, RACHEL. 1793. Born September 9, 1782. 8½″ x 8″. 3 alphabets. Cross-stitch. *Estate of James L. Little, Esq.*

COWING, SARAH.   [Cir. 1793.] Born March 29, 1782.   8½" x 8½".   2 alphabets.   Cross-stitch.
Estate of James L. Little, Esq.

COX, ESTHER.   [Cir. 1768. Near Boston.] Born March, 1759.   9½" x 14".   2 alphabets.   Cross, satin, stem, chain, French knot, and buttonhole-stitch.   Border of conventional flowers, which spring from a basket in middle of border across bottom; peacock in middle of border at top.   "Nothing lovelier can be found in woman than to study household Good and good works in her Husband to promote."   "Remember thy Creator in the days of thy youth," etc.
Mrs. Henry E. Coe

COZZENS, ELIZA.   1795.   Satin, split, eyelet, and stem-stitch.   Border of vine and flowers.   In center, basket filled with fruit and berries; birds flying above.   Illustrated.
Rhode Island School of Design

CRANE, MEHITABLE.   1793.   10" x 16".   4 alphabets.   Eyelet and cross-stitch.   Simple cross-stitch borders.   Verse 641.
Miss Hannah Weston Clap

CREATON, LUCRETIA.   1790. Charleston [S. C.].   16½" x 21½".   Alphabet.   Split, cat, tent, stem, satin, eyelet, and cross-stitch.   Strawberry border.   Cross-borders in Greek fret, diamond, and vase designs.   Verses 92a (2, var.), 627.
Mrs. John F. Bennett

CROSS, BETSY.   1799.   Haverhill [N. H.].   9 yrs.   12½" x 16½".   3 alphabets.   Border design is little rings linked together.
Mrs. Abram Whitcomb

CROW, ELIZABETH.   1747.   12½" x 16".   Cross and satin-stitch.   Double strawberry border.   At bottom, trees, rabbits, basket of flowers, etc.   Verse 131.
Mrs. George E. Dadmun

CROWNINSHIELD, MARY.   1748.   Salem [Mass.].   "Union Academy."   8 yrs.   8" x 8".   2 alphabets.   Cross-stitch.
Mrs. Carl A. de Gersdorff

CUMMINGS, NANCY.   1799.   Westford [Mass.].   18½" x 20".   4 alphabets.   Eyelet, cross, satin, and stem-stitch.   Border of strawberries, carnations, poppies, roses, and vines, also berries.   Trees and vase filled with carnations, roses, etc.   Verse 601 (1, 2, 3, var.).
Mrs. Henry G. Mitchell

CURTIS, LYDIA.   1799.   9 yrs.   10½" x 11½".   3 alphabets.   Eyelet, satin, stem, and cross-stitch.   Carnation border.   Trees on mounds.
Mrs. Thomas A. Lawton

CURTIS, SARAH.   1770.   Salem [Mass.].   8 yrs.   8" x 10".   2 alphabets.   Cross-stitch.   Strawberry border on three sides.   Small, separate designs.
Essex Institute

CUSHING, HANNAH.   [1796.]   10 yrs.   16" x 12".   Cross-stitch.   Flowers tied with a blue bow-knot.
Miss Julia Cushing

CUSHING, JOANNA.   1775.   Hingham [Mass.].   12 yrs.   12" x 14".   Alphabet.   Cross-stitch.   Grecian border.   Verses 128 (1, var.), 607.
Mrs. Frederick Cate

CUSHING, LUCY.   1792.   Turner [Me.].   13 yrs.   12¼" x 16".   3 alphabets and separate letters.   Eyelet and cross-stitch.   Conventional border.   House, grassy terrace, rose bushes, and sunflowers.   Verse 128 (1, var.).   Tailpiece.
Mrs. Paul Blatchford

CUSHING, MARY.   1799.   Scituate.   9⅜" x 9⅜".   2 alphabets.   Drawn-work and cross-stitch.   Verse 527.
A. Stainforth, Dealer, 1917

CUTTER, HANNAH.   1771.   Portsmouth [N. H.].   11 yrs.   10¾" x 22¼".   4 alphabets.   Cross, satin, stem, and eyelet-stitch.   Trees and clover.
Miss Mary Hale Wheeler

DAINTERY, MARY.   1721.   8 yrs.   [Born December 22, 1713. Near New Haven.]   12" x 11".   Stem, satin, and cross-stitch.   Border of vine and strawberry blossoms, and cross-border of the same.   "Publius Lentulus his Letter to the Senate of Rome concerning Jesus Christ."   Illustrated.
Mrs. G. H. Buek

DAVENPORT, ABIGAIL. [Cir. 1750?] 11 yrs. 22" x 8". 2 alphabets. Two crowned lions on either side; two trees topped by birds; strawberries, baskets, etc. Verse 126 (1, 2).
Massachusetts Historical Society

DAVIS, ELES. 1798. 10" x 12". 3 alphabets. Cross-stitch. Simple line border. Verse 490 (var.).
Miss Charlotte M. Smith

DAVIS, LYDIA. 1799. Concord [Mass.]. 10 yrs. 15½" x 17½". 2 alphabets. Eyelet, satin, and cross-stitch. Conventional border on three sides. Conventional designs. Verses 142, 490 (var.).
Mrs. Joseph B. Ross

DAVIS, MARY. 1778. [Burlington County, N. J.] 8" x 12". 2 alphabets. Eyelet and cross-stitch. Strawberry border.
Mrs. Morris D. Wickersham

DAY, DEBORAH. 1777. Methuen [Mass.?]. 10" x 16". 1 alphabet. Stem-stitch. Border of carnations at top and vine with small flowers on sides. House, tree, birds, dog, two ladies, etc. Verse.
Mrs. Charlotte C. Ames

DEANE, SYLVIA. 1784. 17 yrs. 9" x 9". 2 alphabets. Chain and cross-stitch.
Mrs. L. Earle Rowe

DEAVENPORT, MARIAH. 1741. 12 yrs. 16" x 10". 2 alphabets. Eyelet, stem, satin, and cross-stitch. Conventional cross-borders. Adam and Eve and Tree of Knowledge. Illustrated.
Windham Library

DE BANC, SUZANNE LOUISE. 1748. 8 yrs. 18" x 8¼". 3 alphabets. Eyelet, satin, and cross-stitch. Vine border. House, trees, birds, animals, woman, two angels, etc. Verse in French, 588.
Mrs. Rebecca S. Price

DEMING, HANNAH. 1786. Born November 16, 1776. 9½" x 8". 2 alphabets. Cross-stitch. Cross-lines. Verses 205, 206.
Albert C. Bates, Esq.

DEMING, SALLY. 1725. 3½" x 12". 2 alphabets. Cross-stitch. Following additions probably put in by Florence Davis:
> Florence Davis, 1865 Born Dec 19
> Francis Mead Davis 1845 Dec 1
> Elizabeth Deyo Mead 1820 Jan 16
> Sally Deming Deyo 1799 March 15
Mrs. Riley A. Vose

DENNY, POLLY. 1785. Leicester [Mass.]. 12 yrs. 14" x 7". 2 alphabets. Cross, eyelet, and satin-stitch.
Mrs. John A. Sweetser

DERBY, ELIZABETH. 1774. Salem [Mass.]. 10½" x 14". 4 alphabets. Stem and cross-stitch. Conventional border of vine and flowers. Conventional cross-border of flowers. "Idleness is the root of all Evil." "Modesty becomes the fair sex thro life." *Essex Institute*

DEWEY, CHARLOTTE. 1796. 11 yrs. 8" x 12". 2 alphabets. Cross, tent, and chain-stitch. Vine border. Tree design.
Miss Mary Jeannette Tilton

DICK, A[NNA]. 1797. [Salem, N. J. 10 yrs.] 8¼" x 11½". 2 alphabets. Cross, satin, eyelet, buttonhole, and tent-stitch. Strawberry border. [Father and mother] Samuel Dick Sarah Dick. [Sisters and brothers] R. D. [Rebecca] M. D. [Maria] J. D. [Jane] S. D. [Sally] A. D. [Anna] I. D. [Isabel] A. D. S. D. [Samuel] W. D. [William]. Verse 343 (1 var.).
Miss Maria H. Mecum

DICK, A[NNA]. 1799. [Salem, N. J. 12 yrs.] 10⅜" x 11¾". 3 alphabets. Cross, satin, and buttonhole-stitch. Conventional border. Cross-lines. S D [Dr. Samuel Dick, father] S D [Sarah Dick, mother] R D [Rebecca] M D [Maria] J D [Jane] S D [Sally] I D [Isabel] A D [Anna, who made sampler] S D [Samuel] W D [William] M D [Mary]. Verse 240.
Miss Maria H. Mecum

DICKINSON, POLLY. 1798. Hadley, Mass. 11 yrs. Born November, 1787. 8¼" x 9". 2 alphabets. Cross-stitch. Narrow hem. Verse 237. [The linen was woven by Polly Dickinson.]
Mrs. H. H. Wells

DILLWYN, ANN. 1753. 8 yrs. [Born in 1745 at Burlington, N. J.] 8½" x 9". 2 alphabets. Cross-stitch with hole in center.
Miss Susan P. Wharton

DOLE, ELIZABETH. 1752. 9 yrs. Born December 3, 1743. 10½" x 14". 4 alphabets. Eyelet, satin, and cross-stitch. Twenty-two cross-borders.
Newburyport Historical Society

DOLE, POLLY. [1793.] Newbury [Mass.]. 8 yrs. Born January 25, 1785. 7½" x 9". 2 alphabets. Chain and cross-stitch. Sides hemstitched, strawberry vine at top, picture at bottom. Basket of flowers.
Miss Sarah Jackson Leigh

DOLIBER, ANNE S. 1767. [Marblehead.] 16 yrs. 7½" x 10". 1 alphabet. Eyelet and cross-stitch. Saw-tooth border. Carnation cross-border at bottom. Flower designs. Verse 357.
Marblehead Historical Society

DOUBT, SARAH. 1764. 9 yrs. 12" x 20". 1 alphabet. French knot, buttonhole, stem, satin, and cross-stitch. Strawberry border. Cross-borders in various designs. Elaborate pastoral scene at bottom, with trees, birds, flowers, animals, man, and woman. Verse 188.
Mrs. Richard Cobb

DOUGLASS, PEGGY. 1796. [Kent County, Del. Worked at Mme. Capron's School, Philadelphia, Pa.] 15½" x 15½". 3 alphabets. Stem, satin, and cross-stitch. Roses, carnations, and white berry sprays in border. Strawberry wreath at bottom enclosing verse. Verse 488 (var.).
Miss Harriet Clayton Comegys

DOW, RUTH. 1792. 12 yrs. Born May 3, 1780. 18" x 21". 3 alphabets. Cross-stitch. Double strawberry border. Cross-border of carnations. Scene with house, red lion, sheep, birds, etc. Verse 222.
Mrs. Thomas A. Lawton

DRAPER, ELIZABETH. 1773. [Age worn off.] 12½" x 17¼". 3 alphabets. Mostly cross-stitch. Plain border. Trees and animals. "Bless the Lord O My Soul," etc.
Miss Sarah M. Draper

DRAPER, LENDAMINE. [Cir. 1791. 11 yrs.] Born in Dedham, March 30, 1780. 11" x 15". 1 alphabet. Eyelet and cross-stitch. Double border of eyelet and cross-stitch. Birds, cats, vases, trees, etc. Verse 373.
Mrs. George Marsh

DRAPER, LYDIA. 1742. 13 yrs. Born December 16, 1729. 10½" x 15½". 2 alphabets. Eyelet and cross-stitch. Hemstitched border. "Nothing is so sure as Death & nothing is so uncertain as the Time When I may be to old to Live but I can never be to young to Die I will so live every hour as if I was to die the next."
Mrs. Oliver Wyeth

DRAPER, SUSANNA. 1773. [10 yrs.] 12½" x 17¼". 3 alphabets. Mostly cross-stitch. Plain border. Trees and animals. "Bless the Lord O my Soul," etc.
Miss Sarah M. Draper

DRIVER, ELIZABETH. 1795. Salem [Mass.]. 18" x 18". 3 alphabets. Rose border across top. Cross and stem-stitch. Scene with man and woman gayly dressed, hill, dog, and butterflies.
Essex Institute

DUDLEY, ELIZABETH. 1736. Roxbury [Mass.]. 12 yrs. 8" x 18". 3 alphabets. Great variety of stitches. Plain border. Elaborate design with birds, etc. Verse 128 (var.), the Lord's Prayer, and "Remember thy Creator," etc. [Granddaughter of Governor Joseph Dudley.]
Rev. Dudley Richards Child

DUDLEY, LUCY. 1788. Concord [Mass.]. 14 yrs. 10" x 10". 3 alphabets. Eyelet and cross-stitch. Greek fret borders.
Miss Gertrude Pierce

DUNCAN, ESTHER. 1752. 8″ x 21″. Alphabets. Eyelet and cross-stitch. Cross-borders in scroll, vine, point, lozenge, and circle. Verse 495. *Mrs. John H. Morison*

DUNN, HARRIET. 1790. [New Jersey.] 10 yrs. 7″ x 15″. 4 alphabets. Cross-stitch.
Miss Katharine Harriet Graham

DURBOROUGH, PATTY RINGGOLD. [Cir. 1791. Ivy Hall, Kent County, Del.] Born in 1781. 8″ x 8″. Alphabet. Cross-stitch. Vine border. *Mrs. Frederic Tyson*

DYER, PATTY. 1797. Providence [R. I.]. 8 yrs. 12″ x 12″. 4 alphabets. Chain and cross-stitch. Verse 47 (1). *Miss Katherine C. Mitchell*

E——, E. D. 8″ x 10″. 3 alphabets. Cross-stitch. Simple border. Two strawberry plants at bottom. *Groton Historical Society*

EARL, ESTHER. 1797. [Near Pemberton, Burlington County, N. J.] 11 yrs. [Born October 9, 1786.] 12¾″ x 17¾″. 2 alphabets. Cross, satin, eyelet, chain, queen, cat, flat, and stem-stitch. Strawberry border.

> "Esther Earl Daughter of Joseph and
> Theodosia Earl. Her work in her 11th year
> 1797. Sarah Shoemaker." [Teacher?]

Verse 654. *Miss Sarah Rowan Budd*

EARL, MARY. [Cir. 1765.] Born September 9, 175(?). 8¼″ x 20″. Alphabet. Cross-stitch. Cross-borders in various designs. Verse 128 (var.). *Mrs. Fred R. Gibbs*

EASTON, ELIZABETH. 1795. 10 yrs. Born June 8, 1785. 2 alphabets. Cross-stitch. Border, medley of flowers and birds. Square containing her name and date, part of border. In center a house, with a man on the left and a woman on the right. Verse 10 (1 and 2).
Metropolitan Museum of Art, New York

EATON, ELIZABETH A. 1797. Dudley [Mass.]. 7 yrs. 16½″ x 16½″. 2 alphabets. Cross and satin-stitch. Greek fret border. In center, trees with birds; at bottom, house in right-hand corner, basket in left-hand corner, verse in center. Verse 235 (1). [She lived to be one hundred years old.] *Mrs. George M. Thornton*

EDDY, SARAH ANN. 1771. Milbury. 11 yrs. 20″ x 20″. Alphabets. Cross, satin, and outline-stitch. Vine border. House, trees, and birds. Verse 601 (1, 2, var.).
Mrs. Augustus Hemenway

EDGLOW, JANE. 1795. "Begun in the School of Industry, 1795." 16″ x 20″. Cross and chain-stitch. Strawberry border. Man and woman under tree, and various scattered designs such as houses, trees, animals, flowers, etc. Verse 521. *Mrs. Richard H. Hunt*

ELKINS, JEAN. 1796. Marblehead [Mass.]. 14 yrs. 15½″ x 15″. 1 alphabet. Stem and cross-stitch. Rose, trefoil, and strawberry border. Stage scene with curtain, gentleman presenting a flower to a lady, lamb in foreground and pots of flowers. Verse 188.
Mrs. Arthur A. Bamford

ELLERY, MARY GOULD. 1799. 6 yrs. 10″ x 13″. 3 alphabets. Eyelet, satin, and cross-stitch. Borders. Verse 609 (var.). *Heirs of Mrs. Henry Rust Stedman*

ELLIS, ELIZABETH. 1799. [Near Crosswicks, N. J. 14 yrs.] Born October 5, 1785. 10½″ x 13″. 3 alphabets. Cross and flat-stitch. Strawberry and vine border. Sheep and lambs in corner, at bottom; also birds, trees, and large flower-pot between two green plots.
Mrs. Rebecca S. Price

ELLIS, MARY. 1743. Hem, cross, chain, stem, buttonhole, and lace-stitch. Chain-stitch border. Conventional flowers. Middle worked in small squares to leave canvas in rows of diamond shape. Some of these contain faint figures, probably intended for a multiplication table. Illustrated.
Miss Ellen F. Vose

ELLIS, MARY. 1749. 11 yrs. 7¾" x 12". Cross-stitch. Rosebud border. Large vase of flowers and small baskets of fruit. The Lord's Prayer.
Mrs. H. de B. Parsons

ELLIS, MERIBAH. 1793. [Crosswicks, N. J.] 14 yrs. [Born January 8, 1779.] 9" x 13½". 3 alphabets. Great variety of stitches. Strawberry border. At bottom, two green mounds with two trees on each, flowers growing in grass, large flower-pot in center. Small designs of flowers, baskets, houses, fruit, and birds.
Mrs. Rebecca S. Price

ELMER, ESTHER. 1798. [Fairfield Township, Cumberland County, N. J.] 13⅛" x 17⅛". 5 alphabets. Cross, satin, stem, eyelet, queen, tent, and outline-stitch. Border, carnation and Greek fret. Strawberry and rosebud cross-borders. Urns of flowers at sides. At bottom, sprays of detached geometrical designs. Verse 660. J. W. E. E. [Esther Elmer, maker] D. E. [Daniel Elmer, brother] W. W. [William Westcott, half-brother] C. E. [Charles Elmer, brother] B. T. E. [Benjamin T. Elmer, brother].
Mrs. J. Ogden Burt

ELMER, SARAH. 1787. [Bridgeton, N. J.] 7 yrs. 10" x 12". 3 alphabets. Fagot, cross, and satin-stitch. Strawberry plants and bird on branch.
Mrs. Lewis P. Bush

EMERSON, ANNE. 1799. 13" x 22". 2 alphabets. Cross, satin, eyelet, and outline-stitch. Hem-stitched edge. Conventionalized strawberry and carnation border. Rose cross-borders in flat-stitch. Birds and sheep under trees and strawberry plants; sketchy bird, good cow, etc., at bottom. Verse 634A.
For sale at Koopman's

EVANS, ELEANOR. 1797. 13 yrs. 19" x 19". 2 alphabets. Cross, satin, stem, and chain-stitch. Vine border in cross-stitch. In center a vase full of flowers, standing on a table. Names given on sampler, as follows: Samuel Evans, Ann Evans, Edward Morris, Eleanor Morris, Jacob Evans, Hannah Evans, Samuel Evans, Morris Evans, Jonathan Evans, George Evans, Enos Evans, Aaron Evans, Eleanor Evans, Nathan Evans, Elizabeth Evans. 1797 A. E. "Behold King David Tends his flocks A thousand little Lambs Down" . . . [needle with silk at end of this unfinished quotation]. Verse 503 (var.).
Mrs. E. Boyd Weitzel

FARLEY, ELIZABETH. 1767. 10 yrs. 8" x 9". Alphabets. Cross-stitch. Border of different patterns. At bottom, conventional design in fancy stitches. Verse 133.
Miss Florence Farley Caldwell

FARLEY, SALLY. 1794. Hollis [N. H.]. 12 yrs. 15" x 19½". Cross, laid, and stem-stitch. Strawberry vine around three sides. At bottom, house, sky, and trees. Verse 645.
Miss Elizabeth F. Kelly

FEARLESS, SALLIE. 1797. 15 yrs. 20½" x 24". 2 alphabets. Cross, satin, stem, French knot, double-stitch, and hem-stitch. Background, solid split-stitch. Border, Tree of Life, on either side changing into conventional wild rose design; strawberry design at base; three doves in conventional design at top. Figures of man and woman, etc., at base. Verse 40 (var.).
Miss Josephine G. Keniston

FINNEY, ELIZA A. 1703. 13 yrs. 12¼" x 9¾". 3 alphabets. Cross-stitch. Verse 500.
Mrs. Hobart

FISH, MARY ABRAMS. 10" x 10". 3 alphabets. Cross, eyelet, and satin-stitch. Plain cross-stitch border.
Fitchburg Antique Shop, 1917

FISK, AVIS. 1790. Waltham [Mass.]. 12 yrs. 12" x 16". 1 alphabet. Stem and cross-stitch. Greek fret border.
Leah A. Nunn

FITCH, ELIZABETH M. 1718. 9 yrs. 21" x 21½". 4 alphabets. Eyelet, cross, and queen-stitch. Strawberry border. Scattered designs at top of birds, flowers, baskets, etc. Line borders. Verse 340. Lord's Prayer. "Remember now thy Creator," etc. "Follow virtue and she will guide you to happiness." *Mrs. H. de B. Parsons*

FITHIAN, RACHEL. 1756. [Cumberland County, N. J.] 12 yrs. 10" x 12½". 2 alphabets. Cross-stitch. Trefoil border. Cross-borders of roses, tulips, and strawberries. "Samuel Fithian Phebe Fithian E P". Verse 591. *Mrs. Helen Pancoast and Miss Anna C. Smith*

FLETCHER, ANN. 1792. Chelmsford [Mass.]. Born July 20, 1780. 6½" x 5¼". 2 alphabets. Cross-stitch. Hemstitched border. *Miss Elizabeth B. Heald*

FLETCHER, ANNA. 1792. Chelmsford [Mass.]. 12 yrs. Born July 20, 1780. 6½" x 5¼". 1 alphabet. Cross-stitch. Hemstitched border. *Miss Elizabeth B. Heald*

FLETCHER, REBECCA. [Cir. 1790. Hopkinton, N. H. Born in 1776.] 11½" x 12½". Cross-stitch. Narrow border of cross-stitch and laid-stitch. 4-inch strawberry vine at bottom. [Sister-in-law of Daniel Webster.] *Miss Elizabeth T. Kelly*

FLETSCHER, MARY. 1740. 8" x 17½". 185 letters in 14 rows. *Mrs. Siegfried Wachsman*

FLINT, PRISCILLA. 1784. Reading [Mass.]. 9 yrs. 16" x 16". 2 alphabets. Cross and satin-stitch. Border of conventionalized cross. Elaborate design at bottom. Verse 616. *Harriet Parsons Abbott*

FLOWER, REBEKAH. 1785. 12" x 14". [London Grove, Pa.] 3 alphabets. Cross-stitch. Catherine Wheel border, and cross-borders of roses, tulips, and strawberries. "C. M." "Richard and Alice." Verses 360, 622, 623. *F. F. Sharpless, Esq.*

FOLSOM, DEBORAH. 1767. Exeter [N. H.]. 12 yrs. 17" x 21½". 3 alphabets. Great variety of stitches. Borders of rosebuds and leaves, strawberry, Greek fret, vine and berries. At bottom, strawberries, fret, black and white dogs in corners. Verse 128 (var.). *Mrs. Robert S. Morison*

FORD, BETHIAH. 1793. [New Castle County, Del.] 12 yrs. 10" x 16½". 1 alphabet. Cross-stitch. Verse 132 (1, var.). *Mrs. J. Dale Dilworth*

FORD, JANE. [1797.] 14 yrs. 7¼" x 15". 3 alphabets. Cross-stitch. Border of tulips and strawberries. Strawberry border at bottom. Verse 488 (var.). *Mrs. J. Dale Dilworth*

FOSTER, HANNAH. 1743. Evesham [N. J.]. 15 yrs. 11" x 18". Eyelet, satin, cat, and cross-stitch. Vine border with odd designs. 6 different cross-borders. 2 verses, but not legible. "My Grandfathers and Mothers, Josiah and Amy Foster, Enoch and Sarah Core. My parents, William and Hannah Foster." Names of four sisters, but not legible. "Elizabeth Sullivan taught me." *Miss Elizabeth C. Saunders*

FOSTER, MEHITABLE. 1786. 14 yrs. 15" x 18½". 3 alphabets. Cross, eyelet, stem, and satin-stitch. Border of baskets, flowers, birds, etc. At bottom, elaborate basket of flowers, with two large birds eating flowers. *Mrs. Stanley H. Lowndes*

FOSTER, POLLY. 1787. [Canterbury, N. H.] 12 yrs. 16" x 17". Great variety of stitches. 3 alphabets. Saw-tooth border and nine different cross-border designs. At bottom, conventional baskets of flowers, birds, and trees. *Mrs. Vienna Dodge Pearson*

FREEBORN, GIDEON. 1771. 8" x 11¾". Cross-stitch. Design is diagonal bands of black, forming diamonds in which are bright colors, 1¾" in size. *Miss Sophie Pierce Casey*

FREEBORN, MARY. 1743. 13 yrs. 7" x 9". Alphabet. Cross-stitch. Solid-line border. Rosettes and vases of flowers in center, in lower half. Verse 347. *Mrs. George L. Miner*

FREEMAN, DEBORAH. 1774. Born September 13, 1763. 6″ x 8″. 2 alphabets. Cross and satin-stitch. Carnation border and conventional pine-cone border running across middle of sampler.   *Dr. Oliver W. Huntington*

FRENCH, ANN HEULINGS. 1797–1800. [Near Mullica Hill, Gloucester County, N. J.] 9 to 12 yrs. Born September 29, 1788. 12¼″ x 18¾″. 3 alphabets. Cross, satin, eyelet, and queen-stitch. Border, two rows of satin-stitch. Cross-borders, conventional carnations, berries, roses, and strawberries. Verses 132 (1 var.), 656.

"Uriah French was born the 13th of the 7th mo. 1770
Jacob French was born the 30th of the 4th mo. 1773
Agnes French was born the 24th of the 2nd mo. 1776
Charles French was born the 22nd of the 4th mo. 1777
Samuel French was born the 10th of the 4th mo. 1779
Nancy French was born the 12th of the 5th mo. 1781
Sarah French was born the 24th of the 11th mo. 1783
Joseph French was born the 20th of the 7th mo. 1786
Ann Heulings French was born the 29th of the 9th mo. 1788."

Miss Mary H. Clark

FRENCH, ELIZABETH and ANN. 1793. Philadelphia [Pa.]. 13 yrs. and 11 yrs. 18″ x 21″. 2 alphabets. Cross, satin, eyelet, and stem-stitch. Border of vine and small flowers. Roses and violets in a vine and flower enclosure. Names on sampler: "Charles French, Rebecca French [father and mother]; Mary French, Abigal French, Charles French, James French" [children]. Verse 226.   *Clara M. Lukens*

FRENCH, SALLY. 1793. West Dedham. Born June 1, 1781. 8½″ x 11½″. 1 alphabet. Cross-stitch. Vine border. Verse [unfinished]. "Those Trifles That Amuse In Life Promote A higher . . ."   *Mary E. Fisher*

FRENCH, SARAH. 1794. [Near Mullica Hill, Gloucester County, N. J.] 11 yrs. [Born November 24, 1783.] 10¼″ x 15¼″. 3 alphabets. Cross, satin, eyelet, queen, flat, and cat-stitch. Border, double row of cross-stitch. Carnation, strawberry, and diamond cross-borders. Verse 343 (1 var.).   *Miss Mary H. Clark*

FROTHINGHAM, BETSY. 1784. Newburyport [Mass.]. 17 yrs. 12″ x 16″. 2 alphabets. Eyelet, cross, and satin-stitch. Strawberry border. Large tree, vases of flowers, animals, birds, and green bank. Verse 43 (var.).   *Miss Georgie Bassett*

FRY, MARY. 1724. 12 yrs. 9½″ x 15½″. [Born Jericho, L. I., in 1712.] 1 alphabet. Eyelet, cross, and satin-stitch. Cross-lines, conventional cross-borders. Names and initials on sampler: Mary Frye, M. W., H. W., I. W., William Willis. Mary Wil . . . Verses 581, 582.
                                    Mrs. E. C. Tyson

FRYE, HULDAH. 1747. Andover [Mass. 10 yrs. Born May 13, 1737.]. 8″ x 10″. 2 alphabets. Cross-stitch. Greek fret border. Bird, tree, and lion. "Time how short, Eternity how long." Verses 128 (1, var.), 248 (1, var.).   *Miss Charlotte Osgood*

FULLER, ABIGAIL. 1775. [Warner, N. H.?] 19 yrs. 10″ x 13″. 2 alphabets. Eyelet and cross-stitch. Conventional cross-border. Verse 132 (1, var.).   *Mrs. William H. Woodberry*

FULLER, POLLY. 1790. Needham [Mass.]. [4 yrs.?] 8″ x 10″. 2 alphabets. Eyelet, tent, and cross-stitch.   *Miss Emily F. Allen*

FULTON, FRANCES BURNS. 1786. 7″ x 14″. 1 alphabet. Cross-stitch. Plain cross-border.
                                    Mrs. Thomas A. Lawton

FURLONG, ELIZABETH. 1775. 7″ x 8″. 2 alphabets. Cross, satin, and hem-stitch. Hemstitched border, with a solid triangle design inside.   *Mrs. Sarah F. Bayley*

GALE, MARY. 1787. [Bangor, Me.?] 14 yrs. 16½" x 13½". Alphabet. Cross and satin-stitch. Border, Greek vine with leaves. Landscape, with flowers, birds, trees, etc. Verse 496.

Mrs. S. Gale Treat

GANSEVOORT, ——. 1791. 22" x 10½". Alphabet. Cross-stitch. Vase with roses. "Leonard Gansevoort, Mary Gansevoort, Maria Gansevoort, Arietta Gansevoort, Catharine Douw, Eliza Richards, John Gansevoort, Rachel Douw."

Albany Institute and Historical and Art Society

GANSEVOORT, MARIA. 1790. Albany [N. Y. Born February 17, 1778.]. 15" x 20½". Satin and cross-stitch. Strawberry border. "Leonard and Mary Gansevoort, 1790. Maria Gansevoort, Harrietta, Katharine Douw and John Gansevoort." Birds, butterflies, etc. Federal bower with 11 states of the Union, surmounted by gateway with birds.

Mrs. Marcus T. Hun

GARRISON, PATIENCE. 1796. Trenton [N. J.]. 13 yrs. Born [September 30] 1783. 16" x 18". Cross-stitch. Cross-border. House, trees, flowers, etc. *Mrs. George W. Yeandle*

GATCOMB, DORCAS. 1732. Boston [Mass.]. 7½" x 15¼". 3 alphabets. Cross-stitch. Elaborate 5-inch border of animals, trees, birds, and other designs. Verse 490 (var.).

Mrs. Charles E. Cotting

GATES, MARY. 1796. 17 yrs. 1 alphabet. Cross-stitch. Triple strawberry border. Trees, Adam and Eve, flowers and bucks. Verses 384, 385. *Mr. G. H. Buek*

GAY, ELIZABETH. 1787. 11 yrs. 12" x 10". 2 alphabets. Eyelet and cross-stitch.

Mrs. L. A. Arnold

GEER, PETHENY. 1758. 10 yrs. 9" x 31". 4 alphabets. Eyelet, cross-stitch, and other stitches. Cross-border at top. Verse 128 (1, var.). *Mrs. C. S. Cobb*

GERRISH, MARY. 1798. 13 yrs. [Boscawen, N. H.] 12" x 11". Yellow canvas. 3 alphabets. Hem and cross-stitch. Flower borders, growing out of grass at the bottom.

14 Sumner Road, Cambridge

GERRY, CATHERINE. 1796. 9 yrs. 11½" x 20½". 5 alphabets. Eyelet, cross, and 6 kinds of fancy, open-work stitches. Triangular design. *Miss Bessie H. Lyman*

GIBBS, SARAH. 1749. Newport [R. I.]. 11 yrs. 2 alphabets. Satin and cross-stitch. Trefoil border, carnation cross-borders. Elaborate carnation and tulip design in center. Verse 343 (1). *Mrs. J. West Roosevelt*

GIBSON, SARAH. 1784. Pelham [Mass.]. 27 yrs. "Born Sept 26, 1757". 4" x 8". 2 alphabets. Cross-stitch. Verse 200. *Mrs. J. A. Noble*

GIDDINGE, LYDIA. [Ipswich, Mass.?] 12 yrs. 19" x 23". 3 alphabets. Eyelet, satin, and cross-stitch. Strawberry border, with roses in upper corners. Birds in corners, dog running after a deer. *Mrs. Charles Kane Cobb*

GIFFING, HARIOT. 1799. New York City. 7⅝" x 10". 2 alphabets. Cross-stitch. Vine border.

Miss Estelle Clements

GILKEY, SALLY. 1795. Born September 27, 1779. 14½" x 17½". 3 alphabets. All kinds of fancy stitches. Rose border. Divided into 10 sections. Trees, birds, vases, etc. Family names on sampler: "Betty Gilkey, Born July 29, 1775. Martha Gilkey, Born Au 23, 1777. Sally, Born Sep 27, 1779. Phebe, Born June 3, 1782. Ann, Born May 25, 1784. Mary, Born June 11, 1788. Wm & Isaac, Born May 17, 1790. My Daddy was born April 27, 1757. He dyed November the 13, Aged Forty 3 years. My Mamma was born April the 27, 1755. A E Forty 4 years." Verses 606 (1, var.), 609 (1, var.). *Prof. George C. Chase*

GILL, MARY. 1757. 13 yrs. 8" x 10". 3 alphabets. Eyelet and cross-stitch. Vine, bird, and basket. Verse 343 (1, var.). Initials: I G. N G. M S. W S. S G. L G. R G.
Mrs. Henry J. Irick

GILMORE, KEZIAH. 1799. 8 yrs. [Born April 26, 1790.] 11" x 17". 3 alphabets. Cross-stitch. Vine border. Weeping willow, with verse in lower half and inscription, "Sarah Gilmore born Jan. 6th 1797", evidently a younger sister. Verse 528. *Mrs. John V. Craven*

GITHERNON, INCREASE. 1796. 19" x 16". Stem and cross-stitch. Carnation and tulip border. House, sheep, lambs, and trees. Verses 13, 395 (4). *Mrs. Stanley H. Lowndes*

GLASSEL, JANE M. Born November 17, 1785. 28" x 17". 3 alphabets. Strawberry border. Family tree in center. Record of family names and dates: "Andrew Glassel and Elizabeth Taylor were married October 21, 1776. Milly Glassel was born June the 25, 1778; John Glassel was born Oct. the 28, 1780; Mary —— Glassel was born May the 4, 1783; Helen B. Glassel was born (?) the 28, 1785; Jane M. Glassel was born November the 17, 1785; James M. Glassel was born January the 1, 1790; Andrew Glassel was born May 15, (?); Robert was born May 18, 1795; William Glassel was born May the 17, 1797."

GLAZIER, ELVIRA. [West Boylston, Mass.] 11" x 12". Alphabets. Cross-stitch. Strawberry and alphabet border. *Mrs. Melvin W. Longley*

GLOVER, MARY. 1760. [Marblehead.] 10 yrs. 11½" x 16". 2 alphabets. Eyelet, stem, satin, and cross-stitch. Baskets of flowers and trees, also Caleb and Joshua carrying the grapes of Eschol. Verse 352. *Estate of Miss Sarah Haskell Crocker*

GODDARD, HANNAH. [Cir. 1762.] Born October 10, 1750. 6" x 17". 1 alphabet. Eyelet and cross-stitch. *Mrs. John Brooks*

GOODWIN, BECKY. 1774. Charlestown [Mass.]. 14 yrs. 8" x 12". 1 alphabet. Cross-stitch. Simple cross-borders. Verse 128. *Groton Historical Society*

GOODWIN, P[RISCILLA]. 1790. [Salem, N. J.] 8½" x 12". 3 alphabets. Eyelet, satin, and cross-stitch. Line border on sides; rosettes across top. *Mrs. Oakford Woodnutt Acton*

GORE, ABIGAIL. 1797. Boston [Mass. Born July 27, 1784.]. 14½" x 10½". 2 alphabets. Eyelet, satin, and cross-stitch. Greek fret border. House and lamb. Verse 233.
Miss Mary H. Leeds

GORE, ZEBIAH. 1791. Boston [Mass.]. 11 yrs. Born July 27, 1780. 15" x 17½". 2 alphabets. Eyelet, satin, and cross-stitch, and bullion-stitch for sheep. Eyelet-stitch border on three sides. Landscape with house, trees, dog, birds, sheep, and a shepherd and shepherdess. The background above is filled with black cross-stitch, and the bottom is completely filled with fine cross-stitch. "Now we are Caused to Live there's nothing I Esteem Worth learning but the way to Die." Illustrated. *Miss Mary H. Leeds*

GORHAM, SALLY. 1795. 13 yrs. Born December 28, 1781. 11" x 12". 4 alphabets. Stem, satin, and cross-stitch. Strawberry vine cross-border. Scene with house, trees, etc. Verse 228.
Mrs. Herman Daggett Clark, Jr.

GOULD, ESTHER. 17[??]. [Cir. 1798.] "Agusta." Born 1785. 11" x 14". 4 alphabets. Eyelet, satin, and cross-stitch. Hemstitched edge. Basket of flowers. Verses 128 (1, var.), 667.
Miss Caroline F. Ware

GOVE, POLLY. 9" x 13½". 2 alphabets. Cross-stitch. Unfinished. Verse 243.
Estate of James L. Little, Esq.

GRATZ, RICHEA. 1789. [Philadelphia, Pa. Born in 1774.] 9½" x 20". 3 alphabets. Eyelet and cross-stitch. Strawberry-vine border. Verse 621 (1). *Miss Laura Mordecai*

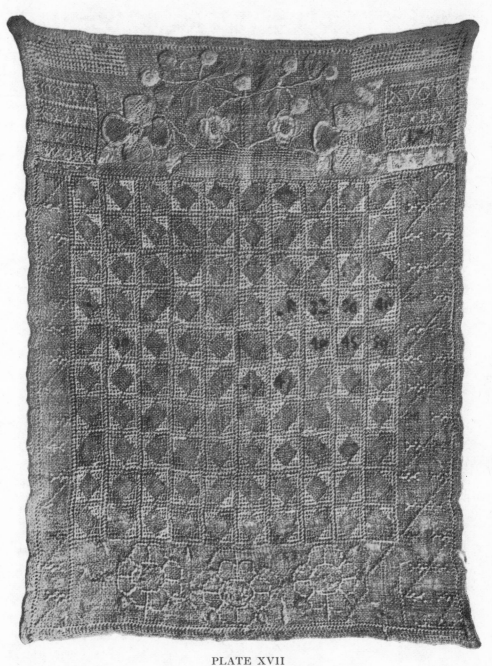

PLATE XVII

MARY ELLIS'S SAMPLER. 1743
Owned by Miss Ellen F. Vose

PLATE XVIII

Elizabeth Pecker's Sampler. 1733
Owned by Mrs. Henry E. Coe

GRAY, ELIZABETH COULTAS. [Before 1760. Gray's Ferry, Philadelphia.] 9¾" x 12¼". Petit-point and cross-stitch. Design, bunch of flowers in basket, fills entire sampler.
Mrs. Robert Bean

GRAY, SALLY ROPES. 1796. Salem [Mass.]. 8 yrs. Born March 27, 1788. 7½" x 16". 2 alphabets. Satin and cross-stitch. Lambs eating strawberries. *Essex Institute*

GREEN, BETSY. 1798. Alexandria [Va.]. 12 yrs. 17" x 20½". 6 alphabets. Great variety of stitches. Border, festoons of eyelets and bunches of strawberries. Verse 202 (1, var.).
Virginia L. Maury

GREENE, CATHERINE. 1785. 11 yrs. 16" x 12". 2 alphabets. Chain and cross-stitch. House with tree on either side. *Charles T. Howard, Esq.*

GREENE, MARY. 1766. 11 yrs. 9½" x 13½". 3 alphabets. Stem, satin, and cross-stitch. Conventional strawberry border. Conventional rose, tulip, and carnation cross-border in middle, small border at bottom. Verses 488 (var.), 598. *Mrs. Henry E. Coe*

GREENE, SARAH. [1760–65.] Boston [Mass.]. 12 yrs. 14" x 7½". 4 alphabets. Stem, eyelet, cat, and cross-stitch. Verse 593. *Mrs. Roger Wolcott*

GREENLEAF, ELIZABETH. 1768. Newburyport [Mass.]. 10 yrs. 8" x 13½". 1 alphabet. Cross-stitch. Fancy cross-border at top. "Deaths terror is the mountain Faith removes Tis Faith discovers destruction. Believe and look with triumph on the Tomb"
Mrs. J. Lewis Stackpole

GREENLEAF, ELIZABETH. 1788. Haverhill [Mass.]. 10 yrs. 17" x 18". Cross, satin, and chain-stitch. 2 alphabets. Leaves and flower border. Two girls, a boy or man with a parasol, a bird, a horse, trees and flowers. Verse 625. *Francis B. Manning, Esq.*

GRENELL, BETSY. 1792. 13 yrs. 6" x 8". 1 alphabet. Cross-stitch. *George Bird, Esq.*

GRIDLEY, ANNA. 1783. 13 yrs. 8" x 21". 3 alphabets. Cross-stitch. Cross-borders. Conventional birds and baskets. Verses 128, 508. *Mrs. Frederick F. Thompson*

GRIGNOR, MARGARET. 1747. 9 yrs. 9" x 18". 2 alphabets. Stem, satin, and cross-stitch. Border of Greek fret, rose, cross, vine, strawberry. "Life is decietful and beauty is vain but a Woman that Feareth the Lord she shall" . . . *Mrs. George A. Plimpton*

GROVER, ELIZABETH. July 16, 1784. Philadelphia, Pa. 17" x 17". Flat and cross-stitch. Carnation border; rose, strawberry, and vine cross-borders. Verses 509, 615.
Mrs. Charles Dickinson

HACKER, REBEKAH. 1786. Salem [Mass.]. 9 yrs. 13" x 16". 4 alphabets. Eyelet, French knot, long, and cross-stitch. Saw-tooth border. Garden of Eden, with Adam and Eve and Cain and Abel in Quaker dress. Verses 128 (1, var.), 248 (var.). *Miss Anna Hazen Howell*

HACKETT, ELIZABETH. [Cir. 1782.] Salisbury Point [Mass.]. Born "Sept. 1771." 9" x 10½". 3 alphabets. Cross-stitch. Conventional design. *Mrs. Dolly C. Ames*

HAIL, MARY. 1763. Born 1754. 10" x 20". 2 alphabets. Eyelets and cross-stitch. Plain cross-stitch border at top. Verse 498. *Mrs. David P. Penhallow*

HALE, POLLY. 1791. [Mass.] 7¼" x 7½". Alphabet. Satin and cross-stitch. Cross-border. Acorn design at bottom. *Mrs. Edwin L. Thompson*

HALL, ELIZABETH. 1750. Dorchester [Mass.]. 12 yrs. Born 1738. 8" x 11". 3 alphabets. Eyelet and cross-stitch. *Miss Marion Stanley Abbot*

HALL, NANCY. August, 1788. Providence [R. I. 12 yrs.]. 14" x 16". "Miss Polly Balch's School." Stem, satin, and cross-stitch. Border, rose, carnation, hyacinth, and myrtle. University Hall, Brown University, in center of oval; President's reception, above, and more people going to President's house, below. Verse 628. Illustrated?
Mrs. W. C. Greene

HALLEN, ABIGAIL. 1750. Mystic [Conn.]. 9 yrs. 8" x 11". Alphabet. Cross-stitch. Vine border. Verse 191.
Mrs. George A. Plimpton

HALLMAN, MARY. Barren Hill, Pa. 13½" x 15". 2 alphabets. Cross-stitch, plain and fancy. Border of diamond shapes. Conventional flower-pots, birds and animals. Verse 490 (var.).
Mrs. Bradbury Bedell

HAMLIN, ANNE. 1790. Providence [R. I.]. Born March 12, 1776. Probably "Miss Polly Balch's School." 9" x 9". 2 alphabets. Stem, satin, and cross-stitch. Greek fret border, top and bottom; straight cross on sides. Strawberry plants. Verse 628.
Miss Sarah S. Mumford

HAMLIN, MEHITABLE. 1798. Providence [R. I.]. 9 yrs. 8" x 12". 2 alphabets. Satin and cross-stitch. Cross-border. Rosebuds. Verse 661.
Mrs. H. M. Preston

HAMMOND, ABIGAIL. 1743. 7 yrs. 8" x 12". 8 alphabets. Cross-stitch. Cross-borders, one conventionalized carnation. Debased carnation.
C. E. Goodspeed, Esq., 1917

HANCE, MARY. 1780. Shrewsbury [N. J.]. 12" x 12". 3 alphabets. Eyelet and cross-stitch. Trees.
Robert H. Oakley, Esq.

HANCOCK, FANNY. 1736. 11 yrs. 3 alphabets. Conventional designs. Hemstitched edge.
In Machias, Me.?

HARDING, PRUDENCE. 1795. 18" x 18". Partial alphabet. Cross, satin, stem, eyelet, queen, and cat-stitch. Rose-wreath border. Cross-border of single-stitch. Verse 647.
Fitchburg Antique Shop, 1917

HARDYMAN, HENRIETTA MARIA. 1765. 2 alphabets. Tent, satin, eyelet, and cross-stitch. Border of vine and strawberry blossoms and berries. Scene with large basket filled with fruit, trees, large deer, and two small dogs.
Mrs. W. W. Richardson

HARIMAN, ELIZABETH. [Cir. 1789.] Born April 23, 1777. 12" x 12". 3 alphabets. Cross-stitch.
Colonial Dames of the State of New York

HARRIS, AMEE. 1767. 12 yrs. 9" x 12". 2 alphabets. Cross-stitch. Trefoil border. Tulip cross-border. Verse 343 (1, var.).
Harriet A. Barstow

HARRIS, BETSY. [1790.] 16" x 12". 3 alphabets. Cross-stitch.
Mrs. F. A. Waterman

HARRIS, HITTY. 1775. Concord [N. H.]. 11 yrs. 8" x 10". Mustard-colored canvas. 2 alphabets. Cross-stitch. Greek fret cross-border.
Miss Annie Haven Thwing

HARRIS, POLLY. [1750. New England.] 9 yrs. 10" x 7½". 1 alphabet. Eyelet and cross-stitch. Saw-tooth border. Horses, grass, shrubs, etc.
Rev. Glenn Tilley Morse

HART, LYDIA. February 4, 1731. 2 alphabets. Tent, eyelet, satin, and cross-stitch. Cross-borders of strawberry, trefoil, scroll, and several different Greek fret designs. Verse 128 (var.).

HART, MARY ELIZA. 1771. Charleston [S. C.]. 7" x 12½". 3 alphabets. Eyelet, hemstitch, satin, stem, and cross-stitch. Hemstitched edge and Greek fret borders. "Remember thy Creator," etc.
Mrs. John F. Bennett

HASKELL, RUTH. [Cir. 1760.] 11 yrs. Alphabet. Eyelet, petit-point, and cross-stitch. Strawberry border on three sides. Adam and Eve scene at bottom. Verse 9. Illustrated.
Society for the Preservation of New England Antiquities

HASKELL, SARAH. 1782. Lunenburg [Pa.?]. Born February 18, 1775. 10" x 14". 2 alphabets. Cross-stitch. Greek fret border. Conventional flowers, etc., in cross-borders. Verses 182 (1), 248 (1, var.), 490. *Mrs. Frank S. Willock*

HASTINGS, DORCAS. 1793. Lincoln [Mass.]. 8 yrs. 7½" x 5". Alphabet. Eyelet and cross-stitch. Simple border. Baskets of fruit. *Miss Caroline L. Manett*

HATHAWAY, ANNE. 1797. 7 yrs. 12½" x 12½". 2 alphabets. Cross-stitch. Plain border. Cross-borders of carnations and acorns. Six deer and three flowers.

I. "Books & needle both content to make a
house wif and a friend"

II. "Fair Philomel she lost her tongue
and in a tedious sampler sewed her mind"
Mrs. Siegfried Wachsman

HATHAWAY, REBEKAH. 1794. 11 yrs. Verses 238, 379. *Miss Helen F. Kimball*

HAVEN, ANNE. 1789. Holliston. 9" x 8". 2 alphabets. Tree design. Verse 129a.
Miss Laura Weeks

HAVENS, MARY CATHERINE. 10 yrs. 8½" x 11½". 1 alphabet. Cross-stitch. "Remember you are in the hands of God". *Miss Cornelia Horsford*

HAWKS, POLLY. 1798. 13 yrs. Born November 4, 1785. 13" x 18". 6 alphabets. Eyelet, outline, chain, cross, satin, and stem-stitch. Sides and bottom, border of vines and flowers; at top, diamonds. Verse 235. *Miss Edith S. Hall*

HAWKS, SIDNEY. 1794. 8 yrs. 8¼" x 10¼". 2 alphabets. Cross-stitch. Strawberry border. Basket of flowers, trees, dogs, etc. *Museum of Pocumtuck Valley Memorial Association*

HAYNES, ANNA. 1775. 8 yrs. 10" x 11¾". 3 alphabets. Satin, stem, eyelet, chain, cross-stitch, and hemstitch. Border, strawberries, dogs, birds, flowers, plants, tree, and sunflower. Crosses at bottom. Verse 363. *Dedham Historical Society*

H[AYNES], A[NNA] M[ARIA]. 1762. Hamburg. 9 yrs. 5" x 16". Lace, and cross-designs in white. *Mrs. G. Clem Goodrich*

HAYNES, SALLY. 1785. Boston [Mass.]. 12 yrs. Born in Boston, June 8, 1773. 9¾" x 10½". 3 alphabets. Eyelet, chain, hemstitch, satin, and cross-stitch. Strawberry border. Verses 10 (1, var.), 92 (1, var.). *Dedham Historical Society*

HAYS, SLOMEY. 1788. Boston [Mass.]. 9 yrs. 7" x 17". 2 alphabets. Eyelet, stem, satin, and cross-stitch. Hemstitched border. Indian design with chickens, animals, basket of flowers, bush, etc. Verse 128 (1, var.). *Mrs. Edward Cohen*

HAZARD, ALICE. 1764. [Little Neck, Narragansett, R. I.] 9 yrs. 13" x 16½". 2 alphabets. Satin, tent, and cross-stitch. Conventional border. Cross-borders. Conventionalized house, tree, fence, bush, and birds. Verses 128 (1, var.), 499. *Miss Mary A. Hazard*

HAZARD, SARAH. 1740. 13 yrs. 8¼" x 16½". 4 alphabets. Eyelet, satin, and cross-stitch. Vine border. Elaborate flower designs with birds. Verse 489. *Miss Susan Woodman*

HAZELTINE, ABIGAIL. 1777. [Salem, Mass.] 14 yrs. 15" x 17". 2 alphabets. Chain, eyelet, stem, satin, and cross-stitch. Strawberries, flowers, lambs in border, also Greek fret design. Dogs, trees, and birds. *Mrs. Edward M. Vickery*

HEARD, NANCY. 1794. [Stepney, Conn.] 13" x 16". Stem, satin, and cross-stitch. Border, detached flowers of different varieties. Basket [unfinished] and 2 plants. Verse 644.

Robert Fridenberg, Dealer

HEATH, JANE. 8 yrs. [Virginia.] 18" x 24". 4 alphabets. Cross-stitch. Strawberry border. Colonial brick house, pine trees, etc. *Mrs. William W. Richardson*

HENDERSON, JANE. 1795. 10 yrs. "Chesterfield School." 17" x 21½". Cross-stitch. Conventionalized vine border. House on top of hill, also man, woman, bushes, trees, and animals. Verses 383, 594 (1). *Miss Susan B. Minor*

HERBERT, ELIZABETH. 1764. Salem, Mass. 12 yrs. 15" x 15". 6 alphabets. Stem, French knot, eyelet, satin, and cross-stitch. Landscape border, showing shepherdess with sheep, fisherman, pond, trees, animals, birds and butterflies, etc. Strawberry cross-border. Verses 194, 495 (var.). *Miss Ellen H. Bailey*

HEYWOOD, HANNAH. [Cir. 1792. Royalston, Mass.] Born January 6, 1781. 8" x 10½". 1 alphabet. Eyelet, feather, and cross-stitch. Slip-stitch border. Conventional design.

Miss Mary Heywood Dean

[HILL, MARY. Cir. 1770.] 7" x 9". 2 alphabets. Cross-stitch and petit-point. Vine, carnation, and Greek fret borders. [Unfinished.] Verse 358. *The Misses Kenyon*

HILL, MARY. 1773. 3½" x 6½". 1 alphabet; parts of others. Cross-stitch. Verses 128 (1), 342.

The Misses Kenyon

HOLBROOK, ALOUA. [1796.] 12" x 7". 2 alphabets. Flat, chain, and cross-stitch. Chain-stitch border. *Miss Edith R. Blanchard*

HOLBROOK, EDENY. 11 yrs. 7" x 14½". 2 alphabets. Cross-stitch. Trees in center.

Miss Edna H. Barger

HOLBROOK, MELLA [MELETIAH. Cir. 1791. Born in Bellingham, Mass., August 23, 1780.]. 8" x 14½". 2 alphabets. Cross-stitch. Baskets of flowers.

Benjamin Stafford Newton, Esq.

HOLDEN, KATHERINE. 1733. 14⅜" x 10". 1 alphabet. Satin and cross-stitch. Rose and bell border. Verses 186, 343. Illustrated.

Miss M. Frances Babcock and Mrs. Winslow Upton

HOLLINSHEAD, BEULAH W. 1797. [Moorestown, N. J.] 13 yrs. [Born July 9, 1784.] 16" x 20½". Stem, tent, flat, and cross-stitch. Strawberry border. "Joshua M. Hollinshead was born —— of July in the year of our Lord 1786. Jane M. Hollinshead was born the 29 September 1792. Departed this life July 31, 1798. Aged 5 yrs. 10 mo. 6 days." House on a terrace, with trees, sheep, and shepherd with his dog. Verse 284.

Mrs. S. A. Cunningham

HOLMES, ELIZABETH. [Cir. 1770.] 10 yrs. 10" x 12". 1 alphabet. Stem, cross, satin, eyelet, and hem-stitch. Simple cross-borders. Bird and strawberries. Verse 129 (var.).

Miss R. Wiswell Ex. Deposited in the Old South Meeting House, Boston

HOLTON, MARY D. 1796. Northfield [Mass.]. 15" x 17". 3 alphabets. Cross-stitch. Hemstitched edge. Large vase of flowers, rose bushes, trees, etc. *Mrs. Elizabeth A. Hubbard*

HOLYOKE, ELIZABETH. [Cir. 1782.] Salem [Mass.]. xiii yrs. 10½" x 12½". Alphabet. Crossstitch. Vine and cross-border. *Miss Susan Ward Osgood*

HOLYOKE, MARY. 1741. 11 yrs. Born April 30, 1730. 8½" x 16". 2 alphabets. Eyelet, stem, satin, and cross-stitch. Cross-borders. Elaborate strawberry at top and bottom, with conventional adaptation of Greek fret. *Estate of James L. Little, Esq.*

HOLYOKE, PRISCILLA. 1752. 12 yrs. 9" x 17". 2 alphabets. Satin, feather, stem, eyelet, and cross-stitch. Inconspicuous cross-lines. Cross-stitch crosses. Verse 128 (var.).
Estate of James L. Little, Esq.

HOLYOKE, SUSANNA. [Cir. 1790.] Salem, Mass. 10 yrs. 8" x 11". Alphabet. Cross-stitch. Cross-border. "Idleness is the mother of vice." *Miss Susan Ward Osgood*

HOOKER, HANNAH. 1728. 7 yrs. 6½" x 17½". Cross-stitch. Verse 492.
Newport Historical Society

HOOKER, RUTH. 1773. Farmington. 5⅝" x 8". 2 alphabets. Cross-stitch. Narrow cross-stitch border. *Mrs. E. Morgan*

HOOTON, SARAH. 6" x 12". 3 alphabets. Satin and cross-stitch. Greek fret border.
M. B. Lemon, Dealer

HOPPING, MARIA. [1796.] 17" x 17". Eyelet, stem, satin, and cross-stitch. Design, First Baptist Church in Providence, R. I. Verse 40. *Miss Caroline E. Briggs*

HOPTON, PERESE. 1786. 6" x 18". 1 alphabet. Cross-stitch. *Mrs. N. James Rouse*

HORNER, ELIZA. 1788. [Philadelphia.] 12 yrs. 16" x 20". 3 alphabets. Eyelet, stem, satin, queen, and cross-stitch. Floral border of strawberry, rose, forget-me-not, violet, etc. Beatitudes at the top. Verse 209. *Edward Horner Coates, Esq.*

HORNSBY, SARAH. [Cir. 1793.] "Williamsburg" [Va.]. Born October 17, 1780. 11¼" x 15½". 1 alphabet. Cross-stitch, very fine. Ornamental vine border. Tree of Life, Adam and Eve, serpent holding apple, and detached figures such as birds, trees, castles, baskets of flowers, etc. Verse 610. Names on sampler: "Hannah Hornsby born March the 21st 1771, Mildred Hornsby born February the 20th 1774, Joseph Hornsby born March the 28th 1777, Thomas Hornsby born January the 12th 1779, Sarah Hornsby born October the 17th 1780." *Mrs. James Henry Watson*

HORTON, POLLY. 1788. 10" x 14". 1 alphabet. Bird's-eye, satin, and cross-stitch. Plain border all around and three more elaborate cross-borders in center. Shepherds, sheep, and trees. Verse 629. *Mrs. Thomas A. Lawton*

[HORWELL, ANN (MAY)]. 1798. [Alexandria, Va.] Made after her marriage to Richard Horwell. Initials: "R x A" 16" x 20". Liberty Tree, flowers, and crowned hearts. "H" Verse 3. *Miss Frances H. Massoletti*

HOWARD, MAIESON. 1787. Bridgewater [Mass.]. 8 yrs. 10½" x 12". 2 alphabets. Flat and cross-stitch. Hemstitched edge, cross-stitch border, flat-stitch cross-border at bottom. Large tree, flowers, and various devices in lower corners. Verse 137.
Mrs. John Rogers, Jr.

HOWELL, LYDIA. 1755. 12" x 9". 3 alphabets. Eyelet and cross-stitch. Strawberry cross-borders. Names on sampler: "Jacob Howell, Mary Howell, Mary Howell." Verse 42.
Miss Sarah Rebecca Nicholson

HOWELL, SARAH. 1731. Philadelphia [Pa.]. 12" x 14". Satin, cross-stitch, and other fine stitches. Carnation border, and rose, carnation, strawberry, and conventional leaf cross-borders. Names given: "Sarah Howell, Jacob Howell, Sarah Howell, Jane Howell." Verses 181, 183, 344 (1), 345 (var.). Illustrated. *Mrs. Clayton McElroy*

HUBBARD, HEPHZIBAH. [1761. Middletown, Conn. About 6 yrs.] 5⅝" x 7½". 1 alphabet. Cross-stitch. Simple dividing lines. *Mrs. Amos Bush McNairy*

Hubbs, Dorothy. 1790. 11½" x 15¼". 4 alphabets. Flat and cross-stitch. Vine border. Verse 343 (1). "Her heart the one thing needfull that good part witch Mary chose withall".
Pennsylvania Museum, Memorial Hall, Fairmount Park

Hughes, Phebe. 1796. Providence [R. I.]. 7 yrs. 11" x 13½". 2 alphabets. Stem and cross-stitch. Strawberry bed at bottom. To the right of verse, two tulips and two birds. Verse 231.   *Miss Mary Anne Greene*

Hughes, Susannah. 1793. 9 yrs. 14" x 18". 1 alphabet. Stem and cross-stitch. Vine border with morning-glories, rosebuds, and passion flowers. Large hearts and crowns. Verses 66 (1, var.), 225, 515 (1, 2, var.).   *Robert R. Jordan, Dealer*

Hull, Rachel. 1795. [14 yrs. Born at Morris(?), N. J.] March 11, 1781. 9" x 10½". 2 alphabets. Eyelet, star, satin, and cross-stitch. Strawberry border at top. Diamonds.
Mrs. J. S. Gale

Humphreys, Ann. 1796. 10 yrs. 9¾" x 15½". 5 alphabets. Stem, eyelet, and chain-stitch. Verses 387 (1), 631.   *Pennsylvania Museum, Memorial Hall, Fairmount Park*

Humphreys, Jane. 1771. 11 yrs. 15" x 12½". Hollie-point, lace, and drawn filet. Large basket with flowers occupies most of sampler. Illustrated.
Pennsylvania Museum, Memorial Hall, Fairmount Park, Philadelphia

Hunt, Content. 1799. Norton [Mass.]. 9 yrs. 16" x 22". 1 alphabet. Stem, satin, and cross-stitch. Carnation and rose border. Man and woman, house, trees, birds, lambs, etc. Verse 129 (var.).   *Mrs. H. J. Gilbert*

Huntington, Hannah. [1766.] 12 yrs. [Born in 1754.] 11½" x 14". 3 alphabets. Eyelet, queen, single, and double cross-stitch. On either side, poles with grapevine running up it and conventionalized bunches of grapes at top; other flowers are growing on vine and the left-hand side is unfinished. Band across center, with conventionalized rose and rose-sprays. At bottom, row of conventionalized thistles, poppies, carnations, strawberry plant, etc. In center, at top, a conventionalized rose-tree. "Be not wise in thine own eyes fear the Lord and depart from evil."   *George H. May, Esq.*

Huston, Esther. 1782. 8 yrs. 5 alphabets. Cross-stitch. "Taught by Mrs. Brunton." "Remember now thy Creator", etc.   *Helen C. Littlefield*

Hutchinson, Lydia. 1727. 13 yrs. 18" x 18". Cross-stitch. Strawberry, quatrefoil, and Greek fret cross-borders. Verse 128 (1, var.).   *Massachusetts Historical Society*

Hyrne, Harriot. 1774. [Clear Spring Plantation on Ashley River, S. C.] 9 yrs. Born July 28, 1765. 8" x 19". 2 alphabets. Eyelet, satin, and cross-stitch. Strawberry border. Three roses in a medallion. "Remember thy Creator", etc. *Mrs. Emma Drayton Grimké*

Hyrne, Harriot. 1774. [Charleston, S. C.] 9 yrs. 18" x 18½". 3 alphabets. Cross-stitch. Pomegranate border at bottom. "Remember thy Creator", etc. *Mrs. J. Drayton Grimké*

Ide, Leafea. [1796?] 10 yrs. 15" x 15". 2 alphabets. Cross-stitch. House with tree on either side. "Let Virtue be made for her."   *Mrs. J. F. P. Lawton*

Ilsley, Charlotte. 1773. Portland [Me. Born 1763.]. 13" x 21". Satin and cross-stitch. Floral and vine border. Verse 355, and about sixteen lines of pious sentiment too faded to be read.   *Miss Clara Mossman Hill*

Ingall, Harriot. 1799. Taunton [Mass.]. 8 yrs. 7½" x 12". 2 alphabets. Tent, cat, and cross-stitch. Angular border of cross-stitch, with triangular trees and ornaments. Large tree, dog, elk, and bird at bottom; in center, Colonial house, trees, and birds.
Mrs. J. S. Rounds

PLATE XIX

DOROTHY LYNDE'S SAMPLER. 1757
Old South Meeting House, Boston
Plate presented by the Worcester members of the Massachusetts Society of the Colonial Dames

PLATE XX

MARY WEBB'S SAMPLER.   York, Pa.   1760
Owned by Mrs. Samuel C. Rumford

INGALLS, RUTHY. 1786. 8″ x 10″. 2 alphabets. Queen and cross-stitch. Cross and vine border. Carnation.   *Miss Caroline M. Burnham*

INGELL, REBEKAH. 1791. Taunton [Mass.]. 8 yrs. 6½″ x 8½″. 2 alphabets. Cross-stitch. Narrow border of cross-stitch. "Let Wisdom direct thy steps."   *Mrs. J. S. Rounds*

IRELAND, PHEBE. 1793. [Cohansey, N. J.] 14 yrs. 12″ x 9″. 3 alphabets. Stem, tent, queen, satin, and cross-stitch. Cross-borders. Geometrical designs and conventionalized flowers. Initials: "S B T E I V A I E I P I D I A I A I." Verse 490 (var.).
Cumberland County, N. J., Historical Society

IVERS, HANNAH. [Cir. 1780.] 1 alphabet. Cross, satin, stem, petit-point, and hem-stitch. Carnation border across top and on sides; rosebud and strawberry cross-borders. In lower section, two shepherds sitting on the ground beneath trees; birds flying above; dogs and sheep in grass. Verse 505.   *Mrs. A. Lawrence Lowell*

IVES, BETSY. July 31, 1778. [Hale Farm, Beverly.] "Sarah Stivour's School" [Salem, Mass.]. 11 yrs. 7½″ x 10½″. 2 alphabets. Cross-stitch and the long-stitch which was characteristic of this school. Hemstitched edge. Scene with 4 sheep standing in grass. Verse 129 (var.).
Mrs. Robert Hale Bancroft

JACKMAN, EMILY E. Yorkshire, Cattaraugus County, N. Y. 12 yrs. 10¾″ x 12¼″. 3 alphabets. Cross-stitch. Cross-stitch border and cross-borders. House, tree, and fence.
A. Stainforth, Dealer

JACKSON, MARIA. 1790. Providence [R. I.]. 12 yrs. 12″ x 15″. Alphabet. Long, knot, cross-stitch, and laid-work. Vine border with ornamental-pink design. Strawberry plants, pinks, roses, and blue flower. Verse 630.   *Miss Ellen Chase*

JACOBS, MARCY. 177(?). [Ipswich, Mass.?] 11 yrs. 17″ x 17″. 2 alphabets. Eyelet, French knot, satin, stem, chain, cross-stitch, and laid-work. Elaborate border in laid-work and stem-stitch of flowers, grass, vase with flowers, and birds on boughs. Verse 600.
Miss Harriet Perkins

JACOBS, MARY. 1776. Scituate [Mass.]. 24 yrs. Born January 27, 1752. 8″ x 10½″. Alphabet. Eyelet and cross-stitch. Simple cross-stitch lines. Verses 187 (var.), 490 (var.).
Miss Edith Tilden

JACOBS, SARAH. 1753. Scituate [Mass.]. 13 yrs. 6½″ x 6½″. 2 alphabets. Cross-stitch. Hemstitched border. Verse 128 (1, var.).   *Miss Antoinette Clapp*

JAMES, MARY. 1798. [New Castle County, Del.] 13″ x 14½″. Stem, satin, flat, and cross-stitch. Detached sprays of strawberries, tulips, roses, etc., and birds, in border. Verses 525, 526 (var.).   *Miss Elizabeth K. Clark*

JAMES, SUSANNAH. 1788. [New Castle County, Del.] 8 yrs. 12″ x 17″. 3 alphabets. Eyelet, tent, satin, and cross-stitch. Rose, carnation, tulip, and strawberry border (worked in detached clusters). Verse 211. [Teacher, Mme. Abigail Giles.]   *Mrs. L. B. Rowley*

JANCY, JUDITH. 1786. 5 alphabets. Eyelet, feather, and cross-stitch. Cross-stitch and feather-stitch border. Bird in lower right-hand corner. Verse 369. *Mrs. Augustus Bailey Small*

JANNEY, HANNAH. 1785. 2 alphabets. Eyelet, chain, tent, and cross-stitch. Rose and vine border rising out of vases at lower corners. Strawberry cross-borders, also vine and small blossoms, small figures of children and animals and insects. Verses 94, 96. Illustrated. [The mother of Johns Hopkins.]   *Mrs. Miles White, Jr.*

JANS, DOROTHY. 1752. 17" x 22". Cross-stitch. Vine and strawberry border outside and Greek fret inside. Scene with Adam and Eve with three children, and tree at bottom; at top, Abraham with his son and the ram at altar. Verses 41 (var.), 152 (1, var.).
The Misses Laura and Lieze Greer

JAQUELLE, KATHERINE WALLACE. 1799. Wilmington [Del.]. 15 yrs. 22" x 18½". Stem-stitch and painted. Hector taking leave of his wife and child. *Mrs. James C. Rogers*

JAQUES, ELIZABETH. [Newburyport, Mass. 12 yrs.] 8½" x 11½". 3 alphabets. Eyelet and cross-stitch. Greek fret border. Verse 203. *Miss Ruth M. B. Macintosh*

JAQUES, MARTHA. [1784. Newburyport, Mass.] "Born July 5, 1772.AE 12 yrs." 17½" x 22". 4 alphabets. Chain, tent, eyelet, satin, and cross-stitch. Elaborate design of trees, flowers, birds, animals, basket of flowers, hills, diamonds, etc. Strawberry and rose vine around verse. Verse 202 (1, var.). *Miss Ruth M. B. Macintosh*

JARVIS, MARY (called Betsy on sampler). 1780. Cambridge [Mass.]. 11 yrs. 7½" x 13". Alphabet. Stem, flat, and cross-stitch. Angular vine border. Horse, dog, etc., at bottom. Verses 490 (var.), 512? *Nathaniel J. W. Fish, Esq.*

JEFFRIES, SARAH. [17]97. [Elsinboro Township, Salem County, N. J., after marriage. 12 yrs.] 7¼" x 13¼". 3 alphabets. Eyelet, queen, and cross-stitch. Vine border and Greek-cross vine at top. *Miss Hannah Hall Acton*

JENKINS, ABIGAIL. 1757. 8" x 10½". 2 alphabets. Eyelet and cross-stitch. Conventional flower and name at bottom. Verse 343 (1, 7, var.). *Miss Susan P. Wharton*

JENNINGS, MARY. 1766. 8¼" x 11". 3 alphabets. Stem, satin, and cross-stitch. Conventional flower border at bottom. In center, large flower and animal on either side of it. Verse 488 (var.). Names on sampler: "Mary Jennings, Josiah Jennings, Temperance Jennings, David Jennings, Mary Jennings." *Mrs. Richard H. Hunt*

JEWETT, NABBY [Abigail]. 1797. Bradford [Mass.]. 12 yrs. 14" x 15". 2 alphabets. Cross-stitch. Cross-stitch border in diamond pattern. Diamond pattern in cross-stitch at bottom. Verse 388. *George Savary Wasson, Esq.*

JOHNSON, ANNA GREENLEAF. 1787. Newburyport [Mass.]. Born March 18, 1780. 22" x 17". 4 alphabets. French knot, chain, eyelet, stem, and cross-stitch. Rose vine border. Landscape with animals, birds, trees, urn with flowering plants, strawberries, and bees. Verse 627 (1). *Mrs. Anne Greenleaf Johnson Rogerson*

JOHNSON, CATHERINE. 1789. Newburyport [Mass.]. 9 yrs. 8" x 10". 2 alphabets. Flat, satin, and cross-stitch. Saw-tooth border. Trefoil cross-stitch borders at bottom. Verse 627 (1). *Miss Eleanor Reed Johnson*

JOHNSON, ELIZABETH. [Cir. 1797.] Born September 9, 1784. Alphabets. Cross, satin, flat, stem-stitch, and French knots. Vine border with blossoms starting from two upper corners going down sides and across top. At bottom, tree in middle, with 2 birds on it, a flowering tree on either side, sheep and strawberries in grass. Verse 617 (var.).
Mrs. Francis A. Goodhue

JOHNSON, EMELEA JANE. 1783. [Baltimore, Md.] 7 yrs. 9" x 16". 2 alphabets. Eyelet and cross-stitch. Carnation border. House, tree, children, and dog at top of sampler. Row of birds on pedestals. Verse 490 (var.). *Miss Mary Winchester*

JOHNSON, HANNAH. 1768. "Newbury Newton." 14 yrs. 18½" x 16½". 2 alphabets. Chain, eyelet, stem, satin, and cross-stitch. Small geometric cross-borders. At bottom, cherry tree, birds, butterflies, cow, deer, and large baskets of flowers. Verse 490 (var.). Illustrated. *Mrs. Henry E. Coe*

JOHNSON, MARY. 1769. 9 yrs. 12" x 20". 3 alphabets. Cross-stitch. "Pitch upon such a course as is excellent and praise worthy and custom will soon make it both easy & delightful." *The Colonial Dames of the State of New York*

JOHNSON, MOLLY. [Cir. 1778. Maine. Born in 1767.] 10½" x 12½". 1 alphabet. Satin and cross-stitch. Hemstitched border and inside border in satin-stitch. Cross-border at top. Verse 128 (var.). *Miss E. L. Alden*

JOHNSON, SALLY. 1799. Newburyport [Mass.]. 12 yrs. 27" x 19". 4 alphabets. Stem, satin, flat, and cross-stitch. Greek fret border. Elaborate design at bottom, with house, mill, ladies and gentlemen, servants, cattle, flowers, vine, trees, birds, etc. Verse 666. Illustrated in color. *Mrs. Francis A. Goodhue*

JONES, FRANCES. 1789. Providence [R. I. Born February 10, 1782. "Miss Polly Balch's School."]. 7½" x 9½". Satin, tent, and cross-stitch. Border of rosebuds and star-flowers. At bottom, State House, Providence, and strawberries. Verse 95 (2). *Mrs. William J. Dyer*

JONES, LUNA. 1797. Great Barrington. 11 yrs. 33" x 24". 5 alphabets. Tapestry, queen, eyelet, chain, and cat-stitch. Names and dates: "Calvin Jones born 1775 April 2, Heman Aug 15, 1777, Horace Feb 15 1780, Atlas Jan 18 1782, Thetis Nov 25 1783, Mithra & Luna Apr 4 1786, Thisbe Feb 21 1790, Andes Apr 30 1792, Sabra May 20 1794, Died Sept 5 1796." "Ebnr Jones my pappa born April 12, 1752. Susanna Jones my mamma born Dec. 11, 1755." Verse 659. *Mrs. William Shippen Jenks*

JONES, MARTHA. 1759. Medford [Mass.]. 9 yrs. 12" x 7¾". Alphabet. Cross-stitch. Cross-borders of strawberries and fruit trees. Verse 490 (var.). *Mrs. Mary H. Hayes*

JONES, MARY. 1792. Vincentown [N. J.]. 9 yrs. 12½" x 18". 3 alphabets. Eyelet and cross-stitch. Strawberry border at top. At bottom, small trees with green leaves and red flowers. Verses 353 (1), 635. *Mary Stretch Frick Drexel*

JONES, MARY. 1795. Vine border. Center bottom, a pot of flowers. Above, six lace circles around a seventh, with a vine interspersed. Stem and satin-stitch and twenty-seven different lace-stitches. *Mrs. Robert W. de Forest*

JONES, RUTH. 1791. 10½" x 13". 3 alphabets. Eyelet, cat, flat, and cross-stitch. Simple cross-stitch border. *Mrs. Joseph W. Knight*

JONES, SARAH. 1763. Savannah [Ga.]. 7 yrs. 13" x 13". Cross-stitch. Flowered vine border. Basket and flowers at bottom. Verse 355 (var.). The Ten Commandments, the Lord's Prayer, and the Apostles' Creed. *Mrs. O. N. Torian*

JORDAN, HANNAH. 1798. Scituate [Mass.]. 18 yrs. 15½" x 19½". 2 alphabets. Eyelet and cross-stitch. Cross-borders. Verses 187, 490 (var.). *Estate of James L. Little, Esq.*

KEATING, RUTH L. 1799. 11 yrs. 12" x 15". 4 alphabets. Eyelet, stem, tent, satin, and cross-stitch. Cross-stitch border. Basket of flowers, birds and vines at bottom. *Mrs. H. C. Bunner*

KEELER, CATHERINE. 1718. 8" x 11". Satin and cross-stitch. Simple border. At bottom, 2 baskets of fruit, bird between, large vase of flowers each side, candlesticks between birds, pine tree on each end. Verse 66 (1, var.). *A. M. Barnes, Esq.*

KEITH, JEMIMA. 1785. Bridgewater [Mass.]. 18 yrs. 5¾" x 5½". 1 alphabet. Cross-stitch. *Miss Julia M. Howard*

KELLAR, BETSY OTIS LEWIS. 1785. 8" x 10". 3 alphabets. Cross-stitch. *Mrs. George T. Brown*

K[EMP], A. M. 11½" x 9". 3 alphabets. Cross-stitch. *Mrs. George R. Southwick*

KEMP, HARRIOT. 9 yrs. 12" x 15". Cross-stitch. Strawberry border. At bottom, large urn in middle, with conventional flowers. Four smaller vases of roses and two bowls of strawberries. Verse 515 (var.). *A. Piatt Andrew, Esq.*

KENT, SALLY [SARA EVELINA]. January 17, 1794. Suffield, Conn. 15" x 21". 3 alphabets. Cross and eyelet-stitch. Eyelet border and conventional flower. "Germanicus Kent Aged 4 years May 31. Arrates Kent Aged 7 months January 17, 1794. Sally Kent Dec 24". Verse 601. *Mrs. Richard Webb*

KILLE, BATHSHEBA. 1790. 13" x 17". Satin and cross-stitch. Hemstitched, with Greek fret border of currants, clover leaves, forget-me-nots, rosebuds, strawberries, etc. Floral spray tied with bow-knot around verse. Verses 631 (1), 633. Names on sampler: "Father John Kille, Mother Mary Kille." *Mrs. John Tyler*

KIMBALL, ABIGAL. 1772. 10½" x 10½". 3 alphabets. Cross-stitch. *Wilbur M. Stone, Esq.*

KING, ELIZABETH. 1788. 12 yrs. 12" x 14¾". Alphabet. Laid-work, cross-stitch, and other fancy stitches. Narrow border outside, and inside border with set patterns of strawberries and animals. Elaborate pattern of animals and strawberries at bottom. Elizabeth King died soon after completing this sampler, and this fact is indicated on the sampler by a black letter E. *Mrs. A. W. Hitchcock*

KING, ——. [After 1795.] 12" x 24". 2 alphabets. Eyelet, chain, and cross-stitch. Family names and dates on sampler: "Martha King born June 11, 1785; Miles King born June 9, 1786; Eliza King born July 29, 1788; Peggy Cara King born Oct. 5, 1792; Maria Custiné born June 25, 1795." *Mrs. John Southgate Tucker*

KING, MARY. 1759. Boston [Mass.]. 11 yrs. 14" x 14". Alphabet. Satin and cross-stitch. Conventional border, with roses on top and sides. Dogs, squirrels, flowers, and peacocks at bottom. *Essex Institute*

KING, RHODA. [Cir. 1780.] Taunton [Mass. Born October 10, 1767.]. 7" x 9". Alphabets. Cross, queen, and tent-stitch. *Miss Emily C. Williams*

KINSMAN, LUCY. 1758. Ipswich [Mass.]. 7" x 9½". 2 alphabets. Cross-stitch. Plain border in cross-stitch, also cross-borders. *Miss Lucy S. Jewett*

KITCHIN, SARAH. 1790. [Solebury Township, Bucks County, Pa.] 13 yrs. 11" x 15". 3 alphabets. Cross-stitch. Cross-borders. *The Misses Ely*

KNEELAND, LYDIA. 1741. Boston [Mass.]. 13 yrs. 10½" x 15½". Cross and satin-stitch. Vine border. Elaborate cross-borders of roses, strawberry plants, trees, birds, animals. Verses 8, 187, 490 (var.). *Miss Charlotte Hedge*

KNEELAND, MARY. 1793. 14 yrs. 14" x 16". Cross-stitch and petit-point. Conventional strawberry border with filled-in background. Trees, birds, and flowers. Verses 40 (var.), 248 (1, var.). *Mrs. Thomas A. Lawton*

KNIGHT, ALES. 1737. 7" x 17". 2 alphabets. Satin and cross-stitch. Strawberry and conventional cross-borders in seventeenth century style. Verse 584. *Mrs. Thomas A. Lawton*

KNIGHT, EUNICE. [Cir. 1752.] Newbury [Mass.]. Born July 2, 1741. 12" x 21". 3 alphabets. Rosette, satin, and cross-stitch. Greek fret border. Hills, trees with fruit, and flowers, birds, baskets, sheep, etc. *Mrs. Ann M. Ilsley*

KNIGHT, EUNICE. 1799. 13 yrs. 11" x 14½". 3 alphabets. Cross-stitch. Hemstitched edge. Cross-border of roses. Birds, trees, dogs, flower-pots, and large basket of flowers. *Eunice Harriet Roery*

PLATE XXI

CATHERINE VAN SCHAICK. Albany. 1763
Owned by the late Mrs. Abraham Lansing

PLATE XXII

SALLY REA'S SAMPLER. 1766
Owned by Mrs. Miles White, Jr.

KNOWLES, SARAH. 1732 or 6. 12 yrs. 6½" x 8½". Cross-stitch. Birds, trees, and the names, Gilpin and Knowles. Verses 39, 92 (1, var.), 345 (1). *Miss Elizabeth J. Hopkins*

LADSON, MARY SMITH. 1789. Charleston [S. C.]. 8 yrs. 10½" x 11½". Alphabet. Cross-stitch, eyelet, and satin-stitch. Eyelet-stitch border. Verse 212. *Miss Isabelle Ladson*

LAKE, SARAH. 7" x 12". 3 alphabets. Bird's-eye, satin, and cross-stitch. Border of roses, bachelor's buttons, birds, etc. Verse 343 (1, var.). *Redwood Library, Newport*

LAMB, LYDIA. 1787. 10½" x 14". 3 alphabets. Eyelet, queen, and cross-stitch. Verse 343 (1, var.). *Mrs. Stanley H. Lowndes*

LAMSON, HANNAH. 1766. Medford [Mass.]. Born in 1756. 8" x 10½". 4 alphabets. Eyelet and cross-stitch. Strawberry cross-border. Names on sampler: "Susanna born Dec. 27 1753; Hannah Lamson born Jan. 2, 1756; Elizabeth Lamson born Dec. 4, 1760; Joseph Lamson born Feb. 2, 1760; Nathaniel [Lamson born] April 10, 1762; William [Lamson born] April 1, 1764." "Whilst we are here . . ." *Mrs. Thomas S. Young*

LANE, FANNY. 1791. Bedford [Mass.]. 10 yrs. 12" x 18". 2 alphabets. Eyelet and cross-stitch. Border in eyelet-stitch. Cross-borders of strawberries and vine and strawberry blossoms and vine. *Mrs. E. A. Rollins*

LANGDON, CAROLINE. 1790. Portsmouth, N. H. Born December 31, 1780. 12" x 20". 4 alphabets. Cross-stitch and variety of fancy stitches. Vine border. Fancy design using diamond shapes. Verse 632. *Mrs. William Gorham Rice*

LANGDON, CATY [Catherine Smith]. 1797. Conventional flowers. Verse 128 (1, var.). [She married Amos Smith, and Washington Allston had his studio in her house.] *Miss Catherine Langdon Rogers*

LARKINS, SUKY. 1792. 12 yrs. 12" x 8". Stem and cross-stitch. 2 alphabets. Verse 362. *Miss Lorimer*

LATHAM, C. W. 13½" x 13". 4 alphabets. Chain, satin, and cross-stitch. Vine border. Verse 515 (var.). *Estate of James L. Little, Esq.*

LATHAM, MARIA P. 8" x 17½". 3 alphabets. Chain, satin, and cross-stitch. Greek fret border. Flowers. Verse 515 (var.). *Estate of James L. Little, Esq.*

LATHROP, LUCY. 11 yrs. 13" x 14". 2 alphabets. Eyelet, satin, and cross-stitch. In border, sprays of roses, pinks, heartsease, tulips, etc., also basket filled with different flowers. *Miss Marian Hague*

LAWRENCE, SALLY CLAY. 1798. Exeter [N. H.]. 7 yrs. 10" x 16". 5 alphabets. Eyelet, cat, satin, and cross-stitch. Sheep, strawberry plants and blossoms. *Mrs. Walter M. Lincoln*

LAWTON, MARY. 1771. Portsmouth [R. I.]. 12 yrs. Born August 28, 1759. 9" x 10". 6 alphabets. Satin and cross-stitch. Strawberry and vine border. Verse 129 (var.). *Mrs. Fred R. Gibbs*

LAYCOCK, HANNAH. 1787. 9 yrs. Cross-stitch. Hearts and hour-glasses. "Remember thy Creator," etc. *Mrs. John C. Munro*

LAYCOCK, SARAH. 1787. 12 yrs. Eyelet and cross-stitch. Verses 198, 345 (var.). *Mrs. John C. Munro*

LEA, ELIZABETH. 1752. [Born at Concord, Pa., January 15, 1745. O. S.] 10" x 14". Cross and stem-stitch. Green grass and flowers. *Miss Anna Lea*

LEACH, BETSY. 1789. Marblehead [Mass.]. 11 yrs. 17½″ x 18½″. Cross-stitch. Strawberry border. Vase with flowers, ram, birds, and flowers. Names and ages given on sampler: "Henry Leach aged 43 yrs, Betsy Leach aged 11 years, Richard Leach aged 6 years, Hannah Leach aged 3 years, Katharine Leach aged 42 years, Nathaniel Leach aged 9 years, Salle Leach aged 2 years. Mary Magery who died September 26, aged 22 years." Verses 128, 213.   *Marblehead Historical Society*

LEAVITT, MARY. 1718. 13 yrs. 8½″ x 16½″. 4 alphabets. Cross-stitch and tent-stitch. Simple cross-borders. Figures of "Ashur" and "Elisha" dancing on green mound and playing on wind instruments, also detached letters and figures. (See tailpiece, p. 8.)   *Miss A. B. Willson*

LEECH, MARY. 1794. Hatboro [Pa.]. 9 yrs. Cross-stitch. Greek fret border. Houses, trees, and birds. Initials of the family. Verse 343 (1).   *Descendants of Mary Leech*

LEES, HETTY. 1799. 9 yrs. 16½″ x 20″. Alphabet. Queen, satin, and cross-stitch. Strawberry vine border in satin-stitch. Design of barn, house, trees, etc. Verse 198. Illustrated.   *Mrs. Henry Eugene Coe*

LEHMAN, ELIZABETH. 1790. 16″ x 17½″. Hollie-point lace.   *Memorial Hall, Fairmount Park, Philadelphia*

LEHMAN, SUSAN. [1799.] 9 yrs. [Born in Philadelphia in 1790.] 14″ x 12″. 6 alphabets. Eyelet and cross-stitch. Simple cross-borders. Parrots and dogs and plant at bottom. Verse 239. Illustrated.   *Mrs. Charles Schäffer*

LEHMAN, SUSAN. [1799.] 9 yrs. [Born in 1790.] 16½″ x 16½″. 2 alphabets. Stem, satin, and cross-stitch. Strawberry border and, inside, saw-tooth border. Scene with house, barn, fence, and trees.

"One Weeks Extremity May Teach Us More Than Long Prosperity
   Had Done Before Death Is Forgotten In Our Easy State But Trou
   ples Mind Us In Our Final Fate The Doing Ill Affects Us not with Fears
   But Suffring Ill Brings Sorrow Woe And Tears."   *Mrs. Charles Schäffer*

LEHMAN, SUSANAH. 1796. [6 yrs.] 2 alphabets. Cross-stitch. Carnation cross-borders.   *Mrs. Charles Schäffer*

LEIGH, MARCY. [Cir. 1784. Newbury, Mass.] Born November 22 [1775]. 7½″ x 9½″. Alphabets. Cross-stitch. Hemstitched border.   *Miss Sarah Jackson Leigh*

LEONARD, FANNY. 1774. 12 yrs. 13″ x 8″. 1 alphabet. Cross-stitch. Verse 604.   *Charles H. Warren, Esq.*

LEVISTONE, OLIVE. 1797. 11 yrs. 12″ x 16″. 2 alphabets. Eyelet, stem, satin, and cross-stitch. Zigzag borders, with eyelets in between. Conventional trees and birds and man in baggy breeches. Verse 128 (var.).   *Miss Mary C. Wheelwright*

LEWIS, ELIZABETH. 18″ x 18″. Stem and cross-stitch. Rose border. Hill with flower garden, peacock, tall vases, sheep, lady with lamb, rose tree with white squirrel under it, white French poodle, rabbit, and bluebird between poplars. Verse 515.   *Mrs. Bradbury Bedell*

LEWIS, MARTHA. 1740. Charleston [S. C.]. 12 yrs. 10½″ x 18″. 2 alphabets. Eyelet, stem, satin, petit-point, cat, tent, and cross-stitch. Border of little trees at top; border of birds and geometrical designs at bottom.   *Mrs. John F. Bennett*

LEWIS, MARY. 1790. Born November 3, 1780. 8″ x 10″. 3 alphabets. Cross-stitch. Narrow cross-borders. Conventional tree, etc.   *Annie Booth Law*

LEWISE, ANN. 11 yrs. 16″ x 17½″. 2 alphabets. Tent, filler, cushion, French knot, and cross-stitch. Flowered vine border. Scene with house, barn, dovecote, doves, trees, fence, and two flower baskets. Verse 494 (1 and 2). *The Emma B. Hodge Collection*

LINCOLN, EUNICE. 1794. 24½″ x 20¼″. Stem, satin, tent, cat, cross-stitch, queen and petit-point. Strawberry border outside, next, wide conventional border in solid cross-stitch; vines and flowers on either side, and across top, scene with shepherd and shepherdess and black and white sheep; just below, angels, birds, trees, and animals; then house and trees, with picture of farmer and his wife in corners; inscription, "Let Virtue be a guide to thee"; and in lower section, lord and lady of the manor on either side of shield bearing name and date; and below that, Verse 646. *Mrs. Miles White, Jr.*

LIPPINCOTT, RACHEL. 1793. 17 yrs. 11″ x 17″. 2 alphabets. Cat, queen, eyelet, and cross-stitch. Strawberry border. Verse 375. *Anna C. Scott*

LIPPITT, JULIA. 1797. 14″ x 12″. ["Miss Polly Balch's School."] Long and short, stem, satin, split, eyelet, and cross-stitch. Basket of fruit, flowers and birds inside of arch.
Miss M. Frances Babcock

LIPPITT, PHEBE. 1787. Cranston [R. I.]. 11 yrs. 9½″ x 13″. 2 alphabets. Tent, chain, eyelet, and cross-stitch. Strawberry border and strawberry and carnation cross-borders. Verses 187, 490 (var.). *Mrs. L. C. Harper*

LITTLE, JANE. 1786. Newbury [Mass.]. 12″ x 13″. Alphabet. Stem, eyelet, and cross-stitch. Strawberry and vine border. Small letters in needlework frames. "General George Washington the ornament example and defense of our nation". *Miss Hannah M. W. Merrill*

LITTLE, RUTH. 1766. Marshfield [Mass.]. 9 yrs. 10½″ x 21″. 1 alphabet. Cross and eyelet-stitch, Greek fret and trefoil cross-borders. Verses 182 (1, 3), 490 (var.).
Miss Florence G. Ford

L[OCKWOOD], P[HEBE]. 1785. Born December 9, 1778. 13½″ x 7¼″. 2 alphabets. Cross-stitch. Verses 10 (1), 201, 617 (var). *Mrs. Lorenzo Sears*

LORD, HANNAH. 1764. 7¼″ x 9½″. 2 alphabets. Petit-point, queen, tent, and cross-stitch. Conventional border of flowers and vines. Conventionalized flower in cross-border.
"Sing unto God, sing praises to his name.
Extol him that rideth upon the heavens
by his name jah and rejoice before him
A father of the fatherless and a judge of
the widow is god in his holy habitation." *Albert C. Bates, Esq.*

LORING, LYDIA. 1794. Born August 31, 1781. "Derby School." 11″ x 15″. 2 alphabets. Cross-stitch. Strawberry border, with different designs in corners. Verse 227. [Massachusetts.]
Mrs. Frederick H. Tappan

LORING, POLLY. 1787. Born February 16, 1778. 1 alphabet. Cat-stitch. Strawberry border. Greek fret cross-border. *Mrs. Frederick H. Tappan*

LYNDE, ANNA. 14 yrs. 10″ x 14″. 2 alphabets. Eyelet, stem, and cross-stitch. Conventional border at top. Verse 132 (1, var.). *Worcester Art Museum*

LYNDE, DOROTHY. 1757. 12″ x 14″. 10 yrs. 1 alphabet and 2 parts of alphabets. Petit-point covering the entire canvas. Eyelet and satin-stitch. Border contains the sun at the top, cherubim at either upper corner, figures on pedestals at either side; below, a scene with house, trees, a black dog, one sheep, and a shepherdess. Verse 132 (1, var.). Illustrated in color. *Old South Meeting House, Boston*

LYNDE, HANNAH. 7″ x 12½″. Alphabet. Cross-stitch. Hemstitched edge. Verse 128 (var.).
Worcester Art Museum

LYNDE, MARY. 1751. 13 yrs. 6½″ x 8½″. 2 alphabets. Cross-stitch. *Worcester Art Museum*

LYON, ELIZABETH. 1791. [New Haven, Conn.] 14 yrs. 18″ x 21″. 2 alphabets. Vine border. Vases in corners at bottom. Picture of an old girls' school on State Street, with ladies and gentlemen and sheep. Verse 218. *Mrs. William Lyon Phelps*

LYON, POLLY. 1786. 5 yrs. 6″ x 10″. 1 alphabet. Cross-stitch. Strawberry design.
Mrs. William Lyon Phelps

LYON, SOPHIA. August 8, 1790. [New Haven, Conn.] 5 yrs. 10″ x 11½″. 2 alphabets. Cross-stitch. At top, bird in nest and flowers. Greek fret at bottom. Verses 216, 340.
Mrs. William Lyon Phelps

M., A. F. 1762. 9 yrs. Hamburg. 11″ x 14″. Twenty imitations of materials, from silk stockings to brocade. Even the selvage is imitated. *Mrs. G. Clem Goodrich*

MACOMBER, ANN. 1799. 11″ x 13″. Alphabet. Stem, satin, and cross-stitch. Scene with "Liberty Hall," Philadelphia, also house, fence, two gates, sidewalk, horse, trees, dog. Illustrated. *Mrs. Lorenzo Sears*

MAKEPEACE, SUKEY. [1750.] 16½″ x 23″. Alphabet. Cross, split, satin, and knot-stitch. Pineapple and rose border. Landscape with peacock, birds, two dogs, and stag. Illustrated. *The Emma B. Hodge Collection*

MANN, ANNA. 1791. 12 yrs. 7″ x 9″. 2 alphabets. Chain and cross-stitch. Crude designs in center. *Estate of James L. Little, Esq.*

MANSFIELD, BETSY ⎫ 1772. 1772–1799. 8½″ x 10½″. 2 alphabets. Cross-stitch. "1. Betsy
PIERCE, ELIZA ⎬ 1796. Mansfield 1772 aged 10. 2. Eliza Pierce 1796 aged 10. 3. Har-
PIERCE, HARRIOT ⎭ 1799. riot Pierce 1799 aged 8." *Mrs. Charles J. White*

MARQUAND, ANN. 1796. Newburyport [Mass.]. 10 yrs. Born October 16, 1786. 11″ x 11″. 4 alphabets. Eyelet, stem, satin, and cross-stitch. Cross-borders: lozenge and diamond, scroll, heart, diamond, and Greek fret. Four baskets and two rose bushes. Verse 617.
Miss Elizabeth Marquand

MARSHALL, BETSY. 1799. [Bridgewater, Mass.] 9 yrs. 7½″ x 10½″. 2 alphabets. Cross-stitch. Vine border. Design of leaves and figures. *Theodore P. Tower, Esq.*

MARSHALL, ELIZABETH. 1724. 11 yrs. 7½″ x 11½″. 2 alphabets. Eyelet and cross-stitch. Scroll, point, and strawberry borders at top. Bird perched on branch of leaves and flowers. ["From the West Indies."] *Mrs. John H. Morison*

MARSHALL, LYDIA. 11 yrs. 3 alphabets. Stem, satin, and cross-stitch. Border, saw-tooth and strawberry vine. In middle, a vase with small tree on either side. Verse 164.
Mrs. Mabel Hurley

MARTIN, MARGARET. 1763. Charleston [S. C.]. 8½″ x 18″. 3 alphabets. Eyelet, hem-stitch, and cross-stitch. Hemstitched and drawn-work border at top and bottom. Verse 356.
Mrs. William Dunkin

MARTIN, NABBY. 1786. 10¼″ x 15″. Petit-point, split, stem, satin, tent, queen, and cross-stitch. Brown University building at top, and at bottom, Old State House, also three groups of ladies and gentlemen. Large flowers on either side in border. Verse 97. ["Miss Polly Balch's School."] *Rhode Island School of Design*

MASCARENE, ELIZABETH. 1762. 11 yrs. 6″ x 9″. Alphabet. Cross-stitch. Simple cross-stitch design at top and bottom. *Edmund M. Dow, Esq.*

MASON, JOHN. [Cir. 1780.] Painted sampler. "Son of Solomon Mason and Anna his wife, was born January the 3rd Anno Domini 1767." Floral design at top, and at bottom, figures of parents, with vase filled with flowers in between them. Verse 365. Illustrated.
Maxcy Applegate, Esq.

MASON, MARY. 1797. [Salem County, N. J.] 12 yrs. 8½" x 17". 3 alphabets. Buttonhole, tent, eyelet, satin, and cross-stitch. Conventional borders. *The Misses Holme*

MASON, POLLY. 1798. Framingham [Mass.]. 9" x 6". Alphabet. Cross-stitch. Unfinished.
Lancaster Library, Massachusetts

MATHER, MARY. 1767. 12 yrs. 4 alphabets. Eyelet, stem, satin, and cross-stitch. Carnation, strawberry, trees, and birds, and conventional cross-borders. Strawberry design.
Mrs. J. Henry Small

MATTHEWS, TEMPERANCE. 1750. 10 yrs. 10" x 12". Eyelet and cross-stitch. Border of pine trees and crowns. Proverbs 31, verses 29–31. *Robert P. Jordan, Dealer*

MAWNEY, AMEY. 1787. Providence [R. I.]. 7½" x 14". 3 alphabets. Satin and cross-stitch. Cross-stitch border. Design of strawberry vine, but incomplete. Verses 617 (var.), 626.
Miss Amey Lemoine Willson

MAY, CATHERINE. 1770. Boston [Mass.]. 13 yrs. 5½" x 19½". 6 alphabets. Tapestry, satin, and cross-stitch. Dog-tooth border. Landscape with house, sheep, figures, trees, etc.
Dr. Zabdiel Boylston Adams

MAY, MARY ANN. April 23, 1793. 11 yrs. 12" x 16". 3 alphabets. Cross, satin, and stem-stitch. Strawberry border. Simple cross-borders. Tree, two baskets of fruit, and two butterflies. Verses 45, 92a (2). *Metropolitan Museum of Art, New York*

MAYHEW, SALLY. 1787. Newburyport [Mass.]. 17" x 8½". 3 alphabets. Eyelet, satin, and cross-stitch. Strawberry border at top. Double lines of cross-stitch at bottom. "I'le praise my maker while I have breath." *Miss Lillian Adams*

McCLURE, NANCY. 1795. 7 yrs. 17" x 15½". 3 alphabets. Chiefly stem and cross-stitch. Vine border. *Mrs I. Tucker Burr*

McCULLOUGH, ELIZABETH. 1787. Newcastle [Del.]. 11" x 15". 2 alphabets. Queen, flat, stem, and cross-stitch. Vine border. At bottom, tree on either side of a flower piece and medallion at right. Verse 511 (1, var.). *Mrs. Edmund K. Goldsborough*

McDONALD, MARY. 1787. Albany [N. Y.]. 12 yrs. 7½" x 10½". 1 alphabet. Cross-stitch. Two peacocks, on either side of basket of flowers. *Mary McDonald Vosburgh*

McGARY, LYDIA JAMES. [1785.] 8 yrs. 7½" x 9". 3 alphabets. Cross-stitch.
Mrs. George Thurber Brown

McLEAN, ELIZABETH H. 1785. [Near Gettysburg, Pa.] 2 alphabets. Outline, eyelet, and cross-stitch. Top border of strawberry; bottom border, old Indian basket pattern. Verse 619. *Mrs. W. P. Stevenson*

McLEAN, MARY. [1773 or 1775.] Border and cross-borders. At bottom, pine tree with bird on top branch. Verse 197. *Maxcy Applegate, Esq.*

McLELLAN, ELIZA. 12 yrs. 11" x 17". 2 alphabets. Queen, tent, and cross-stitch. Cross-borders. Design, basket of strawberries and two plants on either side.
A. Stainforth, Dealer

MEARS, ABIGAIL. 1772. 15" x 19". 2 alphabets. Cross, satin, eyelet, imitation couching-stitch. Border of conventionalized flowers. Strawberry, saw-tooth, and Greek fret cross-borders. At bottom, a hunting scene with a stag and four dogs. Verse 359. Illustrated.
Mrs. Henry Eugene Coe

MERRICK, MARIA. 1798. [Brookfield, Mass.] 8 yrs. Born October 14, 1790. 11″ x 12½″. 3 alphabets. Cross-stitch. Strawberry border. Trees, birds, plants, flowers, fruits, animals, etc., divided by four cross-borders.   *Miss Frances M. Lincoln*

MERRILL, SUSANNA [SUKEY]. 1793. Newburyport [Mass.]. 14 yrs. 16½″ x 21″. 3 alphabets. Eyelet, chain, herring-bone, stem, satin, and cross-stitch. Vine border interwoven with flowers. Vase of flowers with bird on either side, also sheep, trees, and set designs.

> "Sickness may strip you of
> The bloom of the rose
> But the beauties of
> The mind will endear
> Beyond the grave,
> My young friend
> Prepare to meet
> Your God."

Verse 601 (1, 2, 3).   *Mrs. F. D. Greene*

MESSER, NANCY. 1798. New London [Conn.]. 8″ x 8½″. 3 alphabets. Eyelet and cross-stitch.   *Wilbur M. Stone, Esq.*

MICHENER, DEBORAH. 1774. [Plumstead Township, Bucks County, Pa.]. 17 yrs. 8½″ x 11½″. Alphabet. Family initials: "W M [William], J M [John], S M [Sarah], B M [Barak], H M [Hannah], D M [Deborah], M M [Mordecai], H M [Hannah], E M [Elizabeth], R M [?], K M [Katharine], M M [?], S M [?]."   *Captain Capehart, U. S. N.*

MICKLE, SARAH. 1763. 9″ x 10½″. 2 alphabets. Eyelet, flat, and cross-stitch. Cross-borders and small designs.   *Mrs. Edward Dillon*

MILLER, [ANNA] ELIZABETH. 1797. [Kensington, Philadelphia, Pa.] 11 yrs. 16½″ x 17″. 1 alphabet. Queen, eyelet, stem, satin, cross-stitch, and other stitches. Border, Greek fret, strawberries or roses. Cross-borders. Trees, birds, houses, and fences. Initials of father and mother, "C M, M M." Verse 523.   *Miss Anna E. Murphy*

MILLER, LUCRETIA. 1798. 14 yrs. 7″ x 7½″. 2 alphabets. Cross-stitch. Narrow cross-stitch border. Cross-borders of Greek fret. Heart, crown, etc.   *Mrs. John F. Calder*

MILLER, MARY. 1775. Savannah [Ga.]. 10″ x 12½″. Alphabet. Stem, satin, and cross-stitch. Floral border. Scene with ladies, children, servants, tree, fruit, flowers, and insects. Verse 606 (1, var.).   *Mrs. Arthur H. Wright*

MILLER, SALLY. 1783. Middletown [Conn.]. 9 yrs. 16½″ x 17″. 2 alphabets. Cross-stitch. Border, strawberry design on sides, vine with small ball at top and bottom. Verses 41 (var.), 132 (1, var.), 191 (1, var.).   *Mrs. Stanley H. Lowndes*

MONTGOMERY, NANCY. 1798. Middleborough. 9 yrs. 6″ x 8″. Alphabet. Cross-stitch.   *Mrs. George F. Seaver*

MOORE, SIBILAH. 1788. [Mullica Hill, Gloucester County, N. J.] 10 yrs. [Born February 8, 1778.] 12½″ x 17″. 3 alphabets. Eyelet, cat, flat, queen, and cross-stitch. Borders across top and bottom of strawberries, roses, vines. Conventional carnations across bottom. Verse 343 (1). Family names and initials on sampler: father and mother, "Joshua Moore, Rachel Moore;" children, "H M, R M, A M, K M, S M, P M, M M."   *William F. Edwards, Esq.*

MOREY, BETSY JENKINS. 1798. [Vermont. 7 yrs.] 12″ x 4″. 3 alphabets. Satin, stem, and cross-stitch. Border of stem-stitch points. Carnation design.   *Mrs. James N. Bailey*

MORSE, CYNTHIA. 1748. Foxboro. 3″ x 8″. 1 alphabet. Cross-stitch.   *Mrs. Ella G. Church*

MORTON, LYDIA. 1765. 12 yrs. 8" x 14". 3 alphabets. Eyelet, satin, and cross-stitch. Diamond border and plain cross-borders. Strawberry design. Verse 128 (1, var.).

M. B. Lemon, Dealer

MOTLEY, MARY. 1795. 11 yrs. Born August 25, 1783. 1 alphabet. Satin and cross-stitch. Border of vine and strawberries. In center, Mason's square and compass with inscription, "Richard Driver departed this life July the 19 in the year of our lord 1792;" and on either side a large flowering plant, also the words, "Aged seventy seven." In upper part, "Richard Motley was married to Ann Wilson Driver the 14th of July in Year of our lord 1780. Ann Motley Born July 8 1781, Mary Motley Born Aug 25 1783, Sukey Motley Born March 5 1788, Elizabeth Motley Born February 4 1787, James Motley Born Aug 15 1789, William Motley Born October 6 1791, John Motley Born June 5 1794." Verse 613.

Mrs. Frederick F. Thompson

MOUNTFORT, HANNAH. May 22, 1736. [Boston, Mass.?] 12 yrs. Born February 5, 1724. 18" x 9". 3 alphabets. Eyelet, stem, satin, and cross-stitch. Borders of carnation, strawberry, Greek fret, rose, cross, vine, and trefoil designs. Verse 128 (var.).

Mrs. Mary A. Rhodes

MUHLENBERG, HETTY. 1797. Reading [Pa.]. 12 yrs. 21½" x 21½". 2 alphabets. Stem and cross-stitch. Strawberry border and carnation cross-border at top. Round basket out of which are growing carnations, bluebells, rosebuds, and heartsease. Small parrot is perched on top spray. Verse 48.

Mrs. John A. Hoogerwerff

MUHLENBERG, SUSANNA. 1790. Trappe [Pa.]. 11 yrs. 18" x 11". 3 alphabets. Eyelet, stem, satin, and cross-stitch. Borders, Greek fret and strawberry. Cross in two upper corners. Verse 139.

Mrs. John A. Kress

MULFORD, SARAH. 1794. [Alloway, N. J.] 10" x 14". 5 alphabets. Eyelet, tent, queen, and cross-stitch. Vine and carnation border. Cross-border in vine and strawberry pattern. Two trees and grass. Verse 642.

Mrs. William K. Andrews

MUNRO, SALLY. 12" x 17". Queen, satin, and cross-stitch. Border, vine rising out of vases in lower corners, also strawberries and various flowers. Scene 1, Adam and Eve beautifully dressed, and Tree of Knowledge; Scene 2, President's house, Brown University, and people going to the reception. A doctor's gig in front of the house. Verse 4. Illustrated.

Newport Historical Society

MURRAY, DEBORAH. 1777. 6 yrs. Alphabet. Eyelet and cross-stitch. Rows of strawberries, crowns, and saw-teeth. "The Expectation of future Happiness is the Best Relief of Anxious Thoughts the most perfect cure of Milancholy the guide of Life and the Comfort of Death." "Remember thy Creator," etc. Verse 609 (2, var.). *Mrs. I. Edwin Ruggles*

MUTTER, ELIZABETH. [Cir. 1790. Granville County, N. C. 12 yrs.] 16½" x 17". Darning and cross-stitch. Floral border. *Mary Sumner Kingsbury*

NELSON, MARY ANN. 1797. Augusta, Va. 12 yrs. 17" x 21". Flat, eyelet, stem, and satin-stitch. Simple borders. "The Message," St. Luke, Chapter 2, verses 13, 14, and 15. Verse 524. *Mrs. H. C. Skaggs*

NEWCOMB, EDETH. 1795-96. Cohansey, N. J. 17" x 24". 3 alphabets. Satin and cross-stitch. Vine border. Cross-borders of flowers and vines. Potted flowers. Family initials: "T B, E B, E B, E B, A B, S B, R N, E N, E N, K N, E N, R N." Verses 187, 490 (var.).

Mrs. C. May Neeld

NEWELL, MARY. 1792. 10 yrs. 7" x 9". 2 alphabets. Cross-stitch. *Prof. F. P. Gorham*

NEWHALL, LUCY. 1793. Lynn [Mass.]. 11 yrs. [Born July 26, 1782.] 9″ x 18″. 1 alphabet. Eyelet, stem, and cross-stitch. Strawberry border. Verses 490 (var.), 639.

Miss Bertha M. Larkin

NICHOLS, ANNA. 1778. 21 yrs. 7½″ x 6″. 2 alphabets. Herring-bone and cross-stitch. Cross-stitch border.   *Mrs. Emma Cheney Peabody*

NICHOLS, SARAH. 1794. Newbury [Mass.]. 8 yrs. 11″ x 17″. 5 alphabets. Laid-stitch, satin and cross-stitch. Diamond border. Design at bottom consists of trees, large and small birds, animals, baskets of flowers, etc. Verse 380.   *Mrs. Mary F. Hudson*

NICKALLS, SUSANNE. 1792. Londonderry. 12 yrs. 9½″ x 15½″. 2 alphabets. Cross and satin-stitch. Hemstitched edge and strawberry border. Garden of Eden, with Adam and Eve and Serpent. Verse 10 (1).   *Miss Lucasta J. Boynton*

NILES, JANE. 1791. Philadelphia [Pa. 18 yrs. Born July 7, 1773.]. 18″ x 22″. 2 alphabets. Eyelet and cross-stitch. Strawberry, rose, carnation, and vine border. Trees, birds, animals, and baskets of flowers. Verses 219, 490 (var.).   *Hannah Niles Freeland Miller*

NORCROSS, POLLY. [Cir. 1791.] Pittston [Me.]. 7″ x 10″. 3 alphabets. Cat, rope, and cross-stitch. Cat-stitch border. "There is nothing of so much worth as a mind well instructed."

Mrs. Bradbury Bedell

NORTON, ABIGAIL. 1775. 15 yrs. 21½″ x 7″. 2 alphabets. Cross-stitch. "Remember Thy Creator in the days of thy Youth."   *Clarence A. Mathewson, Esq.*

NOYES, KATY. 1787. Newbury [Mass.]. 14 yrs. Born August 17, 1773. 17″ x 22½″. 4 alphabets. Eyelet, French knot, stem, satin, and cross-stitch. Rose and vine border on three sides. Landscape with hills, sheep, lambs, trees, sparrow, and parrot. Verse 368.

Mrs. John F. Pearson

NUGENT, SALLY. 1784. Philadelphia [Pa.]. 21 yrs. 7¾″ x 17″. Alphabet. Buttonhole, stem, eyelet, and cross-stitch. Strawberry border. Vase with unfinished flowers and cluster of flowers. Names of brothers, "Washington, Charles, James," and one too indistinct to make out. "Love best and honor thy mother."   *Miss Mary Hale Coffin*

OLIVER, SARAH. 1755. Boston [Mass.]. Born in 1745. 8½″ x 11″. Alphabets. Conventional trees.   *Hutchinson Collection, sold at American Art Galleries, New York, April 11, 1918*

OLMSTED, ELIZABETH. [Cir. 1736.] East Hartford [Conn.]. Born August 26, 1726. Cross-stitch. Conventional border. Family record: "Ashbel Olmsted born February 10, 1726; Hannah Newberry born October 3, 1729; Married November 3, 1737; Mabel Olmsted born January 21, 1759; died May 19, 1759; Mabel Olmsted born November 7, 1759; Ashbel Olmsted born March 12, 1761; Elizabeth Olmsted born August 26, 1762; Ursula Olmsted born January 29, 1764; Elihu Olmsted born September 7, 1765; Hannah Olmsted born January 21, 1768; Amelia Olmsted born August 19, 1769; Naomi Olmsted born October 13, 1772; Elizy Olmsted's Registry."   *Mrs. A. L. Fanning*

ORMSBEE, ROBE A. 1790. 10″ x 7″. 5 alphabets. Chain and cross-stitch. Verse 617 (1).

The Misses Peck

ORNE, LOIS. 1767. Salem [Mass.]. 8″ x 11″. 3 alphabets. Stem and cross-stitch. Cross-stitch border. Strawberry vine design.   *Mrs. A. G. Bullock*

ORWIN, MARGARET. 1786. 8½″ x 21″. 5 alphabets. Tent and eyelet-stitch. Animals, man and woman, and many initials.   *Miss Anne Lee*

OSGOOD, LYDIA. [Before 1800.] 12 yrs. 8¾″ x 9″. 4 alphabets. Border of Greek fret, strawberry, cross, and chain patterns. Several hearts on right side.   *W. G. Bowdoin, Esq.*

PLATE XXIII

MARGARET CALEF'S SAMPLER. Middletown, Conn. 1767
Owned by Mrs. W. S. Fulton

PLATE XXIV

HANNAH JOHNSON'S SAMPLER. Newburyport. 1768
Owned by Mrs. Henry E. Coe

OWEN, REBEKAH. 1745. [Cambridge, Mass.] 11 yrs. 8″ x 15″. 1 alphabet. Stem, rose-point, and cross-stitch over a single thread. Strawberry border. Conventional cross-stitch cross-borders. Adam and Eve, Tree of Knowledge and Serpent, also detached flowers around scene. Verse 348. Illustrated. *Mrs. George E. Smith*

OWINGS, SARAH. 1799. 4 alphabets. Cross-stitch. Plain border. Verse 241. *Mrs. Sigbee*

PACKARD, SOPHIA. 1791. Providence [R. I.]. 14″ x 12″. ["Miss Polly Balch's School."] 3 alphabets. Chain, stem, satin, queen, and cross-stitch. Carnation border. Oval with inscription inside. Verse 503 (var.). *Mrs. J. H. Hambly*

PADELFORD, SUSAN SARAH LEVETT. 1794. Taunton [Mass.]. 8¼″ x 8¼″. Cross, satin, chain, and flat-stitch. House, with arch over the door and small windowpanes. [Born 1782.]
Mrs. J. Lewis Austin

PAIN, RACHEL. 1792. [Marblehead? Mass.] 8″ x 8″. Chain, stem, satin, and cross-stitch. Chain-stitch border. Plant in flower-pot, bush, and birds. Verse 12. *Mrs. B. F. Stacey*

PAINE, HARRIET. 1787. [St. Johns, New Brunswick.] 12 yrs. 19″ x 19″. Alphabet. Stem and cross-stitch. Vine and flower border. Verse 138. *Mrs. Francis H. Lee*

PAINTER, SUSANNA. 1724. Philadelphia [Pa.]. 7 yrs. 7½″ x 8½″. 2 alphabets. Eyelet and cross-stitch. "The blessing of the Lord: it maketh rich and he addeth no sorrow with it."
Miss Susan P. Wharton

PARKER, BETSY. 1799. 15 yrs. 11″ x 14½″. 3 alphabets. Satin, queen, petit-point, stem, eyelet, and cross-stitch. Border of carnations and cross-borders of rose and trefoil patterns. Humpy green ground, with bush and unfinished rose [?]. Verse 627 (1).
A. Stainforth, Dealer

PARKER, MARY. 1741. 13 yrs. 9¼″ x 18¼″. 3 alphabets. Cross, eyelet, and various other stitches. Strawberry, carnation, and other conventional cross-borders. Scene with Adam and Eve and Tree of Knowledge and Serpent. Illustrated. *Mrs. Henry H. Edes*

PARKER, SALLY. 1796. 11 yrs. 2 alphabets. Satin, eyelet, long, stem, and cross-stitch. Greek fret border. Trees, grass, and flowers. Verse 625 (1). *Mrs. Savary and Miss Parker*

PARKER, SUSANNAH. 1790. Portsmouth [N. H.]. 10 yrs. 9″ x 14″. Alphabets. Eyelet and cross-stitch. Vine border. *Merrill Spalding, Esq.*

PARKHURST, HANNAH. 1781. Newark [N. J.]. 13 yrs. Born December 6, 1768. 7½″ x 9½″. 3 alphabets. Satin and cross-stitch. *Miss Frances C. Force*

PARRISH, DEBORAH. 1784. Philadelphia [Pa.]. 10½″ x 12½″. 2 alphabets. Eyelet, long, and cross-stitch. Rose and strawberry border. Verse 609 (var.). *Miss Susan P. Wharton*

PATTEN, EXPERIENCE. 1799. Hartford [Conn.]. 12 yrs. 15″ x 22″. 5 alphabets. Eyelet, stem, and cross-stitch. Plain border. Scene with house, poplars, fence, and grass.
Verse 74. *The Misses Hill*

PATTEN, LUCINDA. 1794. 8 yrs. 12½″ x 20½″. 2 alphabets. Stem and cross-stitch. Plain border. Rose in center, tulips on either side. Verses 46, 98, 129. *The Misses Hill*

PAUL, JUDITH. [1791.] Providence. 16½″ x 13½″. ["Miss Polly Balch's School."] Chain, satin, and cross-stitch. House, figures, and trees. Verse 606 (1, var.).
Rhode Island Historical Society

PEABODY, SARAH HAZARD. 17——. [Cir. 1765?] 12″ x 15½″. 4 alphabets. Eyelet, satin, and cross-stitch. Double saw-tooth border. Pot of flowers in lower corners, baskets of fruit, with flowers arching over. Verse 95. *Miss Susan Woodman*

PEARCE, LYDIA. 1796. 8 yrs. Alphabet. Cross and satin-stitch. Plain cross-stitch border. Cross-stitch dividing lines. Verse 129 (var.). *Described by Mrs. A. A. Lawrence*

PEARSON, HANNAH. 1793. Ipswich [Mass.]. 10 yrs. 12" x 21". 2 alphabets. French knots, satin, stem, and cross-stitch. Flower and vine border. At top, in center, a bouquet in jar, with large birds on either side. At bottom, flowers and leaves. *John F. Pearson, Esq.*

PEARSON, MARY HOLYOKE.
PEARSON, MARGARETTA BROMFIELD. } 10 yrs. [M.B.P.] 16" x 8½". 4 alphabets. Cross-stitch. Simple zigzag border. Greek fret cross-border at bottom. *Estate of James L. Little, Esq.*

PEARSON, SUSANNAH. 1756. 10¼" x 15¼". 3 alphabets. Eyelet, flat, and cross-stitch. Cross-border at top and bottom. Verse 185. *Miss Caroline M. Burnham*

PECKER, ELIZABETH. 1750. Born July 31, 1735. 15¼" x 20". 4 alphabets. Stem and cross-stitch. Double strawberry border. Elaborate design at bottom, with two trees, large basket of flowers, birds, hens, cat, dogs, and lady. Verse 128 (1, var.). Illustrated. *Mrs. Henry E. Coe*

PEDRICK, ELIZABETH. 1787. [Marblehead, Mass.] 18" x 21". 3 alphabets. Chain, stem, satin, cross-stitch, and seed-stitch. Adam and Eve in Garden of Eden, etc., also many symbols, crowns, doves, animals, trees, vases, etc. "As Soon As We Are Born Then Presently We Cry As If We Knew We Came Into A World Of Music." *Marblehead Historical Society*

PEELE, NABBY MASON. 1778. Boston [Mass.]. 12 yrs. 15½" x 19". "Miss Sarah Stivour's School." Alphabet. Satin and cross-stitch. Hemstitched edge. Floral border. At bottom, plant, man and woman, and animals. Verses 376, 502, 503 (var.). *Essex Institute*

PERKINS, LUCY. 1792. Liverpool, Nova Scotia. 21½" x 24". 2 alphabets. French knot, stem, and cross-stitch. Strawberry border. Green lawn and two rose bushes. Verse 24 (1, 2, 3, 4, var.). *Miss Elizabeth Perkins*

PERKINS, LYDIA. 1774. [Norwich, Conn.] 7 yrs. [Born October 11, 1767.] 8" x 12". 2 alphabets. Cross-stitch. Carnation and Grecian cross-borders. Verse 198 (lines 3, 4, 5). *Miss Anna Perkins Williams*

PERKINS, LYDIA. 1776. [Norwich, Conn.] 8" x 19". 3 alphabets. Eyelet, satin, and cross-stitch. Vine, strawberry, and Greek fret cross-borders. Strawberry plant. *Miss Anna Perkins Williams*

PERKINS, MARTHA. 1773. 13" x 10". Alphabet. Cross-stitch and tent-stitch in silk and wool. House, trees, flowers, sheep, man, and woman. Verse 490 (var.). *Mrs. H. C. Hatch*

PERKINS, MARTHA. [Cir. 1799.] Nobleboro [Me.?]. Born in 1786. 8" x 10". 2 alphabets. Cross-stitch. Plain border. Ornamental embroidery. Verse 490 (var.). *Mrs. Albert G. Ropes*

PERKINS, SARAH. 1779. Newburyport [Mass.]. 11 yrs. 17" x 23". 2 alphabets. Eyelet, stem, satin, and cross-stitch. Trees, rosebush, basket of flowers, lambs, parrots, bluebird, strawberries, etc. Verse 202 (1). *Miss Georgiana Augusta Currier*

PERRY, ALFREDA BAILEY. Easton [Mass.]. 16" x 6". 3 alphabets. Cross-stitch in black. *Sold at Libby's Auction Rooms, Boston, March 1, 1916*

PETERS, CHARITY. 1760. 7" x 20". 3 alphabets. Eyelet and cross-stitch. Bands of cross-stitch. *Miss Grace Hewlett*

PETERSON, SARAH. 1792. Hartford [Conn.]. 8 yrs. Born March 20, 1784. 15″ x 17″. Satin and cross-stitch. Greek border. Cornucopia with fruit and flowers. Family names and dates: "Daniel Peterson born 1757; Catherine Caldwell born April 4, 1761; Married January 18, 1781. Harry Peterson born Feb. 6, 1782; Sarah Peterson born March 20, 1784; Elizabeth Peterson born April 27, 1787; died March 12, 1788; David Peterson lost at sea, aged 29 yrs." *Mrs. Henry P. Briggs*

PETTINGELL, MARY. [Cir. 1780.] Newburyport [Mass.]. Born April 30, 1769. 11½″ x 15¼″. 2 alphabets. Eyelet, satin, and cross-stitch. Greek fret border. Trees, hills, baskets of flowers, and owls. Verse 203. *Miss Helen Pike*

PHILLIPS, HANNAH. 1770. 13 yrs. 9″ x 5″. Cross-stitch. Strawberry design. Verse 1.
Mrs. Josiah Quincy

PHILLIPS, HANNAH. 1793. [Hunterdon County, N. J.] 15 yrs. 8″ x 18″. 2 alphabets. Outline, chain, eyelet, and cross-stitch. *Mrs. L. W. Grover*

PHILLIPS, MARGARET. 1799. [Near Wickford, R. I.] 10 yrs. 8¼″ x 12½″. Alphabet. Crossstitch. Cross and vine border. Birds, trees, and bird-house. *Mrs. G. W. Slocum*

PICKERING, LUCIA. 1759. Salem [Mass.]. 12 yrs. 7½″ x 15½″. 4 alphabets. Eyelet and crossstitch. 7 different cross-borders. Verses 40 (var.), 248 (1, var.).
Mrs. Frederick A. Whitwell

PICKERING, SARAH. 1742. Salem [Mass.]. 12 yrs. 10½″ x 14″. 2 alphabets. Eyelet and crossstitch. Strawberry border. *Mrs. John Pickering*

PIERCE, ELIZA. See BETSY MANSFIELD.

PIERCE, HARRIOT. See BETSY MANSFIELD.

PIKE, NANCY. 11 yrs. 9½″ x 11½″. Alphabet. Yellow linen. Cross-stitch.
Miss Elizabeth F. Kelly

PILLSBURY, EUNICE. 1778. 12″ x 20″. Satin, eyelet, and cross-stitch. Carnation border through center. Adam and Eve and the Serpent, also hearts, baskets, birds, and trees. "It is good for me to draw near unto God." *Miss Caroline C. Tappan*

PINER, ELIZABETH. 1776. Dover [Del.]. 12 yrs. 18″ x 8½″. 2 alphabets. Stem-stitch. Outside border in diamond pattern, and inside, one of large flowers. Cross-lines.
Mrs. Eugene du Pont

PINNIGER, ABIGAIL. 1730. 9¾″ x 16″. Satin and cross-stitch. Vine and flower border. Conventionalized tulip, rose, and carnation cross-borders. Large flower and vine design not quite finished. Verses 186 (2, 3, 4), 343 (3, 4, 5, var.). Illustrated.
Rhode Island School of Design

PIPER, BETSY. 1790. 13 yrs. 8¼″ x 10¼″. 3 alphabets. Satin and cross-stitch. Modified strawberry and other simple borders. *A. Stainforth, Dealer*

PIPER, MIRIAM. 1784. Newburyport [Mass.]. 10 yrs. 18″ x 24″. 4 alphabets. French knot, eyelet, satin, and cross-stitch. Trees, urns, kids, dogs, and birds. Verse 202 (1).
Miss Lucie A. Peabody

PLATT, SARAH. [Cir. 1784.] Painted sampler. "Sarah Platt Daughter of Thomas & Mary Platt his wife Was Born July 25 Anno Domini 1770." Picture of Sarah at bottom surrounded by vines and flowers. *Maxcy Applegate, Esq.*

PLUMMER, MOLLY. 1793. Newbury [Mass.]. 9 yrs. Born October 5, 1784. 7½″ x 10″. 2 alphabets. Cat and cross-stitch. Hemstitched edge. Strawberry design.
Miss Edith D. Newman

POLK, MARGARET JANE. [Before 1775.] Born June 4, 1768. 8″ x 21½″. 2 alphabets. Eyelet, queen, and cross-stitch. Greek fret border at top. Across center, band of strawberries and branches of trees. At bottom, band of saw-tooth design, with little cups in spaces. "Elizabeth Polk died on Tuesday evening at 7 o'clock in the year 1775." Verse 49.

J. Clifford Haines, M.D.

POPE, SARAH E. 1773. 11 yrs. 10½″ x 13½″. Tent, eyelet, and cross-stitch. Border with vine and strawberry blossoms, buds, and berries. Cross-border of flowers, dogs, and angels. Scene with house, fence, gate, trees, animals, birds, arbor, and high-shouldered man and woman. Verse 360 (var.). *Newport Historical Society*

POOR, JUDITH. [1761.] Newbury [Mass.]. 10 yrs. Born October 12, 1751. 4 alphabets. Eyelet, satin, and cross-stitch. Trefoil border on three sides, and carnation, rosebud, saw-tooth, and Greek fret cross-borders. Verse 490 (var.).

POTTER, SARAH. 1775. Ipswich [Mass.]. 7½″ x 8¼″. Alphabet. Cross-stitch. Simple cross-stitch border. Large candelabra in center, birds each side standing on branches; below, sheep and grass. *Mrs. William Dole*

PRAY, MARY. [10 yrs.?] 9½″ x 13″. 2 alphabets. Cross-stitch. Hemstitched edge and cross-borders. Verse 128 (1, var.). *A. Stainforth, Dealer*

PRESTON, ELIZABETH. 1787. 12″ x 8½″. Alphabet. Cross-stitch. Simple border. Strawberry cross-borders. Family initials: "A P, E P, I P, M P, M P, I P, A S, I S, M S, I S, M S, E S, B S, I D, I D, Z P, I P, A P, M P, P P, E P, W , I P, E P, M S, E S, W P, E P, A S, R S, B S, I S, S D, T D, I P, R P, B S, M S, W ."

Mrs. L. D. Samson

PRIOR, MARTHA D. 1795. 5 yrs. 7½″ x 8″. 2 alphabets. Cross-stitch.

Rhode Island School of Design

PRIOR, MARY. 1796. [Priors Mill and Bergen, N. J.] 13 yrs. 9″ x 11¼″. Eyelet, satin, and cross-stitch. Strawberry and vine border. Birds, baskets, and flowers.

Miss Emma Post Denniston

PUTNAM, HANNAH. [Cir. 1764.] Danvers [Mass.]. 10½″ x 16″. 4 alphabets. Outline, long, cross, and other stitches. Clover border. Verse 490 (var.). *Mrs. Robert Hale Bancroft*

PUTNAM, MARTHA. 1797. Worcester [Mass.]. 13 yrs. 11½″ x 17″. 2 alphabets. Cross-stitch. Greek cross in corners, and lozenges between in border. Small, conventional trees. Verse 658. *Miss M. C. Wheelwright*

QUAILES, SALLY. 1793. 8 yrs. 8¼″ x 13½″. Alphabet. Eyelet, outline, cross, and hem-stitch. Several simple motifs. Verses 126 (1), 193. *Wilbur M. Stone, Esq.*

QUASH, SARAH. 1783. Charleston [S. C.]. 10″ x 12″. Alphabet. Eyelet and cross-stitch. Hemstitched edge and simple cross-stitch border. *Mrs. William Dunkin*

R——, S——. 1798. 12″ x 12″. 3 alphabets. Cross-stitch. *Mrs. Brouwer*

RAMSAY, MARGARET. 1789. Albany [N. Y.]. 8 yrs. 8″ x 10″. Cross, tent, stem, chain, split, satin, buttonhole, and a lace-stitch. Adam and Eve, the serpent, and the Tree of Knowledge below; above, a fence with flowers, and above that a cottage. Illustrated.

The New York Society of the Colonial Dames. Van Cortlandt Manor

RAND, ELIZABETH SIMPKINS. 8″ x 6″. 5 alphabets. Cross-stitch. Strawberry border.

Charles W. Jenks, Esq.

RAND, LUCY. 1770. [Born in 1762.] 9″ x 10½″. Alphabets. Cross-stitch. Strawberry, vine, and Greek fret borders. Verse 595. *Mrs. Arthur Crittenden Smith*

RAND, MARY. 1788. 11 yrs. 11½″ x 15¾″. 3 alphabets. Eyelet, satin, and cross-stitch. Borders of double strawberry, birds, baskets, carnations, crowned passant lions, etc. Verses 22, 342. "Fear God and . . ." *Charles W. Jenks, Esq.*

RAND, SUSANAH. 1798. 13″ x 19″. 4 alphabets. Satin, eyelet, and cross-stitch. Simple cross-border. Flower-pots, birds, strawberries, crowned lions, flowers, etc. Verse 128 (var.). *Charles W. Jenks, Esq.*

RANDALL, FANNY. 1794. Annapolis [Md.]. 9 yrs. 8″ x 15″. 2 alphabets. Darning and cross-stitch. Hemstitched edge. Birds. *Judge A. B. Hagner*

RAWSON, CLARA. 1795. Warwick [Mass.]. 10″ x 14″. 3 alphabets. Stem and cross-stitch. Strawberry border. Branches of strawberries. Verse 128 (1, var.). *Mrs. Edgar H. Bucklin*

RAWSON, HANNAH. [About 1799.] 16½″ x 12″. 3 alphabets. Chain and cross-stitch. Cross-stitch border. Verse 5. *Mrs. Fred A. Morse*

RAWSON, HANNAH. [About 1799.] 12⅞″ x 8″. 3 alphabets. Cross-stitch. Simple border. Verse 630. *Mrs. Fred A. Morse*

RAYNER, ELIZABETH. 1789. Newburyport [Mass.]. 12 yrs. [Born March 27, 1777.] 10½″ x 9″. Alphabets. Satin and cross-stitch. Double and triple strawberry border divided in sections. Dogs, sheep, flowers, double strawberries, and birds. Verse 372. *Mrs. R. S. Southard*

RAYNER, KATY. 1793. [Newburyport, Mass.] 12 yrs. [Born July 19, 1781.] 10″ x 18½″. 2 alphabets. Cross-stitch. Strawberry border. Dogs, cats, and strawberries. Verse 224. *Mrs. R. S. Southard*

REA, SALLY. 1766. 16″ x 18″. 2 alphabets. Eyelet, tent, and cross-stitch. Vine and flower border, and cross-borders of carnations and strawberries. At bottom, Adam and Eve and Tree of Knowledge. "If women will not be inclined to seek the Information of the mind, Believe me Sally for its true, Parrots will talk as well as you." Illustrated. *Mrs. Miles White, Jr.*

REYNOLDS, CLARISSA. 1784. 10 yrs. 8″ x 9½″. 3 alphabets. Chain, eyelet, and cross-stitch. *Wilbur M. Stone, Esq.*

RHODES, ELIZABETH. 1776. 8″ x 7″. 3 alphabets. Chain and cross-stitch. *Mrs. Fred A. Morse*

RHODES, ELIZABETH. 1776. 7″ x 5″. 2 alphabets. Chain, stem, and cross-stitch. Verses 186 (1, 2), 343 (1, 3, var.). *Mrs. Fred A. Morse*

RICE, FANNY. 1782. Brookfield [Mass.]. 13 yrs. Born October 29, 1779. 7½″ x 9½″. 3 alphabets. Cross-stitch. Hemstitched edge, with narrow cross-stitch border. Strawberry cross-border. *Miss Frances M. Lincoln*

RICHARDS, CHLOE. 1798. 13 yrs. Born December 8, 1785. 8½″ x 10½″. 2 alphabets. Cross-stitch. Simple border, hemstitched edge. Verse 187. *Mrs. Frederick F. Thompson*

RICHARDS, GRACE ANN. 1794. Verse 517. *Mrs. Frederick F. Thompson*

RICHARDS, SALLY. 1797. 10″ x 12″. 3 alphabets. Cross-stitch. Simple border. *Mrs. H. C. Bunner*

RICHARDSON, ANSTIS E. 1789. 8″ x 12″. 3 alphabets. Cat, chain, queen, satin, and cross-stitch. Strawberry border with roses in corners. *Charles E. Goodspeed, Esq.*

RICHARDSON, JANE. 1790. 9 yrs. 17" x 21½". Punch-work and cross-stitch. Greek fret and zigzag clover pattern in border. Cross-borders of geometric hearts and crowns, tree with birds, man and woman, flower vases and baskets, sailing vessel, fish, bird, etc.

The Emma B. Hodge Collection

RICHARDSON, MARY. 1783. Salem, Mass. 12 yrs. ["Miss Sarah Stivour's School."] 20" x 20½". 5 alphabets. Carnation and vine border, with head of cherub in center at top. Man and woman standing in field of flowers and grass. Verses 128, 129 (var.). Illustrated in "Memories of Old Salem," p. 104. *Mrs. Charles R. Waters*

RICHARDSON, MARY. 1797. 7 yrs. 8" x 10". 2 alphabets. Satin, eyelet, and cross-stitch. Hemstitched edge and Greek fret border. Large tree, birds, and strawberries.

Edmund M. Dow, Esq.

RICHARDSON, SARAH. 1780. 7 yrs. Born April 7, 1773. 6" x 10". 1 alphabet. Satin and cross-stitch. Cross-stitch cross-borders. Rose spray at bottom. Verse 199.

C. E. Goodspeed, Esq., 1917

RICHMOND, RHODA M. 1795. Providence [R. I.]. 6½" x 8". 3 alphabets. Eyelet, tent, and cross-stitch. Cross-border. *Miss Alice L. Washburn*

RICHMOND, RUTH. 1791. 12 yrs. 10" x 4". 2 alphabets. Chain and cross-stitch.

Sydney R. Burleigh, Esq.

RIDGWAY, ABIGAIL. 1795. Cross-stitch. Vine border. Conventional trees, flowers, and dogs, also elaborate carnation and rose through the center. Verse 229.

Formerly one of the Drake Collection

ROBBINS, JERUSHA. 1795. Williamstown [Mass.]. 10 yrs. 10" x 8". Alphabet. Cross-stitch. Plain border. Verse 187 (var.). *Mrs. Charles Read Banks*

ROBINS, ANN. 1730. 12" x 16". Tent, satin, long and short, eyelet, rope, and cross-stitch. Carnation border and cross-borders of roses, strawberries, vines, etc. Verses 67, 181 (1, var.). Names: "Thomas Robins, Sarah Robins, Hester Chandler, John Chandler, Samuel Robins, Ann Robins, Thomas Robins, John Robins, Sarah Robins, Rebecca Robins, Mary Robins, Elizabeth Robins, William Robins, Jacob Robins, Mary Robins, Samuel Robins." Illustrated. *Miss Susan P. Wharton*

ROBINS, DEBORAH. 1750. 10" x 13¾". Alphabet. Stem, eyelet, and cross-stitch. Rose-vine border. Pastoral scene, with shepherdess, sheep, dog, birds, flowers, and trees. Verse 92a (var.). *Mrs. Robert G. Patten*

ROBSON, ANE. 1768. 15 yrs. 5¼" x 6". 2 alphabets. Cross-stitch. Greek fret borders. Verse 128 (1, var.). *Mrs. Gertrude Fuller Nichols*

ROGERS, HANNAH CUTTER. 1793. Portsmouth [N. H.]. 12 yrs. 12½" x 16½". 3 alphabets. Eyelet, stem, satin, and cross-stitch. Trefoil and rose border at sides, scroll and satin-stitch border at top, wide floral design at bottom. *Miss Mary H. Wheeler*

ROGERS, NANCY. 1797. Gloucester [Mass.]. 7 yrs. [Born February 8, 1790.] 8" x 13". Alphabet. Cross-stitch. Hemstitched edge. Verse 129 (var.). *Miss Judith Rogers*

ROYLSTON, DOROTHY. 1731. 12 yrs. 7¾" x 13¼". 3 alphabets. Cross-stitch. Strawberry, Greek fret, and geometrical borders. Verse 128 (var.). *Theodore P. Tower, Esq.*

RUSH, AGNES. 1797. 4 yrs. 3½" x 16". Alphabet. Cross-stitch. Simple cross-stitch dividing lines. *Mrs. Fred W. Smith*

RUSSELL, ABIGAIL. 1782. Very small. Cross-stitch. Only letters on it besides name.

Miss Betty Russell

RUSSELL, ELIZABETH. 1719. Marblehead [Mass.]. 14 yrs. 6½″ x 7½″. 3 alphabets. Eyelet and cross-stitch. 9 different cross-borders. Tree, plants, and squirrels.

Mrs. Frederick A. Whitwell

RUSSELL, MARY. 8″ x 10″. 3 alphabets. Cross-stitch. Very plain sampler.

Belonged to Delano Estate and sold at Libby's, Boston, March 1, 1916

RUSSELL, MARY. 1784. Alphabet. Petit-point, stem, eyelet, French knot, satin, and cross-stitch. Strawberry border. Hunting and milking scene. Very interesting.

The Emma B. Hodge Collection

RUSSELL, TABBY. [Cir. 1789.] Born September, 1779. 19″ x 20″. 5 alphabets. Laid and punch-work and cross-stitch. 3 borders, outside point, black punch-work, vine of conventional-ized rose leaves and Greek fret. Trees, fruit, squirrels, birds, butterflies, turtle, ducks, deer, cow, flowers, etc. Verse undecipherable.

Miss Harriet D. Perkins

SACKETT, SALLY. [Cir. 1796.] Long Island. Born April 21, 1786. 10½″ x 17″. Cross-stitch. Vine border on three sides. Medley of flowers, baskets, and birds. Verse 65. "Stephen Sacket born May 23, 1752; Eunice Lovering Born December 28, 1748; Married Nob 25, 1776. Stepn Sacket jr born Aug 7, 1777; Eunice Sacket born April 25, 1779; Hannah Sacket born Aug 7, 1781; Sally Sacket born April 21, 1786; Daniel Sact born Sept. 23, 1790."

Mrs. Henry Eugene Coe

SALTONSTALL, ANNA. 1799. Haverhill [Mass.]. 11 yrs. 14½″ x 16″. 4 alphabets. Eyelet, stem, and cross-stitch. Rose-vine border. Grass, tree, and shrub. Verse 101.

The Misses Ward

SANDBORN, ELIZABETH DEARBORN. 1786. Meredith Bridge [now Laconia, N. H.]. Born October 18, 1773. 17″ x 22″. 3 alphabets. Stem, flat, cat, satin, and cross-stitch. Hemstitched edge and trefoil border across top. Verse 182 (1).

Mrs. Arthur F. Titus

SANDERSON, HANNAH. 1789. 15″ x 18″. 2 alphabets. Long and short, satin, and cross-stitch. Double border of carnations and scrolls. Cherry tree and strawberry bushes.

The Emma B. Hodge Collection

SANDERSON, SIBBYL. 11″ x 7½″. 3 alphabets. Cross-stitch. Hemstitched edge and simple border.

A. Stainforth, Dealer

SANFORD, BATHSHEBA. 1783. Medway [Mass.]. 12 yrs. [Born February 14, 1771.] 8″ x 9″. Alphabet. Cross-stitch. Simple border.

Mrs. Lyndon Sanford Macy

SANFORD, SARAH. 1786. 20″ x 18″. Long and short, stem, and cross-stitch. Elaborate rose and strawberry border. Shepherd and shepherdess and black slave under a tree. Bees, birds, animals, and flowers fill in spaces. Verse 363.

Mrs. Maynadiere Browne

SAUNDERS, SARAH. 1789. [Salem.] Born March 6, 1779. 9″ x 13½″. Alphabets. Eyelet and cross-stitch. Hemstitched edge. Verses 44, 138.

Mrs. H. A. Everett

SAUNDERS, SARAH DONNA LEONORA. 16½″ x 16″. Cross-stitch. Border of strawberry leaves. Picture of William and Mary College, Virginia, in center. Initials: "S B M, L A M, M L S, L A P, E J N, C N P, P A R, A C, F A B, M C H, E L B, C A M." These are probably the initials of friends and embroidered by them. Also the names: "John S. Mary Saunders."

Mrs. Bradbury Bedell

SAVAGE, JANE. 1747. 12 yrs. Born January 5, 1735. 9¼″ x 16½″. Tent, chain, and cross-stitch. Dogs and flowers in top border. Verse 190.

The Emma B. Hodge Collection

SAWYER, BETSEY. 1798. "Born August 24, 1785." 13″ x 16″. 4 alphabets. Cross, chain, stem, and flat-stitch. Trefoil and saw-tooth borders. Carnation cross-border. Tree, parrot, woman, vase of flowers, and birds. Verse 659a.

Scott, Betsy. 1793. Very large. Map of England and Wales, showing counties. Wreath of flowers in upper right-hand corner, with name, etc. Work done in chain, satin, and cross-stitch.　　　　　　　　　　　　　　　　　　　　　　　　　　　*Mrs. E. L. H. Wood*

Scott, Elizabeth. 1741. Newport, R. I. 5 yrs. 8″ x 10″. Cross, satin, and back-stitch. Vine border. Verse 342 (var.). Also "Lord give me wisdom to direct my ways."
　　　　　　　　　　　　　　　　　　　　　　　　　　　Mrs. Emma J. De Blois

Searing, Bath–sheba. 1766. Dighton, Mass. 9 yrs. 10½″ x 15¼″. 3 alphabets. Tent, stem, cross, and cat-stitch. Border of conventionalized strawberries and flowers. Brick house, tree, gate, bird, etc. Verse 128 (1, var.), and another illegible.　　*Arthur F. Wastcoat, Esq.*

Sears, Hitty [Mehitable]. 1798. Dennis [Mass. Born October 21, 1788.]. 8¼″ x 10¼″. 3 alphabets. Star and cross-stitch. Strawberry-vine border and hemstitched edge. Verse 490 (var.). "This work above my needle wrought
　　　　　May I reflect my life is short."　　　　　　　　　*Mrs. R. F. Graham*

Seaver, Mary G. 1709. 14 yrs. 7¾″ x 8″. Alphabets. Stem and cross-stitch. Plain border. Rose design in stem-stitch.　　　　　　　　　　　　　　　　　　　*Mrs. E. Morgan*

Shanahan, Margaret. 3 alphabets. Petit-point, tapestry, stem, and cross-stitch. Border in tapestry-stitch, with diamond pattern at top and marigolds on sides. House and flower-pots. Verse 367a.　　　　　　*Illustrated in "Memories of Old Salem," p. 104*

Sharpless, Eliza. 1797. Philadelphia [Pa. 8 yrs.]. 9½″ x 10½″. Eyelet, chain, satin, and cross-stitch. Strawberry border. Family initials: "J S, I S, E S, J S, E S, T S, J S, M S." Houses, baskets of flowers, plants, terraced lawn, trees, bushes, dogs, and conventionalized strawberry plant.　　　　　　　　　　　　　　*The Misses Penniman*

Sharpless, Emily. 1796. Philadelphia [Pa.]. 9 yrs. 22½″ x 21½″. Satin and cross-stitch. Conventional vine border. Houses, terraced grass, trees, men, women, dogs, rabbits, birds, butterflies, conventionalized strawberry plant, etc.　　　　　*The Misses Penniman*

Shaw, Mary. 1754. 8″ x 12″. 5 alphabets. Flat, eyelet, and cross-stitch. Vine with flowers across top. Heart.　　　　　　　　　　　　　　　　*Miss Beulah A. Saunders*

Shaw, Priscilla. 1771. Plymouth [Mass.]. 13 yrs. Born January 11, 1758. 7½″ x 10″. Alphabet. Stem and cross-stitch. Borders of rose, carnation, and strawberry designs. "Remember thy Creator," etc.　　　　　　　　　　　*Mrs. J. B. Shurtleff, Jr.*

Sheafe, Hetty. 1773. Portsmouth [N. H.]. 13 yrs. 11″ x 20″. Four alphabets. Eyelet, stem, satin, and cross-stitch. Hemstitched border. 16 border designs.
　　　　　　　　　　　　　　　　　　　　　　　　Miss Lois Sheafe Joslyn

Sheffield, Elizabeth. 1784. Born July 20, 1771. 10″ x 14″. 2 alphabets. Petit-point and cross-stitch. Border of roses, vine, and birds. Man and woman on each side of a house. Cross-borders of strawberries, and below, birds, dogs, and trees.
　　　　　　　　　　　　Koopman's, Boston, for sale February, 1919

Sherburne, Sarah. [Cir. 1761.] Born March 27, 1748. 6 alphabets. Eyelet and cross-stitch. Simple cross-borders. Verse 490 (var.).　　　　　　*Mrs. Charles S. Hamlin*

Sherman, Margaret. [1770.] Jericho [L. I.]. 7¾″ x 11¾″. Alphabets. Cross-stitch. Very meager design.　　　　　　　　　　　　　　　*Mrs. Henry McAllister, Jr.*

Shirlay, Ann. 1776. 10″ x 8″. 3 alphabets. Eyelet and cross-stitch. *Mrs. Arthur G. Beals*

Shoemaker. See also Stevenson.

Silsbee, Content P. 20″ x 17″. 12 yrs. Full-blown rose design in border.
　　　　　　　　　　　　Sold at Walpole Galleries, New York, June 29, 1917

PLATE XXV

GRACE WELSH'S SAMPLER.   1774
The Emma B. Hodge Collection

PLATE XXVI

ABIGAIL MEARS'S SAMPLER. 1772
Owned by Mrs. Henry E. Coe

AMERICAN SAMPLERS

SIMPKINS, MARY. 1757. 12 yrs. 11½" x 16½". 2 alphabets. Satin, eyelet, and cross-stitch. Double strawberry border, also carnation and single strawberry. "Fear God and Love Him." Verses 202, 342, 350, 496. *Charles W. Jenks, Esq.*

SIMPKINS, SUSANAH. 1745. 13 yrs. 8½" x 13½". 2 alphabets. Eyelet, satin, and cross-stitch. Borders of carnation, strawberry, double and single, and tulip designs. Crowned lions, baskets, birds, etc. *Charles W. Jenks, Esq.*

SIMPSON, ANNE. [Cir. 1735.] Boston [Mass. Born 1720.]. 8" x 7". 4 alphabets. Cross-stitch. Greek fret, strawberry, and conventional borders. Verse 128 (1, 2). *Miss Margaret C. Wyman*

SIMPSON, MARGARET. 1755. Born in 1743. 8" x 22". 4 alphabets. Tapestry, stem, and cross-stitch. Narrow hem. Tapestry design in diamond-shaped figures. Verse 589. *Mrs. James Tuckerman*

SIMPSON, MARY. 1725. Boston [Mass. Born October 18, 1714.]. 8¼" x 18". 2 alphabets. Eyelet and cross-stitch. Borders of scroll and strawberry designs. Verse 128 (var.). *Mrs. Mary W. Nichols*

SINNICKSON, MARY. 1794. Salem [N. J.]. Born August 27, 1781. 10" x 12½". 4 alphabets. Eyelet and cross-stitch. Narrow cross-border at each end. Line of flowers. *Estate of Maria H. Eakin*

SLIM, MARIAN. 1780. [Chester Township, Burlington County, N. J. 11 yrs.] 8¼" x 9½". 1 alphabet. Eyelet and cross-stitch. Simple border. Initials of father and mother: "P S, C S." [Her parents were Holland "Redemptioners."] *Mr. Charles Lippincott*

SMITH, ——. After 1797. Sutton [Mass.]. "Born March 11, 1778." "Born Dec. 24, 1797." Names given: "Samuel Smith, Sally Smith." 3 alphabets. 15¼" x 10". Cross-stitch. Border in chain design. *W. G. Bowdoin, Esq.*

SMITH, ABIGAIL. 1755. Fairhaven [Mass.]. 12 yrs. Born June 21, 1743. 7¾" x 7¾". 2 alphabets. Cross-stitch. Simple border. *Miss Mary F. Gill*

SMITH, ANN. 1787. 23" x 22". Map of Europe done in chain and cross-stitch. Festoon at top, bows, cord, and tassel in center, with conventional tulips and small flowers festooned from bow. Small flowers and leaves in lower corners. *Miss F. M. Kerr*

SMITH, CATHARINE. 1798. Born in 1788. [Chester, Orange County, N. Y.] 16½" x 12½". Alphabet. Eyelet and cross-stitch. Simple border. "Make the study of the Sacred Scriptures your daily Practice and principal Concern and Embrace the Doctrines contained in them, as the real Oracles of God and the Dictates of . . ." *Mrs. George S. Hamlin*

SMITH, ELIZABETH. 1794. Plainfield [Conn.]. 4½" x 7". Alphabet. Cross-stitch. Plain, double cross-stitch border. *Mrs. Albert Babcock*

SMITH, ESTHER. 1798. 14 yrs. 17" x 9". 3 alphabets. Chain, stem, and cross-stitch. *Miss Alzada Sprague*

SMITH, LOANN. 1785. 13 yrs. Born September 27, 1772. 12" x 15". 2 alphabets. Satin and cross-stitch. Border at sides of vine and flowers; at top, University Hall at Brown, with figures of man and woman, trees and animals; at bottom, Old State House, with woman, animals, etc. Verse 95 (2). Illustrated. *Rhode Island School of Design*

SMITH, LUCY. 1794. 12¼" x 12½". 9 alphabets. Eyelet, buttonhole, and cross-stitch. Vine and flower border. Elaborate convenfional carnations, strawberries, roses, and vines. Verse 518. *Miss Lucy Dennis Holme*

SMITH, MARY. "17014". 5 yrs. 8½" x 21". Double alphabet. Chain, tent, and cross-stitch. Conventional cross-borders. Verse 128 (1, var.).   *Mrs. Charles M. Morse*

SMITH, MARY. 1782. [Rowley, Mass.] 15 yrs. 16" x 18". 3 alphabets. Stem, satin, flat, eyelet, and cross-stitch. Border of flowers, leaves, birds, vases, buds, or berries. Flower design.   *Miss Caroline M. Burnham*

SMITH, MARY. 1783. [Salem County, N. J.] 13" x 13". Satin, chain, and French knot. Whole sampler is in drawn-work and fine embroidery. Basket filled with flowers in center. Open-work and embroidered circles in lower corners, with gathered ribbon around them. Fine hemstitched border.   *Mrs. Ella Maria Hamilton*

SMITH, POLLY. 1794. Salem [Mass.]. 9 yrs. 12¼" x 16¾". 2 alphabets. Satin, chain, eyelet, tent, and cross-stitch. Border of vine and roses. Farm scene. Verse 129 (var.).   *Miss M. Lizzie Bray*

SMITH, SALLY. Salem [Mass.]. 17" x 17". 2 alphabets. Stem and cross-stitch. Border at top of carnations; at sides, vine with small flowers; in corners, bunches of lily-of-the-valley. Large flower-pot, with rose bush in full bloom.   *Mrs. John Pickering*

SMITH, SARAH. 1794. Newburyport [Mass.]. 11 yrs. Born November 13, 1783. 20" x 20". Alphabets. Eyelet, stem, satin, and cross-stitch. Carnation, rose, and other flowers in border. Landscape, with trees, birds, cow, and sheep. Verse 601 (1, 2, var.).   *The Emma B. Hodge Collection*

SMITH, TABITHA. 1713. Smithtown [L. I.]. 9 yrs. 9" x 10¾". 4 alphabets. Eyelet and cross-stitch. Hemstitched edge. Cross-borders. Verse 180.   *Mrs. Charles E. Sherman*

SNOW, LUCY. 1796. 8 yrs. 5" x 12". 2 alphabets. Eyelet, satin, and cross-stitch. Cross-borders. Verse 660.   *Charlotte M. Smith*

SOUDER, SARAH ANN. [Cir. 1775. Born in 1760.] 12½" x 18". 5 alphabets. Eyelet, cat, and cross-stitch. Strawberry border. Verse 135.   *Mrs. H. C. Jones*

SPECHET, LEONORA LOUISA. 1798. 13" x 17". Map of England.   *Mrs. Thomas A. Lawton*

SPENCER, PHEBE. 1763. 14 yrs. 7½" x 12". Alphabet. Cross-stitch. Simple border. Vine cross-border. Verse 68.   *The Misses Chadsey*

SPOONER, HANNAH. 1785. 10 yrs. 7½" x 12⅛". 1 alphabet. Eyelet, cross, and two variations of buttonhole-stitch. Vine and flower border. Verses 41 (var.), 191, 620.
     W. M. Cooper, Esq.

SPOONER, SARAH. 1781. 11 yrs. 12" x 12½". 2 alphabets. Cross-stitch. Verse 345 (var.).   *Mrs. Sydney R. Burleigh*

SPRAGUE, POLLY. 1798. Petersham [Mass.]. 15 yrs. 8" x 6½". 5 alphabets. Cross-stitch. Simple border. Cocks standing on trees, two sets of two pulling worms apart.
     Estate of James L. Little, Esq.

STAATS, MARGARET. 1795. [Staats Homestead, Bound Brook, N. J.] 14 yrs. 8" x 11". 1 alphabet. Stem, satin, and cross-stitch. Border representing a fence with garden gate. At bottom, trees and baskets of flowers. "Remember thy Creator," etc.
     Eugene DuBois La Tourette, Esq.

STAATS, PHEBE. 1788. 13 yrs. 8" x 11". 2 alphabets.   *Eugene DuBois La Tourette, Esq.*

STARR, MARGARET. 1795. 11" x 14". Parts of alphabets. Tent and cross-stitch. Roman border with acorns. Pine trees, birds, dogs, and vase of flowers. Name "Wm. Cox" worked in with design. Verse 132 (1, var.).   *Miss Julia L. Muirheid*

STEBBINS, CAROLINE. 1798. 9 yrs. 7¼″ x 13″. 1 alphabet. Cross-stitch. Strawberry border. Casual arrangement of animals, birds, flowers, baskets, etc., grouped about a long medallion bordered with hearts. *Museum of Pocumtuck Valley Memorial Association*

STEBBINS, EUNICE. [Cir. 1787.] Springfield [Mass.]. Born January 14, 1775. 8½″ x 22¼″. 2 alphabets. Cross-stitch. Greek fret border. Names and dates on sampler: "Daniel born April 2, 1766. Festus born March 5, 1768, Eunice born April 5, 1770, died August 27, 1771, Quartus born November 21, 1772, Eunice born July 14, 1775, Lois born March 31, 1777." Verse 128, unfinished. *Mrs. Frederick N. Conner*

STERETT, MARY. 1783. Baltimore [Md.]. 11 yrs. 15″ x 9″. Cross-stitch. Strawberry and vine border. Verses 612, 613, 614. *Miss Mary Sterett Gittings*

STEVENS, HENRIETTA. 1788. [Talbot County, Md.] 12 yrs. Born August 14, 1776. 16″ x 20″. Cross-stitch and other stitches. Four different cross-border designs. "A Silent and loving woman is a gift of the Lord." Verses 70, 223. *Edwin J. Stevens, Esq.*

STEVENSON, { MARY / MARTHA / HARRIET }
SHOEMAKER, SARAH. 1794. 13″ x 18″. 2 alphabets. Satin and cross-stitch. Strawberry and vine border, with roses in the four corners. Large urn in center, with roses; also strawberry vines, pine trees, cats, birds, etc. Verses 378, 381. *Mrs. Harriet S. Earl*

STOCKER, LYDIA. 1798. 12 yrs. 17″ x 16″. 1 alphabet. Split, chain, stem, and cross-stitch. Wide and elaborate border, with flowers, butterflies, birds, etc. Scene with house, tree, deer, man, and woman. Verse 73. Illustrated in color. *Mrs. Henry E. Coe*

STOKES, MARTHA. 1799. Boston [Mass.]. 12 yrs. 16″ x 21″. 5 alphabets. Satin and stem-stitch. Vine border. Scene with Colonial house, tile walk, six flower-beds, fence, trees, diamond, heart, and birds, also English crowns. Verse 601 (1, 2, 3, var.). *Mrs. Nellie Wightman Nason*

STONE, MARY LIGHTBOURNE. 1790. Charleston [S. C.]. 12½″ x 18″. 4 alphabets. Eyelet and cross-stitch. Cross-design in border, doubled at top. Cross-borders in scroll design. *Miss Anna Bell Bruns*

STOODLEY, MARY. 1753. Portsmouth [N. H.]. 11 yrs. 16″ x 22″. 7 alphabets. Satin and cross-stitch. Strawberry design. The Lord's Prayer. *Miss Mary L. Gilman*

STOODLEY, MARY. [1753.] Portsmouth [N. H.]. 11 yrs. 20″ x 22″. 2 alphabets. Eyelet, satin, and cross-stitch. Floral design. The Lord's Prayer. *Miss Mary L. Gilman*

STORER, HANNAH. 1747. Groton [Mass.]. 8 yrs. 11¾″ x 15″. Alphabet. Eyelet, satin, and cross-stitch. Elaborate border, with roses and leaves. Two spies bearing the grapes of Eschol, two green trees, trefoil border, and other borders. Verses 65 (var.), 248 (1, var.). *Massachusetts Historical Society*

STROBRIDGE, ANNE. 1764. Middleboro [Mass.]. 10 yrs. 8″ x 10½″. 1 alphabet. Cross-stitch. Saw-tooth border at top. Verse 128 (var.). Unfinished. *Miss Harriet A. Barstow*

STRUDIBO, ANN. 1734. Charleston [S. C.]. 8½″ x 16½″. 2 alphabets. Petit-point, stem, satin, cat, and cross-stitch. Conventional border at top and cross-borders at bottom in Greek fret, trefoil, tree, and strawberry designs. Verse 128 (var.). *Mrs. John F. Bennett*

SUMMERILL, MARY. 1788. [Upper Penns Neck, Salem County, N. J.] 16 yrs. 10¼″ x 15¼″. 3 alphabets. Eyelet and cross-stitch. Plain border. Urns, crowns, and heart. *David C. Holton, M.D.*

SUTTON, ANN. 1789. 17 yrs. 11½" x 17½". 4 alphabets. Eyelet and cross-stitch. Dividing lines in cross-stitch. *Miss Hannah A. Sheppard*

SWAIN, MARGARET. 1754. 8" x 15". 1 alphabet. Cross-stitch. Family initials and dates:

"M S Born ye 5 day of 4 month 1745   O S
T S Born ye 3 day of   month   N S
A S Born the day of 12 month 1749
L S Born ye 13 day of ye 6 month 1752
P S Died the 9 day of May in the yar 1754."

Verses 343 (1, var.), 585. *Rhode Island School of Design*

SWAN, RUTH. 1785. Leicester [Mass.]. 10½" x 7". 2 alphabets. Cross-stitch. Cross-borders in geometrical design. Verse 14 (var.). *Mrs. John A. Sweetser*

SWEETSER, POLLY. [After 1776.] "Born at Lynn, in the County of Essex, State of Mass." 7¾" x 17⅜". 3 alphabets. Flat, tent, stem, outline, and cross-stitch. Simple cross-stitch border. Verse 494. *Miss Harriet E. Cummings*

SYMONDS, LUCY. 1796. Boxford [Mass.]. 11 yrs. 21¼" x 24½". 2 alphabets. Stem and cross-stitch. Border of vine and flowers on three sides. Five hills; on middle one, large vase of flowers, two trees on the next, baskets on remaining two, from which a vine covered with assorted flowers springs and continues as a border around the sampler. Verses 141, 653. *Mrs. Henry E. Coe*

TAGE [probably MONTAGUE], SARAH. 1794. Philadelphia [Pa.]. 18½" x 22". Satin-stitch. Landscape with man and woman and title, "Belville and Rosina." *Mrs. Mary C. Cooley*

TALBOT, MARY. 1796. Providence [R. I.]. 14" x 16". ["Miss Polly Balch's School."] Eyelet, chain, tent, queen, satin, and cross-stitch. Border at sides, rose vine, and at bottom, strawberry. Scene with State House, Providence, lambs, birds, figures of man and woman. Verse 630 (var.). *Miss Helen H. Greene*

TALMAN, KEZIA. 1788. 14 yrs. 11" x 13". [New Jersey.] Double alphabet. Stem, satin, and cross-stitch. Floral border. Verse 343 (1, var.). *Mrs. S. A. Cunningham*

TAPPAN [or TOPPAN], MARTHA. [Cir. 1721. Newbury, Mass. Born 1710.] 8" x 10½". 2 alphabets. Cross-stitch. Strawberry border. *Miss Charlotte M. Smith*

TATNALL, ANN. 1786. 12 yrs. 12½" x 17". Stem, satin, and cross-stitch. Carnation border, with strawberries in four corners. Cross-borders of strawberry, rose, elaborate vine with blossoms, and saw-tooth designs. Verses 132 (1, var.), 204, 344 (var.), 510. Names of paternal and maternal grandparents: "Edward Tatnall, Betty Tatnall, James Lea, Margaret Lea." Names of parents and children: "Joseph Tatnall, Elizabeth Tatnall; Sarah, Margaret, Elizabeth, Edward, Ann, Joseph, Esther, Edward, Thomas; Thomas Lea, Joseph Lea." Name of teacher: "Mary Askew." Illustrated. *Henry M. Canby, Esq.*

TATNALL, ELIZABETH. 1755. Wilmington [Del.]. 11 yrs. 11" x 16". Stem, satin, and cross-stitch. Border a combination of vine, strawberry, and Greek cross in corners. Two large carnations. Verses 132 (1, var.), 181, (1, var.), 192, 590. Initials of father, mother, 3 sisters, and brother: "E T, E T, M T, A T, J T, I T." *Mrs. Alter Megear*

TATUM, SYBIL. 1788. Woodbury [N. J.]. 26" x 26". Satin and cross-stitch. Thirty-three large bunches of flowers. *Miss Sybil T. Jones*

TAYLOR, ALICE. 1798. 10" x 8". 1 alphabet. Cross-stitch. Verse 390. *Mrs. William A. Spicer*

TAYLOR, ELIZA. [Cir. 1796. Born in New York, July 14, 1786.] 12½" x 16". 2 alphabets. Cross-stitch. Strawberry border. Conventional cross-lines in simple designs. Initials on sampler: "I T, M T [John Taylor and Margaret Taylor, father and mother]; E, M T, I S T, I B T, A T, I T, R L T, S T [brothers and sisters]." Verse 652.

Mrs. Henry E. Coe

TAYLOR, ISABEL. 1794. [2 Liberty St., New York City.] 8 yrs. 19″ x 23″. Alphabet. Cross-stitch. 6 cross-borders in different patterns. Birds, beast, trees, and heart. Verse 92.

Mrs. George Thacher

TAYLOR, MARY. 1740. 12 yrs. 9″ x 16″. 2 alphabets. Tulip border with minor borders. Elaborate cross-borders. Verses 184, 489 (2, 3). *Estate of James L. Little, Esq.*

TEACLE, RACHEL BIRCKHEAD. 1798. 11½″ x 12½″. 2 alphabets. Punch-work, queen and cross-stitch. Bits of fret-work and geometric patterns. "The higher character a person suports the more he should regard his minutest action." *Mrs. James Fortescue Giffen*

TENNY, SARAH. 1794. 16 yrs. 12½″ x 16½″. 4 alphabets. Bird's-eye, satin, and cross-stitch. Strawberries and sheep. *Mrs. Thomas A. Lawton*

THAYER, CHARLOTTE. 3½″ x 4″. 1 alphabet. Fine cross-stitch. Design of various figures.

Lancaster Public Library

THOMAS, MERCY. 1797. Plymouth [Mass.]. 8 yrs. Alphabet. Cross-stitch. Carnation border at top. *Mrs. J. B. Shurtleff, Jr.*

THOMAS, PRISCILLA. [1795.] 7 yrs. Born in Plymouth [Mass.], August 23, 1788. 7½″ x 8½″. Alphabet. Stem, satin, and cross-stitch. Hemstitched edge, with rose, carnation, and strawberry border. Carnation design. *Mrs. J. B. Shurtleff, Jr.*

THOMPSON, ISABELLA. 1771. 14 yrs. 19″ x 22½″. 5 alphabets. Stem, satin, and cross-stitch. Strawberry border. 3 green hills covered with sheep, and trees set between the hills, also various birds. Verse 202 (1, var.). *Miss Mary C. Wheelwright*

THOMPSON, ISABELLA. 1797. See MARY WHEATLEY.

THOMPSON, MARY. 1749. 10 yrs. 8½″ x 12″. 2 alphabets. Petit-point, tapestry, tent, and cross-stitch. 7 cross-borders. *Mrs. Theodore Yates*

THOMSON, MARGARET. 1793. 12″ x 18″. 4 alphabets. Buttonhole, stem, eyelet, and cross-stitch. Border. Basket of flowers, crowns, and tree at bottom. *Miss Alice Morton*

THORNTON, ANN. 1798. 9 yrs. 2 alphabets. Cross-stitch. Strawberry border. Carnation, rose, and conventional cross-borders. At bottom, very uneven ground with trees, large and small, animals, butterflies, birds, and detached baskets of flowers. Verse 389.

Mrs. Henry Eugene Coe

THURBER, SALLY. 1799. Born May 13, 1791. 11½″ x 12½″. 3 alphabets. Cross-stitch. Simple border. Fir tree in each lower corner. Verse 4 (var.). *Mrs. Richard Greene Davis*

THURSTON, MEHITABLE. 1795. Born October 5, 1782, at Newbury [Mass.]. 17″ x 21″. 3 alphabets. Stem, satin, and cross-stitch. Carnation, rose, lily, and vine border. Vase of flowers on each side a hill topped by a tree, also bees, bird, goat, lamb, and dog. Verse 25.

Mrs. Maria S. P. Humphreys

THWING, SARAH. 1771. Boston [Mass.]. 12 yrs. [Born in Boston, June 12, 1759.] 7″ x 14″. 3 alphabets. Eyelet, stem, and cross-stitch. Strawberry and Greek fret borders. Vine design. Verse 185. *Mrs. Joseph M. Bright*

TILDEN, JOANNA. 1762. 8¾″ x 14″. 2 alphabets. All kinds of stitches used. Sampler divided into seven sections. At bottom, 9 green mounds in three rows, with strawberries and strawberry blossoms growing among them. *Mrs. Louise J. Horne*

TIPPIT, BETTY. 1774. 18 yrs. 6' x 10". Crewel, satin, and cross-stitch. Designs of ferns and flowers. The lettering is all in cross-stitch along the top, the foliage in sections reaching up toward it. Verse 128. *Mrs. J. A. Noble, Dealer, 1917*

TITUS, POLLY. 1797. 8" x 17". Alphabets. Cross, eyelet, and hem-stitch. Few cross-stitch designs and a tree. *Wilbur M. Stone, Esq.*

TODD, SARAH L. 8 yrs. 11¼" x 7⅞". 3 alphabets. Eyelet, satin, and cross-stitch. Saw-tooth border in cross-stitch, and cross-borders in eyelet and satin-stitch. Green wreath and two baskets of flowers. *A. Stainforth, Dealer*

TOMLIN, DRUSILA. 1793. 8½" x 18". 3 alphabets. Eyelet, tent, and cross-stitch. Cross-stitch border at top and sides, and tent-stitch border at bottom. *J. Clifford Haines, M.D.*

TOMSON, LUCY. 1787. 11 yrs. 7" x 8". 1 alphabet. Cross-stitch. *Mrs. C. M. Eddy*

TOPPAN, MARY. 1762. 12 yrs. Born June 26, 1750. Newbury [Mass.]. 9" x 12". 2 alphabets. Eyelet, satin, and cross-stitch. Greek-fret border across top; triangles of flat-stitch outlined in cross-stitch. Elaborate design in center. "Goodness and Mercy ever follow those that . . ." *Newburyport Historical Society*

TOPPAN, SARAH. 1756. Newbury [Mass.]. Born May 16, 1740. 14" x 20". 3 alphabets. Stem, satin, and cross-stitch. Greek fret, trefoil, and 3rd border on sides and top, also Greek fret cross-borders. At bottom, apple tree, two deer, two rabbits, two bumblebees, two eagles, and Scotch thistle in each upper corner. "Trust in God at all times." *Mrs. Charles H. Atkinson*

TOWNSEND, HANNAH. 1794. 11 yrs. 14" x 17". 1 alphabet. Tapestry, satin, cross-stitch, and hemstitch. Hemstitched edge, with conventional triple strawberry and Greek fret border. Inside frame of saw-tooth and strawberry design, and several different cross-borders. Scene with house and two trees, topped by large birds. Verse 519. *Mrs. Thomas A. Lawton*

TOWNSEND, LYDIA. [Cir. 1750.] Oyster Bay [L. I.]. 7½" x 10". 4 alphabets. Cross-stitch. Simple cross-stitch border, with hemstitched edge. Greek border through middles, and two primitive-looking rods with vines on each side. *Mrs. Henry M. Allister, Jr.*

TOY [or TAY], GRACE. [Cir. 1717. Born in Woburn, May 18, 1704.] 7" x 36". 2 alphabets. Back, cross, and close rope-stitch, also darned and lace-stitch. Sampler consists of cross-bands done in various lace stitches and many different conventionalized flower and vine designs. Illustrated. *Mrs. N. A. Prentiss*

TRAILL, MARY. 1791. [Marblehead, Mass.] 10 yrs. 12½" x 16½". Satin, stem, chain, outline, and cross-stitch. 2 scenes at top, man with rake, man with wife and child, each holding a parasol, and man with cow; below, pastoral scene with trees, house, birds, sheep, shepherd, and shepherdess. Illustrated. *Mrs. Fletcher Hodges*

TRECOTHICK, HANNAH. 1738. Boston [Mass. 10 yrs.]. 8½" x 18". Chiefly cross-stitch. Conventional cross-borders in Greek fret, vine, strawberry, and medley of baskets, hearts, birds in cages, etc. At bottom, figures of animals, birds, conventional trees, and flowers. In center of top border, a crown, with initials G R. Lord's Prayer and Apostles' Creed in cross-stitch frames. Verse 128 (var.). Illustrated. *Miss Jane E. C. Chapman*

TRIPP, ELIZABETH. 1765. Providence, R. I. 12 yrs. Born December 20, 1753. 12" x 8". 3 alphabets. Flat, tent, stem, petit-point, chain, and cross-stitch. *Miss Jessie Tripp*

TROUP, SARAH. 1738. 8 yrs. 9" x 11¾". 4 alphabets. Cross-borders with crowns, etc. Vases of flowers. Verse 186. *Mrs. J. C. Fraser*

PLATE XXVII

BETSY ADAMS'S SAMPLER. Quincy. **1773**

Owned by Mrs. Henry E. Coe

PLATE XXVIII

SAMPLER BY AN UNKNOWN GIRL. 1775
Owned by Mrs. Thomas A. Lawton

TRUMBULL, FAITHY. 1781. Lebanon [Conn.]. 12 yrs. 8¼" x 15½". 2 alphabets. Eyelet, stem, satin, and cross-stitch. Hemstitched edge. Verse 367. *Miss Henrietta W. Hubbard*

T[RUMBULL], M[ARTHA]. 1775. [Said to have belonged to Martha Trumbull of Connecticut.] 5" x 7". Alphabet. Cross-stitch. *Miss Ambia C. Harris*

TRYON, CATHERINE. 1794. Lebanon Springs [N. Y.]. 12 yrs. 11¼" x 9½". 2 alphabets. Cross-stitch. Conventional border in geometrical designs. *Mrs. Albert E. Smith*

TUFTS, SUSANNA. 1789. [Charlestown.] 9 yrs. Born in Charlestown, Mass., December 8, 1780. 8¼" x 9¾". 2 alphabets. Satin and cross-stitch. Simple border. Verse 617 (var.). *Miss Edith Johnson*

TURNER, IRENE. 1799. 8 yrs. 8" x 11". 2 alphabets. Cross-stitch. Hemstitched edge, with border of points in cross-stitch. Small tree with birds and other figures. *Mrs. W. S. Rich*

TURNER, POLLY. 1786. Born February 15, 1775, at Warren [R. I.]. Wrought August 12, 1785, at Providence. Long and short, tent, satin, stem, queen, and cross-stitch. Floral border rising out of vases in lower corners, with birds flying about at top. In each lower corner, small inset, sheep and shepherdess in one, and sheep and shepherd in the other. In center, President's house, Brown University, and ladies and gentlemen going to the reception. Verse 624. ["Miss Polly Balch's School."] *Mrs. Henry E. Coe*

TUTTLE, REBECCA. 1785. Brattleboro [Vt.]. 8½ yrs. 11" x 16½". 2 alphabets. Eyelet, satin, and cross-stitch. Hearts and lozenges. Verse 618 (unfinished). [Linen spun by the maker.] *Mrs. Charles E. Reed*

TUXBURY, LYDIA. 1797. Born November 23, 1787. 8¼" x 8¼". 1 alphabet. Eyelet and cross-stitch. Landscape with two human figures and a very black goat, and an urn in the middle. Strawberries and initials "L. T." at the top. Verse 236. *W. G. Bowdoin, Esq.*

TYLER, DEBORAH. 1756. 9 yrs. 8" x 20½". 4 alphabets. Laid, herring-bone, catch, cross, and other stitches. Fine hem. Cross-borders in chain, Greek fret, vine, pyramid, cube, and diamond designs. Sampler worked in cross-strips, each section divided by different stitches. Verse 193. *Mrs. Alpheus H. Hardy*

TYLER, HANNAH. 1753. Boston [Mass.]. 12 yrs. About 23" x 10½". 3 alphabets. Flat, eyelet, French knot, stem, satin, chain, and cross-stitch. Adam and Eve in Garden of Eden, surrounded by animals and flowers. *Henry Preston Kendall, Esq., and others*

TYLER, LYDIA. 1797. Methuen [Mass.]. 10 yrs. Born June 25, 1787. 18½" x 11½". 3¼ rows of capital letters. Cross-stitch. "This work I wrought when at School to Miss Sally Flint in the Year 1797." *Charles H. Tyler, Esq.*

UNDERWOOD, MARY. 1777. Jamestown [R. I.]. 12 yrs. 10" x 15". 3 alphabets. Cross-stitch. Vine border. Trees, butterflies, etc., near center. Verse 490 (var.). *Miss Edna D. Hammond*

UNKNOWN. 10" x 8". 3 alphabets. Eyelet and cross-stitch. Cross-stitch border at top. *Mrs. Robert Bean*

UNKNOWN. Washington, D. C. 17" x 27". 7 alphabets. Cross-stitch. Festoon border. Strawberry vine and baskets of berries at bottom. *N. H. McRoberts, Esq.*

UNKNOWN. 1704. 8" x 19". Double alphabet. 5 borders across sampler, with three figures, 2 men and a woman, repeated. 2 borders below and a dog. *Francis H. Bigelow, Esq.*

UNKNOWN. 1708. 3 alphabets and letters, M E L B E I W L C E, in very florid and complicated forms. Same on both sides. *Miss Henrietta Paige*

UNKNOWN. 1720. [Sampler came from the Sharpless family, but bears no name.] 8" x 18". 5 alphabets and part of a sixth. Eyelet, satin, and cross-stitch. Cross-borders at top in horizontal designs, used for making card cases, needlebooks, etc. A bird, flower, and dish on lower half of sampler, which appears to be unfinished. *F. F. Sharpless, Esq.*

UNKNOWN. 1722. [Probably Marblehead.] 7" x 7". Stem, satin, and cross-stitch. Saw-tooth border, with corners filled in solid. Blackbird with large tail, perched on vine of green leaves and blue blossoms. *Mrs. B. F. Stacey*

UNKNOWN. '35 [1735], March 18th. [This sampler was handed down to the present owner among papers dating as far back as 1649.] 14 yrs. 11" x 17½". 3 alphabets. Herring-bone, eyelet, satin, and cross-stitch. Strawberry border. Design in center, large blossoms of wild rose and strawberry. At bottom, basket of fruit, dogs on each side, large cedar tree and 2 small cedars, deer with horns, lying on his legs in an upright pose.
Mrs. Anne Pritchett Richardson

UNKNOWN. 1773. 15" x 15". Cross-stitch. Strawberry border; also crown with cup. Flower-pot, roses, and animals. Verse 342. *Mrs. T. Harrison Garrett*

UNKNOWN. 1775. 17½" x 16". Cross-stitch and satin-stitch. Large tree with spreading branches, with leaves and fruit bearing all sorts of names; cow under tree and Christ standing in front of trunk. Verses from Revelation. Illustrated. *Mrs. Thomas A. Lawton*

UNKNOWN. [Cir. 1780. Sampler came from Springfield, Mass.] 12" x 12". 3 alphabets. Cross-stitch. Simple border. Saw-tooth design at bottom. Names and dates on sampler:

"Phoebe, Born April 7, 1751
Lew   bor   feb. 23, 1753
Zebbo   Au   29, 1755
Cal   bor   Jan 29, 1758
Lo.   bo. Au 31 1760
L.   27 1763
T   Au 29 1765
W   Jan 24   1768
M   Feb . 2   1771"   *Mrs. Richard Jones*

UNKNOWN. 1790. 9" x 11". 2 alphabets. Bird's-eye and cross-stitch. Conventional carnation border. Basket of fruit, birds, strawberries growing from pot, etc. [unfinished].
Mrs. Thomas A. Lawton

UNKNOWN. 1790. 8½" x 10½". 2 alphabets. Queen and cross-stitch. Carnation cross-border. Pot of strawberries and birds pecking at a basket of fruit. *Mrs. Thomas A. Lawton*

UNKNOWN. [Cir. 1790.] 16" x 16½". Alphabet. Stem, satin, and cross-stitch. Floral border. Man, woman, animals, and birds. Verse 214. *Mrs. George A. Plimpton*

UNKNOWN. 7¾" x 12". 3 alphabets. Flat, eyelet, and cross-stitch. Strawberry border. Verse 536. *Pennsylvania Museum, Memorial Hall, Fairmount Park, Philadelphia*

UNKNOWN. [Cir. 1799.] 18" x 7½". Alphabet. Petit-point, satin, and cross-stitch. Cross-borders. Adam and Eve in the Garden. Verse 529. *Miss Caroline Franklin*

UNKNOWN. Many different designs done in lace stitches on net. Illustrated.
Mrs. Thomas A. Lawton

UNKNOWN. Cross-stitch. 3 alphabets. Simple cross-stitch border. Two little houses and trees. Verse 622. Unfinished. *From Machias, Me.*

UNKNOWN. A sampler of darned lace on net. Illustrated. *Mrs. Thomas A. Lawton*

UNKNOWN. ["KATHERIN MURY"? Early 18th Century in design.] 1 alphabet. Satin, eyelet, chain, tapestry, flat, stem, back, buttonhole, two-sided line-stitch, queen, and rope-stitch. At bottom, a row of drawn-work filet containing the name. *Mrs. William Cabell Brown*

UNKNOWN. [Early 18th Century.] Upper half, white embroidery, including lace squares; lower half, lace designs and drawn-work. Flat, two-sided line-stitch, and raised buttonhole stitch. *Mrs. William Cabell Brown*

VAN BUREN, ELIZABETH. 1785. New York. 12 yrs. Born August 30, 1773, at New York. 8″ x 12″. 3 alphabets. Cross-stitch. Greek fret border. Small pine tree at bottom. Verse 41 (var.). [Each word separated by single cross-stitch.] *Mrs. G. H. Buek*

VAN FORHIES, SARAH. [Cir. 1742. Blawanburgh, Somerset County, N. J.] Born February 4, 1731. 8″ x 11″. Alphabet. Cross-stitch. Zigzag border. Man, woman, trees, birds, house, and geometric figures. Initials: [father and mother] "C. v. F. A. v. F." [Children] "A. v. F.; M. v. F.; D. v. F.; K. v. F.; S. v. F.; C. v. F.; A. v. F." *Mrs. A. F. Albertson*

VAN MAATER, CATHERINE. 1765. [Monmouth County, N. J.] Born April 5, 1756. 7″ x 8″. Alphabet. Satin and cross-stitch. Vine border, wider at top and bottom. Birds and trees. Names: "Daniel Van Maater [father], Mary Covenhoven [mother], Catherine, Sarah, Gilbert, Micah, Nelly" [children]. *Miss Mary Voorhees*

V[AN] S[CHAICK], C[ATHERINE]. 1763. [Albany, N. Y.] "Out 10." 7½″ x 9¼″. Buttonhole and cross-stitch. Conventional border of strawberries and baskets. House, two fowl, two signs, and many small objects not nameable. Illustrated. *The late Mrs. Abraham Lansing*

VERIEN, ELIZABETH. 1716. [Boston, Mass. 12 yrs.] Born April 16, 1704. 7¾″ x 18″. 4 alphabets. Eyelet, outline, cross-stitch, and one other stitch. Borders run across between the alphabets in rather simple conventional designs, fret, vine, and carnation. 5 conventional cross-borders like those mentioned above. *Mrs. Charles Knowles Bolton*

VICKERY, ANN. 1755. Taunton [Mass.]. 8 yrs. 10″ x 11″. 2 alphabets. Cross-stitch. Cross-stitch border in black. Verse 620. *Miss Harriet A. Barstow*

VICKERY, SALLY CULEY. 1787. Taunton [Mass.]. 7 yrs. 10″ x 14″. 3 alphabets. Cross-stitch. Simple border. Verse 128 (var.). *Miss Harriet A. Barstow*

VILA, ELIZA. 1799. Belmont [Mass.]. 16½″ x 21″. 4 alphabets. Cross-stitch, satin, stem, eyelet, chain, French knot, tent, and punch-work. Border, conventionalized leaf and flower done in punch-work and cross-stitch. Basket of flowers. Verse 669. *Mrs. H. Mortimer Watson*

VINAL, SOPHIA. [Cir. 1799.] Born at Scituate [Mass.], June 30, 1788. 16½″ x 20½″. 3 alphabets. Eyelet, stem, satin, and cross-stitch. Vine border, with bunches of roses, bluebells, and carnations. Sprays of strawberries. Greek cross-border. Verses 242, 663. *Mrs. Lewis Nichols Curtis*

VOSE, LEMUEL. [Cir. 1774.] Born July 20, 1763. 9″ x 10½″. Parts of alphabet. Cross-stitch. Minor border. *Estate of James L. Little, Esq.*

VOSE, NAOMI. 1781. Milton. *The Misses Vose*

WADE, FRANCES. 1798. Savannah [Ga.]. 15 yrs. 17″ x 20″. Stem and cross-stitch. Sampler represents the Western Hemisphere. In upper right-hand corner are the outlines of Europe and Africa; in upper left-hand corner is a compass and spray of flowers; in lower left-hand corner, wreath of flowers with words, "North and South America"; and in lower right-hand corner, wreath with name of maker and date. Illustrated. *Miss Fannie Bleecker Seaman*

WADSWORTH, ABIGAIL. 1730. Hartford [Conn.]. 12 yrs. 10¼" x 13". 3 alphabets. Cross-stitch. Simple border. Verse 515 (var.). *Mrs. Robert A. Wadsworth*

WAGER, MARGARET. 1794. Philadelphia [Pa.]. 8 yrs. 10½" x 15". 4 alphabets. Eyelet, satin, and cross-stitch. Cross and strawberry border. Strawberry design at bottom. *Mrs. Margaret Wager Austin*

WAINE, MARY. 1795. 12 yrs. Lazy-daisy, split, cat, French knot, chain, satin, and cross-stitch. Vine border with roses, peonies, and other flowers. At top, houses, trees, stag, bush, and bird upside down; at bottom, horse, cow, sheep, also huge bird on a tree, vase with flowers, man with a dog, and woman with a chained bird under a flowering arbor. Verse 92 (2, var.). *Francis H. Bigelow, Esq.*

WAKEFIELD, DELIVERANCE. 1757. 10" x 12". 1 alphabet. Cross-stitch. Garden design. Verse 128 (1, var.). *Mrs. Sybil H. Friedley*

WALLAS, SUSANNAH. 1785. [Boston, Mass.] Born in 1773. 10½" x 11½". Alphabet. Chain, stem, satin, and cross-stitch. Strawberry border. Across center, 3 small shrubs, 2 large birds. *Miss Gertrude Whiting*

WARING, DOROTHY. 1774. Charleston [S. C.]. 5 yrs. 8½" x 11". Cross-stitch. Simple border. Verse 362. *Miss Leila Waring*

WARNER, LUCY. 1785. Middletown [Conn.]. 11 yrs. 17" x 16". 2 alphabets. Satin, stem, chain, French knot, queen, tent, and cross-stitch. Vine border with carnations, roses, and small flowers. Bird in each upper corner. Country scene with house, barn, fence, well, horse, trees, grass, and road. Verse 363 (1). Illustrated. *Mrs. Clarence Weart*

WARREN, POLLY. 1798. Northborough [Mass.]. 12" x 12¼". 3 alphabets. Eyelet and cross-stitch. Strawberry border. Pine tree design. Verse 94. *Mrs. John P. Reynolds*

WATERMAN, PHEBE. 1760. Cross-stitch. Unfinished. *Mrs. Lorenzo Sears*

WATSON, LUCY. 1791. Marblehead [Mass.]. 8 yrs. 12" x 15". Alphabet. Cross-stitch. Trefoil border. Sheep and small trees. Verse 98. *George M. Cushing, Esq.*

WATSON, NANCY. [1755.] 8½" x 8". 1 alphabet. Cross and flat-stitch. Verse 248 (1, var.). *Clarence A. Mathewson, Esq.*

WATTS, JANE. 1776. 12" x 16". 1 alphabet. Eyelet and cross-stitch. Quatrefoil and tulip border, and cross-borders of tulips, strawberries, and quatrefoil. At bottom, two large blossoming plants in pots, and mound in center with 5 strawberry plants. Medallion with name and date. Verses 66 (1, var.), 608. *Mrs. Frederick F. Thompson*

WATTSON, ELIZABETH. 1795. [Philadelphia, Pa.] 11 yrs. 10¾" x 12¼". 2 alphabets. Stem, satin, and cross-stitch. Vine border with roses, tulips, and carnations. Small spray of flowers. Verse 382. *Mrs. Victor B. Woolley*

WEAR, ANN. [Cir. 1792.] Norfold [Va.]. Born in 1782. 8¼" x 13". 4 alphabets. Eyelet, cat, and cross-stitch. Cross-border. House. *Miss Ellen Coppuck Curtis*

WEAVER, MARY. 1770. 7" x 9". 2 alphabets. Cross-stitch. Plain border. Design of carnations and tulips. *Newport Historical Society*

WEBB, MARY. 1760. [York, Pa.] 13 yrs. 15" x 17". Tent, satin, and cross-stitch. Carnation and vine border, with tulips in each corner. Inner border in chain design. Sampler divided into 9 squares, with sprays of different flowers in center and four corners, and verses in remaining four. Illustrated. Verses 351, 353, 354, 592. *Mrs. Samuel C. Rumford*

WEEKS, HANNAH. [1787.] Greenland [N. H.]. 9 yrs. [Born in 1778.] 7½″ x 12″. Alphabet and parts of others. Satin, eyelet, and cross-stitch. Hemstitched edge, with trefoil and geometrical designs in border at bottom. Verse 490 (var.). *Miss Hannah Bartlett Rollins*

WEEKS, HANNAH. [1787.] Greenland [N. H.]. 9 yrs. 6″ x 8″. Alphabet. Hemstitched. Satin and cross-stitch. Geometrical designs at the bottom. *Miss Hannah Bartlett Rollins*

WELCH, DORCAS. 1751. Boston [Mass.]. 7½″ x 17″. Cross-stitch. Elaborate border. Verse 490 (var.). *F. C. Welch, Esq.*

WELD, H[ERMIONE]. 1775. [Boston, Mass.] 9½″ x 12″. 1 alphabet. Stem, satin, and cross-stitch. Vine and floral border on three sides. Large conventionalized flower, birds, and small trees in cross-border in center; also scroll and small floral cross-borders. At bottom, grass, trees, farmer with pole, sheep, and cows; flowers growing in grass.
Robert Tracy Jackson, Esq.

WELD, SARAH. 1774. Roxbury [Mass.]. 8¼″ x 11″. 2 alphabets. Cross-stitch. Hemstitched edge. Cross-border of trees and birds at bottom. Verse 490 (var.).
Mrs. Harrison F. Hunt

WELSH, GRACE. 1774. 17″ x 24″. 1 alphabet. Eyelet, stem, satin, and cross-stitch. Elaborate floral border. Scene with trees, hills, deer being chased by dogs, bird of paradise, butterfly, and small birds. Verse 605. Illustrated. *The Emma B. Hodge Collection*

WELSH, MARY. [Cir. 1770.] 12 yrs. 15″ x 21″. 1 alphabet. Eyelet, stem, satin, and cross-stitch. Strawberry border. Strawberry and Greek fret cross-borders. Elaborate pastoral scene, with trees, house, birds, animals, man, and woman. Verse 188. *Mrs. N. A. Prentiss*

WETHERELL, SALLY. 1795. 11 yrs. 17″ x 8″. 3 alphabets. Stem, eyelet, and cross-stitch. Border of leaves and circles. "H.W. dyed February 21. in the year 1794 aged 5 years-6 months." *Rev. Glenn Tilley Morse*

{ WHEATLEY, MARY. 1760.
THOMPSON, ISABELLA. 1797. Alphabets. Eyelet and cross-stitch. Conventional border, in squares. Vase in center at bottom, with a duck on each side. Above Isabella's name, a basket, purple grapes, flowers, and a crown. Below Mary's name, design mentioned above. Verse 497. *Miss Alice Morton*

WHIPPLE, ABBY. 1796. 12 yrs. 8″ x 11″. 3 alphabets. Chain and cross-stitch.
Mrs. H. W. Bradford

WHITACAR, SARAH LEAKE. 1791. [Cumberland County, N. J.] 10 yrs. Born November 1, 1781. 10½″ x 12″. Cross-stitch. Border, double line of cross-stitch, with genealogical data between. Names on sampler: "Recompence and Martha Leake [mother's father and mother]; N. M. Whitacar [father's father and mother, Nathaniel and Mary]; Ambrose and Rachel Whitacar [father and mother]." Design in center, 2 carnations, 1 tulip, and little trees, with border of vine and strawberries. Verses 132 (1, var.), 220, 221, 634.
The Misses Van Meter

WHITE, RUTH. 1765. Newburyport [Mass.]. Born in 1755. 7″ x 10″. Alphabets. Eyelet, satin, and cross-stitch. Cross-stitch border. "Remember I was born to die."
Miss Georgiana Augusta Currier

WHITE, RUTH. 1774. Weston [Mass.]. 13 yrs. 12″ x 10″. 4 alphabets. Eyelet, queen, and cross-stitch. Strawberry border. Simple dividing lines in cross-stitch. Verse 198 (var.).
Rev. Glenn Tilley Morse

WHITE, SALLA [SARAH]. 1787. [Born in 1778, at Longmeadow, Mass.] 8½″ x 7¾″. Alphabet. Cross-stitch and various fancy stitches. Simple cross-stitch border. At bottom, oblong shapes, squares, and triangles. "Salla White her sampler worked by her own hand at Mrs. Horton's Sc. A.D. 1787." *The Misses Edith and Ruth White*

WHITE, SALLY. 1797. Pembroke [Mass.]. 8 yrs. Born July 13, 1789. 6″ x 12″. 2 alphabets. Cross-stitch. Simple border. *Mrs. Louis B. Howe*

WHITE, SALLY. 1795. Portsmouth [N. H.]. 11 yrs. 12¼″ x 14″. 4 alphabets. Eyelet and cross-stitch. Vine border. Two baskets of flowers, with elaborate flower design between them. *Miss Hannah M. W. Merrill*

WHITE, SIBEL. 8¼″ x 7¾″. 3 alphabets. Satin and cross-stitch. Plain saw-tooth border in cross-stitch and satin-stitch. *A. Stainforth, Dealer*

WHITE, SOPHRONIA. Lexington [Mass.]. 9 yrs. 10″ x 12″. 1 alphabet. Border of leaves.
A. Stainforth, Dealer

WHITING, ABIGAIL. 1784. 5″ x 7½″. Alphabet. Simple cross-stitch border.
Estate of James L. Little, Esq.

WHITING, ABIGAIL. 1787. Wrentham [Mass.]. 19 yrs. 13″ x 13″. 2 alphabets. Cross-stitch. Vine border. Verses 246, 490 (var.). *Miss Annie Sanford Head*

WHITMAN, JANE. 1756. 10 yrs. 12″ x 9″. Alphabet. Flat, satin, chain, French knot, and cross-stitch. *Mrs. George E. Miller*

WHITMORE, SUSAN. [1799. Providence, R. I.] 15½″ x 14½″. Satin and stem-stitch. House and basket of fruit. [Probably from "Miss Polly Balch's School."] *George L. Minor, Esq.*

WHITNEY, HANNAH. 1795. Lunenburg [Mass.]. 8″ x 10″. 1 alphabet. Cross-stitch. Simple border. Conventional roses and small flowers. Verse 132 (1, var.). *C. E. Goodspeed, Esq.*

WHITNEY, PATTY. 1796. Boston [Mass.]. 12 yrs. 18″ x 18″. Alphabets. Satin, chain, and cross-stitch. Border, a series of Greek urns, with flowers in corners. Small flowers growing out of three green mounds, with large roses between the mounds, at bottom. Verse 651.
Pauline Emmons Tappan Brown

WHITNEY, SUKEY. 1794. Beverly [Mass.]. 9 yrs. 12″ x 8″. Alphabets. Cross-stitch. Cross-border. Verse 643. *Mrs. Charles Whitney Haddock*

WHITTEMORE, OLIVE. 1797. Sharon [Mass.]. Born February 27, 1784. 14″ x 18″. 3 alphabets. Stem and cross-stitch. Strawberry border, with Greek cross in two upper corners. House, trees, and shrubs at bottom. Verse 129 (var.). *Mrs. Frederick N. Prescott*

WICKS, ELIZABETH. March 6. 15 yrs. 12½″ x 12¾″. Cross and satin-stitch. Vine border. "Tree of Life" in the center, with four small baskets of flowers, birds, etc. "Be zealous to" . . . *William B. Thayer Memorial Collection, University of Kansas*

WIGGIN, MARY. 1797. New Market [N. H.]. 22″ x 18″. 3 alphabets. Tent, satin, and cross-stitch. Conventional border on three sides. At bottom, two apple trees with fruit, conventional rose tree in vase, and two green hills with three lambs at foot of each. Verse 657.
Mrs. Ernest Lovering

WIGGINS, HANNAH. 1730. 12 yrs. 16¼″ x 16¼″. Eyelet, stem, satin, tent, queen, outline, cat, tapestry, and cross-stitch. Cross-borders in various designs of conventional flowers, crowns, crosses, urns, etc. "Ames Wiggins Hannah Wiggin." Verses 182 (1), 343 (1, var.), 493, 583. "Remember thy Creator," etc., and other sayings now undecipherable.
Miss Kate S. Harris

PLATE XXIX

FRANCES BRENTON'S SAMPLER.   Newport, R. I.   1775
Mrs. Thomas A. Lawton

PLATE XXX

John Mason's Sampler. Painted. Cir. 1780
Owned by Maxcy Applegate, Esq.

WILDER, MARTHA. 1794. Lancaster [Mass.]. 10 yrs. 9″ x 17″. 3 alphabets. Eyelet, satin, and cross-stitch. Irregular border, with small crosses on sides and scroll at bottom. Small trees and fancy squares. Verse 639 (var.). "Favour is deceitful and beauty is vain, but a woman that feareth the Lord, she shall be praised." *Mrs. Edward H. Kelly*

WILDES, ELISEY [ELIZABETH. Cir. 1777. Danvers or Topsfield.] Born in 1767. 8″ x 15″. 5 alphabets. Cross-stitch. *Mrs. Samuel Hammond*

WILKINSON, HANNAH. 1747. Smithfield [R. I.]. Born February 1, 1733. 7″ x 7″. Alphabet. Cross-stitch. *Miss Alice A. Razee*

WILLARD, ELIZABETH. [Before 1799.] 8″ x 17″. Alphabet. Satin and cross-stitch. Cross-border at bottom. Verse 128 (var.). *Lancaster Public Library*

WILLARD, SOPHRONIA. [Cir. 1785.] Still River [Mass.]. 12 yrs. Born in 1774. 8½″ x 16″. Alphabet. Cross-stitch. Verses 183 (1, 3), 187 (var.), 490 (var.). *Lancaster Public Library*

WILLES, ROXALANA. 1783. Sampler in shape of the Liberty Bell. Cross-stitch. 2 alphabets and single letters. Illustrated. *Rev. Glenn Tilley Morse*

WILLIAMS, ABIGAIL. 1740. [Deerfield, Mass.] 10 yrs. 5¼″ x 16½″. 2 alphabets. Cross-stitch. Cross-borders in various designs, carnations, trees, squares, etc. At bottom, baskets of fruit, tree, and two crowned lions. Verses 128 (var.), 185. "Favour IS Deceitful And Beauty is Vaine But A Woman That Feareth The Lord She Shall Be Praised." *Museum of the Pocumtuck Valley Memorial Association*

WILLIAMS, DESIER. 1754. 10″ x 15½″. 3 alphabets. Eyelet, knotted, and cross-stitch. Elaborate pattern of conventional flowers, two birds, etc. Cross-border of vine and flowers. Verse 349. "Let not mercy and truth forsake thee. Bind them about thy neck. Write them upon the tables of my heart." *Mrs. Frederick Danforth*

WILLIAMS, HANNAH. 1783. 9½″ x 12½″. 3 alphabets. Eyelet and cross-stitch. Simple border. At top, Noah's Ark, trees alternating with urns filled with flowers. *Mrs. Samuel A. Cunningham*

WILLIAMSON, ANNA. 1788. Albany [N. Y.]. 12½″ x 13½″. 5 alphabets. Cross-stitch. Strawberry border. "John Williams, Marry Williams, Anna Williams." *Mrs. Frederick F. Thompson*

WILSON, ELIZA. 1791. "Concord, County Rockingham" [N. H.]. 7″ x 12½″. 2 alphabets. Petit-point, stem, chain, eyelet, cross-stitch, and hemstitch. Simple cross-borders. 3 conventional plants at bottom. Verse 132 (1, var.). *Mrs. Arthur Williams*

WING, ANNE. 1739. Boston [Mass.]. 13 yrs. 7″ x 11″. Alphabet. Cross-stitch. Strawberry border, with strawberry in middle of sides and corners and rest of leaves. Conventional flowers, sheep, birds, trees, etc. Verses 8 (var.), 187 (var.), 490 (var.). *Museum of Fine Arts, Boston*

WING, CONTENT. 1770. Smithfield. 5″ x 13″. 3 alphabets. Chain and cross-stitch. *Dr. Eugene P. King*

WINGATE, MARY. [Cir. 1719.] Hampton [N. H.]. Born June 7, 1708. 8″ x 15½″. 2 alphabets. Animals and birds. *Mrs. Frederick A. Whitwell*

WINSOR, NANCY. 1786. Providence [R. I. "Miss Polly Balch's School."]. 14″ x 14″. Stem, satin, and cross-stitch. Carnation border. Ship in center, between two points of land. Verse 69. Illustrated in color. *Mrs. John H. Mason*

WINTER, HANNAH. 1796. Tamworth [N. H.]. Border, wreath of vines and flowers. "The noblest employment of the mind of Man, is the study of the works of the Creator. To him whom the science of nature delighteth, every object bringeth a proof of his GoD. Every thing that prayeth it giveth cause of adoration." *Rutherford L. Coerr, Esq.*

WIRE, ELIZA. [Cir. 1800. Philadelphia.] 8" x 8". In each upper corner, basket of fruit, strawberries, house, lawn, trees, rose bushes, and bird. *Mrs. Bradbury Bedell*

WISTER, SARAH. 1773. Cross-stitch. Carnation border, with cross-borders of carnations, straw- berries, and tulips. Verses 342, 361. *Pennsylvania Museum*

WITT, SALLY. 1786. Lynn [Mass. Made at "Miss Sarah Stivour's School".]. 14 yrs. 16" x 17". Alphabet. French knot, stem, satin, and cross-stitch. Elaborate border of flowers, with birds, arbor, trees, and figures of a man and woman. Verse 129 (var.). Illustrated in color. *Mrs. Charles Pearson Coker*

WOOD, ANNA. 1795. Uxbridge [Mass.]. 7" x 8½". Alphabets. Cross-stitch. "C [Cynthia] Wood." *H. W. Erving, Esq.*

WOOD, DOLLY. 1796. 10 yrs. 10¼" x 7½". 2 alphabets. Satin, outline, tent, French knot, hem- stitch, and cross-stitch. Trees and flowers. *Wilbur M. Stone, Esq.*

WOOD, LYDIA. 1793. 11 yrs. 14" x 18". 2 alphabets. Single and cross-stitch. Floral border. Birds and basket full of flowers. Verse 640. *Mrs. Francis Blake*

WOOD, MARY. 1784. Roxbury [Mass.]. 14 yrs. 10½" x 7½". Alphabet. Cross-stitch. Con- ventional cross-borders. Verse 490 (var.). *Christ Church Parish House, Cambridge, Mass.*

WOODBRIDGE, MARY GILMAN. 1779. Salem [Mass. Made at "Miss Sarah Stivour's School".]. 9 yrs. 16" x 20". Alphabet. Satin, stem, and cross-stitch. Wide border with flowers on either side; arbor, birds, and basket of fruit at top; tree, man and woman, and sheep at bottom. Verse 503 (var.). *Frank R. Dow, Esq.*

WOODMAN, APPHA. 1787. 14 yrs. [Born May 2, 1773, at Sanbornton, N. H.] 18" x 20". 3 alphabets. French knot, stem, satin, and cross-stitch. Border made up of flower, tree, bird, and strawberry designs. Vine, strawberry, and Greek fret cross-borders. Illustrated. *Miss Anne B. Hamilton*

WOODNUTT, MARY. 1740. Salem [N. J.]. 13 yrs. 7¾" x 10¼". Eyelet and cross-stitch. *Mrs. Henry J. Irick*

WOODNUT, SARAH. 1792. Salem [N. J.]. 14" x 16". 3 alphabets. Seed, eyelet, stem, satin, and cross-stitch. Border, vine with flowers intersecting, passion flowers, roses, and tulips. In center, spray of roses, 2 birds with branch of cherries in their mouths, and 2 butterflies. Verse 374. *Mrs. I. Oakford Acton*

WOODRUFF, ELIZABETH. 1786. [Born at Princeton, N. J., May 10, 1779.] 8" x 13". 2 alpha- bets. Eyelet, satin, and cross-stitch. Strawberry, tulip, fret, and rosebud cross-borders; at bottom, two trees. Verse 207. *Mrs. John J. Stubbs*

WOODWELL, ALICE. 1760. Newburyport [Mass.]. Born December 16, 1746. 8½" x 8". Done in crewels. *Mrs. George B. Pettingell*

WOODWELL, HANNAH. [Cir. 1754.] Newburyport [Mass.]. Born October 3, 1742. 9" x 6". Cross-stitch. Cross-border of vine and flowers. Names on sampler: "Gideon and Hannah Woodwell [father and mother]." *Mrs. George B. Pettingell*

WRAY, ELIZAETTA. 1767. 14 yrs. 9½" x 13". 2 alphabets. Cross-stitch. Verses 93, 134, 196. *Mrs. George A. Plimpton*

WRIGHT, AZUBAH. 1772. 12 yrs. 7" x 9". 5 alphabets. Cross-stitch. Simple border.

Mrs. Lucy Wadsworth Leavenworth

WYATT, SARAH. 1742. [Salem County, N. J.] 9 yrs. Born June 8, 1733. 12¾" x 21⅝". Flat, outline, queen, stem, satin, and cross-stitch. Greek cross border and cross-borders. A band of tape, one inch wide, with tiny stitches overcast all around. Upper center, gorgeous conventionalized flowers. Initials and names on sampler: "I T H, IT, ST, DT, ET, DT, IT, SR, IS, SS, RS, ES, EE, IS, DS, ES, KS; bartholomew wyatt, sarah wyatt, joseph tomlinson, elizabeth tomlinson [grandparents]; bartholomew wyatt, elizabeth wyatt [father and mother]; robert smith, elizabeth smith; john ann richason, ephraim s tomlinson, joseph l tomlinson, john mary tomlinson; william r tomlinson, ebenezer e tomlinson, othmel richard tomlinson, edward margret batton; samuel mary sharp C E H, bartholomew wyatt, I T I T E T M T S T I T M T L T." Verses 344 (var.), 345 (var.), 346a, 585 (var.), 586 (1), 587.

Miss Hannah Carpenter Reeve

WYMAN, ISSAC. 1796. Charlestown [Mass.]. 16½" x 17½". 2 alphabets. Cross-stitch. Greek border.

Miss Mary J. Maguire

WYMAN, RHODA. 1708. Bedford [Mass.]. 12 yrs. 9½" x 16½". 2 alphabets. Cross-stitch. House and tree. Verse 490 (var.).

Miss Mary J. Maguire

WYMAN, SARAH AUGUSTA. 1792. Ashby [Mass.]. 11 yrs. 10" x 12". 2 alphabets. French knot, stem, and cross-stitch. 2 geometric and strawberry borders. Fruit tree with bird on it, also bowl of fruit. Verse 514.

Mrs. Sidney Harris

YEOMANS, MARY. 1790. 16" x 12". Two birds at top; figures of man and woman at bottom.

Miss Harriet L. Sheldon

ZANE, MARY. 1798. Born October 6, 1778. 18" x 17". 3 alphabets. Eyelet, flat, and cross-stitch. Border, vine and carnations all around, with rose corners. Vine and various other designs at bottom. Family names and dates: "The ages of the Children of William Zane and Sarah and Alice his wives:

"William Zane was Born The 6th of the 3 month 1765
Sarah Zane was Born The 21 of the 10 month 1767
Martha Zane was Born The 7 of the 2 month 1770
Jane Zane was Born The 2 of the 9 month 1776
Mary Zane was Born The 6 of the 10 month 1778
Ester Zane was Born The 29 of the 4 month 1780
Alice Zane was Born The 17 of the 11 month 1781
Rebecca Zane was Born the 15 of the 6 month 1783"

Verses 132 (1, var.), 343 (1, var.). "Fear God and Kep his Commands".

Miss Helen Botsford Clark

NINETEENTH CENTURY SAMPLERS

IN looking over a large number of American samplers, we find the dates between 1800 and 1810 occurring with such frequency that we begin to realize that when embroidery revived with the other arts of peace after the Revolution, it was considered high time to show the mother country that our daughters could produce specimens of fine needlework which were not merely copies of old designs.

In the preceding centuries, when England was producing her most beautiful work, life in the Colonies had been too hard and too serious to allow of much attention to the gentle arts except in rare cases, and the few samplers produced at that time were generally direct copies of English models. But with the opening years of the nineteenth century, our independence and originality were shown by the branching out on quite different lines; and if, at times, we find these early conceptions a trifle crude, it must be remembered that these samplers may not be judged as critically as those of a more mature civilization. Indeed, even in the nineteenth century, Colonial life was no bed of roses. The old Pryor Mill, in Bergen County, New Jersey, the birthplace of the little sampler maker, Sarah Van Horne, 1827, was run by tidewater, and we are told that her father often had to arise in the middle of the night to grind the grain.

In England, the early nineteenth century brought a type of sampler not highly esteemed by English collectors. The specimens abound in small figures and objects not well adapted to needlework, especially when worked in the ubiquitous cross-stitch, and contrast unfavorably with the wonderful samplers of an earlier day, so rich in beautiful designs adapted from all that was best in the patterns brought from Italy and elsewhere. The funny little houses and figures, neat and tidy, but so evidently copied from pattern books, seem trivial compared to the fine, early embroideries, though there is nothing to criticize in the quality of stitchery exhibited. It is wonderfully fine—

we do not like to let our minds dwell on the fearful strain to those young eyes!

It was just the reverse with the American sampler of the same period. Those whose interest is centered entirely on the fine stitchery done on delicate fabrics will find comparatively little to admire, for although fine work does exist, it is, however, not a general characteristic. Such critics should learn to view these youthful efforts from a completely different standpoint, appreciating the handicaps under which they were made, watching the development of the design which reflected the life of that day, and thus getting at the spirit and true character of the American work; or else they would do well to confine themselves to the study of the better regulated sampler of the English schools. It is important to realize the conditions and influences that made the English and American samplers of the nineteenth century so unlike. For one thing, pattern books were exceedingly scarce on this side of the Atlantic, and although the practice of making samplers in schools grew with the years, many children lived in remote villages far away from such advantages, and were forced to draw on their own surroundings for inspiration. Aid in composing the design must have been frequently sought from older friends or members of the family, and as they were not past masters in the art of drawing, it led to many amusing inaccuracies in perspective and proportion. For instance, notice Rebecca Slim's gigantic mouse, 1830. He would have had great difficulty in squeezing through the door of her little house.

Another difficulty lay in the materials available, which did not lend themselves especially well to very fine work, much of the linen being of a coarse, loose weave, with threads that were apt to pull together awkwardly when cross-stitch was used. Occasionally a child was lucky enough to procure fine muslin or tiffany for a groundwork; the latter lends a peculiar lightness and richness to the background, the colors stand out well upon it, but unfortunately it cracks and disintegrates easily. The silk, much of it home-dyed, must have been originally in a very thick twist, which had to be unraveled before being used, for this is the only way we can account for the crinkly floss we see so often in the embroidery of the flowers, lawns, animals, and figures, as well as in the backgrounds, and which lends itself particularly well to the petals of the flowers worked in satin or split-stitch. But when it comes to embroidering a church, where the stitches extend the entire distance from the steeple to the ground without a break, the result is fragile, and such a piece of work should be preserved under glass. Silk of this variety is practically never seen in foreign embroideries. It is different from the floss used occasionally on the English samplers, and is quite peculiar to our country. The kink is very close and not a general wave, and was probably considered pleasing in its effect. If it was a product of China and Japan, and brought home by the old American sea captains, it is strange that the English captains did not do likewise. Why were they less thoughtful of their families' needs?

Usually the designs were drawn directly on the linen with pen or pencil, but sometimes the back of a sampler shows, by the bits of paper still sticking to it, that the outline was drawn on thin paper and placed under the linen, the design showing through, and the paper being torn away after the embroidery was finished. The sampler of Julia Ann Hoffner, where a vivid green bird is to be seen enjoying a meal of scarlet berries growing on an oak, was worked in this way.

From time immemorial, stitchery has been found a difficult medium for the portrayal of the human face. Undoubtedly even the mature embroiderers of the seventeenth century gave sighs of relief as they traced the last eyebrow or curved the final smile on the placid face of the king or queen in their needlework pictures. How much more difficult the problem for the American sampler maker, usually a little girl under twelve years of age! When the canvas was small and the figures so tiny that a black cross-stitch could stand for each eye and a long stitch for the mouth, they could cope with the difficulty; but in the larger and more ambitious scenes, where ladies reclined under a tree or stood in front of a sylvan altar, it was a different matter. It was felt that these pictured people should wear the bland, almost

PLATE XXXI

ROCKSALANA WILLES'S SAMPLER. 1783

Owned by the Rev. Glenn Tilley Morse

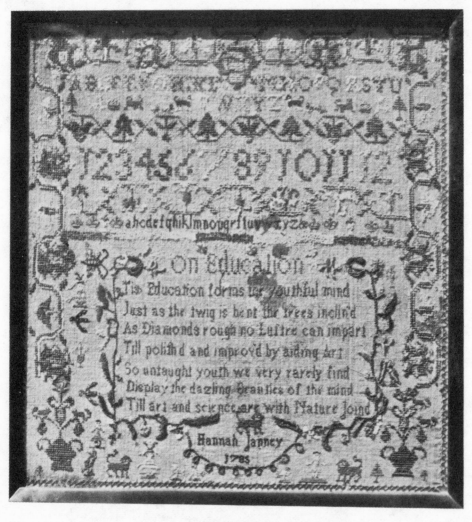

PLATE XXXII

HANNAH JANNEY'S SAMPLER. 1785
Owned by Mrs. Miles White, Jr.

simpering expression considered *"comme il faut"* for females of the period, and so the custom arose of helping out the embroidered design by painting the face and hands.

Wilamina Rine, 1813, and Mary Hamilton, 1812 (Plate xlviii), used watercolor, which possibly gave a satisfactory effect at the time, but their tints have become somewhat faint with the lapse of years; perhaps the tiffany or fine muslin of their samplers would not allow of any other method. Clarissa and Sophia Emerson (Plate xlix), who may have been sisters or relatives, since their work is similar in style and date, used oil paint on the heavy linen, but the effect is a little hard. Laura Bowker (Plate l), 1817, showed a good deal of ingenuity in painting a face for her shepherdess, for she cut it out of paper and pasted it on the linen, and she did the same with some lambs made of kid, and added richness to her cedar trees by embroidering them in chenille. Ann E. Kelly (Plate xcvii), 1825, gives an ethereal look to her damsel, devoutly offering a sacrifice on an altar, by inserting the painted face *under* the thin muslin. The effect is very good; in fact, this is the most successful of all these experiments. In other cases the distant view is helped out by paint, as in the Loring family record, or in the reflection in the water which we see in Lucy Stickney's sampler (Plate li), 1830, showing the house and trees on Charlestown Neck, near Boston. A most realistic effect was sometimes given by applying small squares of mica to represent glass in the windows of houses, the frames being indicated by criss-cross threads, but this idea was borrowed from our English cousins. So we find that our ancestresses evolved ideas of their own for surmounting difficulties, though the paint and other extra touches may not have been applied by the same hands that worked the samplers.

In some sections of the country, quaint old ribbons were used as borders, making a neat and pretty edge. Sometimes two ribbons of different widths and contrasting colors were elaborately quilled, one on top of the other, with rosettes at the corners. Again, loops of the embroidery silk were sewed on in clusters, making tufts or rosettes as a further embellishment. Elizabeth Funk (Plate lii), 1813, uses

a narrow lute-string ribbon, gathered and shaded darker at the
bottom, giving a pretty effect. The custom of using quilled ribbon
as an edging was much in vogue among the German sampler makers,
and the name of Funk suggests Pennsylvania Dutch parentage,
although the sampler is thoroughly—rather peculiarly—American in
design. Elizabeth evidently wished to make the date symmetrical,
so, regardless of accuracy, she embroidered the 3 backward in order
to make it balance with the 8.

Some of the floral wreaths encircling the verses and names of the
less elaborate samplers are very pretty and graceful, as in Sophia
Catherine Bier's work (Plate liii), 1810, and one does not regret
the absence of the more ambitious scenes. In this same category is
one made by Sophia Lamborn (Plate liv), whose design is very
similar to those used in the lamp-wick embroidery or tufted bedspreads
of that day; perhaps she may have appropriated the pattern from her
mother's bed linen.

There is no doubt that the practice of making samplers ran in
families. In one case, five successive generations embroidered them,
the first dating back to 1750, and the fifth a production of the last
decade.

Most of the examples of the nineteenth century were made by
rather young children, the average age being eleven, though some poor
tots mark theirs as having been made at a much earlier age, even as
young as six or seven. On the other hand, many girls put off the task
until they were almost grown. But, on the whole, we think of them
as a product of youth, and it comes as a distinct surprise to find
Hannah Crafts, at the ripe age of sixty, embroidering a rather elaborate sampler, with a picture of her own home at the bottom labeled,
"Sweet Home, the dearest spot on earth to me." Her heart probably
reverted to the days of her youth, when samplers were even more
prevalent, and she doubtless reproduced those she remembered, instead
of copying the work of the young people about her. She started to
cover the canvas like tapestry, but failing eyesight or some other ill
prevented its completion, for this was years ago—before the era of

giddy grandmothers, when a woman of sixty was considered old and was often crippled with rheumatism.

The girls' names appearing on the samplers are a study in themselves, and very different from those now in vogue. Submit Weyman, Remember Emmerton, Electe Phillips are reminiscent of Puritan days. Achsa Clark, Asenath Holman, Keturah Moore, Tamson Mulford are Bible names. Philadelphia Webb suggests a connection with the Quaker city; Lovey and Nabby (the latter occurring rather frequently) are probably nicknames; Britannia Holbrook proclaims her English parentage. But where did Amersha Arnold, Lucinthia Cone, Emirancy Howe, Roxa Tainter, Anzolette Hassan, Oceana Harris, Freelove Turner, Waite Phetteplace, and, most sonorous of all, Amorena D. T. Roberts, acquire their names? One wonders if in large families the stock of names became exhausted and the parents were obliged to draw on their imaginations. In the Field family register, the mother's maiden name was Miss Piana Petty. On a sampler dated 1827, we find the following statement:

> "Brooksania Waters is my name
> Milford is my station
> Milford is my place abode
> And Christ is my Salvation."

Another delightful name is Parley Bates, who in 1811 made a record, with one of the pretty, bright red berry-like borders that were popular in the vicinity of Providence; the berries done in a sort of coarse and effective cat-stitch. Parley's twin brother's name was Nahum, and we come across other men's names that are strange to our ears, such as Mickel Trufry and Friend Collens.

A great many fanciful ways are used for inscribing samplers, the American child not being constant to the expression "Wrought by," so in vogue in Great Britain. Sarah Baker, 1811, uses the expression "marked her sampler"; Anna Brown says, "This I did in the year 1824"; Ruth Davis's sampler, 1817, was "performed in her eleventh year"—she was evidently a motherless child, as her verse runs:

> "This work I did to let you see
> What care my Papy took of me."

One finds the expression, "Lydia Barcalow's sampler work"; also, "This completed." A sad, little faded specimen was begun by Mary Dealy, 1806, who died before its completion, a friend evidently finishing it for her, and adding this inscription:

"She was a blessing here below
The only child of a widow
Subscribed by Sally Parker."

One very human inscription, showing that sampler makers did not always consider their tasks entirely congenial, is found on Patty Polk's work. She states: "Patty Polk did this and she hated every stitch she did in it. She loves to read much more." After all, the youngsters of those times were probably, at heart, pretty much as they are now, only terribly repressed, and this inscription opens a more intimate door than we usually happen upon. She has the letters G. W. inscribed on a tomb in the distance, and as the embroidery was done about 1800, these letters undoubtedly stood for the Father of our Country.

Occasionally we find the word "Exampler"; sometimes short didactic axioms are thrown in, such as "Imitate the Best"; "Sweet is the Counsel of a Friend"; "May Liberty, Peace, and Prosperity ever prevail in America".

A pleasing verse and one of the few that bears a sentiment most admirable for modern as well as bygone days, barring its spelling, is found on Ariadne Hackney's sampler made at Mercer, Virginia:

"Believe not each aspersing tongue
As most week persons do
But still believe the story wrong
Which ought not to be true."

But this is venturing too far into the realm of the verses, and must be left for another chapter.

Elizabeth, the daughter of Captain Peter Harwood, sea captain and Revolutionary soldier, combines many unusual features on her sampler. The central part is a register, in which she makes use of rather unusual phraseology. She adds after her parents' names:

"They married Jan. 22nd, 1787,
He hath by her eleven children, viz:—"

and below are the names of the eleven.   On either side she has tall, slender pedestals surmounted by a pair of celestial and terrestrial globes, such as were used in the schools of that period.   Directly over the register is a very elaborate lambrequin, similar to those used over the tops of windows.   The globes and the lambrequin fore-shadowed the Victorian Era that was so soon to come.   At the bottom, Elizabeth has a landscape.   The largest house which she depicts was erected by her father, and was the first brick house built in North Brookfield, Massachusetts.   A smaller building in the very corner represents a store, with its swinging sign near by.

In 1803, two little New York girls of eight and ten, named Caroline and Elizabeth Grimes, each worked a sampler and sent them across the ocean as gifts, to give pleasure to their English grandmother. Caroline, the younger, worked a quaint poem beginning, "The broad Atlantic rolls between fair England's Isle and me," and made per-fectly lovely portraits of "Nero" the dog and "Tiger" the cat on the canvas.   Elizabeth had a more ambitious huntsman and some didactic poetry headed $\mathcal{LINES}$, in script capitals. This is not the only case in which such a piece of work was embroidered as a token of affection to be sent across this "Broad Atlantic," for in 1799 a sampler signed

"Hannah Wilson Bradford, Yorkshire, Old England
to
Phebe Speakman, Concord, North America"

was dispatched from the other side. If the address outside the package was equally vague, the postman of those days must have had clever brains to have enabled it to reach its destination. Still another instance of a sampler taking a long journey is that worked by Lydia Austin, a little Hindu girl.   Though made in British India, it is a typical New England sampler, which leads us to the conclusion that she had a model from the New World to copy, and the deeply religious verse confirms the belief that she had been brought up as a Christian. We know that she was supported and educated by Miss Lydia Austin, who lived and died in New Haven, Connecticut, and who bestowed her name upon her little *protégée*. It was probably a token of gratitude sent to the benefactress.

Two specimens from Virginia indicate that a custom may have prevailed there of making samplers and giving them as betrothal or wedding presents to a relation or some particularly dear friend. One of these was made for a sister, and the design is rich with turtle doves, a wedding bell, and is marked "an emblem of love".

Still another one from Virginia is the handiwork of "Content Phillips, aged 12 October" (Plate lv). Her alphabets are inscribed on an unmistakable memorial tablet, but this does not interfere with her little dream of romance. For the urns at the four corners of her floral border contain rosebuds tied with true lovers' knots, while under the vines of the lower border the true lovers approach each other with arms outstretched. The antlered animal just between them in the picture, but evidently climbing a hillside, seems utterly oblivious of the proximity of the lovers. Content has succeeded in giving him a sublimely unbiased expression. This charming sampler is worked in bright colors on rich tan linen, and the outline of the tablet gives it distinction.

Many of the sampler makers were descendants or relatives of illustrious people, some of them American patriots, some English nobility. Two cousins of John Adams are on the list. Mary Ann Fenno had as ancestor Governor Thomas Dudley, of the Massachusetts Bay Colony; Sarah Jane Fletcher came of Mayflower stock; Jane Arthur was descended from James Dalrymple, Lord Stair of Scotland. Rebecca Old, born 1808, was the granddaughter of Elizabeth Stiegel and great-granddaughter of Henry William Stiegel, "Baron Stiegel," the pioneer Pennsylvania glass maker. The list of these notables could go on indefinitely.

In 1819, the great-great-great-granddaughter of "Marchant" Richard Dole, the builder of the first public wharf in Newburyport, embroidered a charming sampler, which is still cherished by the family. This little Sarah Dole (Plate lvi), aged nine, certainly did herself proud in her choice of soft and harmonious colors, perhaps having

PLATE XXXIII

ANN BULLER'S SAMPLER. 1786
Owned by Mrs. Charles M. Greene

PLATE XXXIV

MARGARET RAMSAY'S SAMPLER. Albany. 1789
Owned by the New York Society of the Colonial Dames,
Van Cortlandt Manor, New York

inherited this good taste from her mother. The story runs that when Washington visited Newburyport he was entertained at a house where the guest-chamber bed and windows were draped with a beautiful orange-yellow India print. In those days, neighbors and friends were often called in to assist and criticize the arrangements made for housing illustrious guests; and Sarah's mother, happening to see this room, found the effect so charming that she secured the pattern of the curtains, bought the goods in Newburyport, and reproduced them for her daughter's bed when she was married in 1831. Sarah's sampler still hangs in the room adorned by these draperies, and the sprightly bird which she embroidered in the lower left-hand corner, while keeping a watchful eye on a stag facing him from the further side of a basket of flowers, has an air of casting an occasional wink across the room at these cheerful-looking curtains, as much as to say, "You and I are in very good taste, are we not?"

Caroline Maria Welch, the maker of a sampler in 1827, was the descendant of John Welch, the carver of the sacred Codfish so much revered by all Bostonians, which once occupied the proud position of weathervane. It is now preserved in the museum inside of the old State House. This disposes of the story that it fell from Heaven into the Frog Pond.

It gives one real pleasure to find family samplers, long separated by the breaking up of homes, brought together again at last between the covers of this book. This is the case with the work of the Rine sisters, probably Pennsylvania Dutch, who both attended Mrs. Armstrong's school at Lancaster, Pennsylvania, where they did the embroidery. Fanny, having rather the best of it, was twelve years old, while Wilamina had to struggle through hers at the tender age of six. No wonder that the younger child's flowers and vines are a bit clumsier in workmanship.

We know that the Pennsylvania Dutch, as the early German settlers of that region were called, produced many samplers, for the children's names betray their Teutonic origin. Their fathers and mothers must have inspired or exacted awe, for the children often

"Respectfully present" the finished product to their parents. A certain sort of weeping willow must have been indigenous to that part of the country, as it frequently appears on these samplers. Sarah Yeakel (Plate lvii), 1806, shows one growing beside her hilltop house, evidently buffeted by a strong easterly wind. A velvety lawn in different shades of green sweeps down to the bottom of the hill, where some sheep are browsing in the shade of a large tree, while in the distance others are seen. But unfortunately the perspective fails here and the meadow stops at the nearer sheep, leaving the others suspended in mid-air. Near the house, a thoroughly English peacock suns himself—a rather unusual variety, however, boasting only eight large feathers to his tail.

Poplar trees, owing to their contour, always lend themselves well to embroidery; but Anna Sophia Beckwith (Plate lviii), 1829, makes it distinctly understood that *her* farmhouse stood in a "Poplar Grove", and has labeled it accordingly. It conveys the impression that farmers of that day understood the art of placing their houses happily, for although in a valley it looks well swept by breezes, and the dark shutters tightly closed seem calculated to keep out the heat.

Nancy Platt (Plate lix), 1804, presumably lived in a house on a terrace, above a row of poplars. Whether or not she moved, later on, to the home of many windows pictured below the terraced one, outdoor life was evidently to her taste, for we find a cow and a dog of almost equal size; and can it be Herself on horseback?

Another pair of sisters reunited in these pages are Betty and Sally Brierly. They each cut a generous piece of pale blue linen as a groundwork—a departure from the usual white or cream color—which very possibly may have been spun, woven, and dyed in their home, not an unusual task and sometimes done by the maker of the sampler. Both girls were inspired by English ideals, especially Betty (Plate lx), as her chief ornament is "A Representation of the Temple of Solomon or the House of the Lord", a curiously thin-walled edifice which frequently appears on English samplers, but which is rarely seen on those made in this country. Betty's five fruit trees below are very ornamental, and her "Evening Meditation on the Crucification", though serious, is a less lugubrious poem than we usually find. Sally Brierly, two years later, copied her sister's complicated strawberry border and also some of the detached roses, but contented herself with a much smaller and more practical church, which, strange to say, appears unmistakably in an earlier sampler by Sarah Bancroft. How interesting it would be if we could identify it!

Still another child of this period, Faith Walker (Plate lxi), erects a Solomon's Temple on her sampler, but makes up for the absence of the usual court by an ornamental fence with arched gateways. It does not appear that either child tried to follow very clearly the description given in the Bible. Below is a most original representation of Adam and Eve, the latter overshadowed by a huge rooster, and the "grand old gardener and his wife" both sadly in need, not only of clothes, but also of a course in physical culture. Those spindle shanks must have made the journey out of Eden very arduous.

The same couple are much more fully clothed in Elizabeth Rowe Terry's handiwork; as a matter of fact, she goes to the other extreme and has dressed them in the fashion of 1828. Fortunately, as the serpent has been omitted, they are labeled, so one is saved from the error of mistaking them for Elizabeth's relations. Eve's train is very stiff and heavy, as if whaleboned. Adam shows no enthusiasm for the proffered apple.

In the nineteenth century, however, our first parents are not often depicted. They evidently did not appeal to our little countrywomen's taste for original design, though it is amusing to note a decided lack of originality in two samplers of 1820, worked by sisters, Abigail and Mary Harding. They are precisely alike; perhaps the younger girl tried to emulate her sister in everything, as little sisters are apt to do. The Reding sisters, Mary A. and Harriet Biron, embroidered pictures of the same house and distant landscape, simply viewed from a different angle. Another copy was the sampler of Phebe Esther Copp, 1822, which was almost a facsimile of that of her grandmother and namesake, Esther Copp, worked in 1765.

Not only temples and churches, but all sorts of public buildings are found on the samplers of this century. The architecture was frequently curiously modified to suit the whim of the maker or to meet the exigencies of embroidery, but we must not be too critical so long as these scenes bear a sufficient resemblance to the original or are labeled. Unfortunately this is often not the case, and many imposing buildings depicted may be real structures and not merely flights of fancy, although, alas, they cannot now be identified. The earliest samplers of this kind show the public buildings at Providence, Rhode Island, and for those, undoubtedly, our thanks are due to old "Marm" Balch's Select Female Academy, a description of which will be found in the chapter on schools.

On many of these samplers stand the old State House and the buildings of Brown University; some ambitious children combine the two. The First Congregational Church of Providence also proved popular. Sarah F. Sweet has embroidered it with great attention to detail and with the inscription that it was destroyed by fire on June 14, 1814. On another unsigned piece of work we see the same church, minus the towers. The child undoubtedly meant to add them, but my theory is that she started to use too many alphabets above, and realizing when she reached R that she had encroached too far on the space required, she stopped short in discouragement, leaving a long, loose end of silk running down and then upward through the linen, to prevent it from tangling. (See Plate lxii.)

A still more ambitious undertaking is that of Maria Hopping, who essayed the First Baptist Church of Providence. We should be devoutly thankful that this church in real life did not share the fate of its Congregational brother, for in its lovely setting of green it still remains, a delight to the eye. She has erected a rather ungainly arch over the church, with curious bases and capitals, in the nature of some of the Family Record arches or those used in the Balch school samplers, only less graceful.

Another sampler (Plate lxiii) bearing many names, but with that of Saunders predominating, shows the building of the College

PLATE XXXV

SALLY MUNRO'S SAMPLER. Cir. 1790
Probably done at Miss Polly Balch's School
Owned by the Newport Historical Society

PLATE XXXVI

JANE HUMPHREYS' SAMPLER. 1771

Given by Miss Letitia Humphreys to Memorial Hall, Fairmount Park, Philadelphia

of William and Mary at Williamsburg, Virginia. This college shares with Harvard the honor of being a pioneer institution of learning in this country, and dates back to 1681, though it did not receive its charter till 1693. Many illustrious men received their education in this historic place. Their parents may have especially approved of sending their sons to a college whose rules forbade any student keeping a race horse, and ordered that drinking be confined to the moderation that becomes a prudent and industrious student. It is truly appropriate that this college should appear as chief ornament on a piece of needlework, for one of the officials appointed in 1761 was a stocking mender, who received the munificent salary of twelve pounds a year. The buildings are pictured as standing on the banks of a river or lake, upon which float several boats. This must be taken as poetic license, as both the York and James Rivers are some miles away.

The "Old Brick Row" of Yale University, which was the chief feature of the college until about thirty years ago, when all but Connecticut Hall was demolished, is to be found on a most interesting sampler by Emily Clark (Plate lxiv). The whole scene, though so tiny, is unmistakable, for every building is there, as well as some of the elms which in those days overshadowed them. As the colors are beautifully harmonious and the stitchery quite wonderful, this is a specimen which leaves very little to be desired.

"Princeton College" (Plate lxv) is the imposing label at the top of an early nineteenth century sampler. But what a different scene from the Princeton we now know! If the child meant to show Nassau Hall, Princeton's oldest building, she altered the architecture very materially. Whatever building is represented is probably still standing, but at present we cannot discover its identity.

Sally Whittington, who lived at Annapolis, chose St. Ann's Church, a notable bit of early architecture, as the chief ornament of her work made in 1819; and the New York City Hall proved equally decorative as embroidered by Elizabeth Jane Hamil (Plate lxvi) in 1828, with the tall trees on either hand and the charmingly shaded lawn in the foreground—a far cry, indeed, to the same building in the midst of the seething business crowds of today.

Independence Hall, in Philadelphia, birthplace of our Declaration of Independence, lends great dignity to Ann Macomber's (Plate xli) work, 1799, and below it, with only half of the building on the canvas, she gives us a glimpse of Carpenter's Hall, where our First Congress met. As the two views stand alone, without border or alphabet, this sampler has a rather unusual appearance.

Eliza F. Budd (Plate lxvii), 1808, crowned a delightful hillside landscape with the courthouse of Mount Holly, New Jersey. There is some effort at perspective in the broad path leading up to the building on the hill, planted with trees alternating in shape, and with one neat tree on each step of the terrace. There, strange to say, David guards his sheep on one side of the slope and Ruth gleans on the other; though why these Biblical characters should appear in the vicinity of Mount Holly, history does not tell.

This form of sampler, where a building stands directly in the center on a hilltop, with trees or jardinières outlining the slope on either side, is quite characteristic of the period. Sometimes the building looks like a castle or church, sometimes a more humble, homelike structure. A group, consisting of a man and woman and strange varieties of domestic animals, generally occupies the foreground. Little "E. T.'s" sampler man looks as if he had donned an Indian suit and headdress for the occasion. He is shown offering a flower to a lady.

Julia Ann Nivers tastefully arranged on her canvas all the public buildings of the main street of Crawford, New Hampshire, and added a long poem entitled "The Young and Giddy", and in smaller letters, "Invited to Christ". (See tailpiece, p. 254.)

Palmyra M. Keen gives us a large church, a schoolhouse, and two other buildings; not in a row, as in a village street, but detached, with a grapevine wandering between. Sophia Stevens Smith (Plate lxviii), 1818, shows the white church at North Branford, Connecticut, a near-by red farmhouse, and a bridge over which an imposing coach is passing. The whole scene, well composed and crowned by a graceful garland of flowers and bowknots, was easily recognizable until a few years ago, when the church was burned to the ground.

Though beyond the period dealt with in this book, it is interesting to note that by 1839 the custom of sampler making had penetrated as far west as Missouri, for a child from Brunswick, in that state, embroidered one with a picture of the "Methodist Episcopal Church."

Two varieties of sampler, much in vogue in England at the period of which I write, never became popular in our country. I refer to those showing the darning stitches and to the embroidered maps. The Dutch were probably the originators of the darned samplers, those fine pieces of work where squares of the linen groundwork are cut out and the holes filled in with different damask patterns worked in contrasting shades of silk; where "barn door" and "winklehawk" tears, purposely made, are darned so as to be almost invisible unless a colored thread is used. The English embellished this work of "stoppage" still further by using baskets or bunches of flowers as a central ornament, with a different darning-stitch in each flower and leaf. For some unknown reason, very little of this work was produced here. It is distressing to reflect that even at this early period our national sin of extravagance betrayed itself in our failure to train the young in the art of repairing and conserving.

One of the happy exceptions is the work of Julia Boudinot (Plate cxvi), 1800. It is a real darned sampler, giving about thirty different designs of darned damask-stitch, the colored silk threads running only in one direction, and the pattern made by picking up the threads of the groundwork which has not been cut away. This resembles the only French darned sampler which has been brought to my notice, so one is not surprised to learn that the Boudinots were French Huguenots. They lived in Newark, New Jersey, and when Julia's sister married a Baltimorian she was one of the six bridesmaids who accompanied the happy pair to their home in Baltimore, where they all spent a most delightful winter, society being especially gay that season, because of the visit of Jerome Bonaparte and his officers.

The charming Northern girls were evidently a great success, for the story of their merry pranks and many festivities is still remembered by their descendants.

Mary Gill (Plate lxix), of Wilmington, Delaware, 1814, made a similar sampler, but she used white cotton and only made six squares, filling the seventh square in the center with a sort of knitting-stitch, such as could be used for repairing stockings. Hannah Bennet, of Hubbardston, 1800, in addition to a panel in which three boats are being rowed up hill, worked a border across the bottom with some damask patterns, but, following Mary Gill's example, the groundwork is not cut out and the threads run only one way.

It is easier to understand the rarity of our map samplers, as an embroidered map of our whole country would, indeed, be an undertaking. The English children turned out maps of "England, Scotland and Wales" by the dozen, some of which are interesting because of the originality of the geography, embellishments in the way of pretty boats or ships in the surrounding waters, or a figure of Britannia in the corner, guarding a coat of arms. Some are so exact in design as to recall the fact that they were sometimes printed on silk and could be bought in shops ready to embroider, with an inscription such as "A New Map of Scotland for Ladies Needlework, 1797". Mr. Huish, in his book, gives an illustration of a Map of North America made in 1738, but implies that it was an English production. It is amusing as an example of the general conception of our country at that time, the "parts unknown" occupying a very large area.

Only about a dozen maps of American origin have come to light, among them the State of New Jersey; the State of Maryland, by Elizabeth Susannah Bowie; and also one of Massachusetts, by Elizabeth Stevens (Plate cv), made in Public School No. 13 in New York.

Elizabeth Ann Goldin (Plate lxx) exercised her utmost skill, which was considerable, on a map of the State of New York; not only is her stitching wonderful—it is hard to guess how she procured silk fine enough for the curls and tendrils that ornament her capitals—

but she had a turn for statistics and gives valuable information, namely, that the population of New York State in 1829 was 1,392,812 and that "Long Island is the most important Island belonging to the State of New York, 140 miles in length and from 10 to 15 broad, contains three counties and numerous flourishing towns, population 87,000". She gives also this bit of history: "Lake Erie is the celebrated scene of Perry's victory over a British fleet, September 10th, 1813", and "Lake Champlain is celebrated for the victory gained by Macdonough over a British fleet of far superior force, September, 1814". So many of our little sampler makers seemed to have died in early life that it is refreshing to know that Elizabeth Ann lived to a ripe old age and is buried in the cemetery at Watkins Glen, New York.

Betsy Scott made a very large, clear map of England and Wales, and we have also a very pretty little "New Map of France" embroidered by a small American child. But the most original of all is the map of North and South America, by Frances Wade (Plate lxxi), 1798, for the "Great War" has not played such havoc with the map of Europe as did the little needlewoman with the countries of our hemisphere. Chili and Patagonia have changed places; the "Amazon country" occupies a big section of Brazil; Florida is more than half as large as the portion marked "United States". New Mexico is even larger, and Louisiana is tucked in snugly above, right in the heart of the Continent; while Canada, a detached section toward the top of the map, does not touch the United States at all. Altogether it would be difficult to find a more unusual conception of the Western Hemisphere, and one wonders if it was due to a vivid imagination or to ignorance on the part of her instructors.

Two less imaginative but even more courageous children actually embroidered charts of the world, one of them being an ambitious affair, embellished at the corners with allegorical figures of Europe, Asia, Africa, and America. (See Plate xcii.)

I imagine that many of these samplers took many years to work, and in most cases one such effort was considered sufficient to establish a reputation for proficiency in needlework; but cases have been found where one child made two samplers in one year, or two a year or so apart. Mary Hatch, in 1808, set an example in industry by embroidering a sampler and in the same year completing a most elaborate pen-and-ink drawing of the State of New York, the counties being outlined, the rivers and even the turnpikes traced; altogether a most laborious task.

Here and there we find a child incorporating useful bits of information from other branches of learning on her work, such as the "Boundaries of the State of Connecticut" on Lucy Ann Johnson's sampler, 1822, and Frances Parker's multiplication table done at Piny Grove, Charles City County, Virginia, in 1800. Frances did not waste any time on ornamentation, not even as much as did the earlier arithmetical sampler maker mentioned in a previous chapter, but contented herself with marking off the squares in plain cross-stitch and placing a numeral in each.

It was not until the nineteenth century was well on its way that the American Eagle took his place in embroidery as an emblem of patriotism, and even then his appearance is so rare as greatly to enhance the value of any specimen on which he is found. His rarity, however, is less surprising when we reflect that on all the thousands of English samplers we see, the British Lion is generally conspicuous by his absence.

South Carolina contributes the first of the species in a truly patriotic form, for the pennant in the eagle's beak is inscribed with the word "Independence" and he is surrounded by stars. On those of Sarah S. Caldwell, 1806, and Ann Eliza Eyre, 1829, he is suspended in the sky above a rural landscape, his wings outspread and the shield upon his breast. (See Plate lxxii.)

Mary Hallowell, at the very end of this period, made her eagle look so singularly like a dove of peace—even giving him an olive branch to carry—that it requires the surrounding stars and a study of ornithology to identify him positively. However, in those peaceful days he could afford to cultivate this resemblance. Margaret Moss (Plate lxxiii), 1825, makes him resplendent; bearing two American

PLATE XXXVII

MARY CLARK'S SAMPLER. 1789
Owned by Miss Caroline R. Patterson

PLATE XXXVIII

ZEBIAH GORE'S SAMPLER. Boston. 1791
Owned by Miss Mary H. Leeds

flags in his claws and an *E pluribus unum* streamer in his beak. He hovers over an animated scene, in which we see a red house, sheep and shepherd, cows and beehive (around which the bees fly most symmetrically), while the father and mother stroll in the sunshine, watching their three children at play. In a wreath in the upper corner, supported by cherubs clad in dark undershirts, Margaret's name and the date of her work are recorded; and in the pendant the death date, presumably of a grandmother, aged eighty. This sampler came from the vicinity of Philadelphia, and the house is said to represent William Penn's little brick home which stands in Fairmount Park. To be sure, it is a story higher than the original, but that is an unimportant detail. Can it be that the male figure is intended for William himself? It would not be an anachronism to have his wife gayly clad, as she was not a Quakeress.

Another heraldic animal, a cross between a dog and a lion, and wearing a crown, a frequent figure on English work, peeps out from the corner of Emmeline Ivins's attractive house at Mechanicks Town. A crown is another Tory emblem which is rare in this country, and usually indicates an English origin.

Lucy P. Wyman, 1810, uses the aces of hearts, diamonds, clubs, and spades in her design, which strikes one as rather odd in a day when cards were usually taboo in a respectable community.

Other bits of design characteristic of European countries often crop out in American samplers in most unexpected places and apparently without reason, such as the spies bearing the grapes of Eschol or the gnarled pear trees on one of the Brierly samplers, both of which patterns might have been transplanted from the Dutch samplers, where they were favorites. The "West Town" School, near Philadelphia, and "Nine Partners" School, near New York, frequently used the geometric figures characteristic of those from the Vierlande, in Northern Germany. Still others, composed entirely of detached motives—baskets of flowers, wreaths, etc.—need only the addition of a broken column or two, and a Temple of Love or a grotto, to make them resemble the rare early French samplers covered with patterns to be used on embroidered waistcoats.

Early in the last century, the custom arose of making samplers serve the double purpose of decorative needlework and a record of the family births, marriages, and deaths. This idea, in its simplest form, originated perhaps fifty years before, but was never fully developed till later, when it gained rapidly in favor and very many were made. They are generally inscribed, "Genealogy", "Family Register", or "Family Record" (in one case spelled Rechord), and seem to have been a purely American specialty. Many of the records are simply worked on straight lines in cross-stitch, with only a narrow border for decoration—very dull affairs except for the immediate descendants, or where there is some historical interest attached, as in the sampler of Sophia Smith, the founder of Smith College.

Another type manages to be decorative as well as genealogical, for many of them have architectural pillars at the sides and an arch over the top, frequently beautified with garlands of flowers. Dorcas A. Kelly, who was born and lived at Mendon (called Men on the sampler), Massachusetts, and also Betsy Cleveland, inscribed on their floral arches, "Keep sacred the memory of thy Ancestors". On several others, one of them the Loring Family Record (Plate lxxiv), the following lines are found carefully stitched in the lower corners:

The duty
of parents in
bringing up their
children is great and
important no one will deny
that good example set before
children will induce them
to follow the like example
and may lay a founda-
tion for their usefulness
in the world and a
blessing to their
parents.

The duty
of children to-
wards parents is e-
qually great and impor-
tant the great god of heaven
and earth has given a command to children to honour
their parents that their days
may be long upon the land
children would do well
to observe this great
commandment.
* * *

One can imagine that enumerating the duties of parents to their children was a far more congenial as well as important task to the childish mind than the dry recital of their duties to their parents. Usually these genealogies only give the names of two generations, those of the parents and children, but occasionally the grandparents' names also appear.

Harriet Van Wart, in 1822, at the age of thirteen, embroidered a most elaborate Family Record, thirty inches square. It would seem almost the work of a lifetime, as she gives the names of her grandparents, both paternal and maternal, her parents, also those of her thirteen brothers and sisters, with dates of birth and deaths, all of these without abbreviation. Chain-stitching in human hair separates the groups of genealogical data.

Second and third marriages seem to have been very general, and the children bestowed equal care in recording the names of mother and stepmother. Eliza Ann Hunt, in 1824, does this in a pretty way by entwining three hearts. The upper left-hand heart is devoted to the father's name and date of birth; the upper right-hand heart has one lobe assigned to the mother, the other to the stepmother; while the lower inverted heart gives the two marriages, one on each lobe. In addition to the genealogy, this sampler shows an unusually tall house of four stories, surrounded by spacious grounds and lofty trees.

Jane E. Blatchford, 1814, records the birth of seventeen children between the dates of December, 1788, and March, 1811. With so many brothers and sisters, one would think that she, as well as the mother, would have had their hands too full to embark on such a piece of needlework. In our utilitarian age, we do not attempt elaborate phraseology; but a century ago, parents were "United in Marriage" or "Departed this Life", and children occasionally listed under the head of "Progeny", with little economic regard for the number of stitches.

One of the earliest and handsomest of these family registers is that made in 1802 by Harriet Jones (Plate lxxv), the daughter of William Jones, governor of Rhode Island from 1811 to 1817, a man who could boast of a varied career previous to that time. During the Revolution, he first held a commission in Babcock's regiment, then became Captain of Marines on the frigate *Providence,* and was afterwards the bearer of dispatches to Benjamin Franklin in Paris and the first delegate from the United States to be received at the French court. The record is a pathetic one, because of the fact that of his six children only two survived. Four little urns in a row surmount a tomb on which their names are inscribed, with this verse below the dates of their deaths:

"These tender blossoms of the opening year,
Secure from harms still claim a parents tear."

Another sampler records the birth of a still-born child. It is sad to find how great was the mortality among the young children of large families. From Geneva, New York, comes the cry of poor little Catherine Meach, who in 1824 bewails the loss of four small brothers and sisters "all removed from this world in the course of five months"; she adds, "This little tribute of affection is recorded by a sister who deeply mourns their loss".

In many of these genealogies, below the lines of names and dates, willow trees are to be seen shading elaborate monuments, inscribed with the names or simply the initials of departed members of the family. These closely resemble the tombs so often found on the embroidered pictures of the period, or recall the designs of the mourning rings and brooches which were so popular with our ancestors. Little Betsy Cook may have been naturally of a gloomy disposition, or perhaps was depressed by the verse she embroidered, so common on samplers:

"This work in hand my friends may have,
When I am dead and laid in grave."

In either case, she was feeling pretty pessimistic about her future when she placed a little tomb, surmounted by an urn, under the usual willow tree, and carefully labelled it "Miss B.C." Ruthy Trufry, of Portland, 1807, embroidered a row of little tombstones under her weeping willows, all ready for the inscriptions should any one of the family pass away. But only one stone, bearing the parents' initials, evidently was needed in her lifetime. Poor little Ruthy had a hard time with the corners of her rather unusual border and, after all, failed to make the ends of the vine meet at the bottom. Mary A. Gale, 1825, beautified her symmetrical record by placing a tiny wreath of flowers about each name and date. The little Sawyer girl evolved a rather ingenious idea for working in a little genealogical information. She makes a border of elongated, interlacing wreaths, in which she places the births of her brothers and sisters. Her name and date, done in black, have gone the way of most of the black silk of those days, which was dyed in iron rust and disintegrated sooner than the colored threads. Charlot Chadwick recorded the birth of a little brother in slightly different colored silk (probably her silk had given out), just after she had finished the sampler. One finds, frequently, that deaths have been added to the records years after their original completion.

In a few instances, the records take the form of a *real* tree, with the names inscribed on the pendant fruit, such as Lydia Russell's tree, 1809, which grows in a meadow surrounded by an elaborate landscape, and flanked by two large pedestals or tombs on either side, bearing the parents' names and supporting jardinières, from which admirably trained rose vines wander to the top of the sampler, where, in a thoroughly Lord Lovell and Lady Nancy Bell manner, "they entwine in a true lover's knot for all lovers true (of samplers) to admire —mire—mire". Lydia's apples, as well as the names thereon, are painted.

Lucy Wyman (Plate lxxvi), 1807, kept strictly to embroidery. Her tree springs from entwined hearts bearing her parents' names, and she provides for such a contingency as the arrival of a baby brother or sister by supplying an upper branch with one extra apple, left blank. Another quaint and somewhat lugubrious tree has branches bearing portrait heads of the different members of the family instead of fruit.

The Rice family genealogy, and that embroidered by Eliza F. Parker, 1818, can be mentioned in the same category. The former is on dark linen, and the tree grows poetically out of two hearts that form a sort of jardinière. The latter has some delightful shading on the wiggly tree trunk. One wishes that the records more often took this truly decorative form.

Finally, there is a type of register where the genealogical data (generally rather brief) is squeezed into some vacant corner, occa-

sionally seeming the result of an after-thought, as in the work of
Elizabeth McIntire, 1807, where the names and dates crowd a pastoral
scene, in which we see cows grazing under a double row of trees on
the banks of a canal or river, with a row of houses on the farther side.
(See Plate lxxvii.)

The record of the Lamborn family (undated), formerly in Mr.
Alexander Drake's collection, is of this same type, and very elaborate
and beautiful. A large jardinière filled with flowers stands on the
top of a grassy knoll, while three white lambs reposing in the foreground seem rather overawed by the size of the flowers growing in
the meadow about them, the whole being gracefully bordered with
flowers at the sides and a grape vine winding across the top.

Considering that so much of this American needlework came from
states bordering on the Atlantic, it is astonishing that ships and boats
did not figure more often in the designs. We occasionally see them
in distant views, but rarely with such fine effect as on Susan Munson's
skillful work, 1824. Her unique contribution is the good ship *Potosi*,
in black with white sails, American flag and ensign, on a light green
sea. Behind it she shows a blue and white sky, with a rainbow, moon,
and star. She has placed the ship in the center of the sampler, and
on either side of it the words:

From Rocks	O God
Shoals and	Protect the
Stormy	Potosi
Weather	ever.
A	Is a
Rainbow	Sailors
at night	delight. (See Plate lxxxii.)

As we have seen, the samplers of the nineteenth century were used
for all sorts of purposes and to commemorate many different events,
having traveled far from their original purpose of simply preserving
valuable patterns in convenient form. Sarah Hillhouse, 1810, chose
a long poem entitled "The Hermit" as the *pièce de résistance* of her
work, one utterly devoid of interest to a child. Let us hope she did
not realize how dull the poem was. Another sampler, depicting a rural
scene, eulogizes Washington:

PLATE XXXIX

SALLY BALDWIN'S SAMPLER. Cir. 1794
Owned by Edward R. Trowbridge, Esq.

PLATE XL

LOANN SMITH'S SAMPLER. Providence. 1785
Done at Miss Polly Balch's School
Owned by the Rhode Island School of Design

"Mourn Hapless Brethern Deeply mourn,
The source of every joy is fled.
Our Father dear, the Friend of Man,
The Godlike Washington is dead."

It was made by Eliza Thomas, in 1804, but probably was begun nearer the time of Washington's death. Still another one of much later date commemorates the death of McPherson, with a poem of seventeen lines bidding "Columbia mourn".

Hannah J. Robinson (Plate lxxviii), 1818, embroidered what we might call a missionary sampler, in which "every prospect pleases", man, fortunately, being omitted. An eagle perches upon a tablet inscribed with a verse, "The Spread of the Gospel"; flowering vines on either side entwine around tall stakes, making a novel border, the whole surrounded by a solid black band of cross-stitch, on which is Hannah's name in white. This border resembles the black mats painted on glass and edged with gold, so often used in framing old prints and memorial pictures.

In 1821, Lucinda Brooks's sampler took the form of an embroidered Marriage Certificate of herself, aged sixteen, and Ruben Dade, aged twenty-two, on one side, and on the other these words:

"May the cares that bind the covetous never disturb our peace. May we yield therefore one to the other and be equally yoked together in the command of God. May neither of us seek basely to through an undue weight on the other's shoulders. Suffer no interference from any other to interrupt our harmony. We are connected for life, nothing can separate our fate in this world. Oh, let nothing divide our affections. May we regard each other with the fullest confidence, the least spark of suspicion from either might forever blast the comfort of both. There can be no harmony where there is no faith."

Sixteen seems a very early age to commit matrimony, but we find that Elizabeth Floyd, also a sampler maker, was married at Smithtown, Long Island, at the age of fifteen.

A curious effusion is found on the handiwork of Catherine Snyder, of Clarkstown, New York, made in 1800. It reads:

"DIALOGUE"

Men	"Tell us O Woman, we would know
	Whither so fast we move
Women	We called to leave the World below
	Are seeking one above
Men	Whence came ye, sa—"

There it ends, unfortunately, as we would greatly enjoy knowing whence they came.

A romantic interest attaches itself to the three samplers made by a son and two daughters of the Gauffreau family (Plate lxxix), who immigrated to New York from St. Barthelemey, one of the Leeward Islands, in 1815. The oldest girl lived to be eighty-seven, and her account of the family's terrible experiences in San Domingo, handed down from her mother, is still remembered. During the slave insurrection of 1791, the members of the family had a narrow escape, having been saved by a faithful slave, who hid them in an abandoned chicken house and then conducted them by night to the coast, whence they fled to Philadelphia. All these sampler inscriptions are in French, and, indeed, the one embroidered by the boy Fortuné was made before coming to this country, and is therefore not strictly American. It is interesting as being the only one of this period made by a boy, although boys' samplers are sometimes found in Europe and Mexico. The girls, Louisa and Celestine, dated theirs from New York. Louisa seems to have been especially fond of her mother, for she dedicated her work to *"Ma Mère"* and accompanied it with some pretty verses and emblems of affection.

Speaking of boys' samplers, the signature of a boy, George Terrell, is found with her name on the work of Margareta Whann, but one cannot tell whether or not he helped with the embroidery. Possibly he furnished the design, but if so he was not a very skillful draughtsman, for the vine border wanders aimlessly about and the central oval containing the house and landscape is oddly irregular. We forget, however, these shortcomings in the charm of the coloring of the grass, the trees, and the pretty draperies above, held back by little cords and tassels. This feature, *i. e.*, the draperies, is generally reserved for the sampler scenes where it is desired to indicate that the action takes place indoors. We see it on a choice English sampler of 1767, around a group of charming ladies clad in stump-work dresses, with real lace fichus and headdresses, who are sweeping their voluminous trains across a tessellated floor, as though on their way to a repast. In this

PLATE XLI

Ann Macomber's Sampler. 1799
Owned by Mrs. Lorenzo Sears

PLATE XLII

PATTY COGGESHALL'S SAMPLER. Bristol. Cir. 1795
Owned by the Metropolitan Museum of Art, New York
Plate presented by Mrs. Bayard Thayer

case the curtains are also in stump-work. Though never used in as elaborate a way, the American samplers made at Providence quite often resort to this effect, as in the President's Inaugural Reception shown on Nancy Hall's (Plate xcix) sampler.

Among other unusual touches that add interest to different samplers we may mention the coach and four horses on Priscilla Ward's; Melissa Marsh's collection of sampler stitches; a branch of autumn leaves lending a note of color to the background of Sally Oliver's work; the hemstitching and fringing done by Nancy Merrill, and bands of openwork on some others.

Several unusual samplers of a very distinctive type have come to light, consisting of a groundwork of white net, without any border, on which are patterns of needle-run lace, such as was in vogue about 1825 (Plate lxix). One of these samplers, which is in the Philadelphia Museum, though unsigned, has a piece of paper sewed to the net on which a name is written. It would be interesting to know more about these samplers, but very little information is forthcoming. We have to content ourselves with believing that the facts point to their probably being of American production some time between 1820 and 1830.

Having touched on most of the varieties to be seen in the examples of the nineteenth century, one comes to what is perhaps the most attractive type, the design which shows the little girl's own home. Such is the sampler of Sophia Cutter, 1801, where a particularly cosy farmhouse nestles against a hillside shaded by a fine tree, enlivened by three large birds perching near by, all seeming to indicate a happy home in the country; the effect only marred by a dreadfully gloomy verse, which "like a worm i' the bud preys on" the peaceful scene.

Usually the little needlewomen were not ultra-realistic, but allowed a playful fancy to improve upon every-day life; especially on the sampler lawns do we meet most delightful, unusual things. There gigantic strawberries grow in orderly rows; beside them graze many strange animals, such as antlered dogs and sheep; sometimes two white horses make a meal of strawberries. Perhaps a gentleman advances across the lawn, hat in hand, to greet a lady with a fan, or a man is seen fishing from a pond set in the midst of the grass, but all has a charming air of "make-believe"; and it is only occasionally that we come upon a scene such as Polly Parker, of Bradford, embroidered in 1802, which is truly pastoral, and more like the "petit-point" pictures of a far earlier period. In this sampler, the shepherd's expression as he pipes to his lady-love, seated in a bosky dell, is almost too sweet to be borne, and we, as well as the sheep dog, share her embarrassment. We often find incongruities in color as well as in perspective and proportion. A lovely border of pink roses admirably shaded in natural colors will suddenly break out into a bright blue rose at the top. Did the child weary of pink, and take liberties in the absence of her mother or teacher; or had she, perhaps, heard of the legend that a blue rose means happiness or love—or, at least, something pleasant to dream of?

Mary Ann Fessenden Vinton (Plate lxxx), 1814, makes her work as nearly like a memorial picture as possible, and yet keeps it a true sampler, and has cleverly arranged the alphabet and numerals in different styles, so as to form a narrow inner border around the tomb and the weeping female, the ornate rose border being quite different in character from the earlier conventionalized pattern. Olive E. Hewins, of Boston, 1829, has done very much the same thing, except that there is no note of sadness about her wide-awake young lady, clad in the dress and coiffure of the period, and the landscape is enriched with chenille. Elizabeth Williams, of Baltimore, uses a similar border, and depicts a very spacious Colonial house set in a lawn, across which the sun casts shadows that are lovely in coloring. The proverbial Southern hospitality had its influence on the young sampler makers, and nearly all of their productions show generous-sized mansions, capable of housing many guests. Eliza Picket's (Plate lxxxi) canvas has given us a particularly spacious house of this type, with wings on either side; in fact, it is so large that she has not left room for anything else except a rose border and her name and age, even the date being omitted.

Aimena Sherman shows an amusing scene. The imposing house does not take up as much room on the sampler as usual (some of its shutters are invitingly open, showing pretty curtains, while other windows are tightly closed), so there is space for ample grounds, with a barn at one side, a long stretch of fence and a road in front, where a procession is passing. We see a man leading a horse and driving three cows, a nurse pulling a very archaic baby carriage, a laborer going to work, and a woman leading a dog, all combining to make an animated scene, the proportions throughout being surprisingly good.

But of these pictured houses, the one above all others in which I would choose to live is that created by Hannah Kibbes, 1806. It is embroidered on dark green tammy, which gives a mellow, warm tone. The house, viewed from a slight angle, is approached by a winding path leading up to the door, on which hangs an engaging knocker. On one side, an arbor, shaded by a sturdy grape vine, forming the border across the top of the sampler; on the other, a well, with hanging bucket, offers refreshment—how many pleasant days could be spent in such a spot! To be sure, the well is very near the house, and in real life might be infected with typhoid and other noxious germs; but sampler-land has its advantages—disagreeable things simply do not exist. The poets of this happy country are, one must confess, a rather gloomy band, but no doubt their morbid lines have but little effect on the peaceful atmosphere of the embroidered scenes, where large families can live happily in small houses, where flowers never fade, where there is always leisure and every one looks happy. If laborers rest on their rakes it does not trouble us, as the crops are never spoiled; the sunny summer afternoon is just comfortable for sitting out of doors in pretty clothes; though flies and insects sometimes assume large proportions, they never molest. Long live this happy sampler-land, a delightful refuge for the imagination in times of stress and worry!

Soon after 1830, a general deterioration may be noticed in both the quality of workmanship and the number of samplers produced; perhaps the demand for a slightly wider education for girls may have led them to devote less time and care to the art of needlework; but more probably it was due to the craze for Berlin wool-work, with its garish colors, coarse cross-stitch, and banal designs, which spread across the ocean, the mothers and teachers thinking the new patterns and methods more modish, and wishing their daughters to be up-to-date. Whatever the cause, the custom gradually died out, and so ended the most prolific and characteristic period of American samplers.

EVA JOHNSTON COE.

LUCY CUSHING'S SAMPLER. 1792
Owned by Mrs. Paul Blatchford

REGISTER OF SAMPLERS, 1800-1830

ACKERMAN, ELIZABETH. 1808? [Born in 1799.] 8" x 16½". 4 alphabets. Eyelet and cross-stitch. Cross-borders, with tree, birds, dog, chair, woman, and small floral designs. Verse 343 (1).   *Mrs. Lucien Lee Kinsolving*

ADAMS, ELLEN E. 11 yrs. 16¼" x 17". 3 alphabets. Stem, cross, and satin-stitch. Rose and grape borders. House with trees and grass. "Under instruction of C. Rockwood." Verses 179, 394.   *Miss Mary C. Wheelwright*

ADAMS, LYDIA. 1814. [Newington, N. H.] 14 yrs. 8" x 12". 3 alphabets. Cross-stitch. Hemstitched edge. Strawberry cross-border. [Parents, Samuel Adams and Lydia Coleman.]   *Mrs. Paul H. McMillin*

ALDEN, CYNTHIA. 1802. Claremont, Mass. Born August 10, 1784. 13" x 14½". 4 alphabets. Cat and cross-stitch. Cross-lines and cross-borders in simple designs. Verses 40, 247.
                                                                            Mrs. Lathrop C. Harper

ALGER, ABBY. 1802. 11 yrs. 12" x 11". 3 alphabets. Cross-stitch. Verse 676 (1).
                                                                            George H. Havens, Esq.

ALLEN, CHLOE. 1802. 6 yrs. 17" x 8". 3 alphabets. Cross-stitch. Verse 343 (1).
                                                                            The Misses Austin

ALLEN, ELIZABETH W. 1821. 10 yrs. 16" x 16". 3 alphabets. Queen and cross-stitch. Strawberry border. Verse 90.   *The Misses Austin*

ALLEN, MARY. 1824. 14" x 15½". 2 alphabets. Eyelet and cross-stitch. Vine border. Verse 472.   *Pennsylvania Museum, Memorial Hall, Fairmount Park*

ALLEN, POLLY ANN. 1821. Born in 1810. Connecticut. 7¾" x 7⅝". 3 alphabets. Cross-stitch. Simple border.   *Mrs. Harry Hale Goss*

ALLEN, SARAH. 1823. 11 yrs. 8" x 11½". 3 alphabets. Chain and cross-stitch.
                                                                            Vernette R. Mowry

ALLEN, WAITY. 1802. 9 yrs. 18" x 18½". 3 alphabets. Cross-stitch. Verse 343 (1).
                                                                            The Misses Austin

ALLEYNE, DOROTHY DEBORAH FOSTER. 1800. 12½" x 8". 4 alphabets. Cross-stitch. Hemstitched edge.   *Mrs. R. M. Chickering*

ALMY, RUTH. 1803. 9 yrs. 17" x 17". 5 alphabets. Chain, eyelet, and cross-stitch. Verses 612, 614.   *Mrs. Howard I. Gardner*

ALMY, RUTH. 1810–1811. 19" x 17". Cross-stitch. Birds and flowers. Ovals containing initials and dates.   *Mrs. Howard I. Gardner*

ANDERSON, CATHERINE. 1808. [Stockton, N. J. 12 yrs.] 15" x 16". 3 alphabets. Cross-stitch. Border, a single line of cross-stitch with short branches on either side, inclosing a vine on which are leaves, rosebuds, and carnations. In center, at top, is a basket of flowers, and on either side of basket is a square inclosing two initials: "J A" [Joshua Anderson, father], "E A" [Elizabeth Anderson, mother]. Row of birds standing on vine at bottom. In four other squares are the initials: "C A" [Catherine Anderson], "E A" [Eliza Anderson, sister], "J H A" [John Hoppock Anderson, brother], "S A A" [Sarah A. Anderson, sister].   *The Misses Anderson*

ANDERSON, ELIZABETH. 1814. 8 yrs. 11″ x 14″. Alphabet. Cross-stitch and padded-stitch. Strawberry border. Scene with house, lambs, dog, rose bushes, and man, basket of apples, vases and conventional flowers, trees and birds. Verse 343 (1). Initials: "A A, H A, AA, S A." *Mrs. Bradbury Bedell*

ANDERSON, MARY A. E. 1802. 18″ x 17″. Satin, cat, and cross-stitch. Floral border. Scene with house, weeping willow tree with crow, and red tree with robin. Verse 398.
Mrs. Thomas A. Lawton

ANDERSON, MARY ALETTA. 1814. 10 yrs. 12½″ x 21″. 3 alphabets. Satin and cross-stitch. Conventional cross and strawberry vine border. Design at bottom of baskets, peacocks, blue strawberries, and vines. Verse 488. *Estate of James L. Little, Esq.*

ANDERSON, NANCY. 1804. [Hamilton Township, N. J.] 20″ x 24″. Flat, chain, and cross-stitch. Carnation border. Scene with house, lawn, strawberries, trees, and vines. "George Anderson" [father], "Sarah Anderson" [mother]. Verse 594 (1, var., 3).
Mrs. John H. Scudder

ANDERSON, RACHEL. 1803. 10 yrs. 16″ x 17″. "Andrew Anderson, Jane Anderson, Andrew Liburn, Jane Liburn, Robert Anderson, Elizabeth Anderson, Andrew Anderson, Jane Anderson, James Anderson, Thomas Anderson, Ann Anderson, Robert Anderson, Anna Anderson." Verses 252, 403. *Mrs. Bradbury Bedell*

ANDERSON, REBECCA ANN. 1809. Salem [N. J. 11 yrs. Born September 26, 1798.] 10¼″ x 14″. 2 alphabets. Outline, stem, and satin-stitch. Vine border with brilliant clusters. Wreath incloses name. Green mounds surmounted by birds, also baskets of flowers, sprays of pansies, carnations, roses and rosebuds, pine tree and weeping willow.
Mrs. John V. Craven

ANEAR, THOMASIN PAINTER. 1828. 12 yrs. 10″ x 11½″. 4 alphabets. Eyelet and cross-stitch. Saw-tooth border. Two hearts intertwined. *W. G. Bowdoin, Esq.*

ANGELL, SALLY. 1804. 12½″ x 7½″. 3 alphabets. Cross and eyelet-stitch. Verse 18.
Mrs. H. W. Bradford

ANTRIM, ELIZABETH S. 1827. 12 yrs. 16″ x 16″. Cross-stitch in worsted. Strawberries and leaves, 2 bunches of roses, at top; 2 bunches of carnations, pitchers with an aster in each, blue vase with red tulips, 2 birds, at bottom. Verse 482. *Mrs. Bradbury Bedell*

APPLETON, BETSY. 1806. Ipswich [Mass.]. 17″ x 20″. 3 alphabets. Stem and cross-stitch. Floral border. Willow sprays at bottom. "Family Record. Oliver Appleton Married Sarah Cogswell Dec. 19th 1790.

Births of Children.

1st Child a daughter born & died Nov. 21, 1790
Harry Appleton born Jan. 25, 1793, & died Aug. 18, 1793
Betsy Appleton born Nov 17, 1794
Harriet Appleton born July 9th 1796.

Mr. Oliver Appleton died Dec. 11th 1797 aged 40 yrs and 18 days."
Verse 268. *Mrs. Henry Lowell Hiscock*

APPLETON, HARRIET. 1805. Born July 9, 1796, at Ipswich. 15″ x 18″. 3 alphabets. Cross-stitch. Conventionalized clover border. Verse 538. *Mrs. Henry Lowell Hiscock*

ARCHER, LYDIA. 1807. Salem [Mass.]. 12 yrs. 16″ x 24″. 3 alphabets. Eyelet, chain, stem, satin, and cross-stitch. Elaborate border, with clump of strawberry vines alternating with clumps of violets or white flowers. Grass, huge vase of roses flanked by a strawberry vine, large and small trees. Verse 129 (var.). *Mrs. Francis H. Russell*

ARMSTRONG, MARY ANN. 1824. 9 yrs. Baltimore, Md. 20″ x 25″. Split, petit-point, cat, tent, chain, stem, satin, and cross-stitch. Rose border outside, and running design in flat-stitch inside. Three-story brick house, lawn, fence, driveway, dogs, weeping willow trees, and birds. Verse 526 (1). *Mrs. Mary Elizabeth Elmer*

ARMSTRONG, MARY ANN. 1824. Baltimore, Md. 9 yrs. 16″ x 18″. 3 alphabets. French knot, queen, tent, cat, petit-point, split, stem, chain, eyelet, satin, and cross-stitch. Strawberry border. Divided into 8 sections. Tree and vase on either side of verse. Verse 526 (1). *Mrs. Mary Elizabeth Elmer*

ARNOLD, AMERSHA. [1818. Born December 7, 1809, in Somers, Conn.] 9 yrs. 12½″ x 9½″. 3 alphabets. Cross-stitch. Heart design. *Miss Julia Amersha Carpenter*

ARNOLD, ANN L. 1802. Providence. 17″ x 12″. 2 alphabets. Cross-stitch. Verse 676. *Miss Rosamond W. Austin*

ARNOLD, JULIANA. [Before 1830. Born in 1815.] Troy, N. Y. 18″ x 18″. Cross-stitch. Hem-stitched edge, with border of vine and carnations. Verse 177. *Mrs. William H. Walker*

ARNOLD, MARCY. 1801. 13 yrs. 15″ x 15″. 3 alphabets. Stem, cat, and cross-stitch. Basket of flowers. "Favor is deceitful and Beauty is vain. But Woman that feareth the Lord she shall be praised". *Mrs. William A. Spicer*

ARNOLD, MARY ELIZABETH. [After 1825.] 20¾″ x 18″. Long and short and hem-stitch. Arch with landscape at bottom, also monument. "Family Register: Mr. Welcome Arnold born Nov. 15th, 1777; died Feb. 15th, 1821; Miss Mary Peirce born Oct. 22nd, 1779; Married August 8th, 1803. Christopher Bentley Arnold born May 13th, 1804; Sally James Arnold born Dec. 4th, 1805; died Aug. 14, 1825; Welcome Arnold born March 23rd, 1809; William Peirce Arnold born Sept. 3rd, 1811; Mary Elizabeth Arnold born April 4th, 1816." "Sacred to the best of Fathers. May angels guard thy sleeping dust." *Frederick W. Arnold, Jr., Esq.*

ARTHUR, JANE. 1804. 9 yrs. 11½″ x 16½″. 3 alphabets. Cat, satin, stem, and cross-stitch. Strawberry border. In center, 2 cross-borders of flowering bushes. Verse 408. *Miss Anna Dunbar*

ASHBURNER, FANNY. 1811. 17″ x 19″. Outline, stem, tent, and cross-stitch. Border of flowers and vine. At top, spray of flowers; in center, 3 flowering rose bushes; at bottom, roses and other flowers in urns at each end. Verse 515 (1, var.). *Mr. William Boyer*

ATKINSON, MARY C. 1810. Newbury, Mass. 12″ x 16½″. Cross-stitch. Strawberry border.
"Michael Atkinson, born Feb. 14, 1774.
Joanna Lunt   born Feb. 14, 1775.
Married April 17, 1794.
Benj'n Atkinson, born May 28, 1795.
Joana' C. Atkinson, born Dec.   22, 1799.
Mich'l Atkinson, born   Mar'h 18, 1801.
Dyed   Mar'h 22, 1801.
Josh' Atkinson, born   April, 18, 1802.
Eliza Atkinson, born   Mar,   6, 1804.
Dyed   Sept.   1, 1805.
Eliza Atkinson, born   June   5, 1806.
Mary C. Atkinson, born   Dec.   25, 1808.
Dyed   March 27, 1810.
Mary C. A" [unfinished]   *Randolph Haigh, Esq.*

ATWOOD, ESTHER. [Cir. 1820.] Born October 23, 1807. 12" x 16". Cross-stitch. Strawberry border. Pine tree, cherry tree, and 2 birds. *Mrs. Bradbury Bedell*

AUSTIN, MARTHA. 1811. [Buckingham, Berks County, Pa.] 10 yrs. 11½" x 14". Cross-stitch. Border of carnations, flowers, and buds, also 2 birds at top. *Charles Clarke Black, Esq.*

AUSTIN, MARY. [Cir. 1819.] 7 yrs. 13½" x 16". 3 alphabets. Fine cross-stitch. Strawberry border. "Remember thy Creator," etc. Verse 458. *Rev. Glenn Tilley Morse*

AUSTIN, SARAH. 1822. 15" x 8". 6 alphabets. Chain and cross-stitch. *The Misses Austin*

AYER, ABIGAIL. 1808. Haverhill [Mass.]. 14 yrs. 19" x 16". 3 alphabets. Petit-point, tapestry, bullion, stem, satin, and cross-stitch. Green grass at bottom, with basket of flowers in either corner, from which springs a vine covered with flowers, extending all around sides and top; baskets with fruit, and small trees on grass, and strawberries growing in grass. Conventional borders around verse, alphabets, etc. Verse 144. *Mrs. Thomas A. Lawton*

AYER, HARRIET. 1829. 10 yrs. Haverhill [Mass.]. 17" x 12½". 4 alphabets. Stem, eyelet, French knot, cross-stitch, and running cross-stitch. Vine and strawberry border. 2 pine trees in lower corners. *Mrs. J. W. Hunter*

BAGG, MARY. 1811. West Springfield [Mass.]. 9 yrs. 13" x 18". 3 alphabets. Chain and cross-stitch. Cross-stitch border. Trees. Verse 291. *Miss May Bliss Dickinson*

BAGGS, ELIZABETH. 1811. [Queen Anne's County, Eastern Shore, Md.] 9 yrs. Alphabet. Cross, satin, and stem-stitch. Carnation border with birds. House and trees. "This is my Verse. She maketh fine linen and selleth it and delivereth the goods unto the merchant." Verse 424. *Mrs. Frank Rea*

BAILY, RACHEL P. [Cir. 1800.] Born August, 1783. 12½" x 17". Flat, eyelet, and cross-stitch. 2 alphabets. Vine and pointed flat-stitch borders. Wall of Troy at bottom. Conventional flowers at top. *Mrs. Bradbury Bedell*

BAKER, NANCY. 1808. Warren [R. I.]. 8 yrs. 19" x 16". 3 alphabets. Stem, satin, and cross-stitch. Strawberry border. House with terrace; also figures of men, women, and children walking about. Verse 710. [Same style as those done in Miss Polly Balch's School.] *Mrs. Thomas W. Aldrich*

BAKER, SARAH. 1811. Gorham [Me.]. Born May 4, 1800. 17½" x 17". 5 alphabets. Eyelet and cross-stitch. Simple border. Conventional design. *Mrs. William Tenter*

BALDWIN, MARTHA A. 1820. Newark [N. J.]. 8 yrs. 15" x 17". 3 alphabets. Eyelet, satin, and cross-stitch. Strawberry and carnation border, with rosettes in lower corners. Cross-borders in Greek fret and double hemstitching. House, tree, hedge, and flower-bed. Verse 560. *Miss Martha C. Pollock*

BANCROFT, ELIZA A. [1815.] Chelmsford [Mass.]. 9 yrs. 12" x 10". 3 alphabets. Satin, cat, and cross-stitch. Hemstitched edge and simple inner border. *Mrs. Elizabeth B. Heald*

BARCALOW, LYDIA. 1825. [Butler County, O.] 11 yrs. 10" x 14". 4 alphabets. Outline, stem, and cross-stitch. Cross-border of trees, also dividing lines in various stitches.
Mrs. Harvey S. Gruver

BARKER, MARY JANE. 1818. Portland [Me.]. 9 yrs. 8" x 23". Outline, chain, satin, cross, and an odd cluster-stitch. Rose-vine border. Green wreath around verses. Names and dates of children of "Thomas and Sarah Barker": "Susan M. Barker born at Hiram Aprilth 3, 1790; Thomas Barker born at Hiram Oct. 27, 1791; died N 3; Sarah Barker born at Limerick Oct. 18, 1792; Thomas A. Barker born at Cornish Oct. 28, 1794; Pamela Barker born at Cornish Julyth 17, 1796; Asenath Barker born at Cornish Septh 23, 1798; Sophia

PLATE XLIII

LUCY WARNER'S SAMPLER. Middletown, Conn. Cir. 1786
Owned by Mrs. Clarence Weart

PLATE XLIV

Mary Traill's Sampler. Marblehead, Mass. 1791
Owned by Mrs. Fletcher Hodges

Barker born at Hiram Julyth 10, 1800; Noah Barker born at Hiram Augth 10, 1802; Elizabeth P. Barker born at Hiram Augth 27, 1804; Peleg Barker born at Cornish Mayth 29, 1807; Mary Jane Barker and Flavilla Ann Barker born at Hiram Julyth 8, 1809; Caroline Barker born at Hiram Julyth 29, 1812." [Mary Jane went to Mme. Niel's School in Portland with Henry W. Longfellow, hand in hand. They were playmates and near neighbors.] Verse 515 (1, var.). *Mrs. Jesse B. Thomas*

BARNES, SARAH E. 1812. 5½" x 14". 3 alphabets. Cross and hem-stitch. Small motifs. *Wilbur M. Stone, Esq.*

BARNHOTT, MARGARET. 1831. 12 yrs. Cross-stitch. Rose-vine border on three sides. At bottom, church with conventional tree on either side, lawn, fence, shed, animals, and men. Adam and Eve scene. Scene with tombstone, weeping willow, man, woman, and children, and initials "R W" and "E B" on stone. Large basket of flowers. Trees with birds on top, and animals and men and women underneath. Detached flowers, birds, animals, and angels are scattered all about. *Mrs. Henry E. Coe*

BARNUM, ABIGAL. 1822. 12 yrs. 7" x 10". 3 alphabets. Cross-stitch. *Wilbur M. Stone, Esq.*

BARRETT, CHARLOTTE C. 1805. 14" x 11". Chain and cross-stitch. "Family Register: John Barrett Esq. Born Aug. 16th 1756; Miss Martha Dickinson Born Oct. 13, 1761; and were married Oct. 29th 1790. Mary Barrett Born July 19th 1791; Eliza E. Barrett Born Dec. 18th 1792; Martha D. Barrett Born Sept. 12, 1794; Died July 18th 1804; Charlotte C. Barrett Born Feb. 27th 1796; Sarah P. Barrett Born Dec. 3rd 1804; John Barrett Born Feb. 21st 1802; Charles Barrett Born Jan. 6th 1804." *The Misses Vose*

BARRETT, ELIZABETH. 1814. Doddington. 9 yrs. 12½" x 13". Chain, stem, satin, and cross-stitch. Floral border. Large bunch of flowers in lower half. Verse 306. *Mrs. S. A. Cunningham*

BARRETT, ELIZABETH E. After 1816. 16¼" x 12½". Cross-stitch. Rose and vine border. "Family Register: John Barrett Born Aug. 16th 1756; Martha Dickinson Born Oct. 18th 1761; and were married Oct. 29th 1790. Mary Barrett Born July 19th 1791; Elizabeth E. Barrett Born Dec. 18th 1792; [———] D. Barrett Born Sept. 12th 1794; Died July 18th 1804; Charlotte C. Barrett Born Feb. 27th 1796; Sarah W. Barrett Born Jan. 5th 1798; Louisa W. Barrett Born Dec. 3rd 1799; Died May 24th 1804; John Barrett Jun'r Born Feb. 21, 1802; Charles Barrett Born Jan. 6th 1804; Died Dec. 2, 1816; —— Died May ——; —— Died June 19th 181[-]." *The Misses Vose*

BARTLETT, ELIZABETH. 1818. Newburyport [Mass.]. 16" x 10". 3 alphabets. Satin and cross-stitch. Strawberry border. Basket of flowers under an arbor of flowers. *Miss Margaret Bartlet*

BARTLETT, EMILY. [Cir. 1818.] Born June 28, 1807. 18" x 22". Stem, satin, and cross-stitch. Fine strawberry border. Weeping willows over a tomb and urn. Roses growing in the grass. Names and dates: "Daniel Bartlett, Born August 15, 1778
Jemima Smith, Born June 26, 1785
They were married April 10, 1806 and have issue
Emily Bartlett, Born June 28, 1807
Daniel Bartlett, Born April 7, 1809
Eliza Bartlett, Born March 21, 1810
Adaline Bartlett, Born May 6, 1812
Stephen S. Bartlett, Born August 6, 1816."
On the tomb is inscribed: "Daniel Bartlett Died May 2 1809 Altho dead not forgotten." *Miss E. B. Batchelder*

BARTLETT, HANNAH. 1804. Newburyport [Mass. Born September 25, 1791.]. 13 yrs. 17″ x 22″. 5 alphabets. Queen, French knot, eyelet, stem, tent, and cross-stitch. Strawberry border and 8 cross-borders. Scene with shepherd, sheep, and fruit trees. Verse 601 (1, 2).
Newburyport Historical Society

BARTLETT, PEGGY. 1801. "Haverhill, County Essex." 10 yrs. 12″ x 11½″. 4 alphabets. Eyelet, stem, tent, satin, and cross-stitch. Conventional border on sides. At bottom, solid bluish ground on which strawberries are growing, and on tops of mounds are small trees and large basket of flowers. Verse 94. *Mrs. Richard H. Hunt*

BARTON, BETSY. 1813. "Bloomsburg, Columbia County, State of Pennsylvania." 12 yrs. 7⅞″ x 10″. 4 alphabets. Cross-stitch. Conventional border. *Mrs. Frederick E. Barber*

BARTON, BEULAH. 1814. "Laurelgrove School. Hannah Barton, Preceptress." 14½″ x 14″. Stem, satin, and cross-stitch. Rose-vine border at sides. At bottom, green hill with trees, dogs, and bird. Flowers scattered over whole sampler. Verse 742. *Mrs. Richard H. Hunt*

BARTON, HARRIET. July 4 [1809. 9 yrs.]. "Shirleysburgh." 7½″ x 17″. Cat, buttonhole, and eyelet-stitch. 2 alphabets. Strawberry border. A curious medley of eyelet stitches, wavy lines, bars, and an urn done in black, green, and yellow. The effect is that of a lot of Indian signs. *W. J. Kennedy, Esq.*

BASSET, RACHEL. [Cir. 1807.] 12 yrs. 8″ x 10½″. 1 alphabet. Eyelet, stem, satin, and cross-stitch. Geometrical designs in border. Geometrical design in center, and on each side a branch with fruit. *Mrs. Henry J. Irick*

BASSETT, ELIZABETH. 1802. 11 yrs. 12½″ x 17¾″. 3 alphabets. Flat, eyelet, tent, queen, and cross-stitch. Conventionalized carnation border. Cross-lines in different stitches.
Frances D. Smith

BATES, PARLEY. 1824. 13 yrs. 16″ x 17″. Chain and cross-stitch. Family Register: Nathan Bates, born April 7, 1773; Parley Ballou, born July 9, 1778; married June 4, 1797; Varnum G. Bates, born Feb. 28, 1798; married Dec. 2, 1821; Whitman Bates, born Jan. 21, 1800; died Dec. 21, 1802; Calvan Bates, born July 5, 1802; Married Nov. 24, 1824; Whitman Bates, born Mar. 9, 1805; married Dec. 13, 1827; Julia Bates, born Oct. 9, 1807; married Aug. 14, 1827; Parley Bates; Nahum Bates, born Mar. 6, 1811; William W. Bates, born Nov. 15, 1813; Sylvia W. Bates, born Dec. 15, 1818. *Francis H. Anthony, Esq.*

BAYLEY, MARY KING. 1810. Boston [Mass.]. 8 yrs. 8″ x 18″. Alphabets. Cross-stitch. Greek fret design. *Essex Institute*

BAYLIES, AMELIA F. July 26, 1826. [Born in 1817.] Taunton [Mass.]. 16½″ x 16½″. 3 alphabets. Cross-stitch. Conventional border. Verse 786. *Mrs. William Brewster*

BEACH, ANNA MARIA. 1825. 9″ x 8″. 3 alphabets. Cat and cross-stitch.
Miss Anna M. Scholfield

BEACH, ELIZA. [1812.] 10 yrs. 10″ x 7″. 2 alphabets. Eyelet and cross-stitch.
Miss Anna M. Scholfield

BEAKES, LYDIA. [Cir. 1804.] Trenton. [Born April 3, 1791.] 17½″ x 12″. 3 alphabets. Cross-stitch. Chain design in border. Small basket of flowers and 2 darning designs. "Remember thy Creator," etc. Verse 511 (1). *Miss Anna Morgan Rossell*

BEALL, HARRIET. 1801. Georgetown [D. C.]. 3 yrs. 16″ x 22″. Stem and buttonhole-stitch. "A chart of the World." *Jane E. Beall*

BEAN, MARY A. After 1820. Brookville [Mass.]. Born August 21, 1807. 17½″ x 25″. French knot, stem, satin, and cross-stitch. Trees, birds, and baskets of flowers. Family record:

"Simeon Draper, born March 27 1755. Mary Lewis born Jan. 29, 1770. Were married August 24, 1785. Their Children: Abagail born March 12, 1787; Betsy born Sept 6, 1789; Henry born June 10, 1790; Lorenzo born Mach 27, 1792; Horace born Jan. 30, 1794; Mary born Dec. 5, 1796; Sophia born Feb. 14, 1799; William F. born April 2, 1801; Francis born Dec. 26, 180 ; William B. born Feb. 15 1804; Simeon born Jan 19, 1806; Mary A. born Aug. 21, 1807; Benjamin H. born May 9, 1810; Sally A. born Feb. 27, 1812; Joshua born Sept. 3, 1814; Theodore E. born June 15, 1816; Abagail died July 27, 1788; Mary died June 16, 1800; William F. died June 20, 1801; Francis died Dec. 30, 1802." *Miss S. Ross*

BECKWITH, ANN SOPHIA. 1829. "Poplar Grove." 11 yrs. 3 alphabets. Petit-point, satin, and cross-stitch. Solid cross-stitch border. House in a valley, with trees on the hillsides, name "Poplar Grove", and poplars on left. Illustrated. *The Emma B. Hodge Collection*

BEDFORD, MARY ANN. 1817. 13 yrs. [Born at Old Boonton, Morris County, N. J., August 9, 1804.] 8" x 10". 3 alphabets. Cross-stitch. Border in point design.
Miss Frances A. Force

BEECHER, SARAH P. 1822. New Haven [Conn.]. 9 yrs. 20¼" x 17¾". 7 lines of alphabets. Cross-stitch and single-stitch. Carnation border. Cross-borders. Verse 467.
Mrs. H. Croswell Tuttle

BENNETT, ANN MARGARET. 1820. Charleston [S. C.]. 17" x 22". 4 alphabets. Split, flat, satin, eyelet, and cross-stitch. Hemstitched edge with Greek fret border, with stars in corners. Baskets of flowers and stars. "We are in nothing more unhappy than in not being truly sensible of our own happiness in the favor of God under free and easy administration" ". . . . according to the real want of advantage of a liberal Education". Verse 120. *Miss Anna Bell Bruns*

BENNETT, HANNAH. [Cir. 1811.] Born at Hubbardston, July 27, 1800. 17" x 12". 4 alphabets. Catch, darning, chain, satin, and cross-stitch. Strawberry border across middle. Satin-stitch border in a variety of designs. Sea with boats in one section at bottom, name and date in middle, and carnation, bird, hen, and cat in the third. At the bottom, darning stitches. Verse 292. *Mrs. Thomas A. Lawton*

BENNETT, JANE. 1813. Bridgeton [Cumberland County, N. J.]. 8 yrs. 12½" x 17½". 4 alphabets. Eyelet, stem, satin, tent, queen, and cross-stitch. Strawberry and Greek fret borders. Urns of flowers. "Jane Bennett did this work in the 9th year of her age 1813 being the 38th year of American Independence Modesty is one of the chief ornaments of youth. A Contented mind is an inestimable treasure." Verse 736. Initials: " J B " [Jeremiah Bennett], "J B" [Joanna Bennett, *née* Fish, mother], "R S B" [Ruth S. Bennett, sister], "M B", "J B" [Jeremiah Bennett, brother], "S F B" [Samuel Bennett, brother], "J B" [Jane H. Bennett]. *Cumberland County Hist. Society, Bridgeton, N. J.*

BENTHAM, MARY ANN. 1820. [Charleston, S. C.] 8 yrs. 10¼" x 16". 2 alphabets. Cross-stitch. Scroll cross-border. Rose bush in bloom, with tree on each side; bird on mound on each side of trees. *Miss Leila Waring*

BENTHAM, MARY ANN. 1830. 22" x 23". [Charleston, S. C.] Satin, stem, eyelet, and cross-stitch. Carnation border. Tree in a basket; moss roses in an urn; tree in center, with flowers; design repeated. *Miss Leila Waring*

BERR, SARAH MONTGOMERY. 1804. 10 yrs. "Only child of William and Sarah Berr." 22" x 19". Petit-point, eyelet, satin, stem, and cross-stitch. Carnation and tulip border, alternating. At bottom, house with four steep terraces; path in front; barn, fence, and trees flanking house; variety of trees surmounting each terrace edge; man and two ladies with animals on lawn. Conventionalized carnations in vases on either side of picture. Basket of fruit on either side of verse. Wreath around name, age, etc., and trees on either side; tiny birds in each corner. Verse 343 (1, var.).   *Mrs. Thomas A. Lawton*

BERRY, BETSY. 1802. Rye [N. H.]. 12 yrs. 8" x 18". Alphabets. Stem, satin, and cross-stitch. Cross-border of flowers and vines.   *Hannah M. W. Merrill*

BERRY, SARAH. 1813. 13 yrs. 12" x 12". Cross-stitch. Scroll design in border. Conventional scrolls and flowers in cross-borders. Verses 488 (var.), 737.   *Robert P. Jordan, Dealer*

BETHLEM, LUCY GREEN. September 6, 1804. 9 yrs. 11½" x 4⅞". 1 alphabet. Cross-stitch. Narrow hem with simple border in cross-stitch. Maltese cross. "Let Virtue be thy guide."
Mrs. H. H. De Yermand

BICKFORD, LOVEY. 1800. 8 yrs. 8½" x 12". 2 alphabets. Tent and cross-stitch.
Mrs. George C. Fraser

BIER, SOPHIA CATHERINE. 1810. 17½" x 22". French knot, eyelet, stem, tent, satin, and cross-stitch. Strawberry border. 4 alphabets. Verse 722.   *Mrs. Miles White, Jr.*

BILLINGS, SUSANNA. 1805. 11 yrs. 16½" x 21". 2 alphabets. Stem, satin, and cross-stitch. Greek fret border; inside border, vine with flowers issuing from flower-pots in lower corners. House in center; trees; basket of flowers and birds above house. Verse 410.
William B. Thayer Memorial Collection, University of Kansas

BINGHAM, MARY SPRAGUE. 1823. Andover [Conn.]. 10 yrs. 15" x 15". 3 alphabets. Cross-stitch. Simple border. Trees, birds, and baskets of fruit.   *Mrs. Lathrop C. Harper*

BINNS, MARTHA E. 1829. [Silver Hall, New Kent County, Va.] 18" x 17". 4 alphabets. Cross-stitch and eyelet. Strawberry border. At bottom, Greek key, vine, and cross.
Mrs. F. B. T. Hollenberg

BISSETS, ELIZA. 1817. 10½" x 13". 2 alphabets. Cross-stitch. Strawberry border.
Mrs. George Plimpton

BIXBY, JANE. July the 1 [1812]. 13 yrs. 15¼" x 21". 3 alphabets. Satin and cross-stitch. Floral border. Small flowers. Names and dates: "James F. Bixby, Born September 10, 1784; Sarah Bixby Born November 6, 1786; William Bixby, Born February 6, 1788; John Bixby Born September 18, 1789; Thomas Bixby, Born May 12, 1791 and died November the 30 1793 aged 2 years; Phebe Bixby, Born April 30, 1793; Polly Bixby, Born January 11, 1796; Thomas Bixby, Born October 15, 1797; Jane Bixby, Born February 1, 1799; Parker Bixby, Born April 9, 1801; Lydia Bixby, Born August 12, 1803."
Mrs. Thomas A. Lawton

BLACK, REBECCA. 1803. West Town School. [Born in 1792.] 13" x 13". 5 alphabets. Cross-stitch. Vine border. Verse 406.   *Elizabeth Butcher Page*

BLACKHALL, ANN. 1817. 10 yrs. 11" x 12". 3 alphabets. Cross-stitch. Flower-pots, flowers, lions, birds, and strawberry, done in crewel.   *Fitchburg Antique Shop, 1917*

BLANCHARD, ADELINE. 1813. [Billerica, Mass.] 8 yrs. 10½" x 13½". 4 alphabets. Rose border at top and bottom, and vines on sides. Chain, flat, satin, and cross-stitch. Verse 162 (1).
Miss Adèle Blanchard Randall

BLANCHARD, ADELINE. August, 1817. [Billerica, Mass.] 11 yrs. 17¼" x 17¼". 3 alphabets. Chain, flat, satin, cross, and hem-stitch. Rose border on three sides. House in center and flowers across top. Family record: "Jeremiah Blanchard born July 10th, 1764; Mary Gowen born July 22nd, 1769; Married June 17, 1776; Jeremiah Blanchard, junr, born January 29, 1797; John G. Blanchard born January 30, 1799; Mary Blanchard born September 7, 1801;

PLATE XLV

Eliza Cozzens's Sampler. Providence. 1795
Done at Miss Polly Balch's School
Owned by the Rhode Island School of Design

PLATE XLVI

Lydia Stocker's Sampler. 1798
Owned by Mrs. Henry E. Coe

Sophia Blanchard born November 27, 1803; died June 22nd, 1816; Adaline Blanchard born December 8th, 1805; Catherine Blanchard born June 2th, 1810; Rhoda Blanchard born February 19d, 1815; died May 5th, 1817." *Miss Adèle Blanchard Randall*

BLATCHFORD, E. JANE. June 8, 1814. [Lansingburgh, N. Y.] 8 yrs. Born November 23, 1805. 20¼" x 16½". 6 alphabets. Eyelet, flat, and cross-stitch. Names and dates:

"Samuel Blatchford, August 1, 1767. [father]
Alicia Blatchford, Nov. 19, 1767. [mother]
[Children]

Henry Blatchford,	Dec. 4, 1788.
Mary M. W. Blatchford,	Jan. 24, 1790.
Alicia W. Blatchford,	Feb. 14, 1791.
Sarah Blatchford,	April 23, 1792.
Samuel Blatchford,	May 3, 1793.
Thomas W. Blatchford,	July 20, 1794.
Harriet P. Blatchford,	Oct. 25, 1795.
Samuel M. Blatchford,	Jan. 5, 1797.
R. Milford Blatchford,	April 23, 1798.
John Blatchford,	May 24, 1799.
Sophia Blatchford,	Aug. 21, 1800.
Frederick Blatchford,	Dec. 7, 1801.
George Blatchford,	Jan. 7, 1803.
Charles B. Blatchford,	Sept. 6, 1804.
E. Jane Blatchford,	Nov. 23, 1805.
George E. Blatchford,	Aug. 1, 1807.
Edgecumbe Blatchford,	March 24, 1811."

Mrs. Alicia Blatchford Judson

BLISS, REBECCA. 1824. [Marblehead?] 8 yrs. 10½" x 17½". 4 alphabets. Stem and cross-stitch. Strawberry and clover borders. Flower. "O virtue how amiable thou art". Verses 515 (1, var.), 645. *Marblehead Historical Society*

BLISS, SARAH ANN. 1823. 12 yrs. 12" x 16½". 4 alphabets. Stem and cross-stitch. Border in conventional clover leaf. Verses 188, 601 (1, 2). *Marblehead Historical Society*

BLOOD, LUCINDA. 1816. Concord [Mass.]. Born November 18, 1805. 11 yrs. 16" x 16". 3 alphabets. Stem, satin, and cross-stitch. Conventional border on sides and across top. At bottom, two houses, with flowering shrubs between and vines at the side. Verses 308, 691 (var.). *Miss Helen A. Whittier*

BLOOMFIELD, EUNICE. 1803. "Weston School." 13½" x 13½". Cross-stitch. Conventional border, with roses at corners. Groups of flowers. Initials of schoolmates in wreaths. ["West Town School"]. *Eleanor A. Bloomfield*

BOLLER, HARRIOT. 1802. 10 yrs. 9½" x 12". 3 alphabets. Satin and cross-stitch. Saw-tooth border and cross-borders. Verse 248. *Mrs. De Forest Danielson*

BOND, JOANN. 1810. 12 yrs. 19" x 21". 5 alphabets. Bird's-eye, stem, French knot, satin, and cross-stitch. Double strawberry border, with inside border in chain pattern. Vine and flowers on either side of upper half, and a weeping willow tree on either side of lower half. Verse 718. *Mrs. Thomas A. Lawton*

BOOTH, FANNIE. 1807. 9 yrs. 11" x 6½". 3 alphabets. Eyelet and cross-stitch.
Charles F. Smith, Esq.

BOOTH, MARY. 1814. 10 yrs. 18″ x 18¼″. Cross-stitch. Border of fern and autumn leaves, foxgloves, and roses. Basket of flowers. Verse 160.   *Mrs. John H. Hall*

BORTON, LYDIA. 1811. 12″ x 16″. 4 alphabets. Cross-stitch. Strawberry border. Basket of fruit, pair bluebirds, basket of flowers, rose, 3 carnations, tulip plant, rosebuds, urn with 3 flowers. Initials: "R L E".   *Mrs. Bradbury Bedell*

BOSWORTH, ANGELINA. 1818. 11 yrs. 8″ x 10½″. 3 alphabets. Cross-stitch. Verse 88.
     Miss Emeline B. Butts

BOUDINOT, JULIA. April 23ᵈ 1800. 10″ x 7½″. Twenty-five parallelograms of darning-stitch, imitating damask.   *Mrs. Theodore Weston*

BOURN, CELIA SOPHIA. 1822. 12 yrs. 16″ x 17″. 3 alphabets. Stem and cross-stitch. Strawberry border. House. Verse 121.   *Mrs. J. F. P. Lawton*

BOWEN, RACHEL S. 1818. [Alloways Creek Township, Salem County, N. J.] 12½″ x 13½″. Alphabet. Outline, stem, satin, and cross-stitch. Vine border with Oriental design. Willow tree at bottom. "Behold fond man thy pictured life". Verses 119, 448.
     Richard W. Ware, Esq.

BOWEN, SARAH. 1824. 14 yrs. 17″ x 16″. 4 alphabets. Cat and cross-stitch. Strawberry border. Verse 563.   *Old Ladies' Home, Providence*

BOWER, MARY. 1808. 18″ x 16″. Cross-stitch. Double carnation border.
     Mrs. Lathrop C. Harper

BOWIE, ELIZABETH SUSANNAH. 1800. [Howard Grove or Mulberry Hill, Anne Arundel County, Md.] 15 yrs. Chain and cross-stitch. Map of Maryland.   *Allen Bowie Howard, Esq.*

BOWKER, LAURA. 1817. 11 yrs. 21½″ x 17″. 2 alphabets. Stem, satin, and cross-stitch. Floral border. Landscape with trees, woman, lambs, and gigantic basket of flowers. Woman's face painted on paper and glued on. Some of trees are embroidered in chenille. Lambs are cut out of kid and pasted on. Illustrated. Verse 515 (1, var.).   *Mrs. Henry E. Coe*

BOWMAN, HARRIET CARPENTER. [Cir. 1820.] Cambridge [Mass.]. Born August 25, 1811. Cat, stem, and cross-stitch, and drawn-work. 3 alphabets. Bands of cross-stitch and strawberry vines. Large white house with a porch at either end, with weeping willows; barn and poplar trees. Verse 703 (1, 3).   *Mrs. B. Percy Mincher*

BOWNE, ELIZABETH. 1805. [Near Trenton, N. J.] 11 yrs. [Born September 2, 1794.] 12″ x 17″. 2 alphabets. Eyelet, cross-stitch, and other stitches. Rose border. Crown, stars, and dogs at bottom.   *Mrs. Henry P. Mason*

BOYD, CATHARINE WILLSEY VAN CLEVE. 1829. Born May 30, 1819. "Made at Mrs. Haywood's School, Hackensack." 13½″ x 14½″. 3 alphabets. Cat, eyelet, and cross-stitch. Vine border. "Honor thy Father and thy Mother that thy days may be long . . ." "Dilligence, Industry and proper improvement of time are material duties of the young and the acquisition of Knowledge is one of the most honourable occupations of youth." "Remember thy Creator in the days of thy youth." Verse 94 (var.).   *Mrs. Bradbury Bedell*

BOYD, MARGARET. 1827. Baltimore [Md.]. 7 yrs. 18″ x 18″. Cross-stitch. Vine border. Basket of flowers. Landscape on either side under verse. Below, larger landscape. Verse 515.   *Mrs. Bertram North Stump*

BOYNTON, ABIGAIL L. 1810. Newbury [Mass.]. 10 yrs. Born August 19, 1800. 8″ x 8″. 3 alphabets. Cross-stitch. Hemstitched edge. Cross-borders of vine and strawberry.
     Charlotte M. Smith

BRACE, MARY. 1809. Salem [Mass.]. 10 yrs. 18″ x 20″. 2 alphabets. Chain, stem, satin, cross, and hem-stitch. Border of spreading vine, with vase at lower corners. Pillars with double arch, also Horn of Plenty and vine with various flowers. Verse 515 (var.).
Mrs. Charles W. Ward

BRADFORD, ANNA. "September the 8, 1811." Plymouth [Mass.]. 11 yrs. 17½″ x 17½″. 2 alphabets. Two-sided line-stitch, flat, eyelet, stem, and cross-stitch. Border in conventional design of diamond and octagon-shaped units around three sides, with festoon of knots and tassels across the top. Basket with flowers, trees and birds, at bottom. Verses 673, 725.
Miss Bertha Sumner Johnson

BRADFORD, MARIA. 1828. Providence [R. I.]. 9″ x 13″. 3 alphabets. Cross-stitch. "The United States of America, The Eden of the World and the Best of the Nations."
Mrs. William C. H. Brand

BRADFORD, NANCY. 1817. Charlestown [Mass.]. 11 yrs. 17″ x 20″. 4 alphabets. Cross-stitch. Honeysuckle border. "Youth is the time for Improvement and Instruction." Verse 754.
Mrs. Henry E. Coe

BRADFORD, SARAH GREENOUGH. 1802. 12″ x 14″. 2 alphabets. Satin, stem, and cross-stitch. Rose border, with bowknot in center at bottom. Verse 144.

BRADLEY, REBECCA L. 1807. 9 yrs. 2″ x 2½″. 3 alphabets. Vine border, with leaves and flowers in corners. Verse 203.
D. A. R., "Spalding House," Lowell

BRADWAY, SARAH. 1820. [Port Elizabeth, Cumberland County, N. J. Born in 1809.] 13″ x 20″. 5 alphabets. Eyelet, stem, satin, and cross-stitch. Border of vine and buds. Vase with flowers. Verse 511 (1).
Mrs. Elmer Griscom

BRAITHWAITE, EMMA. 1809. 7 yrs. 20″ x 16½″. French knots and cross-stitch. Vine border. Scene with houses, trees, bushes, lambs, dog, etc. Verse 425.
Mrs. Frank Thompson

BRANNUM, ALMIRA BATES. 1828. "Groton Female Seminary." 9 yrs. 19″ x 18″. 5 alphabets. Flat, eyelet, satin, and cross-stitch. Rose vines rising out of cornucopias at the side.
Groton Historical Society

BRANNUM, MARY ELIZA. 1825. "Groton Female Seminary." 10 yrs. 19″ x 18″. 5 alphabets. Flat, eyelet, satin, and cross-stitch. Rose-vine border.
Groton Historical Society

BRAY, SUSAN. 1809. 17½″ x 17⅝″. Outline, fine and heavy cross-stitch. Border of floral and geometrical designs. Cornucopia of flowers. Trees and birds, sprays of carnation and bluebells. Verse 426. Family initials.
Wilmer Moore, Esq.

BRICKETT, ABIGAIL T. September 27, 1827. West Newbury [Mass.]. 10 yrs. 16″ x 17″. 5 alphabets. French knots, stem, satin, eyelet, and cross-stitch. Border of vines rising from vases at lower corners, with roses and other flowers at top. Grass, trees with fruit, basket of flowers, etc. Verse 692.
Mrs. Lizzie Huntington Sargent

BRIDGES, DELIA. 1820. [Warren, Mass.] 12 yrs. 16″ x 18″. 2 alphabets. Satin, cross, and hem-stitch. Vine border. Divided into sections; 1st, alphabets and numerals; 2d, trees, birds, and dogs; 3d, trees, birds, two houses, basket of flowers; 4th, trees, flowering plant, birds; 5th, trees, birds, lions, and name-plate in center.
Mrs. William N. Eaton

BRIERLY, BETTY. 1826. 18 yrs. 26″ x 26″. Blue linen. Cross-stitch. Strawberry border. In center, reproduction of Solomon's Temple, surrounded by various kinds of trees and sprays of flowers. Verse 567.
Mrs. Renwick C. Hurry

BRIERLY, SALLY. 1828. [Delaware.] 15 yrs. 20″ x 22″. Blue linen. Satin and cross-stitch. Triple strawberry border. Two jardinières in lower corners with tulip plants, and tulip sprays in between. Just above, church flanked by birds on branches. Verse in upper half, flanked by conventionalized rose sprays and flowering trees. Verse 484. *Mrs. Henry E. Coe*

BRIGGS, ANNA. 1802. Scituate. 9 yrs. 12½" x 17". 3 alphabets. Eyelet, stem, satin, cross, and hem-stitch. Conventional cross-stitch border. House with fence, trees, and bushes. Verse 609. *Miss Antoinette Clapp*

BRIGGS, ELIZABETH. 1805. Salem [Mass.]. 10 yrs. 3 alphabets. Satin-stitch made with crinkly silk, couching, French knot, stem, eyelet, split, and cross-stitch. Vine border, with flowers starting from vase in center at bottom and ending in large conventional blossom in center at top; the whole border is solid satin-stitch. Bird on either side of blossom at top. Verse 40 (var.). *Essex Institute, Salem*

BRIGGS, LAURENTIA. September 11, 1801. Pembroke [Mass.]. 9 yrs. Born September 20, 1792. 8" x 12½". 3 alphabets. Cross-stitch. Cross-border. *Miss Adeline Collomore Young*

BRIGGS, SARAH ANN. 1828. Dighton [Mass.]. 10 yrs. 15" x 17½". Cross, satin, stem, eyelet, tent, and two-sided line-stitch. 3 alphabets. Verse 279. *Mrs. Albert Paull*

BRIGGS, SARAH JACOB. 1805. 10 yrs. 13" x 16½". 3 alphabets. Cross-stitch. House, fence, garden, and trees. Verse 269. *Mrs. Charles J. White*

BRIGHAM, SUSAN B. 1814. Grafton [Mass.]. 10 yrs. 11½" x 12". 3 alphabets. Flat and cross-stitch. Flowering-vine border. *Albert C. Bates, Esq.*

BROOKS, LUCINDA. 1816. Gloucester [Mass.]. 12 yrs. 8" x 10". 3 alphabets. Eyelet, cross-stitch, and solid embroidery. Greek fret border, with hemstitched edge. Verse 166. *Mrs. W. R. Beecher*

BROOKS, LUCINDA. 1821. 16" x 16¼". Cross-stitch, hemstitch, and solid embroidery. Hemstitched edge and Greek fret border. Large bunch of roses in right-hand corner. "Marriage Certificate between Reuben Dade and Lucinda Brooks, She, 16 yrs, He 22 yrs."
"Mutual happiness our mutual object."
"May the cares that bind the covetous never disturb our peace."
"May we yield therefore one to another and be equally yoked together in the command of God. May neither of us seek basely to throw an undue weight on the others shoulders. Suffer no interference from any other to interrupt our harmony. We are connected for life—nothing can separate our fate in this world. Oh let nothing divide our affections. May we regard each other with the fullest confidence—the least spark of suspicion from either might forever blast the comfort of both.
There can be no harmony where there is no faith."
Verse 166. *Mrs. William R. Beecher*

BROUSE, ELEANOR. 1816. [Hillsboro, O. Born in Berkley Springs, Va., March 8, 1803.] 18" x 17". 6 alphabets. Cross-stitch. Vine and flower border. House with pump at one side, also trees, birds, and a number of conventional designs. *Mrs. Charles P. Lesh*

BROWN, ABIGAIL. 1821. Seabrook [N. H.]. 10 yrs. 12" x 18". 5 alphabets. Eyelet, chain, stem, French knot, cat, flat, solid stem, satin, and cross-stitch. Cross-border. At bottom, scroll, rose and vine, with conventional designs of trees, pyramids, and basket of flowers. Verse 763. *Dr. A. B. Chase*

[BROWN, ANN CARTER.] Providence [R. I.]. 5" x 10". 6 alphabets. Cross-stitch. *Hon. John Carter Brown Woods*

BROWN, ANNA. 1804. Dover [N. H.]. 8 yrs. Born May 19, 1796. 13" x 15". 3 alphabets. Eyelet, satin, and cross-stitch. Conventional strawberry border with flowers in corners. Verse 685. *Miss Anna H. Howell*

PLATE XLVII

SUSAN LEHMAN'S SAMPLER. Philadelphia. 1799

Owned by Mrs. Charles Schäffer

PLATE XLVIII

MARY HAMILTON'S SAMPLER. Maytown. 1812
Done in Mrs. Welchan's School
Owned by Mrs. Henry E. Coe

Brown, Elizabeth. 1813. Seabrook [N. H.]. 11 yrs. 9" x 7½". 2 alphabets. Hemstitch, eyelet, satin, and cross-stitch. Double hemstitched border with cross-stitch inside. Greek fret border at bottom. *Mrs. George L. Greene*

Brown, Elizabeth A. 1826. 10 yrs. 11½" x 18". 3 alphabets. Cross-stitch. Greek fret border. Verse 787. *A. Stainforth, Dealer, 1917*

Brown, Elizabeth M. 1818. [Hartford County, Md.] 16½" x 15½". Alphabet. Solid stem, satin, and cross-stitch. Wide border with roses, pineapples, and trees with birds. Verse 757. *Mrs. John Butterfield*

Brown, Martha. 1829. 11 yrs. 8" x 17". 3 alphabets. Cat and cross-stitch. Cross-borders. 2 baskets of piled fruit. *A. Stainforth, Dealer, 1917*

Brown, Nancy. 1808. 10 yrs. 16" x 19". Alphabet. Satin and cross-stitch. Cornucopias at lower corners, out of which rise vines with roses, tulips, strawberries, etc. 2 trees at top. Verse 503. *Mrs. H. Russell Perkins*

Brownell, Mary Ann. 1816. 11 yrs. 16" x 17". 5 alphabets. Flat and cross-stitch. Strawberry border. Verse 245. *Mrs. Roswell B. Burchard*

Brownell, Pamela. 1803. Westport [Mass.]. 12 yrs. 9½" x 17". 5 alphabets. Eyelet and cross-stitch. Conventional designs in border of squares and trefoils, also cross-border of the same. Verse 343 (1). "Westport School". *Mrs. S. Frank Hammett*

Browning, Rebecca T. 1825. 7" x 14½". 4 alphabets. Queen, flat, stem, and cross-stitch. Cross-border. Flowering trees, birds, and dog. *Mr. Joseph C. Street*

Brownrigg, Mary Ann. July 18, 1805. Warrenton [N. C.]. 8 yrs. 15" x 12". 2 alphabets. Fine cross-stitch. Conventional borders. Birds, trees, and various decorations. Verse 411a. *James Hardy Dillard, Esq.*

Bryant, Cynthia. 1815. Lexington [Mass.]. 9 yrs. 11" x 16". Born October 7, 1806. Satin, stem, and cross-stitch. 3 alphabets. Simple cross-borders. Strawberry plant, bird, insect, and conventional designs. *A. Cynthia Shurtleff*

Bryant, Lusanna Tucker. 1815. Lexington [Mass.]. 12 yrs. 11" x 16". 3 alphabets. Stem, satin, and cross-stitch. Simple cross-stitch borders. Spray of strawberry blossoms and leaves, with bird and bee in opposite corners, also small designs on each side. Conventional flowers across top and bottom. *Mrs. Charles C. Goodwin*

Bryant, Mary. 1812. Portland [Me.]. 4 alphabets. Satin, eyelet, stem, buttonhole, and cross-stitch. Rose border. Verse 144 (var.). *Ross H. Maynard, Dealer*

Bryant, Mary P. 1815. Boston, Mass. 10 yrs. 10" x 13". 2 alphabets. Scroll borders. Verse 749. *Mrs. Edward D. Brandegee*

Bryarly, Elizabeth. 1812. Winchester [Va. 11 yrs. Born March 4, 1801.]. 18" x 18". Alphabet. Stem, satin, and cross-stitch. Border at top of strawberries and at sides of vine. At bottom, turtle doves, harebells, fuchsias, roses, blackberries, and carnations, also baskets of fruit. Names of father and mother: "Robert and Sarah Bryarly." Verse 436. *Mrs. Worthington Hopkins*

Budd, Eliza F. 1808. 9 yrs. Cross-stitch. Strawberry border outside and saw-tooth border on the inside. In center, Mount Holly, N. J., Court House, with terraced steps and lawn, each terrace surmounted by a pine tree; birds flying about. Large sprays of carnations in four corners, and small designs of birds, trees, berries, flowers, etc., on saw-tooth borders, above and below scene. On the left, Ruth gleans the sheaves of Boaz, and on the right, David tends his father's flocks. Verses 422, 708. *Miss M. Eliza Smalley*

BUFFINGTON, MARY. 1801. 9 yrs. 6″ x 5½″. 1 alphabet. Cross-stitch. Verse 10.
Miss Amey L. Willson

BUGBE, MARY. 1803. [Bristol.] 10 yrs. 11″ x 17″. 4 alphabets. Eyelet, stem, satin, and cross-stitch. Cross-border. Scroll of flowers and leaves, also conventional flowers in pots. Verse 526 (last six lines altered). *Mrs. Mary Chapman Stetson*

BULL, ESTHER M[EARIA]. 1813. Hartford [Conn.]. Satin and cross-stitch. Wreath of vine and flowers, open at the bottom, where there is a basket of flowers. Sampler filled in with names and dates of Esther's maternal grandfather's family:

> "William Whetten born Dec. 12, 1730.
> Margaret Amy Whetten born July 4, 1739.
> Were married September 7, 1756.

William Whetten Junr	born	July 10th, 1757.
Sarah Whetten	born	June 16th, 1758.
Margaret Whetten	born	August 23d, 1760.
Jane Whetten	born	January 27th, 1763.
William Whetten	born	June 2d, 1766.
Samuel Whetten	born	January 6th, 1768.
Mary Whetten	born	October 23d, 1771.
Ann Whetten	born	February 3d, 1773.
Joseph Whetten	born	August 23d, 1776.

William Whetten Sr.	died	June 7th, 1778.
Margaret Whetten Sr.	died	April 21st, 1809.
William Whetten Jr.	died	September, 1801.
Samuel Whetten	died	1789.
Joseph Whetten	died	May 1778."

William W. Huntington, Esq.

BULL, MARGARET ANN. April 23, 1811. Hartford [Conn.]. 8 yrs. 10″ x 16¼″. 11 alphabets. Eyelet and cross-stitch. Cross-stitch borders, in chain design. Verses 431, 433, 631.
William W. Huntington, Esq.

BUNKER, ELIZABETH. 1812. 14 yrs. 17½″ x 20½″. 4 alphabets. Cross-stitch. Border of poppies, tulips, and carnations. Verse 733 (2, var.). *Newport Historical Society*

BUNTING, JANE ELIZABETH. 1818. 7 yrs. 15″ x 10″. 3 alphabets. Chain, cat, and cross-stitch. "Give me o Lord thy early Grace to guide me in the paths of life and fit me for celestial scenes where Peace and joy forever reign." *Mrs. David S. Seaman*

BURDEN, MARY. [Cir. 1814.] Born February 25, 1801. 16½″ x 18″. Queen, cat, stem, and cross-stitch. Strawberry border. Inn, with swinging sign on post; another house, three storied, and fences. Bound with tape. Verses 333, 554. *Miss Jennie Allen*

BURNS, ELIZA. 1808. Gilmanton [N. H.]. 8 yrs. 14″ x 17½″. 4 alphabets. Stem, satin, and cross-stitch. Saw-tooth border. Vase of flowers, with birds and flowers on either side. Verse 110. *Mrs. Edward V. Shepard*

BURR, KEZIAH. 1807. 11 yrs. Mt. Holly, N. J. Born July 31, 1796. 18″ x 23″. Cross and satin-stitch. Vine and pink satin rose quilling. House, lawn, trees, men and women, dogs, birds, and flowers. Verse 278a. *Mrs. Hervey Muhlenburg Sperry*

BURROUGHS, LYDIA. 1809. 9 yrs. and 6 mos. 16½″ x 20½″. 4 alphabets. Cross-stitch. Alternate strawberry, rose, and lily border. Initials: "F B, M R, M B, A R."
Mrs. William Howard Crosby

BURROUGH, LYDIA. 1814. "Chesterford School." 16" x 26". Stem, satin, and cross-stitch. Rose-vine border. In upper section, wreath inclosing verse, and on either side detached sprays of flowers and birds. In lower section, a picture of the Chesterford schoolhouse, with poplar and willow trees on either side, path directly in front, lawn, fence, small trees on either side of gate, also swans. Verse 746. *Mrs. Bradbury Bedell*

BURROUGHS, MARY ANN. 1825. "Red Bank School." 10¾" x 7". 3 alphabets. Cat, eyelet, and cross-stitch. Cross-stitch border. Fancy cross-stitch between alphabets.
Miss Annie Middleton

BURROUGHS, MARYANN. 1825. 19" x 15". Satin and cross-stitch. Border of roses and rosebuds. At bottom, rose, carnation, lilies of the valley, tree with birds, etc. In center, rose bush, vine with flowers, and tulips. At top, two baskets of flowers and two birds.
Miss Annie Middleton

BURTON, ABIGAIL. 1829. [Unfinished.] 9 yrs. Trumbull [Conn.]. 12" x 8¼". 2 alphabets. French knot, cat, and cross-stitch. *W. G. Bowdoin, Esq.*

BUTCHER, RUTH. 1804. Salem County [N. J.]. 12 yrs. 16" x 15¼". 2 alphabets. Outline, herring-bone, flat, tent, eyelet, stem, satin, and cross-stitch. Greek fret border with rose-buds. At bottom, band of Greek fret, trees, strawberries, Greek cross, and birds. Verse 683. Initials: "BB, R B, H B, R B, E B, M B, S A B B." *Mrs. John Ogden*

BUTLER, HANNAH. 1812. 13 yrs. 12" x 13". 2 alphabets. Bird's-eye, eyelet, stem, satin, and cross-stitch. Trefoil and scroll cross-borders. Large basket of flowers and butterfly. Verse 157. *Mrs. Thomas A. Lawton*

BUTMAN, SALLY. 1801. [Marblehead.] 1 alphabet. Tulip border. Cross, satin, eyelet, and other stitches. Man, woman with a fan on either side of a rose bush. Four sheep at the bottom. Verse 188. *Miss Martha D. Howes*

BUTTRICK, LUCRETIA. 18—(?). Concord [Mass.]. 12" x 14". 3 alphabets. Flat, satin, and cross-stitch. Unusual strawberry border. Basket and two trees. Verse 92.
Concord Antiquarian Society

BUTTRICK, MIRIAM. [Cir. 1805. Concord, Mass.] 8" x 10". 1 alphabet and part of a second. Cross and satin-stitch. Scroll and saw-tooth borders. *Mrs. W. C. Dunton*

BUTTRICK, MIRIAM. 1812. Concord [Mass. 16 yrs.]. Satin and stem-stitch and French knots. Charity with a child in her arms. Flowering trees. Five Lombardy poplars and three clipped yews. Farmhouse and fence. *Mrs. W. C. Dunton*

BUXTON, ALICE. 1805. 10 yrs. 12" x 8". 3 alphabets. Chain and cross-stitch. Verse 132.
Mr. James W. Craig

BUXTON, LYDIA. 1814. 10 yrs. 13¾" x 14". 3 alphabets. Satin, eyelet, and cross-stitch. Strawberry border. Cross-stitch dividing lines. Verse 553.
William B. Thayer Memorial Collection, University of Kansas

C——, T.) 1800. 17" x 32". Eyelet, stem, satin, and cross-stitch. Carnation and tulip border.
C——, M. > Birds, trees, butterflies, and large conventionalized flower cross-borders. Verse 530.
P——, E.) *Mrs. Thomas A. Lawton*

CAISE, MARY H. 1805. [New England.] 9 yrs. 13" x 16". 3 alphabets. Eyelet, flat, chain, and cross-stitch. Border of unfinished flat-stitch points. Green lawn with rose bushes and conventional flowers. *Mrs. Bradbury Bedell*

CALDER, AGNES ELIZABETH. 1817. 15" x 11". 4 alphabets. Cross-stitch. *Mrs. Ralph V. Hadley*

CALDER, OLIVIA CAROLINE. 1820. Charleston [S. C.]. 13 yrs. 8½″ x 10½″. 3 alphabets. Greek fret border. Cross-stitch. "May I govern passions absolute sway." *Miss Marie Lebby*

CALDWELL, SARAH S. July 7, 1806. Barre [Mass.]. 15 yrs. 17″ x 21″. 2 alphabets. Stem and cross-stitch. Scene with house, barn, fence, trees, birds, owner, American eagle, and colored man. Verse 187 (var.). Illustrated. *Mrs. W. F. Allen*

CANADEY, CLARA. 1802. 9 yrs. Stem and cross-stitch. Verse 24 (3, var.).
Mrs. Christine Thayer Calderwood

CANFIELD, CORNELIA C. 1825. New Haven, Conn. 8 yrs. 16½″ x 16½″. 5 alphabets. Chain, satin, and cross-stitch. Greek fret border. Cluster of roses at top. Conventionalized roses in each corner. Verse 325. *Miss Marion Belden Cook*

CARLETON, CAROLINE. 1819. "Miss Moody's School." 8 yrs. 14½″ x 17″. 5 alphabets. Eyelet, tent, stem, and cross-stitch. Strawberry border. Basket of fruit, pine tree, jardinière, etc., in row at bottom. *Mrs. Lathrop C. Harper*

CARMAN, MARTHA. 1826. Bordentown. 8 yrs. 18″ x 18″. 3 alphabets. Eyelet and cross-stitch. Strawberry border. House, trees, birds, and basket of flowers. Verse 480.
Mary F. Wilgus

CARMICHAEL, ALMIRA MARTHA. 1829. Born October 21, 1814. Sandlake [Rensselaer County, N. Y.]. 13″ x 13″. 3 alphabets. Flat and cross-stitch. Saw-tooth border. At top, house, pine trees, weeping willows, rose, basket of flowers, etc. Verse 703 (1, var.).
Mrs. Bradbury Bedell

CARSON, ANN. July, 1818. Alexandria [Va. 10 yrs.]. Cross and one other stitch. Strawberry border. Colonial house, and two cornucopias filled with flowers.
Miss Ursula Carson Greene

CARTER, ELIZA. 1811. Peterboro [N. H.]. 11 yrs. 17″ x 17″. 2 alphabets. Stem, satin, and cross-stitch. Vine and cherry border. Verse 33. *Mrs. George Plimpton*

CARTER, JOANNA S. 1821. 10 yrs. 16½″ x 17½″. 2 alphabets. Satin and cross-stitch. Border, Greek fret and rose vine. Birds, pots of carnations and leaves. *Charles S. Henry, 2d, Esq.*

CARTER, MARY ANN. 1818. Danville [Ky.]. 8 yrs. 17½″ x 17″. 4 alphabets. Eyelet and cross-stitch. Strawberry border. Tree, baskets, beehives, bees, butterfly, and dogs. Verse 515 (1, var.). *Miss Louisa S. Baird*

CARTER, POLLY. 1828. Killingworth [Conn.]. 9 yrs. 17″ x 13½″. 3 alphabets. Cross-stitch. Strawberry border. Trees. Verse 40 (var.). *Wilbur M. Stone, Esq.*

CARTYS, MARTHA ANN R. [Cir. 1810.] 10 yrs. 17″ x 25½″. Cross-stitch, eyelet, and tent-stitch. Acorn border. House, lawn, trees, birds, butterflies, deer, dogs, etc. Verse 716.
Mrs. Siegfried Wachsman

CARY, HANNAH. 1821. Newburyport [Mass.]. 10 yrs. Born April 28, 1811. 8″ x 8″. 3 alphabets. Cat and cross-stitch. *Abby A. Newman*

CASE, CLARISSA. April 14, 1824. Canton [Conn.]. 10 yrs. Teacher, Miss Lucy W. Case. 13″ x 20″. 4 alphabets. Cat and cross-stitch. Verses 128 (var.), 187 (var.).
H. W. Erving, Esq.

CHACE, ELIZABETH. 10 yrs. 21″ x 8″. 2 alphabets. Chain and cross-stitch. Verse 342.
Mrs. Daniel Beckwith

CHACE, ELIZABETH JONES. 1816. 8 yrs. 15″ x 11″. Cross and stem-stitch. Strawberry design.
Mrs. William C. Greene

CHADWICK, NANCY. 1811. 13 yrs. 10″ x 14″. Petit-point, cross-stitch. Conventionalized carnation border. Landscape with house, trees, man, lady feeding hens, 2 cows lying down, sheep, dog; and below, large basket with conventional flowers, topped on each side by a bird and conventional tulip and pot, with carnation on either side. Verse 726.

Mrs. Bradbury Bedell

CHAMPION, ANN W. 1816. 8 yrs. 8″ x 15¾″. 4 alphabets. Flat, queen, eyelet, stem, and cross-stitch. Cross-border. Trees, dogs, flowers, and birds, also initials.

Mrs. Elizabeth Kay

CHAMPNEY, MARY ANN. 1822. Roxbury [Mass.]. 8 yrs. 6″ x 6″. 3 alphabets. Cross-stitch. Hemstitched edge. *Elizabeth N. Champney*

CHAMPNEY, SALLY. 1801. New Ipswich [N. H.]. 9 yrs. 12″ x 12¾″. 2 alphabets. French knot, stem, and cross-stitch. Conventional border in scrolls and points, also vine cross-borders. Fence, flowers, trees, and birds, also large urn holding leaves and flowers, and on either side a basket of flowers. "May virtue mark my footsteps here. And point the way to Heaven." *Mrs. John H. Morison*

CHANDLER, SALLY. [1805.] Bedford [N. H.]. 9 yrs. [Born March 3, 1796.] 18″ x 18″. 3 alphabets. Cross-stitch. Conventional borders. *Mrs. Sarah C. Baldwin*

CHAPEL, MARY. 1819. 4 alphabets. "Lydia Sata Lee Instructress." Verse 132 (1, var.).

Alexander W. Drake Collection, 1913

CHAPIN, SARAH. 1816. 18″ x 17″. 2 alphabets. Chain, eyelet, stem, and cross-stitch. Strawberry border. Verse 503. *Mrs. Louis W. Downes*

CHAPLIN, ELIZA C. 11″ x 13″. Cross-stitch. Verse 64. *Groton Historical Society*

CHAPLIN, HARRIOT. 1803. 13 yrs. 10½″ x 12″. 2 alphabets. Flat, stem, satin, and cross-stitch. Three urns, one with flowers and two with fruit. *Groton Historical Society*

CHAPMAN, CHARLOTTE. 1814. Greenfield, Mass. 17¼″ x 16½″. 3 alphabets. Cross-stitch. Strawberry border. Tree, dogs, birds, and baskets of flowers. Verse 647.

Mrs. Arthur Clark Nason

CHASE, MARY. 1814. Chester [N. H.]. 11 yrs. 12″ x 16″. 4 alphabets. Tent, cross-stitch, and much solid work. Rose and vine border. Verse 609. *Jennie P. Hazelton*

CHASE, SALLY. 1800. Saco [Me.]. Born May 10, 1793. 16¼″ x 18″. 3 alphabets. Stem, satin, and cross-stitch. Conventional border. Elaborate design of flowers and basket. Verse 606 (1). *Miss Caroline Manett*

CHASE, SALLY. 1810. [Hopkinton, N. H.] 12″ x 16″. 4 alphabets. Cat, feather, tent, satin, herring-bone, and cross-stitch. Hemstitched edge and saw-tooth border. Verse 182 (1, var.). *Arthur Chase, Esq.*

[CHATTIN, ELIZABETH. 1813.] Born April 5, 1804 [at Chattinville, near Mullica Hill, N. J.]. 16½″ x 20″. 2 alphabets. Greek cross-border. Squirrel seated on branch eating a nut, and flanked on either side by large full-blown rose, bud, and green spray. Names and dates: "The age of Clark Chatin and wife and children he was born july the first 1770.

Anne his wife was born April forth 1780.

James Chattin was born may the 11 1798.

Sarah Chattin was born september the 29 1800.

John Chattin was born february the 5 1802.

Elizabeth Chattin was born april the 5 1804.

Jonathan Chattin was born february the 1 1806.

Benjamin Chattin was born november the 4 1807.

Mary and Anne was born March the 28 1810."

Clark Chattin Hewitt, Esq.

CHEEVER, MARY A. 1812. 10" x 10". 2 alphabets. Cross-stitch. *C. W. Goodspeed, Esq.*

CHEEVER, MARY A. 1817. Attleborough. 11 yrs. 16" x 17". Stem, satin, and cross-stitch. Oak-leaf border. Family Register:

"Samuel Blackinton born March 7, A.D. 1753 George Cheever born Oct. 10, 1771
Mehetabel Richards born Nov. 1, 1755 Sally Blackinton born March 7, 1779
They were Married May 23, 1778 They were Married April 27, 1800
Sally Blackinton born March 7, 1779 Samuel B. Cheever born Nov. 18, 1801
Nabby Blackinton born October 26, 1763 George W. Cheever born Augt 19, 1803
Was Married to Henry Maxey Jan. 1, 1806 Mary A. Cheever born Sept. 30, 1806
And Died Dec. 26, 1807 Sally Cheever died 1816"
Samuel Blackinton Died March 14, 1816

"Blessed are the dead that die in the Lord from henceforth. Yea, saith the spirit that they may rest from their labours, and their works do follow them." Verse 310.

Mrs. Lathrop C. Harper

CHEFTON, MARIA. 1810. 16" x 18". Satin and cross-stitch. Double strawberry border. Scene with house, trees, gateway, and flowers. *Mrs. Renwick C. Hurry*

CHEW, FRANCES. 1808. 8 yrs. 9" x 7½". Cross-stitch. Simple border. *Mrs. H. C. Bunner*

CHILD, HARRIOT. 1802. Roxbury [Mass.]. 9 yrs. 11¾" x 17½". 6 alphabets. Eyelet and cross-stitch. Hemstitched on sides, strawberry border at top and bottom, but unfinished. Cross-borders with birds, animals, trees, fruit, etc. Verse 396. *Miss Cornelia P. Stone*

CHOATE, CLARISSA. 1821. Essex. 9" x 12". 4 alphabets. Cat, cross, and hem-stitch.

W. G. Bowdoin, Esq.

CHURCH, SARAH LOUISE. 1824. 5 alphabets. Cross-stitch. Tulip border, and dividing lines in scroll pattern. Verse 515. *Old Dartmouth Historical Society*

CLAPHAM, MARY. 1813 or 15. 7½" x 10½". 6 alphabets. Eyelet and cross-stitch. "Done this 20th day of March by Mary Clapham for Mary Robertson 1813."

Miss Fanny G. Crenshaw

CLARK, ACHSA. 1810. Woodbury [N. J.]. 14 yrs. 17" x 21". Cross-stitch. Flowers and birds. Names and dates: "Thomas Clark was born the 18th of the first mo. 1767. Achsa Clark was born the 26th of the first mo 1767 and departed this life the 10th of the fifth mo. 1808. The ages of their children are as follows: Hannah Clark was born the 18th of the tenth mo. 1787. Thomas P. Clark was born the 17th of the fifth mo. 1789. Mary B. Clark was born the 23rd of the fifth mo. 1791. Beulah Clark was born the 25th of the seventh mo. 1793. Achsa Clark was born the 6th of the second mo. 1796. Eliza Clark was born the 2nd of the fifth mo. 1798. Edith Clark was born the 15th of the ninth mo. 1800. Ann Clark was born the 10th of the third mo. 1804. Achsa Clark wife of Thomas Clark was a Pancoast." *Miss Eliza W. Knight*

CLARK, CLARA. 1816. Pelham [Mass.]. 12 yrs. Born in 1804. 18" x 18". Alphabets. Cross-stitch. Cross-borders. Verse 308a. *Mrs. Mary A. Fisher*

CLARK, SARAH. 1811. Bridgeton [N. J.]. 10" x 12". [10 yrs.] 3 alphabets. Chain, queen, eyelet, satin, and cross-stitch. Basket of conventionalized fruit; 3 trees on each side; bird on central tree. Names: "Arthur Clark, Mary Clark [father and mother]; James C x John C x Susanna C x Elisabeth C x Sarah C x Nicolas C x Thomas D C [children]."

Mrs. I. Smith Reed

CLARK, SARAH. 1811. Bridgeton [N. J. 10 yrs.]. 14" x 17". 1 alphabet. Buttonhole, queen, chain, eyelet, stem, satin, and cross-stitch. Borders in Greek fret, rose, and conventional geometrical flower designs. House surrounded with floral design. Verse 432. "Sarah Clark was born November 10th 1801." *Mrs. I. Smith Reed*

CLARK, SOPHRONIA. [Cir. 1800.] Southampton [Mass.]. 18½" x 16½". Cross-stitch. 3 alphabets. Flower basket, dogs, trees, and geometrical figures. *Edward Clark Bridgman, Esq.*

CLARKE, MARTHA ANN. January 22, 1808. [Westmoreland County, Pa.] Born May 21, 1792. 17" x 17". 3 alphabets. Cross-stitch. Strawberry border. Figures of children at bottom. Verse 707. *Mrs. W. H. Udall*

CLARKE, RACHEL. 1816. Stony Brook [N. J.]. 18 yrs. Born November 10, 1798. 17" x 21½". Alphabet. Cross-stitch. Rose border with two carnations. Initials: "C C [Charles Clarke, father]; M C [Mary Clarke, mother]; TFC [Thomas F. Clarke, brother]; RN C [Robert N. Clarke, brother]." Verse 558. *Charles Clarke Black, Esq.*

CLARKE, RUTH. 1809. 10 yrs. 17" x 12". 5 alphabets. Cross-stitch. Verse 223 (var.). *E. C. Williams, Esq.*

CLARKE, SUSANNA. October 16, 1800. 8½" x 12". 2 alphabets. Petit-point, tent, satin, and cross-stitch. Conventional tent-stitch border, strawberry cross-borders. Terrace in center, with urn, 2 baskets of flowers, flower-bed, bird on tree, 2 swallows flying. Verse 46. *Mrs. Bradbury Bedell*

CLEAVER, HANNAH. May 9, 1814. 11 yrs. 14" x 16". 2 alphabets. Cross-stitch. Vine border. Conventional designs. Verse too faded to decipher. *Robert P. Jordan, Esq.*

CLEMENT, HANNAH ANN. 1823. [12 yrs.] 13" x 12". 3 alphabets. Cross-stitch. *Mrs. Beulah A. Saunders*

CLEMENT, ISABELLA. 1812. Philadelphia. About 7 yrs. 6" x 6½". 2 alphabets. Flat, satin, and cross-stitch. Grapevine border, also saw-tooth border. *The Misses Jennie and Helen Gwynne*

CLEMENT, MARY. 1807. Amesbury [Mass.]. 11 yrs. 12½" x 12½". 2 alphabets. Stem, eyelet, and cross-stitch. Border in stem-stitch. Pointed design at bottom. *Miss Carrie W. Keniston*

CLEVELAND, MARY S. 1823. 14 yrs. 25" x 21". 4 alphabets. Cross-stitch. Realistic strawberry border. Verses 94 (var.), 469. *Mrs. Charles Cleveland*

C[LEWS], E[LIZABETH] A[NN]. 18Z0? Amherst Court House [Amherst County, Va.]. 4" x 17". 3 alphabets. Great variety of stitches used. Border has been cut off. *Mrs. Clementine Watson Boles*

CLOUTMAN, SALLY H. 1807. Marblehead [Mass.]. 11 yrs. 16" x 13½". 1 alphabet. Satin, stem, and cross-stitch. Rose border. Scene with men, women, dog, etc. Verse 188. *Mrs. Theodore Parker Gooding*

COBB, ESTHER G. 1813. Springfield [Vt.]. 11 yrs. 16" x 16". 3 alphabets. Stem and cross-stitch. Border design a cross alternating with strawberry on a criss-cross vine. Urn with flowers, woman, two large trees, two dogs, two cats, and a bunch of roses at bottom. Verse 732. *Mrs. John DeLoss Underwood*

COCKE, ANN BLAWS. 1822. Bremo. 10" x 12". 5 alphabets. Eyelet and cross-stitch. Hemstitched border. *Mrs. Richard K. Campbell*

COFFIN, APPHIA. 1819. Boscawen [N. H.]. 8 yrs. 17¾" x 15¾". 4 alphabets. Eyelet, stem, satin, and cross-stitch. Strawberry and carnation border. Pine trees on either side at bottom. Verse 279 (var.). *Miss Mary F. Sawyer*

COFFIN, MARY. 1801. Newburyport [Mass.]. 10 yrs. Cross, satin, flat, and stem-stitch. Saw-tooth and vine borders. 2 incomplete alphabets. At the bottom a grape arbor, and in front a lady with a train, followed by a Negro slave holding a parasol over her head. In the center, a pond with four ducks, a man fishing, and two women under an orange tree. There are two weeping willows by the pond. Verse 666.   *Miss Helen Pike*

COHEN, BELLA H. October 10, 1806. [South Carolina.] 14 yrs. 1 mo. Cross, eyelet, and satin-stitch. Rose border. American eagle with pennant, with word "Independence" on it, surrounded by stars. At bottom, house, tree, two lambs, rose vine, baskets of flowers. Verse 609 (var.).   *Mrs. M. C. Hammond*

COIT, FANNY. 1801. 9 yrs. 7½" x 10". 2 alphabets. Cross-stitch. Simple border. Small basket, birds, and animals.   *Mrs. H. C. Bunner*

COIT, HARRIET. 1829. [New York.] 9 yrs. [Born in New London, Conn.] 16½" x 16½". Cross, stem, queen, cat-stitch, and petit-point. Carnation and strawberry cross-borders. 2 cornucopias with roses and grapes. Verse 515.   *Mrs. John Lester Keep*

COIT, SUSAN. 1806. 7 yrs. 10" x 11". 3 alphabets. Cross-stitch. Verse 46 (var.).   *Mrs. H. C. Bunner*

COLBY, ELIZABETH. 1803. Haverhill, County Essex. 8 yrs. 8" x 9". Trees and urn.   *Mrs. G. C. Fraser*

COLE, BROOKSEY. 1817. Sutton [Mass.]. 14 yrs. 17" x 18". 5 alphabets. Stem, satin, and cross-stitch. Vine border, with carnations and roses. Verse 168.   *Miss Mary Lavey Riley*

COLE, CAROLINE. [Cir. 1800.] Fayetteville [Oneida County, N. Y.]. 9½" x 6½". Eyelet and cross-stitch. 3 alphabets. Plain border.   *Mrs. Siegfried Wachsman*

COLE, LAURA MARGARET. 1814. 4 alphabets. Eyelet, satin, stem, and cross-stitch. Strawberry border. Verse 734.   *Reported by Mrs. A. A. Lawrence*

COLE, MARY ANN. 1816. Providence. 9½" x 10". Alphabet. Cross-stitch.   *Miss Ellen Chase*

COLE, ZILPHA. 1828. "Carve." 8" x 18". 3 alphabets. Cross-stitch. Borders of Greek fret and trees. Basket of flowers and other conventional designs.   *Fitchburg Antique Shop, 1917*

COLES, MARY. 1818. Ellisburg School [near Philadelphia]. 22" x 21". Stem, satin, and cross-stitch. Floral border on three sides, with name, date, and small birds in center at top. At bottom, house, queer conventionalized trees, and small animals. Detached designs of flowers, baskets, birds, etc., fill in remainder of space. Verse 758.   *Mrs. Henry E. Coe*

COLLAMORE, ADELINE. 1829. Pembroke [Mass.]. 8 yrs. 9" x 12". 3 alphabets. Cross-stitch.   *Adeline Collamore Young*

COLLAMORE, LAURA ANN. 1829. Pembroke [Mass.]. 10 yrs. 9" x 12". 3 alphabets. Cross-stitch.   *Adeline Collamore Young*

COLLENS, HARRIOT. 1804. 14 yrs. 18" x 16". Stem and cross-stitch. Unusual conventional flowers in border at top and sides; at bottom, basket of fruit in center, with baskets of carnations and poppies on either side. Family record: "Friend Collens born September 16, 1726; Philana Norton born September 12, 1761; Married February 20, 1785. John Collens born October 1, 1785; Mary Ann Collens born March 21, 1787; William Henry Collens born Nov. 3, 1788; Harriot Collens born September 2, 1790; George Lemon Collens born Oct. 23, 1792, George Lemon Collens died Sept. 10, 1793; Sophia T. Collens born Sept. 23, 1794, died 1795; Sophia Theresa Collens born June 16, 1797; Jonathan Collens born December 19, 1799; Emily Collens born March 6, 1801."   *Mrs. Henry Eugene Coe*

COLLINS, ANN S. 1801. 17½" x 19". Cross and satin-stitch. Carnation border. Elaborate rose cross-border at bottom, and also cross-border of roses and tulips. Verses 132 (1, var.), 246 (var.), 359 (1).   *Mrs. Algernon Sydney Sullivan*

COLLINS, ELIZA. 1807. 8 yrs. Verse 606 (1, var.). Names and dates:
> "John Collins Born Aug. 30, 1771.
> Rebeckah Collins Born May 1, 1773.
> Married July 3, 1798
> Their offspring.
> Eliza Born Mar 3rd 1799.
> George Born Mar 23rd 1801.
> Caroline W. Born Ap 22d 1803.
> Charles Born Aug 8th 1807."   *Miss Susan Varney*

COLLINS, ELIZA M. 1828. 17" x 17". 3 alphabets. Stem and cross-stitch. Rose border. House. Verse 792.   *The Misses Collins*

COLLINS, SARAH ANN MARRIOTT. 1824. 9 yrs. 12" x 12". 4 alphabets. Chain, stem, queen, and cross-stitch. Verse 60.   *The Misses Collins*

COLQUHOUN, REBECCA BOLLING. [Cir. 1800.] Petersburg [Va.]. 12" x 16". 7 alphabets. Cross-stitch. Simple designs. Verse 393.   *Mrs. James N. Edwards*

COLTON, BETSEY. 1807. Hartford [Conn.]. 11½" x 15". Stem and cross-stitch. Ornamental cross-stitch border. Large design at bottom of fruits, leaves, etc. Design at top, bow-knot and festoon of moss roses, buds, and leaves. Verse 277. Names and dates:
> "Aaron Colton Born December 5, 1758.
> Elizabeth Olmsted Born August 26, 1762.
> Married   April 6, 1787.
> Laura Colton Born May 2, 1788.
> Betsey Colton Born March 18, 1794.
> Anson Colton Born December 23, 1797.
> Nathan Colton Born May 27, 1799."

Miss Bessie Colton Farr

COMBS, ABIGAIL. 1820. 15" x 17". Alphabet. Cross-stitch. Greek fret border and conventional strawberry along 3 sides. Design in center of star, fruit, flowers, birds, and animals. Initials: "SC, AC, EC, RC, SC, MC, LC." Verse 395 (4, var.).   *Miss Anna Bell Weatherby*

COMPTON, HANNAH B. 1826. Port Elizabeth [Cumberland County, N. J.]. 10 yrs. 17" x 18". 1 alphabet. Eyelet and cross-stitch. Greek cross and Greek fret border. Trees, birds, flowers, fruits, sprays of strawberries, cats and dogs, urn of flowers, basket of flowers, crowns, swan, doves, etc., at sides and at bottom. Verse 172.   *Mrs. Japhet M. Fox*

COMSTOCK, E. 1822. 9" x 11". 3 alphabets.   *Mrs. C. D. Owen*

CONE, LUCINTHIA. 1808. Westchester [Conn.]. 11 yrs. 9½" x 7". 2 alphabets. Satin and cross-stitch. Cross-border. At bottom, rosebuds and some large flowers.
Eveline W. Brainerd

CONGDON, MARY I. 1821. New Bedford [Mass.]. 12 yrs. 5 alphabets. Stem, satin, and cross-stitch. Rose border; cross-borders in strawberry, vine, and other designs. Two cornucopias, filled with flowers, in center, at bottom. Verse 515.
Old Dartmouth Historical Society

CONGDON, REBECCA H. 1812. 13 yrs. 11" x 9½". 3 alphabets. Cross-stitch.
Miss Eliza B. Hazie

CONKLIN, AGNES MARY. 1805. Jamaica [L. I.]. 9 yrs. 13″ x 16″. Trefoil border. House, tree, and fence at bottom; dog and tree in center. Verse 693 (1).   *F. C. Thomas, Esq.*

CONOVER, ALICE. 10 yrs. 18″ x 17″. 2 alphabets. Design at bottom, replica of Mechanicstown, also 2 baskets and lions. Verse 576.   *Mrs. Renwick C. Hurry*

CONOVER, SARAH ANN. [Cir. 1809.] Born July 8, 1797. 16½″ x 21″. 3 alphabets. Satin and cross-stitch. Triple strawberry border on sides. Flowers and bird across top and baskets of fruit and animals at bottom. Scene with Adam and Eve and Tree. "Abraham, Abraham here am I and he said lay not thine hand." Verse 515 (1, var.).
Mrs. Thomas A. Lawton

CONOVER, LEAH. 1826. 16 yrs. Middletown [now Holmdel, N. J.]. 15″ x 18″. Made at Middletown Academy. 1 alphabet. Trees. "Favor is deceitful and beauty is vain, but a woman that feareth the Lord She shall be praised. Give her the fruit of Her hands and let her own Works praise her in the gates."   *Miss Anna Lawrence Crawford*

CONWAY, ELIZABETH. 1807. Marblehead, Mass. 11 yrs. 13″ x 11″. French knot, stem, satin, and cross-stitch. Basket of flowers with a spray in each corner.   *Miss F. P. Hammond*

COOK, MARY ANN. 1823. Newburyport, Mass. 9 yrs. 6″ x 12″. 4 alphabets. Flat, satin, and cross-stitch. Verse 150 (1).   *Elizabeth B. Myrick*

COOK, MARY MARIA. 1820. 10 yrs. Born July 16, 1810. 16″ x 20″. Alphabets. Eyelet, stem, satin, cross, and flat-stitch. Strawberry border on three sides; cross-borders in trefoil, heart, carnation, and vine designs. At bottom, weeping willow trees, with tombstone in center bearing inscription: "Sacred to the Memory of Humphrey Cook who died May 18, 1812 Aged 24." Names and dates: "Humphrey Cook was Born March 21st 1788. Died May 18, 1812. Harriet Cook was Born August 8, 1790. Mary Maria Cook was Born July 16, 1810. Humphrey Cook was Born Novᵣ 5, 1811." Verse 315.   *Mrs. Thomas A. Lawton*

COOK, NANCY. 1823. Lyme [N. H.]. 18″ x 18″. 4 alphabets. Cross-stitch. Border in pointed design. Large candlestick design. Cross-borders in diamond, candlestick, or flower tree designs. "S. M." Verse 511 (1).   *Louise Mears*

COOK, SALLY. 1809. 14 yrs. 5 alphabets. Verses 155, 286.

COOK, SARAH. 1814. 7½″ x 13½″. Pineapple border. Scene with house, trees, and deer, also detached birds, trees, butterflies, large dog, and leopard.
On sale at Walpole Galleries, June 29, 1917

COOKE, ELIZABETH. 1818. 16″ x 10″. 3 alphabets. Cross-stitch. Verse 150.
Mrs. Harold W. Oatley

COOKE, FRANCIS REBECCA. [Cir. 1810.] Schenectady [N. Y.]. Born April 7, 1798. 11½″ x 22″. 3 alphabets. Cross-stitch. Greek fret border. Medallion design at bottom. Verse 31.
Mrs. Quincy O'M. Gillmore

COOL, ABIGAIL. 1810. [14 yrs.] Born February 6, 1796. 14″ x 14″. 6 alphabets. Eyelet, flat, and queen-stitch in a square. Zigzag border. Verse 128 (1, var.). *Mrs. Thomas A. Lawton*

COOMBS, ELIZA ANN. 1818. Newburyport. 8 yrs. 26½″ x 20″. Chain, eyelet, stem, satin, and cross-stitch. Greek fret border. Flowery hillside. Family record: "The family of Philip and Ann Jewett Coombs. Philip Coombs was born Dec. 16th, 1779; Ann J. Morse was born May 11th, 1782; (children) Mary, April 6th, 1807; Eliza Ann, July 15th, 1809; John, Sept. 17th, 1812; Philip, July 26th, 1815." Verse 513.   *Mrs. John F. Pearson*

COOPER, ANN P. September 4, 1816. 19″ x 23″. Cat, outline, stem, tent, satin, and cross-stitch. Vine border in double outline with flowers and buds. Scene with terrace, flowering tree, squirrel seated between limbs of tree, at bottom; in center, green bank with 2 weeping willows. Pleated satin ribbon around sampler, with rosette at each corner.

Mrs. Walter Hunt

COOPER, MARTHA ANN. 1826. Baltimore [Md.]. 8 yrs. 18" x 20". Split, chain, cat, stem, tent, queen, satin, and cross-stitch. True lovers' knot with tassels, also carnations with leaves at top; vine with birds and flowers alternating at sides. House with peaked roof, two and one-half stories high; large flower urn on one side; flower boxes and cedar trees on the other side; front lawn inclosed with panel fence and iron gate. Verse 536.

Mrs. Lewis Stewart Elmer

COPP, PHEBE ESTHER. 1822. 8 yrs. 18" x 24". 3 alphabets. Cross-stitch. Double zigzag and strawberry border. Trees and rose bushes, also hearts, tulips, etc., scattered about. Verses 41, 553.

National Museum

CORBIN, JANE VIRGINIA. 1825. The Reeds, Caroline County. 12" x 16". 3 alphabets. Eyelet and cross-stitch. Eyelet border. "Conscious virtue is its own reward."

Fitchburg Antique Shop, 1917

COREY, SARAH. [Cir. 1800.] Born in 1787. 12" x 15". 2 alphabets. Eyelet, satin, and cross-stitch. Conventional border. Vases, trees, flowers, birds, grass, etc.

Mrs. Thomas A. Lawton

CORNELL, ELIZABETH BALDWIN. 1810. White Plains [N. Y.]. 9 yrs. 12" x 12". Alphabet. Cross-stitch. Cross-borders of vine, rose, fret, and cross-stitch designs. Beautiful bouquet of forget-me-nots, jonquils, and roses, also a spray of moss roses, harp in wreath, pot of flowers, and rabbit.

Mrs. Thomas W. Strange

CORNING, PATTY [MARTHA CORNING]. 1803. Londonderry [N. H.]. 12 yrs. Born July 14, 1791. 17" x 17". 4 alphabets. Chain, eyelet, stem, and cross-stitch. Border in tree and diamond designs, and outlined with fancy hemstitching. Verse 679. *Miss Louisa A. Orbeton*

CORNSTOCK, E. 1822. 9" x 11". 3 alphabets. Cross-stitch. *Mrs. C. D. Owen*

CORTLAND, LUCY MARIA RANDALL. 1828. 18" x 18". 3 alphabets. Cross-stitch. Zigzag border.

National Museum

CORTWRIGHT, HANNAH. 1807. [Wilkes-Barre, Pa. Born February 7, 1798.] 9 yrs., 6 mos., and 14 days when finished. 7½" x 8½". 3 alphabets. Cross-stitch.

Mrs. Robert Miner Abbott

COSTILL, REBECCA. 1817. 7½" x 7½". Cross-stitch. Vine border. Flowers and birds.

Louise Burr Taylor

COVELL, LYDIA. [Cir. 1808 or 10.] Glastonbury [Conn. Born in 1800.]. 11" x 11". 3 alphabets. Cross-stitch. Greek border. Verse 163. *Mrs. Eugene C. Stratton*

COX, SUSANA. [Cir. 1802.] "West Town Boarding School." 14" x 13½". [Born in 1785.] Very fine cross-stitch. 28 designs of flowers, fruit, wreaths, and baskets of fruit and flowers. Illustrated. *Miss Susan P. Wharton*

COZZENS, ANNE. [Cir. 1804.] Sherborn [Mass.]. 9 yrs. [Born in 1795.] 9" x 12". 2 alphabets. Cross-border. Lines of feather-stitching between rows of letters. *Augusta Barber*

CRAWFORD, ELIZABETH. 1822. Cape May [N. J.]. 8 yrs. 18½" x 15½". 3 alphabets. Eyelet, outline, and queen-stitch. Silk fringe, vine, and flower design in border. Births of children of Jonathan and Hannah Crowell Crawford: "Jonathan and William Crawford were born May 15th, 1811; Elizabeth Crawford was born July 22nd, 1814, and did this work April, 1822; Rebecca Crawford was born Sept. 4th, 1818; Barnabas Crawford was born Aug. 27th, 1820; Sarah Crawford was born May 7th, 1823; Isaac O. Crawford [no date given]."

Mrs. Thomas Stevens

CRAWFORD, REBECCA. 1829. Cape May [N. J.]. 11 yrs. Born September 4, 1818. 12½″ x 18″. 2 alphabets. Star, eyelet, queen, and cross-stitch. Border of links and diamonds, also Walls of Troy. Vine design. Verse 553.   *Miss Mary Elizabeth Smith*

CRESPIN, JULI ANN. 1830. West Chester School. 16″ x 15″. Satin, couch, and cross-stitch. Strawberry border on three sides. Heart-shaped border of pink rosebuds and leaves incloses verse. In center, at bottom, brick house, trees, lawn, etc. In upper left-hand corner, an aster and rosebud within border; outside border, in upper corners, are stars. Verse 338.
                                                   Mrs. Bradbury Bedell

CROCKER, ELIZA. 1803. "At Mrs. Dobell's Seminary in Boston." 16″ x 18″. Stem, satin, and cross-stitch. In center, picture with house and tree in background and two children under tree in foreground. Picture surrounded by elaborate floral design of roses, carnations, and tulips. Odd conventional strawberry band above picture, forming sort of arch, supported by solid cross-stitch pillars. Verses in lower corners and name, date, etc., in upper corners. Verse 634. Illustrated.   *Susan P. Peabody*

CROCKER, LEONICE H. 1806. 16″ x 20″. Eyelet, cat, satin, and cross-stitch. 4 alphabets. Conventional design in border. Verse 412.   *Miss Lucy G. Peabody*

CROFT, SARAH ELIZA. 1829. Charleston [S. C.]. 9 yrs. 18″ x 18″. Eyelet and cross-stitch. Primrose border. Primrose vine and flowers.

"No trees bear fruit in autumn ✕ unless they blossom in the spring ✕ to the end that our age may be profitable and laden with ripe fruit ✕ let us all endeavour that our youth may be studious ✕ and flowered with blossoms of learning and observation."

"Virtue is the greatest ornament of youth, it is the foundation of honor and esteem and the source of all beauty, order and happiness in Nature. Beauty and wit will die, learning will vanish away and all the arts of life will soon be forgotten, but virtue will remain forever."

"The flower of youth never appears more beautiful than when it bends toward the sun of Righteousness."

Verse 126.   *Miss Georgie L. Gready*

CROSBY, ELIZABETH H. 1812. Born August 12, 1804. 8 yrs. 10″ x 11″. 3 alphabets. Eyelet, stem, and cross-stitch. Rose and vine border. Verse 601 (1, 2, var.).
                                                   Mrs. Horace N. Fisher

CROSSMAN, NANCY. [Cir. 1823. West Boylston, Mass.] 8″ x 10″. 3 alphabets.
                                                   Miss Pamelia H. Parker

CROWNINSHIELD, MARIA LOUISA. 1825. Salem. 9 yrs. 17″ x 17″. 4 alphabets. Single, double, and quadruple cross-stitch. Conventionalized strawberry and leaf design around verse. "Do as you would be done by." Verses 123, 645 (2).   *Mrs. Helen Suzette de Gersdorff*

CUMMINGS, JUDITH. 1805. Topsfield [Mass.]. 13 yrs. 12¼″ x 15¼″. 2 alphabets. Satin and cross-stitch. Hemstitched edge. Rose border at sides and strawberries in center at top and in each lower corner. Fuchsias and other flowers in fancy vase in center. Pine tree and grass on each side of vase. Verse 270.   *Mrs. Horace Plumer*

CUNNINGHAM, SUSANNAH. [Before 1813.] "August 27th." 14 yrs. 15½″ x 18½″. 3 alphabets. Stem, satin, and cross-stitch. Conventional design of leaves and flowers in border. Various designs in cross-borders. Verse 549.   *Mrs. Andrew C. Wheelwright*

CURRIER, ABIGAIL A. 1830. Newbury, Mass. 19 yrs. 10″ x 16″. 5 alphabets. Chain, eyelet, satin, tent, cross, and hem-stitch. Hemstitched edge. Rose border. 14 cross-bands. Roses, leaves, and bow. Verses 178, 236. [Her hands were lame and every stitch was drawn through with her teeth.]   *Newburyport Historical Society*

PLATE XLIX

CLARISSA EMERSON'S SAMPLER. Lancaster, Mass.
Formerly owned by Dwight M. Prouty, Esq.

PLATE L

LAURA BOWKER'S SAMPLER. 1817
Owned by Mrs. Henry E. Coe
Plate presented by Mrs. Barrett Wendell

CURRIER, CHARLOTTE. 1806. Methuen [Mass.]. 8 yrs. 12″ x 5″. 2 alphabets. Cross-stitch. Geometrical designs in border. Rose design at bottom. *Miss Bessie M. Swan*

CURRIER, CHARLOTTE. 1808. Methuen [Mass.]. 10 yrs. 12″ x 10″. 2 alphabets. Cat and cross-stitch. Vine border. *Miss Bessie M. Swan*

CURRIER, SALLY. 1806. Methuen [Mass.]. Born March 7, 1796. 12″ x 10″. 3 alphabets. Satin and cross-stitch. Flat-stitch design in border. *Miss Bessie M. Swan*

CURTIS, ELISABETH. 1826. Beverly [Mass.]. 16″ x 16″. Born August 1, 1815. Stem, satin, and cross-stitch. Border of ivy leaves and berries, also saw-tooth border. Family record: "Mr. William Curtis was born in Beverly, Mass. Sept. 18, 1792. Miss Betsey Dodge was born in Wenham Mass. Nov. 25th, 1792. They were married 1812. Mr. Curtis died in Cape Henry, West Indies, Feb. 17, 1820. Blest be the tie which binds our hearts in nuptial love. Lucy Ann Curtis born May 3, 1813. Elisabeth Curtis born Aug. 1st, 1815. Mary S. Curtis Born Nov. 9th, 1817. Abigail Curtis Born Feb. 17, died 20, 1820." Verse 61.
Mrs. Bradbury Bedell

CUSHING, JANE L. 1825. Hull [Mass.]. 9 yrs. Born December 20, 1816. 12″ x 12″. 3 alphabets. Eyelet and cross-stitch. Triangular design in border. Verse 515.
A. Stainforth, Dealer, 1917

CUSHING, MARY. July, 1820. Hull [Mass.]. 9 yrs. 10″ x 9½″. 3 alphabets. Petit-point and cross-stitch. Elaborate vine in the form of a Greek fret in border. Birds, beast, and plants.
A. Stainforth, Dealer, 1917

CUSHING, MARY ANN. 1822. Newburyport [Mass.]. 6 yrs. 15″ x 16¼″. 5 alphabets. Eyelet, satin, and cross-stitch. Strawberry border. Cross-borders with heart, Greek key, trefoil, and triangular designs. Tree on either side of name. *Miss Ellen Gilliss Todd*

CUSHING, NANCY. 1816. [Probably Hingham, Mass.] 9½″ x 5½″. 1 alphabet. Cross-stitch. Two diamonds and one heart. Initials "S C B" in left-hand corner.
Miss Margaret W. Cushing

CUTLER, ABIGAIL BIGELOW. 1808. Rockingham [Vt.]. 8 yrs. 11″ x 12″. 3 alphabets. Tent, eyelet, satin, and cross-stitch. Border of vine and double tent. Verse 515 (1, var.).
Arthur Chase, Esq.

CUTLER, HARRIET. 1808. Rockingham [Vt.]. 11 yrs. Born November 15, 1796. 12″ x 16″. Cat, eyelet, satin, and cross-stitch. Conventional border. Verse 279 (var.). Names and dates: "Samuel Cutler and Jennett Caldwell were married July 15th 1786. Maria Ann and John Lenox Cutler born April 23rd 1788. James Iredell Cutler born May 20th 1792. Harriet Cutler born Novr 15th, 1796. Abigail Bigelow Cutler born Jany 7th 1799. Abigail B. Cutler died March 15th 1806." [All were born at Hartford, Conn.]
Lawrence Brainerd, Esq.

CUTLER, LYDIA. 1818. Royalston [Mass.]. 11″ x 13″. 2 alphabets. Satin and cross-stitch. Rose border. Basket of roses and several other flowers. Plants in each corner. Wreath of roses. *Mrs. John Brooks*

CUTLER, SOPHIA. [Cir. 1807.] Rindge [N. H.]. Born January 30, 1794. 20″ x 17″. 3 alphabets. Satin and cross-stitch. Three borders, one of solid work and two in Greek fret. Verse 511 (1, var.). *Mrs. Charles H. Atkinson*

CUTLER, SOPHIA. 1801. 8 yrs. 17½″ x 21″. Wide vine border on three sides. Scene with house, bridge over a river, birds, baskets, etc. Verse 222. *The Emma B. Hodge Collection*

DAGGETT, MARIA. 1819. Providence [R. I.]. 9 yrs. 17" x 17". 3 alphabets. Stem, satin, and cross-stitch. Rose border. Verse 57. *Mrs. Joseph H. Jewett*

DAGGETT, MARY M. 1813. Holmes Hole [Mass.]. [8 yrs.] 17" x 15". 5 alphabets. Eyelet and cross-stitch. Rose border. House. Verse 94 (var.). *Mrs. Rebecca D. Getchell*

DALLAS, ANN. 1810. Salem [N. J.]. 10 yrs. Born March 11, 1800. 17¼" x 22¼". 7 alphabets. Buttonhole, outline, tent, stem, satin, and cross-stitch. Vine and strawberry border. Sampler divided into 3 panels, running lengthwise. Designs of blooming plants and buds. "See that ye fall not out by the way." Verses 54, 82, 511 (1, var.).
Miss Adaline Sinnickson

DANA, MARY. 1812. 10" x 8". 1 alphabet. Cross-stitch. Verse 515. *Mrs. B. Ray Phelan*

DANFORD, ELIZABETH PARKER. 1805. 16 yrs. 17" x 12". Flat and cross-stitch. 4 alphabets. Realistic vine border. Verses 220a, 688. *Mrs. William Henry Gilbane*

DANFORTH, REBECCA BROWN. 1820. Newbury [Mass.]. 9 yrs. Born January 8, 1811. 17" x 17". 5 alphabets. Eyelet, stem, tent, flat, cat, French knot, satin, and cross-stitch. Trefoil border. Vase of flowers, trees, lambs, butterflies, and other ornamental designs. Verse 515 (1, var.). *Etta T. Lovett*

DANIELS, NABBY SHILABER. Danvers [Mass.]. 9 yrs. 19" x 25". 3 alphabets. Stem and cross-stitch. Vine border with tulips, carnations, and marguerites. Vase with flowers and vine running upward. Verses 40 (var.), 128 (var.).
Miss Annie S. Symonds and Mrs. Frank M. Goss

DANIELS, SALLY. 1810. Danvers [Mass.]. 10 yrs. 22" x 24". 3 alphabets. Stem, French knots, and cross-stitch. Rose and tulip border. Elaborate cornucopia design at bottom. Verse 515 (var.). *Mrs. Lucy F. Caller*

DANIELS, SARAH P. 1814. Born October 22, 1802. 16" x 20". 5 alphabets. French knots, chain, stem, satin, double and single cross-stitch. Carnation and vine border. Large basket in center, holding roses, pansies, tulips, and forget-me-nots; at left, a smaller basket of fruit; at right, a pitcher with sprays of berries. Verse 609. *Sara Adeline Thompson*

DARE, JANE. 1821. Bridgeton [Cumberland County, N. J.]. 11 yrs. Born January 11, 1810. 17" x 18". 5 alphabets. Stem, eyelet, queen, tent, satin, and cross-stitch. Saw-tooth border done in flat-stitch. Sprays of flowers and buds on either side of rectangle inclosing verse. Verse 819. Initials: "D D [David Dare, father]; R D [Rebecca Dare, mother, daughter of Jonathan and Mary Fithian]; E F D [Enoch Fithian, brother]; S D [Sarah, sister]; W D [William, brother]; E D; M H D [Mary Hay, sister]; J F [Jonathan Fithian, maternal grandfather]; M F [Mary Fithian, maternal grandmother]; A F [Ann, daughter of J. & M. F.]; E F [Elizabeth, daughter]; D F [Daniel, son]; M F [Mary, daughter]; J F [Joel, son]; E F [Emily, daughter]; M F [Mary, daughter]; S F [Sarah, daughter]." *Mr. Charles E. Sheppard*

DARLING, ELIZABETH. 1823. Henniker [N. H.]. 11 yrs. 16" x 16". 4 alphabets. Eyelet, stem, satin, and cross-stitch. Border of vine, roses, carnations, and berries, in clusters. Verse 645 (2). *Julia B. Park*

DAVENPORT, ELIZA. 1818. New Bedford [Mass.]. 11 yrs. 16" x 18". 5 alphabets. Stem, satin, and cross-stitch. Rose border. Verse 104 (2). *Francis O. Allen, Esq.*

DAVENPORT, JOANNA C. 1826. 15 yrs. 16¾" x 16½". Saw-tooth and rose borders. Family register: "Jereme Davenport Born Feb. 1781; Polly B. Davenport Born Aug. 2, 1784. Were married Sept. 19, 1806 and had the following children:—

Jereme Davenport died September 19, 1838. Polly B. Davenport died January 1, 1870.

Warren T. & Rufus	Born Dec. 23, 1807.	Died Apr. 25, 1809.
Jereme B.	Born Jan. 28, 1809.	Died Apr. 7, 1830.
Rufus W.	Born Jan. 30, 1810.	
Joanna C.	Born Mar. 2, 1811.	Died Sept. 13, 1831.
Oliver G.	Born April 30, 1812.	
Ariel H.	Born Nov. 1813.	Died Oct. 13, 1871.
John N.	Born Dec. 10, 1814.	
Aaron K.	Born Feb. 12, 1816.	
Jesse C.	Born Mar. 22, 1817.	Died May 20, 1863.
Mary	Born Aug. 28, 1818.	
Phebe J.	Born Dec. 11, 1819.	
Jonas	Born May 10, 1821.	
Joseph C.	Born June 2, 1822.	
Charles W.	Born Mar. 8, 1826.	
Abner B.	Born May 22, 1827."	

[The dates later than 1826 were put in by some member of the family other than Joanna.]

A. Stainforth, Dealer, 1915

DAVENPORT, LYDIA. 1800. Dorchester [Mass.]. 14 yrs. 13″ x 16″. 1 alphabet. Stem, filler, chain, cat, and cross-stitch. Scene with house, trees, and flowers. Verse 490 (var.).

The Emma B. Hodge Collection

DAVIS, ABIGAIL. 1820. 19½″ x 19½″. Queen, stem, satin, and cross-stitch. Rose border. Scene with house, trees, parrots, and flowers. Verse 532. *Mrs. Renwick C. Hurry*

DAVIS, HANNAH (B.?) 1827. Woodstown [N. J.]. 13 yrs. 21¼″ x 21¼″. Cross-stitch. Rose border. Border of flowers, trees, animals, and birds around the verse. Verse 481.

Mrs. Isabella Smith Lippincott

DAVIS, LUCY ANN. 1808. Newburyport [Mass.]. 11 yrs. 7½″ x 8½″. 3 partial alphabets. Satin and cross-stitch. Greek fret border across top. *Lucie A. Peabody*

DAVIS, MARA ANN. 1816. [Cumberland County, N. J.] 7 yrs. 6¾″ x 9½″. 2 alphabets. Outline and cross-stitch. Vine border. Strawberry and Greek cross designs at bottom. Verse 41 (var.). Initials: "J A, L A, R D, M D, A D, E D, A D, E D, L A D."

Mrs. Jonathan W. Acton

DAVIS, MARY E. 1816. Woodstown [N. J.]. 17¼″ x 21¼″. Eyelet, satin, and cross-stitch. Border of strawberries and sprays of flowers. Urn with flowers, also animals and birds, in design at bottom. Verse 750. *Mrs. Isabella Smith Lippincott*

DAVIS, RUTH. 1817. Cumberland [N. J.]. 11 yrs. 11¼″ x 13½″. 3 alphabets. Eyelet, satin, and cross-stitch. Simple line border. At bottom, tree surmounted by bird and geometrical and floral figures. Verses 41 (var.), 490 (var.), 526 (1). Initials: "R D, H D, J A, L A, S D, L D, D A D, J W D, W D, R D, A D, I D, S D, L D, G B D, H W D." *Miss Josephine McAltioner*

DEACON, ANN [BURR]. [Before 1810.] Weston School. [Born September 22, 1788.] 13″ x 14″. Eyelet, stem, and cross-stitch. 18 sprays of flowers around outside; inside, 11 different designs, baskets of flowers, wreaths inclosing initials, etc. Initials "I D H" stand for John and Hannah Deacon, father and mother. *Gertrude N. Deacon*

DEACON, HANNAH E. 1816. Weston School. [Born June 14, 1799.] 11″ x 11″. Flat, darning, chain, and cross-stitch. Sampler divided into blocks of 7 different designs.

Gertrude E. Deacon

DEALY, MARY. 1806. 7 yrs. Stem, satin, and cross-stitch. Vines intertwined across sampler. Addition made to sampler: "She was a blessing here below. An only child of a widow. Subscribed by Sally Parker." *Mrs. Richard H. Hunt*

DEAN, CATHARINE. 1813. Charlestown [Mass.]. 11 yrs. 12" x 14". 3 alphabets. Cross-stitch. Vine and rosebud border. Strawberry cross-border. Verse 159. *Worcester Art Museum*

DEAN, ELIZABETH. 1806. Taunton [Mass.]. 9 yrs. 14½" x 18½". 5 alphabets. Satin and cross-stitch. Zigzag border and floral border. Verse 647. *Sarah B. Williams*

DEAN, MARY. 1819. 11 yrs. 11" x 11". 3 alphabets. Cross-stitch. Cross-stitch motifs. Verse 79. *Wilbur M. Stone, Esq.*

DEARTH, ELIZABETH B. 1825. 13" x 8". 4 alphabets. Cross-stitch. *Miss Kate Simmons*

DECOW, ABIGAIL. 1821. Chesterfield School. 17" x 19". Outline, flat, satin, and cross-stitch. Rose border with bluebirds, butterflies, and baskets of roses and buds. Large and small pine trees and rose bushes on strip of green grass. Verse 316. *James Linton Engle, Esq.*

DECOW, MARGARET. 1825. Chesterfield [Burlington County, N. J.]. 18" x 16". Cross-stitch. Strawberry border. At top, five plants in pots; at bottom, scene with house, tree, birds, and butterfly. Verses 316, 478. *Mrs. Margaret T. Engle*

DEERING, ELLEN D. 1810. 7 yrs. 17" x 16". 6 alphabets. Eyelet, chain, queen, and cross-stitch. *Mrs. Ellen J. Richardson*

DENNETT, ELIZABETH. 1815. 11 yrs. 8" x 12". 3 alphabets. Cross-stitch. *Mrs. Thomas A. Lawton*

DENNIS, ELIZABETH. 1822. Salem [N. J. 9 yrs. Born in 1813.] Cross-stitch. Vine border. Geometrical design in center, containing 2 birds, name and date, trees, flowers, vases, 2 dogs, and verse. Verse 377. *Miss Elizabeth Dennis Holme*

DENNY, ADELINE. [Cir. 1800.] Leicester [Mass.]. 12 yrs. 17" x 17". 2 alphabets. Cross-stitch. Simple border. Scene with large brick house, one large tree, and two unfinished trees. Verse 511 (1, var.). *Mrs. William Hooper*

DENNY, CAROLINE. 1814. Leicester [Mass.]. 13 yrs. 17" x 12½". 1 alphabet. Satin and cross-stitch. Hemstitched edge with border of rose design. In center, a large brick house with road in front. Verse 41 (var.). *Mrs. John A. Sweetser*

[DE VENT, MARIA CATHERINE ELIZABETH.] 181[2]. New Haven. 7 yrs. 8" x 16". 2 alphabets. Hemstitched edge. Cross-stitch. *Howard M. Chapin, Esq.*

DEVEREUX, MARY. 1804. [Marblehead, Mass.] 10 yrs. 1 alphabet. Stem, satin, and cross-stitch. Verse 407. *The Emma B. Hodge Collection*

DIAMENT, ROSENA. 1801. Jones Island [near Cedarville, Cumberland County, N. J.]. 8 yrs. Born January 11, 1793. 14" x 17". 5 alphabets. Eyelet, stem, tent, queen, and cross-stitch. Carnation border. Strawberry and baskets of flowers at bottom. Verse 662. *Mrs. Rosena Foster Whitlock*

DICK, MARIA. [Cir. 1807.] Salem [N. J. About 11 yrs.]. 7½" x 11½". 2 alphabets. Eyelet and cross-stitch. Vine border. Initials: "S D [Dr. Samuel Dick, father]; S D [Sarah Dick, mother]; R D [Rebecca]; M D [Maria]; J D [Jane]; S D [Samuel]; A D [Anna]; I D [Isabel]; S D [Sally]; W D [William], [children of Samuel and Sarah Dick]." *Miss Maria H. Mecum*

DICKINSON, AME S.   August 28, 1805.   Amherst [Mass.].   9 yrs.   16" x 20".   3 alphabets.
Cross-stitch.   Greek fret border.   Trees, mill, basket, hearts.   *Harriet Carr Loomis*

DICKINSON, MARY.   [Cir. 1809.   Berks County, Pa.]   12 yrs.   Born in 1797.   17" x 21".   1 alphabet.   Queen, outline, stem, and various other stitches.   Elaborate conventional design in
border.   Urn with flowers, rosebuds, birds, stars, and sprays of flowers in design at bottom.
Verses 226, 488 (var.).   *Emily Haines*

DIMOND, ANN.   1808.   8 yrs.   12" x 16".   Flat and cross-stitch.   Red berries falling from top
border and fringe looped across with cord and 3 tassels; large perspective portal looking into a garden, and on either side smaller doors; pine trees and urns of tulips seen
through doors.   Scene with brick house, dog on either side, 2 urns, 2 pine trees.   Underneath, a large windmill, with large bird and squirrel on either side. "The eyes of the Lord
are in every place beholding the evil and the good."   *Mrs. Bradbury Bedell*

DIVERS, ANN.   1813.   13 yrs.   17" x 15½".   Verse 363 (2, var.).   *Mrs. H. E. Gillingham*

DOCKRAY, MARY.   1829.   17" x 14".   5 alphabets.   Stem, satin, and cross-stitch.   Verses 515,
796a.   *Mrs. M. F. Cocroft*

DODGE, ABIGAIL M.   1824.   North Beverly [Mass.].   12 yrs.   16" x 18".   5 alphabets.   French
knot, stem, and cross-stitch.   Rose border.   Design with large jars of roses and a weeping
willow tree.   Verse 471.   *Miss Alice M. Dodge*

DOLE, SARAH.   1819.   9 yrs.   16" x 15".   2 alphabets.   Eyelet, stem, satin, and cross-stitch.
Vine and flowers on either side.   At bottom, basket of flowers, with deer and cow on one
side and 2 birds on the other, also trees.   Verse 559.   Illustrated.   *Leonard Smith, Esq.*

DORRANCE, MARY.   1816.   Providence [R. I.].   10 yrs.   12" x 8".   2 alphabets.   Chain, eyelet,
cat, and cross-stitch. "Life and immortality are brought to light by the Gospel.   Remember
thy Creator in the days of thy youth."   *Mrs. M. L. D. Aldrich*

DORSEY, PRISCILLA MILCAH.   1822.   Ellicott City [Howard County, Md.].   9 yrs.   17" x 17".
Cross and hem-stitch.   Strawberry-vine border.   Peacocks, dogs, and crowns.
                                                        Mrs. Edward M. Hammond

DOSWELL, MARY ELIZABETH PORTHRESS.   1802.   [Va.]   11 yrs.   17" x 17½".   Stem, satin-stitch,
and French knots.   Strawberry and blackberry border, with fruit and blossoms and a kind
of tiger lily.   Bow-knot at top and bottom.   In the center, basket filled with different
flowers. "Taught by Mrs. Woodson."   *J. E. Perkenson, Esq.*

DOUGLAS, ANGELINA. "July the 1, 1823." Wilton [N. H.].   12 yrs.   18" x 16".   Cross, satin,
long and short, and stem-stitch.   3 alphabets.   An oval picture of Wilton, with the back of
the church on the right.   Verses 627 (1), 771.   *Estate of James L. Little, Esq.*

DOUINE, MARGARET.   1826.   Charleston [S. C.].   13 yrs.   18" x 16".   1 alphabet.   Eyelet, tent,
stem, satin, cross, and hem-stitch.   Strawberry border.   Basket of fruit flanked by baskets
of roses; stars at intervals and peacocks in corners.   Verse 783.   *Miss Margaret B. Mure*

DOVER, CATHORINE.   1801.   Philadelphia.   8½" x 17½".   2 alphabets.   Eyelet, herring-bone, tent,
and cross-stitch.   Cross-border.   *Mrs. William E. Black*

DOW, MARY.   1805.   [Cumberland County, N. C.]   13 yrs.   11" x 13¼".   5 alphabets, not all completed.   Eyelet, stem, satin, and cross-stitch.   Vine border with small flowers and a strawberry in each corner.   At bottom, vines crossing and forming two wreaths.   Verse 690.
                                                        Miss Nannie MacQueen

Down, M. 1828. 16" x 18". 6 alphabets. Eyelet, satin, stem, outline, and cross-stitch. Rose, carnation, and vine border.

"Family Record"

M   T.

John . Down . was . born . november . th . 2 . A.D. 1777
Amy . Down . was . born . sePtember . th . 1. A.D. 1782
Mariah . Down . was . born . June . th . 2. A.D. 1803
Mary . Down . was . born . November . th . 1. A.D. 1813
Charity . Down . was . born . July . th . 16 . A.D. 1816
John . W. Down . was . born . may . th . 1. A.D. 1824
Amy Down   deParted this life october . th . 4 A.D. 1828.

E   T"

Verse 187 (var.).

Mrs. William D. Frishmuth, at the Pennsylvania Museum, Memorial Hall, Fairmount Park, Philadelphia

Doyle, Margaret. 1806. 10 yrs. 17" x 20". 3 alphabets. Eyelet and cross-stitch. Strawberry border at top and bottom; wide border at sides of conventionalized corn-flowers and other flowers; inside border of fine green vine with little pink dots; below verse, band of strawberries mounted in four places by little birds. Diamond border incloses verse. Wreath of strawberries incloses name and age, and flanked on each side by conventional pots of flowers. Verse 694.   *Mrs. Bradbury Bedell*

Draper, Harriet. 1829. Providence. 17" x 12". 3 alphabets. Chain and cross-stitch. Verses 113, 150.   *Miss Harriet Sheldon*

Draper, Sophia. 1806. Brookville [Mass.]. 7 yrs. 17½" x 17". 2 alphabets. Stem, satin, tent, and cross-stitch. Small conventional border. Scene with house on a hill, 4 trees to the left, and barn and door-yard to the right. Inset of 2 pitchers of flowers and 5 birds. Verse 601 (1, 2, 3, var.).   *Miss S. Ross*

Draper, Family Register. [Cir. 1808.] 17" x 20½". Chain, stem, satin, tent, and cross-stitch. Grape vine on either side. Tree in lower right-hand corner and tombstone in lower left, bearing inscription: "Mary Draper died Dec. 9, 1800. Dear Babe at Rest we Hope Thee Blest." Verses 53, 83, 287.

"Family Register

Nathan Draper   Born Sept. 18, 1761.
Hannah Whiting   Born April 10, 1768.
    They were married December 28, 1788.
    And have had the following children viz.
Elizabeth Draper   Born April 16, 1790.
Hannah Draper   Born August 23, 1792.
William W. Draper   Born August 18, 1794.
Charlotte Draper   Born Sept. 6, 1796.
Julia E. Draper   Born November 13, 1798.
Mary Draper   Born November 25, 1800.
George W. Draper   Born Nov. 30, 1801.
Emily Draper   Born December 6, 1803.
Caleb E. Draper   Born June 9, 1806.
Catherine Draper   Born May 1, 1808."   *W. K. Draper, Esq.*

Drew, Sarah Snelling. 1823. 9 yrs. 17" x 7". 3 alphabets. Cross-stitch. "Be virtuous and be happy."   *Mrs. Sydney R. Burleigh*

PLATE LI

Lucy D. Stickney's Sampler.   Charlestown, Mass.   1830
View of Charlestown
Owned by Mrs. Henry E. Coe

PLATE LII

Elizabeth Funk's Sampler. 1813
Owned by Mrs. Henry E. Coe

DRUMMOND, MARIA. 1809. Warrenton. 7 yrs. 11" x 13". 2 alphabets. Cross-stitch. Border of conventionalized flowers and cross-stitch scallop. Scene with large house, 3 smaller houses, bird-house, birds, trees, and various other designs. Verse 714.

Dr. William A. Hardaway

DUKES, SARA ELIZABETH. 1815. 9 yrs. 13" x 15⅞". Conventional rose border. Leopard resting between two trees, also two dishes of fruit.

"Love your parents, they claim your love, they love you with great affection. Who is so kind to you as your parents . who supplies all your wants . who provides for your education . who delights to make you happy . who but your Parents Therefore return love for love."

"Endeavour to employ yourself in something useful . Take great pains to learn . Too great a thirst for play is unfavourable to learning."

Verse 515 (var.). *Mrs. George C. Fraser*

DUNBAR, MARY S. 1811. Taunton, Mass. 8 yrs. 8½" x 10". 3 alphabets. Cross-stitch. Cross-border. *Miss M. W. Baylies*

DUNHAM, JANE. 1812. 7" x 10". 2 alphabets. Cross-stitch. In center, wreath of leaves with name and date; birds on one side; flowers at each side of top and a tree on either side at bottom. *Mrs. James Moses*

DUNHAM, LYDIA. 1805. 4¼" x 7¼". 1 alphabet. Cross-stitch. Simple border.

Miss Lucy C. Sweet

DUNHAM, SEMANTHA. 1806. Mansfield [Conn.]. 7 yrs. Born November 25, 1799. 12" x 12". 4 alphabets. Cross-stitch. Hemstitched border. Verse 697. *Miss Julia McAlmont Warner*

DUNHAM, SOPHIA. 1811. [Hartford]. 10½" x 10½". 4 alphabets. Satin and cross-stitch. Pillars and arch design with baskets of flowers. *Wilbur M. Stone, Esq.*

DUPEE, SUSANNAH WALLIS. 1813. Boston. 10 yrs. 12¼" x 12¼". 3 alphabets. Eyelet, tent, and cross-stitch. Simple cross-stitch border. 2 small vases of flowers.

Miss Gertrude Whiting

DURAND, LOUISA. 1827. 18" x 18". Cross-stitch. Border of roses, buds, and leaves. Basket of flowers. *Mrs. Bradbury Bedell*

DURFEE, ABBY W. 1810. New Bedford [Mass.]. 12 yrs. 17" x 12½". 3 alphabets. Satin, stem, and cross-stitch. Carnation border, top and bottom. "Thou shalt love the Lord thy God with all thy heart, and with all thy soul, and with all thy mind, and with all thy strength; thou shalt love thy neighbor as thyself." "Remember now thy Creator", etc.

Miss Abbie W. Covel

DUSTIN, ABIGAIL. 1800. 12 yrs. 9" x 7½". Alphabet. Cross-stitch. [Unfinished.]

Miss McCairnes

DUTTON, ABIGAIL. 1825. Jaffrey, N. H. 16⅞" x 18". Alphabets. Cross-stitch. Trees and basket of flowers. Wide floral design at bottom. Verse.

Sold at American Art Galleries, New York, April 11, 1918

DWIER, MARY H. 1828. Kensington [Philadelphia, Pa.]. 7 yrs. 11½" x 12½". Cross-stitch. Border of vine and strawberries. Scene with brick house, grass plot on either side, and in front, trees and fence. *Mrs. John S. Swoyd*

DYER, ANSTIS. 1812. Providence [R. I.]. 15" x 11". Flat, eyelet, and cross-stitch. Flat-stitch border. "The Ten Commandments." *Mrs. Anstis Pearce Dyer Manton*

DYER, SUSANNA. 1802. 8 yrs. 17″ x 19″. Alphabet. Stem, chain, and cross-stitch. Simple cross-stitch border. Two buildings, one with fence around it, also trees and shrubs.

Mrs. Thomas Baker

EAGER, REBEKAH. 1807. 10 yrs. 13″ x 12″. 3 alphabets. Cross-stitch. Verse 128 (1, var.).

Mrs. R. M. Chickering

EAGLES, BARBARY. 1808. Bristol School [Pa.]. 14″ x 18″. 4 alphabets. Detached sprays of flowers and baskets of flowers around edge. Vine with very few leaves, inclosing alphabets, etc. Initials scattered about: "J E, C E, B E, M E, S E, M E, F G, A E." Illustrated.

Mrs. Arthur M. Waitt

EARLE, FANNY HOLROYD. 1817. Providence [R. I.]. 11 yrs. 13″ x 17½″. 3 alphabets. Cross-stitch. Cross design in border. Family Register:
"Fanny Holroyd Earle Born Tuesday July 8th 1806
William Earle Born Saturday April 16th 1808
George Earle Born Sunday October 1st 1809
Sarah Waterman Earle Born Friday August 31st 1812
Marcy Arnold Earle Born Monday April 12th 1813
Sarah Arnold Earle Born Friday November 11th 1814
Oliver Earle Born Saturday August 17th 1816

Sarah W. Earle Died Sunday May 9th 1813 Ag'd 1 yr 9 m
Sarah A. Earle Died Saturday August 19th 1815 Ag'd 9 m 8 d
Oliver Earle Died Thursday June 26th 1817 Aged 10 m 9 d"

Rhode Island School of Design

EARLE, HARRIOT ADELINE. 1830. Providence [R. I.]. 10 yrs. 17″ x 17″. 5 alphabets. Cross-stitch. Cross design in border. "The Family Register:
Births
"Fanny H. Earle Born Tuesday July 8th 1806
William Earle Born Saturday April 16th 1808
George Earle Born Sunday October 1st 1809
Sarah W. Earle Born Friday August 31st 1812
Marcy A Earle Born Monday April 12th 1813
Sarah A Earle Born Friday November 11th 1814
Oliver Earle Born Saturday August 17th 1816
Sally A Earle Born Friday April 3d 1818
Harriot A Earle Born Thursday Sept 18th 1820
Julia Earle Born Sunday July 22nd 1822"
Deaths
"Sarah Waterman Earle Departed this life Sunday May 9th 1813 aged 1 year 9 months
Sarah Arnold Earle Departed this life Saturday August 19th 1813 aged 9 m 8 d
Oliver Earle Departed this life Thursday June 26th 1817 aged 10 m 9 d
Our dear Father Oliver Earle Departed this life July 5th in the year 1824 in the 55th year of his age.
Providence March 23d A.D. 1830." *Rhode Island School of Design*

EARLE, MARCY A[RNOLD]. 1823. 8½″ x 12¼″. 3 alphabets. Cross design in border. Cross-stitch. For Genealogy, see samplers made by Fanny and Julia Earle.

Rhode Island School of Design

EARLE, SALLY ARNOLD. 1828. 10 yrs. 13½″ x 17¼″. 3 alphabets. Cross-stitch. Cross design in border. *Rhode Island School of Design*

EATON, ——. [Cir. 1805.] 16⅛" x 12⅝". 3 alphabets. Eyelet, cross, long, and short-stitch. Long and short-stitch border. Names and dates:

"Job Eaton Born May 26 1762
Phoebe Eaton Born December 20, 1765
Sarah Eaton Born November 22, 1786
Job Eaton Born January 21, 1789
Moses Eaton Born March 18, 1791
Hannah Eaton Born March 15, 1793
Jonathan M. Eaton Born June 10, 1794
Hannah Eaton Born January 27, 1797
Ezra B. Eaton Born August 24, 1799
Worcester Eaton Born December 17, 1801." *Mrs. George C. Fraser*

EATON, HANNAH. 1813. 10 yrs. 10" x 12". 2 alphabets. Cross-stitch. Saw-tooth design in border. Elaborate baskets of flowers and trees. Verse 373 (var.).
Mrs. Elisabeth B. Hutchins

EAYRE, MARIA. 1814. Eayrestown [N. J.]. 8 yrs. Born May 14, 1806. 8" x 11". 2 alphabets. Cross-stitch. Simple line border. Baskets of flowers and birds. Verse 343 (1, 2).
Laura Clarissa Howell

EDDEY, BETSEY. [Cir. 1815.] 13 yrs. 16¼" x 8". 3 alphabets. Cross-stitch. "Time flies Eternity hastens." *Miss Emily B. Aldrich*

EDDY, MARY. 1816. Providence [R. I.]. 9" x 12½". 3 alphabets. Cross-stitch. Line border. Verse 721. *Miss Elizabeth L. Betton*

EDDY, MARY ANN. 1813. Baltimore [Md.]. 7 yrs. 19½" x 18". 6 alphabets. Cross-stitch. Vine border. Verse 515 (var.). *Mrs. Marvin F. McNeil*

EDES, CAROLINE. 1814. Charlestown [Mass.]. Born October 16, 1805. 12½" x 17". 3 alphabets. Cross-stitch. Border of conventionalized vine and flowers. Verse 692.
Mrs. Caroline H. Nicholson

EDES, ELIZA B. 1815. [Boston?] 7 yrs. 9" x 13½". 4 alphabets. Cat and cross-stitch. Hem-stitched edge. *Mrs. E. G. Cutler*

EDINGTON, MARY ANN. 1812. 11 yrs. 14" x 18". Stem, satin, and cross-stitch. Border of vine with flowers. Scene with house, fence, tree, and to the right, large plant in pot with small animal underneath. Across sampler at top, tree and potted plant, and on ground, chickens and 2 small dogs. Verse 297. *Robert P. Jordan, Dealer*

EDMANDS, MARTHA CAPEN. 1820. Charlestown [Mass.]. 10 yrs. 12" x 17½". 2 alphabets. Satin and cross-stitch. Greek fret border. Basket of fruit, trees, and birds. Verse 35.
Charles S. Henry, 2nd, Esq.

EDWARDS, SARAH ANN J[ACKSON]. 1820. Newburyport [Mass.]. 7 yrs. 8½" x 8½". 3 alphabets. Satin and cross-stitch. Cross-stitch border in triangular design.
Abbie Scott Edwards

EFFINGHAM, SALLY HOBBS. 1824. 19 yrs. 12" x 12". 6 alphabets. Chain and cross-stitch.
Mrs. Herbert E. Maine

ELDER, CATHERINE JONES. 1826. [Harrisburg, Pa.] (7 yrs.) 14½" x 14½". 1 alphabet. Cross-stitch. Strawberry border. House, 2 trees, basket, and dog. ["Litiz School," near Bethlehem, Pa.] *Mrs. Huger Elliott*

ELDER, CATHERINE JONES. 1827. (8 yrs.) 22" x 20". Cross-stitch. Wreath of roses, carnations, and other flowers. ["Litiz School."] *Mrs. Huger Elliott*

ELLET, HANNAH. 1806. Salem [N. J.]. West Town Boarding School. 12½" x 14". 8 alphabets. Cross, stem, and two-sided line-stitch. Vine with leaves in circular shape.

Miss Elizabeth Alford Smith

ELLET, MARIA CHAMBLESS. 1805. Salem [N. J.]. 9 yrs. 17" x 11". 7 alphabets. Single and double cross-stitch. Vine border. Verses 272, 409, 692 (var.).

Miss Elizabeth Alford Smith

ELLET, MARIA CHAMLESS. 1809. Salem [N. J. Born in 1795.]. 26" x 22". 2 alphabets. Satin and stem-stitch. Wreath of carnations, buds, other flowers, and leaves. Horn filled with flowers in center of wreath. *Mrs. Ella Maria Hamilton*

ELLIS, ABIGAIL. 1805. [Born on Biddle's Island in the Delaware River.] 8½" x 11½". 3 alphabets. Flat, eyelet, and cross-stitch. Top border of carnations and bottom of vine. Flower design at bottom. *Abbie Ellis Folwell*

ELLIS, CAROLINE. 1818. Brookfield [Mass.]. 13 yrs. 17" x 17". Cross-stitch and hemstitch. Strawberry and vine border. Crown design. *Mrs. William M. Goorkies or Goodwin?*

ELWELL, ANN MARIA. [Cir. 1826. New Jersey.] Born November 10, 1813. 18" x 16½". 2 alphabets. Flat, outline, queen, eyelet, stem, satin, and cross-stitch. Carnation, strawberry, and vine border. 4 birds in border. In center, urn of flowers and bands of geometrical designs; at bottom, sprays of flowers, birds, and figures. Verses 327, 327a. Initials: "J B [John Brooks, grandfather]; M B [Mary Brooks, grandmother]; D B [Daniel, brother of mother]; R B [Rachel, mother]; J E [John Elwell, father]; R E [Rachel Brooks Elwell, mother]; D B E [Daniel B. Elwell, brother]; G W E [George W Elwell, brother]; J M E [John M. Elwell, brother]; A M E [Ann Maria Elwell, maker]; J B E [James B. Elwell, brother, died aet. 10]; D S [Daniel Simkins, second husband of mother]; R. S [Rachel Simkins, mother's name after second marriage]; S M S [Smith M. Simkins, halfbrother]; D B E [brother, same as above]; M J E [Mary Jane Dane Elwell, wife of D. B. E.]; M A E [Mary Ann Elwell, daughter of D. B. E. and M. J. E.]; G. W. E [George W. Elwell, as above]; L F E [Lovisa Fithian Elwell, wife of G. W. E.]."

Charles S. Sheppard, Esq.

EMERSON, CLARISSA. Lancaster [Mass.]. 14 yrs. 16" x 22". Cross, flat, satin, long and short, stem-stitch, and couching. 2 alphabets. House, hillocks, mother and child. Verse 515 (var.).

Dwight M. Prouty, Esq.

EMERSON, RUTH. 1815. Machias [Me.]. 17½" x 22". 4 alphabets. Stem and cross-stitch. Conventional wreath of strawberries at bottom. Verse 606 (1, var.).

Mrs. Frederick E. Hovey

EMERSON, SOPHIA. 1815. 14 yrs. 18" x 26½". 2 alphabets. Chain, stem, satin, cross, split, and back-stitch. Elaborate floral border. Wreath around name, etc. Two trees with woman sitting underneath and holding bunch of flowers in her hand; birds resting on flowers; more flowers growing in grass. Verse 86. *Mrs. Henry E. Coe*

EMERY, MARY. 1809. [Born February 14, 1800, in New York State.] 17" x 16". 3 alphabets. Cross-stitch and paint russe. Triangular border with star design. Ornamental cross-stitch border lines. Design at bottom unfinished. Verse 712. *Mrs. I. E. Ingle*

EMMERTON, REMEMBER. 1817. Lynn [Mass.]. 8½" x 12". 4 alphabets. Cross-stitch. Greek fret border. *Mrs. Charles E. Reed*

EVANS, FRANCIS M. 1827. 9 yrs. 5½" x 4¼". 2 alphabets. Fine cross-stitch. Narrow hemstitched border. *Rev. Glen Tilley Morse*

EVANS, TULLANIA. 1809. Pinegrove School. 9 yrs. Born October 6, 1799. "Daughter of Jakob and Rachel Evans." 15½" x 17½". 2 alphabéts. Cross, satin, eyelet, and tent-stitch. Carnation and acorn borders. Trees, flowers, baskets of fruit, birds, dogs, etc. Verse 255.

Mrs. Siegfried Wachsman

EVERETT, HANNAH. 1800. Wareham [Mass.]. 12" x 13". 3 alphabets. Satin, stem, and cross-stitch. Plain, double strawberry border. "Beauty as the flowers blossom, soon fades but the divine excellence of the mind like the medicinal virtues of the plant remain in it when all those charms are withered." *Mrs. Thomas A. Lawton*

EVERS, TIRZA. 1827. 14 yrs. 20" x 17". 5 alphabets. Cross-stitch. Verses 569, 788.

Mr. Arthur W. Seavey

EYRE, ANN ELIZA. 1827. 8 yrs. 22" x 16½". Feather, stem, satin, tent, and cross-stitch. Rose border on three sides. Vine around verse in upper section. At bottom, scene with brick house, trees, lawn, ducks, cat, horses, birds on trees, men and women. Large sprays of flowers in pots at either side; detached sprays of flowers fill in remainder of space. Verse 515 (var.). "Daughter of James and Margaret Eyre." *Mrs. Henry E. Coe*

F———, A———. 1804. 18" x 13". Cross-stitch. Border of large green leaves. Scene with house, trees, yard, duck, and hens, street with cow, and 2 horses.

Sold at Libbie's Auction Rooms, Boston, December, 1915

F[REAS], C———. (A fragment, 6" x 6".) Outline, chain, stem, and satin-stitch. Peacock surrounded with flowers, wild roses, strawberries, and conventionalized flowers. [Secured from Freas family near Alloway, Salem County, N. J.] *Mrs. William Johnson*

F———, S. & M[ARIA]. "Begun by S. F——— and made by Maria." 1806. 12" x 14". 3 alphabets. Cross-stitch. Strawberry border. Verse 413. *Robert P. Jordan, Dealer*

FABENS, SARAH. 1806. Salem [Mass.]. 13 yrs. [Born in Salem, October 9, 1793.] 16" x 23". Satin, stem, and cross-stitch. 4 alphabets. Border of flowers starting from cornucopias in lower corners and broken at top by boat-shaped pot of erect strawberries, with bird at each end, and at bottom by spray of carnations; 2 white animals and 4 strawberry clusters also appear in bottom border. Below verse is conventional floral design. Verse 129 (var.). *Mrs. Elizabeth B. Putnam*

FABENS, SARAH. 1807. Salem [Mass.]. 14 yrs. 9½" x 11½". [Born October 9, 1793.] Stem, satin, and cross-stitch. Floral border, starting from cornucopias in lower corners. Carnations in upper corners. Large spray of carnations in center and cluster of flowers at each side. Oblong wreath of leaves incloses name and date. Verse inclosed between pillars supporting double arch; carnation sprays in each arch. Verse 40 (var.).

Mrs. Elizabeth B. Putnam

FARLEY, LUCY MARY. 1807. Ipswich [Mass.]. 10 yrs. 10" x 10". 3 alphabets. Stem and cross-stitch. Strawberry-vine border on three sides. Strawberry plants and blossoms with grass at bottom. *Mrs. Henry Wardwell*

FARRA, SUSSANNAH. 1809. 22" x 23". Cross-stitch. Conventional border on three sides. At bottom, maple tree in pot and smaller potted maple trees on either side, also baskets of flowers. Vine with carnations and strawberries surrounds name. Family names: "[grandparents] Christianna Ann Dunnet, Samuel an Hannah Dunnet; [parents] John and Sussannah Farra [worked in hair]; [brothers and sisters] Daniel, Ann, Sussannah, John, Chalter, Carter, Benjamin, Christian, Hannah, Farra Dunnet." Verses 187 (var.), 226 (var.). "Hannah Hollingswort." *Mrs. Edward Twaddell*

FAY, MARIA. 1811. 9 yrs. 16½" x 16½". 3 alphabets. Eyelet, cat, satin, cross-stitch, and a long cross-stitch that runs over 2 squares. Greek fret border. Vase with 2 flowers;

2 vases with strawberry plants; 3 birds and a crowned lion, in design at bottom. Verse 92 (1, var.). *A. Stainforth, Dealer, 1917*

FEASTER, RACHEL. 1823. 17″ x 17″. Rose border. Scattered flowers, with birds, at bottom. "The Wish I sigh not for beauty nor languish for wealth", etc. *Mrs. H. E. Gillingham*

FENNO, MARY ANN. 1801. Salem, Mass. 11 yrs. 8″ x 11″. 2 alphabets. Cross-stitch. "Then let my heart at once attend Thy all sufficient"— *Frank R. Dow, Esq.*

FENWICK, TERESIA. 1802. "St. Mary's County in Maryland." 15″ x 18½″. 4 alphabets. Cross-borders. Urn with strawberries; eight-pointed star in each corner; 2 flowers below; Calvary cross above. "I glory in the Cross of Jesus Christ." "When this you see, Pray for me." "Virtue is the sweetest jewel that can adorn the fair." "Eleanor Morland" [governess]. Verse 128 (var.). *Miss Madge Fenwick*

FIELD FAMILY REGISTER. [Cir. 1816.] Northfield [Mass.]. 11″ x 13″. Eyelet and cross-stitch. Conventional border. "Family Register"

> "Mr. Walter Field Born November 24th 1758
> Miss Piana Petty Born June 26th 1762
> Married May 12th 1782
> Nancy Field Born July 14th 1783
> Paul Field Born Jan. 22nd 1785   Died Sept 28th 1810
> Roxana Field Born July 2nd 1787
> Mrs. R. Janes Died Nov. 5th 1810
> Philana Field Born Sept 17th 1789 Died June 22nd 1813
> Erastus Field Born Dec. 24th 1791
> Sarah Field Born Dec. 4th 1793   Died Oct. 23rd 1794
> Sarah Field Born Sept. 11th 1795
> Gratia Field Born March 3rd 1798
> Piana Field Born April 20th 1800   Died Aug. 15th 1803
> Eloiza Field Born Sept. 19th 1802
> ————, Born Aug. 19th 1803
> Walter Field Jun'r Born June 30th 1804 Died July 1st 1804
> Walter Field Junr. Born Oct. 22nd 1805
> Eloiza P. Field Born June 4th 1808
> Lucretia F. Janes Born Dec. 17th 1808
> Roxana Janes Born Sept 28th 1810 Died March 20th 1811"
> *Mrs. Frank A. Hubbard*

FIELD, ZILPHA. 1812. Bridgewater [Mass.]. 9 yrs. 7½″ x 6½″. 2 alphabets. Cross-stitch. *Julia M. Howard*

FILLMORE, HARRIOT. 1814. Franklin, New London County, Conn. 14½″ x 8½″. 3 alphabets. Bird's-eye and cross-stitch. *Mrs. Thomas A. Lawton*

FISHER, ELIZA. 1824. 24″ x 24″. Eyelet and cross-stitch. Elaborate carnation and strawberry border. In one top corner, white dove, 2 stars, bunch of carnations in vase, 2 large butterflies, conventional bunch of flowers. Directly under this, 2 birds picking a strawberry; baskets of strawberries on each side; on either side of baskets, one large red rose with buds; below, bunches of bluebells; on either side, pot of carnations; under these, bunches of strawberries; under berries, elaborate baskets of strawberries, and on either side the name a half-wreath; on either side of wreath a little pine tree in triangle of lawn on which stands a little dog. Large Colonial house with fence, gate, 2 weeping willows, and lawn. Bunches of grapes and strawberries are also in design around house. Verses 132, 778. Initials: "J S, M S, W S, V S, J S, J D, E D, S S, J S, R S, J S, G S, S A F, S F, E W F, M D, J F, H F, S D, E F, M F, E D, W S F, M F, J D, J C F, J A F, J D, R F." *Mrs. Bradbury Bedell*

FISHER, MARIA ANN. 1811. Franklin [Mass.]. 9 yrs. 8" x 13". 3 alphabets. Cross-stitch. Vine border. *Miss Annie Sanford Head*

FISHER, S. 1804. 18" x 17". 1 alphabet. Queen, satin, and cross-stitch. Double strawberry border. Basket of flowers just above border. Verse 682. *Miss H. L. Parrish*

FISK, ELIZABETH T. 1830. 8" x 16". 4 alphabets. Cat and cross-stitch. Verses 28, 609, 700. *Miss Kate Simmons*

FISK, MARY. November 2, 180[5?]. [Cambridge, Mass.] 8" x 12". Alphabet. Cross-stitch. Greek fret border. [Probably the work of the grandmother of John Fiske the historian.] Verse 689. *Albert C. Bates, Esq.*

FISK, SUSANNA. Cambridgeport [Mass.]. 8 yrs. 12½" x 14". 3 alphabets. Cross-stitch. Vine border. Verse 578. *Mrs. Bradbury Bedell*

FITCH, CAROLINE M. 1816. Boston. 8 yrs. 7" x 9". 3 alphabets. Cross-stitch. Greek fret border. *Charles W. Jenks, Esq.*

FITZGERALD, SARAH. 1810. Portsmouth [N. H.]. 17" x 17". 2 alphabets. Stem and cross-stitch. Vine, with clover-leaf border. Conventional cross-borders. "Sacred to the Memory of Mrs. A. Fitzgerald. In memory of an affectionate mother, who died March 1st 1808, aged 40 years." This inscription is overshadowed by weeping willow, and on either side are small trees, dog, bird, large basket of tall flowers, all on a straight green base. "Wrought by her daughter Sarah Fitzgerald under the inspection of Mary E. Hill." On either side of verses, basket of fruit, with bird perched on spray above. Verse 289. *Harriette E. Jones*

FLAGG, GEORGIANNA. 1811. Charleston [S. C.]. 8 yrs. 15" x 15". Alphabets. Eyelet, satin, and cross-stitch. Rose-vine border. At bottom, Greek fret border, with a carnation at each end. Verse 547. *Mrs. St. John P. Kimloch*

FLAGG, SALLY. 1802. 10 yrs. 11" x 16". 2 alphabets. Satin and cross-stitch. Wide design at bottom. Verse 60. *Lancaster Public Library*

FLETCHER, SARAH JANE. 1829. Albany [N. Y.]. 10 yrs. 17" x 17½". 5 alphabets. Cross-stitch. Strawberry-vine border. Great variety of cross-lines. Verse 475. *Mary McDonald Vosburgh*

FLITCRAFT, ANN. 1831. 32" x 20". Vine and rosebud border. In each corner conventional floral design, with birds, dog, urns, basket of fruit, etc. Brick house just below center, with willow trees on either side; also 2 little dogs, 2 chickens in the grass, and scattered through the sampler are rosebuds and butterflies. Three-sided border of leaves around verse, and above verse is a vine with a bird at each end. Verse 392. *Mrs. Bradbury Bedell*

FLITCRAFT, MARY. 1800. Eldridge's Hill [N. J.]. 21" x 21". Satin and cross-stitch. Vine, coral, and honeysuckle border. Large bunch of flowers, with smaller spray at corners; tulips at top and roses at bottom. Verse 132 (1, var.). *Mrs. William T. Flitcraft*

FLOYD, ELIZABETH. 18" x 15½". Cross-stitch. Rose and tulip border. Vases of flowers, squirrel, duck, butterfly, 2 small dogs, house, and other detached designs. Verse 579. *Mrs. Thomas S. Young*

FOLLEN, MARY. 1812. Needham [Mass.]. 12 yrs. 12" x 16½". 3 alphabets. Eyelet, satin, and cross-stitch. Vine border. House and flowers, at bottom; 2 large birds and conventionalized plant, at top. Verse 410. *Mrs. James Y. Noyes*

FORD, CLARISSA. 1801. 10 yrs. 12½" x 8". 2 alphabets. Cross-stitch. *Mrs. George Plimpton*

FORD, ELIZABETH M. "Miss Damon's School, Boston." 13 yrs. 4 alphabets. Stem, satin, and cross-stitch. Odd flowers on vine in border. Flower-pots, trees, and stars. Verse 577.

The Emma B. Hodge Collection

FORD, SARAH. 1810. Philadelphia, Pa. 13″ x 12″. Cross-stitch. Greek fret border. Verse 647.

Mary Hall Pennock

FOSTER, ———. 1808. 14″ x 13½″. Satin and split-stitch. Figures of weeping man and woman dressed in mourning, leaning over two urns; weeping willow tree in background. "To the memory of Samuel Foster. He was born July 9th A.D. 1789 and died Nov. 24th A.D. 1803"; also, "To the memory of Mary Foster. She was born May 8th A.D. 1799 and died Aug. 30th A.D. 1803." *Wilbur M. Stone, Esq.*

FOSTER, SABRA. 1811. 5″ x 8″. 2 alphabets. Cat and cross-stitch. *Sabra Batchelder Harwood*

FOWLER, MARY ANN. 1817. 11 yrs. 12″ x 11″. 3 alphabets. Cross-stitch. Strawberry design. Verse 515 (var.). *Mrs. Louise Cranston*

FOWLER, MEHITABLE. 1809. Pembroke [N. H.]. 10 yrs. 12″ x 16″. 4 alphabets. Back-stitch, satin, and cross-stitch. Saw-tooth border. Basket, trees, and birds.

Miss Clara Fowler

FOX, MARION. 1802. 10 yrs. 11″ x 15″. 2 alphabets. Cross-stitch. Strawberry border. Green bush in center, with small dog on each side, at bottom; in center, 2 bay trees on either side of name, with bird at top; underneath, 2 baskets of flowers. Verse 343 (1, var.).

Mrs. William Holland Wilmer

FOX, MARY. 1826. Hartford [Conn.]. 9 yrs. 18″ x 16″. 3 alphabets. Cross-stitch. Greek fret border. Strawberry design at bottom. Verse 356. Names and dates:
   "Gurdon Fox, born Jan'y 30th 1791; Sophia Kendall, born Feb'y 4th 1796; Married Oct'r 27st 1814; Edward Fox, born May 2, 1828; Mary Fox born Sept'r 21st 1816; Henry Fox, born March 8th 1826." *Albert C. Bates, Esq.*

FOX, NANCY. 1824. "Woodstoc." 12 yrs. 17″ x 15″. 3 alphabets. Satin and cross-stitch. Lozenge border. Elaborate conventional design of branches, topped by diamond-shaped figures; underneath, row of sheep, dogs, and basket with rose branches. On topmost branch is large pigeon and bird's nest; on another branch, a small bird; in center of basket, a bird's nest with egg; above basket, row of 5 conventional figures. Verse 465.

Mrs. Bradbury Bedell

FOX, SOPHIA M. 1827. "Waterford, Washington, Ohio." 9 yrs. 10¾″ x 12½″. 4 alphabets. Herringbone, queen, French knot, chain, and cross-stitch. Vine, strawberry, and rose border. Fir tree, with jardinière on either side, holding rose vines. *Mary Allen Taylor*

FRANKLIN, AMELIA. 1818. [Berlin, Worcester County, Md. Born in 1802.] 18″ x 17″. Split, satin, and cross-stitch. Vine and strawberry border. Scene with house, grass, ducks, geese, men feeding them, and flowering shrubs; on either side of house are tall, pointed trees topped by birds. Verse 733 (2, var.). *Mrs. J. W. McIlvain*

FRANKLIN, AMELIA. 1818. [Maryland.] 13 yrs. 18″ x 19½″. Split, satin, and cross-stitch. Vine border with leaves. Landscape with house, tall trees, gate, fence; dark strip of silk inserted, with man and two women feeding ducks, cow, and pig. Flowers around house and birds flying above it, also butterflies. Verse 733 (2, var.).

Miss Louisa Amelia Covington

FRANKLIN, MILOCH E. 1818. 18″ x 18″. Stem, satin, and cross-stitch. Strawberry border. Scene with house, trees, man, children, cows, geese, and dogs. Verse 733 (1, var.).

Mrs. Renwick C. Hurry

FRAZER, REBEKAH. 1816. Duxbury [Mass.]. 8 yrs. [Born September 23, 1808.] 10″ x 9″. 3 alphabets. Cross-stitch. Narrow hemstitched border. At bottom, small rectangle of solid cross-stitch and initials "F F". *Mrs. A. McK. Gifford*

FREDERICK, DEBORAH. 1830. 17″ x 17″. 2 alphabets. Satin, queen, and cross-stitch. Conventionalized strawberry border. Scene with house with railing in front, large rose bush on one side and 2 queer colored birds on the other side. *Mrs. Renwick C. Hurry*

FREEBORN, HANNAH. 1817. 11 yrs. 12¼″ x 17½″. 4 alphabets. Chain, eyelet, stem, and cross-stitch. Double trefoil border. "H. L. F. Born 1st mo. 9th 1806", inclosed in wreath with strawberry below, and on either side two triangular conventional designs. Verse 453. *Rhode Island School of Design*

FREEBORNE, MARY G. 1826. 10 yrs. 15″ x 13″. Chain and cross-stitch. Rose border. Verse 784. *Herbert O. Brigham, Esq.*

FRENCH, HANNAH. 1805. 13 yrs. [Born in West Dedham, Mass., in 1792.] 12¼″ x 12″. 3 alphabets. Satin and cross-stitch. Strawberry border. Verse 609 (var.). *Miss Mary E. Fisher*

FRENCH, HANNAH. 1822. [Mullica Hill, N. J.] 9 yrs. 8″ x 19″. 4 alphabets. Flat, eyelet, tent, and cross-stitch. Simple cross-stitch border. One dog. *Mrs. John Gill Whitall*

FRINK, ISABEL. [Before 1830.] Rutland [Mass.]. 10½″ x 10½″. 2 alphabets. Stem-stitch. Vine border. Verse 660 (1). *Miss Isabella H. Dana*

FROST, HARRIET. [1820.] 6½″ x 9½″. 2 alphabets. Cross-stitch. *Mrs. Herbert E. Maine*

FROTHINGHAM, BETSY. 1801. Newburyport [Mass.]. Born July 28, 1790. 11 yrs. 10″ x 15½″. 2 alphabets. Cross-stitch. Strawberry border. Verse 667. *Miss Georgie Bassett*

FROTHINGHAM, DEBBY. 1803. 15½″ x 20½″. 3 alphabets. Chain, cross, long and short-stitch. Vine, roses, carnations, and other flowers in border. Wreath around inscription. *The Emma B. Hodge Collection*

FUDGE, SALLY. [Cir. 1801. Born in 1790.] 11″ x 11″. 2 alphabets. Eyelet, satin, and cross-stitch. Hemstitched border with rosebud design at top and bottom. *Edmund M. Dow, Esq.*

FULLER, CORNELIA. 1809. New York City. 7 yrs. 12″ x 18″. 3 alphabets. Satin, chain, French knot, and cross-stitch. Strawberry, flower, and vine border. Village scene, with church, several houses, trees, stream, and boats. Verse 94. *Mrs. C. H. Nelson*

FULLER, ESTHER G. August, 1823. Charlestown [Mass.]. 11 yrs. 18″ x 17½″. 3 alphabets. Cross, satin, and buttonhole-stitch. Cross-borders. House, vine with blue flowers, and 3 small trees. 4 sprigs of pink flowers below. Verse 515 (var.). *William B. Thayer Memorial Collection, University of Kansas*

FULLER, SUSANNAH. [Cir. 1817.] 14 yrs. [Born in Francestown, N. H., June 4, 1804.] 23″ x 20″. 3 alphabets. Satin stitch. Border of roses, pansies, strawberries, and carnations. Basket of flowers and vine at bottom. *Lillie Fisher Brokaw*

FUNK, ELIZABETH. 1813. 17″ x 21½″. Satin and cross-stitch. Border of flowers and leaves at top and bottom. Large flowering plant in pot takes up most of space, the remainder filled in with flower sprays and animals. Quilled ribbon border and rosettes on corners of the sampler. *Mrs. Henry E. Coe*

FURLONG, MARY. 1806. 10 yrs. 20″ x 16″. 2 alphabets. Cross and satin-stitch. Verse 19. *Owner not recorded*

G——, C——. 1802. Boston. 4½" x 3¾". Partial alphabet. Cross-stitch.
Miss Marette Longley

G——, H. M. 1800. 8½" x 12". 2 alphabets. Long and short, and tent-stitch. Done in memory of the birth of Lovey Bickford. *Mrs. George C. Fraser*

GAILLIARD, EMMA ANNA. 1823. Charleston [S. C.]. 9 yrs. 11" x 18". 3 alphabets. Flat, cat, eyelet, cross-stitch, and hemstitch. Hemstitched edge with scroll border. Various cross-borders. Verse 773. *Mrs. J. Waring Witsell*

GALBRAITH, JANE ELIZABETH. [Cir. 1830.] Birmingham [Pa.]. Born June 17, 1818. 18" x 20½". 3 alphabets. Stem, eyelet, satin, and cross-stitch. Strawberry border at sides and vine at top. Scene with two houses, fence, trees, vases of flowers, lion, and birds. Verses 490 (var.), 796. *Carolyn Scribner Barnes*

GALE, ELIZA W. 1813. 12 yrs. Worked at Mrs. Tuft's School, Charlestown [Mass.]. 18" x 22". 2 alphabets. Cross-stitch. Elaborate rose and carnation border. Verse 741.
Estate of James L. Little, Esq.

GALE, MARY A. 1825. 11 yrs. Great variety of stitches. Elaborate floral border on sides. At bottom, basket of flowers in center, and on either side, trees and small sprays of flowers. Verse at top. Verse 780. 9 wreaths, 5 of which contain family register in rows of three, and between rows and in 2 end wreaths sprays of flowers. "Mary Richards Born Dec. 17, 1790; Samuel Gale Born Apr. 7, 1793; Were married May 15, 1814; Mary A. Gale Born Oct. 27, 1814(*sic*); Samuel Gale Born Nov. 12, 1821; Eliza E. Gale Born June 8, 1824; died Oct. 30, 1824." *Mrs. H. de B. Parsons*

GALE, SALLY J. 1810. 13 yrs. 2 alphabets. Stem, satin, and cross-stitch. Vine border. Strawberry cross-border at top. Trees, man, and woman. Birds, flowers, and baskets of fruit, at bottom. Verse 287a. *Mrs. Daniel Webster Sanborn*

GANO, ELIZA. 1814. 9 yrs. Pattenburg [N. J.]. 20" x 20". 3 alphabets. Cross-stitch. Greek fret border and cross-borders. Large and small trees, and baskets of flowers. Verse 745.
Ella Felmly

GARDINER, ESTHER. 1813. Evesham [N. J.]. (12 yrs.) 19" x 23". Satin and cross-stitch. Vine and floral border. Plot of grass, sheep and lambs, geese, weeping willow and poplars, numerous small plants. Clumps of flowers all around. 8-pointed star at top. Verse 442.
Abigail E. Willitts

GARDINER, HANNAH. 1820. 12 yrs. "Evesham School" [N. J.]. 19" x 23". French knot, chain, tent, queen, stem, satin, and cross-stitch. Rose border with leaves; upper corners filled with flowers and baskets of flowers. Grape vines and grapes, in center; roses, white half-moon, baskets of flowers, and bunches of flowers fill in remainder of space. Verse 316 (var.).
Esther G. Evans

GARNER, CATHERINE. 1805. 15 yrs. 12" x 19". 4 alphabets. Outline, chain, satin, knot, loop, chrysanthemum, and cross-stitch. Greek floral border. Verse 271. Names: "John Garner, Frances Garner, Hendly Garner, I. Garner, E. Garner, J. Garner." *Mrs. D. D. Cameron*

GASKILL, MARY ANN. 1810. 12 yrs. 12" x 15". 4 alphabets. Cross-stitch. Strawberry border. Basket of fruit; rosebud and strawberries. *Josephine B. Osmond*

GAUFFREAU, CELESTINE. 1822. New York. 8 yrs. 16½" x 17". 2 alphabets. Cross-stitch. Strawberry border. House, dogs, cows, baskets of flowers, and several small birds. "Celestine Gauffreau agée de 8 ans fait le 2 d'aout 1822 à New York."
Mrs. J. Herbert Johnston

PLATE LIII
SOPHIA CATHERINE BIER'S SAMPLER. 1810
Owned by Mrs. Miles White, Jr.

PLATE LIV

MARIA LAMBORN'S SAMPLER.   1827
Owned by Mrs. Henry E. Coe

GAUFFREAU, FORTUNÉ. 1816. 12 yrs. St. Bartholomew (an island of the West Indies belonging to France). 13″ x 14″. 2 alphabets. Cross-stitch. Small cross-stitch border. House, birds, dogs, cows, vases of flowers, and clover. "Fortuné Gauffreau agé de 12 ans fait a St. Barth'my le 24 de Juillet 1816" (a boy).   *Mrs. J. Herbert Johnston*

GAUFFREAU, LOUISA. 1821. New York. 8 yrs. 15″ x 13″. Cross-stitch. Rose border. House, peacock, vases of flowers, pitcher, and dog. "Louisa Gauffreau agée de 8 ans, New York 1821." Verse (in French) 58. Illustrated.   *Mrs. J. Herbert Johnston*

GAY, MARY. 1808. 9 yrs. 16″ x 17″. 3 alphabets. Cross-stitch. Trefoil border. House, weeping willow, cow, lion with curly tail, and baskets. Verses 153, 511 (1, var.).
          Mrs. Thomas A. Lawton

GAY, MARY OTIS. 1809. Hingham [Mass.]. 8 yrs. 8″ x 12½″. Cross-stitch. Conventional border. "Apply thine heart unto instruction and thine ears to the words of knowledge."
          Mrs. Oliver Fiske

GEORGE, ISABELLA. 1826. Baltimore. 8 yrs. 9″ x 17″. 6 alphabets. Chain, eyelet, satin, cross, cat, tent, hem-stitch, and two-sided line-stitch. Strawberry, Greek fret, cross, and vine borders.   *Elizabeth C. Lee*

GEORGE, ISABELLA. 1827. Baltimore [Md.]. 9 yrs. 17″ x 17″. 2 alphabets. Satin, eyelet, chain, queen, tent, and cross-stitch. Borders of Greek fret, cross, vine, and strawberry designs.   *Elizabeth C. Lee*

GEORGE, MARIA LOUISA. [1827.] 8 yrs. Newburyport [Mass.]. 8¼″ x 8½″. 3 alphabets. Cross-stitch. Simple cross-stitch border. "Be virtuous and you will be happy."
          Miss Charlotte M. Smith

GEORGE, MARY ELIZABETH. 1817. Newburyport [Mass.]. 8 yrs. 18″ x 22″. 3 alphabets. Satin and cross-stitch. Rose-vine border, with 2 willow trees. Trees, bush, leaves, and flowers. Verse 515 (1, var.).   *Mrs. Emma F. Stephenson*

GERRISH, CAROLINE. 1809. 11 yrs. 17″ x 21″. 4 alphabets. Satin, catch, crow-foot, and cross-stitch. Hemstitched edge. Design at bottom like steps to courthouse.
          Miss Caroline L. Manett

GERRY, SOPHIA. 1810. Stoneham. 13 yrs. 19″ x 24¾″. 3 alphabets. Stem, satin, and cross-stitch. House, yard, trees, sheep, and fowl. Verse not given.   *Mrs. B. C. Hall*

GIBBON, SARAH ANN. 1825. Salem [N. J.]. 10 yrs. 9″ x 16½″. 6 alphabets. Queen, eyelet, and cross-stitch. Simple cross-stitch border. Short vine with tree and 2 strawberries.
          Mrs. Robert D. Hughes

GIBBS, ELIZABETH. 1812. [Near Crosswicks, N. J. Born October 26, 1798.] 14 yrs. 10½″ x 14″. 4 alphabets. French knot, tent, chain, eyelet, stem, satin, and cross-stitch. Fancy cross-border at bottom of strawberries, trees, and flowers, with hearts in each corner.
          Rebecca S. Price

GIBBS, LUCINDA. 1814. Sturbridge. 9 yrs. 18″ x 8″. 3 alphabets. Cross-stitch.
          Mrs. Henry Lowell Hiscock

GIBBS, MERCY. 1808. Birmingham [N. Y.]. 14 yrs. 9″ x 18″. 3 alphabets. Eyelet, satin, and cross-stitch. Twelve rows of different stitches at bottom. "Love the path of truth."
          Miss Bertha Gibbs

GIBBS, RACHEL B. 1812. 11 yrs. Born May 14, 1801. 10½″ x 16″. 4 alphabets. Great variety of stitches. Vine border. Double row of strawberries at bottom. Verse 94 (var.).
          Rebecca S. Price

GIBSON, ELIZABETH. 1800. Farmville [Va.]. 10 yrs. 12″ x 15″. 3 alphabets. Weaving, eyelet, satin, and cross-stitch. Vine border. Wide floral design at bottom. Verse 66.
Mrs. Wallace Delafield

GIBSON, HANNAH. [1815.] 12 yrs. 14″ x 19½″. Born August 11, 1803. Hemstitch and cross-stitch. Triple strawberry, rose, and carnation border, on top and sides. Verse 307. "Register of Mr. Barnabas Gibson and family. He was born July 12, 1767 and married Miss Hannah Tate Feb. 26, 1788. She was born 17— and died Aug. 31, 1801. He married Miss Betsy Chase July 16, 1802. She was born June 24, 1770. By him they have the following children:—

Names	Born	Died
Samuel Gibson	April 26, 1794	July 30, 1864
Mary Gibson	Sept. 6, 1795	
Robert Gibson	Nov. 4, 1797	
Hannah Gibson	Aug. 31, 1801	Dec. 2, 1801
Hannah Gibson	Aug. 11, 1803	
Luther Gibson	March 1805	April 16, 1805
Elizabeth Gibson	April 6, 1806	
David Gibson	March 24, 1809	Sept. 16, 1865
Sarah Gibson	Nov. 12, 1810	
William Gibson	July 12, 1812	May 4, 1854"

(Dates of three of the deaths filled in later on.) *Mrs. Thomas A. Lawton*

GIBSON, MARY. 1800. Lexington [Ky.]. 14 yrs. 16½″ x 17½″. 3 alphabets. Cross-stitch. Strawberry border. Carnations at bottom. Verse 665 (var.). *Mrs. G. W. Cain*

GILBERT, HANNAH. 1811. [Near Doylestown, Pa. 12 yrs.] 22″ x 22″. Cross-stitch. Waving line of cross-stitch as a border. In top corners are octagons inclosing swan and vines, also small bunches of roses and carnations, with squirrel in center of top row. Two doves above name. Small detached bunches of roses and carnations and sprays in baskets here and there on sampler. *Mrs. Bryan H. Taylor*

GILBERT, NANCY. 1800. 10 yrs. 10½″ x 14″. 1 alphabet. Cross and satin-stitch. Double strawberry border. House, hillside, tree, sheep, and people. Verse 595 (var.).
Mrs. Thomas A. Lawton

GILBERT, NANCY. 1806. Born September 20, 1793. 13 yrs. 15½″ x 12″. 3 alphabets. Eyelet and cross-stitch. Greek fret and strawberry borders. 2 vases at the bottom and 3 at the top. Verse 46. *Rev. Glenn Tilley Morse*

GILBERT, REBECCA SWISS. 1825. 10 yrs. 12″ x 10″. 3 alphabets. Chain, queen, and cross-stitch. Strawberry border. *Miss Bassell*

GILES, NARCISSA. 1802. 11 yrs. 12″ x 13″. 5 alphabets. Cross-stitch. Straight-line border. Cross-borders of strawberries, hearts, vines, diamonds, etc. *Arthur Leslie Green, Esq.*

GILL, ELIZABETH. 1805. Boston. 9 yrs. 10½″ x 17½″. 4 alphabets. Cross-stitch. Vase of flowers in center, a double strawberry on either side, then 2 trees, 2 shrubs, and 2 potted plants. Border patterns between alphabets. Verse 128 (1, var.).
Miss Marette Longley

GILL, MARY. 1809. Clarksboro [N. J.]. 12 yrs. 17″ x 17″. 4 alphabets. Eyelet, satin, and cross-stitch. Carnation and vine border. "See the time for sleep is before sun rise."
Mrs. Joseph W. Merritt

GILL, MARY. 1814. Wilmington [Del.]. 10″ x 10″. Cross-stitch. Seven square white designs worked in cotton, six of darning and one of knitting-stitch. Illustrated.
Mrs. Charles C. Jessup

GILLET, MARY ANN. 1827. 10 yrs. 8¼" x 7½". 2 alphabets. Cross-stitch. Greek fret border. House, dog, figures, and double hearts at bottom. *Mrs. Wallace Holcomb*

GILMAN, SARAH HIDDEN. [1826.] Meredith [N. H.]. 11 yrs. 8" x 10". 3 alphabets. *Mrs. George H. Williams*

GILSON, MARY. 1826. 17½" x 15¼". 2 alphabets. French knot, outline, satin, and cross-stitch. Elaborate rose border. Roses in pots. Verse 328. *Wilbur M. Stone, Esq.*

GITHENS, MARY. 1814. [Moorestown, Burlington County, N. J.] Born in 1806. 12" x 12½". Stem, cat, satin, and cross-stitch. Vine and floral border. Grass with dog and sprays of roses above and birds on each side. In center, a vine wreath with tiny flowers inclosing the following: "J.G., J. G., J.G., Mary Githens 1814." The rest of sampler filled in with floral designs. *Mrs. Henry I. Budd*

GLADDING, SUSAN CARY. 1805. Providence, R. I. (5 or 6 yrs.) 13" x 16". 4 alphabets. French knot, chain, stem, satin, and cross-stitch. Rose border, with tulip and leaves in one corner. At bottom, very correct (though unfinished) representation of First Congregational (Unitarian) Church in Providence. Verse 40 (var.). ["Miss Polly Balch's School," perhaps.] *Mrs. Charles W. Lippitt*

GLASIER, ABIGAIL. 1806. 13 yrs. Born August 26, 1793. 18½" x 21". 3 alphabets. Chain, stem, satin, and cross-stitch. Border has elaborate design of vine, flowers, and fruit starting from two vases and meeting in true lover's knot. Basket of flowers, at bottom. Verse 538 (var.).

"Family Record: Benjamin Glasier married Deborah Pinder October 20, 1792. Births of their children: Abigail Glasier born June 26, 1793; Lydia and Mary Glasier born January 9, 1795; Lydia died January 25, Mary, February 25, 1795; Mary Glasier born February 8, 1799; Salome Glasier born Sept. 4, 1800, died Sept. 17, 1801; Edmund H. and Elizabeth O. Glasier born April 25, 1802; Elizabeth O. died July 19, Edmund H. August 25, 1802; Lydia H. Glasier born July 19, 1804; William P. Glasier born November 19, died December 6, 1806."

Ipswich Historical Society

GLASS, SALLY. 1823. 14 yrs. 16" x 16". 4 alphabets. Stem and cross-stitch. Strawberry border. Border of conventional flowers and strawberries surrounds verse. Verses 188, 601 (1, 2, var.). "Praise ye the Lord all his Works". *Mrs. Bradbury Bedell*

GODARD, MARCY. 1811. Born November 7, 1803. 6" x 15½". 3 alphabets. Plain border. *Newport Historical Society*

GODARD, MARY. 1803. Cambridge, Mass. 11 yrs. 11" x 14¼". 2 alphabets. Chain, stem, and cross-stitch. Vine border with conventional flowers. Verse 259. *Mrs. Thomas G. Kent*

GODMAN, MARGARETTA ARABELLA. 1808. [Baltimore.] (8 yrs.) 16½" x 20". Satin and cross-stitch. Wreath of flowers, and below verse small green wreath. Design copied from brocade of her mother's wedding gown. Verse 709. *Mrs. Davis C. Buntin*

GODWIN, RACHEL. 1808. 20" x 16". Cross-stitch. Entire sampler, except oval in center, covered with running rose design coming out of a cornucopia at the bottom. Oval of green vine and leaves around verse. Verse 416. *Mrs. Marguerite du Pont Lee*

GOLDIN, ELIZABETH ANN. 1829. New York. 20" x 17½". Stem, back, and cross-stitch. Map of the state of New York. "Lake Erie is the celebrated scene of Perry's victory over a British fleet, September 10, 1813." "Lake Champlain is celebrated for the victory gained by Macdonough over a British fleet of far superior force, Sept. 11, 1814." "Long Island is the most important island belonging to the state of New York 140 miles in length and from 10 to 15 broad, contains three counties and numerous flourishing towns, population,

?7,000." "population of the State of New York in 1820 was 1,372,812. Albany is the Capital." Illustrated. *Mrs. Henry E. Coe*

GOODMAN, ELIZA. 1821. 11 yrs. Born April 13, 1809. 1 alphabet. Cross-stitch. Simple border. Scene with farmhouse with two ells, birds, and conventional tree. Verses 41 (var.), 764. *The Emma B. Hodge Collection*

GOODRIDGE, JANE. 1813. Lynn [Mass.]. 11 yrs. 17″ x 16½″. Alphabets. Seed, outline, stem, satin, and cross-stitch. Rose border. Wreath of forget-me-nots. Other vines of forget-me-nots elsewhere. Verse 129 (var.).

"Family Register"
"Mr. Moses Goodridge, born Nov. 27, 1768.
Miss Hannah Graves, born Jan. 22, 1774.
Married Aug. 7, 1795.

Childrens names	Births	Deaths
Hannah Goodridge	April 6, 1797.	
Polly Goodridge	Dec. 18, 1798.	Sept. 10, 1821.
Jane Goodridge	Dec. 3, 1801.	[d. 1906, 104 years old.]
Rand G. Goodridge	Feb. 25, 1804.	March 17, 1804.
Sally B. Goodridge	Feb. 12, 1805.	
Eliza Goodridge	Dec. 29, 1806.	Jan. 7, 1807.
Moses Goodridge	May 12, 1808.	
Joseph B. Goodridge	March 20, 1810.	
Eliza G. Goodridge	March 23, 1812."	

Mrs. Frederick C. Leslie

GOODWIN, ELIZA. 1801. [South Berwick, Maine.] 7 years. Born September 21, 1794. 18″ x 24″. 3 alphabets. Satin, stem, chain, French knot, and cross-stitch. Rose and vine border, starting from small baskets on either side and ending in large basket in center at top. Trees and birds across bottom. Rows of fancy stitches and narrow bands in strawberry designs. Verse 601 (1). *Mrs. William S. Whitney*

GOODWIN, ELIZABETH. 1805. Salem [N. J. 16 yrs.]. West-Town Boarding School. 9¾″ x 12¼″. Satin and outline stitch. Vine border. Verse 515 (var.). *Miss Anna Elizabeth Woodnutt*

GOODWIN, SARAH. 1824. Marblehead [Mass.]. 9 yrs. 6 mos. 18″ x 12½″. 3 alphabets. Stem, satin, and cross-stitch. Strawberry border. Panel at bottom with figures of boy and girl, also sunflower plant with bird flying about. Verse 776. *Mrs. Robert B. Dixon*

GORHAM, LUCY TAYLOR. 1801. Boston. 12″ x 15″. 2 alphabets. Cross-stitch. Vine border. Design in shape of peaks. Initials "G. W." underneath verse. Verse 5a.
Mrs. Shepherd Brooks

GOULD, LUCY H. [After 1803.] 9 yrs. 12″ x 16″. Cross, satin, stem, eyelet, long and short-stitch. 3 alphabets. Flowering vine border on solid embroidery. At bottom, two urns with willow branches, and under both "Eliza Gould Æ 9 Ys Died August 6, 1803." Verse 261. *Owner not recorded*

GRAHAM, SOPHIA. 1803. Mobile [Ala.]. 7½″ x 9″. 2½ alphabets. Cross-stitch.
Mrs. John Adams Dix

GRAVES, MARY McNERAN. 1810. Philadelphia. 7 yrs. Born March 9, 1803. 8″ x 18″. Cat, eyelet, and cross-stitch. Verse 342 (var.). *Miss Ellen Coppuck Curtis*

GRAY, SUSAN (YOUNG). 1803. Boston. 13 yrs. 16½″ x 18″. 2 alphabets. Stem and cross-stitch. Strawberry-vine border. Strawberry design at top and bottom, inside border. Verse 718. *The Misses Sophia and E. Frances Morton*

GREELY, MARY ANN. 1814. Newburyport [Mass.]. 10 yrs. 12″ x 15″. 5 alphabets. Chain, satin, eyelet, and cross-stitch. Strawberries and grass at base. "The family of Stephen and Betsy Greely; Benjamin born Dec. 11, 1793; Nathaniel born Nov. 11, 1795; John born June 19, 1798; Alice born Nov. 14, 1800; John B. born July 20, 1802; Mary A. born Nov. 19, 1804; Elizabeth born July 20, 1810." *Lucius H. Greely, Esq.*

GREEN, ELIZA. 1805. Stoneh—. 10 yrs. 16″ x 23½″. 4 alphabets. Chain, stem, satin, and cross-stitch. Elaborate floral border in satin-stitch. Picture of a house with trees and two little dogs. Verse 147. *Estate of James L. Little, Esq.*

GREEN, MARY. 1813. 7 yrs. 15″ x 14″. 3 alphabets. Stem and cross-stitch. Strawberry border. Verse 515 (var.). *The Rhode Island School of Design*

GREEN, MARY. 1814. Cambridge, New York. 14 yrs. 9½″ x 13″. 5 alphabets. Eyelet and cross-stitch. *Marguerite Emery*

GREENE, MARTHA. 1807. Born the 23rd of June, 1797, at Coventry, R. I. 8″ x 8″. 3 alphabets. Cross-stitch. Border, two designs in cross-stitch, also cross-borders in different designs. Verse 92a. *Emma A. Davis*

GREENLEAF, DOLLY. 1804. Newburyport [Mass.]. Born March, 1796. 11″ x 15″. 3 alphabets. Satin, stem, and cross-stitch. Border of saw-tooth design. Vase with flowers; tulips, roses, and bachelor buttons. *Mrs. Francis R. Allen*

GREENLEAF, ELIZA ANN. 1808. Newburyport [Mass.]. 10 yrs. 18″ x 17″. 4 alphabets. Satin, eyelet, stem, and cross-stitch. Garland of flowers around verse, also 2 lines of Greek key pattern. Verse 202 (1, var.). *Mrs. Francis R. Allen*

GREENOUGH, ELIZA. 1809. Essex County, Haverhill. 10″ x 14″. 3 alphabets. Stem, tent, satin, and cross-stitch. Grape-vine border, with rosebuds. Tulip design at bottom. Verse 111. *Mrs. Edward Webster*

GREENWALT, ELIZA. 1822. Cumberland [Md.]. 14½″ x 16″. Flat, chain, stem, satin, and cross-stitch. Flat-stitch border. Pastoral scene. Verse 435. *Mrs. Lloyd Lowndes*

GRIFFIN, FRANCES LOUISA. 1810. Boston. 8 yrs. 4 alphabets. Hemstitch and cross-stitch. Hemstitched edge, with scroll border. Narrow cross-border designs. *Miss F. L. Smith*

GRIMES, CAROLINE. 1803. New York. 8 yrs. 14″ x 16″. Cross-stitch. Border design something like a sweet-pea. At bottom, house, 2 fir trees, man, weeping willow, and monument; detached designs on sides, birds on branches, sprays of bluebells, and rosebuds, dog, "Nero," cat, "Tiger," with basket of flowers in between. Made and sent to Grandmother in England. Verse 16. *Marshall Cutler, Esq.*

GRIMES, ELIZABETH. 1803. New York. 10 yrs. 14″ x 16″. Cross-stitch. Narrow border in diamond design. At bottom, house with tree on either side, bird on one side and dog on the other, baskets of flowers at each end. Detached designs around verse of man shooting at birds, with a dog at his side, conventional tree, sprays of flowers, colored man, etc. Initials above verse: "L I N E S." Sent to maker's grandmother in England. Verse 145. *Marshall Cutler, Esq.*

GROFF, DEBORAH. 1807. Woodstown, N. J. 10 yrs. 18″ x 20″. 2 alphabets. Satin and cross-stitch. Border, Walls of Troy with carnations. Names: "John and Deborah Groff (parents); Thomas Groff (deceased), Asa, Sarah, Letice Martha, John, William, Benjamin (brothers and sisters)." Verse 52.
Mrs. I. Oakford Acton

GROSS, ELIZA. 1820. 13 yrs. 20″ x 10″. 2 alphabets. Cross-stitch. Verse 317.
Mrs. Arthur Durfee

GROW, ELIZA. 1810. Ipswich [Mass.]. 11 yrs. 16¾″ x 22¼″. 2 alphabets. Stem, satin, and cross-stitch. Border of vines running up each side and across top and starting from flower-pots at lower corners. Verse 538 (var.). Family names and dates: "John Grow born Sept. 3, 1772; Elizabeth Caldwell born Aug. 17, 1772; Married June 19, 1798. Eliza Grow born April 3, 1799."
Mrs. Charlotte M. Jones

GUILD, ABIGAIL. 1802. Dedham [Mass.]. 11 yrs. 10½″ x 15½″. 2 alphabets. Cross-stitch. Vine and rose border. Rose trees at bottom. Verse 249.
Miss Isabel Russell Brown

GUILD, LUCY. 1802. 10 yrs. 14″ x 9″. 2 alphabets. Chain and cross-stitch. Strawberry border. Verse 250.
Miss Louise Cranston

GUILD, MARIANN. 1819. Dedham [Mass.]. 13 yrs. 17½″ x 16½″. 4 alphabets. Satin and cross-stitch. Verses 152, 249.
Mrs. Howard M. Chapin

GUILD, REBEKAH. 1801. Dedham [Mass.]. 8 yrs. 12″ x 13″. 3 alphabets. Eyelet and cross-stitch. Strawberry border. Design at top of trees, flowers, and bouquets. Verse 532.
Annie R. Thayer

HACKNEY, ARIADNE. May 8, 1817. Mercer [Pa.]. 12″ x 12″. French knot, stem, satin, and cross-stitch. Vine border, with pink flowers. Four bunches of roses, an urn, and wreath of roses in center around verse. Verse 755.
Miss Addie Venable

HACKNEY, MARIA. April, 1819. Mercer [Pa.]. 10″ x 10″. Satin, flat, and cross-stitch. Vine border. Sprays of roses in each corner with 2 blocks in between; roses at top and bottom and 1 block on each side. Verses 733, 761.
Miss Jane Reid Venable

HACKNEY, MARIA. 1819. Mercer [Pa.]. 10″ x 10″. French knot, chain, stem, satin, and cross-stitch. Tulip border. Four bunches of roses, with verse between. Verse 733.
Miss Jane Reid Venable

HAINES, JANE. 1807. 18″ x 17″. Chain, satin, and cross-stitch. 2 alphabets. Oval incloses verse and alphabets; initials around the border. Verse 415.
The Misses Chace

HALL, ABBY D. 1821. 11 yrs. 11″ x 11″. 3 alphabets. Chain, stem, and cross-stitch. Rose border, with violets in corners.
Mrs. William H. Bradford

HALL, ELIZA. [1801?] Westmoreland [N. H.]. 9 yrs. [Born December 21, 1792, in Raynham, Mass.] 10″ x 17″. 3 alphabets. Eyelet, cross, and hem-stitch. Strawberry border. Basket of flowers, trees, and birds.
Miss Cora E. Pierce

HALL, LUCY JONES. 1820. Medford [Mass.]. 7 yrs. 14″ x 15¾″. 2 alphabets. Satin, tent, and cross-stitch. Narrow cross-borders with trees and hanging fruits.
Mary H. Hayes

HALL, M. [Cir. 1820.] 10″ x 11″. 3 alphabets. Cross-stitch. Two strawberries. Initials: "M.W.H. and S.S."
Mrs. Bradbury Bedell

HALL, M. H. [Cir. 1812.] [Ann Arundell County, Md.] [Born in 1799.] 5½″ x 6½″. 2 alphabets. Hem and cross-stitch. Hemstitched edge.
Miss Stockett

PLATE LV

CONTENT PHILLIPS'S SAMPLER
Owned by Florence C. McKenny

PLATE LVI

SARAH DOLE'S SAMPLER.   1819
Owned by Leonard Smith, Esq.

HALL, MARGARET. 1823. 14″ x 19″. 1 alphabet. Stem, satin, and cross-stitch. Elaborate floral border, with pineapple at top, large red poppy at bottom, roses, poppies, tulips, and carnations on sides. Large weeping willow on lawn, two large butterflies, and tulips in grass. Grape vines on either side of verse. Verse 774. *Mrs. Bradbury Bedell*

HALL, MARTHA. 1808. Medford [Mass.]. 16″ x 21″. 3 alphabets. Vine and flower border. Cross-borders. Basket of flowers in each corner and circular design of flowers and leaves in center.

> "Friendship is like a debt of honour, the moment it is talked of it loses its name and assumes the ungrateful form of obligation."

> "Virtue is the noblest ornament of humanity and a true sense of sublime pleasure. It is a solid foundation of honour and esteem." *Mary H. Hayes*

HALL, NABBY L. 1804. Pembroke [Mass.]. 10 yrs. 21½″ x 16½″. 3 alphabets. Stem, eyelet, and cross-stitch. Vine and rose border at sides and basket of roses at top and bottom. *Charles H. Tyler, Esq.*

HALL, PHEBE. 1812. 11 yrs. 7¾″ x 17¼″. 2 alphabets. Chain and stem-stitch. Trefoil border at top; small alternating squares, containing conventionalized trees and flowers across bottom. Verse 441. *W. G. Bowdoin, Esq.*

HALL, PRUDENCE. 1805. Salem [N. J.]. [16 yrs.] 7¾″ x 8¾″. Cross-stitch. Dove inclosed in wreath tied with bow-knot. Detached designs of birds, flowers, and fruit on balance of sampler. *Miss Adaline Sinnickson*

HALL, R———. 1813. 10″ x 8″. Cross-stitch. 3 alphabets. *Mrs. I. Oakford Acton*

HALLET, MARY. 1803. 8 yrs. 13″ x 15″. Alphabet. Queen, satin, and cross-stitch. Strawberry border. Cross-borders. In upper corners, crowns and rabbits; across center, house, trees, deer, bushes, and chickens; underneath, flowers in vases, design with name and date; in lower corners, bowls of roses, and in center of bottom, 2 trees. Verse 535. *Mrs. Frederic R. Kellogg*

HAMIL, JANE. 1802. 10½″ x 17½″. 3 alphabets. Eyelet, satin, and cross-stitch. Strawberry border. 2 small ships and 2 baskets of fruit. Verses 41 (var.), 128 (1, var.), 447, 534. *Mrs. Day Brookmire Hebard*

HAMILTON, CATHERINE. 1808. 3 alphabets. Eyelet and cross-stitch. Tulip border. Wreath around name. Narrow borders across. 2 flowers in the lower corners. Verse 424. *Memorial Hall, Fairmount Park, Philadelphia*

HAMILTON, E———. 1819. 12″ x 16½″. 3 alphabets. Eyelet and cross-stitch. Narrow cross-borders. Verse 29 (2). *Memorial Hall, Fairmount Park, Philadelphia*

HAMILTON, MARY. 1812. Maytown, Mrs. Welchan's School. 18 yrs. 17″ x 17″. Satin and cross-stitch. Border made up of series of squares, containing different designs of baskets and sprays of flowers. Oval picture in center, with woman standing under tree; her face and arms are painted. Inscription in center square at bottom: "Mary Hamilton a daughter of John and Catherine Hamilton was born in County Antrim February the 1 in the year of our Lord 1794 and made this sampler in Maytown in Mrs. Welchan's School in the year of our Lord 1812." Illustrated. *Mrs. Henry E. Coe*

HAMILTON, SARAH. [Cir. 1800.] Philadelphia. 7½" x 10". Alphabets. Variety of stitches. Cross-borders. *On sale by American Art Association, December 12, 1917*

HAMMOND, ANN J. [Cir. 1805.] 17" x 18". 2 alphabets. Eyelet, queen, and cross-stitch. Unusual strawberry border. Verse 515 (var.). *Mrs. Algernon Sydney Sullivan*

HAMMOND, ELIZABETH H. September 3, 1823. Ashford [Conn.]. 9 yrs. 11" x 15½". 3 alphabets. Satin and cross-stitch. Saw-tooth design in border. Conventional cross-stitch design at bottom. Flower-pot and bird. Verse 772. *Mrs. Grace Buchanan Reynolds*

HAMMOND, LYDIA A. October, 1829. Wickford [R. I.]. 17½" x 18". 3 alphabets. Cross-stitch. Rosebud border. "Hope Eternal Hope! Where yonder Spheres sublime." *Abby C. Bullock*

HAMSON, ANN. 1808. 11" x 13½". 3 alphabets. Eyelet, flat, and cross-stitch. Border has strawberries on the outside and cherries on the inside, with interesting corners. Eyelet-work borders. 4 pine trees separated by conventional stalks of flowers; rose tree in center. Verse 418. *Mrs. Bradbury Bedell*

HANCOCK, E. C. 1826. Salem [N. J.]. 14 yrs. 8½" x 9½". 1 alphabet. Cross-stitch. Strawberry border. Flowers and animals. *Mrs. James F. Barr*

HANCOCK, EMILEA. 1800. 8 yrs. Cross-stitch. Carnation border and strawberry cross-border. Scene with house, trees, butterflies, and below, trees, stags, birds, lady, dog, and gate. Verse 515 (var.). *The Emma B. Hodge Collection*

HANNERS, ELIZABETH JANE. 1812. 18" x 14". Design at bottom, New York City Hall. *Mrs. Arthur Curtis James*

HARDEN, ELIZA. October 12, 1803. Portland [Me.]. 11 yrs. 17" x 24". 6 alphabets. Eyelet, satin, and cross-stitch. Rose border. Scene at bottom with house, garden, trees, birds, sheep, fence, shrubs, and girl. Spray of roses around verse. Verse 404. *Mrs. Pearl Wight*

HARDENBROOK, REBEKAH. Decbr the 20, 1800. 7 yrs. 4 mos. 7" x 12". 3 alphabets. Eyelet and cross-stitch. Waving line border. "Margaret Hardenbrook, William Hardenbrook x 1800." *Mrs. Samuel A. Cunningham*

HARDING, ABIGAIL. 1820. Medway [Mass. Born October 24, 1808.]. 10¾" x 11". 3 alphabets. Cross-stitch. Simple border. 3 baskets of flowers, with 2 trees between, at bottom. Verse 515 (var.). *Mrs. Mary H. Wilder*

HARDING, MARY. 1820. Medway. [Born March 17, 1811.] 10¾" x 11¾". 3 alphabets. Cross-stitch. Simple border. 3 baskets of flowers and two trees, at bottom. Verse 515 (var.). *Mrs. Mary H. Wilder*

HARDMAN, ANN. 1816. 6" x 10". 3 alphabets. Cross-stitch. *Sold at Libbie's, March 1, 1916*

HARDY, CLARISA. 1816. Stem, satin, and cross-stitch. Elaborate floral design starting from cornucopia in center at bottom. In center is the "Family Register: William Hardy Born Aug th 2 1779; Clarisa Worcester Born January th 5 1786; They were married November the 30 1803. A list of the name birth and deaths of their children: Clarissa W. Born Dec. th 11 1804; William Born May th 20 1806; Hannah W. Born Oct 12th 1808.

William the husband of Clarisa Hardy died Oct 2, 1808. Ebenezer Hunt the second husband of Clarissa Hardy Born March th 3. They were married Dec th 29 1809." "Now hear you read that death has call my parent Dear and may we all for that day prepare." Verse 55.   *Mrs. Thomas A. Lawton*

HARFORTH, HANNAH. 1808. 13 yrs. Alphabets. Flowers and urn. Verses 41*a*, 420, 541.
Mrs. J. F. Linder

HARRINGTON, HANNAH. 1815. Worcester [Mass.]. 9 yrs. 12½" x 13". 2 alphabets and other letters. Cross-stitch. Verse 490 (var.).   *Philip Hope Baker, Esq.*

HARRINGTON, MARY. 1812. Worcester [Mass.]. 8 yrs. 3 alphabets. Cross and eyelet stitch. Zigzag border.   *Philip Hope Baker, Esq.*

HARRINGTON, RUTH. 1809. 9 yrs. 12" x 7¾". 2 alphabets. Satin, cross, and hem-stitch. Rose border. Several conventional figures.   *Wilbur M. Stone, Esq.*

HARRIS, ADELINE ELEANOR. 1816. Cranston [R. I.]. Born December 3, 1803. 17" x 18". 2 alphabets. Stem, satin, and cross-stitch. Hemstitched edge. Flower design at bottom. Verse 680.   *Adeline Harris Sears*

HARRIS, ELIZABETH. 1806. Born July 27, 1796. 10" x 10½". 3 alphabets. Stem, satin, tent, and cross-stitch. Strawberry border. Flowering branches and small trees in bloom.   *Mrs. Lyman Daniels*

HARRIS, HENRIETTA C. 1829. 13¼" x 13¼". 5 alphabets. Cat and cross-stitch. Zigzag border. Cross-borders in conventional designs. "C. L. A."   *W. G. Bowdoin, Esq.*

HARRIS, MARIA L. 1816. 3 alphabets. Two hillocks with pine trees. "B. C. Harris. A. E. Harris." "Daughter of Joseph and Sussina Harris." Verse 515 (var.).
Owner not recorded

HARRIS, OCEANA. May 8, 1805. Providence [R. I.]. 8 yrs. 8" x 19". 3 alphabets. Cross-stitch and satin-stitch. Simple cross-stitch border. Pyramid design at bottom. Verse 537.   *Miss Emma A. Taft II*

HARRIS, POLLY. Before 1830. 10 yrs. 6" x 10". 1 alphabet. Cross-stitch. Greek fret border. Two white horses eating strawberries.   *Rev. Glenn Tilley Morse*

HARRIS, S. 1808. 13" x 15". 4 alphabets. Cross-stitch. Strawberry border around lower half. Two doves with branches in mouths. Verse 421.   *Mrs. Frederick F. Thompson*

HARRISON, ELIZABETH. [Cir. 1800.] "Born August the 5, 1791." 8½" x 16½". 4 alphabets. Eyelet and cross-stitch. Verse 187.   *Mrs. H. B. Leary, Jr.*

HARRISON, MARY. 1822. 9 yrs. 3 alphabets. Cross, eyelet, and satin-stitch. Strawberry border. Vase of flowers, log hut, and an animal under a tree. Birds. Verse 561.
Mrs. Mary Harrison Snow

HARTH, CAROLINE. 1824. 10 yrs. 8" x 10". 3 alphabets. Eyelet and cross-stitch. Strawberry and Greek key borders.   *The Misses Laura and Lieze Green*

HARWOOD, ELIZABETH A. 1814. [Massachusetts.] 17 yrs. 15½" x 20". Cross, satin, chain, stem, cat, and tent-stitch. Rose-vine border. The Register is framed between two posts, with balls at the top. Between them is a draped curtain with tassels.

" Register
Capt. Peter Harwood was born Sept 16 AD 1766. Miss Elizabeth Airmet was born
June 12 A D. 1770. They Married Jan 22 1787. He hath by her the following
children. Viz.

Names	Births	Deaths
Thomas Airmet	Feb 6th 1789	
Fanny Russell	Feb 7th 1791	
Sarah Ann	May 27th 1793	
Esther Brazier	May 3, th 1795	
Elizabeth Airmet	May 28, th 1797	
Clarisse	June 16, th 1799	Died June 15th 1803
Ebenezer	Dec 21th 1801	Died Feb 13th 1807
William Brazier	April 21th 1803	
Ebenezer	June 28th 1805	
Peter Branscome	May 21th 1807	Died April th 22
Clarisse Branscome	June 16, th 1812 "	

At the bottom two houses, trees, and a garden. The right-hand house was built by
Captain Peter Harwood, and was the first brick house in North Brookfield, Mass. Verse
744. Illustrated. *Mrs. Grace Craig Stork*

HASKELL, HANNAH PRIEST. "March 2." [Cir. 1815. Boston.] 6 yrs. 16″ x 20″. 4 alphabets. French knot, satin, and cross-stitch. "Modesty and Truth To Piety add Modesty
and Docility Show reverence and submission to those who are your superiors in Knowledge or Station and note that Dependance and obedience belong to youth. Modesty is
one of the chief ornaments and tokens of piety. Truth is a precious adornment."
Mrs. Delano Wight

HASKELL, LUCY S. 1816. 12 yrs. 18½″ x 17″. 3 alphabets. French knot, stem, and cross-
stitch. Conventional strawberry-vine border with potted strawberry plant in center at
bottom, flanked by sprays of star flowers. Detached spray of strawberries and baskets
of flowers. Conventional cross-borders. Verses 194 (var.), 751.
Miss Mary O. Longfellow

HASKELL, SARAH K[IDDER. 1811. Boston. Born September 28, 1805.]. 6 yrs. 18″ x 16″.
3 alphabets. Satin and cross-stitch. Strawberry border. Verse 724.
The Late Miss Sarah Haskell Crocker

HASKINS, MARY ANN. 1828. Rehoboth [Mass.]. 14 yrs. 16″ x 20″. 3 alphabets. Flat,
stem, satin, and cross-stitch. Rose border. House and flowers. Verse 794.
Sara Lawrence White

HASSEN, ANNZELETTE. 1821. 8 yrs. 24″ x 20″. 3 alphabets. Chain, stem, and cross-stitch.
Strawberry border with flowers. Large basket of flowers in center at bottom, and on
either side an octagon inclosing name and dates; garland and tassels hang from inside
of each octagon, and underneath are solid cross-stitch pyramids.
National Museum, Washington, D. C.

HATCH, MARY. 1808. Paris [N. Y.]. 10 yrs. 17″ x 9″. 5 alphabets. Chain, eyelet, satin,
and cross-stitch. Eyelet and cross-stitch border. Sprays of roses in corners. Verse 154.
Ella M. Russell

HATFIELD, EMELINE. [Cir. 1823 New York.] 14 yrs. 22½″ x 22½″. Cross, satin, queen, flat,
and split-stitch. Grape and diamond border. Two cornucopias and a basket of roses.
Verse 515. *Mrs. John Lester Keep*

HATFIELD, MARY. 1828. [New York.] 11 yrs. 17½″ x 16½″. Cross-stitch. Rose-vine border. Large basket at the bottom. *Mrs. John Lester Keep*

HATFIELD, SARAH. [New York.] 22½″ x 22½″. Cross, satin, queen, flat, and long-stitch. Grape-vine and diamond border. Large basket of fruit. The handles are gracefully curved. *Mrs. John Lester Keep*

HATHAWAY, BETSEY. 1828. Freetown, Assonet Village. 14 yrs. 16″ x 16″. 4 alphabets. Cat, eyelet, queen, stem, tent, and cross-stitch. Rose border at bottom and on sides, and poppies across top. Cross-borders in variety of designs and stitches. Verse 483. *Mrs. Mary B. Pierce*

HATHEWEY, LUCY. Freetown [Mass.]. 14 yrs. 19″ x 20″. 3 alphabets. French knot, chain, stem, and cross-stitch. Carnation border at sides. House, two figures, basket of flowers, sprays of flowers, etc. Verse 109. *Mrs. Charles A. Clark*

HAWKES, ELIZABETH. [Cir. 1815.] Windham [Me. Cir. 20 yrs.]. 20″ x 29″. Cross and hem-stitch. Strawberry and vine border. Births, marriages, and deaths of Hawkes family:

Births

Ebenezer Hawkes   April 25, 1766
Rebecca Legrow   September 9, 1772
Married November 20, 1794 in Windham, Maine

Their children born in Windham

Elizabeth Hawkes	July 27, 1795	Mary Hawkes	March 29, 1804
Ebenezer Hawkes	February 23, 1797	Lydia Hawkes	March 29, 1806
Sarah Hawkes	October 8, 1798	William Hawkes	February 12, 1809
Joseph Hawkes	July 7, 1800	Elias Hawkes	April 6, 1811
Anna Hawkes	May 1, 1802	Jeremiah Hawkes	April 17, 1815

Deaths

Rebecca Hawkes   July 12, 1819
    Aged 46
Sarah Purrington   July 28, 1825
    Aged 26
Elias Hawkes   September 23, 1825
    Aged 14

Mrs. Franklin P. Shumway

HAWTHORNE, RHODA. 1806. Born November 21, 1791. 12″ x 15½″. 2 alphabets. Bird's-eye and cross-stitch. Plain border. Verse 105. *Mrs. Thomas A. Lawton*

HAYDEN, HARRIOT F. 1812. Fitzwilliam [N. H.]. 8 yrs. 17″ x 16½″. 3 alphabets. Cat, stem, flat, and cross-stitch. Strawberry border at top and bottom, with vine on sides. Verse 107. *Mrs. Roger Johnson*

HAYS, ELLEN. 1808. Philadelphia. 8 yrs. 16″ x 18″. 11 alphabets. Cross-stitch. Vine border with strawberries. *Miss Rosa Mordecai*

HAYS, ROSA ELIZABETH. 1813. Philadelphia. [10 yrs.] 13″ x 13½″. 6 alphabets. Greek fret border with conventional designs. 3 flower-pots with flowers, also small sprays, at bottom. *Miss Rosa Mordecai*

HAZWELL, FRANCES. 1828. 12 yrs. 18″ x 12″. 6 alphabets. Chain, eyelet, and cross-stitch. House. Verse 515. *Mrs. W. B. Vine*

[HEACOCK, EVALINE. (?) Bucks County, Pa.]. 8″ x 13″. Alphabets. Variety of stitches. Cross-stitch border. At bottom, dog, bird on flowering plant; bird on plant in upper left-hand corner and conventional flower in upper right-hand corner; in center, conventional design with two birds, beak to beak, bell flower, carnations, and crown.

Mrs. J. Raufmann

HEATH, RACHEL A. 1829. Pittsfield, Ill. 11 yrs. 17″ x 17″. 2 alphabets. Cross, satin, and eyelet-stitch. *F. Maude Smith*

HEATON, ROSAMOND P. 1824. Berlin [Vt.]. 10 yrs. 17″ x 17″. 3 alphabets. Stem, chain, and cross-stitch. Tree and flower design. *Miss M. Louise Gladding*

HEBBARD, HARRIOT. 1812. 10 yrs. 17″ x 14½″. 3 alphabets. Satin and cross-stitch. Small zigzag border. Conventional trees and baskets at bottom. *Miss Mary C. Wheelwright*

HEMPSTED, CAROLINE. 1823. New London [Conn.]. 9 yrs. 13″ x 13″. 2 alphabets. Cross-stitch. Greek fret and strawberry border. Rose in fancy square in corners at bottom. Verse 515 (var.). *Dr. Elmer Hempstead Ames*

HENDRICKSON, ALICE. 1807. [Monmouth County, N. J. Born March 18, 1795. Daughter of John and Alche.] 12 yrs. 12½″ x 17″. Cross-stitch. Strawberry border. Basket of flowers, birds, rosebuds, berries, and diamond-shaped designs, etc. Verses 10 (1), 395 (4). *Mrs. Elwood Davis*

HENDRICKSON, GERTRUDE. 1805. [Monmouth County, N. J. Born December 28, 1792.] 13 yrs. 15½″ x 18″. 2 alphabets. Eyelet and cross-stitch. Strawberry border. Basket of flowers with branches and berries on each side. *Letitia E. Davis*

HEPBURN, ANN. 1828. 10″ x 9″. Back-stitch and cross-stitch. Strawberry border. House, fence, trees, and sheep. *Mrs. Bradbury Bedell*

HERRHER, ELIZABETH. 1824. 8 yrs. "Done in Ruth H. Redman's School, Strawsburg." 12½″ x 17″. Alphabets. Cross-stitch. Strawberry border. Flower-pots, birds, and two dogs at top. *Charles S. Henry, 2d, Esq.*

HERRICK, EUNICE. 1801. 11 yrs. 5½″ x 6½″. Alphabet. Cross-stitch. Variety of cross-stitch designs in border. Two hearts at bottom. *Mrs. E. L. Mark*

HEULING, MARTHA. 1806. Moorestown [N. J. 13 yrs. Born October 27, 1793.]. 21″ x 22½″. Chain, satin, and cross-stitch. Border of roses, baskets of fruit, birds, stars, and carnations. Picture of the West Town School, with tree on either side and birds above it. Verses 77 (var.), 399 (var.). Illustrated. *Hannah F. Gardiner*

HEULINGS, MARY C. 1821. Burlington [N. J.]. 10 yrs. 21″ x 18½″. 4 alphabets. Outline, chain, and cross-stitch. Rose border. 13 bunches of flowers and several small flowers; also 2 large baskets of flowers. Verse 765. *Miss Margaret S. Bedell*

HEWINS, OLIVE E. 1829. Boston. 4 alphabets. Great variety of stitches. Wide and elaborate rose border. Picture in center, with tree and lady in foreground, and house, trees, pond, cow, grass, etc., in background. *Mrs. Thomas A. Lawton*

HEWLING, REBECCA ANN. 1826. 15½″ x 17½″. 6 alphabets. Eyelet, chain, cat, queen, satin, buttonhole, two-sided tent, and cross-stitch. Strawberry-vine border. Large diamond in four parts, pair of love birds, baskets of flowers, dogs, hearts, tree, and rosebud.

Frances D. Smith

HIBBARD, ELIZABETH. 1813. 15 yrs. 18″ x 22½″. French knot, flat, outline, petit-point, stem, and cross-stitch. Strawberry and rose border. Baskets of flowers, trees, birds, etc. Verse 132 (var.). "My parents, William and Jane Hibbard; My Brothers, Walter, Thomas & William Hibbard; My Grandparents, Caleb and Phebe Hibbard, John and Elizabeth Williamson; My Sisters, Esther, & Phebe Hibbard."

Miss Josephine Parry Amos

HIGGINS, SARAH. 1803. Cape May City, N. J. 9½″ x 17½″. 2 alphabets. Eyelet and cross-stitch. Top border of crowns and trees. Rose trees, bunches of flowers, and dog. Verse 256. *Mrs. Henry B. Diverty*

HILDRETH, ADALINE S. 1820. Hopkinton [Mass.]. 9 yrs. 8″ x 10″. 2 alphabets. Satin and cross-stitch. Simple pyramid border. [Lived in the house where Sir Harry Frankland and Agnes Surriage once lived.] *Mrs. H. O. Stearns*

HILLHOUSE, SARAH G. 1800. 16″ x 7½″. 3 alphabets. Cross-stitch. Verse 673. *Sarah G. F. Hillhouse*

HILLS, ABIGAIL. 1802. New Bedford [Mass.]. 12 yrs. 13″ x 18″. 3 alphabets. Cross-stitch. Strawberry border. *The Canandaigua Historical Society*

HINCHMAN, MARTHA ENGLE. 1821. [Mannington Township, Salem County, N. J.] 13 yrs. 14¼″ x 19¼″. Queen, cat, satin, and cross-stitch. Border of vine and strawberry. Vase with large bluebird, sprays of strawberries, rosebuds, tulips, birds, baskets of flowers, horses, lions, goose, etc. Initials: " [father, mother, and children, E.H. done in black, had died] L.H. C.H. M.H. T.H. E.H. A.H. M.H. R.H. M.H. R.H. C.H." Verses 399, 617. *Miss Martha Richman*

HINCKLEY, ELIZABETH K. 1816. Hingham [Mass.]. 7 yrs. 10″ x 12″. 3 alphabets. Cross-stitch. "Let Virtue be my Guide." *Mrs. John Laidlaw Buel*

PUPILS OF SALLY HINSDALE. [Cir. 1825.] New Hartford and Harwinton [Conn.]. 7 to 15 yrs. 16 small samplers, 4½″ x 6″ to 1¾″ x 3″. Alphabets on some of them. Cross-stitch. Simple borders. Names of different children. *Albert C. Bates, Esq.*

HITCHCOCK, ABAGAIL M. A. 1809. 9 yrs. 13¼″ x 15¼″. 3 alphabets. French knot, chain, stem, satin, and cross-stitch. Strawberry and Greek fret border. Festoons of roses at top; trees, cornucopias, and basket of flowers at bottom. Verse 515 (var.). *Mrs. David P. Coffin*

HODGE, LYDIA. 1770. 3″ x 8½″. Alphabet. Cross-stitch. *Mrs. Eugene C. Stratton*

HOES, CATHERINE ANN. 1827. 7 yrs. Kinderhook. 10″ x 14″. 2 alphabets. Cross-stitch. Verse 175 (1). *National Museum, Washington*

HOLBROOK, ANN P. 1810. Medfield [Mass.]. 10 yrs. 16½″ x 16½″. 3 alphabets. Loop, stem, and cross-stitch. Geometrical design in border, with row of tassels at top. House, fence, garden, potted plants, weeping willow trees, and two tombstones. *Mrs. Abby Alice Bishop*

HOLBROOK, BRITAINIA. 1819. 14 yrs. 17″ x 17″. 3 alphabets. Queen and cross-stitch. "Honour thy Father and Mother that it may be well with thee and thou live long on the Earth." Verse 119. *Mrs. William Henry Gilbane*

HOLBROOK, JULIA. [Cir. 1801.] Born May 7, 1790. 10¼″ x 15¾″. 4 alphabets. Satin, cross, and fagoting-stitch. Block pattern in border. *Benjamin S. Newton, Esq.*

HOLBROOK, MARY W. [Cir. 1813.] Grafton [Mass.]. Born May 6, 1800. 8″ x 18″. 3 alphabets. Eyelet, chain, and cross-stitch. *Fitchburg Antique Shop, July 1, 1917*

HOLLINGSWORTH, REBECCA H. 1827. 7 yrs. 7¾″ x 9¾″. 2 alphabets. Cross-stitch. Vine border at bottom. *Pennsylvania Museum, Memorial Hall, Fairmount Park*

HOLLISTER, POLLY. 1808. [Born in Glastonbury, Conn., 1798.] 10 yrs. 10½″ x 11″. 3 alphabets. Cross-stitch. Simple border. *Mrs. Robert A. Wadsworth*

HOLLOWAY, MARGARET. 1807. Waynesville, O. 8 yrs. 18″ x 18″. Cross-stitch. Birds and roses in border. At top of sampler, "Waynesville School," and beneath two baskets of fruit and blue paraquet on small flower-pot. At bottom, four conventional designs, resembling houses with vines over them. Verse 704.   *Mrs. Charles R. Miller*

HOLLYDAY, ANNA MARIA. [1814. "Radcliffe" near Easton, Md.] 9 yrs. [Born in 1805.] 16½″ x 16½″. Alphabet. Cross, stem, eyelet, French knot, queen, tent, and double cat-stitch. Strawberry border. In center at bottom, bird on tree in wreath of roses, and on either side, basket of flowers with bird flying over. Verse 693.   *Clara G. Hollyday*

HOLMAN, ——. [Cir. 1814.] 13″ x 14″. 3 alphabets. Stem, satin, and cross-stitch. Vine and flower border on three sides. Tomb, willow tree, and two smaller trees at bottom. "Sacred to the memory of Polly Holman who died May 31, 1814, aet. 24." Verse 289 (1).   *Mrs. Thomas A. Lawton*

HOLMAN, ASENETH. 1804. 10 yrs. 11½″ x 21″. 2 alphabets. Cross-stitch. Conventional design in border. Trees and birds in two rows. "Teach us to live."   *Lancaster Public Library*

HOLMAN, ASENETH. [1806.] 12 yrs. 15″ x 18″. 2 alphabets. Fine cross-stitch. Border of vine and flowers. Verse 274.   *Lancaster Public Library*

HOMER, ALMIRA. [1826.] Boston. 24″ x 18″. Satin and cross-stitch, also slanting-stitch used for dividing lines. Rose border, saw-tooth border. "The family record of Eleazer and Mary Homer. Eleazer Homer born March 22, 1761; Mary Bartlett born Jan. 8th, 1770. Eleazer Homer and Mary Bartlett married Nov. 12, 1786."

"Names	Births	Marriages	Deaths
Jacob Homer	Aug. 18, 1787.	Aug. 13, 1816.	Sept. 10, 1829.
Eleazer Homer	Mar. 6, 1789.		Sept. 18, 1795.
Mary C. Homer	Apr. 21, 1790.	Jan. 8, 18—	
Sarah M. Homer	June 17, 1792.	July 27, 1814.	
Harriet Homer	July 16, 1794.	May 26, 1816.	
Eleazer Homer 2nd	June 28, 1796.	June 8, 1828.	
Eliza B. Homer	Sept. 16, 1798.	June 1st, 1821.	
Abraham B. Homer	Oct. 18, 1800.	Dec. 2, 1821.	
William F. Homer	Nov. 12, 1802.	Sept. 1, 1831.	
James B. Homer	Sept. 16, 1804.	Apr. 14, 1833.	
Henry Homer	Jan. 24, 1807.		
Charles S. Homer	Mar. 7, 1809.		
Almira	Aug. 1, 1811.		Oct. 26, 1811.
Almira	Oct. 26, 1812."		

Grenville Norcross, Esq.

HOMER, SALLY S. 1804. 6 yrs. 7½″ x 17½″. 2 alphabets. Cross-stitch. Scroll border. Trees and a flower-pot.   *Sold at Libbie's, Boston*

HOOPER, ELIZABETH. 1814. Marblehead [Mass.]. 10 yrs. 12″ x 15½″. 2 alphabets. Cross and hem-stitch. Vine and carnation border. Verse 445.   *Mrs. C. G. Betton*

HOPKINS, ELIZA. 1810. 17″ x 15½″. 2 alphabets. Stem, satin, and cross-stitch. Vine, straw-berry, carnation, and rose border on top and sides; conventional flower in vase in each lower corner and tiny trees in between. Verse 504.   *Mrs. Miles White, Jr.*

PLATE LVII

SARAH YEAKEL'S SAMPLER. 1806
Owned by Mrs. Henry E. Coe

PLATE LVIII

ANN SOPHIA BECKWITH'S SAMPLER. 1829
The Emma B. Hodge Collection

HOPKINS, SARAH. 1816. [Baltimore, Md.] Born December 8, 1805. 10 yrs., 4 mos. 18¼" x 17". 3 alphabets. Satin, stem, eyelet, and cross-stitch. Floral border outside and saw-tooth design on inside. Verse 515 (var.). *Miss Fanny G. Crenshaw*

HORNER, SUSANNA. 1830. 16 yrs. 18" x 24". 6 alphabets. Eyelet, satin, and cross-stitch. Rose border. Basket of flowers across top with birds above it. Little dog in alphabet row. House, weeping willows, lambs, and dog. On right of house, 2 turtle doves inclosed in octagon surmounted with vase of strawberries and columbine. On left of house, swan floating on water and a vase of flowers near by. Bowl of flowers. Names and dates: "Susanna Horner, Daughter of Elijah Horner and Elizabeth his wife, was born in the year 1814." Verse 337. *Mrs. I. Oakford Acton*

HORSFUL, REBECCA. 1814. Allentown [N. J.]. About 12 yrs. 10" x 17½". 4 alphabets. Eyelet and cross-stitch. Vine border. *Hannah S. Cook*

HORTON, MARY ELIZABETH. 1815. Newburyport [Mass.]. 9 yrs. 9½" x 8". 3 alphabets. Eyelet, satin, and cross-stitch. Cross-borders. *Mrs. Eben Bradbury*

[HORWELL, ANN. 1819. Alexandria, Va. Made for her sister, Sarah May Horwell, on her marriage in 1819.] Petit-point and cross-stitch. Tulip and strawberry border; cross and trefoil borders at top and bottom. Scattered flowers, hearts, baskets, etc. "An emblem of love." *Miss Frances H. Massoletti*

HORWELL, SARAH M[AY]. 1807. Alexandria [Va.]. 8 yrs. 9½" x 15". 5 alphabets. Tapestry, four-sided line-stitch, rope, star, queen, and cross-stitch. Cross-stitch border. Strawberry cross-border. Verse 702. *Miss Frances H. Massoletti*

[HORWELL, SARAH MAY. Before 1819. Alexandria, Va.] 16" x 19". Petit-point, stem, tent, satin, and cross-stitch. Tulip border. Trees, flowers, vines, baskets, etc. *Miss Frances H. Massoletti*

HOSMER, ELIZABETH JANE. 1828. Cross-stitch. Narrow conventional outside border, and rose and vine border on inside. Picture of "City Hall," New York City, and grounds. Above building and repeated on either side: "EDUCATION." "It is a companion which no misfortunes can depress, no clime destroy, no enemy alienate, no despotism enslave. At home a friend, abroad an introduction, in Solitude a Solace and in Society an ornament. It chastens vice, it guides virtue it gives at once a grace and government to genius." Illustrated. *Mrs. Arthur Curtis James*

HOUSTOON, ELIZA. 1819. 3 alphabets. Eyelet and cross-stitch. Simple cross-border designs. *Communicated by Mrs. A. A. Lawrence*

H[OWARD], C[AROLINE] B[LANCHE] and J[ULIANA] W[EST]. 1808. [About 11 and 10 yrs., respectively.] "Sherwood" [Baltimore, Md.]. 22" x 17". 3 alphabets. Cat, stem, cross, and other stitches. Row of cat and cross-stitch combined for border. Various objects such as chairs, birds, cats, crowns, trees, flowers, etc. Family initials. *Miss Victoria Elisabeth Gittings*

HOWARD, ELIZABETH. 1824. 8 yrs. 8" x 9". 3 alphabets. Eyelet, French knot, and cross-stitch. Small flower designs. *Wilbur M. Stone, Esq.*

Howe, Charlotte. 1818. 11 yrs. 16" x 17". Cross-stitch. Strawberry border. Trees, stars, and baskets of flowers.

"Family Register"

"William Howe Born Nov. 15, th 17—
Abigail Crosby born May 27, th 1762(59)
were married Nov. 2, 1780

Sally	born August 8, th A. D. 1782	George	born April 9, th A. D. 1795
Nancy	" Nov. 5, th A. D. 1784	Amos	" April 2, th A. D. 1797
Jabez	" Feb.ry 5, th A. D. 1787	Francis	" March 14, th A. D. 1799
Otis	" Oct.r 27, th A. D. 1788	Oliver	" August 22, th A. D. 1801
Otis C.	" June 26, th A. D. 1790	Charlotte	" Sept. 17, th A. D. 1804
William	" Nov.r 20, th A. D. 1792	Charlotte A.	" Jan. 18, th A. D. 1807

Mrs. Abigail Howe Obt. Feb. 14th, 1816. Otis Obt. Mar. 15, 1790. Charlotte Obt. Sept. 19, 1708."

Mrs. Wolcott Howe Johnson

Howe, Emiramcy. 1821. Vernon, Vt. 12 yrs. 10" x 14". 4 alphabets. Cross-stitch. Chain design in border. Small trees and fancy motifs. "Win gold and wear it."

Mrs. Hiram W. Moore

Howe, Louisa. 1816. Strawberry border. Trees. *Miss Abbott*

Howe, Sally G[edney]. 1807. 2 alphabets. *Miss Abbott*

Hugg, Eliza. 1806. Camden [N. J.]. 12 yrs. 8" x 18". 3 alphabets. Eyelet and cross-stitch. Strawberry and vine border. Across bottom, grass and picket fence; woman and dog in front; tree and shrubs in back. *Mrs. Joseph W. Merritt*

Hugg, Lucy. 1806. Camden [N. J.]. 10 yrs. 8¼" x 18". Eyelet and cross-stitch. Vine and strawberry border on three sides; cedar trees in top corners. Grass, picket fence, dog, trees, flowering shrubs, and vine with flowers. *Mrs. Ella P. Housell*

Huggins, Sally. 1809. Granby [Conn. 9 yrs. Born at Branford, Conn., February 2, 1800.]. 12" x 12". 3 alphabets. Cross-stitch. Cross-border. Verse 711.

Herbert M. Lloyd, Esq.

Hughes, Mary Ann. 1825. Cape May. 12 yrs. 16½" x 15½". 3 alphabets. Outline, eyelet, queen, and cross-stitch. Strawberry and vine border. At bottom, jars of flowers and honeysuckle vine. "Daughter of James Hughes and Tryphena his wife was born Sept. 20th in the yr of our Lord 1813." Verse 564. *Miss Tryphena Blake*

H[ughes], M[ary] V. [1821.] Greenwich School. 8" x 16½". 3 alphabets. Eyelet, stem, tent, cat, queen, and cross-stitch. Strawberry and vine border.

Miss Helen Botsford Clark

Hughes, Rosana. 1824. Germantown. 13 yrs. 22" x 21". Queen, chain, stem, and cross-stitch. Carnation and strawberry border. 2 dogs and a basket. *Mr. Charles Willing*

Hull, Evelina. 1806. Charlestown [Mass.]. 10 yrs. 16½" x 16½". 1 alphabet. Cross, satin, and tent-stitch. Hemstitched edge. Vine border with large flowers. Verse 695.

Mrs. Joshua M. Van Cott

Humphrey, Lucy. 1800. Weymouth [Mass.]. Born December 31, 1789. 7½" x 12½". 2 alphabets. Chain and cross-stitch. Cross-stitch borders. Dove in center with flower-pot on each side. *Mrs. Susan C. Humphrey*

HUMPHREY, R. 1807. 7½″ x 9¾″. 2 alphabets. Eyelet and cross-stitch. Strawberry border at bottom. *Pennsylvania Museum, Memorial Hall, Fairmount Park*

HUMPHREYS, ELIZA [Elizabeth, from family record.]. 1807. Sharptown [Salem County, N. J. 11 yrs. Born February 3, 1796.]. 8″ x 10″. Satin and cross-stitch. Vine border. Upper part of sampler filled in with floral designs, birds, and little dogs; lower half filled in with stars, birds, baskets of flowers, and cornucopia filled with flowers.
Miss M. Elizabeth Hilliard

HUNNEWELL, CAROLINE E. 1826. 13 yrs. 17″ x 17″. 3½ alphabets. Stem, satin, and cross-stitch. Two garlands of flowers meeting at top, and below, simple arch supported by columns; grapevine runs across from tops of columns, dividing alphabets from " Family Register." Names and dates: " Mr. William Hunnewell Born Sept. 28th 1782; Mrs. Anna Hunnewell Born May 8th 1787; Married Apr 6 1809. Sarah A. Hunnewell Born March 5th 1810; Caroline E. Hunnewell Born June 12th 1813; Harriot C. Hunnewell Born June 17th 1816; Susan M. Hunnewell Born June 1st 1820." *Mrs. Henry E. Coe*

HUNT, ELIZA ANN. 1824. 9 yrs. 17″ x 15½″. 4 alphabets. Split, back, stem, satin, and cross-stitch. Simple conventional border. Across bottom, row of single strawberries and strawberry plants. In lower left-hand corner, house with fence in front and 6 trees; in lower right-hand corner, large willow tree drooping over tombstone with inscription, " Sacred to the memory of Mrs. Eliza Hunt who died Jan. 6, 1817; Mrs. Sarah Hunt died Sept. 28, 1823." Two large rose sprays on either side of three hearts twined together inclosing inscriptions, " Reuben Hunt bn Jan. 11, 1783; Eliza Tuft bn June 27, 1788; Sarah Snow bn Dec. 14, 1785; Married to E T Oct. 27, 1814; to S S March 10, 1819." Below, " Eliza A. Hunt bn Sept 20 1815; Reuben Hunt Jr bn Dec. 19 1816; Sarah Hunt bn Feb 8 1820; Martha A. Hunt bn Nov 7 1822. Sacred to the memory of Mrs. Eliza Hunt who died Jan 6 1817. Mrs. Sarah Hunt died Sep. 26, 1823." Verse 515 (var.).
Mrs. Henry E. Coe

HUNT, MARIA L. 1814. 10 yrs. [Date said to have been pulled out and reworked later to make Maria appear younger.] 14″ x 12½″. 3 alphabets. Cross-stitch. Greek fret, strawberry, and carnation cross-borders. Large house, bird, vase, tree, flowering plant, and small animal. Verse 515 (var.). *Albert C. Bates, Esq.*

HUNT, SARAH. 1804. [1804. Salem?] 9 yrs. 18″ x 22″. 1 alphabet. Stem, satin, and cross-stitch. Floral and vine border. Flowers from a satin-stitch base. *Miss M. E. Stanley*

HUNT, SARAH. 1812. Woodstown [N. J.]. 13 yrs. 16¾″ x 21¾″. Queen, satin, flat, and cross-stitch. Border of Greek fret, rosebuds, leaves, and carnations. Upper half, star, large spray of carnations. Another spray in a cornucopia, strawberry plant, baskets of fruit and flowers, birds, trees, etc. Lower half, names and dates: " William, January 14th, 1761; Mary Hunt, April 15th, 1774; Margaret Hunt, January th 1st, 1798; Sarah Hunt, Nov. 6th, 1799; Jacob Hunt, November 16th, 1801; William Hunt, June 20th, 1804; Mary Hunt, January 7th, 1807; Eliza Hunt, June 11th, 1809; James B. Hunt, William Hunt, March 17th, 1811." *Mrs. Sarah Hunt Bridgman*

HUNT, SARAH ANN. 1818. Providence [R. I.]. 13 yrs. 15½″ x 17″. 2 alphabets. Stem, satin, and cross-stitch. Border at bottom of vine, trees, and strawberry. Trees. Verse 759. *Irene Borden Butler*

HUNTINGTON, ANN M. 1824. New London [Conn.]. 11 yrs. 7¼″ x 10½″. 4 alphabets. Cross-stitch. Trees and vines at bottom. Cross-borders. *Mary Saltonstall Hebard*

HUNTINGTON, ANNA. Feb. 1816. Snowdon Hill, New Hartford [Conn.]. "Worked at Miss L. P. Mott's School." 14″ x 14″. 3 alphabets. Cross-stitch. Herringbone-stitch in border. Verse 87a. *Miss Cornelia Horsford*

HUNTINGTON, CATHERINE. 1807. 9 yrs. 9¾″ x 14½″. 2 alphabets. Great variety of stitches. Buttonholed edge, with vine and flowers on sides. Turkey work in gay colors at bottom. "Honor thy Father and thy Mother that thy days may be long upon the land which the Lord thy God giveth thee." *Miss Cornelia Horsford*

HUNTINGTON, FRANCES. 1807. 7 yrs. 11¼″ x 9¾″. 2 alphabets. Cross-stitch and turkey-stitch. Outer border in cross-stitch and inner border in turkey work. Alphabets and numerals inclosed in heart-shaped design. Turkey work at top. Sprays of roses on each side. Border patterns. "Be religious, be virtuous, be industrious and be happy." *Miss Cornelia Horsford*

HUNTINGTON, GLORIANA. "June 25, 1818. Miss Orpha Crane's School, Rome." 10¾″ x 16″. 4 alphabets. Tent and cross-stitch. Border, two rows of herringbone-stitch. Edge bound with green ribband mounted on paper. "Let Virtue be a guide to thee." Verses 617 (var.), 756. *Miss Cornelia Horsford*

HUNTINGTON, LUCY. 1818. "Miss Orpha Crane's School, Rome." 10¾″ x 16″. 4 alphabets. Bound with green silk ribband. Two rows of herringbone-stitch all around. Tent and cross-stitch. Verse 202. *Miss Cornelia Horsford*

HUNTINGTON, NANCY. July 8, 1814. 8½″ x 9″. 2 alphabets. Cross-stitch. Simple border. House, barn, and man on horseback. *Mrs. H. C. Bunner*

HUSE, JOANNA. 10 yrs. "Under the tuition of Maria S. Aiken." 18″ x 15″. 4 alphabets. Satin and cross-stitch. Saw-tooth border all around and cross-borders. *Frederick W. Huse, Esq.*

HUTCHINS, PERSIS. Oct. 4, 1814. Bath [N. H.]. 13 yrs. 17″ x 17½″. 5 alphabets. Eyelet, stem, and cross-stitch. Vine border. Two trees. Verse 94 (var.). *Mrs. Edward W. Hutchins*

HUTTON, ELIZABETH HELEN. February 18, 1823. [New York City.] 10 yrs. 7¼″ x 8″. 2 alphabets. Cross-stitch. Hemstitched edge. Strawberries at bottom. "Great minds conquer difficulties by daring to attempt them." *Mrs. H. H. Colburn*

HYDE, ELIZABETH A. H. 1812. 17½″ x 20″. 4 alphabets. Cushion, long and short and cross-stitch. Double border, geometric and floral. Strawberry panel around verse; two flower urns and tablet. Verse 438. *The Emma B. Hodge Collection*

HYDE, MARY. 180–. 10 yrs. 17″ x 20″. 4 alphabets. Eyelet and cross-stitch. Carnation and strawberry border. Strawberry vine around verse. Verse 162. *Mrs. Thomas A. Lawton*

HYDE, MARY K. [Cir. 1828.] 9 yrs. [Born 1817.] 11½″ x 17″. Cross-stitch. Strawberry border, top and sides. Verse 793. *Miss Mary Frances Bigelow*

HYDE, SARAH. 1813. 10 yrs. 16″ x 20″. 4 alphabets. Petit-point and cross-stitch. Strawberry border outside and carnation border inside, around three sides. Conventional border around verse. Baskets of flowers. Verse 443. *Mrs. Thomas A. Lawton*

IDE, NABBY KOLLOCK. July 16, 1804. Wrentham. 14 yrs. 12½″ x 17″. 2 alphabets. Cross-stitch. Hemstitched edge, with strawberry border. "Embroidery decks the canvas round and yields a pleasing view, so virtue tends to deck the mind and form its blissful state." At the bottom in cross-stitch is the following : "Nabby K. Ide died December the 5th 1813. Aged 23 yrs. Mrs. Mary I. Wheaton died July 28th 1817." *Miss Alice W. Hunt*

ISLEY, ANN. 1810. Newburyport. 11 yrs. 17½″ x 18½″. 3 alphabets. Eyelet, satin, and cross-stitch. Strawberry and Greek fret border. Verses and trees unfinished.

Ipswich Historical Society

INGRAHAM, MARY A. 1811. 12 yrs. 9″ x 10″. 3 alphabets. Chain and cross-stitch.

Clarence A. Mathewson, Esq.

INGRAM, MARILLA S. 1825. Amherst [Mass.]. 11 yrs. 3 alphabets. Strawberry border. Columns with drapery between; two baskets of flowers. Verses 124, 326. " The liberal Arts and Sciences are seven: Grammar, Logic, Rhetoric, Arithmetic, Geometry, Music." " Important branches of a polite Education: Botany, Chemistry, History, Philosophy, Mineralogy, Drawing, Painting." " Mr. John Ingram was born May 28, 1788; Miss Lucy Hubbard born April 11, 1788; married Feb. 4, 1813. Marilla Sophia born Jan 18, 1814; Cordelia Maria born Jan 15, 1815; Austin born Feb. 27, 1818; died March 2, 1819; Harrison born April 8, 1820. Mrs. Ingram died June 28, 1822."

Frederick Smith Richards, Esq.

IRWIN, ELIZABETH. 1814. 14 yrs. 8″ x 17″. Alphabets. Cross-stitch. Cross-stitch line-border. Verse 444. *Mrs. George L. Miner*

IVINS, EMMELINE. July 4, 1823. Mechanicks Town. 12 yrs. 22″ x 21″. Queen, chain, and cross-stitch. Strawberry border. At bottom, house, fence, trees, barn, dogs, and birds. Large basket of flowers between verses at top, and conventional baskets of fruit with birds and animals on either side of third verse. Verses 468, 591 (var.).

Mrs. Henry E. Coe

J——, A. C. 1820. Charleston [S. C.]. 11″ x 13″. 3 alphabets. Eyelet and cross-stitch. Simple border. At bottom, church, parish house, and trees. Detached designs of baskets of flowers, vase of flowers, lion, dog, andiron, windmill, woman, cradle, chair, etc.

Mrs. George Moffett

JACKMAN, EMILY E. December 21. Yorkshire, Cattaraugus County, N. Y. 12 yrs. 10¾″ x 12¼″. 3 alphabets and the vowels. House with green blinds, tree, fence, etc.

A. Stainforth, Dealer

JACKSON, SARAH DUBOIS. 1811. Rockaway, N. J. 11 yrs. 10″ x 15″. 3 alphabets. Stem, satin, and cross-stitch. Simple cross-stitch border. Medallion in cross-stitch, also medallions in stem-stitch and in strawberry design. Strawberry vine below. Verse 728.

Mrs. F. R. Kellogg

JACOBS, ELIZABETH CUTLER. 1817. 7 yrs. 17″ x 17″. 4 alphabets. Cross, stem, and satin-stitch. Rose border. Verse 387 (1). *Mrs. Robert C. Root*

JANVIER, MARY FRIES. 1828. Pittsgrove [Salem County, N. J.]. 10 yrs. 13″ x 18″. 5 alphabets. Vine and strawberry border. Flower baskets, strawberry plant, little birds, and various conventional designs. Verse 486. *Miss Louise Janvier*

JANVIER, MARY GAW. 1824. [Wilmington, Del.] " Wilmington Boarding School." 13 yrs. 10″ x 12″. *Miss Mary F. Janvier*

JAQUES, ANNA. 1810. Newbury [Mass.]. 10 yrs. 8½″ x 8½″. 2 alphabets. Cross-stitch. Simple border. *Mrs. W. O. Downs*

JAQUES, ANNA. 1812. [Newbury, Mass.] 12 yrs. 13″ x 18½″. Satin, French knot, and cross-stitch. Floral border all around, starting from vase in center at bottom, and in lower corners. Row of trees and baskets of fruit at base. Vines cross sampler in center. Verses 114, 298. "Enoch Jaques born February 13th, 1763; Joanna Plumer born June 18th, 1768; Married February 9th, 1797; Their children, Joseph born September 22, 1798;

Anna born May 8th, 1800; Enoch born January 19th, 1802; Eliza born July 11th, 1804."

Mrs. W. W. Downs

JAQUES, EUNICE. [Cir. 1805.] Newbury, Mass. [Born in 1795.] 8½" x 13". Partial alphabets. Eyelet, satin, and cross-stitch. Cross-border. Two trees with urn in center. Verse 617 (var.). *Mrs. David T. Woodwell*

JARRETT, ALICE. 1810. Jarrettown, Pa. Worked at West Town Boarding School. 10½" x 13". Flat, outline, stem, and cross-stitch. Vine border. "From purity of thought all pleasure springs and from an humble spirit all our peace." Verse 723. *Mrs. William Stokes*

JARVIS, ELIZABETH HART. Before 1816. 10 yrs. 18" x 17". 3 alphabets. Cross-stitch. Double strawberry border. Verses 115, 450. *Mrs. Thomas A. Lawton*

JEFFERIS, ANN. 1804. West Chester, Pa. 11 yrs. 17" x 19½". Cross and over-and-over stitch. Rosebuds and vine on sides, and conventionalized carnations across top and bottom. Conventionalized pine and willow trees, vases and baskets of flowers, wreath of flowers, basket of fruit with birds nibbling at it, and fragment of tulip border fill in spaces across top and bottom, sides, center, etc., between verses. "My Parents Jacob Jefferis & Elizabeth; My Brother & Sisters Joseph Sarah Hannah & Rachel Jefferis; My GrandParents James Jefferis & Ann Joseph Coope & Ann." Verses 132 (1, var.), 226 (var.), 536. *F. F. Sharpless, Esq.*

JENKS, LYDIA. 1802. Born May 13, 1793. 8" x 17½". 4 alphabets. Eyelet, chain, satin, stem, long, short, and cross-stitch. Hemmed edge on two sides and two rows of cross-stitch all around. Elaborate design; house, large trees, strawberries and blossoms, etc. Verse 401 (1). *Mrs. Harrison F. Hunt*

JEWETT, ELIZABETH. 1805. [Elm Street, Northampton, Mass.] 9 yrs. 11" x 12". Alphabet. Satin and cross-stitch. Strawberry border. Trees, flowers, and animals. Verse 687.

Mrs. George D. Jewett

JEWETT, HITTY JANE. 1818. Newburyport, Mass. 9 yrs. 17" x 18". 5 alphabets. Eyelet, chain, satin, and cross-stitch. Broad base in satin-stitch; vine on each side and between alphabets. "The family of William and Hitty Hobson Jewett. William Jewett born Aug. 13, 1773. Hitty H. Dole, June 15, 1778. Married 1797. William Jewett, Feb. 21, 1798. Clarissa Jewett, Sept. 29, 1803. Mary A. Jewett, June 14, 1807. Ebenezer Jewett, Jan. 31, 1808. Hitty Jane Jewett, April 20, 1809." *Lucius H. Greely, Esq.*

JOHNSON, ELIZA R. 11" x 13½". 2 alphabets. Eyelet and cross-stitch. Vine border. Verse 798. *Pennsylvania Museum, Memorial Hall, Fairmount Park*

JOHNSON, FANNY. June 8, 1823. Hollis. 12 yrs. 18" x 19". 6 alphabets, not complete. Eyelet, stem, satin, and cross-stitch. Rose border with bunches of grapes in each corner. Across bottom, house, fence, and 4 trees. Wreaths around name, age, and "Sweet is the counsel of a friend." *Mrs. Henry E. Coe*

JOHNSON, LUCY ANN. Oct. 8, 1822. 11 yrs. 17¼" x 11¼". 4 alphabets. Cross-stitch. Three houses separated by trees and bushes. "Connecticut bounded north by Massachusetts east by Rhode Island south by Long Island Sound west by New York."

Rhode Island School of Design

JOHNSON, LYDIA. 1819. Salem [Mass.]. 9 yrs. 8" x 8". 2 alphabets. Cross-stitch. "Love Learning." "Wrought at L. Johnson's School." *Mrs. Davis P. Coffin*

JOHNSON, SALLY. 1813. 13 yrs. 14" x 17". 2 alphabets. Satin and cross-stitch. Border of conventional squares. Flowers at bottom. "The names and births of Mr. William and Mrs. Lucy Johnson's children. Lucy born April 17, 1791; Rebecca born May 16, 1793;

Nancy Platt's Work 1804

PLATE LIX

NANCY PLATT'S SAMPLER. Wrightstown, N. J. 1804
Owned by Miss Fanny Lippincott

PLATE LX

BETTY BRIERLEY'S SAMPLER.   1826
Owned by Mrs. Renwick C. Hurry

Sally born Feb. 29, 1796 and died Nov. 21, 1800; William born March 2, 1798; Sally born Jan. 2, 1801; Mary born July 22, 1804 and died June 20, 1807; Eliza born Feb. 4, 1807 and died Feb. 2, 1811; Urania born July 12, 1810; Harriet born April 23, 1813. In memory of the three sisters." Verse 300. *Mrs. Thomas A. Lawton*

JOHNSTON, ELIZA S[USANNA]. 1809. Boston [Mass. Born December 12, 1800.]. 9 yrs. 13″ x 17½″. 3 alphabets. Stem and cross-stitch. Border of roses and carnations. Verse 284. *William E. Barnard, Esq.*

JOHNSTON, ELIZA S[USANNA]. 1809. Boston [Mass. Born December 12, 1800.]. 9 yrs. 12″ x 12″. 3 alphabets. Cross-stitch. Strawberry border without leaves. Basket of flowers, shrubs, trees, and bird. *William E. Barnard, Esq.*

JOHNSTON, JANE E. 1827. [New Hartford, Oneida County, N. Y.] 9 yrs. 11⅝″ x 12¼″. 4 alphabets. Cross-stitch. Strawberry border on sides and across top. The background of the sampler is entirely filled in with cross-stitch. *Mrs. Amos Bush McNairy*

JOLLEY, ELIZABETH. 1824. 25½″ x 22″. Stem and cross-stitch. Carnation border and cross-border. In upper section, small basket of fruit and vines in center, with large basket of flowers on either side. In lower section, brick house, fence, three willow trees, lawn, sheep, birds, flowers growing in grass, man and woman, with large spray of roses between them, etc. *Mrs. H. de Berkely Parsons*

JONES, ABIGAIL GREENLIEF. 1806. North Yarmouth [Mass.]. 10 yrs. 18″ x 24″. Satin and cross-stitch. Vine border on sides, with a few rosebuds on one side. " The Genealogy Of David and Elizabeth Jones of North Yarmouth. David Jones born at Wrentham March 21, 1748; Elizabeth Hobart at Abington Feb 6 1761. Married at Abington January 26 A D 1778.

> Mary Jones born at Abington Nov 7 1778.
> Jacob H. Jones born at Abington March 6 1780.
> Elizabeth Jones born at N. Yarmouth Jan 17 1784.
> Sarah Jones born at N. Yarmouth Oct 18 1785.
> David Jones born at N. Yarmouth Aug 11 1788.
> Esther B. Jones born at N. Yarmouth Oct 2 1790.
> A Son born December 28 1793 lived 36 hours.
> A Son born December 25 1794 lived 18 hours.
> Abigail C. Jones at N. Yarmouth Sept 29 1795.
> Elias Jones born at N. Yarmouth Nov 30 1799.
> Jane T. Jones born at N. Yarmouth Jan 8 1805.
> Executed by Abigail Greenlief Jones aged 10-
> Northyarmouth September 6 AD 1806. [years."

Mrs. George McLauchlan

JONES, ELIZA PEARCE. [Cir. 1810.] Providence, R. I. [Miss Polly Balch's School.] 10″ x 16″. 3 alphabets. Eyelet, queen, tent, and cross-stitch. Strawberry border. Cross-borders with flowers, sheep, trees, strawberries, dog, etc. Verse 721.

Mrs. William J. Dyer

JONES, HANNAH. 1801. Cross, eyelet, and satin-stitch. Border of hearts and flowers. " May Liberty Peace and Prosperity Ever Prevail in America." *Mrs. John Emerson*

JONES, HANNAH B. 1824. 9 yrs. 16″ x 16″. 4 alphabets. Cat, eyelet, stem, satin, cross, and hem-stitch. Greek fret and trefoil borders on three sides, hemstitched edge. Three-story house with a tree on either side. *Albert Harrison Hall, Esq.*

JONES, HARRIET. 1802. 10 yrs. 18″ x 20″. Stem, satin, long and short, tapestry, petit-point, French knot, and cross-stitch. Rose vine on two sides; upper corners, angels with trumpets; at bottom, two trees and tombstone with four urns on top; tomb has names inscribed on it as follows: "In Memory of Samuel D. Jones, Cary D. Jones, William W. Jones, And Sophia Jones." In center, an arch supported by three columns, dove perched on central column and two other birds flying about. Family Register of William Jones between columns, as follows:

"William and Ann Jones were Married in Boston Feb. 28, 1796, in the Evening by the Rev. Samuel Parker, D.D.

Samuel Dunn Jones their first Child was born July 1, 1787.
    And died April 17 1789. Aged 21 months.
Cary Dunn Jones, their second Child was born July 13, 1791.
    And died the 22. Aged 9 days.
Harriet Jones their third child was born June 14, 1792.
Elizabeth Pearce Jones their fourth child was born August 19, 1794.
William Washington Jones their fifth child was born Dec. 30 1796.
    And died May 29, 1799. Aged 2 years and 6 Months.
Sophia Jones their sixth child was born March 8, 1801.
    And died Feb. 16, 1802. Aged 11 months and seven days."

Verse 251.   *Mrs. William J. Dyer*

JONES, MARCY H. 1810. Charlestown [Mass.]. 11 yrs. 17¼″ x 21½″. 4 alphabets. Cross-stitch. Vine border. "Modesty is an ornament to the female sex." Verse 29 (1).
                                                            Miss Sarah M. Draper

JONES, MARTHA MELVINA MILLEDGE. 1810. Louisville [Ky.]. 9 yrs. 6 alphabets. Eyelet and cross-stitch. Strawberry border. Conventional design across bottom. Verse 511 (var.). "Taught by Mrs. Mary Scott at Louisville."
                                                    Communicated by Mrs. A. A. Lawrence

JONES, MARY ANN. 1814. Vincentown [N. J.]. 11″ x 15″. Alphabets. Blanket and cross-stitch. Simple border. Conventional bush with flowers.   *Mary Irick Drexel*

JONES, SALLY. 1804. Wrentham [Mass.]. 9 yrs. "I was born March 21, 1795." 8″ x 4½″. 1 alphabet. Cross-stitch.   *Mrs. W. S. Kimball*

KAY, HENRIETTA. 1816. [Born near Haddonfield. Greenville School.] 18″ x 13″. Satin and cross-stitch. Rose border at sides and strawberry border across top. Elaborate tree, flowers, and bird in bush. Verses 409, 451.   *Miss Helen Moore Fogg*

KAY, FAMILY AND GENEALOGY. [Cir. 1809.] 23″ x 22″. Eyelet, stem, satin, and cross-stitch. Rose border at sides and strawberry border across top. Elaborate scene with white animals, sheep, dogs, cow, rising from green base, with foliage and white flowers. Verses 488 (var.), 543. In a square in center is the following: "M Wood   R Thom   Ages of Josiah and Elizabeth Kay and their children. Josiah Kay was born the 2nd mo 12th 1751. Elizabeth Kay born the 5th mo 5th 1771. Martha S. Kay born 3rd mo 11th 1787. Ann T. Kay born the 10th mo 21st 1791. Elizabeth H. Kay born the 1st mo 7th 1794. Henrietta Kay born the 3rd mo 26th 1805. 1809   E Heulings S Heulings M Ba(?)   E Wood."   *Miss Helen Moore Fogg*

KEEN, PALMYRA M. 1824. 11 yrs. 3 alphabets. Cross-stitch. Strawberry border across bottom. In lower half, large grapevine, church, barn, two houses, various kinds of trees, and initials "J M K." Verses 206, 279, 325a.   *(Owner ?)*

KEIGLE, SARAH. [Cir. 1809.] Carlyle, Pa. Born in 1796. 10" x 17". 3½ alphabets. Eyelet and cross-stitch. Chain design in border. Narrow cross-borders. *William D. Pratt, Esq.*

KEITH, DEBORAH. 1810. Grafton [Mass.]. 11 yrs. 17" x 17½". 2 alphabets. Satin, stem, chain, and cross-stitch. Rose and carnation border on three sides, and at bottom a basket with vine. Verse 112. *Miss Emma A. Taft*

KELCEY, CAROLINE. 1814. "Huntington Academy." 8½" x 12½". 2 alphabets. Cat and cross-stitch. Strawberry border. At bottom, picture of Huntington Academy and church. Verse 743. *Mrs. Stanley H. Lowndes*

KELLEY, MARY ANN. July 31, 1826. Portland [Me.]. 11 yrs. 13½" x 15". 3 alphabets. Chain, flat, satin, stem, and cross-stitch. Greek fret border with flowers in between. Trees and birds. *Mrs. J. H. Kimball*

KELLY, ANN E. 1825. 11 yrs. 18" x 18". Chain, buttonhole, satin, and cross-stitch. Border made up of series of squares containing different designs, such as birds, sheep, sprays of flowers, strawberries, bunches of wheat, etc. In center, woman with garland of flowers in her hands standing beside pedestal; pitcher at her feet; her face is painted and inserted under the muslin. Border of wheat sprays around this picture. In one of the lower squares is the inscription: "Ann E. Kelly was born in Halifax April 20 in the year of our Lord 1814 and made this sampler in Mrs. Leah Meguier's School in Harrisburg January 21, 1826." "O may the Lord instil good principles in me and make me a good and faithful servant." Illustrated. *Mrs. Henry E. Coe*

KELLY, DORCAS A. 1830. Men[don, Mass.]. 11 yrs. 16" x 17". Cross, satin, stem, and a very close cat-stitch. Wide conventionalized strawberry border, with rose sprays in upper corners. Arch supported by columns. Inscription on arch, "Keep Sacred the Memory of thy Ancestors." Family names and dates: "David Kelly Bn. Men. 12 mo. 13, 1781; Amy Comstock Bn. Providence 8 mo. 19, 1788; They were married Men. 1 27 1807. Their childrens Births Deaths Marriages: Eliza A K Born 4 mo. 1 1809; Mar. 10 mo. 20 1821; William A K Born 12 mo 31 1812; Dorcas A K Born 10 mo. 30 1818." Weeping willow tree in center. In lower section between columns, vine with large leaves inclosing verse. Verse 574. *Mrs. Henry E. Coe*

KELTER, CECILIA. 1829. 17 yrs. 25" x 21". Fine cross-stitch. Trefoil and strawberry borders. Large basket of flowers in upper corners. Circle of flowers at top containing name, date, etc. Scene with house, perspective lawn, sheep, rabbits, dogs, men, bushes, trees, flowers, birds on trees, and cornucopias of flowers. *Mrs. Bradbury Bedell*

KEMP, SOPHIA. [Cir. 1800.] 8 yrs. 8¾" x 11¾". 4 alphabets. Herringbone and cross-stitch. Cross-border. *Mrs. William E. Black*

KEMPTON, EMILY MARIA. 1824. Fairhaven [Mass.]. 10 yrs. 5 alphabets. Stem, satin, and cross-stitch. Rose border. Verse 777. "Remember thy Creator."
Old Dartmouth Historical Society

KENDAL, TRYPHENA. 1815. Woodstock, Conn. 12 yrs. 3 alphabets. Cross-stitch. Vine border. Strawberry. Verse 556a. *Edward L. Child, Esq.*

KENDALL, SARAH A. 1810. [Billerica, Mass. ?] 10 yrs. 8" x 10¼". 2 alphabets. Cross-stitch. At top, cross-stitch frame around Verse 617 (1, var.), and on either side a plant in a basket. At bottom, a house, tree on either side and tops of two others showing above roof, and a large spray of flowers in basket at either end. *Mrs. Charles J. White*

KENNEDY, MARY ANN. 1823. Baltimore [Md.]. 9 yrs. 12″ x 21″. Split, chain, cat, tent, stem, satin, cross, queen, and hem-stitch. Verse framed by border of hem-stitching. Strawberry border at bottom. Two-thirds of sampler consists of a town mansion of brick, two stories and a half high; also large weeping willow trees, lawn inclosed by iron fence; outside on walk two neighbors talking together (man and woman), with dog and goose beside them; moth or butterfly between trees. Lower third of sampler contains framed dates, etc., on either side of which are large urns filled with blooming flowers. Verse 23. *Mrs. Hugh P. Mohler*

KENNEDY, REBECCA. 1817. 12½″ x 13½″. 3 alphabets. Cross-stitch. Strawberry tree, birds, lily, and basket of flowers at bottom. *Wilbur M. Stone, Esq.*

KENNEY, ELIZABETH. [Cir. 1808.] "Born May 15, A. D. 1797, North Yarmouth." 12¼″ x 16″. 4 alphabets. Cross-stitch. Simple border. Verse 423. *Elizabeth B. Hutchins*

KENNEY, LYDIA. [Cir. 1815.] 9 yrs. 17½″ x 17″. 3 alphabets. Eyelet, flat, and cross-stitch. Zigzag and moss-rose border. Flowering trees, basket, parrot, dog, and birds. Verse 515 (var.). *The Emma B. Hodge Collection*

KENT, JUDITH. 1809. Cape May. 12 yrs. [Born August 29, 1797.] 12″ x 17″. 3 alphabets. Outline, queen, and cross-stitch. Vine and honeysuckle border. At bottom, pots of flowers. *The Misses Hannah and Jane Smith*

KERLIN, MARGARET. 1801. Burlington. 17½″ x 20½″. Long, tent, and cross-stitch. Carnation border; carnation and strawberry cross-borders. At bottom, house with terraced lawn; willow and pine trees on terraces, birds on trees and on ground; sheep grazing on lawn. Detached sprays of flowers, baskets of flowers, and trees here and there, filling in spaces between verses, etc. Verse 395. Illustrated. *Mrs. Frederick F. Thompson*

KEYES, ELIZABETH. 1806. 14″ x 18″. 2 alphabets. Italian open-work stitch and cross-stitch. Zigzag and clover border. Pine trees and basket of flowers at bottom. Verse 79. *The Emma B. Hodge Collection*

KIBBE, MARGARET. 1806. 17″ x 22″. 3 alphabets. Green linen. Rope, French knot, stem, satin, and cross-stitch. Scene with brick house, well-house, fence, gate, tree, animals, birds, and large grapevine. Verse 698. *Mrs. Thomas A. Lawton*

KIMBALL, LYDIA. 1818. 7 yrs. 10″ x 16½″. 3 alphabets. Satin and cross-stitch. Saw-tooth border. Border at bottom of little pink flowers and leaves. Saw-tooth border around name. Verses 455, 652. "Wrought by her ingenuity and industry in the 8th year of her age by my superintendency N. L." *Mrs. Bradbury Bedell*

KIMBALL, SARAH. 1806. 13 yrs. 11″ x 16″. 3 alphabets. Chain, stem, satin, and cross-stitch. Strawberry border. At bottom, vine and flowers in vase. Verse 538 (var.). *Mrs. Frank Keyes*

KING, EXPERIENCE. 1805. Suffield [Conn.]. 10 yrs. 7½″ x 17″. 3 alphabets. Eyelet, stem, and cross-stitch. Eyelet and stem-stitch border. *Charles L. Spencer, Esq.*

KING, HARRIET. [Cir. 1813.] Boston [Mass. Born in 1801.]. 3 alphabets. Cross-stitch. Conventional border. Verse 272 (var.). *Mrs. M. G. Goodwin*

KINGSBURY, SUSAN. 1811. Walpole [Mass.]. 11″ x 9½″. 2 alphabets. Vine border. Verse 128 (2, var.). *Mrs. George Plimpton*

KIRKLAND, ELIZA. October 13, 1802. 11″ x 9½″. 2 alphabets. Tent and cross-stitch. Plain cross-stitch border. House and small tree at bottom. Verse 677. *Mrs. Stanley H. Lowndes*

KITTREDGE, SALLY. "Sept th 3 1804." Walpole [N. H.]. 10 yrs. Born April 27 [1794]. 11½" x 11½". 2 alphabets. Cross-stitch. Name and dates in border around three sides. Irregular figures across bottom. Small birds at intervals. *Mrs. Francis B. Austin*

KITTREDGE, SARAH. 1811. 10 yrs. 17" x 15". 1 alphabet. Satin and cross-stitch. Elaborate rose border. Basket of roses and tree at bottom. Verse 129 (var.).
Mrs. J. Fred Temple

KNAPP, JULIA. [Cir. 1823.] Stamford. [Born in 1816.] 9" x 11". 3 alphabets. Eyelet and cross-stitch. Cross-stitch border. Verse 41 (var.). Initials "J. aA. K."
Mrs. William H. Walker

KNIGHT, JULIA. 1808. "Pleasant Hill Boarding School." 14½" x 12". 3 alphabets. Cross-stitch. Spray of flowers in each corner. Irregular oval line, with here and there a small leaf inclosing alphabets, name, date, etc. Small wreath on either side of verse, one inclosing a bird and the other the initials "SK and MK." Verse 185.
Mrs. Henry E. Coe

KNIGHT, MARGERET. August 21, 1805. Boscawen [N. H.]. 12½" x 15½". 5 alphabets. Cross and flat-stitch. Saw-tooth border and simple cross-borders. *Owner not recorded*

KNIGHT, MARY L. January 1st, 1830. New Haven [Conn.]. 8 yrs. 18" x 17". 3 alphabets. Cross-stitch. Conventional diamond pattern in border. Flowers and baskets alternating at bottom. Verses 335, 515 (var.). *Mrs. Mary Knight Staples*

KNOWLES, HARRIET. [Cir. 1829.] Eastham. Born July 8, 1816. 17¼" x 7½". 5 alphabets. Eyelet and cross-stitch. Cross and vine border. Stars and hearts. *Mrs. R. Chapman*

LADD, SOPHIA B. July 18, 1827. Haverhill [Mass.]. 7 yrs. 13" x 17". 3 alphabets. Cross, stem, outline, flat, and solid stem-stitch. Floral border. In lower right-hand corner, a tree in full leaf. Verse 329. *Mrs. George Wright Briggs*

LAING, MARTHA. 1810. Verse inclosed in oval with birds at top, and 2 animals drinking from vessel at bottom; in four corners are initials "J L M L P C H C." Initials around outside of oval are "M C P E E C M T L P H W M H A L." Verse 226.
Maxcy Applegate, Esq.

LAIRD, BARBARA L. [Cir. 1807. Georgetown. Born in 1795 at Bladensburg, Md.]. 15½" x 17¼". 5 alphabets. Eyelet, double and single cross-stitch. Rose border. At bottom, vase in center with fuchsia, and vases on either side with roses; terrace with pine trees; bushes on either side with birds. Verse 80. *Mrs. William Laird Dunlop*

LAIRD, MARGARET. [Cir. 1809. Born in 1797 at Bladensburg, Md.] 17" x 18". 5 alphabets. Eyelet and cross-stitch. Rose border. At bottom, 3 vases with flowers and 2 baskets with flowers; above, wreaths with birds. Strawberry vine above verse, with large trees topped by birds on either side of verse and 2 smaller trees below. Verse 274.
Mrs. William Laird Dunlop

LAKE, MARGARET. "May the 1817." "Great Eggharbor School." 2 alphabets. Cross, eyelet, and queen-stitch. Line of stitching across top and bottom. Initials "J L x A x A Jx D M x S x S Ax L J x H L." *Miss S. N. Doughty*

LAKE, FAMILY RECORD. [After 1818.] 1 alphabet. Cross-stitch. Greek fret border. Designs outside of border. Urn of fruit in each corner. Tree on each side and sheaf of wheat on one side. Bird on branch on each lower side. Names and dates "John Lakes wosBorne 21 of December the 1773. Abigail Lake Wos Born 11 of January 1775. Armenia Lake Wos Born 26 of April 1797. John Lake Wos Born the 12 of Jenuary 1799. Aseneth Lake Wos Born the 24 of Dec 1801. Daniel Lake Wos Born the 5 of

May 1803. Margaret Lake Wos Born the 30 of November 1804. Sarah Lake Wos Born the 23 of March 1808. Jesse Lake Wos Born the 16 of December 1810. Simon Lake Wos Born the 3 of September 1813. Lucas Lake Wos Born the 25 of April 1814. David Lake Wos born the 17 of Oct 1818." Verses 343 (1), 800.   *Miss S. N. Doughty*

LAMBERSON, CATHERINE. 1803. Jamaica, Long Island. 10 yrs. 7½" x 11½". 3 alphabets. Eyelet and cross-stitch. Eyelet border across bottom.   *Mrs. C. E. W. McDonald*

LAMBERT, HANNAH D. 1812. "North-School, Philadelphia." [Born January 4, 1796.] 16½" x 13½". 7 alphabets. Stem and cross-stitch all in black. Vine with leaves; inverted tulip hanging from center at top.   *The Misses M. L. and H. C. Anderson*

LAMBORN, MARIA. 1827. 21½" x 17". Queen, stem, satin, and cross-stitch. Basket in center at bottom, out of which grow elaborate rose vines; sprays of roses joined together at top; small baskets of fruit on either side of verse. Verse 790. Illustrated.

Mrs. Henry E. Coe

LAMSON, SUSANNA. [Cir. 1805.] Charlestown [Mass. Born in 1792.]. 16" x 16". French knot, satin, chain, cross-stitch, and hem-stitch. Cross and satin-stitch border. At bottom, house (unfinished), tree on either side. In center, conventional flowers and birds. Wide band on top and sides of diagonal chain and conventional flowers or ornaments. Verse 691.   *James M. Hunnewell, Esq.*

LANCASTER, ELIZA. [1802.] Born January 11, 1786. 16 yrs. Alphabet. Basket of flowers with verse on either side. Verses unreadable.   *Mrs. W. M. Tenney*

LANE, JUDITH. 1811. 7 yrs. 9" x 10½". 2 alphabets. Eyelet, back-stitch, and cross-stitch. Band of flowers across bottom, vine border across top, and other cross-borders of rose, strawberry, carnation, honeysuckle, and Greek designs. Tall tree on either side of verse. Below, three panels, one with name and age, second and third with pine tree, dog, and birds. Verse 515 (var.).   *Mrs. John F. Calder*

LANE, LUCY A[NN. 1824.] Boston. 8 yrs. 12" x 16". 2 alphabets. Hem-stitch and cross-stitch. Trefoil and conventional cross-borders. " 'Tis Education forms the common mind."   *Grenville Norcross, Esq.*

LARNED, EUNICE. 1801. Conway. 10 yrs. 8" x 13". 3 alphabets. Satin and cross-stitch. Green vine with red flower or berry in border. At bottom, house with tree on either side, also woman and other trees. Below this is a basket of flowers with potted plant on either side, and in each corner a sheep.   *Mrs. Jane Allen Crawford*

LATHROP, LUCY. 11 yrs. 13" x 14". 2 alphabets. Wide border of tulips, pinks, and other flowers. Cross, satin, and eyelet-stitch. Background covered with black cross-stitch.

Mrs. Marian Hague

LAURENCE, LAURA MATILDA. [1822. Born in 1815.] 7 yrs. 13" x 18". 2 alphabets. Vine border. Two cups of flowers, tree on either side; 2 wreaths with a bird above; lovingcup on a pyramid.   *Mrs. A. W. Whitaker*

LAVERTY, MARY. 1802. [Chester County, Pa.] 16 yrs. 18" x 23". 2 alphabets. Cross-stitch. Vine border. Clusters of strawberries and flowers at bottom. Initials of 9 brothers and sisters. Three parallel panels, first with fruit, second with trees, and third with flowers.   *Miss Mary Hutchin*

LAWRENCE, ELIZA. 1808. Groton [Mass.]. 12 yrs. 13½" x 17". 3 alphabets. Stem, chain, satin, and cross-stitch. Vine and flower border. At top, 3 flower-pots; at bottom, 2 flowers. Verse 690.   *Massachusetts Historical Society*

PLATE LXI

FAITH WALKER'S SAMPLER. 1820
Owned by the Estate of James L. Little, Esq.

PLATE LXII

SARAH F. SWEET'S SAMPLER. Providence, R. I.   After 1814
Owned by Miss M. Frances Babcock

LAWRENCE, POLLY [MARY.] 1803. Groton [Mass.]. 13 yrs. 13½" x 21". 4 alphabets. Eyelet, satin, cross, and hem-stitch. Conventional flowers in cross-stitch border. At bottom, house, garden, and two tall strawberry plants standing on pyramids.
Mrs. Charles S. Minot

LAWRENCE, MARY OAKES. 1819. 12 yrs. 3 alphabets. Cross-stitch. Stiff strawberry border. House, fence, garden, and flower-pots. Verse 515 (var.). *Miss Charlotte S. Tower*

LAWRENCE, SARAH IVINE. 1827. 9 yrs. 6½" x 8¾". 3 alphabets. Eyelet and chain-stitch. Line border. Words "Virtue" and "Youth." *W. G. Bowdoin, Esq.*

LAWRENCE, SUKEY. 1800. 12 yrs. 12¾" x 18¾". 3 alphabets. Eyelet and cross-stitch. Zig-zag border with conventional flowering plant. Flowers in pots at bottom.
Mrs. W. A. Lawrence

LEA, MARY. 1802. "West-Town School." 10½" x 13½". 2 alphabets. Stem-stitch. Vine border with leaves. Verse 678. *Mrs. Hampton L. Carson*

LEACH, ELIZABETH. 1800. Beverly [Mass.]. 11 yrs. 10" x 10". Eyelet and cross-stitch. Conventional border. *Mrs. Charles Whitney Haddock*

LE BARON, HANNAH G. 1826. [Bristol, R. I., or Scituate, Mass.] 9 yrs. 14" x 16½". 4 alphabets. Satin and cross-stitch. Strawberry border. Her mother's tombstone on either side with inscriptions: "M. L. B. Born Sept th 24 1787 M. L. B. Died Dec th 24 1825." "Enumbered Blessings from Above Encompass us Around." Verse 568.
Miss Anne Le Baron Drumm

LE BRETON, CHARLOTTE. 1809. Newburyport [Mass.]. 15" x 15". 4 alphabets. Eyelet and cross-stitch. Scroll border. Various cross-stitch cross-borders.
Dr. Charlotte Le Breton Baker

LEE, ELIZA J. Before 1816. Worcester [Mass.]. 8" x 8½". 3 alphabets. Cross-stitch. Vine border. *Esther H. Bucklin*

LEE, SARAH. 1800. 10 yrs. 11" x 17". 2 alphabets. Cross-stitch. Acorn border. Strawberry border at bottom. *Mrs. H. de B. Parsons*

LEE, SARAH. 1803. 8 yrs. 9¾" x 19¾". 4 alphabets. Cross-stitch. Strawberry border.
Edward Hicks Bassett, Esq.

LEGG, LOUISA. 1824. 10 yrs. 16½" x 8". 3 alphabets. Cross-stitch. *Vernette R. Mowry*

LEGGETT, JANE. 1807. West Farms [N. Y. Born July 27, 1797.]. 10 yrs. 9" x 13". Cross-stitch. Greek border. Verse 276. *Robert H. Oakley, Esq.*

LEIPER, MARY ANN. 1824. Philadelphia [Pa.]. 16" x 17". 4 alphabets. Variety of stitches. Floral-vine border at top and bottom. Verses 473, 474. "August 11th 1824 Washington and Lafayette Welcome." *Mrs. Georg A. Leiper*

LESTER, LUCINDA. 1803. 10 yrs. Born December 16, 1783. 11½" x 13". 2 alphabets. Cross-stitch. Vine border. 3 large conventional flower patterns at bottom. Verse 17.
Mrs. H. C. Bunner

[LETSON, MARY. Cir. 1816. Three Mile Run, 3 miles from New Brunswick, N. J. Born November 7, 1792.] 5" x 5½". 1 alphabet. Cross-stitch. Cross-lines. Greek fret across bottom, also Greek cross. Letters on sampler: "A N E H I L L Y."
Miss Hannah A. Sheppard

LEVIS, KITTY ANN. 1809. Springfield [Delaware County, Pa. 16 yrs.]. 8½" x 9¾". 3 alphabets. Cross and eyelet-stitch. Rose border. Basket of flowers, two trees, and animals.
Mrs. Charles Lippincott

LEVY, MARIA. 1828. 7 yrs. 16" x 12". 2 alphabets. Cross-stitch. Vine border. "I will praise God for he is exceeding great. I will bless God for he is very good and thy heart shall love him. The little birds sing praises to God, when they warble sweetly in the green shade. The brooks and rivers praise God when they murmur melodiously among the smooth pebbles. I will praise God with my voice for I may praise him though I am but a little child. A few years ago and I was a little infant and my tongue was dumb within my mouth and I did not know the great name of God for my reason was not come unto me. But now I can speak and my tongue will praise him. I can think of all his kindness and I will obey him." *Mrs. Steinert*

LEVY, MARTHA. 1803. Philadelphia. 5 yrs. 8½" x 10". 2 alphabets. Cross-stitch. Simple line border. Various patterns in dividing lines. *Mrs. Robert Hale Bancroft*

LEWIS, ANN. 1800. Born October 12, 1790. 10 yrs. 12½" x 15". 2 alphabets. Satin and cross-stitch. Strawberry border. At bottom, scene with shepherd and shepherdess, strawberry tree, birds, and sheep. Verses 575, 594 (1, var.). *Mrs. Thomas A. Lawton*

LEWIS, ANNA. 1811. Athol [Mass.]. 10 yrs. 14" x 16". 3 alphabets. Cross-stitch and hemstitch. Hemstitched edge. Three small trees at bottom. *Miss Emma F. Rhodes*

LEWIS, ANNE. 1813. 11 yrs. 13" x 15½". Carnation border. Satin, stem, and cross-stitch. In upper section, shepherd and shepherdess with sheep; in center section, scene with barn, windmill, haycock, trees, birds, insects, etc. Verse 550. *Mrs. Frederick F. Thompson*

LEWIS, MARY ANN. [Cir. 1820.] New Haven [Conn.]. 8 yrs. At Miss Pierce's School, Litchfield, Conn. 3 alphabets. A row of stiff cross-stitch flowers and strawberries at the bottom. "Diligence and Perseverance are the Keys to improvement and Subdue all difficulties." *From an illustration*

LEWIS, MIRANDA. 1812. Walpole [Mass.]. 10 yrs. 12½" x 12½". Cross-stitch. *Mrs. A. B. Wallace*

LEWIS, SARAH HOBART. 1813. 13" x 15". 3 alphabets. Stem, satin, and cross-stitch. Small crosses in side borders, and elaborate trees and flowers across top. Verse 551. *Estate of James L. Little, Esq.*

L'HOMMEDIEU, MARY CATHERINE. 1813. Middletown. 6 yrs. 7" x 9". 2 alphabets. Crossstitch. Line border. At bottom, cross-border of lozenge design. *Miss Cornelia Horsford*

[L'HOMMEDIEU, MARY CATHERINE.] 8" x 16". 2 alphabets. Tent and cross-stitch. 20 different cross-border patterns. *Miss Cornelia Horsford*

LILLIE, PATIENCE HOLBROOK. 1800. Milton. 11 yrs. 7¾" x 10". 2 alphabets. Cross-stitch. Simple border. Verse 669. *Mrs. Lydia Bowman Taft*

LINCKLAEN, HELEN A. L. 1821. Cazenovia [N. Y.]. 10 yrs. [Born November, 1811.] 18" x 16". 4 alphabets. Eyelet and cross-stitch. Rose border. Verse 169. *Mrs. Charles S. Fairchild*

LINCOLN, BETSY. 1804. Cohasset [Mass.]. 10 yrs. 10" x 11". 2 alphabets. Cross-stitch. Three strawberries in vases, also birds. Verse 146. *Mrs. Walter M. Lincoln*

LINCOLN, MEHITABLE. 1829. Hingham [Mass.]. 10 yrs. 9½" x 13". 4 alphabets. Crossstitch. Vine border. Verse 487. *Lancaster Public Library*

LINCOLN, NANCY. 1801. Norton [Mass.]. 9 yrs. [Born November 28, 1792.] 13¾" x 12¾". 6 alphabets. Stem and cross-stitch. Vine border with colored corners. In lower half, scene with house, trees, birds, cats, dogs, bushes, and flowers; over all is an arch and extending over arch is a vine with flowers. Verse 617 (1, var.). *Miss Olive Lincoln Guild*

LINDSAY, MARY T. 1828. Hillsboro [N. C., at school; home at Greensboro, N. C. About 14 or 16 yrs.]. 17″ x 19″. 8 alphabets. Eyelet, buttonhole, stem, satin, queen, two-sided line-stitch, and cross-stitch. Cross-borders in Greek fret and cross designs. 2 ribbon scrolls. *Miss Emma Morehead Whitfield*

LIPPINCOTT, ANN F[OLWELL]. 1828. [Near Bridgeport, N. J. 16 yrs.] 16″ x 16″. 4 alphabets. Eyelet, chain, tent, queen, and cross-stitch. Cross-borders in various stitches. Basket of fruit and flowers, rose sprays, and blackbirds. Verse 571. Initials: "N Y L [Nathan Yarnall Lippincott]; S L [Samuel Lippincott]; G L [George Lippincott]; [brothers]." *Mrs. Lydia Davis*

LIPPINCOTT, ANNA. 1820. Riverton [N. J.]. 19″ x 22″. Chain, satin, and cross-stitch. Vine and rose border. At bottom, farmhouse with weeping willow tree on one side and pine on the other. In the yard are sheep, a mouse, swan, bird, horse, rooster, duck, etc. Verses 430, 460, 544. *S. Frances Moore*

LIPPINCOTT, MARY. 1828. 10 yrs. 17″ x 17″. Cross and solid stem-stitch. Vine border with leaves and flowers on three sides. Conventional scene at bottom, with brick house, fence, six trees, terraces, and animals. Just above house, two hearts enclosing initials "C P L" and "A L." Wreath in center at top inclosing name and age, and on either side baskets of fruit. Sprays of flowers fill in remainder of space. *Mrs. Fred W. Smith*

LIPPINCOTT, SARAH. 1810. "Westfield School" [N. J.]. 13″ x 14″. Chain, stem, satin, and cross-stitch. Rose-vine border, with bunch of strawberries in each upper corner. At bottom, lawn with trees and flowers. In center, lake with swan sitting under overhanging bush. Vine around verse. Verse 395 (1, 2). *Mrs. Lewis D. Horner*

LIPPITT, MARY. 1804. Cranston [R. I.]. 9 yrs. 9½″ x 18″. 2 alphabets. Cross-stitch. Hemstitched on two sides. Conventional flower and bird design at top, and narrow border at bottom. Flower and bird design above verse. Verse 92a (1). *Mary Lippitt Mason*

LITHGOW, MARY. 1807. Augusta [Me.]. 9 yrs. 13″ x 15″. 5 alphabets. French knot, tent, chain, stem, satin, and cross-stitch. Strawberry and Greek fret borders. Vase of flowers, birds on top of pine trees, and large strawberry plants. Verse 81. *Mary Devens*

LITTLE, ABBIE N. 1829. Georgetown [Mass.]. 12 yrs. 16½″ x 16½″. 4 alphabets. Satin, stem, flat, tent, cat, and cross-stitch. Morning-glory vine on two sides and halfway across the top. Wreath of strawberries in center at top. Across bottom, basket of flowers in center; on each side two mounds, one with two trees on top, and in corners two larger trees. Verse 515 (1). *Mrs. Charlotte H. Howard*

LITTLE, MARY. 1800. Newburyport [Mass.]. 14 yrs. 22½″ x 18½″. 3 alphabets. Stem, satin, and cross-stitch. Greek fret and floral borders. At bottom, trees, fruit, flowers, children, lady, gentleman, colored servants, dog, large insect, arbor, and vine. Verse 666 (var.). *Mrs. Charles H. Atkinson*

LITTLE, RUTHA. 1801. West Newbury [Mass.]. 10 yrs. 13″ x 16½″. 3 alphabets. French knot, stem, satin, and cross-stitch. Cross and satin-stitch border. At bottom, solid satin-stitch. Verse 674. *Mrs. J. B. Nutter*

LIVINGSTON, JANE. August, 1813. Born September 4, 1804. [Livingstone, N. Y.] 13″ x 13″. 2 alphabets. Bird's-eye, satin, and cross-stitch. Strawberry-vine border. Verse 511 (1, var.). *Mrs. Harold Wilson*

LLEWELLYN, RACHEL. [Cir. 1816.] 10½″ x 13½″. Lace stitches on fine net. *Mrs. Thomas A. Lawton*

LOCKE, ELIZA. 1813. 13 yrs. Satin, eyelet, and cross-stitch. Floral border. Elaborate landscape at bottom. Verse 305.   *Mrs. J. Hamilton Woodsum*

LOCKE, SUSANNA BROWN. 1814. Woburn [Mass.]. 11 yrs. 11″ x 11″. 4 alphabets. Satin and cross-stitch. Narrow hemstitched edge with pointed border. At bottom, spray of roses with leaves, and two little birds and two urns at each.
                          Mrs. Albert F. Swaine

LOCKE, SUSANNA BROWN. 1819. Woburn [Mass.]. 16 yrs. 17″ x 20″. Locke family record:

"Mr. Josiah Locke Born
  December the 23rd 1779
Mrs. Susanna Locke
  August the 27th 1779.

Names and Births of their Children

Susanna Brown Locke Born
  November the 15th 1803
Elizabeth Locke born
  May the 8th 1805
Cherry Adams Locke born
  January the 13th 1807

Mary Locke Born
  May the 13th 1808
Josiah Locke Born
  Aug the 20th 1810
Louisa Locke Born
  Sept the 18th 1811
Rebekah Ann Locke Born
  July the 13th 1813
Frances Frost Locke Born
  October 27th 1815
Lucy Frost Locke Born
  February 9th 1818

Deaths
Mr. Josiah Locke Died August 21st 1818
Aged 38 years
Josiah Locke Died October 11th 1810
Aged 7 weeks."
                          Mrs. Albert F. Swaine

LOGAN, SARAH B. 1826. 7½″ x 9″. 2 alphabets. Cross-stitch.   *Mrs. Hampton L. Carson*

LOMBARD, ELSA. 1800. [Springfield, Mass.]   10 yrs. 10¾″ x 11¾″. 4 alphabets. Herringbone and cross-stitch. Border, double row of cross-stitch. "Improve in virtue and be happy."
                          Mrs. Edward W. Hutchins

LONG, FANNY. 1801. Newburyport [Mass.]. 11 yrs. [Born July 8, 1790.] 22″ x 18″. 4 alphabets. Stem, eyelet, satin, and cross-stitch. Strawberry border. Vine of wild roses around verse; below verse are violets, tulips, roses, butterfly, and goldfinch. Verse 515 (var.).   *Miss Georgiana Augusta Currier*

LONGFELLOW, ELIZA. 1828. Machias [Me.]. 9 yrs. 4 alphabets. Satin, eyelet, petit-point, and cross-stitch. Arch supported by two columns, and twined around it are vines and roses. Verses 148, 795.   *Sold. Owner unknown*

LONGFELLOW, SARAH. 1813. Machias [Me.]. 15 yrs. 7½″ x 8″. 3 alphabets. Cross-stitch.
                          W. B. Parlin, Esq.

LOONY, MARTHA. 1828. [Charleston, S. C.]   8 yrs. 17″ x 16″. Cross-stitch. Border of clover, leaves, and vine, with roses in each corner. In center, large house, grass, fence, trees, and two dogs. "Children obey your parents in the Lord for this is right. Eph. Chap VI, 1 verse."   *Miss Mary Miller*

LORD, HANNAH. 1816. Ipswich, Mass. 12 yrs. 10″ x 8″. 2 alphabets. Cross-stitch. Hemstitched edge and Grecian border inside. Verse 116.   *Miss Lucy S. Jewett*

PLATE LXIII

<small>SARAH : DONNA : LEONORA : SAUNDERS</small>
View of William and Mary College, Virginia
Owned by Mrs. Bradbury Bedell

PLATE LXIV

EMILY CLARK'S SAMPLER
View of Yale College
Owned by Mrs. A. J. Downs

LORD, HANNAH NOBLE. 1804. South Berwick, Me. 11 yrs. 20½" x 14". 4 alphabets. Cross-stitch. Modified Greek fret border. Verse 601 (1, 2).   *Mrs. Ellen Rollins*

LORING [FAMILY RECORD]. 1804. 19" x 22". Stem, satin, and cross-stitch. Vine border, with brilliant flowers and leaves. At bottom, 2 black weeping willows and a black wreath. Verse 262.

> " Jerom Loring and Mary Hodgkins were married November 6th 1787 at Bath."
> " Progeny "
> " John Loring was born August 16th 1783
> Jerom C. Loring was born October 28th 1789
> Mary Loring was born October 11th 1791
> Rachel Loring was born November 25th 1794 "
> " Death "
> " John Loring died February 25th 1804 "

Estate of James L. Little, Esq.

LORING, ANN M. 1822. Boston. 11 yrs. 13½" x 19½". 2 alphabets. Fine cross-stitch. 14 rows of rainbow design. Verse 769.   *Mrs. Henry P. Briggs*

LORING, HANNAH. 1812. Made " At Miss Perkin's Academy, Boston." 12 yrs. 17" x 26". French knot, satin, and cross-stitch; part of background painted. Arch supported by tall pillars; clock set at six o'clock in center of arch; funeral urn flanked by weeping willows in center at base, and birds on pedestals close to pillars. Two circles at base, one bearing dissertation on " The Duty of Parents in bringing up their children " and the other on " The Duty of children towards parents." Under urn is inscription " Sacred to Memory of Ebenezer Loring Obt. July 22, nd 1791, AEt 19 mo; Mrs. Nancy Loring Obt. March 28, th 1798, AEt 31 yrs; Mrs. Sarah Loring Obt. Oct. 30, th 1800, AEt 37; Mrs. Sarah Newcomb Obt. Jany 11, th 1812, AE 24." In center of sampler are the names, births, and marriages of

> " The
> Family
> of Matthew Loring &
> Nancy, Sarah & Mercy Loring
> ___
> Matthew Loring Born Hull Jan 17, 1751
> Nancy Floyd Born Boston May 18, 1767
> Married by the Rev. Doct. Stillman Boston January 1st 1768
> ___
> Sarah Blake Born Boston April 4, 1763
> Married by the Rev. Doct. Baldwin Boston June 17th 1799
> ___
> Mercy Bates Born Bath June 16, 1765
> Married by Rev. Doct. Baldwin Boston June 6th 1801

Sarah Loring	Born	Boston October	20th 1787
Ebenezer Loring	Born	Boston January	23d 1790
Nancy Loring	Born	Boston Sept	11th 1792
William P. Loring	Born	Boston January	28th 1795
Jane B. Loring	Born	Boston May	15th 1797
Hannah B Loring	Born	Boston October	22d 1800
Joseph B Loring	Born	Boston May	15th 1802
Caroline M Loring	Born	Boston Decem	8th 1806
Francis M Loring	Born	Boston Aug	27th 1811

Verse 437. Illustrated.   *Mrs. Lathrop C. Harper*

[Louks, Rachel.] 1830. [Pennsylvania.] 10½″ x 11″. 4 alphabets. Cross-stitch. Vine at top. Carnations, birds.   *Mrs. Edgar Henry Summerfield Bailey*

Lovejoy, Sally C. 1811. Born March 10, 1801. 5½″ x 6¼″. 3 alphabets. Cross-stitch. Simple border. Verse 295.   *Mrs. Thomas A. Lawton*

Lovell, Lydia D. 1820. East Medway. Born February 27, 1810. 10 yrs. 8½″ x 12¾″. 2 alphabets. Cross-stitch. Cross-border. Verse 377 (var.).   *Mrs. E. C. Butler*

Lowe, Abigail. Ashburnham [Mass.]. 10¾″ x 12½″. Cross-stitch. Border of vine and Greek fret designs, with flower-pots on each side. At bottom, an inn with swinging sign, trees, and bird. Verse 797.   *Mrs. Edwin L. Thompson*

Lumess, Patty N. 1810. 11″ x 20″. 5 alphabets. Satin and cross-stitch. Verse 717.   *Mrs. Thomas A. Lawton*

Lynde, Eliza. 1807. 8 yrs. 14″ x 17″. 5 alphabets. Cross, chain, eyelet, French knot, and satin-stitch. Simple border design. Floral design at bottom.   *Miss Helen Lynde Sullivan*

Lyon, Mary W. 1821. Milton [Mass.]. 11 yrs. 17″ x 17″. Chain, satin, and cross-stitch. Heavy vine border, springing from two large vases in lower corners; third large vase filled with flowers in center at bottom. Verses 320, 767.
"Family Register
Reuben Lyon was born November 7th 1785
Abigail W. Dalie was born August 23rd 1789
Married April 22d 1810
Mary Willis Lyon was born July 16th 1811
Catherine Manly Lyon was born Sepptm 8th 1813
Charles Reuben Lyon was born Octbr 10th 1816
Susan Abigail Lyon was born September — 1819
Charles Lyon died Jany 26th 18—."
    Miss Anne F. Randall

Lyons, Sally. 1800. New Haven [Conn.]. 10 yrs. 8 mos. 12½″ x 12½″. Alphabets. Satin, stem, and cross-stitch. Cross, vine, and strawberry border. At top of sampler is a large house with fence and trees on either side. Verses 24 (2, 3), 245.   *Mrs. George A. Hill*

M——, A. 1810. Cross-stitch. Scattered conventionalized flower and Greek fret designs, with wreath in center, inclosing initials and date; bird at lower left-hand corner of wreath. Made at a Pennsylvania school.   *Metropolitan Museum of Art, New York*

M——, I. R., also I. C. S. 1803. 12½″ x 19″. 2 alphabets. Cross-stitch. Cross-borders in trefoil, strawberry, double strawberry, and several Greek fret designs. At top, isolated animals, flowers, etc.   *Delano Estate. Sold at Libbie's, March 1, 1916*

Mack, Esther Clarke. 1820. 8 yrs. 18″ x 17″. 6 alphabets. Eyelet, cat, and cross-stitch. Verse 129.   *Miss Esther Stone*

Mackubin, Elizabeth. [Cir. 1801.] Born April 29, 1788. 22″ x 16″. 4 alphabets. Eyelet and cross-stitch. Vine border. House, and fence across bottom. "The grace of our Lord Jesus Christ and the fellowship of the Holy Ghost be with us ever mo." Verse not legible.   *Miss Caroline Franklin*

[MALCOLM, MARIA K.] 1800. [Hanover Street, Boston, Mass. Born in 1792.] 6¼" x 23". 3 alphabets. Chain, satin, and cross-stitch. 7 cross-border designs. *John Taylor, Esq.*

MANNING, HANNAH P. [Cir. 1818.] 14½" x 10½". 2 alphabets. Cross-stitch. Vine border. House and birds. 2 willow trees with an urn under each, and initials: "Mr. A. P. Mrs. H. M." *Mrs. Eva R. Greeley*

MANNING, SARAH H. [Cir. 1818.] 15" x 11". Cross-stitch. 2 alphabets. Vine border. House with a cupola. One willow tree and a conventional tree with tablet: "Died in 1818. Mrs. H. M. A D 31." *Mrs. Eva R. Greeley*

MARCH, LYDIA. 1806. Salisbury [Mass. 7 yrs.]. 18" x 18". 3 alphabets. Satin and cross-stitch. Cross-borders of vines and forget-me-nots. At bottom, meeting house and trees. Names and dates: "Mary March born Dec. 25, 1785; Lydia March born March 25, 1799; Susanna March born Feb. 6, 1802; Samuel March born June 21, 1804." *Newburyport Historical Society*

MAREFORD, ABBY. Jencks Street School, Providence. 21" x 17½". 5 alphabets. Chain and cross-stitch. Verse 127. *Mrs. John H. Mason*

MAGARGE, SUSANNA. 1827. "Bristol School." 12" x 15". Petit-point, stem, and cross-stitch. Greek fret border inside and strawberry border outside. Verse 511. [Made at Quaker School at Bristol, Pa.] *Mrs. Arthur M. Waitt*

MARGARGE, SUSANNA. 1827. "Bristol School." 17" x 18". 3 alphabets. Cross-stitch. Strawberry border. Baskets of flowers and sprays of flowers in upper and lower corners; wreath in center at bottom, with bird standing on twig inside. *Mrs. Arthur M. Waitt*

MARIS, ALICE. Marple. 20" x 21". Floral border. Arbor, animals, etc., at bottom. *Mrs. H. E. Gillingham*

MARSH, ELIZABETH HANNAH. 1823. 11 yrs. 11" x 12¼". 3 alphabets. Stem and cross-stitch. Roses and garland in border. At bottom, deer, birds, trees, pots and baskets of flowers; hearts, squares, and diamonds complete end of lines. Verse 59. "Under her mother's tuition." *Mrs. Blanton C. Welsh*

MARSH, MELINDA. 1812. 10 yrs. 9¼" x 9¼". 2 alphabets. Eyelet, queen, buttonhole, line, and satin-stitch. Cross-border. Collection of sample stitches. *Mrs. Blanton C. Welsh*

MARSH, REBECCA. 1803. "West Town School." 15" x 12". 4 alphabets. Stem-stitch. Verse 405. Initials: "M B, A L, R B, M S." *Anthony Morris Tyson*

MARSHALL, ELIZABETH PILSBURY. 1823. West Newbury [Mass.]. 10 yrs. 3 alphabets. Satin, stem, and cross-stitch. Elaborate floral border. Verse 562. *Mrs. Thomas A. Lawton*

MARSTERS, HANNAH. 1818. Manchester [Mass.]. Born October 8, 1818. 16" x 17". 4 alphabets. Cross-stitch. Conventional border. At bottom, small trees and birds, also four peacocks. Verse 104. *Miss Helen L. Marsters*

MARTIN, CORDELIA. 1830. 7 yrs. 13" x 11". 3 alphabets. Cross-stitch. 2 houses, trees, jardinière on table; 2 female figures, etc., at bottom of sampler. "Youth is the season for improvement." *Albert C. Bates, Esq.*

MARTIN, MARY ANN. 1806. Verona [N. J.]. 15" x 18". 4 alphabets. Cross-stitch. Three kinds of strawberry designs in border. At bottom, large basket of flowers, small basket of flowers, 6 fancy trees, 3 sprays of flowers, black dog, peacock with spread tail, etc. Verse 150 (1). *M. Anna Sickley*

MATHEWSON, AMY ANN. 1828. 11 yrs. 17" x 17". 3 alphabets. Chain, stem, and cross-stitch. Strawberry border. "A record of the family of Mr. Obediah and Mrs. Susannah

Mathewson: George Mathewson was born January 3, 1816; Amy Ann Mathewson was born July 9, 1817; Brockholst L. Mathewson was born October 2, 1818; Charles R. Mathewson was born October 28, 1820. Mr. O[bediah] Mathewson was born Jan. 22, 1793; died April 27, 1822 - - - Mrs. S[usannah] Mathewson was born Oct. 22, 1796; died Aug. 27, 1824."
Mrs. George M. Smith

MAXWELL, ANN. 1808. Carlisle [Pa.]. 13″ x 18″. 3 alphabets. Eyelet, stem, chain, flat, and cross-stitch. Conventional border design resembling daisies done in eyelets. Fancy bands across in hemstitching. Verse 706.
Maxwell Cathcart, Esq.

MAYHEW, SARAH. 1825. Daretown [Salem County, N. J. 23 yrs.]. 19¼″ x 26¼″. 1 alphabet. Variety of stitches. Greek fret and carnation borders. Peacocks, birds, bowl of fruit, geometrical figures, branches of strawberries, urns with sprays of flowers, fruit, branches of roses and forget-me-nots. Verse 662 (var.).
Owner not recorded

McALTIONER, RACHEL E. 1830. [Pilesgrove Township, Salem County, N. J.] 10 yrs. 17″ x 16″. Flat, satin, and cross-stitch. Strawberry border across top and on sides. Band of flat-stitch across bottom. In center, large basket of fruit and flowers; on right side, tulip plant; and on left side, rose bush and small tree. Bunch of roses in center at top. In right corner, carnation plant in urn; in left corner, bouquet of drooping flowers. On each side of verse, basket of fruit and flowers, small basket, and a tulip. Verse 573.
Mrs. Elizabeth McAltioner Coles

McCARTHY, SARAH. 1802. 15 yrs. 16″ x 17″. 3 alphabets. Eyelet, tapestry, satin, and cross-stitch. Elaborate carnation border.
Estate of James L. Little, Esq.

McCLAIN, MARY. 1820. 18″ x 22½″. Chain and cross-stitch. Acorn border. At bottom, flowers dotted around. Wreath around name. Verses 79, 532.
Mrs. Renwick C. Hurry

McCLURE, EMILY JANE. 1816. Baltimore. 7 yrs. 27″ x 15″. 2 alphabets. Chain, eyelet, cat, queen, and cross-stitch. Greek fret and strawberry border. House, trees, and birds. Verse 515 (var.).
Miss Ella Howard Hardie

McCLURE, LUCRETIA. 1800. 7 yrs. 9½″ x 9½″. 2 alphabets. Cross-stitch. Verse (unfinished) 670.
Mrs. I. Tucker Burr

McGILLIARD, ELISA. 1816. 17″ x 13″. 3 alphabets. Japanese stitch, crewel and cross-stitch. Vine and flower border, and cross-borders in varied patterns. Lower left-hand corner, pot containing flowers. "The things unseen do not deceive us." Verse 526.
Mrs. Bradbury Bedell

McINTIRE, [ELIZABETH P.] 3 alphabets. Satin, stem, cat, French knot, and cross-stitch. Elaborate grapevine and rose border on sides and across top. Village scene (Fitchburg), trees, and animals in foreground, a village street with church; across a pond houses, men, women, etc., and several boats on pond. Detached spray of flowers and willow tree in center section. Verse 760. Names and dates: "Mr. Elijah McIntire Jr born Wedny Feb th 10 1784; Miss Sophia Cowdin born frid Sept th 24 1779; Married in Fitchburg by Revd T. T. Barton May 28 1806; Elizabeth P. McIntire born frid April th 24, 1807; Farrington McIntire born tues^d Feb th 4, 1818. Died 21st." Verse 461. Illustrated.
Mrs. Thomas A. Lawton

McKELLAR, CATHERINE WYRES. 1828. Machias, Me. 3 alphabets. Vine and flower border at sides. Verse (unfinished) 606 (1, var.).
Owner not recorded

McKIM, MARGARET. 1827. [Fairfax Court House, Va.]. 12½″ x 12½″. Cross-stitch. 2 alphabets. Vine across top. Church with weathervane in center at bottom; remainder of sampler filled in with detached baskets, flowers, wreaths, angels, two men carrying large bunch of grapes on a pole, small house and part of fence, and small scene with houses and trees.   *Mrs. William Ayres Cook*

McLELLAN, MARY ANN. 1816. Portland. [12 yrs.] 16½" x 21½". Eyelet, satin, cross, and various other stitches. Conventional border design, also inside floral border with bunches of flowers in each corner. Genealogy: "Stephen McLellan born at Portland Feb. 26, 1766. Charlotte Ilsley wife of Stephen McLellan born at Portland Jan. 25, 1763; died Sep. 22, 1802. Hannah Ilsley wife of Stephen McLellan born at Portland Jan. 19, 1771. The Births of their Ofspring: Mary Ann McLellan born at Portland Nov. 27, 1803; Isaac Ilsley McLellan born at Portland Feb. 6, 1806; Augusta Ilsley McLellan born at Portland March 16, 1808, died August 16, 1812; Charlotte Ilsley McLellan born at Portland Oct. 28, 1810." Verse 703 (var.).   *Miss Clara Mossman Hill*

MEAD, HARRIET. 1804. 12 yrs. 12" x 16". 3 alphabets. Satin and cross-stitch. Conventional flower design in border. At bottom, rose bush with conventional pot of flowers on either side.   *Mrs. William D. Eaton*

McCRACKIN, MARGARET. 1815. 16" x 21". Stem, satin, split, and cross-stitch. Rose border. Two large willow trees, one pine tree, and two lambs at bottom. Flowers in pots, baskets of fruit, and sprays of flowers scattered around. "Parents Names, George and Mary A. Mecrakin; William Rebecca Mecrakin, James Margaret Bodly, Brother and Sisters, Rebecca, Mary Ann, William, Hannah Sidney, Susanna Mecrakin." Verses 448, 557.
                                                                    Mrs. H. de Berkeley Parsons

MEDHAM, MARY ANN. 1802. Lynnfield [Mass.]. 10 yrs. 16" x 14½". 3 alphabets. Stem, satin, and cross-stitch. Greek design in border. Jars and plants at bottom, and flower in center.   *Mrs. Frederick W. Hatch*

MELTON, MARY ANN. [Early 19th Century.] 9 yrs. 12" x 15¼". Cross-stitch. Carnation and vine border. Basket of flowers, deer, and pine trees. Verse 515.
                              William B. Thayer Memorial Collection, University of Kansas

MENDINHALL, HANNAH. 1810. Westown [Pa. West Town School.]. 16 yrs. 12" x 13". Cross-stitch and pen-and-ink lettering. Vine around verses. Verses 430, 544.
                                                                          Mrs. A. D. Warren

MERRILL, MARY W. 1817. Portland [Me.]. 14 yrs. 18" x 20½". Chain, eyelet, satin, and cross-stitch. Rose-vine border. Verse 753. "The Genalogy of John and Martha Merrill. John Merrill born July 9, 1769; Martha Merrill born Oct. 16, 1775; Lydia Merrill born Dec. 2, 1799; Died June 22, 1802. So fades the lovely blooming flower. Mary W. Merrill born Mar. 15, 1803; Lydia Merrill born Feb. 19, 1805; John M. Merrill born Dec. 5, 1807; Martha Merrill born July 9, 1810; Susannah Merrill born July 9, 1810." Two geometrical designs in lower corners, with initials "L M" and "P W."
                                                                             Susan I. Merrill

MERRILL, NANCY. 1813. Born in 1796. 5½" x 3". 1 alphabet. Cross-stitch. Hemstitched and fringed edge.   *Elizabeth C. B. Bradbury*

MERRITT, JANE. 1803. 12¾" x 14¾". Sampler is an all-over design of plants, flowers, and birds.   *Mrs. James Richardson*

MERSEILLES, HANNAH SMITH. 1812. Bridgeton [N. J.]. 13 yrs. 14" x 19". 3 alphabets. French knot, eyelet, stem, satin, tent, and cross-stitch. Strawberry border. At bottom, 2 baskets of flowers. Verse 236 (1).   *Mrs. H. B. Pierce*

METCALF, FRANCES CALDER. 1817. 10 yrs. 21" x 20". Eyelet, satin, stem, and cross-stitch. Strawberry border. Columned arch inclosing family register. "Mr. Samuel Metcalf, born Dec. 29, 1783; Miss Frances Calder, born Sept. 10, 1785. They were married in Providence by the Rev. Stephen Gano July 13, 1806. Their first child Frances Calder Metcalf, March 31, 1807; their second child Julia Metcalf, April 29, 1809; died January 31, 1823; their third child Samuel Augustus Metcalf, March 21, 1811; their fourth child Sophia Perin Metcalf, February 18, 1813; their fifth child Harriet Newell Metcalf, February 28, 1815; their sixth child Sarah Calder Metcalf, Sept. 12, 1816; died Dec. 13, 1822; their seventh child Eliza Gray Metcalf, Dec. 20, 1818; their eighth child Albert Metcalf, January 31, 1821; died August 16, 1822; their ninth child Caroline Julia Metcalf, Dec. 25, 1824; their tenth child Cornelia Sarah Metcalf Dec. 25, 1824 (twins); their eleventh child Levi Lincoln Metcalf, June 11, 1825." Verse 309.

Miss F. G. Ormsbee and Mrs. E. C. Harrington

METCALF, MELIA. 1801. Franklin [Mass. Born in 1783.]. 18" x 18". 2 alphabets. Cross-stitch. Cross-stitch borders. Verse 490 (var.).   *Mrs. Lena Fisher Wyman*

METCALF, RHODA. 1811. [Ashburnham, Mass.]. 12 yrs. 10¼" x 12". 3 alphabets. Mostly cross-stitch. Conventionalized flower bands around register of names. Family names and dates:

" Mr. Ezekiel S. Metcalf born   Oct 13th 1769
  Mrs. Eunice Metcalf   Oct 20 1768
       Eunice Metcalf   Oct 10 1782
       Ezekiel Metcalf   Nov 7 1784
       Joseph Metcalf   Jan 21 1786
       Dinah Metcalf   June 7 1787
       Jeremiah Metcalf   May 24 1789
       Lucy Metcalf   July 26 1791
       Asa Metcalf   June 8 1793
       Rhoda Metcalf   May 4 1799
       Asa Metcalf died Sept 8th 1794 "

Mrs. C. E. Corwin

METTISS, MATILDA CATHERINE. [Cir. 1829.] 18" x 22". Born November 10, 1817. Eyelet, satin, and cross-stitch. Conventional flower border with two yellow stars. Green lawn with long, low, red building with belfry, 2 spruce trees, and steps on to lawn. Verse 331.

Mrs. Bradbury Bedell

MICKLE, KEZIAH. 1800. [West Town School.] 10" x 13". 2 alphabets. Cross-stitch. Vine at top with flowers in center.   *Mrs. Edwin Dillon*

MIDDLETON, MARY. 1804. Worked at "Southern Boarding School." 13½" x 16". Verse 264. Genealogical data: "Robert Middleton and Mary Armitage were married the 19th of the 8th month 1788. Dorcas Middleton was born the 8th of the 10th month; Mary Middleton was born the 30th of the 6th month 1791; John Middleton was born the 14th of the 11th month and deceased the 25th of the 4th month 1795; Robert Middleton was born the 19th of the 1st month 1796; Marianne Middleton was born the 14th of the 7th month 1798; William Middleton was born the 11th of the 11th mo. 1801; Joseph Middleton was born the 22nd of the 8th mo. 1804; Mary Middleton was deceased the 31st of the 8th mo. 1804; Robert Middleton was deceased the 2nd of the 1st month 1805."   *Mrs. Eleanor Armitage Whelan and Miss Mary B. Zellar*

MILES, MARIA. 1804. 9 yrs. [New Haven.] 3 alphabets. Cross-stitch. Hemstitched edge with simple cross-stitch cross-borders. Double strawberry border across top. Verse 340.

Mrs. Jack Ross Bowdre

MILES, MARY D. 1807. Leicester [Mass.]. 8 yrs. 8" x 7¾". 3 alphabets. Cross-stitch.

Mrs. John A. Sweetser

MILLER, ANNE. 1815. [Near Greenwich, N. J.] 15 yrs. 17″ x 17″. 2 alphabets. French knot, chain, eyelet, tent, stem, satin, cross, and other stitches. Vine border. At bottom, house and grounds. *Mrs. H. B. Pierce*

MILLER, EUPHEMIA. 1823. [Near Allentown, N. J. Born November 12, 1812.] 11 yrs. 14″ x 16″. 2 alphabets. Chain, long and short, outline, stem, satin, and cross-stitch. Strawberry and vine border. House, tree, flowering bushes, butterflies, man, woman, dog, and double terrace of grass. Verse 775. *Euphemia Augusta Grover*

MILLER, EXCY. 1816. 9 yrs. 16½″ x 17″. 2 alphabets. Variety of stitches. Strawberry, rose, leaf, and other flower designs in borders. Verse 452. *Albert C. Bates, Esq.*

MILLER, HANNAH. July 14, A. D. 18[25]. 11 yrs. Born 18[14]. Middlefield [Conn.]. 12½″ x 7½″. 5 alphabets. Cross-stitch. Cross-borders.
Mrs. Edgar Henry Summerfield Bailey

MILLER, HANNAH. [1826. Middlefield, Conn.] 12 yrs. 10″ x 9½″. 2 alphabets. Cross-stitch. Cross-stitch border. House, basket of flowers, birds, and trees. Worn and frayed.
Mrs. Edgar Henry Summerfield Bailey

MILLER, HANNAH MARY. August 30, 1830. Middletown [Conn. 16 yrs.]. 17″ x 19″. 2 alphabets. French knot, chain, stem, satin, and cross-stitch. Greek fret border. Divided into three sections: upper section, inverted cornucopias of flowers in each corner; middle section, "Register" with births and deaths, also verses; lower section, landscape with four houses, pine, maple, weeping willow, and fruit trees, fence, gates, and tombstone bearing letters "C S M." "Register: Seth Miller born November 2nd 17 77; Charity Birdsey born May 9th 1779; United in marriage December 16th 1802 and have the following children: Mila born October 1st 1803; Alma born September 18th 1808; Hannah Mary born June 21st 1814; Caroline Sarah born December 15th 1818; Deaths: Caroline Sarah died March 7th 1819; Mila died January 16th 1856*; Hannah Mary died August 17th 1865; Alma died July 27th 1877. Mr. Seth Miller died April 7th 1831; Mrs. Seth Miller died Nov. 15th 1845." Verse 334. *Mrs. Edgar Henry Summerfield Bailey*

MILLER, HANNAH N[ILES]. 1808. Philadelphia. 10 yrs. 13″ x 17″. 2½ alphabets. Eyelet, cross-stitch, and hem-stitch. Strawberry border. The Niles was omitted by the child. As punishment her sampler was never framed. *Hannah Niles Freeland Miller*

MILLER, MARIA. 1820. [Near Deerfield, Cumberland County, N. J.] 13 yrs. 10″ x 12″. 4 alphabets. Flat, outline, eyelet, and cross-stitch. Strawberry-vine border. At bottom, small basket of flowers with 2 birds on it. *Mabel H. Turner*

MILLER, S[ARAH] W[YATT]. 1802. Salem [N. J. 11 yrs. Born September 24, 1791.]. 6½″ x 8″. Cross-stitch. Vine border. Verses 77, 399. "West-town School" inscribed at top. "S. W. Miller to E. W. Miller " [her mother]. *Miss Hannah Hall Acton*

MILLS, SARAH. [Cir. 1800.] 11 yrs. 16¼″ x 16¾″. Stem, satin, and cross-stitch. Vine border with roses in corners; roses and carnations alternate with leaves in rest of border. Carnation cross-border. Basket of flowers on either side of verse. Basket of flowers in lower section. Verse 108.
William B. Thayer Memorial Collection, University of Kansas

MISKEY, ELIZABETH. 1822. Philadelphia. 11 yrs. 24″ x 16″. Chain, stem, queen, and cross-stitch. Carnation border. Large basket of grapes embroidered in crewel in center, with spray of flowers on either side. Vine and flowers around panel containing verse. At bottom, "Respectfully presented to Anthony and Elizabeth Miskey by their affectionate daughter Elizabeth Miskey." Verse 720. *Mrs. Henry E. Coe*

These dates are evidently a later insertion.

MITCHELL, MARIE SUTHERLAND. 1818. [Charleston, S. C.] 8 yrs. 10½" x 8". 2 alphabets. Eyelet and cross-stitch. Strawberry border. Two small houses at bottom connected by fence; trees at either end. Verse 454.   *Mrs. Robert Bee Lebby*

MITCHELL, MARY. 1803. Bridgewater [Mass. 7 or 9 yrs., indistinct.]. 15" x 21". 3 alphabets. Stem and cross-stitch. Conventional cross-stitch border. Rosebuds in stem-stitch at bottom. Verse 647.   *Miss S. Lizzie Dunbar*

MONKS, SUSANNA. 1822. 16" x 14". 2 alphabets. Satin and cross-stitch. Carnation border at top and strawberry on sides; saw-tooth border inside. Sprays of carnations and wild roses, baskets of flowers, large vase with conventional carnations, bunches of lilies of the valley, bunches of strawberries, sprays of tulips, crowns, and green wreath. In one corner, Wall of Troy design with conventionalized design.   *Mrs. Bradbury Bedell*

MONTGOMERY, HARRIOT. 1804. Middleborough. 11 yrs. [Born in 1793.] 12" x 15". 4 alphabets. Eyelet, stem, and cross-stitch. Stem-stitch border. At bottom, vine with flowers in lower corners.   *Mrs. George F. Seaver*

MOODY, FAMILY RECORD. [Cir. 1830.] 15" x 18". Eyelet, stem, and cross-stitch. Border of heavy green stem with roses, etc., held at top center by large, true lovers' knot with small ones on ends. Across bottom, 2 paths in a hilly lawn, one leading to 3 poplars and one to 3 pines. In center, a huge basket of flowers. "Family Rechord: Cutting Moody born November 6, 1780; Mary Penny born June 10, 1781; Mary A. born April 20, 1808; Moses V. born April 30, 1818 [Married May 1807]. Faith, Hope, Charity."
                         Mrs. Bradbury Bedell

MOORE, FANNY. 1826. New Town. 10 yrs. 17" x 17". 5 alphabets. Cross-stitch. Strawberry-vine border. Verse 173.   *Miss Frances Moore Dickinson*

MOORE, HANNAH E. 1822. "Easton School." 28" x 30". Stem, tent, satin, and cross-stitch. Floral border on three sides. House, trees, path, fence, birds and sheep on terraced lawn. Wreath of flowers around verses, and flowers in pots and detached sprays in remainder of space. Initials E. M., D. M., E. M., J. R. M. Verse 387.
                         Mrs. F. Leonard Kellogg

MOORE, KETURAH. 1800. [Mullica Hill, Gloucester County, N. J. 12 yrs.] 10½" x 17". 3 alphabets. Flat, queen, and cross-stitch. Cross-border. Cross-borders of strawberry and carnation, strawberry and rose. In each corner there is a tulip spray. "Joshua Moore and Rachel Moore" [parents]. Verses 49a, 244.   *Elizabeth G. Borton*

MOORE, LAURINDA. 1819. Acworth. Born November 22, 1810. 20" x 20". 4 alphabets. Eyelet, tent, stem, satin, and cross-stitch. Saw-tooth border. Flower-pots, hearts, trees with birds, etc. "Remember thy Creator," etc. Verse 314.
                         Fitchburg Antique Shop, July 1, 1917

MOORE, LYDIA. 1807. [Lumberton, N. J.] 9 yrs. 14½" x 17". 4 alphabets. Eyelet, stem, and cross-stitch. Strawberry border at top and Greek fret on sides. At bottom, 2 pine trees, 2 birds, 2 tulips, 2 roses, also basket of flowers. Initials of brothers and sisters: "M M, H M, L M, A M, M M, S M, A M." Verse 343 (1).   *Mrs. Adelaide Joyce*

MOORE, MARY A. 1828. 7 yrs. 18" x 17". 5 alphabets. Eyelet, queen, and cross-stitch. Carnation border at top and bottom. Verse 37.   *Mrs. Renwick C. Hurry*

MORSE, LUCY. 1810. Boston. 12 yrs. 5 alphabets. Petit-point, cat, stem, and cross-stitch. Strawberry cross-border and wreath. Formal garden with trees and peacocks. "There's no dependance upon a mind that wants feeling and . . . of nature." Verse 720 (var.).   *The Emma B. Hodge Collection*

PLATE LXV

ANN WATSON'S SAMPLER. 1808
Princeton College
Owned by Miss Anna Reed

PLATE LXVI

ELIZABETH JANE HOSMER'S SAMPLER. 1828
New York City Hall
Owned by Mrs. Arthur Curtis James

MORTON, MARY. 1809. 9 yrs. 13" x 17". 1 alphabet. Cross-stitch. Strawberry border. Rose and saw-tooth cross-borders. Baskets of flowers and fruit, sprays of flowers, deer and dogs in cross rows; a lion in each lower corner. Verse 198.

Canandaigua Historical Society

MOSS, MARGARET. 1825. [Philadelphia.] 11 yrs. 26" x 27½". Tent, stem, satin, and cross-stitch. Elaborate conventionalized passion-flower border. In center, scene with brick house, weeping willows on either side, and tops of pine trees showing above roof; beehive, boy guarding sheep, 2 girls, ducks, dog, cows, man, and woman. Above scene, American Eagle with wreath on either side, inclosing name and age of maker in one and inscription "Elizabeth Wiert, aged 80, died 1825" in the other. Words "E Pluribus Unum" above eagle, and detached figures of angels and stars in rest of space. Illustrated in color.

Mrs. Henry Eugene Coe

MOWRY, ALCY. 1825. Providence. 8" x 11". 3 alphabets. Cross-stitch. "Let Virtue be a guide to thee."

Mrs. Nicholson

MUHLENBERG, SUSANNA. 1790. Trappe [Pa.]. 11 yrs. 18" x 11". 3 alphabets. Eyelet, stem, satin, and cross-stitch. Strawberry border on three sides, also fret border, and a cross in upper corner. Verse 139. Family record: "Henry M. Muhlenberg born 1711, died 1787; Ann Mary Weifer born 1727. Phillip Hall B. 1733 and Catharine Seckel Born 1728; Henry Muhlenberg Born 1753; Catharine Hall Born 1756; Catharine Muhlenberg Born 1776; Susanna B. 1779; Henry Born 1782; Phillip B 1784; Peter Born 1786; Maria Born 1789; Elisabeth Born 1791; F. Augustus B. 1795."

Mrs. John A. Kress

MULFORD, EMMA. 1806. [Cumberland County, N. J.] 10 yrs. [Born in 1796.] 18½" x 14½". 3 alphabets. Flat, eyelet, satin, and cross-stitch. Greek cross and Greek fret borders. Line of flat-stitch all around. At bottom, floral spray, 2 pine trees, 2 fir trees, small geometrical designs. Initials of father and mother and brothers and sisters: "H M [Henry Mulford]; P M [Phebe Mulford]; H M [Henry]; C M [Charles]; E M [Edward]; E M [Emma]; I S M [Isaac]; D M [record lost]." Verse 540.

William C. Mulford, Esq.

MULFORD, PHEBE. 1803. Roadstown [Cumberland County, N. J.]. 8 yrs. 11" x 15". 3 alphabets. Eyelet, satin, and cross-stitch. Greek fret border. At bottom, apple tree, rose bush; in center, urn of mixed flowers.

"When Abraham's servant
To procure a wife for Isaac, went,
He met Reckah, Told his wish
Her parents gave Consent
Then 'twas for ten days urg'd the man
his journey to delay
Hinder me not I must be — — —"

Verses 253, 254. Family names: "Isaac Mulford [father]; Phebe Ludlum [mother]"; other names and initials: "J. S. Mulford L. H. Polin, I. M., S. M., W. B., T. B., G. Washington, John Adams."

Mrs. Edgar Haas

MULFORD, TAMSON. 1803. Salem [N. J.]. 13 yrs. 11" x 13". 3 alphabets. Eyelet, satin, and cross-stitch. Simple cross-stitch line-border. Band of trees and stars across center. Verses 255, 488 (var.). Family initials: "F R M [Furman and Rhoda Mulford, parents]; H M [Hannah]; L M [Lewis]; I M [Isaac]; D M [David]; T M [Tamson]; W M [record lost]; F M [Furman]; T M [Thomas]; F M [Furman]; R M [Rhoda]; [brothers and sisters]." "Remember now thy Creator," &c.

Mrs. Clark H. Thompson

MUNSON, GRACE. August 14, 1803. 10 yrs. 16″ x 21″. Dark green linen. 3 alphabets. Chain and cross-stitch. Border of grapes and flowers. At bottom, house, fence, trees, birds, butterfly, man, and sailboat on small pond. Verses 78, 260.

Mrs. Douglas C. Despard

MUNSON, SUSAN H. 1824. 15 yrs. 18″ x 17″. Cross and satin-stitch. A ship in full sail, called the "Potosi."
> "From rocks and shoals and stormy weather
> O God protect the Potosi ever."
> "A rainbow at night
> Is sailor's delight."

George S. McKearin, Esq.

MURDOCK, BEULAH. 1800. Newton [Mass.]. 12 yrs. 8″ x 12½″. 2 alphabets. Hemstitch, satin, stem, and cross-stitch. Cross and vine borders. At bottom, flowers and vase with rosebud. Verse 182 (1, var.). *Mrs. Edward F. Jackson*

MURDOCK, BEULAH. 1812. Newton [Mass.]. 24 yrs. 22″ x 24″. 2 alphabets. Petit-point and cross-stitch. Borders of strawberry and conventional rose, scroll, and Greek fret designs. Design of blue crescent with sun, moon, and planets; below is a landscape [unfinished, she evidently intended to make a church]. Verse 729.

Mrs. Edward F. Jackson

MURPHY, RHODA. 1803. Born October 25, 1787. 16 yrs. 8″ x 11″. 2 alphabets. Queen, stem, and cross-stitch. Strawberry and Greek fret borders. At bottom, two pots of tulips with leaves. *Rhoda Lee*

MURRAY, ADDELAIDE M. 1825. Providence [R. I.]. 16″ x 12″. 3 alphabets. Stem, cat, satin, and cross-stitch. Verse 515 (var.). *Mrs. W. C. Angell*

NASH, NANCY K. July 18, 1821. Williamsburgh, Mass. 11 yrs. 8″ x 17″. 2 alphabets. Cross-stitch. Simple border design. Basket of flowers, two ornaments, dog, and watering-pot. Verse 162 (1, var.). *Mrs. Lorenzo Sears*

NEAL, SARAH C. 1826. Newmarket, N. H. 18 yrs. 3 alphabets. Stem, satin, chain, eyelet, and cross-stitch. Conventional borders. Three jardinières at base, out of which grow archaic rose vines; two birds also at bottom. *Mrs. Henry E. Coe*

NEALON, ISABELLA. 1816. Paradise Row, St. John, N. B. 11 yrs. 8″ x 17½″. 3 alphabets. Cross-stitch and other stitches. Narrow cross-borders. "Remember now thy Creator in the days of thy youth. While the evil days come not nor the years draw nigh when thou shalt say, 'I have no pleasure in them.'" *Anna W. Jordan*

NEWBOLD, ANN. 1810. 13⅝″ x 18″. Cross-stitch. Strawberry-vine border. At bottom, scene with house, trees, and shrubs. Verse 32.

Mrs. George C. Fraser, Formerly in the Drake Collection

NEWBOLD, ANN T. 1813. [Springfield Township, Burlington County, N. J.] "Weston School." 13 yrs. [Born November 17th, 1799.] 9¼″ x 9½″. Darning and cross-stitch. Blocks done in different stitches. *Mrs. John B. Atkinson*

NEWELL, ELMINA. Shirley Shaker Community. 14 yrs. 17½″ x 10½″. 4 alphabets. Cross-stitch. *Mrs. William E. Barnard*

NEWHALL, MARY. [1815.] 12 yrs. 3 alphabets. Solid stem, satin, French knot, long and short, and cross-stitch. Roses, other flowers and leaves, and bleeding hearts in border. Family register: "Mr. David Newhall born May 13, 1757; married Miss Elizabeth Goss Sept. 1, 1779; Died Sept. 19, 1807. Childrens' names: Elizabeth born May 28, 1780;

died June 17, 1814; Thomas Goss born May 15, 1782; Frances born Feb. 13, 1784; Gustavus born April 11, 1786; Nancy born March 27, 1789; Abigail born May 10, 1791; David born Feb. 22, 1795; Susan born March 2, 1797; Samuel Coats, born Sept. 23, 1799. Mr. David Newhall married Miss Mary Holman Sept. 19, 1802; died Sept 11, 1815. Mary born Oct. 18, 1803." *Mrs. George B. Walton*

NEWMAN, MARY HALE. 1820. Newbury [Mass.]. 7 yrs. 8½" x 10½". 3 alphabets. Flat, cat, chain, eyelet, and cross-stitch. Hemstitched edge. *Etta T. Lovett*

NEWMAN, PHEBE. 1815. Newbury [Mass. Born April 9, 1804.]. 11 yrs. 12" x 17". 5 alphabets. Eyelet, satin, chain, flat, tent, and cross-stitch. Strawberry border. Trees, vase of flowers, and other ornamental designs. Verse 449. *Edith D. Newman*

NEWMAN, SARAH. 1806. 9 yrs. Born November 2, 1797. 10½" x 15¼". 3 alphabets. Chain, stem, tent, satin, and cross-stitch. Strawberry border. Flowers with true lovers' knot at bottom. Verse 538 (var.). *Miss Abby Newman*

NEWTON, SOPHIA. 1807. Woodbridge. 12 yrs. 10" x 15". 3 alphabets. Verse 278.
Annie B. Law

NICHOLL, LUCY E. 1826. Salem [Mass.]. 14 yrs. 16¼" x 16¼". Chain, stem, satin, and cross-stitch. Elaborate cross-borders; around edge, solid chain and cross-stitch; inside, two rows of detached 8-pointed stars and a Greek fret border. Two plants. "Sincerity and truth form the basis of everything." Verse 94 (var.). *A. Stainforth, Dealer*

NICHOLS, ELIZA ARNOLD. 1829. [Providence, R. I.] 12 yrs. 17" x 15½". 3 alphabets. Cross-stitch. House and trees in lower section. Verse 332. *A. W. Claflin, Esq.*

NICHOLS, LYDIA. 1802. Salem [Mass.]. 12 yrs. 1 mo. 22 dys. 18" x 20½". 3 alphabets. Stem, cross-stitch, and long, loose stitches. Rose border. Vase with flowers on green base. Design like a pineapple in each lower corner. Verse 40 (var.).
Mrs. W. H. Varney

NICHOLSON, REBECCA. 1801. 14 yrs. 14" x 28". 1 alphabet. Cross-stitch. Carnation border with two designs at top; carnations growing in pots. At bottom, 2 trees, bowl of flowers, spray of rosebuds, strawberries and plant. Upper center, 2 doves in circlet with names under them, "Abel and Mary Nichoson." Verses 132 (1, var.), 143, 226 (var.), 617. Names and dates:

"Rebecca Nicholson was Born the 18th of 12 month 1787
Isaac Nicholson was born the 18th of 2 month 1790
Samuel Nicholson was Born the 18th of 4 month 1793
Abel Nicholson was Born the 11th of 10 month 1795
Joseph Nicholson was Born the 18th of 5 month 1798
Mary Nicholson was born the 15th of 12 month 1801"
Miss Sarah Rebecca Nicholson

NIGHTINGALE, SUSAN ELIZABETH. 1820. 11 yrs. 5½" x 8". 3 alphabets. Cross-stitch.
Charles H. Warren, Esq.

NOBLE, MARY. 1808. South Berwick [Me.]. 11 yrs. 23¾" x 22". 2 alphabets. Stem-stitch. Modified Greek fret border. Rose bushes, a memorial urn and weeping willow, under which is inscription, "An affectionate child pays this tribute of respect to the memory of her father who died 19th June 1808. Aet 48." Verse 542. *Mrs. Ellen Rollins*

NORRIS, ELINOR. [Early 19th Century.] Born March 20th, 1789. 8" x 15". 2 alphabets. Cross-borders. *William B. Thayer Memorial Collection, University of Kansas*

NORWOOD, HARRIET G. 1822. Camden [Me.]. 11 yrs. 11½" x 18½". 4 alphabets. Hemstitch, eyelet, stem, queen, tent, chain, and cross-stitch. Hemstitched border. House in lower center, with trees, pots of flowers, and tulip plants on either side.

Mrs. Nathan Atherton Middleton

NOURSE, ABIGAIL. Before 1830. 6" x 6". 3 alphabets. Petit-point and cross-stitch. Elaborate hemstitched border. Cross-borders. "Honour the Lord with thy substance and with the first fruit of all thine increase." *A. Stainforth, Dealer*

OAKES, SARAH B. 1826. [Probably Cohasset, Mass.] 7 yrs. 12" x 17". 2 alphabets. Stem, satin, and cross-stitch. Strawberry border. Two willows drooping over monuments, separated by a rose and leaves with love knot above. "Josiah Oakes Born Aug. 20, 1789; Mary C. Oakes born Jan. 6, 1798; Their daughter, Sarah B. Oakes Born Aug. 18, 1819." Verses 62, 782. *Heirs of E. S. Remington*

OAKLEY, ELIZA. 1803. White Plains [N. Y.]. 14 yrs. [Born December 5, 1789.] 17" x 18". 2 alphabets. Eyelet, stem, and cross-stitch. Border of flowers, leaves, apples, and birds. Apple tree and vases. Verse 27. *Robert H. Oakley, Esq.*

O'BRIEN, CYNTHIA. 1807. 12¼" x 19¼". 3 alphabets. Stem, tent, eyelet, and cross-stitch. Vine and floral border. "Lean not on earth, twill pierce the to the heart. A broken reed at best but oftn spear. On its sharp point, peace bleeds and hope expires." *Mrs. George E. Claplin*

O'BRIEN, JULIA. 1812. Washington City. 20" x 20". Cross-stitch. Border of conventionalized tulips and roses. At bottom, large brick house with garden, trees, woman, duck, etc. Verse 435. *A. Piatt Andrew, Esq.*

ODIORNE, SARAH CATHERINE MOFFATT. 1802. Portsmouth, N. H. 12 yrs. 3 alphabets. Stem, satin, petit-point, tent, and cross-stitch. Simple cross-stitch border in waving design and dots. In upper half, 2 vine wreaths inclosing verses, with flower sprays under verses and birds perched on twig at top; the Ten Commandments in between. In lower half, funeral urn on pedestal in center, with initials "S C M"; and underneath, "In memory of Mrs. Sarah Catherine Moffatt Obiit. December (?) 1802 A E (? ?)." On either sides wreaths of leaves, with flower on mound at bottom. In one is the name and date of maker, also the inscription, "Worked at Miss Ward's School New Hampshire; Fear God Honor your Parents." In the other is a verse. Above urn is a short band of loops and tassels. Verses 190, 397, 647. Illustrated. *Mrs. John Fremont Hill*

ODIORNE, ELLEN MARIA. 1822. 9 yrs. 16½" x 21". 3 alphabets. Stem, satin, and cross-stitch. Elaborate grapevine border on three sides. Large basket of flowers in center at bottom, with two trees on either side topped by birds. Verse 770.

Mrs. Henry Eugene Coe

OFAY, ELIZA. 1818. 11 yrs. 11¼" x 8". 3 alphabets. Cross-stitch. Strawberry border.

W. G. Bowdoin, Esq.

OGDEN, ELIZABETH. 1810. Swedesboro [N. J.]. 9 yrs. 16½" x 17". 4 alphabets. Eyelet and cross-stitch. Vine border with trees and other designs. In center an eight-sided design with two birds. Initials: "S O, M A O, J T, E T, J O, S O, D O, S O, E O, J O, M O."

Miss Sibyl T. Jones

OGDEN, LAURA E. [Cir. 1828. New Germantown, N. J., at "Barnet Hall."] 16" x 18". 3 alphabets. Chain, eyelet, tent, and cross-stitch. Vine and strawberry border. Grapevine cross-border. Verse 515 (var.). *Laura Ogden Ross*

OLIVER, SALLY. 1801. 14 yrs. 21½" x 22¾". 2 alphabets. French knot, stem, satin, and cross-stitch. Satin-stitch border in saw-tooth design. Border at bottom of trees, vine, tulips, carnations, fruit, and other flowers. Also at bottom, trees with fruit on lower branches, rose tree in center; on one side a man, dove, and two lambs; on the other side a woman with bouquet of roses, and behind her a bough of colored leaves. "Establish unto Thyself Principles and See that Thou Ever Act According to Them."

Mrs. John Walker

OLMSTEAD, ANJINETTE. [Cir. 1819. Bridgewater, Conn.] Born June 13, 1809. 6" x 6". 2 alphabets. *Mrs. J. Herbert Redding*

ORCUTT, ADELINE. [Cir. 1820.] 13 yrs. Born in 1807. 20" x 24". Eyelet, satin, and cross-stitch. Scroll border with long satin-stitch leaves. Willow trees, tablet, and woman weeping. "Record of Jonathan Orcutt family. He was born Oct. 2, 1769 and married May Humphrey 1783. She was born Nov. 14, 1766 and they hath the following children:

Names	Births	Deaths
" Rebecca	Feb. the 15, 1783	
Sophia	June the 20, 1786	
Mary	May the 4, 1789	
George	March 9, 1791	June 6
Silvia	Oct. the 24, 1793	
David	Sept. the 19, 1796	
Silence	May 11, 1802 "	

" Mrs. Orcutt died June 20, 1805. Death where is thy sting o grav."
" Capt Orcot Miss Alice Graves Married Oct 1806."

" Adeline	July 6, 1807	
Abner G.	Feb. 20, 1808	April 13, 1813
Alice A.	April 8, 1809	
Azuba	Dec. 9, 1811	
Abner G.	March 5, 1815	
Jonathan	Dec. 26, 1816."	

Fitchburg Antique Shop, July 1, 1917

OSBORN, SOPHIA B. 1829. Ware [Mass.]. 10 yrs. 16" x 16". Satin and cross-stitch. Strawberry border. Two baskets of flowers with weeping willow tree.

" Family Register

Names	Births	Marriages	Deaths
John Osborn, Jr.	Sept. 29, 1783		
Eunice Bemis	April 23, 1790	May 9, 1808	
John H. Osborn	Sept. 11, 1809		
Eliza B. Osborn	Sept. 27, 1811		Jan. 16, 1813
Thomas D. Osborn	Sept. 8, 1816		
Sophia B. Osborn	Nov. 7, 1819		
James Osborn	July 31, 1822		
David W. Osborn	Sept. 24, 1828		
George C. Osborn	Sept. 28, 1830 "		

Graydon Stetson, Esq.

OSGOOD, CHARLOTTE. 1817. Newburyport [Mass.]. 11 yrs. 15" x 16". 5 alphabets. Flat, chain, and cross-stitch. Verse 601 (1, 2). Family record: " Alfred Osgood Born March 7, 1773; Mary Osgood Born April 4, 1778; Nathaniel Osgood Born April 23, 1801; John Osgood Born Sept. 1, 1803; Charlotte Osgood Born Jan. 30, 1806; Alfred Osgood Born June 1, 1809; William H. Osgood Born Sept. 5, 1811; Mary Ann Osgood Born Dec. 14, 1814."

Mrs. H. Anthony Dyer

OSGOOD, LYDIA. 1823. 12 yrs. Born December 12, 1811. 9" x 8¾". 4 alphabets. Chain-stitch. Greek border at top, strawberry at bottom. 2 hearts, panel and strawberry pattern alternating. *W. G. Bowdoin, Esq.*

OWEN, ADA. 1809. 9½" x 8". 2 alphabets. Cross-stitch. Verse 377. *Mrs. Daniel Beckwith*

[OXIY], NANCY. 1814. 25" x 21½". Eyelet and cross-stitch. Strawberry border. Verses 10 (1), 40, 556. *Mrs. Arthur Barker*

PAIN, LAURA. 1826. 16¼" x 8". 3 alphabets. Cross-stitch. House and tree at bottom. Verses 125, 692. *A. Stainforth, Dealer*

PALMER, ELIZABETH C. [1820–25.] Boston [Mass. 9 to 12 yrs.]. 8" x 8". 2 alphabets. Cross-stitch. Simple border. Stars in corners.
Mrs. William B. Stevens and Miss Mary Foster Light

PALMER, SUSAN M. 1826. Boston [Mass.]. 10 yrs. 18" x 18". 3 alphabets. Chain, stem, satin, and cross-stitch. Grapevine border. At bottom, house, trees, and grass. On each side, flower-pots with flowering plants, and wild rose design in between. Verse 515 (var.). *Miss Martha A. Palmer, Mrs. William B. Stevens, Miss Mary Foster Light*

PARKER, ANN. 1815. 7 yrs. 16" x 8¾". 5 alphabets. Cross-stitch. Double line of cross-stitch all around. Small detached design. *Anne Parker Appleton*

PARKER, CATHARINE. [1826.] 9 yrs. 11" x 13". 3 alphabets. Cross-stitch. Hemstitched edge. Verse 601 (1, 2, 3). *Anne Parker Appleton*

PARKER, ELIZA E[LEANOR]. 1818. [Lexington, Mass.] 16½" x 19½". Satin, stem, and cross-stitch. Wreath of vine and flowers around edge. Large tree in center, with fruit inscribed with names and dates. At base of tree, two hearts with the inscriptions: "Robert Parker born April 15, 1771" and "Elizabeth Simonds born July 4, 1772." Under-neath, "Married Oct. 25, 1793." Apples bear names of children: "Mary born Dec. 25, 1794; Josiah born July 6, 1798; Thomas born March 16, 1800; Eliza E. born Sept. 20, 1804; Almira born Aug. 30, 1806; Jonathan S. born Aug. 8, 1808; Jonathan S. born July 30, 1812; William B. born Jan. 13, 1817." *The Misses Robbins*

PARKER, ELIZABETH T. 1819. 8 yrs. 16" x 8¾". 5 alphabets. Cross-stitch. Simple-line border. "Life is but a dream." *Anne Parker Appleton*

PARKER, HARRIOT. 1808. [Pepperell, Mass.] 10 yrs. 22" x 26". 2 alphabets. Cross, satin, stem, chain, cat-stitch, and petit-point. Clover vine and Greek fret. Three-story house with Captain's walk, fence, gate, weeping willow, and many birds. Verse 601 (1, 2, 3, var.). *Miss Harriet E. Freeman*

PARKER, MARIE ANTOINETTE. 9 yrs. 4 alphabets. Cross-stitch. Hemstitched edge and narrow floral border. Verse 129 (var.).

PARKER, MARY MORSE. 1826. Keene [N. H.]. 9 yrs. 17½" x 12½". 3 alphabets. Cat, satin, cross, and hem-stitch. Strawberry border; trefoil and conventional cross-borders. In center of lower half, a standard basket of fruit flanked by trees, an evergreen and a flowering fruit tree. Below basket, an oblong space containing name and date, and guarded on each side by small black dog with yellow collar. *Mrs. George Sheffield*

PARKER, POLLY. 1802. Bradford [Mass. 15 yrs.]. 22½" x 17½". 3 alphabets. Stem, satin, and cross-stitch. Garland of flowers around upper section, tied at top corners and in center at bottom with bowknots. In center at top, drapery with fringe and tassels, on which is inscribed name, date, etc. In lower part of sampler is pastoral scene, with lovers in one corner sitting under tree and playing on instruments; sheep and dogs are wandering around in front of them. Verse 601 (1, 2, 3, var.).
Mrs. Alice C. Savary and Miss Elizabeth Parker

PARTRIDGE, CATHERINE. 1813. Boston [Mass.]. 8 yrs. 12" x 18". Cross-stitch. Strawberry border. Basket of flowers and two peacocks at bottom. Verse —. [Not on description.] *Dr. James C. White*

PARVIN, LYDIA. 1809. Deerfield [N. J.]. 9 yrs. 6½" x 8½". 2 alphabets. Eyelet, outline, and cross-stitch. Strawberry-vine border. Initials: "J. P. [Jerry Parvin, father]; S. P. [Sarah Parvin, mother]; [Children], L. P. [Lydia]; J. P. [Jerry]; A. R. P. [Anna R.]; H. P. [Harriet]." *Anna M. Jaquette*

PATTERSON, SARAH ANN EWALT. 1819. "Pittsburg." [13 yrs.] 18" x 17". Stem, satin, and cross-stitch. Strawberry border. House, trees, fence, birds on trees, and cat on fence. Upper verse flanked by basket of fruit and bushes in flower; lower verse flanked by jar of flowers and basket of flowers. Verses 226 (var.), 511 (1, var.). *Elzeria Allen*

PAYNE, SARAH ANN. 1825. 14 yrs. 20" x 20". 3 alphabets. Cross and queen-stitch. Ribbon border. Verse surrounded by flowers. Basket of flowers with parrots on either side; growing flowers and bowknots. Verse 565. *National Museum, Washington, D. C.*

PAYSON, ABIGAIL WELSH. 1808. Chelsea. 8 yrs. 6½" x 8". 2 alphabets. Cross-stitch. Greek fret border across top. Verse 30. *Mrs. N. A. Prentiss*

PEABODY, LUCRETIA. [1810?] 10 yrs. 13" x 16". 5 alphabets. Tapestry, petit-point, eyelet, stem, satin, and cross-stitch. Solid tapestry all around. Cross-borders. At bottom, urn of flowers flanked by two baskets of fruit. "Just as the twig is bent the tree inclined." *Mrs. William S. Eaton*

PEABODY, MARY. 1800. Ipswich. 11" x 20". 4 alphabets. Eyelet and cross-stitch. Greek fret border. *Mrs. H. C. Lazelle*

PEABODY, ROXCENA. 1808. Bradford [Mass.]. "Bradford Academy." Born March 6, 1793. 17" x 22". 4 alphabets. Stem-stitch. Outside border of triangular design; inside border, vine with bunches of flowers. Verse worn away.
The Misses Eleanor and Grace Kimball

PEARCE, SUSANNA STEVENS. [Cir. 1804. Born about 1793.] 11½" x 12". 4 alphabets. Tent and cross-stitch. Vine border. Verse 265. *Mrs. D. P. Penhallow*

PEARSE, HANNAH S. April 15, 1814. 10 yrs. 12½" x 17". 3 alphabets. Cross-stitch. Double strawberry border. At bottom, tree, birds, and flower-pots. Verse 515.
Mrs. Thomas A. Lawton

PEARSE, MARY. July 22, 1810. Portsmouth. 8 yrs. 8½" x 16". 3 alphabets. Satin and cross-stitch. At bottom, basket of strawberries, and four strawberries growing on mounds. Verse 515 (var.). *Mrs. Thomas A. Lawton*

PEARSE, MARY. 1812. Portsmouth. 11 yrs. 8¼" x 8½". 3 alphabets. Cross-stitch. At bottom, birds, baskets, and strawberries in pots. Verse 731. *Mrs. Thomas A. Lawton*

PEARSON, ABIGAIL. 1802. 10 yrs. 7¾" x 9¾". 2 alphabets. Cross-stitch. Conventional rose or strawberry-vine border. *Mrs. George C. Fraser*

PEARSON, EUNICE. 1813. [Newburyport, Mass.] "Born January 23, 1801, AE 12 yrs." 9¼" x 12½". 3 alphabets. Chain, eyelet, satin, and cross-stitch. "Let virtue be your guide." *Ruth M. B. Macintosh*

PEARSON, LYDIA. 1802. Born in Newburyport, Mass., June 24, 1791. 11 yrs. 12" x 16½". 3 alphabets. Satin and cross-stitch. Clover border. At bottom, vase with flowers. Verse 601 (1, 2, var.). *Mrs. George F. Poor*

PEASE, EMILY. 1806. Suffield [Conn.]. 10 yrs. 11″ x 17½″. 5 alphabets. Eyelet and cross-stitch. Eyelet border. Verse 696.   *Mrs. E. A. Fuller*

PECK, AMANDA M. 1828. 10 yrs. 8″ x 17″. 3 alphabets. Cross-stitch.   *Mrs. E. A. Cary*

PECK, HARRIET. 1825. Coventry. 11 yrs. 12″ x 8″. 2 alphabets. Cross-stitch. Verse 779.   *Mrs. Willis H. White*

[PECK], LYDIA. 1807. 15″ x 10¾″. 3 alphabets. Chain and cross-stitch. [Verses too indistinct to read.]   *Mrs. Ralph V. Hadley*

PECK, LYDIA WICKES. 1822. Coventry. 11 yrs. 12″ x 8″. 2 alphabets. Chain and cross-stitch. Verse 91.   *Mrs. Willis H. White*

PECK, MARTHA E. 1819. 11 yrs. 4 partial alphabets. Petit-point, satin, and cross-stitch. Elaborate rose border. Design is Town of Ipswich, Mass. Verse 144 (1).   *The Emma B. Hodge Collection*

PECK, MARY ANN. 1825. Coventry. 10 yrs. 12″ x 8″. 2 alphabets. Chain and cross-stitch. Verse 171.   *Mrs. Willis H. White*

PECKHAM, ESTHER. 1806. 10 yrs. 12″ x 17″. Tent, chain, and cross-stitch. Strawberry and rose-vine border. At bottom, strawberry and rose design in tent-stitch. Verse 273. Names and dates: "Augustus Peckham born January 1, 1761; Esther Peckham born March 21, 1762; married June the 10 1792. Their issues is as followeth: James Hervey Peckham born May 22, 1793; Esther Peckham born May 6, 1796; Sarah Peckham born March 12, 1797; Augustus Peckham born October 28, 1798; George Peckham born November 8, 1800."   *Antoinette S. Peckham*

PEIRCE, HANNAH. 1814. Somerset. 13 yrs. 8″ x 16″. 3 alphabets. Chain and cross-stitch.   *Mrs. Stephen O. Metcalf*

PEIRCE, REBECCA B. 1813. Philadelphia, Pa. 17″ x 21″. Stem and cross-stitch. Elaborate floral border of roses, carnations, lilies, and leaves. At bottom, cornucopia and floral designs. Verse 85.   *Emily Haines*

PENNIMAN, MARY OLIVE. [1813. Machias, Me.] 10 yrs. 15½″ x 16½″. 3 alphabets. Tent, stem, satin, and cross-stitch. Vine and flower border. Verse 735.   *Owned in Machias, Me.*

PERKINS, NANCY S. 1821. 14 yrs. 16″ x 17″. Satin, stem, and cross-stitch. Rose border. Landscape in center. Verse 766.   *Mrs. Philip B. Sumner*

PERKINS, NANCY S. 1821. 14 yrs. 17″ x 18″. Satin, stem, queen, and cross-stitch. Rose border. Square in center of sampler containing scene with shepherdess tending flock of sheep. Verse 766.   *Mrs. Edith M. Noble*

PERKINS, SARAH. 1808. South Kingston. 14 yrs. 9″ x 12″. 3 alphabets. Cross-stitch.   *Emily J. Anthony*

PERRY, ALICE H. 1807. "Nantucket" [Mass.]. "Born Novr the 28, in 1797." 15″ x 19″. Satin and cross-stitch. Vine and floral border. Carnation cross-border. Floral design in center, with birds and trees. Verse 345 (1, var.).   *William B. Thayer Memorial Collection, University of Kansas*

PERRY, ANN CATHERINE. [Cir. 1800.] 8 yrs. 13″ x 16″. 2 alphabets. Stem, satin, and cross-stitch. Vine border with flowers. Ornamental cross-borders. Border of flowers around verse. Lower section, pastoral scene with trees, gate, lambs, and shepherds. Verse 594.   *William B. Thayer Memorial Collection, University of Kansas*

PLATE LXVII

ELIZA F. BUDD'S SAMPLER. 1808
Court House, Mount Holly, N. J.
Owned by Miss M. Eliza Smalley

PLATE LXVIII

SOPHIA STEVENS SMITH'S SAMPLER. 1818
View of North Branford, Conn.
Owned by Mrs. Henry E. Coe

PERRY, JERUSHA, MARY, AND SARAH. Before 1830. Miss Pierce's School in Litchfield, Conn. 19″ x 19″. Long-stitch and French knots. Oak leaves and acorns in border. At bottom, 3 girls with man and woman standing by tombstone; hands and faces painted; big urn on top of stone. In background, weeping willow tree, house, stream, waterfall, grass, and sky (painted in). Inscription on stone: " In memory of Florilla daughter of the Rev. David and Mrs. Jerusha Perry, who died May 28th 1807 aged 16 years. Although dead she still forcibly yet silently repeats her dying admonition ' Prepare for Death.' " *Mrs. Lewis S. Rice*

PERRY, SYRENA. 1811. Putney [Vt.]. 12 yrs. 12½″ x 15¼″. 4 alphabets. Cross-stitch. Cross-border. At bottom, conventionalized tree, houses, bowls of flowers, and smaller trees. Verse 490 (var.). *Mrs. Edgar M. Morsman, Jr.*

PETERS, HANNAH. 1818. Marlborough [Mass.]. " Under the care of L. Brigham." 14 yrs. Born April 25, 1804. 4 alphabets. Stem, satin, and cross-stitch. Broad vine and flower border on three sides; three baskets filled with flowers across base. Verse 56. *Mrs. Charles J. White*

PETERSON, ELIZABETH. 1824. [Millville and Port Elizabeth, Cumberland County, N. J.] 11 yrs. 16¾″ x 21¾″. 5 alphabets. Chain, outline, petit-point, flat, stem, and cross-stitch. Rosebud and carnation border. At bottom, house, birds, pheasant, peacocks, flowers, and vase. " Make good use of your time for this life will not be long. The Lord is good and Kind to us and we must pray to him for help." Verse 594 (1, var.). Names and dates: [father and mother] " Hollingshead Peterson was born September the 24, 1789; Elcey Peterson was born January the 29, 1795; [children] Elizabeth Peterson was born December the 14, in the year of our Lord 1813; Aaron Peterson was born January the 31, 1816; Mary Peterson was born May the 31, 1818; William Peterson was born November the 25, 1820; Hollinshead Peterson was born July the 6, 1824." *Mrs. John H. Ballinger*

PETERSON, REBECCA. 1813. " Haines Neck School." [Born in 1798.] 10″ x 17″. 4 alphabets. Eyelet, queen, and cross-stitch. Triangles in solid cross-stitch in lower corners. Cross-border. At bottom, 2 urns of flowers, rose in center with small rose on either side. Space left unfinished. *Miss Rebecca Webber Austin*

PETIT, RACHEL. 1813. 9 yrs. 22¾″ x 18¾″. Carnation, strawberry, and rose border. Basket of fruit at top corners; strawberries in lower corners; flower in pot at sides. Six trees at bottom. Verse 299. Initials in circles, doves facing them, and words " Emblem of love 1813," " W P, S P " and " M S, S P." *Mrs. Warren W. Flitcraft*

PETTENGELL, CHARLOTTE. [Cir. 1820.] Newburyport [Mass.]. 9½″ x 9½″. 5 alphabets. Stem, satin, and cross-stitch. Rose border at top, vine at bottom. *Mrs. John Wheeler*

PETTINGILL, OLIVE. 1828. Newburyport [Mass.]. 13 yrs. 17½″ x 17″. 3 alphabets. Cross and satin-stitch. Saw-tooth design in border. Two bunches of roses. Verse 572. " Family Record: Cuttin Pettingill and Olive Smith were united September 1808. Cuttin Pettingill born July 4, 1809; died December 7, 1810, Age 17 months; Cutting Pettingill Jr. born July 16, 1812; Olive Pettingill born Nov. 14, 1815; Moses Pettingill born Oct. 14, 1818; Lydia S. Pettingill born Nov. 9, 1821; Lucy S. Pettingill born July 5, 1823." *Mrs. E. C. Pearson*

PEYTON, MARY DENT. 1822. 12″ x 15″. Partial alphabets. Eyelet and cross-stitch. Strawberry border, top and bottom; side border in scroll design. At bottom, lawn with 7 large and 10 small fir trees in distance. Verse 515 (var.). *Mrs. Kensey John Hammond*

PHETTEPLACE FAMILY. [About 1818.] 17" x 17". Cross-stitch. "We feel to lament yet we will silence every murmur that our first born brother before he was three years of age fell asleep in the arms of death, also our much beloved brother Riley while in his 25th year of age to our great distress he fell in her cold icy arms. It has so pleased our Savior to call for these in the bloom of life we would wish not to recall thee thoughg *(sic)*." "Record of the children of Eber and Waite Phetteplace. The former was born 1765; the latter 1775. Dexter Phetteplace was born . . . . ; Clarke Phetteplace was born . . . . ; Amy Phetteplace was born Nov. the 18 . . . . ; Celia Phetteplace was born Jan. . . . . ; Riley Phetteplace was born April 18th . . . . ; Miranda Phetteplace was born June 8th 1811; Dexter S. Phetteplace was born April 28, 18—; . . . . A. Phetteplace was born April 30, 18—." *Mrs. P. R. Kendall*

PHILLIPS, AMY ANN. 1811. Waterford [Va.]. 12 yrs. 18" x 24". 1 alphabet. Chain and cross-stitch. In border, cross-stitch forming running monogram A. P. Vase with flowers, strawberry design, and a drooping fuchsia. T. P. [Thomas Phillips, father]; S. P. [Sarah Phillips, mother]. Names of two teachers Amelia Hough and Mary Lawrence. Verse 413 (var.). *Miss Amy P. Miller*

PHILLIPS, ELECTE. September 1st, 1803. Bridgewater [Mass.]. 10 yrs. Born February, 1793. 12" x 16". 3 alphabets. Satin and cross-stitch. Vine of rosebuds and leaves, starting from a basket at the top and falling down two sides. Two robin redbreasts on a large bough of a small tree looking at each other. Verse 606 (1, var.).
Mrs. Bradbury Bedell

PHILLIPS, HARRIET JANE. 1817. Portland [Me.]. 9 yrs. 17½" x 16½". 3 alphabets. Rose border. House with tall trees. Verse 752. *Fanny L. Emerson*

PHIPPS, SALLY. [1813.] 10 yrs. [Born in Framingham, Mass., November 25, 1803.] 12½" x 12½". 3 alphabets. Eyelet and cross-stitch. Hemmed all around. Greek design in border. Elaborate scroll design around verse. Verse 739. *Mrs. Harrison F. Hunt*

PICKERING, ELIZA C. 1815. 9 yrs. 13" x 16". 3 alphabets. Satin and cross-stitch. Pillars with arched top rising out of vases, flowers along the side. *C. E. Goodspeed, Esq.*

PICKET, ELIZA. 1823. Baltimore [Md.]. 9 yrs. 24" x 17". 6 alphabets. Eyelet, tent, and cross-stitch. Greek fret and rose and vine borders. Sprays of flowers and leaves, rose spray. Verse 36. *Miss Lida Bartlett*

PICKET, ELIZA. 1825. Baltimore, Md. 11 yrs. 21" x 18". Chain, stem, tent, satin, and cross-stitch. Border of acorns and oak leaves. Large brick house, fences, and flowering trees. Illustrated. *Miss Lida Bartlett*

PIDGEON, HANNAH SOPHIA. 1813. [Born at Chews Landing, N. J., May 11, 1803. Lived at 5th St., below Washington Ave., Philadelphia, where Wharton School now stands.] 10 yrs. 17½" x 17½". Cross-stitch. Strawberry-vine border. In center, three-story brick house showing front and back doors; on lawn below, a lady, an armchair, 2 dogs, 3 lambs, 6 bees, birds on trees, chicken, etc. Other designs are urns, baskets of flowers, and border around name. *Mrs. Edward Ogg*

PIERCE, MARY. 1824. Newburyport [Mass.]. 13 yrs. 13" x 8". Stem, satin, and cross-stitch. Double cross-stitch border. At bottom, large basket of flowers in center, with two smaller baskets and two bushes in bloom; also grass and flowers. Five rows of embroidery. *Old Newbury Historical Society*

PIERCE, SILVIA. [Cir. 1809.] 23" x 29". Satin, stem, cross, and many other stitches. Large tomb with funeral vase on top bearing verse, willows drooping over it and woman in black leaning on it; child in white at her side wrapped in black, shroudlike drapery. On another tombstone, with pillars on either side, is the inscription, "Sacred to the memory of Mr. Thomas Tingley who died Jan. 9, 1809 in the 77 year of his age and Mrs. Martha Tingley, his wife, who died Nov. 22, 1805 in the 74 year of her age." On a smaller tomb is the inscription, "Inscribed to the remains of Miss Ruth Tingley, daughter of Mr. Thomas Tingley, who died Nov. 30, 1803 in the 39 year of her age." Verse 283.

Mrs. Otis Tingley

PIKE, ELEANOR S. 1826. Salisbury [R. I.]. Born August 22, 1816. 17" x 17". 3 alphabets. Satin and cross-stitch. Ròses and leaves in border and Grecian work inside the border. At bottom, "The Homestead," house, wharf, trees, bushes, and small flowers. Seven rows of cross-stitch in different designs. Verse 174. On either side of verse is a vase filled with a mixed bouquet.

Mrs. John C. Rolfe

PIKE, RUTH. [1809. North Providence, R. I.] 13 yrs. 8" x 10". 2 alphabets. Satin, cross, queen, and three openwork stitches. Simple cross-stitch border. At bottom, three trees. Seven different cross-lines.

Miss Elizabeth H. Snow

PILSBURY, BETSY. [Cir. 1800.] 7½" x 10½". 3 alphabets. Chain, satin, eyelet, cross-stitch, and hem-stitch. Row of cross-stitch all around.

Mrs. R. H. Little

PIPER, MARTHA. 1829. Dublin [N. H.]. 12 yrs. [Born November 23, 1817.] 9½" x 9½". 3 alphabets. Flat and cross-stitch. She pulled threads to keep her lines straight. Verse 128.

Mrs. W. J. Stewart

PITMAN, MARY A. 1812. 12 yrs. 10" x 8". 3 alphabets. Cross-stitch.

Mrs. Clarence A. Matthewson

PITTEE, MARY W. 10 yrs. 10" x 8". Tapestry and cross-stitch. Conventional cross-borders at top and bottom and across center. House and four fir trees; house is white at bottom and yellow at top.

Mrs. Thomas A. Lawton

PITTMAN, ABIGAIL. 1830. 8" x 11". 2 alphabets. Cross-stitch. *Mrs. Lydia Satterthwait*

PITTMAN, LYDIA. 1810. [New Jersey.] 18" x 18". Satin and cross-stitch. Strawberry and rose border. At bottom, house, birds, cattle, fowl, chicken house, trees, and flowers in pots. "Daughter of Aaron Pittman and Elizabeth his wife." Verse 290.

Mrs. Lydia Satterthwait

PLATT, NANCY. 1804. [Wrightstown, N. J.] 16 yrs. 20" x 20". Eyelet, flat, stem, satin, and cross-stitch. Design represents large country estate. Across top is farmhouse set on knoll, tree on either side, fence running down banking, 10 fir trees, one lady standing and another seated on mound. In center is the residence, with large willow tree on either side and one fir tree. Below, a lady on horseback, cow eating grass, dog, trees, and bird. In lower right-hand corner is distant view of the spring house, with fence and trees. Illustrated.

Miss Fanny Lippincott

PLUMER, ELIZA. 1809. Newburyport [Mass. Born October 20, 1799.]. 10 yrs. 9" x 12". 3 alphabets. Eyelet and cross-stitch. Hemstitched edge with band of eyelets inside. At bottom, animals, trees, and baskets of flowers. *Miss Judith Rogers*

PLUMER, LYDIA. 1812. Newburyport [Mass.]. 10 yrs. 8½" x 11". 3 alphabets. Cross and eyelet-stitch. Cross-stitch border. *Miss Judith Rogers*

PLUMER, MARY. 1816. Newburyport [Mass.]. 11 yrs. [Born November 20, 1805.] 8½" x 11". 4 partial alphabets. Satin, eyelet, and cross-stitch. Hemstitched edge. At bottom, elaborate design consisting of three hills with two trees; between the trees a horn of plenty filled with roses and buds. *Miss Judith Rogers*

POLK, MARTHA SURBOROUGH. [Kent County, Md.] 9 yrs. 12″ x 14″. Vase of roses and leaves; one rose has fallen over the vase. *Mrs. Frederic Tyson*

POLK, PATTY. [Cir. 1800. Kent County, Md.] 10 yrs. 16″ x 16″. Stem-stitch. Large garland of pinks, roses, passion flowers, nasturtiums, and green leaves; in center, a white tomb with "G W" on it, surrounded by forget-me-nots. "Patty Polk did this and she hated every stitch she did in it. She loves to read much more." *Mrs. Frederic Tyson*

POMEROY, ROSAMUND PORTER. 1806. Burlington [Vt.]. 9 yrs. 17″ x 15″. 3 alphabets. Flat, outline, stem, and cross-stitch. Greek fret border. Above verse, 3 vases of flowers, and below, 3 sprays of flowers. Verse 106. *Mrs. Charles W. Baker*

POND, CHLOE. 1811. Walpole [Mass.]. 13 yrs. 16″ x 12½″. 3 alphabets. Flat and cross-stitch. Border has a basket in each lower corner, from which runs an elaborate vine bearing large pink flowers. Across top are four trees and a large bird. Verse 162 (1). *Albert C. Bates, Esq.*

POND, CYNTHIA. 1816. Burlington [Conn.]. 12 yrs. 14″ x 17″. 4 alphabets. Eyelet, herringbone, and cross-stitch. Border done in herringbone-stitch. Strawberry design across bottom, with two vases of flowers, small bird, and animal. Verse 95. *Albert C. Bates, Esq.*

PORTER, HANNAH. 1800. Bridgewater [Mass.]. 13″ x 16″. 4 alphabets. Cross-stitch. Conventional border. Saw-tooth design at bottom. Initials "C B R" in left lower corner. Verse 672. *Mrs. Francis Collamore*

PORTER, HANNAH S. 1823. 14 yrs. 16″ x 16″. Cross-stitch. Small conventional border. House in right-hand corner; scattered trees; stars and baskets. "Family Register: Nathaniel Porter born April 4, 1760; Nancy Porter born June 12, (1864) *sic*; Benjamin A. Porter born June 12, 1864 (*sic*); Nathan Porter born May 12, 1767 (87?); George Porter born June 12, 1769 (89?); Betsy Porter born March 12, 1792 (1892 *sic*); Elizabeth Porter born Feb. 4, (1813)?; Joseph Porter born April 20, (1810?); William Porter born Oct. 22, 1800; Warren Porter born July 23, 1803; Edward P. Porter born April 31, 1809; Hannah S. Porter born June 12, 1812; Nancy A. Porter born Sept. 23, 1813; Betsy Porter died March 19, 1794; Warren Porter died February 17, 1810." *Wilder's Bookshop, 1920*

PORTER, RACHEL A. 1829. 9 yrs. 7″ x 16″. 5 alphabets. Split, stem, hem, cat, tent, and cross-stitch. Double border; vine interlined with a border of solid stem-stitch. *Mrs. G. Clem Goodrich*

PORTER, SALLY. 1808. Born in Danvers, March 15, 1797. 11 yrs. 14″ x 17″. 3 alphabets. French knot, chain, eyelet, stem, satin, and cross-stitch. Vine border with smaller cross-stitch design inside. Lower third of sampler is a rose pattern over a conventional design, with trees on either side. Five different cross-borders. *Winthrop Porter Abbott, Esq.*

POTTER, ELIZABETH. 1801. [Philadelphia.?] 17″ x 20″. 4 alphabets. Cross-stitch. Simple conventional flower border. Above name, 17 little trees arranged on steps. In lower corners, two jardinières full of flowers. Near center, two birds in wreaths of flowers. Verse 533. *Mrs. William Nelson Marye*

POTTS, SERENA M[ATILDA]. 1823. 7″ x 20″. 2 alphabets. Eyelet and cross-stitch. Conventional border. 9 different cross-borders. 2 large and 1 small conventional flowers at bottom. Verse 515 (var.). *Mrs. Mary T. Schaffer*

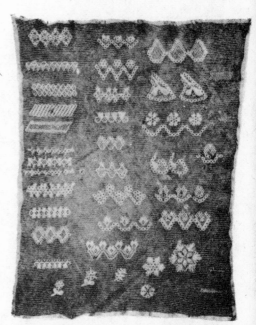

PLATE LXIX

MARY GILL'S SAMPLER. Wilmington, Del. 1814
Owned by Mrs. Charles C. Jessup

SAMPLER BY AN UNKNOWN GIRL
Owned by Mrs. Thomas A. Lawton

PLATE LXX

ELIZABETH ANN GOLDIN'S SAMPLER. New York. 1829
Owned by Mrs. Henry E. Coe

POTTS, SERENA MATILDA. 1822. 8" x 8¼". 2½ alphabets. Eyelet and cross-stitch. Simple cross-stitch lines.   *Mrs. Mary T. Schaffer*

POYAS, ELIZABETH C. 1800. Charleston [S. C.]. 6 yrs. 11" x 13". 2 alphabets. Eyelet, tent, satin, and cross-stitch. Hemstitched edge, with strawberry and carnation border at top and bottom.   *Mrs. William Ball*

PRANDALL, SUSAN. 1808. [Born at Gloucester, Mass., 1799.] 16½" x 12". 3 alphabets. Satin and cross-stitch. Greek fret border. Elaborate bow and garland over the verses. Verse 152 (var.).   *William H. Swasey, Esq.*

PRATT, ELIZA. 1822. [13 yrs.] 22" x 30". Petit-point, couching, long, short, cat, stem, satin, cross-stitch, and appliquéd satin pieces. Large design of arch with 2 columns. Clock at top set at 3 minutes past 4. At bottom, tomb with urn on top. Other designs are baskets of flowers, spray of roses, and 8-pointed stars. Appliquéd satin piece on tomb, inscribed with deaths of Thomas and Eliza. Appliquéd satin circles on either side of tomb; one has "Duty of Parents to Children" and the other has "Duty of Children to Parents." In between columns is family register. "Family of Thomas B. and Betsy Pratt. Parents ages, Thomas Brooks Pratt born January 8, 1774; Betsy Smith born April 13, 1776; Married March 16, 1796. Children's ages: John Foster adopted son born July 26, 1796; Mary Pratt born July 12, 1796; died Aug. 9, 1796; Mary Pratt born July 29, 1796; died July 30, 1796; Thomas Pratt born Dec. 28, 1798; died Aug. 12, 1800; Thomas Pratt born Dec. 26, 1800; Eliza Pratt born Oct. 8, 1802; died Dec. 26, 1807; Caleb Pratt born Dec. 2, 1804; Mary Pratt born Dec. 25, 1806; Eliza Pratt born Jan. 21, 1809; John Murray Pratt born Feb. 23, 1811; Samuel Pratt born April 29, 1813; Nathan Pratt born May 20, 1817." Verses 21, 322.   *Carbone's, December 10, 1919*

PRESBREY, ABBY B. 1828. Taunton [Mass.]. 10 yrs. 18" x 12½". 3 alphabets. Cross-stitch. Plain border. 5 diamond-shaped designs at bottom. "Happy is the man that findeth wisdom's length of days is in her right hand and in her left hand riches and honour. Her ways are ways of pleasantness and all her paths are peace."

Mrs. George W. Barrows

PRESCOTT, EMILY. September 1, 1804. 16" x 20". 3 alphabets. Cross, satin, stem, and flat-stitch. Broad and elaborate carnation border. Two rose and other simple cross-borders. Verse 47 (1, 2).   *Metropolitan Museum of Art, New York*

PRESTON, ELIZA. [1824.] Boston [Mass.]. 6 yrs. [Born in 1818.] 6" x 12". 3 alphabets. Cat, flat, and cross-stitch. At bottom, two bowls of flowers.

Henry Preston Kendall, Esq., and His Sisters

PRESTON, MARY. [1805.] Roxbury [Mass.]. 7 yrs. 12" x 14½". 3 alphabets. Hem-stitch, chain, and cross-stitch. Flowers in pots alternate with trees on sides and across bottom; birds sitting on treetops; other birds and bees flying about. Cross-borders of small flowers. Verse 411.   *Miss Alice Wetherbee*

PURINTON, EUNICE. [1810.] 11 yrs. Born September 28, 1799. East Harpswell [Me.]. 23¼" x 17½". 5 alphabets. Long and short and cross-stitch. Double border; long and short on outside and strawberry border inside. Hourglass surmounted by basket of flowers; also, man, woman, dogs, cats, sheep, birds, tree, and vine. "Samplar completed when child was eleven years old. Certified by Temperance P. Jackson Instructor." Verse 257. The register not received.   *Mrs. George Carroll Smith*

PURINTON, PRISCILLA. 1805. Harpswell [Me.]. Born September 7, 1795. 15½" x 17½". 5 alphabets. Eyelet, stem, satin, and cross-stitch. Strawberry-vine border outside and saw-tooth design inside. Strawberry-vine cross-border at bottom. Also at bottom, large tree with birds on several branches, and under tree are sheep, dog, man and woman in Colonial dress shaking hands. In center is a large basket filled with flowers, and on the right side a large bush with a bird on top and a cage hanging from a branch. Various cross-borders.   *Mary Chapman Stetson*

PUTNEY, HARRIOT. 1809. Boscawen [N. H.]. 10 yrs. 16" x 22". Partial alphabets. Eyelet, stem, satin, and cross-stitch. Strawberry border at top and sides and Greek fret at bottom. Stiff-looking tree in each lower corner. Verses 285, 715.   *Esther D. Gill*

QUIGLEY, ANN. 1814. 17" x 17". Satin and cross-stitch. Elaborate wreath of small flowers and leaves. A black octagonal frame incloses an acrostic. Verse 446.
      Mrs. Henry Eugene Coe

RAMSDELL, MARY. 1815. Lunenburg [Mass.]. 15 yrs. 17" x 17½". 3 alphabets. Chain, satin, and cross-stitch. Rose border. Triangular border in satin-stitch. At bottom, upright strawberries; in center, 2 baskets of flowers; below, 3 baskets with 2 dogs between. Verse 164 (var.). Names and dates: "Freedom Ramsdell born May 25, 1794; Mary, born Feb. 28, 1800; Lydia born Dec. 14, 1801; Lucy born Nov. 23, 1803; Allaseba and Lucinda born June 6, 1805; Abagail born Feb. 9, 1807; John born June 29, 1810."
      Frank J. Lawton, Esq.

RAND, JANE. 1811. Newburyport [Mass.]. 9 yrs. 9" x 17". 2 alphabets. Seed, satin, and cross-stitch. Cross-stitch border. Basket of flowers at bottom.   *Miss Jane Rand Wood*

RANDALL, ELIZABETH PALMER. 182?. 8 yrs. Partial alphabets. Cross-stitch. Scroll design in border. Simple, narrow cross-borders. Verse 515 (1, var.).
      Communicated by Mrs. A. A. Lawrence

RANDALL, MARY A. 1818. Smithfield. 8" x 9". 3 alphabets. Chain and cross-stitch. Verses 94, 117.   *Mrs. H. W. Bradford*

RANDALL, MARY O. 1822. 18" x 17½". 5 alphabets. Chain, stem, and cross-stitch. House. Verse 122.   *Mrs. H. W. Bradford*

RANDELL, FRANCES D. 1830. North Providence. 8" x 12". 3 alphabets. Cat and cross-stitch.
      Mrs. H. W. Bradford

RANDEL, MARY AMANDA. 1826. [Harlem, New York City.] 9 yrs. 17" x 17½". 2 alphabets. Cross-stitch. Greek border with strawberry design. At bottom, urn with tulips and leaves, basket, and bush. Verse 515 (var.).   *Mrs. Charles G. Trumbull*

RANDOLPH, SALLY FRENCH. 1812. 16½" x 20½". 3 alphabets. Chain, stem, satin, and cross-stitch. Violet and vine border. Same runs across center. Inner border in conventional design. In lower section, two-story house with sheds on one side and garden on the other; ladies in garden and on path in front of house. In middle section, verse flanked by two pedestals topped by urns. Verse 434.   *Max Williams, 1916*

RANSOM, SOPHIA ANN. 1824. 12 yrs. 17½" x 16". 4 alphabets. Cross-stitch. Strawberry border.   *Albert C. Bates, Esq.*

RAPP, MARY ANN. 1827. 8" x 11". 5 alphabets. Eyelet and cross-stitch. Scroll and other designs in cross-borders.   *Mrs. Henry Eugene Coe*

RAPP, CATHERINE. 1827. 7" x 12½". 1½ alphabets. Eyelet, tent, queen, and cross-stitch. In lower half, basket of fruit and detached flowers.   *Mrs. Henry Eugene Coe*

RATHBUN, LYDIA. 1812. 11 yrs. 11½" x 11½". 3 alphabets. Cross-stitch.
      Mrs. Barton A. Ballou

RAYNER, CATHERINE. 1818. Boston [Mass.]. 9 yrs. [Born in 1809.] 9" x 12". Cross-stitch. Double strawberry border. 3 alphabets. *Mrs. R. S. Southard*

READ, RUTH. 1812. 12 yrs. 12¼" x 13¾". 5 alphabets. Cross-stitch. Conventional border in cross-stitch and drawn-work. Conventional design of same at bottom. Verse 439. *Mrs. Octavia Pickens*

READING, MARY A[NN]. 1820 or 22. [Born June 23, 1810.] 10½" x 10½". 3 alphabets. Eyelet and cross-stitch. Cross-stitch border. *Miss Mary Reading Scofield*

REDING, HARRIET BIRON. [Portsmouth, N. H.] 4 alphabets, not all complete. Satin, stem, and cross-stitch. Conventional border and three cross-borders. Scene at bottom with three-story house, fence, trees, lawn, harbor, sailboat, and man fishing from banking. Verse 323. *Mrs. Thomas A. Lawton*

REDING, MARY A. April 3, 1824. Portsmouth [N. H.]. 2 alphabets. Stem, satin, tent, and cross-stitch. Rose border with wreath around name, date, etc., in center at top. Scene with large white house, fence, barn, trees, pond, boats, and houses in the distance. Verses 323, 324. *Mrs. Thomas A. Lawton*

REED, ELIZA. 13 yrs. " Under the tuition of Harriet Ellis." 16" x 15". 4 alphabets. Border of conventional flowers inside squares that are joined together. At bottom, large house, tree, fence, small house, and baskets of flowers. Verse 94 (var.). *Miss Harriet Perkins*

REED, PHEBE. 1805. 14 yrs. 17" x 20". 1 alphabet. Chain, stem, and cross-stitch. Grapevine border around three sides. Wreath, oblong in shape, at bottom. House, tree in blossom on either side. Verse 601 (1, 2, var.). *Arthur Leslie Green, Esq.*

[REMINGTON], [CYNTHIA T.] [1825.] 8½" x 8½". 5 alphabets. Cross-stitch. *Mrs. A. W. Love*

REMINGTON, SALLY ANN. 1818. Coventry. 6" x 8½". 3 alphabets. Chain and cross-stitch. *Mr. Arthur W. Claflin*

RENDOIS, SARAH C. 1828. Boston [Mass.]. 12 yrs. [Salem Street Academy.] 18" x 18". 3 alphabets. Satin and cross-stitch. Vine border. Verse 485. *Mrs. Graydon Stetson*

REYNOLDS, LUCRETIA C. 1822. Shepardtown, Va. About 10 yrs. 16" x 16½". 3 alphabets. Eyelet, satin, and cross-stitch. Strawberry design in border. Greek fret cross-border and several others. At one side of verse is an urn. Verse 515 (var.). *Estelle Lucretia Wheeler*

RHODES, MARY. 1806. Southampton [L. I.]. 11 yrs. 11" x 12". 3 alphabets. Queen and cross-stitch. Queen-stitch border in saw-tooth design. Band of solid embroidery across the bottom, with geometric figures in queen-stitch. Verse 699. *Mrs. Thomas B. Clarke*

RHODES, PHEBE. 1820. 10 yrs. 16" x 17". 3 alphabets. Stem, chain, French knots, and cross-stitch. Flowers and strawberries. Verse 515. Family record: " Robert Rhodes born Apr. 22, 1804; William P. Rhodes born Apr. 8, 1807; died Jan. 5th, 1808; Mary M. Rhodes, March 5, 1807; died February 18th, 1812; Phoebe Rhodes born December 18th, 1810; Sally A. Rhodes born August 8th, 1813; died September 14th, 1813; Mary H. Rhodes born September 12th, 1815; Sally A. Rhodes born August 11th, 1819; died August 7th, 1820." *Mrs. George Arnold*

RICE, ELMIRA. [Cir. 1813.] Ashby [Mass. Cir. 10 yrs. Born January 31, 1803.]. 16½" x 23". 2 alphabets. Italian, laid, satin, and cross-stitch. Strawberry vine on sides, flower-pots at top and bottom. Inscriptions on two hearts at bottom of sampler are: "John Rice, born in Ashby, Mass., March 18, 1768," and "Lucy (Hubbard) Rice born in Concord, Mass., Aug. 16, 1775." Births of children are inscribed on the fruit on family tree as on Lucy Rice's Sampler, below. Verses 552, 738.   *Miss Elizabeth F. Kelly*

RICE, LUCY. 1811. Ashby [Mass.]. 12 yrs. 16" x 19½". 2 alphabets. Stem, laid, and cross-stitch. Strawberry vine on three sides and scroll design. Verse and 5 floral designs at bottom. Verse 727. "Mr. John Rice born March 18th, 1768; Mrs. Lucy Rice born Aug. 16th, 1775; [children], Rebecca [born Feb. 20], 1793; Lucy [born March 11], 1799; Almira [born Jan. 31], 1803; John H. [born Aug. 13], 1806."   *Miss Elizabeth F. Kelly*

RICE, MARY. 1810. 12 yrs. 15½" x 21½". 3 alphabets. Satin, stem, and cross-stitch. Cross and diamond designs in border. Baskets of flowers on each side of tree at bottom. Verse 40 (var.). Family record of Samuel and Mary Rice [father and mother of maker].
                                                      Heirs of E. G. Remington

RICE, PERSIS. September, 1815. Marlborough [Mass.]. 11 yrs. 14½" x 18". 3 alphabets. Stem and cross-stitch. Hemstitched edge with strawberry-vine border. Tree in center at bottom. Verses 165, 515 (1, var.).   *Mrs. William H. Hackett*

RICE, PHEBE. 1815. 9 yrs. 10" x 8". 3 alphabets. Cross-stitch.   *Mrs. Brouwer*

RICHARDS, NANCY. August 20. Newton [Mass.]. 9 yrs. Alphabets. Verse 799.
                                                      Estate of James L. Little, Esq.

RICHARDS, SALLY. July 8, 1805. Dedham [Mass.]. 11 yrs. 10¼" x 16½". 2 alphabets. Chain, eyelet, satin, and cross-stitch. Double hemstitching on three sides. Greek design at bottom. Elaborate design at bottom of large pot of flowers and leaves, and two urns with handles on either side. Fancy design underneath.   *Mrs. Harrison F. Hunt*

RICHARDS, SALLY. [Cir. 1806.] Dedham [Mass. Born in 1794.]. 5½" x 7¾". 2 alphabets. Satin and cross-stitch. Hemstitched edge. Spaces left for age and date.
                                                      Mrs. Harrison F. Hunt

RICHARDSON, MARY. 1812. Westford [Mass.]. 13 yrs. 17" x 17". 3½ alphabets. Stem and cross-stitch. Grapevine border. At bottom, house with trees, deer, dog, birds, garden seat, vines, and plants. Verse 732 (1, var.). Under the design at bottom, "Mary Cummings, Instructress."   *J. V. Fletcher Library, Westford*

RIDGWAY, ABIGAIL. Done in the year 1795. 17" x 18". Tent and cross-stitch. Decorative and unusual design arrangement. Verse 229.   *Miss Belle Skinner*

RIDGWAY, ELIZABETH. 1830. Alphabets. Cross-stitch. Verse 337.   *Maxcy Applegate, Esq.*

RIDGWAY, MARY J. May 24, 1822. [New Jersey.] 8 yrs. 19¼" x 21¼". Cross-stitch. Strawberry border. House, trees, arbor, deer, dog, and 3 doves. Entire sampler covered with flowering shrubs in jars and flowers in bowls. Verse 515 (var.).
                                                      Mrs. R. A. Rodrick

RIEMAN, SOPHIA. 1812. Baltimore [Md.]. 9 yrs. 16" x 17". 9 alphabets. Cat, eyelet, and cross-stitch. Conventional border, with alternate roses and carnations.
                                                      Mrs. Michael B. Wild

RIGGS, ——. [Cir. 1809.] 17" x 20". Eyelet, stem, satin, and cross-stitch. Vine border with red ends. Elaborate flower in each corner. Family Register: "William Riggs born

May 2, 1769; Mary Riggs born Octr 18, 1772. Married December 13, 1792; Nabby Gootch born Decr 3, 1753.

Births				Deaths			
"Fanny Riggs	born	sep^r	10, 1793	"Daniel Riggs	died	oct^r	28, 1795
Daniel Riggs	born	Aug^t	11, 1796	Hannah Riggs	died	feb^y	28, 1805
Eliza Riggs	born	Aug^t	22, 1797	Mary Riggs	died	march	5, 1805
Mary Riggs	born	Aug^t	13, 1799	Mary Riggs	died	march	30, 1806
Hannah Riggs	born	Nov^r	12, 1801	Hannah Riggs	died	aug^t	22, 1809
Joann Riggs	born	feb^y	14, 1804	Eliza Riggs	died	oct^r	28, 1809 "
Mary Riggs	born	feb^y	4, 1806				
Hannah Riggs	born	jan^y	24, 1807				
William Riggs	born	jan^y	14, 1810				
Jane Riggs	born	March	5, 1813				
Eliza Riggs	born	March	11, 1815 "				

Estate of James L. Little, Esq.

RINE, FANNY. 1808. Borough of Lancaster [Pa.]. "Made at Mrs. Armstrong's School." 14 yrs. 17½" x 18½". 2 alphabets. Satin and cross-stitch. Vine and flowers on three sides, and narrow frame inside. In upper section, wreath inclosing girl with lamb, sitting under a willow tree; sprays of flowers in four corners of frame. Inscription, alphabets, and verses in lower section. Verses 282, 417. Inscription as follows: "Fanny Rine a daughter of Christian and Barbara Rine was born in the borough of Lancaster the 26th day of Sept. 1796 and made this sampler in Mrs. Armstrong's School A. D. 1808." *Mrs. Frederick F. Thompson*

RINE, WILLAMINA. 1813. "Mrs. Armstrong's School," Lancaster [Pa.]. 12 yrs. 19" x 15½". Stem-stitch. "Willamina Rine a daughter of Christian and Barbara Rine was born November 6th 1801 and Made this Sampler at Mrs. Armstrong's School, Lancaster." Verse 282 (var.). In center, oval with girl (painted face) standing under a weeping willow tree, and above and below oval are sprays of leaves and flowers tied with bow-knots to form a wreath. *Mrs. Henry E. Coe*

RING, ELIZA. 1808. Salem [Mass.]. 10 yrs. 15" x 18". Partial alphabet. Stem-stitch. Rose-vine border at sides. Roses and tulips in vase in center at bottom; horns of plenty on either side, filled with flowers; small trees in vases in each upper corner. Verse in center at top. Verse 40. *Edward Rivers Lemon, Esq.*

RINGWALT, HARRIET A. 1806. 7 yrs. 20" x 18". 3 alphabets. 20" x 18". Cross-stitch. Strawberry and carnation border, with basket of flowers in upper corners and birds in lower corners. At bottom, house on a terraced lawn, with fence on either side, at end of which are two huge vases of flowers; small pine trees on either side at bottom of terrace; a buck and two lambs on lawn. *Mrs. Lathrop Brown*

RIPLEY, LUCY. 1802. Hartford, Conn. 13 yrs. 16" x 12½". 3 alphabets. Cross-stitch. Simple cross-stitch border. Verses 76, 515. *Miss Laura M. Ripley*

RIPLEY, SARAH SHURTLEFF. [Cir. 1804.] Born February 1, 1794. 7" x 12¾". Alphabet. Cross-stitch. Across center, 3 rows of conventional flowers, and at bottom, 2 large and totally different trees. *Mrs. Charles J. White*

RISING, SALLIE M. September 22nd, 1812. Rupert [Vt.]. 12 yrs. 7" x 8½". 2 alphabets. Cross-stitch. Greek fret border in three styles of cross-stitch. *Miss Agnes M. Arnold*

ROACH, HARRIOT. March 25th, 1805. Charleston [S. C.]. 12½" x 18". Hem-stitch, satin, petit-point, stem, and cross-stitch. Tulip border all around and across upper center. In center, house, trees, sheep, dog, and eight-pointed stars. At bottom, baskets of flowers with birds on either side of them, and a large vase of flowers in between. Large insects on either side. Sprays of flowers on either side of verse at top. Verse 104 (1, 2, 3, var.).

Mrs. Middleton Guérard Fuller

ROBERDEAN, SUSAN. 1811. 9″ x 12″. 2 alphabets. Eyelet and cross-stitch. Hemstitched edge. At bottom, large green tree in center, with 2 smaller trees on either side with a bird on top. *National Museum, Washington, D. C.*

ROBERTS, AMORENA D. T. 1828. Born August 28th, 1818. 18″ x 18″. 4 alphabets. Eyelet, stem, satin, queen, tent, petit-point, and cross-stitch. Conventional border. In lower left-hand corner, scene with house, orchard, fence, and large blossom growing in grass. Wreath of roses and basket, fruit, and leaves over verse. Verse 515.

Mrs. Thomas A. Lawton

ROBERTSON, ELIZABETH. September 30th, 1817. 14″ x 16″. Alphabet. Cross-stitch. Conventional diamond-shaped design in border. Strawberry-vine cross-border at top, and scroll across center. Oblong wreath of vine and flowers at bottom, with a basket in top center. Over it are the words, "It is no shame to learn, the shame is to be ignorant." Verse 720 (var.). *Mrs. W. B. Gillican*

ROBERTSON, LYDIA. 1807. 14″ x 17″. Alphabet. Satin and cross-stitch. Conventional rose-vine border. At bottom, child standing on hilltop, with large flowers in pots at either side; butterflies, birds, etc., also in picture. Verse 601. *A. Piatt Andrews, Esq.*

ROBINSON, ADELINE E. [Cir. 1800.] 12 yrs. 17½″ x 16½″. Satin and cross-stitch. Rose-vine border. Floral border inclosing verses and acrostic; spray of roses below. Verses 539, 701. Acrostic. *William B. Thayer Memorial Collection, University of Kansas*

ROBINSON, HANNAH J. 1818. 18″ x 16″. Satin, stem, and cross-stitch. Heavy black line around edge. High green hill, with weeping willow on top; maple tree at right and rose-bush at left; flowers growing in grass at foot of hill; on either side of hill are brown poles with vines. At top of sampler is a spread eagle holding framed verse in claws. Verse 456. Illustrated. *Mrs. Bradbury Bedell*

ROBINSON, MARY. 1814. Exeter. 10 yrs. 7½″ x 11″. 3 alphabets. Cross-stitch. Simple border. Strawberry design at bottom. Verse 161. *Boston Museum of Fine Arts*

ROBINSON, MARY. 1820. 13 yrs. 13″ x 15½″. 3 alphabets. Cross-stitch. Greek fret and triangular figure in border. At bottom, 2 birds on bush; strawberry bush below them; strawberry vine on each side and in between; basket of fruit on one side and basket of flowers on the other; also, spray of rosebuds and bunch of grapes. Initials: " B R [Benjamin Robinson, father]; E R [Elizabeth Robinson, mother]; J R [Joseph]; M R [Mary]; W R [William]; A R [Angeline]; C R [Caroline]; E R [Emaline, brothers and sisters]." Verse 546 (1). *Miss Emma R. Burt*

ROBINSON, MARY A. June 27, 1804. 13 yrs. 8″ x 10″. 2 alphabets. Cross-stitch. Cross-border. At bottom, little animals. Verse 91a (1, var.). *Mrs. J. S. Brace*

ROBINSON, SUSAN. 1809. 7 yrs. Augusta [Me.]. 8″ x 11″. 3 alphabets. Cross-stitch. Simple cross-borders. *Mrs. Henry P. Briggs*

ROGERS, AMELIA. 1830. Baltimore [Md.]. 15 yrs. 17″ x 22″. 4 alphabets. Tent, stem, and cross-stitch. Cross-stitch border. At bottom, urns with flowers and willow trees.

Nannie Dryden Kensett

ROGERS, DEIDAMIA S. 1826. 10 yrs. Border at sides and top of rose vine, and of solid work across bottom. Corners filled (?) in bunches of berries, and in between is inscription:

"Family Record   Mr. Josiah Rogers born April 28, 1759; Miss Diedamia Reed born Dec.   Married June 1, 1813." Below, in 3 circles of tiny flowers weaving into each other, are names and birth dates of children: "Lucy J. Rogers born Dec. 22, 1814; Deidamia S. Rogers born Jan. 16, 1816; Martha Rogers born March 20, 1819." At bottom, in saw-tooth medallion from which sprout weeping willow branches, is inscription, "Josiah Rogers died Dec. 4, 1822."   *Mrs. L. I. Hathaway*

ROGERS, ELIZABETH. 1810. Burlington. 18" x 22". 5 alphabets. Cross-stitch. Tulip and carnation border. Flowers and baskets of fruit. Verse 515 (var.).
    Mrs. Siegfried Wachsman

ROGERS, JOANNA. 1807. Newbury [Mass.]. 10 yrs. 6 mos. Born February 14, 1797. 15½" x 22½". 3 alphabets. French knots, petit-point, stem, satin, and cross-stitch. Greek fret border. Design of trees, animals, and men. At bottom, a square on either side filled with geometrical figures. Verses 128 (var.), 187.   *Mrs. John F. Hibbs*

ROGERS, MARTHA. 1824. 17" x 20". [Born at Hainesport, N. J.]. 17" x 20". 4 alphabets. Cross-stitch. Design of tree, basket of flowers, ship, and turtle doves.
    Deborah J. Peacock

ROGERS, MARY A. 1826. 11 yrs. 10" x 20". 3 alphabets. Cross-stitch. Vine border on three sides. Simple cross-borders. Across bottom, house, trees, basket of fruit, basket of flowers, sprays of flowers, windmill, birds, etc. Above house, in center at bottom, are two white birds holding band on which is inscribed name, age and date.
    Mrs. Thomas A. Lawton

ROGERS, PATIENCE. 1801. Warren. 10 yrs. 12½" x 17½". Alphabet. Stem and cross-stitch. Greek fret border. Verse 606.   *Lyra Brown Nickerson*

ROGERSON, ——. 1808. 15¼" x 14¾". French knots, long and short, and cross-stitch. Willow tree, urn, and weeping figure. "Sacred to the Memory of Dr. Robt. Rogerson Obt. April 1st, 1806 AE 49 yrs; Lucy Rogerson Obt. March 4th, 1807 AE 39; Danl H. Rogerson Obt. March 25th, 1808 AE 14; Lucy H. Rogerson Obt. 1803 AE 11 months."
    Mrs. George C. Fraser

ROLFE, RHODA C. 1824. Concord [N. H.]. 12 yrs. Born May 26, 1812. 17" x 17". 6 alphabets. Flat, cat, satin, eyelet, stem, cross-stitch, and Van Dyke stitch. Cat-stitched hem all around. Large basket with plant in center at bottom, and on either side large plants in pots. Verse 703 (3).   *Miss Lydia Rolfe Farnum*

ROLLINGS, SALLY. 1800. 9½" x 12½". 3 alphabets. Satin and cross-stitch. At bottom, large spray of flowers, with two smaller sprays on each side.   *Mrs. Bradbury Bedell*

ROSSELL, MARY T. 1828. Trenton [N. J.]. 17" x 15". 4 alphabets. Cross-stitch. Strawberry-vine border. In center, vine inclosing verse and name; star on each side; large flowers and basket of flowers in rest of space. Verse 791.   *Margaret Rossell*

ROWAND, SARAH W. 1810. [Southampton Township, Burlington County, N. J.] 14 yrs. [Born November 10, 1796.] 18" x 16¾". 5 alphabets. Cat, queen, flat, eyelet, and cross-stitch. Cross-border. At bottom, strawberries, flowers, birds, and crown.
    Miss Sarah Rowand Budd

ROWE, A[NNE]. 1814. Milton. 7 yrs. 7½" x 8". 3 alphabets. Cross-stitch. Hemstitched edge.   *Mrs. Caleb Loring Cunningham*

ROWE, P. 9 yrs. 1814. Milton. 7½" x 8". 3 alphabets. Cross-stitch. Hemstitched edge. A. 7 yrs.   *Mrs. Caleb Loring Cunningham*

ROYAL, POLLY. 1811. [Salem County, N. J.] 11 yrs. [Born October, 1800.] 12" x 12¼". 3 alphabets. Outline, eyelet, chain, satin, and cross-stitch. Strawberry-vine border. At bottom, butterflies, trees, birds, plants, stars, diamonds, strawberries, rosebuds, baskets, and baskets of flowers. Initials: "D R [David Royal, father]; R R [Ruth Royal, mother]; P R [Phebe]; P R [Polly]; J R [John]; D R [David]." Verse 594 (1, var.).
Miss Mary E. Hives

RUDDEROW, ANNA. 1816. 9" x 14". 4 alphabets. Cat, eyelet, and cross-stitch. Border of straight and irregular rows of cross-stitch. Initials: "E. Jones [Elnora Jones, grandmother]; J R [Jane]; AR [Abigail]; C R [Catharine]; B R [Beulah, sisters]."
Mrs. Gustavus M. Murray

RUE, HANNAH. 1827. 10 yrs. Born December 3, 1817. "Time swiftly flies. Improve each passing moment."
Maxcy Applegate, Esq.

RUNDLETTE, OLIVE H. C. 1830. Newcastle [Me.?]. 16¼" x 8¼". 4 alphabets. Eyelet and cross-stitch. Key pattern in border done in eyelet and cross-stitch. Strawberry design at bottom. Initials: "S R, R R, D R, J R, F R, P R, R R, H C, O C."
A. Stainforth, Dealer, August, 1917

RUSSELL, AMANDA. November 12, 1829. [Ohio.] 17½" x 16". 4 alphabets. Eyelet and cross-stitch. Conventionalized rose and tulip border. Small urns and geometrical designs at bottom. Verse 487a.
Mrs. Walter L. Milliken

RUSSELL, AMEY. 1808. Providence [R. I.]. 12½" x 15½". 3 alphabets. Stem, outline, and cross-stitch. Vine and flower border. Verse 503.
D. A. R. Museum, Kingston, R. I.

RUSSELL, LYDIA. 1809. Born February 26, 1791. [West Cambridge, now Arlington, Mass.] Satin, stem, French knots, long and short stitch. Tombstones in each lower corner with urn on top, out of which rises a vine with blossoms forming arch, and tied at the top with ribbon. In center at bottom is a large apple tree, each apple bearing the name and birth of a child. Underneath tree is a tiny house, trees, animals, etc. On one tombstone is inscription, "Edward Russell Born Octr 5th, 1764. Was Married May 11th, 1786. Died Novr 3rd, 1808." On the other is the inscription, "Lydia Adams Born Sept. 2d, 1767. Lydia R. 1st *—. Died Augst 28, 1790." On the apples are the following: "Jeremiah born Augst 28th, 1786; Leonora born February 24, 1787; Lydia 1st born Jany 22, 1789; Lydia 2nd born Febry 26th, 1791; Sophia born Sept. 2d, 1793; Edward born October 15, 1795; Mary born March 12, 1801."
Russell Carter, Esq.

RUSSELL, MARIA. 1808. Gettysburg [Pa.]. About 7 yrs. 8½" x 22". 4 alphabets. Eyelet and cross-stitch. Verse 281.
Marianne W. Stevenson

RUSSELL, MARY JANE. 1827. 10 yrs. 18" x 15¼". 4 alphabets. Satin and cross-stitch. Fine strawberry border and cross-borders. At bottom, two baskets of strawberries and two diamonds. Verse 176.
A. Stainforth, Dealer, 1917

RUSSELL, SUSAN. 1820. Newburyport [Mass.]. 9" x 12". 3 alphabets. Cross-stitch. Drawn-work border.
Miss Mary E. Wills

RUTHERFORD, JANE. 1804. 10 yrs. 17" x 12". Alphabets. Variety of stitches. Yellow bird, tree, and foliage. Diamond-shaped shields with name and date. (Six-line verse not given in sales catalogue.)
Walpole Galleries, New York City, sold June 29, 1917

RUTHVEN, MARION. [1803 or 4.] Charlestown. [7 yrs.] 9" x 17". 5 alphabets. Buttonhole and cross-stitch. Strawberry-vine border. Initials repeated often: "H C, M R, J R, S R, B R, I R." "Quintilian, an accurate judge of men was pleased with children who wept when their schoolfellows outdid them, for the sense of disgrace would make them emulous,

PLATE LXXI

FRANCES WADE'S SAMPLER. Savannah, Ga. 1798
Owned by Miss Fannie Bleeker Seaman

PLATE LXXII

SARAH S. CALDWELL'S SAMPLER. Barre, Mass. 1806
Owned by Mrs. W. F. Allen

and emulation would make them, schoolars." "The best school for a good life, is the frequent meditation upon a happy death." *Miss Mary H. Deane*

SAGE, EMMELINE. 1816. [Middletown, Conn., or Northampton, Mass.] 8 yrs. 11½″ x 12½″. 3 alphabets. Cross-stitch. Vine border. At bottom, 2 baskets of flowers with tree in between. Verse 515 (1, var.). *Elizabeth Sage*

SAKER, SUSAN AND ELIZABETH. 1826. 10 yrs. 18″ x 24″. 3 alphabets. Cross-stitch. 3 borders of Greek fret, strawberry, and zigzag designs. Two small baskets of flowers. "Remember thy Creator in the days of thy youth, while the evil days come not nor the years draw nigh, when thou shalt say, I have no pleasure in them."
Louise Salter Codwise Collection, National Museum

SALTONSTALL, SARAH. 1810. Haverhill, Essex County. 18″ x 15″. 3 alphabets. Petit-point, stem, satin, and cross-stitch. Dark green grass, with strawberries, 3 trees, and baskets of apples. *Mr. and Mrs. Edwin Garcia*

SANDERS, ANNA. "September the 1, 1801." Warren [R. I.]. "Born April 20, 1791 at Warren." 13″ x 17″. 2 alphabets. Cross, satin, stem, flat-stitch. Vines growing up the sides from flower-pots. At the top, two birds holding a heart in chains perhaps. Under the arch is a house, with steps down right and left. A tree stands on either side, with a woman under one and a man under the other. In front, a group of men, women, and children. A shepherd, shepherdess, and lambs. The verse is labeled, "An acrostic Presented To Miss Anna Sanders by her very affectionate friend Luther Bayer." Verse 675. [Taught by the same teacher who instructed at Polly Balch's School.]
Mrs. Thomas A. Lawton

SANDERS, MARTHA. March 25, 1825. Central Falls [R. I.]. 9 yrs. 16¼″ x 17¼″. 3 alphabets. Eyelet and cross-stitch. Verses 150 (last 2 lines of verse 1), 476, 566, 655.
Miss Harriet L. Smith

SANDERSON, C. 1809. "Frankford School." Stem, cross-stitch, and needle etching. Design is the World showing 2 hemispheres. In four corners are figures representing America, Europe, Asia, and Africa. Illustrated. *Mrs. Robert Garrett*

SANDERSON, MARY. 1818. 16″ x 16½″. 13 yrs. Variety of stitches. Elaborate border containing house, trees of various kinds, and serpentine floral side-borders. "A Family Record" containing the birth dates of her father, mother, and their six daughters.
Sold at Walpole Galleries, New York, June 29, 1917

SANFORD, ELENER. [Cir. 1800.] Berkley [Mass. Born in 1791.]. 12″ x 12″. 2 alphabets. Cross-stitch. *Mrs. George W. Colby*

SARISH, ABIGAIL ANN. 1828. [Salem County, N. J. Born March 31, 1814.] 17″ x 14½″. 1 alphabet. Eyelet, flat, outline, queen, satin, and cross-stitch. Greek fret and Greek cross borders. At bottom, meetinghouse with weeping willow tree. Lines of drapery with hanging tassels. *Miss Sarah Krom*

SARLE, JULIA ANN. 1814. 14″ x 10″. 3 alphabets. Chain and cross-stitch. Verse 747.
Miss A. C. Westcott

SAUNDERS, FRANCES RESPASS. 1803. Leesburg [Va.]. 12 yrs. 18″ x 24″. 5 alphabets. Eyelet and cross-stitch. Tulip and vine border. House with trees on each side.
Jeannette R. White

SAUNDERS, LUCY D. [Cir. 1810.] 11 yrs. Newburyport [Mass.]. 16½″ x 17″. 3 alphabets. French knots, chain, satin, and cross-stitch. Vine border, with leaves and berries. A figure with six curved rays in all four corners. Verse 113 (var.). *Lucie A. Peabody*

SAUNDERS, SARAH. 1789. Salem [Mass.]. 10 yrs. 10" x 14". 3 alphabets. Hem-stitch, eyelet, and cross-stitch. Hemstitched edge. Verse 44. (This sampler went through the Salem fire in 1914. The frame is scorched by great heat.) *Mrs. H. A. Everett*

SAUNDERS, SARAH DONNA LEONORA. 16½" x 16". Vine leaves framing a circle, in which is a representation of William and Mary College, Virginia. There are two boats in the stream in the foreground. The names "John S. Mary Saunders" and the initials "S. B. M. L. A. M. M. L. S. L. A. P. E. J. N. C. N. ዋ. P. A. R. A. C. F. A. B. M. C. H. E. L. B. C. A. M." Illustrated. *Mrs. Bradbury Bedell*

SAWYER, MARY. 1815. Sterling [Mass.]. 12 yrs. Cross-stitch. Floral border. Verse 748. *Mr. George T. Tilden*

SCHRACK, ELIZABETH. 1802. 9 yrs. 18" x 11½". Stem, satin, and cross-stitch. Carnation border all around. Scene with house, trees, shepherd, dog, sheep, barn, etc. Verse 132 (1, var.). *Mr. H. L. Stowell*

SCHRACKS, CATHERINE. 1812. 15½" x 18". 3 alphabets. Eyelet and cross-stitch. Rose and tulip border. Verse 187 (var.). *Pennsylvania Museum, Memorial Hall, Fairmount Park*

SCOT, MARY A. 1808. Winchester [Va.]. 8 yrs. 13" x 18". 5 alphabets. Cross-stitch. Carnation and Greek fret borders. Trees and plants at bottom. *Mrs. Harry R. Maybin*

SCOT, MARY A. 1808. Winchester [Va.]. 13" x 18". 5 alphabets. Eyelet, satin, and cross-stitch. Cross-border. At bottom, birds, geese, trees, vine, tulips, and roses. *Mrs. Harry R. Maybin*

SCOT, MARY A. 1808. Winchester [Va.]. 10" x 18". 4 alphabets. Eyelet and cross-stitch. Vine and Greek fret border. Strawberry design at bottom. *Mrs. Harry R. Maybin*

SCOT, MARY ANN. [Cir. 1810.] Winchester, Va. Born April, 1799. 18" x 24". Eyelet, stem, satin, and cross-stitch. Across top and bottom, tulips, birds, strawberries, vine, and leaves. Elaborate wreath of roses and morning-glories around verse. Verse 545. *Mrs. Harry R. Maybin*

SCOTT, HANNAH. [Cir. 1807.] Newburyport [Mass.]. Born September 1, 1796. 18" x 16½". 5 alphabets. Eyelet, stem, satin, and cross-stitch. Greek fret border. Rose tree, other trees, plants, butterflies, birds, and other designs. "Names of the family of Joel and Mary Scott. John born Jan. 8 1790; Mary born Jan. 6, 1792; Elizabeth born Dec. 1, 1794; Hannah born Sept. 1, 1796; Sylvanus born Sept. 1, 1798; Sylvanus born July 7, 1799; Sylvanus died Oct. 21, 1799; Sally A. born Jan. 27, 1801; Abraham Tyler born Oct. 1, 1803; Sally born Sept. 12, 1805; Caroline born Aug. 16, 1807; Rufus born July 11, 1809; Sally A. died Oct. 18, 1803; Rufus died Jan. 29, 1810." *The Misses Sarah, Annie, and Effie Tenney*

SCRIPTURE, SARAH. 12 yrs. 13" x 16". 4 alphabets. Bird's-eye, stem, satin, and cross-stitch. Conventional border. Flower design at bottom. Verse 150 (1). *Mrs. Thomas A. Lawton*

SEAVER, HERTILLA. 1817. Taunton [Mass.]. 11 yrs. 13" x 8¼". 3 alphabets. Stem, chain, and cross-stitch. Cat-stitch border top and sides, and chain-stitch across bottom. Design at bottom of sprays of flowers, tree, and pot of flowers. *Mrs. W. H. Boynton*

SEAVEY, REBECCA. 1811. 12½" x 16". 3 alphabets. Eyelet, stem, satin, and cross-stitch. Vine border with pink flowers. "From purity of thought, all pleasure springs. And, from an humble spirit, all our peace." *Mrs. Willis N. Allen*

SELLMAN, ANN. 1807. [Ann Arundel County, Md.] 8¼" x 11¼". 3 alphabets. Eyelet, cat, tent, and cross-stitch. Initials: "A S. A S. A S. J S. J. H. Sellman, ... [Har]wood." (Harwood was mother's family name.) *Miss Stockett*

SERGEANT, SARAH. 1830. [Philadelphia. 10 yrs.] 11″ x 13″. 8 alphabets. Eyelet and cross-stitch. Strawberry border across top, and smaller twin berries on longer stems at bottom.   *Mrs. W. T. Oppenhimer*

SEWALL, MARY. 1804. 7 yrs. 12½″ x 14″. 4 alphabets. Satin and cross-stitch. Border of vine and conventional rose design. Grass at bottom, out of which border-vines seem to spring.   *Mrs. Herbert A. Coffeen*

SHANAHAN, MARGARET. 2 alphabets. Tapestry. Cross, stem-stitch, and petit-point. Tapestry diamonds top and bottom. House and flower-pots at bottom. Verse 580.
" Reminiscences of Old Salem," page 114

SHARP, JAN. 1827. "Northern Liberty School." 22″ x 18″. Cross-stitch. Tulip border, with rosebud and bird in middle. Vases of flowers and sprays scattered about; also 2 butterflies.   *Mrs. Renwick C. Hurry*

SHARP, KEZIAH. 1825. 23½″ x 24″. Stem, satin, and cross-stitch. Rose border. At bottom, large house with 2 men and 2 women, sheep, ducks, birds, trees, dogs, swan, and man on horseback. "K. S. daughter Isaac Sharp and Hannah Sharp his wife was born 12 day 12 month." Verse 132 (1, var.).   *Mrs. Bradbury Bedell*

SHATTUCK, MARY ANN. [Cir. 1824.] West Cambridge [Mass.]. 10 yrs. 12″ x 17″. Alphabets. Stem and cross-stitch. Two-inch embroidered space with rose in the center, strawberry plants on each side, and pot of flowers in each lower corner. Alphabets and genealogical matter inclosed in an arch 11 inches wide, supported by a Corinthian Column 8 inches high. Over the arch are 2 sprays of wild roses and leaves. "Family Record: Isaac Shattuck April 9, 1778; Hannah Shattuck Oct. 21st, 1788; Isaac Shattuck April 17, 1809; Hannah Shattuck May 10, 1812; Mary A. Shattuck April 18, 1814."
Col. A. L. Varney

SHATTUCK, SALLY. 13 yrs. 20½″ x 22″. 4 alphabets. Feather-stitch, petit-point, satin, stem, cat, and cross-stitch. Floral border on three sides. Scene with house, barn, and shed all joined together, trees in background, fence at one end, lawn and path in front. Verse 601 (1, 2, var.). Illustrated.   *Rhode Island School of Design*

SHAW, ABIGAIL. [1808.] Chester [N. H.]. 11 yrs. Born April 8, 1797. 10″ x 14″. 3 alphabets. Greek fret border.   *Jennie P. Hazelton*

SHAW, CHARLOTTE. 1819. 17″ x 26″. Alphabet. Satin and cross-stitch. Half Greek cross, border design. At bottom, weeping willow tree behind and above garden wall, also gray house with gold roof, flower pots. "Motto: In youth the tear of sympathy is graceful." Verse 432 (1st 2 lines of 2d verse).   *Charles S. Henry, 2nd, Esq.*

SHAW, LUCY [WOODS]. 1822. Denmark, Lewis County, N. Y. 10 yrs. 8½″ x 10″. 3 alphabets. Cross-stitch. Simple line border. Three weeping willow trees.
Lucy Shaw Maxwell

SHEAPARD, HANNAH WOOD. 1830. 10 yrs. 17½″ x 16½″. 7 alphabets. Verses 515, 647.

SHEARMAN, PEACE. 1822. 14 yrs. 4 alphabets. Cross-stitch. Conventional diamond design in border. Verse 488 (var.).   *Old Dartmouth Historical Society*

SHELDON, CELIA. 1806. Cranston. 12 yrs. 21″ x 21″. 3 alphabets. Cross-stitch. Verses 28, 609, 700.   *Mrs. Kingman*

SHELDON, MARY. 1808. Deerfield [Mass.]. 10 yrs. 9″ x 16½″. 3 alphabets. Cross-stitch. Strawberry border. Most of sampler given up to well-balanced arrangement of birds, hearts, flowers, baskets, and trees, that surround an oblong framed by a heart border, containing the name and date.   *Museum of the Pocumtuck Valley Association*

SHELDON, MARY. 1810. Suffield [Conn.]. 10 yrs. 8½" x 13". 3 alphabets. Eyelet and cross-stitch. Hemstitched edge and cross-stitch border in conventional design.
Miss Alena F. Owen

SHERMAN, R. 1808. [Jericho, Long Island. Made at West Town School. 16 yrs.] 12½" x 12½". Cross-stitch. Very elaborate floral and geometrical border on three sides. Individual designs of flowers, wreaths, birds, etc., in the manner of the Pennsylvania School.
Mrs. Henry McAllister, Jr.

SHERMAN, SARAH. November 3, 1811. 9 yrs. 8¾" x 3½". 2 alphabets. Cross-stitch. Simple border.
Miss Lena H. Clarke

SHINN, ADELAIDE H. 1827. New Egypt [N. J.]. 9 yrs. 8" x 12". 3 alphabets. Variety of stitches. Cross-stitch border. Flower in each lower corner. Dividing lines in different stitches.
Blanche S. Jobes

SHINN, MARTHA N. 1801. [Near Pemberton, N. J.] 13 yrs. 9½" x 12". 5 alphabets. Stem, cat, flat, queen, eyelet, cross, and two-sided line-stitch. Strawberry border. At bottom, tree, basket of fruit, birds, and flowers.
Mrs. William Wills

SHURTLEFF, ABBY ATWOOD. 1815. Boston [Mass.]. 11 yrs. 13" x 16". 4 alphabets. Cross-stitch. Verse 734 (var.).
Miss Eleanor Shaw

SHUTE, REBECCA. 1830. 24" x 16". Tent and solid stem-stitch. Top border of strawberries with 2 birds; side borders of flowers; bottom border of flat-stitch. In upper half, roses, 2 butterflies, wreath around verse, 2 more butterflies, basket of roses, tulips, poppies, and basket of fruit. Wreath is made up of strawberries on sides and top, with birds and myrtle below. Verse 132 (1, var.).
Mrs. Bradbury Bedell

SIANIHO, LUCY A. 1819. "Stonington, State of Connecticut, U. S." 14 yrs. 8¼" x 8¾". 2 alphabets. Cross-stitch. "Lucy Sianson." Verse 89.
"DETH IS CERTIN AND ROOST THAT AN
IF THE CAT AND DUST INDUSE"
W. G. Bowdoin, Esq.

SICKFRITS, ELIZABETH. 1824. 10 yrs. 22" x 16". Chain and cross-stitch. Carnation border. Scene in center with brick house, fence, and large and small trees. Inscription: "Respectfully presented to Joseph and Sarah Sickfrits by their affectionate daughter . . . . "
Mrs. Henry E. Coe

SIPPLES, ELIZA TATNALL. 1804. Wilmington [Del. Born in 1795.]. 10" x 12". Southern Boarding School. Cross-stitch done on one thread. Strawberry vine at sides; carnation in lower corners. Greek fret border around verse. Verse 263.
William M. Canby, Esq.

SISSON, HANNAH. 1812. 10 yrs. 11" x 9". 2 alphabets. Flat, chain, stem, and cross-stitch. Flat-stitch border. House with man, two women, and a child. Verse 548.
Miss Lois Anna Greene

SISSON, LOIS. [1819.] 15 yrs. 7" x 8". 3 alphabets. Chain, stem, and cross-stitch. Verse 457.
Miss Lois Anna Greene

SISSON, SUSSANA. 1811. 9 yrs. 12" x 10". 2 alphabets. Flat, stem, cross, and queen-stitch. Flat-stitch border. House with man and woman standing on each side. Verse 294.
Miss Lois Anna Greene

SKELTON, JUDITH O. [1819.] 18½" x 15". 1 alphabet and part of 2 others. Tulip border and simple cross-border. Cross and eyelet-stitch. At bottom 2 roses with birds perched upon them and a carnation plant in the center.
Mrs. Walter Carter Moore

SKINNER, MARY HURD. 1815. Charlestown [Mass.]. 7 yrs. 10″ x 11″. 3 alphabets. Eyelet, cat, cross, and hem-stitch. Simple zigzag border design. "Be virtuous while thou art young." *Katharine French*

SKINNER, REBECCA. 1824. Philadelphia. 8 yrs. 22″ x 25″. 5 alphabets. Flat, eyelet, and cross-stitch. Vine and strawberry border, with flat-stitch inside. Near the base, a brick house with 2 rabbits and a dog in front; at one side, a boy and bush with birds; under a willow tree, a girl with crook and dog tending 5 sheep, 2 trees back of house; above house, 3 birds with twigs in bills, an eagle, the sun, pair of birds with strawberry between them, and other fancy designs. "God is love." Initials: "W E S" [William and Esther Skinner, parents]. *Miss Mable Adaline Stiles*

SKINNER, REBECCA. 1826. Philadelphia. 10 yrs. 26″ x 27″. Outline, chain, stem, satin, and cross-stitch. Border of heavy passion flowers. Wreath around name and age. *Mrs. Clement Reeves*

SLADE, RUTH G. August, 1806. "Swanzy" [now called Swansea]. Born in Swanzy, January the 4th, 1796. 10″ x 12″. 4 alphabets. Pineapple, feather, chain, eyelet, satin, cross, and over-and-under stitch. Cross-stitch border. At bottom, conventional trees and fruit. Dividing lines in different stitches. *Anna H. Borden*

SLIM, REBECCA. 1830. 25″ x 21½″. Satin and cross-stitch. Vine border, with leaves and blossoms on three sides; two birds nibbling at spray in center at top. At bottom, scene with brick house, trees, huge mandolin, lawn, cows, hens, dogs, geese, sheep, etc. Remainder of space filled in with detached birds and flowers. *Mrs. Henry E. Coe*

SLUMAN, MARY. 1807. 13 yrs. 15½″ x 23″. Stem, satin, and cross-stitch. 3 alphabets. Floral border in satin-stitch. Flowers, sheep, and a vase at bottom. Verse 703 (3). *Mrs. Thomas A. Lawton*

SMALL, SALLY D. July 28, 1818. Portland [Me.]. Born December 28, 1804. 17″ x 21″. Flat, stem, satin, and cross-stitch. Rose border. In lower left-hand corner, monument surmounted by bust and bearing inscription "A. Small" on the base; willow tree in background and weeping woman in foreground. Remainder of sampler contains, "A Genealogy: Alexander Small born Dec. 27, 1777; Sarah Mariner born Apr 21, 1779; Married Sept. 16, 1799. Moses Mariner born June 17, 1742; Rebecah Parker born July 2, 1746; Married Nov. 27, 1766. Abagail Mariner born Sept. 12, 1767; Died Jan. 7, 1769. Abagail Mariner born Nov. 31, 1769. Joseph Mariner born Sept. 12, 1772. Hannah Mariner born Apr 21, 1775. Sarah Mariner born Apr 21, 1779. Moses Mariner Jun. born May 27, 1782. Joseph Mariner died Sept. 8, 1784. Rebecah Mariner born Jul 4, 1786. Joseph Mariner born Oct. 26, 1791. Joseph Mariner born Oct. 26, 1791. Moses Mariner Jun. died March 1, 1803. Arthur M. Small born Sept. 12, 1800. Alexander Small jr. born Dec. 3, 1802. Sally D. Small born Dec. 28, 1804. Alexander Small died Sept. 16, 1806." *Marshall Cutler, Esq.*

SMITH, BETSY K. 1818. 12 yrs. 17″ x 17″. 3 alphabets. Chain and cross-stitch. Realistic strawberry border. House with an animal on either side. Verse 118. *Mrs. Leroy A. White*

SMITH, ELECTRA. 1809. Bristol [R. I.]. 10 yrs. 17″ x 14½″. Cross-stitch. Pointed cross-stitch design at bottom. Festoon of roses and bowknot. Family register: "John Smith born April 10th, 1764; Anna Smith born May 23rd, 1773; Married August 7th, 1791. George Smith born May 5th, 1793; Anna Cook Smith born April 23rd, 1796; Electra Smith born June 16th, 1799; John Smith Jr. born April 3rd, 1801; Richard Smith born Dec. 3rd, 1804; John Atwood Smith born Sept 29, 180?; Richard Dimoch Smith born September

20, 1808. John Smith Jr. Son of John & Anna Smith died Dec. 25th, 1801; Richard Smith Son of John & Anna Smith died Jan. 23rd, 1809." *Miss Jane L. Anthony*

SMITH, ESTHER. 1823. Born April 21, 1811. "Brookhaven, Long Island, Suffolk County, State of New York." Cross-stitch. Dividing lines in different designs. 4 partial alphabets. Large baskets of flowers at bottom, and smaller ones elsewhere. Verse 169a.
Dr. James W. Walker

SMITH, HANNAH H. [Cir. 1824.] Hampstead [N. H.]. Born April 6, 1813. 6" x 6". 2 alphabets. Satin and cross-stitch. Three baskets at base, one with flowers and two with blocks. *Miss Harriet M. Smith*

SMITH, ISABEL. 1811. 11 yrs. 7" x 12½". 2 alphabets. Chain and cross-stitch. Scroll design on three sides. *Lancaster Public Library*

SMITH, LUCY. 1806. Sterling [Mass.]. 11½" x 11½". 2 alphabets. Satin and cross-stitch. Narrow border with satin-stitch points. Strawberry design at bottom.
Lancaster Public Library

SMITH, LYDIA C. 1828. Holmes Hole [Mass.]. 9 yrs. 17" x 17". 4 alphabets. Stem, eyelet, satin, cross, and hem-stitch. Conventional rose-tree border. At bottom, picture of birthplace, showing house, garden, fence, and trees. *Mrs. F. LeBaron Monroe*

SMITH, MARY. 1821. 9½" x 9". 3 alphabets. Cross-stitch. Birds, flowers, and acorn designs. [Found in Tarrytown.] *Wilbur M. Stone, Esq.*

SMITH, MARY AMANDA. 1813. Hanover [N. H.]. 10 yrs. 17½" x 11". 3 alphabets. Top border, heavy trefoil; side borders, outline trefoil; lower border, zigzag shell design.
Mrs. Edward C. Wood

SMITH, SOPHIA STEVENS. 1818. 14 yrs. 23" x 17". 3 alphabets. Chain, stem, satin, and cross-stitch. Elaborate scene with church, farmhouses, stream, boats, bridge, coach and horses on bridge, trees, etc. Scene represents the North Branford (Conn.) church, which was burned down recently. Elaborate garland of flowers across top, and caught up by bowknots. Verse 311. Illustrated in color. *Mrs. Henry E. Coe*

SMITHHER (?), EMMA. [Cir. 1810.] 8 yrs. 9¼" x 10½". Petit-point, tent, and cross-stitch. Conventional border. House, little girl, and dogs. *Mrs. Siegfried Wachsman*

SNEAD, SARAH H. 1818. Worcester [Mass.]. 7 yrs. 9½" x 13½". 3 alphabets. Cross-stitch. Greek fret border outside, saw-tooth design next, and third border of Greek fret. Dividing lines in different designs. *Mrs. D. W. Kuhn*

SNODGRAS, MARY. 1802. Harrisburgh [Pa.]. Born in Philadelphia, August 13 A D 1787. 14" x 14". 3 alphabets. Stem, satin, and cross-stitch. Border has squares, with strawberries, roses, bachelor buttons, and conventional designs. In center, lady under a tree writing; tree to the left with apples; at bottom, a house with a large bird on the right and tree on the left. An intertwined vine around central picture. *Dr. Mary G. Hood*

SNIVELY, MARY. 1814. [Cumberland County, Pa.] 13 yrs. Born May 13, 1801. 10" x 12". 4 alphabets. Eyelet and cross-stitch. Strawberry border. Strawberry vine at bottom. Verse 20. *Mrs. Frederick D. Rose*

SNYDER, CATHERINE STRINGHAM. 1800. [Clarkstown, Orange County, N. Y.] 15" x 18". Alphabet. Cross-stitch. Vine border. Geometrical figures at bottom.
  "Dialogue:
      Men: Tell us O women, we would know whither so fast we move.
      Women: We call'd to leave the world below are seeking one above.
      Men: When came ye, sa."
Mrs. William H. Dickson

SOUTHWORTH, MIRA. 1818. 7 yrs. 14¾" x 15". 3 alphabets. Cross-stitch. Strawberry border. Verse 129 (var.).   *Mrs. Lewis Bass*

SPALDING, MARIA E. 1819. Brooklyn [N. Y.]. 10 yrs. 3 alphabets. Rope, satin, queen, and cross-stitch. Strawberry border across top, with solid pillars on sides. Two trees and lozenges.   *The Emma B. Hodge Collection*

SPAULDING, EMELINE. 1828. Hillsboro [N. H.]. 8 yrs. 10" x 11". Cross-stitch. Greek fret border.   *Mrs. Nettie Spalding Ferebee*

SPAULDING, MARY. 1823. Lowell [Mass.]. 11 yrs. Born January 24, 1812. 13" x 13". 3 alphabets. Stem, French knots, satin, and cross-stitch. Rose and vine border.
Mrs. Nettie Spalding Ferebee

SPEAKMAN, PHEBE ANN. 1820. "West Town School." 22" x 21". Cross-stitch. Geometric figures cut in half-form border. Scattered vines at bottom. Verses 462, 762.
Mrs. Edward H. Johnson

SPEER, POLLY. 1804. [Near Gettysburg, Pa.] 12" x 12". 2 alphabets. Eyelet and cross-stitch. Top border of strawberries.   *Mrs. William Paxton Stevenson*

SPICER, ABIGAIL. 1808. 11 yrs. 12" x 9". 4 alphabets. Flat, chain, and cross-stitch. Cross-stitch border. Verse 280.   *Mrs. C. R. Stark*

SPOONER, MARY ANN. 1808. 9 yrs. Born in Boston, October 18, 1799. 16" x 21". 3 alphabets. Satin and cross-stitch. Rose border. Verses 162 (var.), 187 (var.), 419.
Mrs. Frederick Cate

SPRAGUE, ESTHER S. 1823. 9 yrs. 16" x 17". 4 alphabets. Chain, stem, satin, and cross-stitch. Rose border. Verse 515 (1, var.).   *Miss Alzada J. Sprague*

SPRAGUE, MARY. 1807. 16" x 16". 3 alphabets. Chain and cross-stitch. Trees and birds. Verses 28, 609, 700.   *Mr. Arthur W. Claflin*

SPRAGUE, PHEBE. 1807. 11 yrs. 16" x 16". 3 alphabets. Cross-stitch. Verses 28, 609, 700.
Mr. Arthur W. Claflin

SPROGELL, MARY CATHARINE. [Cir. 1814. 10 yrs.] 17½" x 17". Birds, flowers, and baskets of flowers. Strawberry border. Verse 555.   *Mrs. J. F. Barr*

SQUIRE, ABIGAIL. 1821. New Bedford [Mass.]. 12 yrs. 4 alphabets. Satin and cross-stitch. Roses and six-pointed stars inclosed in squares in border. Verse 104 (var.).
Old Dartmouth Historical Society

STANIFORD, SARAH. 1808. 11 yrs. 22" x 22". 3 alphabets. Tent, stem, and cross-stitch. In center at bottom is a basket of roses, tulips, and leaves, from which a wreath of flowers tied with blue bowknots extends around the sampler. Family register: "Aaron Staniford born March 10th, 1754; Lucy Lord born October 4th, 1765; They were married March 18th, 1787. Aaron Staniford born January 4th, 1788; Lucy Staniford born May 22, 1790; Mary Staniford born July 22d, 1794; Sarah Staniford born October 15th, 1797; Mr. Aaron Staniford died July 22 1801 aged 47."   *Thomas Todd, Esq.*

STANLEY, ELIZA MATILDA. 1829. Hamilton [Mass.]. 12 yrs. 16½" x 16½". 5 alphabets. Satin, eyelet, chain, and cross-stitch. Rose border; bouquets separated by triangular line.   *Charles T. Gallagher, Esq.*

STANLEY, PHEBE M[ARIE. 1828. Norton, Mass.]. 13 yrs. [Born October 21, 1815.] 17½" x 17¼". 3 alphabets. Cross-stitch. Cross-stitch border. House in Norton, Mass., with curving fence, unfinished.   *Ralph M. Messinger, Esq.*

STANTON, MARY. 1825. 11 yrs. 20" x 17". 4 alphabets. Flat, chain, and cross-stitch. House, with man and woman under a tree at one side. Verse 272. *Mrs. Alfred H. Wilkinson*

STARRY, MARY E. 1824. Charlestown. 18" x 17½". 7 alphabets. Queen, back, eyelet, stem, satin, and cross-stitch. Strawberry border; larger pattern on sides. Cross-borders in crescent, scroll, and other conventional designs. At bottom, 2 roses, 1 clover plant, and 1 rose plant. Verse 515 (var.). *Mrs. S. E. Cunningham*

STEARNS, MARY HALL. 1810. Lunenburg [Mass.]. 7 yrs. 18½" x 15½". 3½ alphabets. Eyelet and cross-stitch. *Mrs. Alexander S. Porter*

STEARNS, NANCY. 1805. 16" x 20". 2 alphabets. Stem, satin, eyelet, and cross-stitch. Climbing rose-vine on three sides. At bottom, cluster of flowers with fruit trees on each side. Verse 645 (2). *Miss Mary Louisa Adams Clement*

STEER, RACHEL. 1800. Frederick County, Va. 9 yrs. Born in 1791. 14" x 17". 2 alphabets. Cross-stitch. Strawberry border at bottom. *Elma C. Collins*

STEER, SARAH. 1806. 9 yrs. 12" x 20". Stem, satin, and cross-stitch. Vine and floral border. Floral border around verses. Verse 275.
William B. Thayer Memorial Collection, University of Kansas

STERLING, PATTY KENDALL. 1806. 12 yrs. 18" x 17¼". 3 alphabets. Herringbone and satin-stitch. Strawberry beds at bottom. Verse 107 (var.). *The Emma B. Hodge Collection*

STETSON, HULDAH. May 18th, 1809. Bridgewater [Mass.]. 12 yrs. 21" x 21". 3 alphabets. Chain, cross, and flat-stitch. Conventional designs. *The Misses Ford*

STEVENS, ANNE. [Cir. 1803.] Marblehead [Mass.]. 8" x 8½". 2 alphabets. Cross-stitch. Simple line border. At bottom, 2 girls with floral design between and birds perched around bottom. Fancy cross-borders. *Mrs. Fletcher Hodges*

STEVENS, ELIZABETH. 1810. New York City. 9" x 12". French knots, chain, stem, tent, satin, and cross-stitch. Cross-stitch border. Map of Massachusetts. " New York Public School No. 13." *Mrs. F. E. Wallace*

STEVENS, ELIZABETH H. 1820. 16" x 17". Satin and cross-stitch. Strawberry border. At bottom, house, trees, and grass. Verse 655 (2). *Mrs. John Wahl Queen*

STEVENS, EMMA A. [Cir. 1825.] Salisbury [N. H.]. 21½" x 21". Stem, satin, French knots, and cross-stitch. Elaborate rose border. Border and wreath around name. Verse 477.
Shreve, Crump & Low, March, 1919

STEVENSON, MARY ANN. 1829. Philadelphia. 13 yrs. 17½" x 21½". Satin and cross-stitch. Greek fret border, also flower and tree border. Three white roses with leaves in upper center; cherries, grapes, currants, and basket of strawberries in lower center. Verses 515 (var.), 622 (var.). *Mrs. Charles H. Tindall*

STICKNEY, LUCY D. 1830. Charlestown [Mass.]. 12 yrs. 23½" x 25". 3 alphabets. French knots, stem, satin, and cross-stitch. Elaborate rose border on three sides, caught up with bowknots in upper corners. At bottom, scene with Charlestown Neck House, trees, marsh, wharf, and water. Sky and reflection in water are painted. On either side of verse in center are sprays of flowers. Verse 38. *Mrs. Henry E. Coe*

STICKNEY, SARAH ANN. 1813. Newburyport. 11 yrs. 18" x 21½". Chain, stem, satin, and cross-stitch. Clover border. At bottom, three tombstones with three weeping willow trees, bearing inscriptions: " In memory of Thomas Adams, Obt. Oct. 11, 1795, aged 37; In memory of Wm. Stickney Obt. Sept. 22, 1802, aged 20 months; Sacred to the memory of Thomas Stickney Obt. Sept. 6, 1803, aged 30." Family register: " Thomas Adams

PLATE LXXIII

MARGARET MOSS'S SAMPLER. Philadelphia. 1825
Owned by Mrs. Henry E. Coe
Plate presented by Mrs. Henry E. Coe

PLATE LXXIV

HANNAH LORING'S SAMPLER. Boston. 1812

Made in Miss Perkins's Academy, Boston

Owned by Mrs. Lathrop C. Harper

born December 22, 1758; Alice Moody born January 11, 1768; Married May 28, 1789. Thomas Adams born March 11, 1790; James Adams born January 27, 1794; Thomas Stickney born May 28, 1773; Alice Adams married September 22, 1798; David Stickney born June 24, 1799; William Stickney born January 7, 1801; Sarah Ann Stickney born Oct. 16, 1802; Silas Moody born Dec. 5, 1775; Alice Stickney married June 9, 1808." Verse 302. *Mrs. Alice Genn*

STILES, ELIZABETH S. M. 1810. 15" x 17". 3 alphabets. Birds'-eye and cross-stitch. Small and queer strawberries in border. Unfinished vase of flowers at bottom. Verse 288.
Mrs. Thomas A. Lawton

STITES, RHODA. 1826. [Beasley's Point, Cape May County, N. J.] 17" x 17¾". 4 alphabets. Flat, cross, and other stitches. Strawberry-vine border. Flowers in vase. Verse 781.
Mrs. M. V. B. Scull

STOCKTON, ANN. 1804. [Springfield Township, N. J.] 17" x 18". Cross, satin, stem, chain, solid stem-stitch. Flat-stitch border. At top a house with fence, two poplar trees, willow tree, and basket of plums. At bottom, fence, girl on horseback, dog, and cow. Tenant house in corner, with lambs, hill and trees. *Miss Nancy Brown*

STOCKTON, LYDIA. 1803. [Springfield Township, Burlington County, N. J.] 10 yrs. Born October 30, 1793. 8¾" x 11½". 4 alphabets. Cross-stitch. Cross-border.
Miss Mary Taylor Black

STOCKTON, MARGARET. 1802. Marlton [N. J.]. 17" x 23". 3 alphabets. Eyelet, queen, and cross-stitch. Vine border. Rose, carnation, duck, and bird at bottom. Verse 633 (1, var.). *Dr. J. C. Haines*

STOCKWELL, ANN C. 1802. 10 yrs. 9½" x 11½". Alphabets. Cross-stitch. Small church in center. *For Sale May 29, 1917, at The Walpole Galleries*

STODDARD, ANN. 1801. Hingham. 11 yrs. 12" x 12". 3 alphabets. Trefoil border. "Industry is the law of our nature, the indispensible condition of a possessing of a sound mind and a sound body." *M. Anna Pierce*

STOKES, CAROLINE. 1818. 21½" x 23". Edged with ribbon. (This sampler is very similar to Sarah Cole's.) *Mrs. H. E. Gillingham*

STONE, MARY. August 20, 1806. Topsham [Me.]. 7 yrs. 19" x 17". 2 alphabets. Cross-stitch. Strawberry border. Verse 693 (1). *Mrs. George Plimpton*

STONE, MARY. 1808. Cambridge [Mass.]. 11 yrs. 13" x 14". 2 alphabets. Border of double cross-stitch, with drawnwork between all around, scroll design at top and sides; conventional border in cross-stitch and drawnwork also at top. Square in center with 5 trees, each with dove on top. Wide band of flat-stitch around square.
Nathaniel J. W. Fish, Esq.

STORER, HANNAH. 1821. Waldoboro [Me.]. 9 yrs. 12" x 14". 3 alphabets. Stem, satin, and cross-stitch. Hemstitched edge with vine border. At bottom, basket, cross, urn with flowers, tree; also elaborate design of plant in receptacle, on which are leaves and flowers. Verse 515 (1, var.). *Mrs. William H. Shurtleff*

STRATTEN, SARAH B. September 26, 1813. Northborough. 14 yrs. 3 alphabets. Great variety of stitches. Spray of flowers in each corner; then wreath of vine and berries with inner circle of conventional pointed design. Basket of flowers at top and vase o berries and leaves at bottom. Dividing lines between alphabets and Greek fret borde inclosing verse. Verse 40 (var.). *Mrs. Richard H. Hur*

STRETCH, ANN W. [Salem County, N. J.] 13½" x 14". Cross-stitch. Grapevine border. At bottom, mound surmounted with vase containing carnation and 2 strawberries, and flanked on each side with vases of flowers and fruit. Design in center, 2 doves with branch in mouths surrounded by octagonal inclosure, with words "Emblem of Love." Trees, bowls of fruit, sprays of flowers, etc., scattered all over sampler. Verse 377 (var.).

Miss Kate S. Harris

STRONG, FRANCES. 1821. [Northampton, Mass.] 10 yrs. [Born February 4, 1821.] 18" x 13". 3 alphabets. Chain and cross-stitch. Alternate squares in borders. At bottom, large basket of flowers in each lower corner and five trees in a row, three large and two small. Fancy stitches in dividing lines. Cross-stitch shield around name. Verses 321, 768.

Miss Harriet J. Kneeland

STURGES, NANCY A. 1830. Vassalborough, Me. 12 yrs. 9" x 19". 4 alphabets. Cross-stitch. Two alternate rows of cross-stitch in border.

Mrs. Charles Vose

SULLIVAN, ELMIRA. 1818. Portsmouth [N. H.]. 10 yrs. 12" x 15". 3 alphabets. Flat, eyelet, and cross-stitch. Greek fret border. Beneath row of eyelets are the words, "Youth is the time to improve." Verse 601 (1, 2, var.).

Caroline Stavers

SWEET, SARAH F. Before 1814. 10½" x 9". Stem, satin, and cross-stitch. Picture of the First Congregational Church in Providence. The Church was destroyed by fire June 14, 1814. Illustrated.

Miss M. Frances Babcock

SWEETLAND, HARRIET. 1811. Heebson [Conn. Born November 20, 1798]. 11" x 12". 1 alphabet. Stem, satin, and cross-stitch. Cross-stitch border at top. At bottom, house with a rose bush on each side, fence around green space, more rose bushes, white pot of roses, and green wreath around letters "S B" [initials of a cousin living with her].

Mrs. John L. Jerome

SWEETSER, CORNELIA. February 22, 1807. Newburyport [Mass.]. 7 yrs. 18" x 13". 4 alphabets. Eyelet and cross-stitch. Narrow saw-tooth border. Dividing lines in various designs.

Miss Frances W. Sweetser

SWEETSER, MARY JANE. August 28, 1813. 8 yrs. 13" x 9¼". 4 alphabets. Cross-stitch. Strawberry border. Verse 680 (1).

Mrs. John A. Sweetser

SWEETSER, SALLY. April 18, 1808. Newburyport [Mass.]. 6 yrs. 18" x 13". 3 alphabets. Eyelet, satin, and cross-stitch. Narrow saw-tooth border. Verse 639.

Mrs. John A. Sweetser

SWIFT, ROSANNAH. September 10, 1817. 9¾" x 8". Chain and cross-stitch. 3 alphabets. Various different cross-borders in conventional designs. Verse 182 (1).

W. G. Bowdoin, Esq.

T——, E. 1810. 20" x 18". Cross-stitch. Elaborate carnation border. Hill with house on top; four trees on either side of hill; birds on first tree on either side; man in Indian costume and a woman standing with hands clasped, with deer and sheep around them; baskets of flowers hang in mid-air on either side of house. Verse 428. Wreaths inclosing single initials "E" and "T."

Mrs. Henry E. Coe

TAINTER, ROXA. June 20, 1806. Leicester [Mass.]. 13 yrs. 8" x 16". 2 alphabets. Cross-stitch and hem-stitch. Hemstitched edge. Verse 414.

Myra M. Gilbert Morrill

TALBOT, ELIZA. 1810. "West School." 16" x 17". Chain and cat-stitch. 3 alphabets. Verse 515 (var.).

Mrs. Howard Gardner

TALLMAN, LYDIA. 1808. New Bedford [Mass.]. 10 yrs. 17" x 21". 4 alphabets. French knots, stem, and cross-stitch. Tulip border. Verse 104 (var.).

Miss Belle Skinner

[TAWN, MARY ANN. 1812. Philadelphia, Pa.] 26″ x 18″. Long and cross-stitch. Scene at bottom with three-story brick house, tall poplars, bushes, groups of men and women on lawn at either side, sheep, and urn of flowers in front, and two flocks of birds.

Mrs. Edward Twaddell

TAYLOR, ELIZA. September 1, 1804. Little Compton [R. I.]. 8 yrs. 17″ x 11″. Cross-stitch. 3 alphabets. Scene with house and rose bushes. *Miss Alice Martin Morgan*

TAYLOR, ELIZABETH. 1812. Baltimore [Md.]. 9 yrs. 18″ x 20″. 3 alphabets. Eyelet, cat, tent, and cross-stitch. Double border, strawberry and crow-foot; also cross-borders.

Miss Grace Evelyn Bouldin

TAYLOR, EUNICE. 1817. 11 yrs. 12″ x 16″. Alphabets. Cross-stitch. 2 lines of a proverb.

Sold at American Art Galleries, N. Y., April 11, 1918

TAYLOR, HESTER DASHIELL. 1800. Alexandria [Va.]. 17″ x 17″. Alphabets. Satin, stem, and cross-stitch. Strawberry border. At bottom, house with trees and cornucopia of flowers. Verses 103, 671. *Mrs. John Van Rensselaer*

TAYLOR, JULIAN. 1804. 10 yrs. 16½″ x 10″. 3 alphabets. Eyelet, satin, and cross-stitch. House. *Mrs. William H. Miller*

TAYLOR, SALLY. 1800. Providence. 8 yrs. 21″ x 8″. 5 alphabets. Chain and cross-stitch.

Mr. Elisha H. Howard

TEACKLE, ELIZA CUSTIS. January 12, 1804. 11½″ x 14½″. Satin and cross-stitch. Geometrical design in border and cross-borders. " Prepare to meet Thy God." Verses 266, 681.

Mrs. James Fortescue Giffen

TEMPLE, LYDIA ANN. 1821. 16″ x 16″. 3 alphabets. Cross, satin, stem, queen, long and short, two-sided line-stitch, and French knots. Verse 464. *Rhode Island*

TENCHES, NANCY R. S. [Before 1830.] 3 alphabets. Satin, stem, and cross-stitch. Wide floral border. Wreath of roses around name and date. *Mrs. Thomas A. Lawton*

TERRY, ELIZABETH ROWE. 1828. [Cutchogue, L. I.] 16″ x 15½″. Cross-stitch. Simple border. Sampler divided into 4 sections: at top, conventionalized basket of fruit in center, and baskets of flowers on either side; 2d section, conventionalized " Adam and Eve " scene, flanked by huge plants and small trees; 3d section, odd-looking structure in center, with lady carrying flowers on one side and unfinished figure of man on the other side, and small trees topped by birds at ends, also small dogs following man and woman; at bottom, baskets of fruit, flowers, peacock, and small birds. *Mrs. Henry E. Coe*

THACKREY, EBNA ANN. 1822. 21½″ x 21½″. 2 alphabets. Eyelet and cross-stitch. Vine and flowers on sides; green mound at bottom, topped by small trees and animals; birds and sprays of flowers at top; detached sprays of flowers and baskets of fruit and flowers, and birds scattered all about. Verse 466. " Joseph Thackrey " and " Abigail Thackrey " inscribed across top. *Mrs. H. de B. Parsons*

THAW, ANN MARGARET. May, 1819. 17″ x 21½″. Satin, tent, and cross-stitch. Carnation and tulip border all around, and cross-borders of rosebud, carnation, and strawberry designs. In upper section, large pots with flowering plants, vines, etc. In lower section, house, fence, gate, trees, and sheep. *Mrs. Lathrop C. Harper*

THAYER, HARRIOT A. [1811. Greenfield, Mass. Born in 1800.] 11″ x 15″. 3 alphabets. Flat and cross-stitch. Flat-stitch all around, with strawberry vine across top.

Elizabeth DeKalb Peace

THAYER, LEVINA K. [1824. Mendon.] 8″ x 10″. 3 alphabets. Cross-stitch.

Mr. Francis H. Anthony

THOMAS, ELIZA. 1804. Media [Pa.]. 16" x 18". Satin, stem, and cross-stitch. Strawberry border, with stars in the corners and a canopy above. Two baskets of fruit, with leaves at bottom. Scene with brick house on a hill bordered by trees, under which are two stags and a dog; also an arch bordered by trees and a fence. Verses 6, 684.

Mrs. V. S. Chinn

THOMPSON, ANN. 1801. [Near Repaupa, N. J.] 17 yrs. 15" x 17". Cross-stitch. Strawberry and vine border. Wild-rose design at bottom. "Love the Lord and he will be a tender father unto thee." (Children of Isaac and Ann Thomson as recorded on sampler): "Margaret born Jan. 23, 1777; Benjamin born Aug. 18, 1779; Isaac born Nov. 21, 1782; Ann born Nov. 11, 1784; Mary born April 6, 1787; Charles born March 14, 1790; Nathan born Feb. 9, 1793; Jane born Dec. (?) 1798." Verse 343 (1). *E. Arlington Jones*

THOMPSON, ANN. "Σrd moth 9th 18010." 1810. 11 yrs. 18" x 16". Outline, stem, and satin-stitch. Conventional floral border, with roses and leaves. In center, basket of rosebuds and carnations. *Miss Linda Lippincott*

THOMPSON, HANNAH E. W. 1817. Stratham [N. H.]. 11 yrs. 8¼" x 17". 4 alphabets. Flat, eyelet, and cross-stitch. Hemstitched edge, with conventional cross-borders.

Miss Hannah Bartlett Rollins

THOMPSON, RACHEL. 1800. 3 alphabets. Simple cross-borders. Cross and eyelet-stitch.

Mrs. Herbert E. Black

THORNTON, DIANA. 1813. 19" x 17". Eyelet, stem, satin, and cross-stitch. Strawberry and floral border. Verse 515 (var.). "In thy fair book of life devine."

Mr. Arthur W. Claflin

TIDEY, MARY ANN. 1830. 8" x 12". Cross-stitch. Floral border. Three divisions on sampler; upper third contains picture of Adam and Eve with serpent, tree, bushes, and birds; center division contains conventional pot of flowers, flanked by rose bushes and animals; lower third contains row of plants in pots, a cock, crowns, etc.

Mrs. S. Van Rensselaer Thayer

TILESTON, ——. [After 1814.] Satin and cross-stitch. Conventional design on three sides. Three sprays of flowers at top. Names and dates: "Nathaniel Tileston born Feb. 16, 1764; Elizabeth Draper born Sept 10, 1767; Married Nov. 9, 1790. Nathaniel Tileston Junr. born June 14, 1798; George Tileston born Nov. 21, 1795; Eliza Tileston born May 10, 1793; Draper Tileston b. Jan 20, 1801; John Tileston b. Feb. 16 1803; William D. Tileston born Aug. 16, 1806; Charles Tileston born Nov. 1, 1810; Catherine S. Tileston born Sept. 30, 1814." *The Emma B. Hodge Collection*

TILTON, AMELIA. 1814. Hopkinton [Mass.]. 9 yrs. 12½" x 13". 4 alphabets. Eyelet, tent, and cross-stitch. Greek fret border. *Mrs. Charles M. Morse*

TISDALE, RHODA. 1816. Taunton [Mass.]. 10 yrs. 7" x 12". Cross-stitch. Zigzag design in border. *Emily C. Williams*

TISE, SARAH ANN. 1827. 10 yrs. [Born November 1, 1817, at Bergen, N. J.] 17" x 19". 3 alphabets. Cross-stitch. Greek fret and strawberry borders. "Honor thy Parents." "Fear God." Verse 63. *Mrs. Vincent R. Schenck*

TODD, L. [Cir. 1814. Born in 1800. Salisbury, N. Y.] 30" x 24". Quilting-stitch. Cornucopia quilted all in white fruits and flowers. Grapevine at bottom and on sides. Name in circle of knots. *Mrs. Edward S. Isham*

TOPLIFF, SARAH. 1810. Dorchester [Mass.]. 12" x 12". 3 alphabets. Cross-stitch. Pointed design in border. Verse 669 (var.). *Harriet M. Cutler*

PLATE LXXV

HARRIET JONES'S SAMPLER.   1802
Owned by Mrs. William J. Dyer

PLATE LXXVI

LUCY P. WYMAN'S SAMPLER. 1807
Owned by Mrs. Bradbury Bedell

TOPPAN, ELLEN M. 1814. 8" x 10". 3 alphabets. Cross-stitch. Cross borders in chain design. Verses 515, 714 (var.). *Miss L. Gertrude Winship*

TOPPING, HARRIET NEWELL. 1828. Bridgehampton [L. I.]. 11 yrs. 18" x 13½". 3 alphabets. Herringbone, queen, and cross-stitch. Rose-vine border. Verse 515.
Helen Topping French

TOWNE, ELIZABETH. 1820. Shepards Town, Va. 4 alphabets. Eyelet, herringbone, and cross-stitch. Border in cross-stitch and herringbone-stitch. Strawberry design in cross-borders. *Mrs. Knox Taylor*

TOWNSEND, CHARLOTTE. 1827. [Seaville, Cape May County, N. J.] 11 yrs. [Born October 1, 1816.] 8½" x 16". 3 alphabets. Cat, eyelet, tent, queen, and cross-stitch. Diamond patterns. Cross design in border. *Mrs. Isabelle Townsend Keeney*

TRASK, NABBY. 1804. 8 yrs. 22" x 18". 3 alphabets. Leaves and flowers in border. Scene with house, fence, garden, and flower-beds. Verse of eight lines.
On sale at Walpole Galleries, May 29, 1917

TREADWELL, LUCY A. 1809. Ipswich. Born August 4, 1802. 7¾" x 8". Hem-stitch and cross-stitch. 3 alphabets. Greek fret border. Rows across of single and double cross-stitch.
Miss Lucy S. Jewett

TREAT, SALLY ANN. 1813. South Britain, Conn. 8 yrs. 10½" x 10½". 2 alphabets. Stem, satin, and cross-stitch. At top, house, trees, flowers, and fence. Verse 303.
Mrs. Pitts H. Burt

TREAT, SARAH. 1818. Milford, Conn. 10 yrs. 10" x 14". 4 alphabets. Cross-stitch and eyelet. Verse 312. *Mrs. Henry Champion*

TRUFRY, RUTHY. 1807. Portland [Me.]. 12 yrs. 16" x 21". Great variety of stitches. Conventionalized vine and flower border. Squares in lower corners, with pictures of tombs and weeping willow trees, one bearing initials " H T, P T " and the other " B T." " The Genealogy of Mickel and Mary Trufry. Mickel Trufry born dec. 25, 175 ; Mary Trufry born sept. 18, 1766; [Mic]kel Trufry born feb. 11, 1781; Polly Trufry born oct. 30, 1791; Ruthy Trufry born aug. 20, 1787; Sarah Trufry born oct. 9, 1789; Ruthy Trufry born jan. 22, 1795; Mary Trufry born jan. 22, 1795; Mary Trufry born oct. 19, 1798; Eliza Trufry born nov. 10, 1801." *Mrs. G. H. Buek*

TRUMAN, SARAH. 1820. Providence [R. I.]. 7 yrs. 4 alphabets. Long and short, eyelet, chain, and cross-stitch. Cross-stitch border. Verse 515 (var.).
Frederick W. Arnold, Jr., Esq.

TUBBS, MARY. 1814. 12 yrs. 22" x 9". 4 alphabets. Cross-stitch. Dividing lines in various designs. At bottom, basket of fruit flanked by birds and trees; below, three tiny dogs.
Miss Mary Reading Scofield

TUCKER, ELIZABETH CROSMAN. 1800. 11 yrs. Stem and cross-stitch. Border of buds, flowers, and birds. *Miss Rebecca Tucker*

TUCKER, LYDIA. 1809. Andover [Mass.]. 12 yrs. 15½" x 18". 3 alphabets. Chain, seed, stem, French knots, and cross-stitch. Conventionalized rose border. Verse 616.
Mrs. J. S. Andrews

TUCKER, MARY. 1807. Milton [Mass.]. 9 yrs. Verses 40 (var.), 151. " Virtue is amiable."
Mrs. Stephen A. Tucker

TUCKER, RHODA. [1818.] New Bedford. 12 yrs. " Born 27th 11th month, 1806." 18" x 17". 4 alphabets. Mostly cross-stitch. Conventional border with leaves. Various cross-borders. Leaves and flowers on either side of verse. "Benjamin Tucker born 1781 Lucretia Tucker Born 1778." Verse 2a.   *Mrs. George H. Davenport*

TUFTS, ABIGAIL. 8 yrs. 12″ x 17″. Stem, satin, and cross-stitch. Conventionalized floral border on three sides. Three houses in center; above, tree with birds and basket of flowers; below, wreath around name and date, with baskets of flowers and two birds nibbling at strawberry above it. "The fairest flower will soon decay."
                    Mrs. Thomas A. Lawton

TURNER, FREELOVE. 1823. 12 yrs. 17″ x 15″. 3 alphabets. Stem and cross-stitch. Cross-stitch border. "In all my past concerns with thee." Verse 470.
                    Mrs. G. Richmond Parsons

TURNER, LOUISA. 1811. Medway [Mass.]. 10 yrs. 20½″ x 21¼″. 3 alphabets. Outline, satin, and cross-stitch. Leaf border. Vine with small star-shaped flowers at bottom. Verse 293.   *Mrs. W. S. Rich*

TURNER, LUCY. 1806. Salem [Mass.]. 13 yrs. 21″ x 23″. Alphabet. Stem, satin, and cross-stitch. Vase with roses and vine in border. Verses 40 (var.), 128 (1, var.).
                    Mrs. Lavinia T. Snow

TURNER, MARY. [Cir. 1803.] Fort Covington, N. Y. Born in 1792. 11″ x 11″. 3 alphabets. Eyelet and cross-stitch. At bottom, tree, animal, and vase with plant. Sixty-six sets of initials beginning with "A T" [Alexander Turner], "S T" [Susan Turner, parents of maker].   *Mrs. Samuel Elliott Perkins*

TUTTLE, L. August 29, 1810. New Hampshire. 13 yrs. 13″ x 12″. 2 alphabets. Cross-stitch. Pyramid design in border.   *Mrs. S. G. Stevens*

TUTTLE, LYDIA. 6½″ x 17½″. 3 alphabets. Cushion, long and short, satin, eyelet and cross-stitch. Six narrow rows of designs at top. Verse 40 (var.).
                    The Emma B. Hodge Collection

TYLER, MARY. 1804. [Made in a Boston School.] 7 yrs. 14″ x 13″. 4 alphabets. Stem, satin, and cross-stitch. Vine and flower border. Strawberry design at bottom. Verse 274.   *Harvard Historical Society*

TYLER, NABBY S. 1805. 14 yrs. 22″ x 17½″. Stem and cross-stitch. Rose vine at sides and across top. Three-story house, with trees and lamb. Verse 267.   *Charles H. Tyler, Esq.*

TYSON, R. C. 1825. [Germantown, Pa.] 16″ x 17″. Stem and cross-stitch. Vine border with leaves and tulips on three sides. Verse in center, with "J & K Tyson" just below it, and underneath this, wreath inclosing name of maker. Remainder of sampler filled in with detached sprays of flowers, trees, and basket of flowers. Verse 418 (var.).
                    Mrs. Harley L. Stowell

ULRICH, ELIZABETH. 1803. [She came from Hamburg, Germany, in 1795.] Baltimore [Md.]. 9 yrs. 8″ x 17″. 4 alphabets. Tent and cross-stitch. Elaborate cross-borders in strawberry and other designs. Crown, and urns filled with flowers.
                    Mrs. G. Clem Goodrich

UNKNOWN. 1801. 12″ x 10½″. Split and satin-stitch. Elaborate tombstone, with weeping willow tree in background. Inscription on stone: "M. T. OB. Oct. 19, 1801. AE 8." Verse 15.   *Wilbur M. Stone, Esq.*

UNKNOWN. 1804. 11″ x 13″. Cross and tent-stitch. Fret border. Bird on a bough, flowers, leaves, deer, and a rabbit.
                    William B. Thayer Memorial Collection, University of Kansas

UNKNOWN. 1818. Boston [Mass.]. 2 alphabets. Eyelet and cross-stitch. Conventional border. Verse 363 (1, var.).   *The Emma B. Hodge Collection*

UNKNOWN. 1820. 13 yrs. Alphabets. Stem, satin, chain, cross, long and short stitch. Elaborate floral border. Cross-borders. Verse almost completely worn off. Verse 538 (var.).   *Mrs. Thomas A. Lawton*

UNKNOWN. 1821. 10″ x 12½″. Flat, eyelet, and cross-stitch. Conventional design in border. 4 alphabets. "Remember now thy Creator in the days of thy youth. Eccl. 12th 1st." *Mrs. John R. Varney*

UNKNOWN. 1824. 5¾″ x 12½″. 6 alphabets.   *Wilbur M. Stone, Esq.*

UNKNOWN. 1825. 8¾″ x 6¾″. Satin and cross-stitch. Tree, urn, and tombstone. "In Memory of Miss Nancy Chamberlain who died May 12, 1825 aged 21 years." "Memento Mori."   *Wilbur M. Stone, Esq.*

UNKNOWN. 1829. Double strawberry and carnation border.   *Miss Abbott*

UNKNOWN. [Before 1830.] 10″ x 16½″. 2 alphabets. Mostly cross-stitch. Tent-stitch in border. Little pyramids in different colors between letters and numerals. *Miss Elizabeth E. Dana*

UNKNOWN. 6½″ x 10″. 2 alphabets. Cross-stitch. Simple border. [Design unfinished.] *Groton Historical Society*

UNKNOWN. 3 alphabets. Cross-stitch. Scroll design around edge with conventionalized rosebud sprays on sides and at top, with basket of flowers in center at top. "There is a world where souls are free. Where tyrants taint not natures bliss. If in . . . . ." *Mrs. Henry E. Coe*

UNKNOWN. 6½″ x 11″. 1 alphabet. Cross-stitch. Conventionalized strawberry border. Strawberry design at bottom in queen-stitch. "Remember Thy Creator in the days of thy Youth Before the Evil Days."   *Newport Historical Society*

UNKNOWN. 16″ x 15¼″. 3 alphabets. Bird's-eye, stem, satin, and cross-stitch. Carnation cross-border. Basket of fruit in center, with a bird and spray of flowers on either side. Below, strawberry plant in large pot and small plants growing in grass. *Mrs. Thomas A. Lawton*

UNKNOWN. 3 alphabets. Cross-stitch and satin-stitch. Hemstitched edge, with simple cross-stitch line-border. Saw-tooth design across sampler. Verse 536.

UNKNOWN. [Before 1810, in Vermont.] 12½″ x 16¼″. 2 alphabets. Tent, satin, stem, and cross-stitch. Strawberry border across top; geometrical design on sides; hourglass in upper corners. Basket of flowers in center at bottom, flanked by geometrical designs. *Mrs. Amos Bush McNairy*

UNKNOWN. [After 1812.] 16″ x 13″. 2 alphabets. Cross, satin, stem and tent-stitch. Border of detached sprays of flowers. At the bottom an unfinished picture of the First Congregational Church, Providence, R. I., which burned in 1812 or 14?

[VALUE, JANE CATHERINE LOUISE. 1827.] 8″ x 10″. 3 alphabets. Cross-stitch. *Howard M. Chapin, Esq.*

VAN ALLEN, EUPHEMIA ANTONNETTE. 1830. [Belvidere, N. J.] 7 yrs. 8½″ x 17″. 3 alphabets. Cross-stitch. Strawberry and vine border. Large strawberry border at bottom, with house, tree, flower in pot, basket of fruit, bird, butterflies, and daisies. *Mrs. George A. Walter*

VAN DOREN, MARY. 1801. [Bedminster, Somerset County, N. J.] 10 yrs. 12″ x 17″. 2 alphabets. Outline, herringbone, and cross-stitch. Waving line in border, with straw- berries. *Mrs. William Johnston Taylor*

VAN HORN, SARAH. 1829. [Bergen County, N. J.] 11 yrs. 8″ x 6½″. Cross-stitch. Cross and vine border. *Miss Clara Post*

VAN RENSSELAER, CATHERINA VISSCHEL. [1827?] Cherry Hill, Albany, N. Y. 7 yrs. 19″ x 17″. 4 alphabets. Cross-stitch. Strawberry-vine border. At bottom, house and barn with trees, and man with gun aiming at bird. Verse 515 (var.). *Emma C. Bonney*

VAN RENSSELAER, HARRIET MARIA. 1826. Cherry Hill, Albany, N. Y. 8 yrs. 19″ x 17″. 4 alphabets. Cross-stitch. Strawberry-vine border. At bottom, house, barn, tree, and man shooting at bird. Verse 515 (var.). *Mrs. Harriet V. R. Gould*

VAN WART, HARRIET. 1822. 13 yrs. 30″ x 30″. Chain, queen, satin, and cross-stitch. Cluster of roses and other flowers in center at top. Clover blossom, etc., at bottom. Chain- stitching, done in hair, separates different genealogical groups. " A record of the births and deaths of Isaac Van Wart and Forster Families."
" Isaac Van Wart was Born October 25, 1762
" Isaac Van Wart died May 23, 1828.
Rachel his Wife was Born June 4, 1760
Anna their daughter was Born March 24, 1782
Anna their first daughter died Oct. 30, 1820.
Abraham their son was Born Aug. 12, 1785
Abraham their first son died May 15, 1823.
Fanny their daughter was Born May 12, 1793
Fanny their second daughter died May 2, 1824.
Alexander their son was Born Sept. 28, 1799
Marmaduke Forster was Born July 29, 1738
Marmaduke Forster died Aug. 13, 1825.
Jemima his wife was Born June 29, 1743
Jemima his wife died July 20, 1825.
Annah their daughter was Born Nov. 13, 1762
Annah their daughter died March 24, 1762[-3.]
John their son was Born March 27, 1764
Mary their daughter was Born May 6, 1766
Mary their daughter died Aug. 5, 1767.
Elizabeth their daughter was Born Jan. 10, 1768
Elizabeth their daughter died June 19, 1772.
Jane their daughter was Born Sept. 17, 1769
Jane their daughter died Aug. 16, 1770.
James their son was Born May 13, 1771
James their son died June 15, 1772.
Elizabeth their daughter was Born Apr. 16, 1773
Rachel their daughter was Born Sept. 27, 1775
Rachel their daughter died March 1, 1828.
William their son was Born Oct. 30, 1777
James their son was Born July 17, 1779
James their son died Jan. 5, 1790.
Isaac their son was Born July 5, 1781
Isaac their son died Feb. 1819.

Jane their daughter was Born Aug. 29, 1783
Phebe their daughter was Born Aug. 16, 1785
Sarah their daughter was Born Oct. 9, 1788
A Record of the Births and Deaths of Abraham Van Warts family
Abraham Van Wart was Born Aug. 12, 1785

Abraham Van Wart died May 15, 1823.

Phebe Foster, his wife was Born Aug. 16, 1785
Adelia their daughter was Born June 5, 1808
Harriet their daughter was Born Jan. 11, 1810
Sarah their daughter was Born July 16, 1812
Jane their daughter was Born Oct. 21, 1815
Isaac Foster their son was Born Nov. 14, 1819
Anna their daughter was Born Sept. 21, 1821."

VAN WYCK, ELIZABETH. 1807. Huntington. "Born March 15, Anno Domini 1796."
17" x 15½". 2 alphabets. Cross-stitch. Conventional border. Verse 10 (1, 2, var.).

Miss Grace Hewlett

VANZANT, JANE. 10 yrs. 8½" x 21". Alphabets doubled and trebled. Cross-stitch. Verse
198 (var.). *Mrs. Thomas A. Lawton*

VARNEY, SUSANNAH. 1808. Danvers [Mass.]. 14 yrs. Verse 248. *Miss Susan Varney*

VAUGHAN, CAROLINE. October 28, 1818. 10 yrs. "Worked at Mary Walden's School."
18" x 15½". 3 alphabets. Chain, eyelet, stem, tent, and cross-stitch. Conventional border
of flowers and Greek fret. Basket with flowers on either side of verse, and below, small
house, barn, trees, fence, birdhouse, and several birds. Verse 515 (var.).

Mrs. Miles White, Jr.

VICKERY, SALLY AMY. 1807. Taunton [Mass.]. 10 yrs. 8" x 12½". 3 alphabets. Cross-
stitch. Border in black cross-stitch. "Imitate The Best." *Harriet A. Barstow*

VINING, EMILY. [Cir. 1827. Weymouth, Mass.] 10 yrs. Stem, cat, satin, couching, and
cross-stitch. Floral border, with two small baskets of flowers in center at top. Funeral
urns in each lower corner, one "In memory of Delia Vining who died Aug. the 1st aged
7 months," and the other "In Memory of James Vining who died June the 6th aged 38
years." "Family Register: James Vining was born Feb. the 10th A. D. 1779; Lucy
Cushing was born Oct. the 27th A. D. 1781. Jared Vining was born July the 17th A. D.
1800; Elias Vining was born June the 24th A. D. 1802; Lydia B. Vining was born Nov.
the 23rd A. D. 1804; Martin Vining was born Mar. the 20th A. D. 1806; Lucy Vining
was born Oct. the 2nd A. D. 1810; Emily Vining was born Feb. the 8th A. D. 1814;
Delia Vining was born Jan. the 2nd A. D. 1817." *Mrs. Fifield*

VINTON, ESTHER E. 1813. 11½" x 11". 3 alphabets. Cross-stitch. Cross-border. At bottom, 2 houses and 5 small trees. *Albert C. Bates, Esq.*

VINTON, MARY ANN FESSENDEN. 1819. 3 alphabets. Petit-point. Border of heavy rose-
sprays repeated. Tomb, urn, weeping willow, and weeping lady. "M S of John Vinton
Obt. April 14, 1813 Aged 43 years." Illustrated. *The Emma B. Hodge Collection*

VOSE, ELIZABETH ELIOT. 1820. 7 yrs. 13" x 10". 3 alphabets. Cross-stitch. Verse 515 (1,
var.). *The Misses Vose*

VOSE, EUNICE. 1807. Watertown. 11 yrs. Cross-stitch. Verse 104 (3). *Mrs. John Emerson*

VOSE, SARAH ANN G. 1808. Milton. 8 yrs. Verse 669 (var.). *The Misses Vose*

VREELAND, MARTHA. 1800. Newark [N. J.]. 10 yrs. 18″ x 18″. 4 alphabets. Cross-stitch. Greek fret border. *Mrs. Charles F. Lonergan*

WADLEIGH, MARY ANN. 1824. Salisbury [Mass. 18 yrs.]. 22″ x 24″. 4 alphabets. Stem, flat, cat, eyelet, satin, and cross-stitch. Outside border in cross design; inside border of flowers, worked in silk and chenille. Landscape with houses, trees, pond, and boat. Verse 475. *Mrs. George H. Williams*

WADSWORTH, JULIA ANN. [1806.] Hartford [Conn.]. 23½″ x 16¼″. French knots and stem-stitch. Design is the south front view of Lord Oxford's seat in England. Background is done in water-colors. *Mrs. Robert A. Wadsworth*

WADSWORTH, MARY. 1810. Milton [Mass.]. Cross-stitch. Hemstitched edge. *Mrs. E. D. Wadsworth*

WALDRON, BETSY. 1816. Taunton [Mass.]. [Born February 22, 1800.] 16 yrs. 3⅝″ x 13⅛″. 1 alphabet. Cross-stitch. *Ruth A. Tew*

WALDRON, HANNAH. 1810. 11 yrs. 14″ x 10″. 1 alphabet. Chain and cross-stitch. House. "O God I beg The to impart Thy Grace to sanctify my heart." *Mrs. Frank L. Bowen*

WALDRON, LYDIA DEAN. 1815. Taunton [Mass.]. 13 yrs. 17½″ x 17″. 3 alphabets. Eyelet, flat, and cross-stitch. Zigzag design in border. Verse in center, and on either side are figures of boys and girls, also birds on perches, shrubs, bowls, and squares in lower corners. Verse 515 (var.). *Ruth A. Tew*

WALKER, ELIZABETH. 1813. 8½″ x 17″. 3 alphabets. Cross-stitch. Hemstitched edge. Hearts, diamonds, birds, and trees worked at end of alphabets. Verse 440. *Mrs. W. H. Walker*

WALKER, FAITH. [After 1800.] Design at bottom is a building marked "Solomon's Temple," and underneath picture of Adam and Eve. Verse 258. *Estate of James L. Little, Esq.*

WALKLEY, ELIZA. 1814. 10 yrs. 8¼″ x 7½″. 5 alphabets. Cross-stitch. [Probably Hartford.] *Wilbur M. Stone, Esq.*

WALLIS, CAROLINE. 1827. Salem [Mass.]. 8 yrs. 19″ x 16½″. Alphabets. Satin, cross, and many fancy stitches. Greek fret border outside, with fancy inner border. Wreath of roses and purple grapes. Verse 330. *Miss Carrie M. Lefavour*

WALLIS, ELIZA. June 23, 1817. Brookline [Mass.]. 16 yrs. 1 alphabet. Great variety of stitches. Elaborate vine border, with leaves and blossoms. At bottom, two trees, with huge sprays of roses in between. Verse 318. *Mrs. Thomas A. Lawton*

WALTON, CAROLINE. November 18, 1806. Lebanon. "Polly Huntington, instructoress." 9 yrs. 4 alphabets. Cross-stitch.

WALTON, ELIZABETH. 1825. 25″ x 20½″. Stem, satin, and cross-stitch. Vine border, with leaves and blossoms. Thirteen different sprays of flowers occupy most of space. *Mrs. Henry E. Coe*

WANDEL, SARAH. 6¾″ x 17½″. 3 alphabets. Cross-stitch. *Pennsylvania Museum, Memorial Hall, Fairmount Park*

WARD, MATILDA. 1808. [Washington, Ky.] 2 alphabets. Cross-stitch. "Domestic Academy." Names and initials: "Susan P. G; L C Keets; T Keets; HL; FB; CP; BE; PL; FD; GE; FE; BD." "A grateful mind by owing owes not, but still pays at once indebted and discharged." *Mrs. Mary Ward Holton*

PLATE LXXVII

ELIZABETH McINTYRE's SAMPLER. Fitchburg, Mass. Cir. 1820
View of Fitchburg
Owned by Mrs. Thomas A. Lawton

PLATE LXXVIII

HANNAH J. ROBINSON'S SAMPLER. 1818
Owned by Mrs. Bradbury Bedell

WARD, PRISCILLA. 1812. Providence [R. I.]. 9 yrs. 26" x 20". 3 alphabets. Cross-stitch. Ivy and strawberry border. A coach and four horses, a road, and fruit trees.

Once owned by Henry D. Sleeper, Esq.

WARD, SARAH B. 1822. 11 yrs. 16" x 17". 3 alphabets. Stem, chain, satin, and cross-stitch. Vine and flower border. House with trees, grass, and flowers. Verse 601 (1, 2, var.).

Pennsylvania Museum, Memorial Hall, Fairmount Park

WARDELL, MARY. 1812. 23" x 22". Satin and cross-stitch. Rose border on three sides. Central design of carnations in low basket, with pedestal flanked by trees, topped by birds; and below, yellow cowslips. *Mrs. Sabin W. Colton, Jr.*

WARE, ——. [Cir. 1805.] 12½" x 16". Satin and cross-stitch. "A Register of the Family of Joseph Ware who was born October 15th 1753 and Esther Ware his wife who was born January 15th 1756."

"Births			Marriages	Deaths
Joseph Ware	Nov.	9th, 1772		
William Ware	Aug.	3th, 1774	Jan. 1, 1812	
George Ware	June	25, 1785		
Dolly Ware	June	10th, 1789		April 5, 1796
Abigal Ware	Sept.	10th, 1791		
Ralph Ware	July	19, 1793		March 20, 1800
Mary Ware	April	12, 1795		
Joseph Ware deceased Nov. 12, 1805				
Esther Ware "				

Verse 50. *Miss Angelica C. Post*

WARING, CATHERINE SOPHIA. 1815. Charleston [S. C.]. 9½" x 10". 4 alphabets. Cross-stitch. Cross-stitch lines around edge. *Miss Leila Waring*

WARNER, POLLY. 11 yrs. 17¾" x 21". 2 alphabets. Satin, stem, and cross-stitch. Wide rose-border with wider border at bottom. Verse 168 (1, var.). *Lancaster Public Library*

WARREN, BETSY. 1805. Portland [Me.]. 14 yrs. 16" x 21". 4 alphabets. Eyelet, satin, and cross-stitch. Rose-vine border, with rosebuds in corner. At bottom, three-story brick house, fence, garden, and tree; also two-story wooden house, fence, garden, and trees. (Made at a young ladies boarding school in Portland Me.) Verse 686.

Mrs. Pamelia Washburn Crane Agry

WARREN, SARAH CURTIS. 1828. 3 alphabets. Cross-stitch. Rose border. Verse 175 (var.).

The Emma B. Hodge Collection

WASHBURN, LATIETIA M. 1825. 8" x 8½". 9 yrs. [Born September 3, 1816.] 3 alphabets. Eyelet, stem, and satin stitch. Conventional border. Verse 785. *Mrs. J. W. Hawkins*

WASHBURN, LATIETIA M. 1826. Orange. 10 yrs. 20½" x 17¼". Cross-stitch. Elaborate border. Six varied conventional designs and three fancy division lines. Verses 7, 479.

Mrs. J. W. Hawkins

WASHBURN, LOUISA. 1818. Taunton [Mass.]. 14 yrs. 12" x 6". 3 alphabets. Eyelet, cat, tent, and cross-stitch. "Virtue the best treasure." *Harriet B. Monroe*

WASHBURN, MARY A. 1818. Middleborough [now Lakeville, Mass.]. 14 yrs. 8" x 15". 4 alphabets. Eyelet and cross-stitch. *Mrs. George F. Seaver*

WATERMAN, BETSY. 1808. 12 yrs. 17" x 17". Cross-stitch. Strawberry-vine border. "Family Record: Eliphalet Waterman born January th 15, 1764 aged 44 years; Silvina Waterman born June 19th, 1772 aged 37 years; Married November th 25, 1790; Sophronia Waterman born December th 16, 1791; died January th 17 1792 aged 4 weeks, 4 days; Martin Waterman born October th 1, 1793 aged 15 years; Betsy Waterman born July th 12, 1796 aged 12 years; Ela B. Waterman born November th 24, 1803; died January th 20, 1804 aged 1 year 2 months; Thomas H. Waterman born October th 9, 1807 aged 2 years."

New England Historic Genealogical Society

WATKINSON, MARY. [Cir. 1815.] New York City. 9″ x 13″. 3 alphabets. Cross-stitch. Greek border. Scroll design at bottom. "The Golden Rule Be unto others just and true, As you would have others be unto you. Think twice before you speak once."

William H. Walker, Esq.

WATSON, ANN. 1808. Cross, satin, and stem-stitch. Greek fret border. Representation of Princeton College. *Miss Anna Reed*

WATSON, BETTY. 1803. Leicester [Mass.]. 11 yrs. 10½″ long. 2 alphabets. Cross-stitch. Hemstitched edge. Conventional cross-border, and another with dogs, birds, plant, etc.

Mrs. E. T. Draper

WATSON, CAROLINE B. 1824. Leicester [Mass.]. 10½″. 2 alphabets. Tent and cross-stitch. Hemmed edge. Two-story house with fence, trees, and paths. Strawberry cross-border.

Mrs. W. A. Dick

WATSON, HANNAH. 1803. Jamestown [R. I.]. 11 yrs. 16½″ x 18″. 4 alphabets. Tent, satin, eyelet, and cross-stitch. Strawberry border. Flowers and conventional figures at bottom. "In all thy desires let religion go along with thee. Fix not thy hopes beyond the bounds of possibility nor the reach of thy fortune." "Every one should mind their own business for we only torment ourselves with that of other people." *Hannah Watson Tefft*

WATSON, LYDIA. 1813. Princeton [Mass.]. 11 yrs. [Born December 17, 1802.] 17½″ x 15¾″. Stem, buttonhole, laid, and cross-stitch. Conventionalized pinks in border. At bottom, house, fruit tree, willow tree, and 3 small trees. *Mrs. A. B. Curtis*

WATSON, MARY. October 6, 1804. Jamestown [R. I.]. 10 yrs. 17″ x 16″. 2 alphabets. Eyelet, satin, and cross-stitch. Rose border. Wreath. *Mrs. G. A. Clarke*

WATSON, SABRA B. May 30, 1821. Barrington [R. I.]. 10 yrs. 17½″ x 22″. 2 alphabets. Chiefly cross-stitch. Rose border. Verse 94. *Mrs. W. E. Byerly*

WATSON, SUSANNA M. 1809. [Bristol, Pa.] 10 yrs. 12″ x 15″. 4 alphabets. Satin and cross-stitch. Greek fret border at top, and strawberry border across bottom.

Mrs. S. H. Shearman

WEBB, PHILADELPHIA. 1818. 13½″ x 8″. 4 alphabets. Triangle, darning and cross-stitch. Cross-border. "Thou shalt love the Lord thy God with all thy heart and with all thy mind. This is the first and great Commandment. And the second is like unto it. Thou shalt love thy neighbor as thy self." "St. Matthew, Chapter 22nd, Verse 37th, 38th and 39th," also, "All things whatsoever ye would that men should do to you, do you even so to them." "St. Matthew, Chapter 7th, Verse 12th."

Woman's Club, Elizabeth, N. J.

WEBSTER, ABIGAIL. 1802. 11 yrs. 24″ x 17″. Alphabets. Elaborate border filled in to represent grass, through which runs a serpentine pattern in leaf and flower. Five lines, worked by another hand, state the death of Adelaide and her little brother.

Sold at Walpole Galleries, June 29, 1917

WEBSTER, ELIZA ANNE. 1816. 12 yrs. [Born December 31, 1804.] 2″ x 1¾″. 2 alphabets. Eyelet, satin, catch, and cross-stitch. Verse 87. *Mrs. Charles T. Upton*

WEBSTER, LYDIA B. 1819. [12 yrs.] Woodbury [N. J.]. 17" x 19". Flat and cross-stitch. Rose border on three sides. At bottom, mound with 3 trees topped by birds, and 2 bushes. Sprays of flowers, vases of flowers, birds, duck, basket, etc., fill in spaces around verse. Verse 459. *Sara Webster Stokes*

WEEDEN, SALLY. 1803. Jamestown [R. I.]. 12 yrs. 16" x 17½". 3 alphabets. Tent, stem, eyelet, and cross-stitch. Strawberry border. Wreath around name and date. "Endeavor to be first in thy calling, let not any one go ahead of thee in well-doing. Envy not the merits of another, but improve thine own talents. In the practise of piety is satisfaction on earth and its reward is on high, in the regions of bliss and immortality." *Carr Homestead*

WELCH, CAROLINE MARIA. 1827. Boston [Mass.]. 8 yrs. 15½" x 16". 4 alphabets. Cross-stitch. Strawberry, Greek fret, and scroll borders. Trefoil design across bottom. *Mrs. Carl A. de Gersdorff*

WENTWORTH, ELIZA. 1807. Bridgewater [Mass.]. "Bridgewater Academy." 10 yrs. 15½" x 17½". 3 alphabets. Queen and cross-stitch and drawnwork. Strawberry-vine border. Bands of queen-stitch and drawnwork. Verse 104 (3). *Mrs. Cassander Gilmore*

WETHERBY, MARY. 1813. Harvard [Mass.]. 10 yrs. 10" x 11". 3 alphabets. Cross-stitch. Simple border. Verse 301. *Harvard Historical Society*

WHANN, MARGERETA. Satin, stem, chain, and cross-stitch. Strawberry and vine all around; outside vine, on sides, detached sprays of flowers, birds, and butterflies. Oval frame in center, with fringe at top inclosing picture of small house, four trees, fence, and lawn. Remainder of sampler filled in with detached baskets with fruit and flowers, birds, etc. At bottom are the names, "Margereta Whann" and "George Terrell." *Mrs. Henry E. Coe*

WHEATON, MARY. [Cir. 1804.] Cumberland County, N. J. [Born in 1789.] 9½" x 9". 3 alphabets. Eyelet and cross-stitch. Cross-design in border, with intersecting lines across. *Mr. William C. Mulford*

WHEATON, MARY W. P. 1805. [15 yrs.] 17½" x 17". 5 alphabets. Stem, eyelet, cat, and cross-stitch. Rose border. Trees. Verse 135 (var.). *Juliet Hammond Price*

WHEELER, ALMIRA. 1828. 12 yrs. 17" x 16". 2 alphabets. Flat, stem, satin, and cross-stitch. Flat-stitch border. *Mrs. George Tilden Brown*

WHELDEN, RUTH M. 1812. 12 yrs. 18" x 17". 4 alphabets. Cross-stitch. Conventional carnation border. Houses and trees at bottom. Verse 515 (1, var.). *Mrs. Thomas A. Lawton*

WHIPPLE FAMILY. [Cir. 1806.] 18" x 23". 2 alphabets. Feather and cross-stitch. Verse 372 (1st two lines). Vine and flower border. "Family Record of Whipple Family: John Whipple born Octr the 11, 1743; Martha Cogswell born March the 30, 1742; they were United in marriage Jany the 8 1767; Martha Whipple born October the 11, 1768; John Safford born Octr the 15, 1750; United in marriage Dec'r the 30, 1785; Edward Whipple born Dec'r the 8, 1771; deceased Jan'y the 8, 1772; Susannah Whipple born March the 16, 1774; John Botang born Sept'r the 16, 1769; United in marriage Feb'y the 28, 17—; J. B. departed this life August the 14, 1797; Philip Cilley born August the 19, 1774; United in Marriage June the 21, 1801; Polly Whipple born Sept'r the 5, 1777; Isaac Warding born Dec'r the 10, 1770; United in marriage Nov'r the 29, 1796; I. H. [M.?] departed this life March the 27, 1801; Edward Whipple born June the 23, 1780; Clarissa Brimmer born Feb'y the 9, 1783; United in marriage June the 27, 1802; Bridget Whipple born April the 17, 1782; David Giddings born March the 18, 1771; United in marriage May the 28, 1804." "Is their ambition in my heart Search Gracious God and see."

Ipswich Historical Society

WHIPPLE, PRUSIA. 1801. 10 yrs. 8½" x 8½". 2 alphabets. Chain and cross-stitch.

Miss Emily B. Aldrich

WHITAKER, JANE MARIA. March 3, 1814. 7 yrs. Tapestry and cross-stitch. Greek fret border. Verse 545 (var.). *The Emma B. Hodge Collection*

WHITCOMB, NANCY ANN. Before 1816. Keene [N. H.]. 7 yrs. 6" x 14". 4 alphabets. Eyelet and cross-stitch. Cross-stitch border. *Lucy H. Bucklin*

WHITCOMB, SALLY. [Cir. 1814.] Randolph [Mass.]. 15" x 14". 3 alphabets. Cross-stitch. Verses 40 (var.), 490 (var.). Parents' names and births: "Moses Whitcomb was born April 8, 1789; Rachel Whitcomb was born June 30, in the year 1765." Names and births of children: "Bathsheba Whitcomb was born September 24, 1788; Moses Whitcomb was born January 3, 1791; Clarissa Whitcomb was born May 6, in the year 1794; Sally Whitcomb was born August 17, in the year 1800." "Robert Harris was married to Bathsheba Whitcomb April 30, in the year 1809." *Mrs. Clara Wales Alden*

WHITE, ANN. 1828. Taunton [Mass.]. 14 yrs. 16" x 20". 4 alphabets. Stem and cross-stitch. Rose border. House and trees at bottom. Verse 794. *Dora I. Tetlow*

WHITE, CLARISSA. [Cir. 1822.] Mansfield [Mass.]. 14" x 18". Stem, queen, and cross-stitch. Conventional flowers at bottom. Scene with house, trees, birds, sheep, flowers, man, woman, and angels. Verse 648. *Mrs. Charles T. Hubbard*

WHITE, ELIZABETH. 1823. [Pilesgrove Township, Salem County, N. J.] About 8 yrs. 9¾" x 9¾". 4 alphabets. Queen, eyelet, and cross-stitch. Conventional strawberry and rose border. *Gertrude W. Callahan*

WHITE, MALVINA. 1804. 9½" x 8". Cross-stitch. Strawberry border on sides. Divided into three sections: at top, basket of flowers, strawberry plants, and trees; in center, conventional tree flanked by potted plants; in lower third, tall tree in center, with birds on fences at either side, also two insects flying about. *Mrs. Florence S. Babbitt*

WHITE, MARY ELIZABETH. 1828. Leesburg, Va. 12 yrs. 18" x 20". 3 alphabets. Eyelet, stem, satin, and cross-stitch. Vine border. Pope's Universal Prayer on right side, and hymn on left side. *Jeannette R. White*

WHITE, RIBA. 1806. Newport [R. I.]. 10" x 12". Queen, French knots, satin, stem, and cross-stitch. Rose border done in queen-stitch. Elaborate house, birds, trees, and people. Verse 606 (1, var.). *Newport Historical Society*

WHITELEY, KITTY. 1807. Newark [Del.]. 18½" x 21". 2 alphabets. Stem, satin, fagot, and cross-stitch. Elaborate border with bunches of roses in corners, bird and strawberries in center at bottom, basket and 2 large butterflies in center at top, and sprays of wild honey on sides. At bottom, 2 rabbits on grass and conventional tree. Sprays of lilies around verse. Verse 29 (1, var.). *Mrs. Lewis P. Bush*

WHITING, ELIZABETH. 1817. Billerica [Mass.]. 9 yrs. 16" x 16¾". 3 alphabets. Cross-stitch. Conventional border. Verse 732 (1, var.). *The Misses Cummings*

WHITING, ELIZABETH. 1817. Billerica [Mass.]. 9 yrs. 12½" x 17¼". 6 alphabets. Stem, eyelet, and cross-stitch. Two trees with birds in each, and several border patterns.

Mrs. Stephen H. Blodgett

WHITING, JULIA ANN. 1817. 10 yrs. 17" x 17". 4 alphabets. Flat, stem, satin, and cross-stitch. Realistic carnation border. Verse 515 (var.). *Mrs. Thomas W. Aldrich*

WHITING, SARAH. May 8, 1818. Billerica [Mass.]. 8 yrs. 16¾" x 15¾". 3 alphabets. Cross-stitch. Conventional border. Verse 732 (1, var.). *The Misses Cummings*

WHITNEY, ABIGAIL C. 1821. 11 yrs. 19" x 20". 1 alphabet. Darning, satin, chain, French knots, and cross-stitch. Vine and parrot border. Baskets and rosettes. Parrots and baskets scattered around the verses. Verses 463, 635 (var.). Initials of parents: "S W, B W." *Mrs. Albert Caldwell Manning*

WHITNEY, CYNTHIA. [After 1800.] Winchendon [Mass.]. 3 alphabets. Cross-stitch. Heart and crosses. *John H. Edmands, Esq.*

WHITNEY, HARRIOT F. March 24, 1812. Roxbury [Mass.]. 15 yrs. 16" x 16". 3 alphabets. Stem, tent, and cross-stitch. Border of diamonds on sides and top. Three-story house in center, with tree, plant, shrubs, and women. Dish of fruit at top. Vines and vases on each side. Verse 158. *Mrs. Edward Mock*

WHITNEY, LYDIA. 1807. Bolton [Mass.]. 11 yrs. 11½" x 12½". Cross-stitch. Line of squares inside a scroll border. Alphabets. *J. V. Fletcher Library*

WHITNEY, MARTHA. 1815. Warwick. 11 yrs. 16" x 16¼". 3 alphabets. Stem, cross, and four-sided line-stitch. Diamond design in border. Three-story house in center, with potted plants, trees, and women on each side; child and pet dog or cat on left side. Vase of flowers on each side of alphabets. Dish of fruit in center at top. Vine around verse. Verse 40 (var.). *Mrs. Edward Mock*

WHITNEY, PERMELIA. 1812. Needham, Mass. 13 yrs. 17" x 12½". 2 alphabets. Eyelet, tent, cross, and hem-stitch. Hemstitched edge with rosebud border; also line of herring-bone design with narrow set designs; strawberry border with birds in between. Verse 40 (var.). *Miss Emily F. Allen*

WHITON, MARY ANN. 1825. Hingham [Mass.]. 8 yrs. 13" x 14". 3 alphabets. Greek fret border. Spray of roses at the bottom. "Diligence, industry and proper improvement of time are the material duties of the young. The acquisition of knowledge is one of the most honorable occupations of youth." *Miss Anna Pierce*

WHITTIER, HANNAH. 1805. 14 yrs. 12" x 16". 4 alphabets. Cross-stitch. Basket of flowers at bottom. Verse 149. *M. B. Lemon, Dealer, Boston*

WHITTINGTON, SALLY. 1819. [Annapolis, Md.] Born January 15, 1809. 13½" x 16½". 2 alphabets. Tent, stem, chain, and cross-stitch. Strawberry border. Scene at bottom, with church surrounded by stone wall and trees on either side. *Mrs. E. C. Mallison*

WICKS, ELIZABETH. March 6 [Cir. 1800]. 15 yrs. 12½" x 12¾". Cross and satin-stitch. Vine border, with small pink and blue flowers. Tree of life in center, four baskets of flowers, birds, and flowers. "Be zealous to . . . . "
William B. Thayer Memorial Collection, University of Kansas

WILCOX, FRANCIS. 1820. 14 yrs. 17½" x 16". 4 alphabets. Chain, eyelet, tent, and stem-stitch. Vine border. 4 rosettes in the corners. Verses undecipherable. 2 caskets. *W. G. Bowdoin, Esq.*

WILDER, LYDIA. September, 1813. Hingham [Mass.]. 12 yrs. Born January 24, 1801. 3 alphabets. Eyelet, stem, and cross-stitch. Cross-stitch border. 3 bells or tassels at top. *Mrs. Elliott Bradford Church*

WILEY, ELIZABETH W. 1812. Philadelphia. 10 yrs. 3½" x 16". Alphabet. Eyelet, stem, satin, and cross-stitch. Cross-borders in vine, rose, and strawberry designs. Verses undecipherable.
Elizabeth Wiley Cheney

WILEY, PHOEBE LOUISA. September 24th, 1800. 13½" x 15". 3 alphabets. Very fine cross-stitch. Strawberry and vine border. Conventional border across bottom, with baskets of fruit, two plants, pyramid, and a section on each end of solid tapestry-stitch in conventional designs. Verse 531.
Historical Society, Canandaigua, N. Y.

WILKINS, HESTER ANN. 1815. Baltimore [Md.]. 6 yrs. 18" x 18". Alphabets. Eyelet, cat, single and double cross-stitch, petit-point, and hemstitching. Greek fret border and strawberry vine. Verse 515.
Mary Dorsey Davis

WILKINSON, LYDIA. 1817. Pawtucket [R. I.]. 9 yrs. 12½" x 17½". 2 alphabets. Cross-stitch. Verse 167.
Mrs. Amory Eliot

WILKINSON, RUTH. 1808. Walpole [Mass.]. 11 yrs. Cross-stitch. Verse 162 (1, var.).
Mrs. Nathan Bill

WILLARD, MARY ANN. 1830. Cambridge [Mass.]. [Born October 21, 1821.] 11" x 12". 3 alphabets. Tent, flat, and cross-stitch. Simple cross-stitch border.
Miss Elizabeth E. Dana

WILLARD, PHEBE S. [Cir. 1817.] Francestown [N. H.]. 9 yrs. Born February 4, 1808. 21½" x 21½". 3 alphabets. Stem, tent, chain, satin, and cross-stitch. Floral border with vine, beginning at lower corners; drooping spray in center at top; large roses in lower corners; above, strawberries with leaves and blossoms, pinks, pansies, etc.; in upper corners, conventionalized roses, peas, etc.; in center at bottom, a basket with roses and drooping sprays of strawberries and blossoms. On either side of verse a heavy stem, ending in drooping grasses. Verse 732 (1, var.).
Edna A. Clark

WILLIAMS, ANN ELIZABETH. June 5th, 1801. Baltimore. 27" x 25". Petit-point, flat, and cross-stitch. Rose and geometric borders. Three-story brick house in center, with two weeping willow trees, two large flower urns, and one basket of fruit.
The Emma B. Hodge Collection

WILLIAMS, ANNA. September 26th, 1815. Taunton [Mass.]. 12 yrs. 6½" x 14". 3 alphabets. Cross-stitch.
Sarah B. Williams

WILLIAMS, MARILLA G. 1827. Plainfield [N. J.]. 15" x 17½". Cross and tent-stitch. 4 alphabets. House and cup. Verses 570, 789.
Wilbur M. Stone, Esq.

WILLIAMS, MARY PAIN. 1816. 10 yrs. 12" x 14". 4 alphabets. Cross-stitch. Border of running vine with flowers.
Mrs. Lettie Carlile Strader

WILLIAMS, MATILDA ANN. June 6, 1822. [Culpepper County, Va. 10 yrs.] 9" x 17". Eyelet, stem, and cross-stitch. Hemstitched edge. Alphabets.
Elizabeth Hill Gentry

WILLIAMS, SARAH. 1801. 16" x 8". Satin and cross-stitch. Battlemented border. Verse 515 (var.).
Dealer

WILLIAMS, SUSAN MCPHERSON SIBLEY. 1820. Providence, R. I. 7 yrs. 9" x 8½". 3 alphabets. Chain and cross-stitch. "Behold the child of innocence how beautiful is the mildness of its countenance and the diffidence of its looks." "Be good and be happy."
Miss Emily H. Crouch

WILLIAMS, VIRGINIA F. [Lunenburgh County, Va.] 16" x 16". 3 alphabets. Eyelet and cross-stitch. Conventional border and cross-borders. Verse 594 (1, var.).
J. E. Perkinson, Esq.

WILLINGTON, LUCRETIA G. [Cir. 1814.] Worcester [Mass.]. Born January 4, 1803. 8¼" x 17". 4 alphabets. Cross-stitch. Hemstitched edge. Vine and tree at bottom. Verse 401.
Miss Dora Janette Brown

WILLS, ANN. 1812. Rancocas [N. J.]. "Rancocus School." [Born December 23, 1799.] 16" x 21". Outline, stem, and cross-stitch. Vine border, with inner border of various designs, carnation, rose, birds, urns, baskets, etc. At bottom, basket of flowers, rose sprays, and lilies of the valley. Verse 730.
Rachel A. Williams

WILLS, RACHEL ANN. 1811. Rancocas [Burlington County, N. J. Born February 21, 1797]. 11" x 18". 4 alphabets. Eyelet, queen, and cross-stitch. Carnation border. Verse 725a.
Rachel A. Williams

WILLS, SARAH. 1803. 12 yrs. 17½" x 15½". Alphabets. Tent, eyelet, and cross-stitch. Strawberry border, with flowers and leaves. Love-birds, basket of flowers, tulip, strawberries, and diamond. Verse 399 (var.).
Frances D. Smith

WILLSON, LYDIA A. 1803. Newark, N. J. Born September 2, 1797. 12" x 10½". 2 alphabets. Cross and vine border. Verse 402.
Miss Frances C. Force

WILLSON, RACHEL. 1802. Windsor, N. J. [16 yrs.] 22" x 24". 2 alphabets. Long and short, outline, chain, eyelet, stem, satin, and cross-stitch. Border of vine with flowers. At bottom, pine tree, house, flowering bush in vase, man, woman, children on see-saw, other children, deer, dog, butterfly, birds, and sheep. Verses 187 (var.), 400, 490 (var.).
Mrs. L. W. Grover

WILSON, ALICIA ANN. 1812. [Clermont, N. Y.] 13 yrs. 16" x 20½". Cross-stitch. Strawberry border. At bottom, 2 vases with flowers, basket with fruit, birds, and ornaments. Verse 84.
Miss Anne Lee

WILSON, CLARISSA. 1805. 10 yrs. Cross-stitch and eyelet. Verse 129. *Mrs. Samuel Lord*

WILSON, DOVEY WINSLOW. [Cir. 1805. Mecklenburg County, N. C. 14 yrs.] 9" x 12". Satin-stitch and oil painting. Vine border. Tree, figure of woman, with face done in oil painting, weeping at tomb; inscription on tomb done in ink, "M. W. W. Born Oct. 26, 1804. Died Oct. 30, 1805"; also an oval space with verse done in ink. Verse 51. [Done at Salem Female Academy, Salem, N. C.] *Miss Violet Graham Alexander*

WILSON, HANNAH. Canaan Family [Shakers]. Teacher, Emma Johnson. 7½" x 3½". 2 alphabets. Cross-stitch.
Mrs. H. C. Bunner

WILSON, MARY. 1808. [Jewett City, Conn.] 9 yrs. 12" x 16". 4 alphabets. Stem, eyelet, and cross-stitch. Conventional border.
Mrs. George B. Hatch

WILSON, RACHEL. 1812. 12 yrs. 16½" x 17½". 4 alphabets. Chain, knot, cushion, filling, and cross-stitch. Trees, houses, and wild roses in borders. At bottom, wreath, two houses, and shrubbery. Verse 242 (1).
The Emma B. Hodge Collection

WINANS, MARY FITZ RANDOLPH. 1810. Morristown [N. J.]. 9 yrs. 12" x 16". 2 alphabets. Cross-stitch. Cross-border. Verse 429.
Mrs. Frederic R. Kellogg

WIRE, ELIZA. [Cir. 1800.] Philadelphia. 8" x 8". Upper corners, baskets of fruit, strawberries. House with pea-green front door, red door with knocker. Pink side of house, sky-blue door, blue lawn, and blue trees.
Mrs. Bradbury Bedell

WISNER, MARY. 1801. New York. [Born in 1781.] 9" x 12". Alphabets. French knots, stem, tent, and cross-stitch. Rose, briar, and saw-tooth borders. Crosses inclose date. Verse 226 (var.).
Laura Ogden Ross

WITHCIM, CATHARINE. 1813. Easton [Pa.?]. 8 yrs. 8" x 8". Queen and cross-stitch. Border of vine and buds. House and 2 birds at bottom. 3 roses in a tub in center.
Mrs. Adelaide Moore Joyce

WOLF, MARY MAGDALEN. [1819 or 1820. Born in 1812.] Philadelphia, at a kindergarten. 10″ x 13″. 3 alphabets. Cross and eyelet-stitch. Cross-borders.

The Misses Wilhelmina M. and Catherine Brown

WOOD, ELIZA C. March 21, 1810. Mullica Hill [N. J.]. 18″ x 22″. Flat, stem, satin, and cross-stitch. Outside border of Greek fret; inside border of carnations, roses, and vine. Tree, squirrel, and animals at bottom. Verses 187 (var.), 490 (var.), 546 (var.).

Miss Anna Belle Weatherby

WOOD, FRANCES WOLCOTT. [Cir. 1821.] 16″ x 19″. 3 alphabets. Eyelet and cross-stitch. Strawberry border. "Joseph Wood was born at Stanwick Mar. 24th, Frances Wood, wife of Joseph Wood, was born at Windsor Aug. 31, A. D. 1784. Their children — Frances Wolcott Wood was born at Stamford Mar. 25 A. D. 1810, Oliver Ellsworth Wood was born at Stamford April 14 A. D. 1812, George Ingersoll Wood was born at Stamford May 20 A. D. 1814. Their third son was born at Stamford Nov 30th A. D. 1816 and died Dec 5 A. D. 1816. Delia Williams Wood was born at Stamford Sept 13th [1819]."

Chester W. Lyman, Esq.

WOODEN, MARY. 1810. 11 yrs. 20″ x 7″. 4 alphabets. Eyelet and cross-stitch.

Mrs. William H. Seaman

WOODNUTT, M. 1813. "Wilmington Boarding School." 11 yrs. 13⅝″ x 11″. 3 alphabets. Stem, satin, and cross-stitch. Oval done in stem-stitch with an occasional leaf. Verse 304.

Mrs. Warren W. Flitcraft

WOODNUT, MARGARET. 1805. 11 yrs. 16″ x 16″. 4 alphabets. Eyelet, petit-point, and cross-stitch. Border of vine with berries. Two birds on a branch, 2 baskets of fruit. 1 basket of flowers, 2 sprays of roses, 2 strawberry vines. Initials of father, mother, brothers, and sisters.

Mrs. Bradbury Bedell

WOODNUT, MARTHA. 1814. Weston. 12¾″ x 9″. Stem, satin, and cross-stitch. Grapevine border; oval in black. Verses 430 (var.), 692.

Mrs. Warren W. Flitcraft

WOODS, LAURA ANN. 1828. Westford [Vt.]. 17½″ x 15½″. 4 alphabets. Cross-stitch. Rose border. Verse 647.

Mrs. George B. Walton

WOODS, MARGARET. "May the 9, 1825." 6 yrs. [Coila, now Cambridge, N. Y.] 7½″ x 10½″. 5 alphabets. Cross-stitch. Cross-borders.

Miss Gertrude Gilmore

WOODS, MARGARET OLIVER. 1824. 11 yrs. 15½″ x 16¾″. 4 alphabets. Eyelet, stem, satin, and cross-stitch. Double trefoil border. Large basket of flowers with fruit designs each side, apples, strawberries, and elderberries. Rows of fancy stitches. Verse 692.

Marblehead Historical Society

WOODWARD, ANN. 1824. Baltimore. 12 yrs. Alphabet. Floral border and cross-borders. Central design is that of house on Fayette Street, Baltimore, with large tree on either side and steps and fence in front; two gates, one at each end of fence; driveway; scattered rose-sprays. Verse 170.

Miss Anna E. Brown

WOOLEY, ATTYLANTA SHAFTER. 1819. Grafton [Vt.]. 15 yrs. 17″ x 17″. 4 alphabets. Stem, cat, and cross-stitch. Tree design. Verse 515 (1, var.).

Mr. Leon Wyman

WOOLLEY, RUTH. 1816. [Rumson, Monmouth County, N. J.] 8 yrs. 9″ x 15″. 4 alphabets. Cross-stitch.

Edna R. Kennedy

WRIGHT, ABIGAIL. 1811. Medfield [Mass. Born December 21, 1792.]. 18″ x 27″. 3 alphabets. Stem and cross-stitch. Tassel and fringe. Two urns at bottom, with inscriptions: "In memory of E. M." and "In memory of J. M." Two-story brick house with fence, front yard, four flower-pots with plants in bloom, and two weeping willow trees over urns. Verses 34, 296.

Mrs. Marcia M. Winslow

WRIGHT, ANN. January 27, 1830. Trenton. 20" x 23". Cross-stitch. Conventional tulip border. Willow tree, tombstone, and large baskets of flowers. "Sacred to the memory of S. Wright." Box trees, with birds perched on branches. Above, horn of plenty filled with flowers; and on each side, sprays of flowers. Verse 336.   *Frances D. Smith*

WRIGHT, E——. August, 1803. 9 yrs. 11" x 15". Alphabet. Queen, satin, and cross-stitch. Carnation border. House, gate, trees, and birds.   *Mrs. Hampton L. Carson*

WRIGHT, NANCY. September 4, 1800. [Lower Penns Neck, Salem County, N. J. Born in 1789.] 8½" x 15½". 3 alphabets. Satin, cat-stitch, chain, herringbone, buttonhole, French knot, and cross-stitch. Cross-stitch dividing lines. Conventional design at top. "Virtue Excelleth Vice as Far as Light Exceeds Darkness."   *Miss Maria H. Mecum*

WRIGHT, PRISCILLA CAROLINE. 1813. Wilton [N. H.]. Born October 23, 1804. 9" x 14". 4 alphabets. Cross-stitch. Vine and clover border.   *Mary Priscilla Bunce*

WYCKOFF, MARIA. [Cir. 1800.] Millstone [N. J.]. Born September 17, 1789. 8" x 10". 2 alphabets. Cross-border.   *Catharine L. A. Brokaw Staats*

WYMAN, LUCY P. 1807. Born September 21, 1791. 13" x 17". Satin and stem-stitch. Vine with leaves around edge. Three hearts at bottom, from which springs fruit tree. Inscribed on hearts: "Abel Wyman bn. April 1, 1747; Ruth Putnam bn. March 28, 1751; Married Oct. 20, 1772." On fruit names and births of children: "Elizabeth bn. June 25th, 1773; Samuel bn. April 15th, 1775; Ruth bn. July 5th, 1776; Abel bn. Sept. 28th, 1778; Pamela bn. Jan. 24th, 1781; Abel bn. Aug. 31st, 1783; William and Levi born March 18th, 1786; Sarah bn. July 8th, 1789; Francis bn. July 30th, 1790; Lucy P. bn. Sept. 21st, 1791."   *Mrs. Bradbury Bedell*

WYMAN, LUCY P. 1810. Jay [Me.]. 9 yrs. 7¼" x 12". 2 alphabets. Bordered with hem and divided into fourteen sections. At bottom, tree, horse, house, dog, and another tree. Section 4 contains four characters, corresponding to ace of hearts, diamonds, clubs, and spades. Verse 490 (var.).   *George C. Wing, Esq.*

WYMAN, SOPHIA. 1807. Charlestown. 12 yrs. 15½" x 17½". 2 alphabets. Chain, stem, and cross-stitch. Conventional pomegranates, roses, feathers, etc., in border. "Virtue hath secret charm, which all men love. And those that do not choose her, yet approve." Verse 705.   *Marblehead Historical Society*

WYMAN, SUBMIT. 1805. 12 yrs. 12" x 16". Stem and cross-stitch. 2 alphabets. Rose and carnation border on three sides.   *Lancaster Public Library*

YEAKELS, SARAH. 1806. 22" x 16½". 1 alphabet. Queen, stem, satin, and cross-stitch. Strawberry border. Hill on right-hand side with house on top, shaded by a curious tree; bush and large peacock beside house; fence running down ridge of hill; large bush and weeping willow tree, with sheep underneath; birds flying about; detached trees in open space. Illustrated.   *Mrs. Henry E. Coe*

YEATES, HARRIET. 1813. 13½" x 16½". Cross-stitch. Strawberry border. Conventionalized fruit trees, flowers, and animals. Verse 531 (6).
     William B. Thayer Memorial Collection, University of Kansas

YERRINGTON, CATHERINE B. 1819. 21" x 17". Satin, chain, and stem-stitch. Rose border. Arch containing family register, with fruit basket at base. "Mr. James Yerrington was born Decbr 31, 1772; Miss Catherine Brown was born April 11, 1768; They were married by the Rev. Mr. Hitchcock August 25, 1796." "Births: James B, December 4, 1800; Barker T, April 20, 1803; Catherine B., March 22, 1806; Sarah W., December 25, 1807."
     Mrs. Preston Yerrington

Young, Elizabeth Loring. 1812. Boston [Mass.]. 8 yrs. 2 alphabets. Cat-stitch.

Elizabeth Loring Tappan

Young, Elizabeth. 1826. [Cumberland County, N. J.] 13″ x 16″. 4 alphabets. Cross, eyelet, queen, and stem-stitch. Walls of Troy on sides and across bottom, and cross-design in border across top and bottom. At bottom, gable end of house inclosing initials, flanked on each side by shallow urns of flowers, buds, single conventional flowers, geometrical designs, etc. Initials in house: "J Y, R Y"; and outside, "S Y."

Mrs. Trueman H. Clayton

Young, Elizabeth. 1823. Baltimore. 17″ x 20″. 5 alphabets. Intricate strawberry border. Flowers in pots, trees, and birds. Verse 733 (1). *Mrs. William Nelson Marye*

Young, Polly. [1801.] "Aged 11, born in the year of our Lord 90." 12½″ x 15¼″. Cross, satin, eyelet, chain, and cat-stitch. Saw-tooth cross-borders. Verse 187 (var.).

William B. Thayer Collection, University of Kansas

Z——, S. E., and C——, M.* 1816. 21″ x 21″. 7 alphabets. Eyelet and cross-stitch. Tent-stitch border all around, with carnations, strawberries, birds, etc. Inscription: "Through the industry of two dear girls I have been made the proprietor of this very excellent sampler to whom I feel much indebted. M. Robertson. Mary Robertson her sampler."

Mrs. Edward Dillon

* Perhaps Mary Clapham.

These three Registers were compiled from description blanks, from photographs, and sometimes from "viva voce" descriptions by Mrs. Wolcott West Treadway, and their excellence is largely due to her.

PLATE LXXIX

LOUISA GAUFFREAU'S SAMPLER. New York. 1821
Owned by Mrs. J. Herbert Johnston

PLATE LXXX

MARY ANN FESSENDEN VINTON'S SAMPLER. 1819
The Emma B. Hodge Collection

SAMPLER VERSE

MY DEAR MRS. BOLTON:

Fantastically enough, the first thought which comes to mind as I glance through the verses laboriously stitched into your century and a half of samplers is one of devout thanksgiving that you did not submit them to me when I was still a practicing professor. For, while so employed, I might have been tempted to discern in them good material for a thesis tending toward the degree of Doctor of Philosophy; and, if such degree had thus been attained, the winner thereof would have been apt presently to offer, wherever he chanced to be employed, elaborate courses of instruction in Sampler Poetry.

Nothing short of this intensive study could so deal with the matter as to result in any definite contribution to literary history. Were I a little younger, or a good deal stronger, your wish would tempt me to undertake it; except that, as it would demand patient months, if not years, it could hardly be completed in time for the first edition of your book. This consideration, which somewhat consoles me, must be my excuse for comments so cursory that you may rightly find them unworthy of place in your pages.

To begin with, the evidence on which not long ago I based a message to you that, so late as 1812, the verses on a sampler in my possession were composed by the poetastic father of the rather weak-minded stitcher—whom I remember as an old woman—proves worthless. I possess the draft in her father's handwriting:

> "Tell me, ye knowing and discerning few,
> Where I may find a friend both firm and true,
> Who dares stand by me in my deep distress,
> And then her love and friendship most express?"

The normal answer, I suppose, would have been "My Mother"; in this case, domestic circumstances altered it to "My Ant". Until I saw your collection of verses, I had supposed it original. To my dismay,

I discover a version of it there as early as 1718; and it is repeated five times—last in 1827. The conclusion I draw from these incomplete premises I believe tenable: namely, that throughout the whole range of sampler-poetry the only trace of originality to be found is in the signatures and the dates.

By far the most frequent of the rhymes tends to confirm this opinion. Among the examples you have sent me it is the only one which occurs frequently before 1700. So nearly as I can make out, it first appears in 1675, somewhat as follows:

> "Isabel Ercy is my name
> And with my needle I wrought the same".

With variations, you will find it repeated more than a hundred times before 1830, most frequently in some such form as this:

> "Hannah Weeks is my name,
> New England is my nation,
> Greenland is my dwelling-place,
> And Christ is my salvation".

The next most usual, also with many variations, appears to be the familiar couplet, perhaps metrically based on the New England Primer:

> "When this you see
> Remember me,"

duly followed by signature and date, though generally lacking the precise local address. The two are more than once combined, by adding to something like the first a third couplet:

> "And which whenever you chance to see
> May kind remembrance picture me."

These examples fairly indicate the general poetical and literary quality of the species of expression which they represent.

To pass to the substance of these artless epigrams, a great many of them concern religion, mostly of Calvinistic shade, sometimes pretty deep. Whoever has classified them for you has put seventy-eight, of which a dozen or so are often repeated, under the head of Christ, and one hundred and ten, of which ten are repeated more or less, under that of the Old Testament. Among the latter, by the way, are two

rhymed versions of the Ten Commandments, and among the former
two of the Lord's Prayer, by no means so skillful as that in the Divine
Comedy. For general purposes, the subdivision appears needless; it
were better to say that at least one hundred and eighty-eight of these
rhymes directly concern the orthodox principles of New England
religion, and that a great many more imply them. Death and Sorrow,
for example, are represented by no less than one hundred and sixty-
eight examples between 1730 and 1830; and Virtue, which appears to
have become increasingly popular with the rise of Revolutionary
sentiment, by two hundred and twenty-eight, between 1730 and 1829.
Patriotism, though, was of late growth; there are only nine classified
examples, the first of 1770 and the last of 1826; and at least two of
these might just as well have been placed under Death and Sorrow.
The shorter runs thus:

> "Mourn, hapless brethren, deeply mourn!
> The source of every joy is fled;
> Our Father dear, the Friend of Man,
> The God-like Washington is dead."

A comparison of this quatrain, probably composed in 1799 or 1800,
with the earlier verses I have happened to set down, instantly shows
what is generally true: on the whole, the later verses—those which first
appear after 1760, let us say—are apt to be a little smoother, a bit
more sophisticated, than those formerly found satisfactory. Not many,
however, display any memorable degree of literary culture. Quite
possibly, to be sure, some of them might be traced by study to higher
origin than I have happened to detect. Pope is often quoted: in 1785
occurs the couplet

> " 'Tis education forms the common mind;
> Just as the twig is bent, the tree's inclined;"

and in 1794, the following lines are specifically referred to him:

> "Virtue outshines the stars, outlives the tomb,
> Climbs up to heaven and finds a peaceful home".

One could find many traces of him on later samplers, but none, I think,
in contemporary ones. When the first of these couplets was stitched,
he had been dead forty-one years, and the second was stitched nine

years later. Of Johnson I have discovered no evident influence, and but a little of Goldsmith or of Gray. Minute scrutiny does reveal a gloomy ray or two from Young.

And here are a few casual examples, from more or less similar origin. Whoever cares to find out where they came from can probably do so from the Anthology which follows, without excessive pains:

1. (1766) "Beauty and Pride we often find
            Betray the weakness of the mind;
            He handsom is and merits praise
            That handsom does, the Proverb says."

2. (1787) "Teach me to feel another's wo,
            To hide the fault I see;
            That mercy I to others show
            That mercy show to me."

3. (1798) "So let me live, so let me die,
            That I may live eternally."

4. (1805) "Man wants but little here below", etc.

5. (1805) "My thoughts on awful subjects roll,
            Damnation and the dead," etc.

6. (1812) "Good when He gives, supremely good,
            Nor less when he denies,
            Even crosses from his sovereign hand
            Are blessings in disguise".

7. (1820) "Hark, from the tombs a doleful sound", etc.

8. (1824) "When I can read my title clear
            To mansions in the skies,
            I bid farewell to every fear
            And wipe my weeping eyes."

9. (1827) "Jesus, Lover of my Soul", etc.

The familiar poets, though, seem chiefly to have been the native Yankee classics—Wigglesworth and the New England Primer—and the writers of popular hymns. I have been so careless as to mislay my reference to one sampler clearly based on Wigglesworth's "Day of Doom". The rhythm of the New England Primer reveals itself fourteen times between 1724 and 1821 in the lines

"Let virtue be
A guide to thee,
And innocence
Be thy defence."

The 76th Hymn, on the other hand—I know not from what collection—occurs twice, once in 1795 with six stanzas, of which the first begins, "Lo, He comes with clouds descending".

As I have turned over your hundreds of slips, very few have impressed me as at all exceptional.   Here are some of these:

1. (1757) "In Mother's womb Thy fingers did me make,
            And from the womb Thou didst me safely take;
            From breast Thou hast me nurst my life throughout.
            I may say [that] I never wanted ought."

2. (1795) "I've been to church and love to go,
            'Tis like a little heaven below;
            Not for my pleasure or my play
            Will I forget the Sabbath Day."

3. (1796) "Adam alone in Paradise did grieve,
            And thought Eden a desert without Eve,
            Until God pitying of his lonesome state
            Crowned all his wishes with a loving mate.
            What reason then hath Man to slight or flout her,
            That could not live in Paradise without her?"

(Mary Gates)

(Incidentally, one may hope that the heavenly joys of Mary Gates, who stitched these germinal lines, are enhanced by the rapid growth of female suffrage nowadays.)

4. (1810) "God counts the sorrows of His saints,
            Their groans affect his ears,
            He has a book for their complaints,
            A bottle for their tears".

(A hundred and ten years ago, of course, the deplorable view of stimulants implied by the Second Chapter of the Gospel according to Saint John had not yet been irradiated by the light of constitutional prohibition.)

5. (1817) "Father of light and life! Thou God supreme!
            O, teach me what is good! Teach my Thyself,
            Save me from folly, vanity and vice,
            From every low pursuit, and feed my soul,
            With knowledge, conscious peace, and virtue pure,
            Sacred, substantial, never-fading bliss."

(This is noteworthy as almost the only unrhymed verse in your whole collection.)

6. (1828) "Could we with ink the ocean fill,
            Were the whole earth of parchment made,
            Were every single stick a quill,
            And every man a scribe by trade,
            To write the love of God above
            Would drain the ocean dry,
            Nor could this scroll contain the whole
            Though stretcht from sky to sky.
            Were the whole realm of Nature mine,
            That were a present far too small;
            Love so amazing, so divine,
            Demands my soul, my life, my all."

One might go on like this forever, remarking, for example, that in 1819 Mary Austin, at the end of a long celebration of the glories of God, reveals extensive knowledge of infant prayer in the lines

> "I lay my body down to sleep;
> Let angels guard my head,
> And through the hours of darkness keep
> Their watch about my bed."

We should never get away from where we began. It seems like an atmosphere of stiflingly priggish formalism, saved from hypocrisy only by unintelligence, and refreshed—if at all—only by occasional whiffs of lukewarm sentimentality. You will find counterparts of these verses in the commencement parts of our Yankee colleges throughout the generations when the faded lines were stitched. You will find epitaphs to match them on plenty of gray slate Yankee gravestones. You will find dreary models for all these conventions in the long unread and no longer deeply revered Yankee sermons which make sleepy the shelves of our older libraries. You may smile, or chafe, as you choose, rejoicing that we breathe air more free than ever invigorated our ancestors. But, after all is said and done, you can hardly deny that they bred a race earnest, strong, and—so far as humanity may be—pure of heart. In moods like this, the prayer on the seal of Boston city comes to mind:

> "Sicut patribus sit Deus nobis".
> (As to our fathers so be God to us.)

It is impossible, you see, to plunge into old New England without falling to moralizing, which does no harm here; for until one begins flatly to moralize, one cannot imagine what manner of beings the dead and gone children were who stitched the samplers.

Forgive me for not writing about them more learnedly, and believe me always

Sincerely yours,

(Signed)   Barrett Wendell.[1]

---

[1] Mr. Wendell did not live to read the proof of the letter which he so kindly contributed to the book.

Under the stimulus of Mr. Wendell's letter, it was almost impossible to refrain from delving into contemporary literature to see what a short digging in that unaccustomed soil would produce in the way of authorship for the verses following. The ordinary quotation books have proved themselves almost useless in the search. Moreover misquotation, quotations adapted to the youthful mind, and paraphrased quotations have proved a great stumbling block in the progress of the searcher. A girl in those days thought nothing of blending Pope and Edward Young in one uneasy whole, which it is hard for the would-be identifier to detect.

But there is one result too evident to be ignored by any who study these verses, and that is the overwhelming influence of the Rev. Isaac Watts. He is by far the oftenest quoted writer, and if the local ministers or school-teachers wrote a verse to be put upon the children's samplers, they were sure to copy Watts as nearly as they dared—and sometimes nearer than they ought. The strange part is that the children in their quotations from Watts seldom chose his cheerful verse. "Hark from the tombs a doleful sound" was much more to their taste than one of his triumphal psalms. Truly the terror of the law and of death was early inculcated, in those days. After a prolonged contemplation of these lugubrious expressions, one turns to our own time with a sense of relief, and the reflection that, though we may not be so intent on saving our own souls, we may contribute by joy and good cheer to the saving of others.

Of secular authors, Alexander Pope leads all the rest. The same uneasy feeling again assails the searcher after knowledge, for one is entirely unable to distinguish at a glance or even after much study the real Pope from his close imitators. His style of verse and his somewhat cynical outlook are imitated again and again. Edward Young, Goldsmith, Cowper, Congreve, Thompson, John Bunyan, Gay, and Milton all have their admirers, but only one girl so far quoted Shakespeare. She embroidered the famous sampler quotation from Titus Andronicus—perhaps because she hated doing her sampler so—and remains the only user of the works of the great poet.

There are, of course, many crude verses which must have been the work of local poets, and in a few cases the tradition has come down that the sampler maker wrote her own. One and all, however, reflect the philosophy of the time. As Margaretta Arabella Godman wrote:

> "By virtue ripened from the bud
> The flowers angelic odors breathe,
> The fragrant charm of being good
> Makes gaudy vice to smell like weeds."

ETHEL STANWOOD BOLTON.

JULIA ANN NIVERS'S SAMPLER. 1831
View of Crawford, New Hampshire

PLATE LXXXI

Eliza Pickets's Sampler.   Baltimore, Md.   1825
Owned by Miss Lida Bartlett

PLATE LXXXII

Susan H. Munson's Sampler. 1824
Owned by George S. McKearin, Esq.

AN ANTHOLOGY OF SAMPLER VERSE

IN PRAISE OF PATRIOTISM

1

1770

The Love of Liberty with life was given
And Life itself is the inferior gift of heaven.

2

1781

While hostile foes our coasts invade,
In all the pomp of war arrayed,
Americans be not dismayed,
Nor fear the Sword or Gun.

While innocence is all our pride,
And virtue is our only Guide
Women would scorn to be defyd
if led by Washington.

2a

1788

LINES ON PEACE BY AN ENGLISH LADY

Janus has closed his blood-stained door
And war and carnage rage no more
Long may sweet Peace her olive twine
Round Britain and Columbia's line
May generous friend hip's ardour strive

To keep her kindred smile alive
Nor envy's breath nor blast be near
To force from virtue's eye to war
But each brave country prove this creed
That truth and honour best succeed

ANSWER BY A DAUGHTER OF COLUMBIA

Thus sung a muse of Britains Isle
Columbia's goddess with a smile
   Responded to the lay

Yes from henceforth let discord cease
And all the world be wrapt in peace
   And shine in Heaven's own day.

3

1798

ON WAR

Why these scenes that would the feeling mind
This sport of death, this cockpit of mankind
Why sobs the widow in perpetual pain
Why cries the orphan x oh my father's slain
Why hangs the sire his paralytic head

And nods with manly grief x my son is dead
Oh could I paint the passion I can feel
Or paint a horror that would wound like steel
To the unfeeling unrelenting mind
I'd send a torture and releive mankind

4

1799

With love she is queen
ye American fair

to adorn your mind
bend all your care.

5

After 1799

ON THE DEATH OF GENERAL GEORGE WASHINGTON
WHO DIED DECEMBER 14, 1799

Illustrious Shade if artless hands are mine
Could for the Hero's now a chaplet twine.
The muse for thee would cull each opening bloom.
And with unfading garlands deck thy Tomb.

5a

1801
G. W.

Mute be the voices of Eulogy
For who can justly speak his praise

But the sad tear that fills each eye
A deathless monument shall raise

6

1804

Mourn Hapless Brethren Deeply Mourn
The Source Of Every Joy Is Fled

Our Father Dear The Friend Of Man
The Godlike Washington Is Dead.

7

1826
[ON LIBERTY]

Oh Liberty! thou Power supremely bright,
Profuse of bliss, and fragrant with delight,
Perpetual pleasures in thy presence reign,
And smiling plenty leads thy wanton train.

Religion smiles beneath thy heavenly light,
And Industry looks cheerful in thy sight,
Thou mak'st the gloomy face of nature gay,
Giv'st beauty to the sun, and pleasure to the day.

Nathaniel Low's Almanack. Boston. 1775.

IN PRAISE OF LOVE

8

1739

One did commend me to a Wife Fair and Young
That had French Spannish and Italian Tongue
I thankd him kindly and told him I loved none such
For I thought one tongue for a Wife too much
What love ye not the Larned Yes, as my Life
A Learned Schollar, but not a Larned Wife.[1]

9

1769

When in love I do commence
May it be with a man of sense

Brisk and arey may he be,
Free from a spirit of jealousy.

10

1785

1. When this you see, remember me . . .[2]
2. And bear me in your mind.

What others say when I'm away
Speak of me as you find.

11

1790

Little Bud of opening red
Where the blooming Graces dwell,
Nodding o'er thy dewy bed,
In thy verdant mossy cell.

With lovers hand should some fond youth
To Delia's breast thy beauties bear,
Go and learn this sacred truth,
That greater beauties flourish there.

[1] "Samplers bearing this verse are known as the 'Milton's Daughter' samplers, in reference to his sentiments as to women knowing foreign tongues."
[2] (If sleeping in the icy arms of death. Susanne Nickalls.)

12

1792

No Star so bright
As my delight.

13

As on some lonely building top
The sparrow tells her moan

1796

Far from the tents of joy & hope
I sit and grieve alone

14

When this you see
Think of me
Tho many a mile
We distant be

1796

The gift is small
But love is all
Death only parts
Unighted[1] hearts

15

1801

Belov'd till life coul'd charm no more
And mourn' I till life shall thee restore.

16

Tho broad Alantic rolls between
Fair England's isle and me
On Fancy's wings I fly unseen
And oft converse with thee.

1803

No barrier Ocean can divide
Affection's kindred love
And that I've ne'er forgotten thee
Let this Memento prove

17

Kind heaven O grant me but this
I would not by many be known

1803

And to fill up my measure of bliss
I ask the esteem of but one

18

O let my name engraven stånd
Both on thy heart and on thy hand

1804

Seat me upon thine arm and wear
That pledge of love forever there

19

Sweet bud to Myra's bosom go
And live beneath her eye
There in the sun of beauty blow

1806

Or taste of heaven and die
Sweet earnest of the Blooming year
Whose dawning beauties speak

20

1814

The rosey red, the violet blue,
Sugar is sweet my dear and so are you.

21

1822

When two fond hearts as one unite,
The yoke is easy and the burden light.

[1] United.

IN PRAISE OF NATURE

22   **1788**

O what a pleasant sight it is to see
The fruitful Clusters Bowing down the Tree.

23   **1790**

The industrious bee extracts from evr'y flower
It's fragrant sweets, and mild balsamic pow'r
Learn thence with greatest care and nicest skill
To take the good, and to reject the ill
By her example taught, enrich thy mind
Improve kind nature's gifts, by sense refind.
Be thou the honey-comb in whom may dwell
Each mental sweet, nor leave one vacant cell.

24   **1792**

1. When snow descend, and robes the fields
   In winters bright array
   Touched by the sun the lustre fades
   And weeps itself away

2. When Spring appears—when violets blow
   And shed a rich perfume
   How soon the fragrance breathes its last
   How short lived is the bloom.

3. Fresh in the morn the summer rose
   Hangs withering ere tis noon
   We scarce enjoy the balmy gift
   But mourn the pleasure gone.

4. With gilding fire an evening star
   Streaks the autumnal skies
   Shook from the sphere it darts away
   And in an instant dies.

25   **1795**

In native white and red
The Rose and Lilly stand

And free from Pride their beauties spread
To Shew thy skilful Hand.

*"A Collection of Hymns" for "use of the West Society in
Boston." 1803. (Hymn 29, verse 3. No author given.)*

26   **1798**

First SPRING advancing with her flowery train
Next SUMMER'S hand that spreads the sylvan scene
Then AUTUMN with her yellow harvest crownd
And trembling WINTER close the annual round

27   **1803**

[UPON THE PROMISING FRUITFULNESS OF A TREE]

A comely sight indeed it is to see
A world of blossoms on an apple tree
Yet far more comely would the tree appear
If all its dainty blooms young apples were

But how much more might one upon it see
If all would hang there till they ripe should be
but more of all in beauty would abound
if every one should then be truly sound

John Bunyan. "Divine Emblems."

PLATE LXXXIII

Margaret Kerlin's Sampler. Burlington. 1801
Owned by Mrs. Frederick F. Thompson

PLATE LXXXIV

FANNY RINES'S SAMPLER. Lancaster, Pa. 1808
Made at Mrs. Armstrong's School
Owned by Mrs. Frederick F. Thompson

28   **1806**

I have seen the bright azure of morn   I have found that the rose has a thorn
With darkness and clouds shadowed o'er   Which will wound when its bloom is no more

29   **1807**

1. How fair is the rose what a beautiful flower
   The glory of april and may
   But the leaves are beginning to fade in an hour
   And they wither and die in a day

2. [Yet] The Rose has one powerful virtue to last
   Above all the flowers of the field
   When its leaves are all dead and the colors lost
   [Still,] How sweet a perfume will it yield.

         Rev. Isaac Watts. Moral Songs. III, "The Rose."

30   **1808**

The flowers in varied colours drest
Proclaim their author's high behest

31   **1810**

Down in a greend & shady bed   And yet it was a lovely flower
A modest violet grew   It's colors bright & fair
It's stalks was bent, it hung it's head   It might have graced a rosy bower
As if to hide from view.   Instead of hiding there.

Then let me to the vally go
This pretty flower to see
That I may also learn to grow
In sweet humility.

32   **1810**

Sweet bird thy bower is ever green   Thou hast no sorrow in thy song
Thy sky is ever clear   No winter in thy year.

33   **1811**

From natures beauteous works are fitly drawn
The buding forest & the spreading lawn
These please the eye and lead the aspireing mind
To nobler scenes of pleasure more refind

34   **1811**

Fair Verna lovely[1] village of the west
Of every joy and every charm possessed.

     *   *   *   *   *   *   *

Hail[2] smiling village happiest of the hills
How green thy grove[s] how pure thy [glassy] rills!

     "Picture of a New England village." Timothy Dwight, D.D.,
         in The Columbian Muse. 1794.

[1] Loveliest.
[2] Sweet.

35
1820
BUDDING ROSE
[THE ROSEBUD]

Queen of fragrance, Lovely Rose
The beauty of thy leaves disclose;
The winter's past, the tempests fly,

Soft gales breathe gently thro the sky;
The lark sweet warbling on the wing
Salutes the gay return of spring

Dr. William Broome.

36
1823
[THE ROSE]

The rose had been washed just washed in a shower,
Which Mary to Anna conveyed
The sleuthful moisture encumbered the flower
And weighed down its beautiful head. [haid]

The Columbian Songster. Thomas and Waldo, Brookfield, Mass. 1795.

37
1828

See the early blossoms springing
See the jocund lambkins play

Hear the lark and linnet singing
Welcome to the new-born day

38
1830
A MORNING IN SPRING

To the bright the rosy morning
Calls me forth to take the air
Cheerful spring with smiles returning
Ushers in the new born year.

Praise to thee thou great Creator
Praise be thine from every tongue
Join my soul with every creature
Join the universal song.

IN PRAISE OF PARENTS AND FAMILY

39
1732 or 6

Francis & Sarah Knowles My parents dear
Paid for this which I have heare

40
1747

Next unto God dear parents I address
My self to you in humble thankfulness
For all your care and charge on me bestowd

The means of learning unto me allowd
Go on I pray and let me still pursue
The golden art the vulgar never knew

41
1752

This I did to let you see
what care my parents took of me.

41a
1808

Behold And See
What My Parents Has Don For Me

42

1755

Can I forget that hand that first did lay
My mean foundation out of dust & clay

43

1784

Respects to parents always must be paid
Or God is angered and they are disobeyed

44

1789

How happy is the lovely child
Of manners gentle, temper mild
Who learns each useful pretty art

Sure pleasure to her friends impart
Tis thus my Parents sweeten toil
And my reward is in your smile.

45

1793

Bless Lord my parents who for me Provide
let grace and virtue ever be thy Guide

46

1794

Thanks be to my friends for their care of my breeding
Who taught me betimes to love Working and Reading

Rev. Isaac Watts. Moral Songs. "The Sluggard."

47

1797

1. Happy the child whose green unpractised years
   The guiding hand of parent fondness rears
   To rich instructions ample field removes
   Prunes every fault and every worth improves.

2. Till the young mind unfolds each secret charm
   With genius bright with cherished virtue warm
   Like the Spring's boast the lovely plant shall rise
   In grateful odors to the nurturing skies.

48

1797

TO THE MOTHER

Say, while you press with growing love,
The darling to your heart,
And all a mother's pleasures prove,
Are you entirely blest?
Ah no! a thousand tender cares
By turns your thoughts employ
Now rising hopes, now anxious fears
And grief succeeds to joy
Dear innocent her lovely smiles
With what delight you view,
But every pain the infant feels
The mother feels it too!

Then wispers busy cruel fear
The child, alas, may die
And nature prompts the ready tear
And heaves the rising sigh
Say! does not Heaven our comforts mix
With more than equal pain
To teach us if our hearts we fix
On earth we fix in vain
Then be our earthly joys resign'd
Since here we can not rest,
For earthly joys were ne'er design'd
To make us fully blest—

49 Before 1800

Accept dear shade if Heaven it wills
an infants artless tear,
who loosing the with grief it fills
my heart, altho of tender years

49a 1800

Joshua Moore and Rachel Moore Is my Parents Names
And I do hope to Honor Them while Life Remains.

(See also Number 52)

50 1805

The Father fled to Worlds unknown
When aged fifty two
The Mothers left and may we all
Her virtuous steps pursue.

51 1805

With Garlands of Roses,
I'll daily entwine
The tomb of my brothers
That sacred shrine,
And over the green bank
I'll hourly strew,
Forget-me-nots
Vieing with the sky
In their hue.

52 1807

John and Deborah Groff is the name my parents bare
To love, honor and obey them be it my constant care

53 Cir. 1808

When soon or late we reach that coast
O'er life's rough ocean driven
May we rejoice no wanderer lost
A Family in Heaven.

54 1810

1. When young, life['s] Journey I began
The glittering prospect charm'd my eyes
I saw along the extended Plain
Joy after Joy successive rise—
2. The drooping spirit you can raise
And make objection gay
It is your Power, be it your praise
To banish care away.

55 1816

Now hear you read that death has call my parent Dear,
and may we all for that day prepare

56 1818

All they that worship God and give
Their parents honour due
Here on this they long shall live
And live hereafter too.

57 1819

The God of Heaven is pleased to see
A little Family agree
And will not slight the praise they bring
When loving children join to sing.
For love and kindness please him more
Than if we give him all our store
And children here who dwell in love
Are like his happy ones above.

58

1821

A MA MERE

La rose nait en un instant
En un moment elle sot flétrie

Mais ce que pour vous mon cœur sent
Ne finira qu'avec ma vie.

59

1823

Thank's to my mothers tender care
Who these materials did prepare
And taught my hands to sew

And thanks to God who reigns above
For all the blessings of His love
And all the good I know

60

1824

My parents care points out the way
And I as cheerfully obey

And with my needle let you see
What pains my tutor took with me.

Cowper.

61

1826

Children like tender osiers take the bow,
As they first are fashioned grow.

62

1826

Remembrance gives to childrens sorrows vent
A granddaughters love inscribes the monument.

63

1827

When first my lisping accents came,
And called Father beloved,
Who felt transport fill his frame,
My Father.

Who taught my bosom to rejoice
In God above who hears my voice,
And make his ways my pleasant choice,
My Mother.

64

Me let the tender office long engage
To rock the cradle of declining age

* * * * * * * *

Explore the thought explain the asking eye
And keep awhile one parent from the sky

Alexander Pope. "Epistle to Dr. Arbuthnot."

IN PRAISE OF FRIENDSHIP

65

1684

In prosperity friends are plenty
In adversity not one in twenty.[1]

[1] Supposed to have been written at the time of the Civil War, when families were divided between the adherents of Cromwell and the King. Miles Fleetwood, whose name, with that of Abigail Fleetwood, appears on a sampler containing this verse, was a follower of King Charles, and his brother was a General in Cromwell's army.

66

1718

1. Tell me ye knowing and discerning few
   Where I may find a friend thats firm and true
   Who dares stand by me when in deep distress
   And then his love and friendship most express

2. Who by a secret sympathy can share
   My joy, my grief, my misery my care
   He must be prudent, faithful, just and wise,
   Who can to such a pitch of friendship rise.

67

1730

Despair of nothing that you would attain
Unwearied diligence your point will gain

Diligently practice what is good and then
Great will be thy reward in Bliss—amen

Refrain much talk, you seldom hear of any
Undone by hearing, but by speaking many.

Make spare in youth, least age should find thee poor
When time is past and thou canst spare no more.

Remember well & bear in mind
A faithful friend is hard to find.

68

1763

[PRECEPT I]
[HOW TO GET RICHES]

In things of moment on thy self depend.
Nor trust too far thy servant or thy friend.
With private views thy friend may promise fair.
And servants very seldom prove sincere.

Printed in Nathaniel Low's Almanack for 1772.

69

1781

1. Look on these flowers
   So fade my Hours.

2. Honour and Renown
   Shall the ingenious crown

3. Your friend sincerely love
   And imitate the Dove.

70

1788

To each unthinking being, heaven, a friend
Gives not the useless knowledge of its end;
To man imparts it; but with such a view
As, whilst he dreads it, makes him hope it too,
The hour concealed, and so remote the fear
Death still draws nearer, never seeming near.

Alexander Pope. "Essay on Man." Epistle III.

71   **1792**

Give me a House that never will decay   Give me a Friend that never will depart
And Garments that never will wear away—   Give me a Ruler that can rule my Heart

72   **Cir. 1794**

Let Us Be Friends, In Tender Years   To Share The Early Joys And Prove
When Infant Genius First Appears,   The New Born Votary Of Our Love.

73   **1798**

Happy is the man that hath a friend,   Well may he feel and recommend
Form'd by the God of nature,   Friendship to his creator

74   **1799**

How much to be prized and esteemed is a Friend
On whom we may always with safety depend
Our joys when extended will always increase
And griefs when divided are hushed into peace.

76   **1802**

The world my dear Mary is full of deceit
And friendships a jewell we seldom can meet
How strange does it seem that in searching around
The source of content is so rare to be found.

77   **1802**

Absent or dead still let a friend be dear
A sigh the absent claim, the dead a tear

78   **1803**

Friendship outlives the stars survives the tomb
Climbs up to Heaven & finds a peaceful home
Joys beyond joys in endless circles rise
Till thought can't follow and bold fancy dies.

79   **1806**

And what is friendship but a name   A shade that follows wealth & fame
A charm that lulls to sleep   But leaves the wretch to weep.

                       Oliver Goldsmith. "The Hermit."

80   **1807**

Friendship's a pure a Heav'n descended flame
Worthy the happy region whence it came
The sacred eye that virtuous spirits binds
The golden chain that links immortal minds

81   **1807**

A generous friendship no cold medium knows,
Warms with one love—with one resentment shows,
One should our interests, one our passions be,
My friend must slight the one that injures me.

82   **1810**

Farewell my friend a long farewell
A mornful sad adieu
I call to mind the happy hours
So Sweetly Spent with you

Your gayety inspir'd delight
And made the moments fly
quick as the radiant beams of light
That Sparkle in your eye

83   **1810**

How pleasing t'is to view
The only happy few
Whom friendship's bands unite

Brothers and sisters joined
In social love refined
Give and receive delight.

84   **1812**

Love is but a moving shade
Oft [changing?] with the sun

Valued friendship n'er will fade
Till our earthly course is run

85   **1813**

A solitary blessing few can find
Our joys with those we love are intertwined
And he whose wakeful tenderness removes
The obstructing thorn which wounds the friend he loves
Smooths not anothers rugged path alone
But scatters roses to adorn his own.

86   **1815**

Friendship's a name to few confin'd,
The offspring of a noble mind.

A generous warmth which fills the breast,
And better felt than e'er exprest.

87   **1816**

Be thine those feelings of the mind
That wake to honour friendship's call.

Benevolence that unconfined
Extends her liberal hand to all.

87*a*   **1816**

[I show thee] Friendship is delicate, as dear,
[Of tender violations apt to die?]
Reserve will wound it, and distrust, destroy.
Deliberate on all things with thy friend.
But since friends grow not thick on every bough
Nor every friend unrotten at the core,
First, on thy friend deliberate with thyself,
Pause, ponder, sift; nor eager in the choice,
Nor jealous of the chosen; fixing fix;
Judge before friendship, then confide till death.

Dr. Edward Young. "Night Thoughts." Night II, line 559.

88

1818

Ann thou art fair divinely fair
Nor can I in this work declare
Near half the beauties of thine

89

1819

Except this posey from a Friend
Whose Love will never end.

90

1821

Give me a mind to range the silvan scene   While social joys and friendly intervene
And taste the blessings of the vernal day   To chase the gloomy cares of life away.

91

1822

Friendship of origin divine   And lighten all my load of care
O mayest thou warm this heart of mine   Through this dark veil of doubt and fear
So it shall cease to beat   And give a blest retreat.

IN PRAISE OF LEARNING

92

1732 or 6

1. Labor for learning before you grow old   2. When silver is gone and money is spent
   for it is better than silver or gold   then learning is most excellent

or

92a

1750

Learning is an ornament   When land is gone and money spent,
a portion never to be spent.   then learning proves most excellent.

93

1767

Adorn thyself with grace & truth
And learning prize now in thy youth.

94

1785

1. Tis education forms the tender[1] mind
   Just as the twig is bent the tree's inclin'd

   Alexander Pope. "Moral Essays." Epistle I, line 149.

95

1785

1. Vain are the hopes of those who think to gain
   This noble treasure without taking pains

2. Youth is the time for progress in all arts
   Then use your youth to gain the noblest parts.

[1] "Common" is correct. Evidently changed to "tender" and "youthful" to drive the lesson home.

96 **1785**

As diamonds rough no lustre can impart
Till polish'd and improv'd by aiding Art
So untaught youth we very rarely find
Display the dazzling Beauties of the mind
Till art and science are with nature joined

97 **1786**

To Colleges and Schools ye Youths repair
Improve each precious Moment while you're there

98 **1791**

If to learning you will attend,
Learning will be your surest friend

Dunces ever meet with shame
And never rise to work or fame.

99 **1797**

Delight in Learning Soon doth Bring
a Child to Learn the Hardist Thing.

100 **1797**

Each pleasing Art lends softness to the mind
And with our Studies are our lives refined

As soft refinements flow from works of Art
Our virtuous Actions real Bliss impart.

101 **1799**

Rear'd by blest Education's nurturing hand
Behold the maid arise her mind expand

Deep in her heart the seeds of virtue lay
Maturing age shall give them to the day

102 **1799**

Vain, very vain my weary search to find
That bliss which only centres in the mind
Why have I strayed from pleasure and repose
To seek a good each government bestows
In every government though errors reign
Though tyrant kings or tyrant laws refrain
How small of all that human heart endure
That part which laws or kings can cause or cure

103 **1800**

O Praise thy language was by heaven designed
As manna to the faint bewildered mind
Beauty and diffidence whose hearts rejoice
In the kind comfort of thy heavenly voice
In this wild wood of life wert thou not nigh
Must like the wandering babes lie down and die
But thy sweet accents wake new vital powers
And make this thorny path a path of flowers.

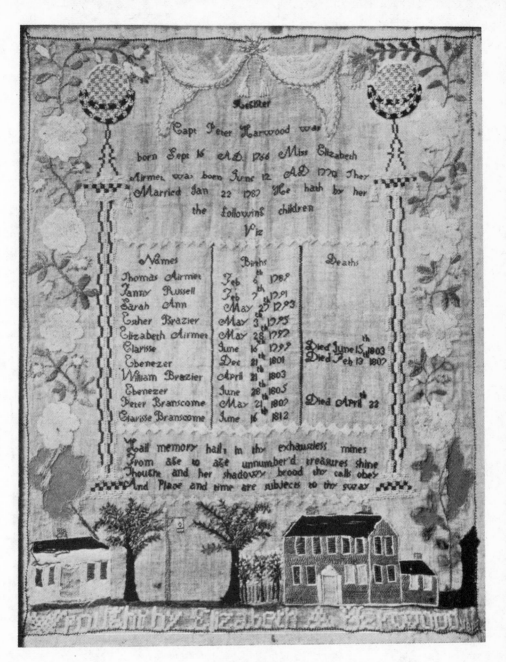

PLATE LXXXV

Elizabeth A. Harwood's Sampler. Massachusetts. 1814
Owned by Miss Grace Craig Stork

PLATE LXXXVI

The Down Family Record. 1828
Made by "M. D."
Owned by Mrs. William D. Frishmuth

104

1805

1. Plain as this canvas was, as plain we find,
   Unlettered unadorned the female mind.
   No fine ideas fill the vacant soul,
   No graceful coloring animates the whole.

2. With close attention carefully inwrought,
   Fair education paints the pleasing thought,
   Inserts the curious line on proper ground,
   Completes the whole, and scatters flowers around.

3. My heart exults, while to the attentive eyes
   The curious needle spreads the enamell'd dyes,
   While varying shades the pleasing task beguile,
   My friends approve me, and my parents smile .

105

1806

Learning do but try to love
And then you surely will improve

106

1806

Get learning tis the grace of science fair
That give the lib'ral mind its noblest air

Get Wisdom in her train the vertues shine
Thy guides with hope and faith to bliss divine

107

1806

The Youth with greatest talent born
Is rough, while unrefined.

Learning will every heart adorn
And polish every mind.

108

Cir. 1806

Industry taught in early days
Not only gives the teacher praise
But gives us pleasure when we view
The works that Innocence can do

The Parents with exulting joy
Survey it as no childish toy
But as a prelude that each day
A greater genius will display

109

1807

Learning is a beauty bright,
In learning take great delight,

Beauty will soon fade away,
But learning never will decay.

110

1808

Adorn your heart, adorn your mind
With knowledge of the purest kind

111

1809

While thus we practice every art
To adorn and grace our mortal part

Let us with no less care devise
To improve the mind that never dies.

112

1809

Sweet is the morning of youth
Inspired with knowledge and truth.

113   **1810**

As memory o'er this task shall wake   Oft shall I wish but wish in vain
And retrospective pleasure take   To enjoy youth's careless hours again

114   **1812**

Youth if set right at first with ease go on
And each new task is with new pleasure done
But if neglected till they grow in years
And each fond Mother her dear children spares
Errour becomes habitual and you'll find
Tis then hard labour to reform the mind

115   **Before 1816**

In this early life to me oh Lord   And while my mind is early taught
Thy pard'ning mercy show   May I in knowledge grow

116   **1816**

Let the mind your noblest thoughts engage
Its beauties last beyond the flight of age

117   **1818**

Delightful task, to rear the tender thought
And teach the young idea how to shoot
          James Thomson. "The Seasons." Line 1149.

118   **1818**

Let solid sense her mind inform   Let her be void of foolish pride
Let gentle love her bosom warm   And modesty her bosom guide.

119   **1819**

Let wreaths of laurel twine the brow   But Education should endow
Of him who strides in arms   With grace the female charms.

120   **1820**

LEARNING

From art and study true content just [must?] flow
For 'tis a God-like attribute to know:
He most improves who studies with delight
And learns sound morals while he learns to write.

121   **1822**

Here the fair form by nobler views refind
Shines the bright mirror of the faultless mind
With pity's dew the eye of radiance flows
With Learnings gem the breast of beauty glows.

122

1822

Science adorns and virtue beams divine
How bright their radience when they both combine.

123

1825

By degrees The human blossom blows
and every day Soft as it rolls along shows
some new charm Then infant reason grows
apace and calls
The kind hand of an assiduous care.

124

1825

The feast of reason which from reading springs
To reasoning man the highest solace brings
Tis books a lasting pleasure can supply
Charm while we live and teach us how to die

125

1826

May improvement stamp each hour
Well employed each Day be found

Each Month new stores of Knowledge yield
With added worth each year be crowned

126

1829

True dress is this, be not to modes confined,
True ornament's a well instructed mind.

127

CELESTIAL WISDOM

How happy is the youth who hears
Instructions warning voice
And who celestial wisdom makes
His early only choice
For she has treasures greater far
Than east or west unfold
And her reward is more secure
Than is the gain of gold
In her right hand she holds to view

A length of happy years
And in her left a prize of fame
With honour bright appears
She guides the young with innocence
In pleasures path to tread
According as her labours rise
So her rewards increase
Her ways are ways of pleasantness
And all her paths are peace.

IN PRAISE OF SAMPLERS

128

Cir. 1630

1. ———— ———————— is my name
    And with my needle I rought the same

2. And if my skil had been better
    I would have mended every letter.

129

1707

This needle work of mine can tell
When I was young I learned well

And by my elders I was taught
Not to spend my time for naught.

129*a*   **1789**

This needlework of mine was taught
not to spend my time for naught.

130   **1738**

Not pleasing objects which soon pass the sight,
Or richest food that highest tastes delight.
Not numbered music which captivates the ear,
Or gayest dress that pleases much the fair,
With virtue equal are, my greetings, maid,
These clog our sense, this to the mind gives aid,
This New Year's gift your sampler may adorn,
And pattern be to others yet unborn.

131   **1747**

Behold the labour of my tender age
And view this work which did my hours engage
With anxious care I did these colours place
A smile to gain from my dear parents face
Whose care for me I ever will regard
And hope that heaven will give a kind reward
My little faults I hope you will excuse
Then your commands on me I'll not refuse.

132   **1752**

1. This work in hand my friends may have
   When I am dead and in my grave

2. And which wheneer you chance to see
   May kind remembrance picture me
   While on this glowing canvas stands
   The labour of my youthful hands

133   **1767**

Blame not my work, if fault you see
Few earn with + + you ————

134   **1767**

My friends I hope you are pleased & so shall I
If this my work I may get credit by
Much labor & much time it hath me cost
I will take care that none of it be lost

135   **Cir. 1775**

[Sarah Ann Souder] worked this in great speed
And left it here for you to read.

136

Oft as thine eye shall fondly trace
Those few lines I here exact

137

138

Behold when I try
My needle can vie
With my pen and my pencil to prove

139

Behold this early sampler may
Show Readers at a future day

140

Olive Bosworth is my name
and with my needle I work the same

141

142

143

144

1. Of female arts in usefulness
The needle far excels the rest
In ornament there's no device
Affords adornings half so nice

145

While I my needle ply with skill
With mimic flowers my canvas fill
O may I often raise

146

Betsy Lincoln is my name
At ten years old I wrought the same

[1] Coarse.

1784

Whate'er the time where'er the Place
Remember me my Friends.

1787

Though young in age And small in stature
Yet I have skill To form a letter.

1787

My very fond wish
Is centerd in this
To gain my dear parents your love

1790

That I was taught before too late
All Sorts of idleness to hate

1795

A time to work my parents give
I will ne'er forget it while I live

1796

These pollish'd arts, have humaniz'd mankind
Soften'd the rude and calm'd the boistrious mind.

1799

Here you may see my work tho course[1]
When I lie moulding in the dust.

1801

I cannot perceive This business design'd
For anything more Than to pleas a raw mind

1802

2. While thus we Practice every art
To adorn and grace our mortal part
Let us with no less care device
To improve the mind that never dies.

1803

My thoughts to Him who made the flowers
And gave us all that we call ours
And render youthful prais

1804

What days more happy mark lifes busy stage
Than those when education forms our age

147   **1805**

[ON THE INVENTION OF LETTERS—THE ANSWER]

The noble art to Cadmus owes its rise   The airy voice and stopp'd the flying sound
Of painting words and speaking to the eyes   The various figuers by his pencil wroght
He first in wondrous maggick letters bond   Gave colour form and body to the thought

Nathaniel Low's Almanack. 1806. No author given.

148   **1828**

Whence did the wondrous mystic Art arise   That we by tracing magic lines are taught
Of painting speech and speaking to the eyes   How both to colour and embody thought.

149   **1805**

This to my friends when I am gone   Remember that I wrought the same
I leave for them to look upon   For underneath you find my name.

150   **1806**

1. When Youth's soft season shall be o'er   2. As memory o'er this task shall wake
And scenes of Childhood charm no more   And retrospective pleasure take
My riper years with Joy shall see   How shall I wish but wish in vain
This proof of infant Industry.   To enjoy Youth's careless hours again.

151   **1807**

Mary Tucker Is My Name   And Practice Every Useful Art
May I Excell in Deeds Of Fame   That May My Happiness Impart.

152   **1808**

In fair proportion see the letters stand
A beauteous equal and impressive band
With eye of care we must their structure raise
A point too much the hand unskilled betrays
A thread misplaced their symmetry despoils
And the fond hope of excellence beguiles
So my sweet girl the path of life survey
And tread with caution o'er devious way
An erring step would blast thy budding fame
And with dishonor stamp my Mary's name
From rules of virtue shouldst thou careless stray
Nor sighs nor tears can e'er the forfeit pay
For female reputation wounded dies
No blest Panaceas this wide world supplies.

153   **1808**

When I was young and quite untaught   But when Im older and know more
These letters I with needle wroght   Ill make them better than before

PLATE LXXXVII

ELIZA CROCKER'S SAMPLER. 1803
"At Mrs. Dobell's Seminary in Boston"
Owned by Miss Susan P. Peabody

PLATE LXXXVIII

SALLY SHATTUCK'S SAMPLER
Owned by the Rhode Island School of Design

154

1808

Thus when my draught some future time invades
The silk and figure from the canvas fades
A rival hand recalls from every part
Some latent grace & equals art with art
Transported we survey with dubious strife
Each form & figure starts again to life.

155

When with the needle I'm imploy
Or whatsoever I pursue

1809

Teach me O Thou Almighty Lord
To keep my final end in view.

156

Dear Mother I am young and cannot show
Such work as I unto your goodness owe

1811

Be pleased to smile upon my first endeavor
And Ill strive to be obedient ever

157

1812

Industrious ingenuity may find
Noble employment for the female mind

158

1812

Parents and patrons of my age I now present to you
This work in which I do engage for you to read and view.
I ask your counsel seek your love and approbation too
And beg a blessing from above on all the works I do.

159

In vain my sampler does assume
To paint the garb of nature to the eye

1813

Art can imitate, tho she presume
The noblest work of nature to outvie

160

This sampler which appears in view,
When first begun cost many a tear;
The merit to my friends is due,
Who taught me the right course to steer.

The silken threads both long and fine
Did often break and make me sigh;
At crosses oft we do repine,
But still our hope's in him on high.

1814

Oh heavenly Father bless my friends
Oh bless them with peculiar care
For I can ne'er make them amends
Oh heavenly Father hear my prayer.

The thread of life may soon decay,
The knot may slip—then all is o'er;
Oh: may the needle ne'er give way,
Until we reach the happy shore.

161

1814

Now while my needle does my hours engage
And thus with care I mark my name and age
Let me reflect though few have been my years
Crowded with sins this narrow space appears

162

1808

1. While rosy cheeks their bloom confess
   And youth thy bosom warms
   Let Virtue and let Knowledge dress
   Thy mind in brighter charms

2. Daily in some fine page to look
   Lay meaner sports aside
   And let the needle and the book
   Thy useful hours divide.

163

Cir. 1808

In the soft scenes of life
When cares are small and few

I'll show to others of my age
What busy hands can do.

164

1815

The book the needle and the pen
Each hours of all will divide

And Virtue with her Peaceful train
Within my breast reside.

165

1815

Please to survey this with a tender eye
Put on good nature and lay judgment by.

166

1816

An idler is a watch that wants both hands.
As useless when it goes as when it stands.

William Cowper. "Retirement." Line 681.

167

1817

By this Exemplar I am taught
How letters great and small are wrought

So by the example of the wise
May I true virtue learn to prize

168

1817

1. Ye sprightly are whose gentle mind incline
   To all that's joyous innocent and fine
   With admiration in your works are read
   The various texture of the twining thread.

2. Then let the needle whose unrivalled skill
   Exalts the needle above the noble quill.

169

1821

This little piece of work I've done
And finished to my mind

And when I've this life's journey run
I hope a heaven to find.

169a

These letters which you now behold
May serve to guide a feeble hand

When many years away have rolled
These letters will securely stand

170

1824

This early labor of my hand
A sacred monument shall stand
And speak when years have flown away
The efforts of an infant day.

Should bounteous nature kindly pour
Her richest gifts on me
Still, O my God, I should be poor
If void of love to Thee.

O grant me then this one request
And I'll be satisfied
That love divine may rule my breast
And all my actions guide.

171

This sampler wrought with so much care
Adorned with colours rich and fair
My little friend let it impart
A moral lesson to thy heart

172

In the glad morn of blooming youth
The varied thread I drew
And pleas'd beheld the finished piece
Rise glowing to the view

173

May you dear Fanny with your needle trace,
A small memorial of your youthful days.
When learnings page, with useful arts combined,
To engage your fancy and improve your mind,
And from this source may you each pleasure know,
Which from wise precepts and industry flow,
And as through life's inconstant scenes you wave
In duties pathway ever humbly move
Of virtue, Innocence and truth possessed,
By friendship cherished by religion blessed.

174

Happy the maid whose artless mind
In works of innocence can find
Amusement and delight

175

1. Accomplishments by heaven were first designed
   Less to adorn Than to amend the mind
   Each should contribute To the general end
   and all to virtue, as their centre bend.

2. Th' acquirements which our best esteem invite
   Should not project but soften mix unite
   In glaring light not strongly be displayed
   But sweetly lost and melted into shade.

176

The canvas thus in colours laid
Gives a just emblem of mankind

177

1825

With like industry may it thou gain
That Peace which will thy mind sustain
In every trying time of need
Then wilt thou happy be indeed.

1826

When gay youth shall charm no more
And age shall chill my blood
May I my life review and say
Behold my works are good.

1826

1826

The landscape on this canvass lay
By which the blended colors may
Give charm and please the sight

1827

1827

Thus education good or bad
Shows on the canvas of the mind.

Before 1830

INDUSTRY

Tho age may shew life's best pursuits are vain
And few the pleasures to be here enjoy'd
Yet may this work a pleasing proof remain
Of youth's gay period.

178

1830

Whoever thinks a faultless piece to see
Thinks what ne'er was, nor is, nor e'er shall be.

Alexander Pope. "Essay on Criticism." Part II.

179

My youthful days will soon be o'er   Laid in the grave we all must be
And time with me will be no more   And this I have wrought for you to see

REFLECTIONS ON DEATH AND SORROW

180   **1713**

DEAR CHILD DELAY NO TIME   THE LONGER THOU DOST LIVE
BUT WITH ALL SPEED AMEND   THE NEARER TO THY END

181   **1730**

1. If All Mankind Would Live In Mutual Love
This World Would Much Resemble That Above.

2. Remember Time Will Come When We Must Give
Account To God How We On Earth Did Live.

182   **1730**

1. The rose is red the grass is green   2. My friends when you Those lines do see
The days are past That I have seen   In reading This remember me.

3. And when the bell begins to toll
The Lord have mercy on my soul

183   **1731**

My Life Is A Flower The Time It Hath To Last
Is Mett With Frost And Shook With Every Blast

184   **1737**

It is no wonder that men turn to Clay
When Rocks and Stones and monuments decay

185   **1737**

Remember time will shortly come   To God the righteous Judge of all
When we a strict account must give,   How we upon this earth do live.

186   **1738**

Did we but know our nearness to the grave
What thoughts what cogitations should we have

187

When I am dead and in my grave
And all my bones are rotten,

188

On earth let my example shine
And when I leave this state,

189

No room for mirth or trifling here,
For worldly hope or worldly fear,
    If life so soon is gone;

190

Our days begin with trouble here
Our life is but a span,
And cruel death is always near
So strange a thing is man.

191

192

As One Day Goes Another Comes
And Sometimes Shew Us Dismal Dooms
As Time Rolls On New Things We See
Which With us Seldom Do Agree
Tho Now And Then a Pleasant Day,

193

194

195

Redeem the mispent life that's past,
Live each day as it were thy last.

1739

When this you see, remember me
That I mant be forgotten.

1741

May heaven receive this soul of mine,
To bliss divinely great.

Rev. Isaac Watts. Hymn for his 39th sermon, verse 6.

1743

If now the Judge is at the door,
And all mankind must stand before
    The inexorable throne!

1747

Then sew the seeds of grace whilst young
That when thou comest to die
Thou'll sing that triumphant song
Death where is thy victory.

1750

Despise the world with all its fading joys
Compared with Heaven are but trifling toys.

(See also Verse 248)

1755

Its Long A Coming, Soon Away
Wherefore The Everlasting Truth
Is Good For Aged And For Youth
For Them To Set Their Hearts Upon
For What Will Last When Time is Done

1756

Remember man thou art but dust
From Earth thou came to Earth thou must

1764

Awake, Arise, Behold. Thou hast
thy life; a leaf, thy breath, a blast.

1767

Then of thy talents take great care,
For the last day thyself prepare.

196   **1767**

Nothing is so sweet and beautiful as a flower
But yet it blows and fades all in an hour
For life as fairest flowers soonest fades
So God takes home the most beautiful maids
Therefore in blooming youth pray now be wise

197   **1773 or 5**

How oft the laughing brow of joy   And thro the cloisters deth in pain
A sick heart conceals   No sorrow feels

198   **1774**

Fragrant the rose is but it fades in time,
the violet Sweet but quickly past the prime
While lilies Hang their heads and soon decay
and whiter Snow in minutes melt away
such and so with'ring Are our early joys
which time or sickness speedily Destroys.

199   **1780**

How soon the [wheel?] of Fortune turns
they late who smiled in Sorrow mourns.

200   **1784**

Time cuts them all
Both great and small.

201   **1785**

Why should I say 'tis yet too soon
to seek for heaven or think of death,
When I may fade before 'tis noon.

202   **1771**

1. Swift as the Sun Revolves the Day   2. 'Tis air that lends us life when first
we hasten to the Dead   The vital billows heave.
Slaves to the wind we Puff away   Our flesh we borrow of the dust
and to the ground we tread.   And when a mother's care has nurst
                                           The babe to manly size, we must
                                           With usury pay the grave.

203   **1780**

While God doth spare
For death prepare.

204   **1786**

Aim not in gaudy cloathes to shine,   Reflect how short must be thy stay,
let dress take up but little time,   How vain to deck a piece of clay.

205

1786

Death is a debt to nature due
that i must pay and so must you.

206

1786

When this you see
Remember me.

207

1786

Make the Extended skys Your Tomb
Let Stars record your Worth

Yet Know Vain Mortals all must die
As Nature Seeketh Birth.

208

1787

You whose fond wishes do to Heaven aspire
Who make those blest abodes yr. sole Desire
If you are wise & hope that Bliss to gain
Live well yr. Time, live not an hour in vain
Let not the Morrow yr. vain thoughts employ,
But think this Day the last you shall enjoy.

209

1788

Sleep by night and cares by day
Bear my fleeting life away

210

1788

Keep Death and Judgment always in y^r eye
None's fit to live that is not fit to die.

Make much of precious time because y^u must
Take up your Lodging shortly in the dust
Its dreadful to behold the setting Sun
And Night approaching e'er your work is done.

211

1788

Why should this Earth delight us so
Why should we fix our Eyes
On this low Ground where Sorrows grow
And every Pleasure dies.

Nature shall be dissolv'd and die
The Sun must end his Race
The Earth and Sea for ever fly
Before my Saviour's Face.

While Time his sharpest Teeth Prepares
Our Comforts to devour
There is a Land above the Stars
And Joys above his Power.

When will that glorious Morning rise
When the last Trumpet sound
And call the Nations to the Skies
From underneath the Ground.

Rev. Isaac Watts. Hymns. Book II, 144.

212

1789

Soft Sleep be thou companion of my bed
Tho' thou bear'st the image of the dead
Oh lovely rest my weary eyes compose

And lull my senses in a sweet repose
For oh! how charming thus intranc'd to lie
Live without life and without death to die.

213

1789

The wise the foolish and the brave,
must try the cold and silent grave.

214

Cir. 1790

My soul come meditate the day
And think how near it sta[n]ds

When thou must quit this house of clay
And fly to unknown lands.

Rev. Isaac Watts. Hymnal. Book II, 61, verse 1.

215

1790

How vain are all thy earthly treasures
Created beauty cannot long last—

The time diminishes at leasure
What human hands can form or cast.

216

1790

There is an hour when I must die
Nor do I know how soon 'twill come

A thousand children young as I
are called by death to hear their doom

217

1791

Death like an over flowing stream sweeps us away
Our life's a dream an Empty tale
An empty tale, a moving flower
Cut down and withered in an hour.

*"A Collection of Hymns . . . for the use of the West Society
in Boston." 1803. (Hymn 146, verse 2. No author given.)*

218

1791

The brightest beauty fades
The fairest flowers decay

The inevitable hour of death
there is none can keep away

219

1791

My flesh shall slumber in the ground
Till the last trumpets joyous sound

Then burst the chorus with sweet surprise
And to my Saviour's image rise

220

1791

Life is uncertain
Death is sure

sin is The death
Christ The cure.

220*a*

1805

Life is short
Death is sure

Sin is the wound
Christ is the cure.

221

1791

Still a new spring shall Bless the earth
and a New harvest rise
But the last year shall Never again
revisit Mortal eyes

Each year fulfils Some new event
that Heaven long decreed Before.
Removes Unnumbered lives aWay
and gives unNumbered more

222

1792

[A THOUGHT]

How like the fleeting wind away
Whole years of joy depart

But oh how slowly does one day,
Move to the mournful heart.

Nathaniel Low's Almanack. 1778.

223

1792

Lord when i Leave this
Mortal ground and thou
Shall bid me rise and come

Send a beloved angle down
Safe to conduct my spirit home

224

1793

Death at a distance we but slightly fear
He brings his terrors as he draws more near
Through poverty pain slavry we drudge on
The worst of beings better please than none
No price too dear to purchase life & breath
The heaviest burdens easier borne than death

225

1793

Remember maid for die thou must
And all thy glory turn to dust.

226

1793

May I with innocence and peace,
My fleeting moments spend;

And when this vale of life shall ceace,
With calmness meet my end.

"Hannah Hollingswort."

227

1794

When my short glass its latest sand shall run
& Death approach to fright the lookers on
Softly may I sigh out my soul in air
Stand thou my pitying guardian Angels there.

Nathaniel Low's Almanack. 1770.

228

1795

Yet shall thy grave with rising flowers be drest
And the green turf lie lightly on thy breast
There shall the morn her earliest tears bestow
There the first roses of the year shall blow

229

1795

How can I weep or mourn at all
For one that fell asleep

Oh was I fit for that same call
That I might cease to weep.

230

1796

Religion should your thoughts engage
Amidst your youthful bloom.

To fit yourself for ———— age
And for the awful tomb.

231   **1796**

When tides of youthful blood run high,   Health presuming, beauty blooming,
And scenes of greatest joy are nigh,   Oh how dreadful 'tis to die!

232   **1797**

Gay dainty Flowers go Swiftly to decay   we eat drink we sleep but lo anon
Poor wretched Life Short Portion flies away   old Age Steals on us never thought upon

233   **1797**

He that Knows how to Live say I
Will easily learn the way to Die.

234   **1797**

s

Her Morning Sun Gone Down   Where All Our Toils Are O'er
Her Noon Her Suffrin Time Is Oer   Our Suffrin And Our Pain
She Shouts Salvation to her King   Who Meet On That Eternal Shore
On Zion's Peaceful Shore.   Shall Never Part Again.

235   **1797**

1. O God how swift my moments fly   2. O God of love almighty Power
How great the thought that I must die   May I improve this present hour
How shorts a day a month a year   Devote myself to thee in time
How fast my moments disappear   And ripen fast for joys sublime.

236   **1797**

This Life is like a morning Flower
Cut Down & Withered in an hour.

237   **1798**

So let me live so let me die
That I may live eternally

238   **1798**

1. Short is the longest day of life   2. Yet equal to our beings aim
And soon its prospect ends,   The space to virtue given
Yet on this days uncertain date   And every minute well improved
Eternity depends.   Secures an age in heaven

239   **1799**

One Weeks Extremity May Teach Us More
Than Long Prosperity Had Done Be Fore
Death Is Forgotten In Our easy State
But Troubles Mind Us In Our Final Fate
The Doing Ill Affects Us not with Fears
But Suffring Ill Brings Sorrow woe And tears

PLATE LXXXIX

NANCY WRIGHT'S SAMPLER. Lower Penns Neck, N. J. 1800
Owned by Miss Maria H. Mecum

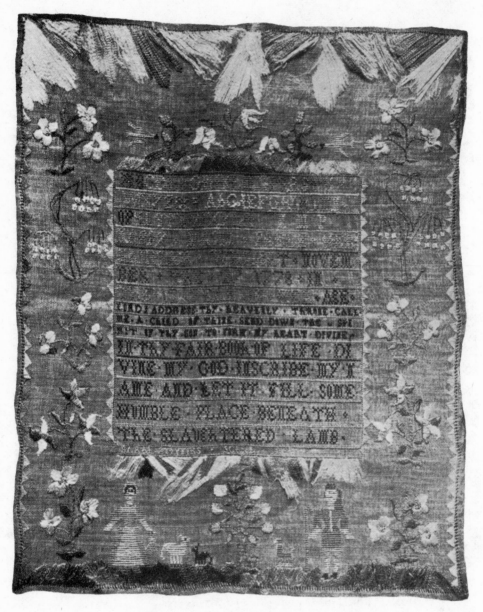

PLATE XC

NABBY MASON PEELE, of Boston. 1778
Miss Sarah Stivour's School
Owned by the Essex Institute, Salem

240   **1799**

To God above and to your friends below
Still let your breast with zeal and duty glow
Time well employed is a most certan gain

Earnest of pleasure remedy for pain
Seize on the winged hours without delay
Nor trust to morrow while we live to day

241   **1799**

Ah! why so vain, though in thy spring,
Thou shining, frail adored and wretched thing;
Old age will come, disease may come before,
Fifteen is full as mortal as threescore.
Thy fortune & thy charms may soon decay,
But grant those fugitives prolong their stay,
Their bases totter, the foundation shakes
Life that supports them in a moment brakes,
Then wrought into the soul let virtue shine
The ground eternal as the work divine.

242   **1799**

1. When death transfers me to the dust,
   May I be numbered with the just
   My soul ascend to World of bliss
   Where dwells immortal happiness

2. Ere here I leave my name behind,
   Forgetful mortals to remind.

243

Lo the young tribes of Adam rise
And thro all natur[e rove?]
Fulfill the wishes of their eyes
And taste the joys they love

They give a loose to wild desires
But let the sinners know
The strict account that God requires
Of all the works they do

The Judge prepars his throne on high
The frighted Earth and seas
Avoid the fury of his eye
And flee before his fall

How shall I bear that dreadful day
And stand the firey test
I'd give all mortal joys away
To be for ever blest.

Rev. Isaac Watts. Hymns and Spiritual Songs. Book I, XC.

244   **1800**

Oh if my days should be but few
Then I would freely bid adue

To all things that are here below
There is nothing surer than I must go

245   **1800**

When Spring appears when violets blow
And shed a rich perfume
How soon the fragrance breathes its last
How short lived is the bloom

Fresh in the morn the summer rose
Hangs withering ere tis noon
We scarce enjoy the balmy gift
But mourn the pleasure gone

246   **1787**

When I am dead and worms me eat
here you shall se my name complete

247   1802

The eye findeth   The hand bindeth
The heart chooseth   And death looseth

248   1747

1. Behold alass our days we spend   2. May useful arts employ my youth
How vain they are how soon they end   with love of vertue & of truth
     That when these fleeting moments end,
     A Crown imortal I may find.

249   1802

We stand exposed to every sin   But business holds our passions in
While idle and without employ.   And keeps out all unlawful joy.

Rev. Isaac Watts.
"The Inscription on several small French Pictures, translated."

250   1802

Great God how frail a thing is man   His age contracts within a span
How swift his minutes pass   He blooms and dies like grass.

251   1802

These tender blossoms of the opening year
Secure from storms still claim a parents' tear.

252   1803

When I am dead   When this you see
And laid in Grave   Pray think on me
And all my flesh decayd   A poor young harmless maid

253   1803

When the solemn mandate fly
The Father and the infant die

254   1803

Death often nips the tender bloom
And vows the blossom to the Tomb

255   1803

And Must this body die   And Must these active limbs of Mine
This Mortal frame decay   Lie mould'ring in the clay

Rev. Isaac Watts. Hymns and Spiritual Songs. Book II, CX, verse 1.

256   1803

Grant me O God A day of rest   In the Heavens Where Angels Dwell
When time shall Cease may I be Blest   And not be Summoned Down to Hell

257

Cir. 1803

As runs the glass
Our lives do pass.

258

Cir. 1803

Teach me to live that I may dread   Teach me to die that so I may
The grave as little as my bed   Triumphing rise at the last day

Bishop Thomas Ken. 1709. 3d verse.
("Glory to Thee, My God, this night")

259

1803

O! Death
As those we love decay we die in Parts
String after String is severd from the hearts
Till loosend life at last but breathing Clay
Without one pang is glad to fall away

260

1803

An hour will come when you will bless
Beyond the brightest dreams of life
Dark days of our distress

261

After 1803

Earthly cavern to thy keeping   Keep it safely, softly sleeping
We commit Eliza's dust   Till the Lord demands the trust

262

1804

Rest lovely youth escap'd this mortal strife   Tir'd with vain life, will close the willing eye
Above the joys, beyond the woes of life   'Tis the great birthright of mankind to die.
Yes we must follow soon, will glad obey

263

1804

O God of Grace and God of truth   Reluctant nature thinks it soon
Who formed me by thy power   But if my morning sun
It is thine hand arrests my youth   Must set in darkness ere its noon
And nips the opening flower   Thy sovereign will be done

From thee I had my life at first
'Tis thou supports my frame
At thy command I turn to dust
And bless thy holy name.

264

1804

How loved how honored once avails thee not   A heap of dust alone remains of thee
To whom related or by whom begot   Tis all thou art & all the proud shall be

265   1804

> To Thee, O Death, my fleeting moments tend,
> In Thee the hurricane of life must end.
> For tho' the seas have leave to ebb & flow,
> The streams of life must always forward go.

266   1804

Quickly will my glass of life be run
And with it all my gain and sorrow gone

No more shall I these Earthly Toys desire
But cold and peaceful to the grave retire

267   1805

Happy the maid who privileged by fate
Too shorter labour and a lighter weight

Received but yesterday the gift of breath
Order'd tomorrow to return to death

268   1805

Farewell my friends who die so soon.
My earthly friends adieu

No more to us will ye return
But we must follow you.

269   1805

Then mortal torn thy cares forgo.
All earthborn cares are wrong.

Man wants but little here below.
Nor wants that little long.
            Oliver Goldsmith. "The Hermit."

270   1805

Our life is ever on the wing
And death is ever nigh

The moment when our lives begin
We all begin to die.

271   1805

My thoughts on awful subjects ran
Damnation and the dead
What horrors seize the guilty soul
Upon a dying bed

Lingering about these mortal shores
She makes a long delay
Till like a flood with rapid force
Death sweeps the wretch away.

272   1805

Seize mortals seize the transient hour
Improve each moment as it flies

Life's a short Summer, man a flow'r
He dies, alas how soon he dies.

273   1806

Life is the time to serve the Lord
The time to improve the great reward
And while the lamp holds out to burn

The vilest sinner may return.
He tells them of Gods service them regard
The eternal crown of life is their reward.
            Rev. Isaac Watts. Hymn 88.

274   1804

The fairest forms that nature shows
Sustain the shortest doom

Beauty is like the morning rose
That withers in its bloom

PLATE XCI

SALLY WITT'S SAMPLER. Lynn, Mass. 1786
Miss Sarah Stivour's School
Owned by Mrs. Charles Pearson Coker
Plate presented by Mrs. C. H. W. Foster

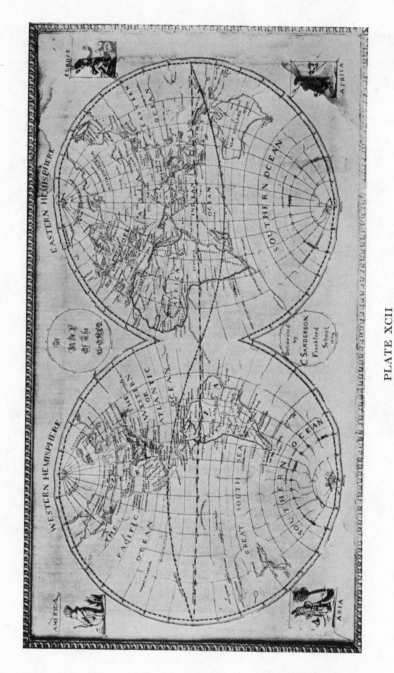

PLATE XCII

C. SANDERSON'S SAMPLER. 1809
The Frankford School
Owned by Mrs. Robert Garrett

275
1806
ON THE DEATH OF A ONLY SON

1

Here drooping by thy lifeless side
Pensive, retir'd, with grief o'erborne
Lovely in death my darling pride,
Thee, the long weeping Muse shall mourn.

2

Farewell thou dearest in my heart,
Whom neither tears nor prayers could save:
Tis death's redoubled pain to part,
And leave such beauty in the grave.

3

Strong was thy wisdom wondrous child
Active and bright its early ray
Thy temper grateful, winning mild,
And love rul'd all the smiling day.

4

Ah me: that once such sweetness gracd
Those winning smiles that angel form
Corruption's greedy train shall waste
The mouldering dust the feasting worm.

5

By night my eyes the search repeat
Sad to the glittering skies they roll
Tell me, I say the happy fate
Say where resides the blissful soul.

6

That day shall bring thee to my sight
Thy presence shall my joys restore
Fill me thou thought with vast delight
When death shall never part us more.

276
1807
ON DEATH

When we have once resigned our sinful breath
for we can die but once
then after Death the immortal Soul immediately goes
to endless joys or everlasting Woes.
Wise thens the Man who labours to secure
His passage safe and his Reception sure.

277
1807

Our God how faithful are his ways!
His Love endures the same:
Nor from the promise of His Grace:
blot out Thy Children's name:

Thus to the Parents and Their Seed
Shall Thy Salvation come
and num'rous Households Meet at last,
In One Eternal Home.

277a
1807

This work in hand my friends may have
When I am dead and in my grave.

278
1807

Youth you must not on numerous years depend,
For unknown accidents your steps attend
Some sudden illness soon may stop thy breath
And prove an inlet to Eternal Death.

278a
1807

From Stately Pallaces we Must remove
The narrow lodgings of a grave to prove
Leave this fair train of this Light guilded room
To lie alone Beneathed in a tomb

279   **1808**

So fades the lovely blooming flower   So our transient comforts fly
Frail smiling solace of an hour   And pleasure only blooms to die

Belknap. In Middlesex Collection of Church Music. Boston, 1808.

280   **1808**

Death cannot make our soul afraid   We may walk through her dark[est shade]
If God be [with us] there   And never yield to fear.

Rev. Isaac Watts. Hymns and Spiritual Songs. Book II, XLIX.

281   **1808**

Take comfort Christian when your friends in Jesus fall asleep
Their better being never ends, why then defeated weep.
Why inconsolable as those, to whom no hope is given.
Death is the messenger of Peace, and calls the soul to heaven
The saints of God from death set free, with Joy shall mount on high
The heavenly hosts with Praises loud shall meet them in the sky
A few short years of evil past, we reach the happy shore
Where death divided friends at last shall meet to part no more.

282   **1808**

Teach me the measure of my days   I would survey life narrow space
Thou maker of my frame   And learn how frail I am

283   **1809**

The wise, the just, the copious and the brave
Live in their deaths, & flourish from the grave.
Grain hid in earth, repays the peasants care
And evening suns but set to rise more fair.

284   **1809**

"THE YOUTHS MANUEL, &C"

In the short season of thy youth,   Remember thy Creator God
        s   For him thy powers employ
In nature   smiling bloom   Make him thy fear thy love
Ere age arives & trembling   Thy hope thy confidence & joy.
Waits its Summons to the Tomb

285   **1809**

All our gaiety is vain   Only lasting and divine
All our laughter is but pain   Is an innocense like thine.

286   **1809**

When with the needle I'm imploy'd   Teach me O Thou Almighty Lord
Or whatsoever I pursue   To keep my end in view

287

1810

Dear Babe at rest
We hope thee blest

287a

1810

B is a beauty all cheerful and gay
But her beauty soon fades like a flower in May

288

1810

E'en while we speak the envious time
Doth make swift haste away

Then seize the Present use thy Prime
Nor trust another day.

289

1810

[THE DEATH OF THE RIGHTEOUS]

1. Sweet is the scene when virtue dies
   When sinks a righteous soul to rest
   How mildly beams the closing eyes
   How gently heaves the expiring breast.

2. A holy quiet reigns around
   A calm which nothing can destroy
   Nought can disturb that peace profound
   Which their unfettered souls enjoy.

*   *   *   *   *   *   *

Printed in "The Clergyman's Almanack for 1814."

290

1810

This work in hand my friends may have
To look upon when I am dead
When days are short, but longer be our rest
Our Saviour calls us home because he thinks it best

291

1811

The finest mould the soonest will decay
Hear this ye fair for you yourselves are clay

May this a warning be to all
That God will judge both great and small.

292

1811

Death will desolve the tenderest tie
Our dearest friends are call'd to die

That nature forms below
And we are left in wo

293

1811

ON TIME

See see the moments how they pass
How swift they speed away
Louisa here as in a glass
Behold thy life's decay.

O waste not then thy youthful prime
In folly's crooked road
Be circumspect redeem the time
Acquaint thyself with God.

So when the pulse of life shall cease
Its throbbing transient play
Thy soul to realms of endless peace
Shall wing its joyful way.

294

That awful day will surely come
The appointed hour makes haste

1811

When I must stand before my judge
And pass the solemn test.

295

Come now let us forget our mirth
And think that we must die

1811

What are our best delights on earth
Compared with those on high

296

May day improve on day and year on year
Without a sigh a trouble or a fear.

1811

Till death unfelt this slender frame destroy
In some soft dream or extacy of joy.

Alexander Pope. Epistle to Mrs. M. B.

297

1812

Why start men at death, so vain a thing.
When Christ himself hath taken out the sting
Live unto him in godliness and fear
And then believe me there's no cause to fear
It's but a passage and a step to be crown'd
With a crown of immortality.

298

1812

Behold alas our days we spend
But it is in vain they soon will end.

299

Make use of present time
Because thou must
Shortly take up thy
Lodging in the dust

1813

Learn to avoid
What thou believest is sin
Mind what reproves
Or justifies within

300

1813

IN MEMORY OF THREE SISTERS

Cold is their form once fill'd with youthful bloom,
They sleep alas within the lonely tomb,
Commingling with the dust they wear away,
Companion only for their fellow clay.

301

Come Muse and lend your mournful aid
Dressed in pale sorrow's sable shade

1813

Come mourn with me a lovely flower
The smiling comfort of an hour

302

Years like mortals wear away
Have their birth and dying day

1813

Youthful spring and wintry age
Then to others quit the stage

303

When I have bid a long adieu
To life and all things here below

Look here my friend and think of me
That I may not forgotten be.

304

Why all this toil for triumph of an hour?
What though we wade in wealth, or soar in fame,
Earth's highest station each in "Here he lies,"
And "dust to dust" concludes her noblest song

305

When sin and sorrow fear and shame
My trembling heart dismay.

My feeble strength alas how vain
It sinks and dies away.

306

When the pure soul is from the body flown
No more shall Night's alternate reign be known
The sun no more shall rolling light bestow
But from the Almighty streams of glory flow
Oh may some nobler thought my soul employ
Than empty transient sublunary joy

307

Fate steals along with silent tread
Lays the fond mother in the dead
Two lovely babes ......

308

Behold the blooming rose
Behold the fading flower

The fairest prospect how it goes
To vanish in an hour

308a

The fairest flowers of the Spring
Has faded fled away

So blooming youth as time glides on
Swift hastens to decay.

309

These various branches rising from one root
May soverign mercy bless, and guard the fruit;
Till the great harvest when our souls shall be,
Ripe, and prepared to live in Heaven with thee.

310

ON THE TRUTH WE BELIEVE

Gr[ant] rem[emb]ranc[e well t]o paint
The moment after death
The glory that surround the saint
When yielding up their breath

While they have gained we loose ....
We miss them day by day
But thou canst ev'ry breach ....
And wipe our tears away.

311

Alas the brittle clay
That built our body first

1818

And every month and every day
Tis mouldering back to dust.

312

Swept with a hasty torrent hence
Like a vain dream we pass

1818

Spring up and grow and wither soon
As doth the short-lived grass

313

See the leaves around us falling,
Dry and wither'd to the ground,
Thus to thoughtless mortals calling,
In a sad and solemn sound.

1819

On the tree of life eternal,
Maid let all thy hope be staid,
Which alone for ever vernal,
Bears a leaf that will not fade.

314

And am I born to die
To lay this body down

1819

And must my trembling spirit fly
Into a world unknown.

Rev. Charles Wesley.

315

Soon as we draw our infant breath,
The seeds of sin grow up to death,

1820

Rise then my thoughts to God on high,
For we are mortals born to die.

316

Enough had Heaven indulged of joy below,
To tempt our tarriance in this loved retreat,

1820

Enough had Heaven ordain'd of useful woe
To make us long for a happier seat.

317

Hark from the tombs a doleful sound
My ears attend the cry

1820

Ye living men come view the ground
Where you must shortly lie.

Tate & Brady's Hymnal. Hymn 66.

318

1820

My days just hastning to there end
Are like an evening shade
My beauty does like wither'd grass
With waning lustre fade

319

The rising morn can't assure
That we shall end the day

1821

For death stands ready at the door
To take our lives away.

320

1821

O'er thy grave shall friendship lingering pause
And view the weeping flowerets there that bloom
Shall heave the generous sigh in virtuous cause
While resignation points beyond the tomb.[1]

[1] Tradition tells us that this verse was composed by the maker of the sampler, Mary W. Lyon.

PLATE XCIII

MARTHA HEULING'S SAMPLER.   Moorestown, N. J.   1809
The West Town Boarding School, and containing a picture of the School
Owned by Hannah F. Gardiner

PLATE XCIV

Susana Cox's Sampler. Cir. 1802
The West Town Boarding School
Owned by Miss Susan P. Wharton

321

1821

Ye whose fond wishes do to heaven aspire,
Who make those blest abodes their souls desire
If you are wise and hope that bliss to gain
Use well your time spend not an hour in vain
Let not tomorrow your vain thoughts employ
But think this day the last you shall enjoy

322

1822

In the deep corners of the grave
Love lingers though it cannot save.

Yes, ——— ——— of the dust
Affection springs and ever must.

323

1824

There is a calm for those who weep,
A rest for weary Pilgrims found,

They softly lie and sweetly sleep,
Low in the ground.

324

1824

Time well employd is a most certain gain
Earnest of pleasures remedy of pain

The chief of blessings on its course attends
Since on its use eternity depends

325

Cir. 1825

Life is short, the wings of time
Bear away our early prime,
Swift with them our spirits fly,
The heart grows chill & dim the eye.

Seize the moment, snatch the treasure,
Sober haste is wisdom's leisure;
Summer blossoms soon decay,
Gather the rose-buds while you may.

325a

1824

Of joys in perspection how fondly you dreamed
While the visions of fancy were ready to fade
And the day star of hope how resplendant it beamed
While swiftly descending to death's silent stream

326

1825

Youth is not rich in time, it may be poor
Part with it as with money, sparing pay
No moment but in purchase of it's worth
And what its worth, ask death-beds, they can say

327

Cir. 1826
"VERSES OF ANN MARIA ELWELL"

Thou God of love thou ever blest
Pity my suffering state
When wilt thou set my soul at rest
From lips that love—

Hard lot of mine my days are cast
Amongst the sons of strife
Whose never ceasing brawlings waste
My golden hours of life.

Not from the dust affliction grows
Nor troubles rise by chance
Yet we are bound to care and woes
A sad inheritance

As sparks break out from burning coals
And still are upward borne
So grief is rooted in our souls
And man grows up to mourn.

Isaac Watts. Psalm CXX.

328   **1826**

Lord what is life Tis like a flower
That blossoms and is gone
We see it flourish for an hour

With all its beauty on
But death comes like a wintry day
And cuts the pretty flower away

329   **1827**

The grass and flowers which clothe the field,
And look so green and gay

Touched by the sythe defenceless yield
And fall and fade away.

330   **1827**

Mortal be wise, imProve the Present hour
The last is gone the next beyond thy Power.

Thy time e'en while advancing speeds away,
Mortal be wise nor risk an hour's delay.

331   **1829**

My flying years time urges on
Who is human must decay

My friends my young companions gone
Can I expect to stay.

332   **1829**

Sweet spring of days and roses made
Whose charms for beauty vie

Thy days depart thy roses fade
Thou too alas must die.

333   **Before 1830**

Tis true twas long ere I began to seek to live forever
But now I run as fast I can, tis better late than never

334   **1830**

THE UNCERTAINTY OF LIFE

How short the connexions we form
 In a world so uncertain as this
How soon will eternitys storm
 Sweep away all the phantoms of bliss

Tho' pleasure may charm with her breath
 And point to her magical bowers
Yet she hides the keen dagger of death
 In a sheath made of blossoms and flowers

335   **1830**

The Sun that Lights the World shall fade
The Stars shall pass away

But I a Child imortal made
Shall Witness this decay.

336   **1830**

Here the beauteous slumberer bear
Soft ye zephyers smooth the air
Earth thy fragrant breast unfold
Lightly lay the hallowed mould
Twine ye woodbines round his tomb

Rosses Lilies lend your bloom
Yet no flowrets eer can shew
Half the charms that fade below
Feet unhallowed shun this shade
Here an angel form is laid.

337   **1830**

Dear youth prepare tho in thy prime
Death may be near and short thy time
O dear youth prepare against the call
For death does cut down, both great and small

338

1830

Oh stranger let your melting heart,
Mark well this fresh, and verdant sod

And eer you from this earth depart;
O let your soul, commune with God.

RELIGIOUS VERSE — OLD TESTAMENT

339   **Cir. 1636**

Lord guide my Heart that I may do thy will
And fill my hands with such convenient skill

As will conduce to Virtue void of shame
And I will give the Glory to Thy Name

340

1718

God loves the child
whose words are mild

341

1723/4

Lord Thou from dust didst raise me
when I no being had

and I in flesh to praise the
a living soul was made

342

1725

Lord give Me Wisdom to Direct My Ways
I beg not riches nor yet length of days

343

1730

LOVE THOU THE LORD

1. O love the Lord and He will be,
   A Tender (faithful) Father unto Thee

2. His glories shine with beams so bright
   No mortal eye can bear the sight

3. Slep downey slep come clos my eyes
   Tired with upholding vanityes

4. Sweet slumbers come and chase away
   The toyles and Follys of the day.

5. On thy soft bosom let me lie
   Forget The world and learn to die.

6. A Mother's Want God can Supply
   And may he Guard You With a Watchful Eye.

7. Neglect not thou thy doing well
   But strive in virtue to excell.

344

1731

1. The bed was earth the raised pillar stone
   whereon poor Jacob rested his head and bones
   Heaven was his Canopy the shades of night
   were his drawn Curtains to exclude the light.

2. poor state of jacob hear it seems to me
   his cattle found as souft a bed as he
   yet god appeared their joy his crown
   god is not always found in beds of down

345

1731

1. See how the Lillies flourish white and fair
   see how the Ravens fed from Heaven are

2. then ne'er distrust thy God for Cloth and Bread
   whilst Lillies flourish and the Ravens fed.

An adaptation of an "Epigram on Providence" by John Hawkins of Boston.

346

I Have A God In Heaven
Who Care For Me Doth Take

1737

And If I To Him Constant Prove
He Will Not Me Forsake.

346a

That truth my tongue might alway tie
from ever speaking foolishly
That no vain thoughts might ever rest
or be conceivéd in my breast

1742

that by each word, each deed, each thought
glory to my god be brought
but what are wishes lord on the!
   (2 lines undecipherable)

347

My heart resolve, My tongue obey
While Angels shall rejoice

1743

To hear thine Heavenly Maker praise
Long from a feeble voice.

348

Adam and Eve in paradise
that was their pedigree.

1745

They had a grant never to die,
wold they obedient be.

349

But how my childhood runs to waste
My sins how great their sum

1754

Lord give me pardon for the past
& strength for days to come

350

1757

In Mothers womb Thy fingers did me make
And from the womb thou didst me safely take
From Breast Thou hast me nurst my life through out
I may say I never wanted ought.

351

Let us my Friend all peevish self withstand
And in the meekness of the spotless lamb
Lead one another gently by the Hand

1760

And travel forward to the Holy Land,
Where the Redeemed on Mount Zion stand,
With Harps of living praises in their Hands

352

1760

MY CHILD TO YOVR CREATOR GOD
YOVR EARLY HONOVRS PAY
WHILE VANITY AND YOVTHFVL BLOOD
WOVLD TEMPT YOR THOVGHTS ASTRAY

THE MEMORY OF HIS MIGHTY NAME
DEMAND YOR FIRST REGARD
NOR DARE INDVLGE A MEANER FLAME
[T]ILL YOV HAVE LOVED THE LORD

353
1760

1. Oh if My Mind
   Should be inclined
   This would increase my fear
   Lord from above
   Thou God of love
   Reveal thy counsel near

2. That I may know
   That I may do
   Thy ever blessed will
   Ah! thine alone
   And not mine own
   Great King! do thou fulfil

354
1760

1. One look of mercy from thy eye
   One whisper of thy voice
   Exceed a whole eternity
   Employ'd in carnal joys

2. Could I the spacious earth command
   Or move the boundless sea
   For one dear hour at thy right hand
   I'd give them both away.

355
1763

THE TEN COMMANDMENTS.

I. Adore no other gods but only me.
II. Worship not God by anything you see.
III. Rever Jehovahs name swear not in vain.
IV. Let Sabbaths be a rest for beast and men.
V. Honour thy parents to prolong thy days.
VI. Thou shalt not kill nor murdring quarrels raise.
VII. Adultry shun in chastity delight.
VIII. Thou shalt not steal nor take anothers right.
IX. In bearing witness never tel a ly.
X. Covet not what may damnify.

356
1763

In life's gay morn when sprightly youth
With vital ardor glows
And smiles with all the fairest charms
Which beauty can disclose
Deep on thy heart before its powers
Are yet by vice enslaved
Be thy creator's glorious name
And character engraved

For soon the shades of grief shall cloud
The sunshine of thy days
And cares and toils in endless round
Encompass all thy ways
Soon shall thy heart the woes of age
In mournful groans deplore
And sadly muse on former joys
That now return no more.

357
1767

Lord let the Sonshine of thy face
So clear my Eyes and Clense my heart

That being seasoned with thy grace
My soul may tast how sweet thou art.

358
1769

Thine eye my bed and path survey
My public haunts and privit ways.

359   **1772**

From my beginning may the almighty powers,
Blessing bestow in never ceasing showers;
Oh, may I happy be and always blest,
Of every joy, of every wish possessed.
May plenty dissapate all worldly cares
And smiling peace bless my revolving years.

360   **1773**

Give unto God the flower of thy youth
take for thy guide the blessed word of truth
Adorn thyself With Grace, Prize Wisdom more
Than all the Pearls upon the Indian shore
Labour to have a conscience Pure
When all things fade that will endure.

361   **1773**

Oh happiness our being end and aim   Plant of celestial seed of dropd below
Good pleasure —— e'er thy name   Say in what mortal soul thou —— to grow

362   **1774**

1. Why should I love my sport so well,   3. How senseless is my heart and wild
   so constant in my play   How vain are all my thoughts
   And lose the thoughts of heaven and hell   Pity the weakness of a child
   and then forget to pray,   And pardon all my faults

2. What do I read my bible for   4. Make me thy heavenly voice to hear
   but Lord to learn thy will   And let me love to pray
   And shall I daily know thee more   Since God will lend a gracious ear
   and less obey thee still   To what a child can say.

               Rev. Isaac Watts. Divine Songs for Children. XXIV.

363   **1775**

1. When we devote our youth to God   2. To Thee, Almighty God, to Thee
   'Tis pleasing in his eyes   Our childhood we resign
   A flower when offered in the bud   Twill please us to look back and see
   Is no vain sacrifice   That our whole lives were Thine

            Isaac Watts. Divine Songs. XII, verses 2 and 5.

364   **1780**

My soul lies cleaving to the dust   From vain desires and every lust,
Lord give me life divine—   Turn off these eyes of mine.

365   **1780**

Nothing I ask but which include   But let me kneel and pray
Of all thy earthly power   That I may live today.

366

1781

Care use with all thy power,
To serve God every hour.

367

1781

Duty, Fear & Love
We Owe to God Above

367a

178–

Sweet are thy works my God, my King   To show thy works by Morning Light
To praise Thy name give thanks and Sing   And talk of all thy truths at Night

"Select Psalms and Hymns: Adapted to the use of Christians."
Dublin, 1762. (No author given.)

368

Cir. 1785

It grieves me Lord it grieves me sore
That I have lived to thee no more.

Rev. Isaac Watts. Lyric Poems sacred to Devotion.

369

1786

All things from nothing to their Sovereign Lord
Obedience tole at his commanding word.

370

1787

Jehovah speaks the healing word   Fevers and plagues obey the law
And no disease withstands,   And fly at his command

371

1789

O. Give my soul thy welfare to his trust   Can raise thy sleeping dust
He that hath raised the world   He wil when nature . . . . . .

372

1789

Is there ambition in my heart   or do I act a haughty part
Search gracious God and see   Lord I appeal to the.

373

1791

O God of Mercy, Grace and Truth   Thro' Life's perplexing thorny road
Guard & Protect an Orphan Youth,   Conduct me safe to thine abode.

374

1792

Still as Thro Life's Meanaring[1] Path I Stray   A Kind Conductor To The Blest Abode,
Lord Be The Sweet Companion On My Way   Of Light Of Life Of Happiness And God

[1] Meandering.

375   **1793**

During the time of life alotted me   I ask no more if more thou'rt please to give
grant me great God my health and liberty,   the overplus Ill gratefully receive

376   **1793**

First give to God the Flower of thy youth.
Take for thy guide the blessed word of Truth.

377   **1793**

Give me O Lord thine early Grace   That the young morning of my days
Nor let my soul complain   Has all been spent in vain.

378   **1794**

Oh keep in fear and lend an ear   Oh come retire and heal inspire
To what the Lord doth say   Thy soul in Wisdom's Way

379   **1794**

A few more rolling seas at most   Where I shall sing my song of Grace
Will land me on fair Canaan's coast   And see my glorious Hiding Place

380   **1794**

Get Thou the Lord & prize him more   for when thy worldly treasures past
than shining gold & silver orr—   The fear of God will ever last?

381   **1794**

Read thou the scriptures let them be thy rule
So shall the fear of God Reign in thy Soul

382   **1795**

Adieu ye fanciful delights   A nobler good my soul invites
Ye fleeting vanities   To soar above the skies.

383   **1795**

I've been to church and love to go,   Not for my pleasure or my play,
Tis like a little heaven below;   Will I forget the sabbath day.

384   **1796**

Adam alone in Paradise did grieve
and thought Eden a desert Without Eve
Until God Pittiing of his lonesome state
Crowned all his Wishes with a Loveing mate
What reason than hath Man to slight or flout her
That Could not Live in Paradise without her.

385

Adam and Eve whilst innocent
in Paradise was placed

386

Thus fair tis well you Read you Pray
You Hear God holy word

387

1. Religion's sacred lamp alone,
   Unerring, points the way
   Where happiness forever shines
   With unpolluted ray:

1796

but soon the serpent by his viles
the happy Pair disgraced

1796

You hearken what your Parent say
and learn to Serve the Lord.

1796

2. Oh! may the everlasting truth,
   My staff, and standard, be.
   The best companion for a youth
   Join'd with humility.

*Anne Steele. "Searching after Happiness." (Verse 5—the
second verse appears not to be hers.)*

388

Glittering Stones and golden things,
Wealth and Honors that have wings
Ever fluttering to be gone,
I could never call my own;
Riches that the world bestows
She can take, and I can lose;

1797

But the treasures that are mine,
Lie afar beyond her line;
When I view my spacious soul,
And survey myself awhole,
And enjoy myself alone,
I am a Kingdom of my own.

389

1798

God give me grace I ask no more
Contentment is a constant store

390

Oh Heaven kind new form my mind.
And give me view divine.

1798

That my small sum of days to come
With nobler deeds may shine.

391

Religion what treasures untold
Reside in that Heavenly word

1798

More precious than Silver or Gold
Or all that the world can afford.

392

Be it my only wisdom here
To serve the Lord with filial fear
With loving gratitude

1800

Superior sense may I display
By shunning every evil way
And walking in the good

393

1800

As pants the wearied hart for cooling streams
That sinks exhausted in the summer's chase
So pants my soul for Thee great King of kings
So thirsts to reach Thy sacred dwelling place

Bishop R. Lowth. 1753.

394

After 1800

Fear & Love
God above

395

1801

1. Teach me oh thou! that teacher art,
Of every duty here below
The number of my days impart
Be thou my guide where'er I go

2. I ask no gold nor length of days
I meet thy will thy will be done
I know that time itself decays
And gold but sparkles in the sun

3. When chastend let me kiss the rod
I wish no transient joy to claim
Be thou my portion oh my God
Thro heavens eternal year the same

4. The Lord can change the darkest skies
Can give us day for night
Make floods of sacred sorrows rise
To rivers of delight

5. Let those that sow in sadness wait
Till the fair harvest come
They shall confess their sheaves are great
And shout the blessing home

6. Adversity is virtue's school
To those who right discern
Let us observe each painful rule
And each hard lesson learn.

396

1802

Give Glory unto God above
He Only Doth Deserve Our Love

397

1802

THE
TEN COMMANDMENTS

1 Thou shalt have no God but me,
2 Before no Idoll bow thy knee;
3 Take not the name of God in vain:
4 Nor dare the Sabbath to prophane
5 Give both thy parents honor due
6 Take heed that thou no murder do
7 Abstain from words, and deeds unclean,
8 Nor steal, tho thou are poor, and mean
9 Nor make a wilful lie, nor love it
10 What is thy neighbours, dare not covet.

Rev. Isaac Watts. Divine Songs for Children.

398

1802

Thou art O Lord my only trust
When friends are mingled with the dust
And all my loves are gone

When earth has teaching to bestow
And every flower is dead below
I look to thee alone

399

1802

Almighty power! whose tender care
Did infancy protect,

Let riper years thy favor share,
And every step direct

PLATE XCV

LYDIA BURROUGHS'S SAMPLER. 1814
The Chesterford School, and containing a picture of the School
Owned by Mrs. Bradbury Bedell

PLATE XCVI

JULIA KNIGHT'S SAMPLER. 1808
Pleasant Hill Boarding School
Owned by Mrs. Henry E. Coe

BARBERRY EAGLE'S SAMPLER. 1808
Bristol School, Pennsylvania
Owned by Mrs. Arthur M. Waitt

400

There is a land of pure delight
  Where saints immortal reign
Eternal day excludes the night
  And pleasures banish pain
There everlasting spring abides
  And never fading flowers
Death, like a narrow sea, divides
  This heavenly land from ours

401

1. To be resign'd when ills betide,
   Patient when favors are denied
   And pleased with favors given,
   Dear Lord, this is Wisdom's part.

402

Though I am young, a little one
If I can speak and go alone

403

The Lord my pasture shall prepare
And feed me with a shepherd's care

404

May my fond genious as I [w]rite
Seek the fair fount where knowledge lies

405

Be sovereign grace the guardian of my youth
May Heaven-born virtue in my breast preside

407

The spacious firmament on high
  With all the blue etherial sky
And spangled heaven a shiny frame
  The great original proclaim

408

409

Grant I may ever at the morning ray
Open with pray'r the consecrated day

1802

Bright fields beyond the flood
  Stand dressed in living green
So to the Jews fair Canaan stood
  While Jordan rolled between
But timorous mortals start and shrink
  To cross the narrow sea;
And linger trembling on the brink
  And fear to launch away.

Rev. Isaac Watts.

1802

2. This is that incense of the heart
   Whose fragrant silence is heaven

1803

Then I must learn to know the Lord
And learn to read his holy words.

1803

His presence shall my wants Supply
And guard me with a watchful eye

Joseph Addison.

1803

On wings sublime trace heavens abode
And learn my duty to my God.

1803

While wisdom, honor, innocence, and truth
Attend my steps, and all my actions guide.

1804

The unwearied sun, from day to day
  Does his creator's pow'r display
And publishes to every land
  The work of an Almighty hand.

Joseph Addison. 1712.

1804

Young children in their early days
shall give the God of Abram Praise

1805

Tune the great praise and bid my soul arise
And with the morning sun ascend the skies.

410

In Paradise within the gates
An higher entertainment waits

1805

Fruit new and old laid up in store
Where we shall feed and thirst no more

411

Not in thyself, in God confide
Let reason all thy actions guide
Thy prayers to heav'n be daily sent
And with thy portion be content.
Speak seldome but attentive hear

1805

Ever superior worth revere
An equal without envy bear.
Ne'er on inferiors look disdain
Entrusted secret close retain.

411a

Not to my wish, but to my Want
Do thou thy Gifts apply

1805

O GOD!

Unasked what good thou knowest grant
What ill thou'rt asked deny

"A Collection of Hymns" for "use of the West Society in Boston."
1803. (Hymn 25, verse 8. No author given.)

412

Parent of all! Omnipotent,
In Heaven and earth below,
Thro' all creation's bounds unspent,
Whose streams of goodness flow.

Teach me to know from whence I rose
And unto what design'd;
No private aims let me propose,
Since linked with human kind.

1806

But chief to hear fair virtue's voice,
May all my thoughts incline:
'Tis reason's law,—'tis wisdom's choice,
'Tis nature's call and thine.

Teach me to feel a brother's grief,
To do in all what's best,
To suffering man to afford relief,
And blessing to be blest.

413

Grant me great God, a heart to Thee inclin'd.
Increase my Faith to rectify my mind
Conduct the steps of my unguarded youth

1806

And point my motions to the paths of Truth.
Teach me betimes to tread Thy sacred ways
And to Thy service consecrate my days.

414

1806

To wake the Soul by tender strokes of art,
To raise the genius, and to mend the heart.

415

1807

Grant me to live and if I live, to find
The dear lov'd portion of a peaceful mind
That health, that sweet content, that pleasing rest
Which God alone can give, as suits me best.

416 **1808**

MEDITATION

Arise my soul, survey the morn,
And purple beauties of the dawn
The herbs that with the dew-drops glow

The grass, the shrubs, the flow-rets show,
Their maker all divine

417 **1808**

The Lord my Shepherd is
I shall be well supply'd
Since he is mine and I am his
What can I want beside

He leads me to the place
Where heav'nly pasture grows
Where living waters gently pass
And full salvation flows

The stars which in their courses roll
Have much instruction given
But thy good word informs my soul
How I may get to heav'n

Rev. Isaac Watts. Psalm XIII. Short metre.

418 **1808**

Preserve me Lord amidst the crowd
From every thought that's vain and proud

And raise my wond'ring mind to see
How good it is to trust in thee

419 **1808**

God of my life and author of my days
Permit my feeble voice to lisp my praise
Teach me to quit this transitory scene

With decent triumph and a look serene
Teach me to fix my ardent hopes on high
And having live'd to thee in thee to die.

420 **1808**

My Thirteenth Year Of Age Is Past
O Lord Point Me The Way

To Anchor In Thy Narrow Path
And Never From It Stray.

421 **1808**

My God the steps of pious men
Are order'd by thy will
Tho they should fall they rise again
Thy hand supports them still

I choos the path of heavenly truth
And glory in my choice
Not all the riches of the earth
Could make me so rejoice.

422 **1808**

Of all the sorows that attend mankind
With patience bear the lot to thee assign

Nor think it chanc nor murmur at the Load.
What man calls fortune if from God.

423 **1808**

Great God Create my Soul Anew
Conform my hea[r]t to thine
Melt down my will and let it flu—

424   **1808**

When all thy mercíes O My God,
My rising soul surveys,

Transported with the view, I'm lost
in wonder, love and praise.

Joseph Addison, 1712.

425   **1809**

Keep silence all created things and wait your Makers nod.
My soul stands trembling while she sings the honours of her God.

426   **1809**

Lord let thy spirit witnefs bare
That I am all thy own

Still make my precious soul thy care
And guard it to thy throne

428   **1810**

God counts the sorrows of his saints
Their groans affect his ears

He has a book for their complaints
A bottle for their tears.

429   **1810**

Great is the Lord His works of Might,
Demand our noblest songs.
Let His Assembled Saints unite
their harmony of tongues

Great is the mercy of the Lord
He givs his children food,
and ever mindful of His [word,]
[he makes his] Promise good
His Son the great Red[eemer, came.]

Rev. Isaac Watts. Psalm CXI. (Part 2, verses 1 and 4, and line 1 of verse 5.)

430   **1810**

Yield to the Lord with simple heart
All that thou hast, and all thou art

Renounce all strength, but strength Divine
And peace forever shall be thine

431   **1811**

"Live while you live," the Epicure would say
And seize the pleasures of the present day
"Live while you live," the sacred Preacher cries
"And give to God each moment as it flies"
Lord in my views let both united be
I live in pleasure when I live to Thee

"On Dr. Doddridge's motto, 'Dum vivimus vivamus.' By Himself."

432   **1811**

Though heaven afflict I'll not repinè
Each heart felt comfort still is mine
Comforts that will oer deth prevail
and journey with me through the vale

amid the various scene of ills
Each stroke some kind design fulfils
And shall I murmer at my god
when soverign love directs the rod

433   **1811**

Conscience distasteful truths may tell
But mark her sacred lessons well

Who ever lives with her at strife
Loses his better friend for life.

434   1812

Long as I live I'll bless thy name
My King and God of love

My work and joy shall be the same
In the bright worlds above

Rev. Isaac Watts. Psalm CXLV. Part first, C. M.

435   1812

Oh may I live to reach the place
Where he unveils his lovely face

Where all his beauties you behold
And sing his name to harps of gold.

436   1812

"BLISS OF CELESTIAL ORIGIN"

Restless mortals toil for nought
Bliss in vain from earth is sought
Bliss a native from the sky

That never wanders. Mortals try,
Then you can not; seek in vain
For to seek her is to gain.

437   1812

There is a land of pure delight
Where friends once parted shall unite

And meeting on that blessed shore
With fond embrace shall part no more

438   1812

Father of light conduct my feet,
Through life's dark dangerous road
Let each advancing step still bring
Me nearer to my God.

Let heavenly[1] prudence be my guide
And when I go astray
Recall my feet from folly's path
To wisdom's better way.

Smart. Hymn 57. Manning & Loring Collection. Boston, 1799.

439   1812

Good, when he gives, supremely good
Nor less when he denies

Even crosses from his soverign hand
Are blessings in disguise.

440   1813

I want a heart to pray
To pray & never cease

Never to murmur at thy ———,
Or wish my sufferings less.

Rev. Charles Wesley.

441   1812

To thee again my gracious God
I lift my heart and eyes

Thou art my only safe abode
Thou only just and wise

442   1813

Mysterious Heaven how wondrous are thy ways
Let us not presume thy ways to scan
Nor dare 'gainst God a murmuring thought to raise
For resignation is the part of Man.

[1] heav'n ey'd.

443

Oh Source of wisdom! I implore
Thy aid to guide me safely o'er
The slippery paths of youth:
O deign to lend a steady ray
To point the sure, the certain way
To piety and truth!

1813

Let thy unerring influence shed
Its soft blessings on Sarahs head,
While piety and peace
Thy genuine offspring round her wait
And guard her through this transient state,
To joys that never cease.

444

There is a land of pleasure
Where streames of joy forever roll

1814

Tis there i have my treasure
And there i hope to rest my soul.

445

Give thanks aloud to God
To God the heavenly King

1814

And let the spacious earth
His works and glories sing.

446

Amidst my learning and my care
Nothing can equal God most dear.
Nor ought with him my heart to share
Quick as my fingers move this thread
Under just rules do act with speed

1814

In wisdom paths still may I tread
Giving to virtue constant heed
Love to be good and therefore wise
Youth finds in these the greatest prize

447

Before 1815

I can be safe and free from care
On any shore if Thou be there.

448

By Babels Streams we sat and we

When Zion we thought on | pt

1815

In the midst thereof we hung our

The willow tree upon. | harps

137th Psalm.

449

Grace is a plant Where eer it grows
Of Pure and Heavenly root

1815

But Fairest in the Youngest Shows
And Yields the Sweetest Fruit.

450

In this early life, to me, Oh Lord
Thy pard'ning mercy show

Before 1816

And while my mind is early taught
May I in knowledge grow.

451

Look gently down Almighty Grace
Prison me round in thy embrace

1816

Pity the heart that would be thine
And let thy power my love confine.

PLATE XCVII

Ann E. Kelly's Sampler. Halifax. 1825
Mrs. Leah Meguier's School, Harrisburg, Pa.
Owned by Mrs. Henry E. Coe

PLATE XCVIII

Sarah Catherine Moffatt Odiorne's Sampler. 1802
Miss Ward's School, Portsmouth, N. H.
Owned by Mrs. John Fremont Hill

452

1816

Then let me Love my Bible more
And take A fresh Delight

By day To read These wonders o'er
And meditate By night.

Rev. Isaac Watts. Divine Songs for Children. VII. Verse 7.

453

1817
STUDIOUS

Father of light and life! thou God supreme
O teach me what is good! teach me thyself.
Save me from folly, vanity, and vice,
From every low pursuit, and feed my soul
With knowledge conscious peace and virtue pure
Sacred substantial never fading bliss.

454

1818

Oh how unlike the Complex works of Man
Heavens easy artless unincumbered plan
Its meretricious graces to beguile
No clust'ring ornaments to clog the pile

From ostentation as from weakness free
It stands like the Cerulean arch we see
Majestic in its own Simplicity

455

1818

Where'er I turn my ravish'd eyes
new scenes of beauty round me rise
and my heart exulting glows

and while I view the wondrous whole
to the creative power o'er flows
my soul with gratitude

456

1818

To distant lands thy Gospel send
And thus thy empire wide extend

To Gentile, Turk, and stubborn Jew
Thy Almighty grace and salvation show.

457

[1819]

Know God and bring thy heart to know
The joys which from religion flow.

458

Cir. 1819
SONG XXV.

My God who makes the sun to know
his proper hour to rise
and to give light to all below—
Doth send him round the skies—
When from the chamber of the east
his morning race begins
He never tires nor stops to rest,

But round the world he shines;
so like the Sun would I fulfill
the business of the day
Begin my work [betimes, and still]
[March on my heavenly way]
Young morning of my days
has all been spent in vain

SONG XXVI.

And now another day is gone,
I'll sing my Makers praise;
My comforts every hour make known.
His Providence and grace,
but how my childhood runs to waste,
my sins how great their sum—

Lord give me pardon for the past
and strength for days to come.
I lay my body down to sleep
Let angels guard my head,
and thro the hours of darkness keep
their watch around my bed.

Rev. Isaac Watts. Divine Songs for Children.

459

My God my all sufficient good
My portion and my choice
In thee are all my hopes renewed
And all my powers rejoice

1819

In God place all thy confidence
And make his word thy guide
He will protect thy innocence
And for thy wants provide

460

1820

Behold the path that I have trod
My path till I go home to God

461

O may their natal morn
Be registered in heaven

1818

And they this life adorn
With every blessing given

462

1820

God of my soul without thy strengthening grace
How weak how blind is human race

463

Author of good, to thee I turn
Thy ever wakeful eye

1821

Alone can all my wants discern
Thy hand alone supply.

Merrick.

464

1821

I read his awful name, emblazoned high
With golden letters on th' illumined sky:
Nor less, the mystic characters I see
Wrought in each flower; inscrib'd on ev'ry tree;
In every leaf that trembles on the breeze,
I hear the voice of God among the trees.

465

Religion, fair descendant from above
Eternal source of happiness and love
Low at thy throne I fall and do implore
In my soft bosom all thy grace store

1821

Grant me a heart obedient to thy laws
Incline to reverence and maintain thy cause
O grant my steps to your celestial skies
Nor leave me here till I to them shall rise

466

1822

Be mine a calm a thankful heart
From every murmur free
The blessings of Thy grace impart
And make me live to Thee

If thou my father Still art nigh
Cheerful I live and peaceful die
Secure when mortal comforts flee
To find ten thousand worlds in Thee

Anne Steele. 1760. 2nd and — verses.

467

1822

As heat increases with the rolling hours
Draws up the vapours and expands the flowers
So with my childhood may my follies cease
So may my wisdom with my years increase
So may religion early warm my soul
Encourage, actuate and cheer the whole.

468

1823

A charge to keep I have
A God to glorify
A never dying soul to save
And fit it for the sky
To serve the present age
My calling to fulfil
O may it all my powers engage
To do my masters will.

Arm me with jealous care
As in thy sight to live
And O thy servant Lord prepare
A strict account to give
Help me to watch and pray
And on thyself rely
Assur'd if I my trust betray
I shall for ever die.

Rev. Charles Wesley. 1762.

469

1823

Author of being sourse of light
With unfading beauty bright
Fullness goodness rolling round
Thy own fair orb without a bound

Whether thy suppliants call
Truth or good or all or all
God or father thee we hail
Essense that can never fail

Grecian or Barbarick name
Thy steadfast being still the same
Thee when morning greets skies
With rosy cheeks and humid eyes

Then when sweet declining day
Sinks in purple waves away
Thee my lips shall still proclaim
And teach the world to bless thy name.

470

1823

In all my vast concerns with thee
In vain my soul would try

To shun thy presence Lord or flee
The notice of thine eye.

471

1824

I ask not gold or length of days,
I ask for wisdoms brighter rays.

O clasp me in thy arms when yours
Accept hosannas from my tongue.

472

1824

Ah lend me the wings of a dove,
To fly from these regions of woe,

My hopes and my joys are above
And thither my spirit would go.

473

When I can read my title clear
To mansions in the sky

1824

I bid farewell to every fear
And wipe my weeping eyes.

Rev. Isaac Watts. Book II, Hymn LXV.

474

Still the orphan & the stranger
Still the widow owns thy care

1824

Screened by the in every danger
Heard by the in every prayer

475

Now in thy youth beseech of Him
Who giveth upbraiding not
That His light in thy heart become not dim

1824

And His love be unforgot
And thy God in the darkest of days will be
Goodness and beauty and strength to thee.

476

One day amidst the place
where my dear god hath been
is sweeter than ten thousand days
of pleasurable sin

1825

My willing sould would stay
in such a frame as this
i sit and sing myself away
to everlasting bliss.

477   **Cir. 1825**

HEAVEN BRIGHTER THAN EARTH.

Those skies no night that wear
  Nor cloud nor tempest know
Those flowers no blight that bear
  Those streams that stainless flow
Are they not brighter far
  Than all that lures us here
Where storms may fright each timid star
  From midnights lonely sphere.

Here Hope of Sorrow drinks
  Here fades with care
And Virtue from Temptation shrinks
  And Folly finds Despair
But mid that world above
  No baneful step may stray
The white winged seraphs glance of love
  Would melt each ill away.

Friendship is there the guest
  Of chilling doubt no more
And Love with thornless breast
  Whose Pangs and fears are o'er
There is no farewell sigh
  Throughout that blessed clime
No murmuring voice nor severed tie
  No change of weary time

Why plant the Cypress near
  The Pillow of the Just
Why dew with murmuring Tear
  Thier calm and holy dus[t]
Rear there the roses Pride
  Bid the green myrtle bloom
Pic[k] emblems of their joys who bide
  Beyond the insateate tomb.

Mid that celestial Place
  Our searing thoughts would glow
E'en while we run this Pilgrim race
  Of Weariness and Woe.
For who would shrink from death
  With sharp and icy hand
Or heed the paths of ——— while breath
  To win the glorious land.

478

1825

Heaven notes the sigh afflicted goodness heaves,
Hears the low plaint by mortal ear unheard,
And from the cheek of patient sorrow wipes
The tear by mortal eye unseen or scorned.

479

1825

When all thy mercies o'er me roll,
Thy favors, Lord! surprise my soul.

480

1826

Now in the heat of youthful blood,
Remember your Creator, God;
Behold the days come hastening on,
When you shall say, My joys are gone.

When we give up our youth to God
'Tis pleasing in his eyes,
A flower thats offer'd in the bud
Is no mean sacrifice.

Rev. Isaac Watts. Book I, Hymn XCI.

481

1827

Lift up thy Thoughts and let thine heart
a grateful sence To God impart

From the earliest mornings dawn
To the latest setting sun

482

1827

Prepare me Gracious God!
To stand before thy face.

Thy spirit must the work perform
For it is all of grace

483

1828

Tis useless that the fingers learn to draw
And soaring reason scans all natures law

If innate virtue's not a welcome guest
And pure religion glows not in the breast.

484

1828

[SUBLIME THOUGHT. *Said to be written by nearly an idiot.*]

Could we with Ink the Ocean fill
Were the whole earth of parchme[n]t made
Were every single stick a Quill
And every man a scribe by trade
To write the Love of GOD above
Would drain the Ocean dry

Nor could this Scroll contain the whole
Tho stretcht from sky to sky
Were the whole realm of nature mine
That were a present far too small
Love so amazing so divine
Demands my soul my life my all

From The Clergyman's Almanack for 1812.

485

1828

Fountain of being! Teach us to devote
To Thee each purpose, action, word and thought!
Thy grace our hope, thy love our only boast.
Be all distinctions in the Christian lost!
Be this in every state our wish alone.
Almighty, wise and good. Thy will be done!

486

Tis religion that can give
Sweetest comfort while we live

1828

Tis religion must supply
Solid comfort when we die.

487

Guide of my youth to thee I cry
Great God to me be ever nigh

1829

Lighten mine eyes convert my heart
Nor let me from thy ways depart

487a

Save me alike from foolish pride
Or impious discontent

1829

At aught thy wisdom has denied
Or aught thy goodness lent.

RELIGIOUS VERSES—NEW TESTAMENT

488

The loss of a father is much
The loss of a Mother is more

1700

The loss of Christ is such a loss
As no other can restore

489

1. Love God, love not gold,
   Love God both young and old;

1700

2. Arise, awake, your lamps to take
   And do no longer slumber;

3. You must them trim to wait on him,
   Unto his wedding chamber.

490

———— ———— is my name
———————— is my nation

1708

———— is my dwelling place
And Christ is my salvation

491   **1715**

Behold and have regard
ye servants of the Lord
which in his house of night do watch.
Praise him with one accord.
Lift up your hands on high unto his holy place.
Give the Lord his praises due, his benefits embrace.
In every land
there none shall stand
and happy be indeed
but only those whom God hath chosen That on Christ Jesus Feed.

492   **1728**

Run thou Christs race
be swift like to the sun

have not they work to do
when ten is done   etc.

PLATE XCIX

NANCY HALL'S SAMPLER. 1788
Miss Polly Balch's School, Providence, R. I.
Owned by Mrs. W. C. Greene

PLATE C

NANCY WINSOR'S SAMPLER.   1786
Miss Polly Balch's School, Providence, R. I.
Owned by Mrs. John H. Mason
Plate presented by the Rhode Island Society of the Colonial Dames

493

Twelve tribes their were in days of old
Twelve Articles of faith we hold

494

Hosanna to Jesus our King
Who comes in the name of the Lord

495

The Waikful Shepherds Hear Their Flocks
Where Watchful of The Morn

496

O may I always ready stand
With my lamp within my hand

497

Christ when our nature He assumed
redeemed the world from sin,

498

To God the Father, God the Son,
and God the Spirit, Three in One,

499

500

501

502

Lord I address Thy heavenly throne
Call me a child of Thine

1730

Twelve gates in new jerusalem their be
unto which city christ bring the and me

1750

By children he's welcom'd on Earth
By angels in Heaven ador'd

1752

But Better News from heaven Was Brought
Your Saviour Christ Is Born—

1757

May I in sight of heaven rejoice
Whence I hear the bridegrooms voice

Thomas Ken. "Midnight Hymn," verse 6.

1760

& by his burial in the grave,
to life we rise again.

1763

Be honor, praise and Glory given
By all on Earth and all in Heaven

Rev. Isaac Watts. Doxology in "Divine Songs for Children."

1764

Cheer up my Soul redeem thy life with mine
My soul shall smart my heart shall bleed for thine
Sinner, Oh Groundless deeds, O Love beyond decree
the offender dies to set the offender Free

1770

Zaccheus short of stature fain would see
his Saviour pass and climb into a Tree,
if we by Faith would see this glorious King,
Our thoughts must mount on contemplations Wing.

1770

Dear Saviour oh! What ails this heart, sure tis of stone
it cannot 'nor yet resent the death of thee
whose death alone could ransom me.

1778

Send down the spirit of Thy Son
To form my heart divine.

503   **1778**

In thy fair book of life divine   There let it fill some humble Place
My God inscribe my name   Beneath the slaughtered Lamb

Rev. Isaac Watts. Lyric Poems Sacred to Devotion. Verse XII.

504   **1779**

Father of all in Heaven and earth supreme
Praisd blessed & hallowed be Thy awful name
Thy Kingdom haste Thy soverign will be done
Alike on earth as near Thy radient throne
Give daily bread & may our sins receive
Of Thee forgiveness even as we forgive
From all temptation guard our steps we pray
And turn from vice to virtues better way
To Thy blest Kingdom every heart incline
For goodness power & glory all are Thine.

505   **Cir. 1780**

While Shepherds watch'd their flocks by night   "Fear not," said he, for mighty dread
All seated on the ground   Had seized their troubled mind
The angel of the Lord came down   "Glad tidings of great joy I bring,
And glory shone around   To you and all mankind" etc.

Nahum Tate. 1703.

506   **1781**

Who walk below In Light and Love
Are sure to live With Christ above.

507   **1781**

May works of nature and of art   And Jesus Christ his grace impart
Combine to raise our thoughts to God   To guide us to his blest abode.

508   **1783**

When our Nature he assumd   and by his Burial in the grave
Redeemd the world from sin   to Life We rise again.

509   **1784**

Our Father who in Heaven art,   As we forgive our enemys,
All hallowed be thy name.   Thy pardon Lord we crave,
Thy Kingdom come, thy will be done,   Into temptation, lead us not,
Throughout this earthly frame.   But thus from Evil save.

As chearfully as by those,   For Kingdom, power and glory
Who dwells with thee on high,   All belong, O, Lord to thee,
Lord, let thy bounty day by day   Thine from Eternity they were
Our daily food supply.   And thine shall ever be.

Tate & Brady's Hymnal. Hymn XXXI.

510

Wash Lord and purify my heart
and make it clean in every part

1786

And when its clean, Lord keep it to,
for that is more than I can do.

511

1. Teach me to feel another's woe
To hide the fault I see
That mercy I to others shew
That mercy shew to me.

1787

2. While some in Folly's Pleasures roll,
And seek the joys that hurt the soul,
Be mine that silent calm repast
A Peaceful conscience to the last.

Alexander Pope. "The Universal Prayer."

512

1788

In his blest life
I see the path and in his death the price
And in his great ascent the proof supreme
Heare it, O ye Nation, hear it O ye dead
He rose, he rose, he burst the bars of death

513

The loss of gold is great
The loss of time is more

1792

The loss of Jesus is so great
That no more can restore.

514

Nothing beneath the sun can give
That bliss to which our Souls aspire

1792

If God we love, if Christ we live
Our joys shall equal our desire.

515

1. Jesus permit thy gracious name to stand
As the first efforts of an infants hand

1793

2. And while her fingers o'er this canvass move
Engage her tender heart to seek thy love.
With thy dear children let her share a part
And write thy name thyself upon her heart.[1]

516

Hosanna to King David's son
Who reigns on a superior throne
We bless the prince of heavenly birth
Who brings Salvation down to earth.

1793

Let every nation, every age
In this delightful work engage
Old men & babes in Zion sing
The growing glories of her King.

Isaac Watts. Hymnal. Book III. XLII.

517

1794

By Truth conducted, and by Scripture taught
To Christ the Door, the humble Youth is brought,
Sees and admires him, as the Rose: the Vine;
The Tree; the Shepherd; and the Ark divine.

[1] English Notes and Queries says that this verse was written by the Rev. John Newton for his niece, Miss Elizabeth Catlett. He was at the time Rector of St. Mary's Woolnooth, London.

518

1794

Within the Rock the Rock Himself Was Laid
Which Both the tomb and the tomb Maker Made
He Was a Man No Such Man Beside
Lived Without Sin And yet for sin He dyed

519

1794

Virgins and youth engage
To sound his praise divine

While Infancy and age
Their feeble voices join

520

1795

2. Jesus who reigns above the sky
And keeps the world in awe
Was once a child as young as I
And kept his father's law.

6. Then why should I so long delay
What others learnt so soon
I would not pass another day
Without this work begun

Isaac Watts. Divine Songs for Children. XXV. Verses 2 and 6.

521

1795

"THE 76 HYMN

Lo He Comes With Clouds Descending
Once For Favor'd Sinners Slain
Thousand Thousand Saints Attending
Hallelujah Hallelujah Amen

Ev'ry Eye Shall Now Behold Him
Rob'd In Dreadful Majesty
They Who Set At Nought And Sold Him
Pierc'd And Nail'd Him To The Tree
Deeply Wailing Shall the true Messiah be

Ev'ry Island sea And Mountain
Heav'n And Earth Shall flee Away
All who Hale Him must Confounded
Hear the Trump Proclaim the Day
Come To Judgment Come Away

Now Redemption Long Expected
See in Solemn pomp Appear
All His Saints By Man Rejected
Now Shall Meet Him in The Air
Hallelujay See The Day of God Appear

Answer Thine Own Bride And Spirit
Hasten Lord The Gen'ral Doom
The Low Heav'n And Earth Inherit
Take Thy Pining Exile Home
All creation Travails groans and Bids The
    Come

Yea Amen Let All Adore Thee
Rigt On Thine Eternal Throne
Saviour Take The Pow'r And Glory
Claim The Kingdom For Thine Own
O Come quickly Hallelujah
Come Lord Come"

Rev. J. Cennick, 1752; Rev. Charles Wesley, 1758.

522

1796

1. Give to your God immortal praise.
Mercy & Truth is all his ways
Wonders of Grace to God belong.
Repeat his mercies in your song.

2. Give the Lord of Lords renown
The King of Kings with glory crown.
His mercies ever shall endure
Where Lords & Kings are known no more.

Isaac Watts. Psalm 136.

3. Now begin the heavenly theme
   Sing aloud in Jesus name
   Ye who Jesus kindness prove
   Triumph in redeeming love.

4. Ye who see the earthly grace
   Beaming in the Savior's face
   On to Canaan on ye move
   Praise & bless redeeming love.

Verses 3 and 4. Author unknown.

523   **1797**

Keep far from a careless heart
From which my Saviour would depart

O, Bless and prosper all my ways,
That they may issue in thy praise

524   **1797**

Swift fly the years & rise the expected morn
O spring to light, auspicious Babe be born
See nature hastes her earliest wreathe to bring
With all the incense of the breathing spring
See lofty Lebanon his herd advance,
See nodding forests on the mountain dance
See spicy clouds from lowly sharon rise
And carmels flowery top perfumes the skies.
Hark a glad voice the lonely desert cheers,
Prepare the way a God a God appears
A God a God the vocal hills reply
The rocks proclaim the approaching Deity,
Lo earth receives him from the bending skies
Sink down ye mountains, & ye vallies rise
With heads declined ye cedars homage pay
Be smooth ye rocks ye rapid floods give way
The Saviour comes by ancient bards foretold,
Hear him ye deaf & all ye blind behold
He from thick films shall purge the visual ray
And on the sightless eye-ball pour the day
Tis he the obstructed paths of sound shall hear
And bid new musick charm the unfolding ears,
The dumb shall sing the lame his crutch forget
And leap exulting like the bounding roe.

525   **1798**

Ye Hearts with youthful Vigor warm
In smiling Crowds draw near
And turn from every mortal charm
A Savior's Voice to hear.

He Lord of all the Worlds on high
Stoops to converse with you
And lays his radiant Glories by
Your Friendship to Pursue.

The Soul that longs to see my Face
Is sure my Love to gain
And those that early seek my Grace
Shall never seek in vain.

What Object Lord my Soul should move
If once compar'd with thee
What Beauty should command my Love
Like what in Christ I see.

Away ye False delusive Toys
Vain Tempters of the Mind
Tis here I fix my lasting Choice
For here true Bliss I find.

Hymn 660. John Dobell's Collection. Morristown. 1810.

526   **1798**

1. Beset with snares on ev'ry hand
   In life' uncertain path I stand
   Father Divine! diffuse thy light,
   To guide my doubtful footsteps ri[gh]t

2. Engage this roving treacherous Heart
   To fix on Mary's better Part
   To scorn the Trifles of a Day
   For Joys that none can take away.

Philip Doddridge.

527   **1799**

Upon his head shall honours rest
And every age pronounce Him blessed.

528   **1799**

In vain doth earthly life afford
A momentary shade
It rises like the prophet's gourd,
And withers o'er my head

But of my Saviour's love possest,
No more for earth I pine
Secure of everlasting rest
Beneath the heavenly vine

529   **Cir. 1799**

If you know Christ you need no little more
If not all's lost that you have learnt before.

530   **1800**

LoVing . Jesus . Gentle . Lamb
In . thy . Gracious . hands . I . am
Make . Me . Saviour . What . Thou . Art
Live . Thyself . Within . My . Heart

I . Shall . Then . Shew . Forth . Thy . Praise
Serve . Thee . All . My . Happy . Days
Then . The . World . Shall . Always . See
Christ . The . Holy . Child . In . Me.

Rev. Charles Wesley. "For A Child." Verses 3 and 4.

531   **1800**

Come Lord and never from me go
This world's a darksome Place
I find no Pleasure here below
When thou dost veil thy Face

There's no such thing as Pleasure here
My Jesus is my all
As thou dost shine or disappear
My Pleasures rise and fall

Come spread thy Saviour on my Frame
No sweetness is as sweet
Till I get up to sing thy name
Where all thy Singers meet.

532   **1801**

Teach me to feel anothers smart,
And teach my tears to flow

Teach me to sooth the sorrowing heart
And give relief to woe.

533   **1801**

Almighty Power whose tender care
Did infancy protect,

Let riper years thy favour share
And every step direct.

534

1802

I can be safe and free from care
On any shore if thou be there

535

Jesus invites young children near
Oh, may we straight Obey

1803

Give us, O Lord, the attentive ear
And teach our hearts to pray.

536

Be Christ my pattern and my guide
His image may I bear

1804

O may I tread his sacred steps
And his bright glories share

537

The Saviour who in glory reigns
Who made the earth & sea
Whose arm unnumbered worlds sustains
Was once a child like me.

1805

He stooped so low that I might rise,
To dwell with him above
Lord send thy blessing from the skies
To teach a child thy love.

538

As this fair sampler shall continue still
The guide and model of my future skill

1805

May Christ the great exemplar of mankind
Direct my ways and regulate my mind.

539

AN ACROSTICK

Love O Love thine origin are divine
Of all human emotions the most sublime
Verily thou first came down from above
Ever thy name will be known for Gods love

540

Yonder amazing sight I see
The incarnate Son of God

1806

Expireing on the accursed tree
And weltering in his blood

Mrs. Barbauld. Hymn on the "Death of Christ."

541

Bear Thou In Mind
The Saviour Kind
Who Did Upon A Tree

1808

His Body Rent
His Blood Was Spent
And All For Love Of The.

542

Precept may teach, example move
And living pattern, lead to love;
N'or love alone; but imitate
The truly Good and therefore great;
And dost thou pant, dear girl, to find
To best examplar for the mind?
Which n'eer shall lead thy yough astray;
To follow vice in pleasured way,

1808

N'or tempt thy feet to heedless rove
Where Serpent man in ambush sleeps
N'or heed the ruined girl that weeps.
Is this thy wish, my lovely friend,
On Mary's steps do thou attend,
She leads to Jesus sacred feet
And there is Virtues peaceful seat.

543

No man's tongue can tell
What grief to him befell

1809

When he was doomed to die
On Mount Calvary

544

Silence and thought the mind improve
They kindle joy in pious hearts

1810

On them descends the mystic dove
And every Christian grace imparts

545

1810

ON CHRISTMAS DAY

What words, what voices can we bring,
Which way our accents raise,
To welcome our mysterious King,
And sing a Saviour's praise.

O 'tis too little all we Can,
For this unbounded Love,
All that was ever wrote by Man,
Or sung in Hymns above.

546

1810

1. Tho youth may fade with all its bloom
   And nervous strength decline
   Yet age shall yield a rich perfume
   If innocence be thine

2. He carve my passion on the bark
   And every wounded tree
   Shall droop and bear some mystic mark
   That Jesus died for me.

547

The Lord is come the heavens proclaim
His birth the nations learn his name
An unknown star directs the road
Of eastern sages to their God.

1811

All ye bright armies of the skies
Go worship where the saviour lies
Angel and Kings before him bow
Those gods on high and gods below.

Let idols totter to the ground
And their own worshippers Confound
But Judah shout but Zion sing
And earth confess her sovereign king.

Isaac Watts. Hymnal. Book II. CVII.

548

The soul who seeks me shall obtain
Immortal wealth and heavenly gain

1812

Immortal life is his reward
Life and the favor of the Lord.

549　　　**Before 1813**

All ye faithful servants are of our almighty King,
both high and low and small and great, His praise devoutly sing.
Let us rejoice and render thanks to his most Holy name.
Rejoice rejoice for now is come the marriage of the Lamb.
His bride herself has ready made How pure and white her dress
Which is her saints Integrity and spotless holiness.
O therefore blest is every one who to the marriage feast
and Holy Supper of the Lamb is called a welcome guest.

PLATE CI

LYDIA CHURCH'S SAMPLER. New Haven, Conn. 1791
Mrs. Mansfield's School
Owned by the Hartford Historical Society

PLATE CII

HETTY LEES' SAMPLER. 1799
Owned by Mrs. Henry E. Coe

550 **1813**

SHEPHERDS rejoice lift up your eyes,   Go shepherds where the infant lies,
And send your fears away,   And see his humble throne,
News from the region of the skies,   With gladness sparkling in your eyes,
The saviour's born to day.   Go and behold the son.

Tate & Brady's Hymnal. Hymn XXXIII. Verses 1 and 4.

551 **1813**

May grace and truth preserve my youth   And I be led by Christ my head
From sin and danger free.   To fountains rich and free.

552 **Cir. 1813**

Attend dear Girl the words of truth   Inclind to feel a Savior's love
Let no false way deform thy Youth   Rest not thy hope beneath the skies
Make every thought obedient move   A heart renewed to Heaven will rise.

553 **1814**

Let the sweet work of prayer & praise,   Thus I am prepared for longer days,
Employ my youngest breath,   Or fit for early death.

Isaac Watts. Divine Songs for Children. XII. Verse 6.

554 **Cir. 1814**

Tis true tis long ere I began   But now I run as fast as I can
To seek to live forever   Tis better late than never

555 **Cir. 1814**

Jesus all hail, Thou risen Savior hail
At thy command the seventh trump shall sound
The sun retires, the moon, the stars turn pale
And heaven and earth and sea no more be found etc.

556 **1814**

Break Forth into singing ye trees of the Wood
for Jesus is bringing Lost sinners to God.

556a **1815**

O, may I stand before the lamb   And hear the judge pronounce my name
When earth and sea are fled   With blessings on my head

557 **1815**

O Lord regard me from above   And lead me on by faith and love
And grant me my request   To lean upon thy breast

558

May I now in the morning of my day
Resolve to choose the narrow way
The way that leads to life and peace
Where all trouble and sorrow cease.

559

Some listen to the scripture's voice
Its sacred truths obey

560

Behold the Savior at thy door
He gently knocks, has knocked before
Has waited long, is waiting still

1816

Engage this frail and wavering heart
Wisely to choose the better part
To scorn the trifles of a day
For those that never fade away

1819

With wisdom then ye shall rejoice
In Christ the only way.

1820

You treat no other friend so ill
Admit him or the hour's at hand
When at his door denied you'll stand.

Hymn 326. John Dobell's Collection. Morristown. 1810.

561

In Sharon's lovely rose
Immortal beauties shine

562

1822

Its sweet refreshing fragrance shows
Its origin divine

1823

Observe the rising lily's snowy grace;
Observe the various vegetable race
They neither toil nor spin but careless grow,
Yet see how warm they blush how bright they glow!
Will he not care for you ye faithless say?
Is he unwise? or are ye less than they

563

Now in thy youth attend to truth
let Jesus be thy guide,

564

1824

Be always mindful of the lord
Prepare to be his bride.

1825

O Render thanks to God above,
The fountain of eternal love.

565

In other men we faults can spy
And blame the mote that dims the eye
Each little spark and blemish find

566

Welcome sweet day of rest
that saw the *lord* arise
Welcome to this reviving breast
and these rejoicing eyes

1825

To our own stronger errors blind
Ere we remark anothers sin
Let our own conscience look within

1825

The king himself comes near
and feasts his saints to day
here we may sit and see him here
and love and Praise and Pray

Isaac Watts. Hymns and Spiritual Songs. XIV. Verses 1 and 2.

567

1826

EVENING MEDITATION ON THE CRUCIFIXION

My Lord my Saviour died, For guilty sinners sake:
The tokens of his love Oft keep mine eyes awake.
I cannot chuse but mourn, That He should suffer so;
And yet it is the source Whence all my comforts flow.
I cannot chuse but mourn, Whose sin made him To bleed;
And yet such sacrifice My soul from death hath freed.
Twas not the treacherous Jews That did my Lord betray;
It was heinous sins, More treacherous far than they.
Twas not the soldier's spear That pierc'd my Saviour's side,
Twas my Ingratitude. My unbelief, my pride.
These were the bloody thorns That did his temples wound.
And caus'd those sacred drops, That did bedew the ground.
And when his Father's wrath Drew forth that bitter cry.
He yielded up his life For rebels such as I.
And can I chuse but mourn, When skies and rocks did rend.
And Nature veil'd her face, At sight of such an end.
But haste My soul to view. Thy happiness restor'd,
And death and hell subdu'd. By the triumphant Lord.
Put off thy mourning weed, Thy Jesus reigns on high.
Receiving gifts for men, For rebels such as I.

568

And must I Part with all I Have
My dearest Lord for Thee.
It is But right since Thou hast done
Much more than this for me.

569

Jesus lover of my soul
Let me to thy bosom fly

570

Hopes vivid beams the fancy cheers
As down the slopes of ills we stray

571

Mary loved her Master
And washed his holy feet

572

Happy the soul where innocence does reign
Where pure religion does its right maintain

573

To God who guards us all the night
And gives us length of days

1826

Ill Let It go, One Look from Thee
Will more than make Amends
For all the Losses I Sustain
Of Credit, Riches, Friends.

1827

While the billows near me roar
While the tempest still is nigh.

Rev. Charles Wesley.

1827

Smiles through the wilderness of tears
The sunshine of a brighter day

1828

Here I am coming after
His blessing may I greet

1828

Where truth and piety its actions sway
And all its pleasure is its God t'obey.

1830

To God who sheds the morning light
Be honour, love and praise.

574   **1830**
                    RELIGION

Beyond the narrow vale of time,   To scenes eternal scenes sublime,
Where bright celestial ages roll,   She points the way and leads the soul.

575

Firm as a rock elevated mind   Soft smiling hope thou anchor of the mind
Stand[s] Faith the comforter of human kind.   And only comforter the wretched find
Against each earthly evil we endure   All fly to thee when troubles wring the heart
She points at one an everlasting cure   To soothe by future prospect present smart

576

Let all my thoughts & actions rise   O Lord will not despise
From innocence & truth & thou   The Prayrs of early youth.

577

                Jesus thy gracious name I will inscribe
                Be Thou my Counsellor, my Friend and guide
                Protect me from the dangerous snares of youth
                And write upon my heart thy word of truth.

578

To Thee my God will I devote   Oh keep me from the snares of youth
The morning of my days   And I will sing Thy praise.

579

Lord how delightful tis to see   At once they sing at once they Pray
A whole assembly worship thee   They hear of heaven & love the way
                Isaac Watts. Divine Songs for Children. XXVIII.

580

Sweet are thy works my God my King   To show thy works by Morning Light
To praise thy name give thanks and sing And talk of all thy truths at night
                Isaac Watts. Psalm XCII. (Not quoted quite correctly.)

IN PRAISE OF THE VIRTUES

581   **1724**

                Be not wise
                in thy own eyes.
                Be just and wise
                and virtue prize

582

1724

Beauty and virtue when they do meet
with a good education make a lady complete

583

1730

Vertuous Man Needs No Great Dangers Fear
No troubled Conscience Nor Black Despair
Can th[e]re Find Place Or Room to harbour there

Vertue in Man guides him the safest way
as the bright son that rules the gracious day
Doth on his head as beauteous rays display

584

1737

VIRTUE AN[D] LOVE
IS FROM A[BOVE]

585

1742

The winter tree resembles me
Whose sap lies in the root,

The spring draws nigh; as it, so I
Shall bud, I hope, and shoot.

586

1742

1. O that Mine Eye Might Closed Be
To What Becomes Me Not To See
That Deafness might Possess Mine Ear
To What concerns Me Not To Hear

2. That Truth My Tongue Might Alway Tie
From Ever Speaking Foolishly
That No Vain Thought Might Ever Rest
Or Be Conceived In My Breast

3. that by each word each deed each thought
glory to my god be brought
but what are wishes lord on the!

587

1742

Where The Contented Mind Is Known
There Is As well Increas
Of Solitude Where Thy Son Lies Down
In Everlasting Peace

True Peace And Joy Not To Be Found
In Vain Thirristial Things
True Holy Praises Doth B---- V----
The King of Kings

588

1748

Les enfants son comme des jeune plante
Avec grand soint il faut les cultivez

Cest un devoir qui nous doit captivez
pour les remplire de vertus excellente

589

1755

Force may indeed the heart invade
but Kindness only can perswade

Shun the ———
With the ———
                    (rest undecipherable)

590

1755

Modest Attire And Meekness Signify
a Mind Composed of Native Purity

Yea Modesty Doth Many Ways Express
To All Beholders Innate Comeliness.

591

1756

Lay All the Steps of Pride Aside
Let Truth And Wisdom Be Your Guide

Let All Thy Homage be To Wisdom Paid
Seek Her Protection and In Love Her Aid

592

1760

Consider well some by past days
On former Times reflect

And see if thou in all thy ways
Are truly Circumspect.

593

[1760–5]

Make much of precious Time While in your power.
Be careful well to husband every Hour
or Time will come when you shall sore lament
The unhappy minutes that you have mispent.

594

1761

"ON RELIGION"

1. If I [am right, O teach my heart]
    Still in the right to stay
If I am wrong thy grace impart
    To find that better way

2. Save me alike from foolish pride
    Or impious discontent
At aught thy wisdom has deny'd
    Or aught thy goodness lent

3. This day be bread and peace my lot
    All else beneath the Sun
Thou know'st if best bestowed or not
    And let thy will be done

595

1762

In books or work and healthful play,
Let my first years be past,

That I may give for every day,
    A good account at last.

Isaac Watts. Divine Songs for Children. XX. Verse 4.

596

1763

To vindicate my Works and Tell
I'll make no more pretence

Not one of all my thousend Faiths
Can bear a just Defence

597

1763

Let not thy mind be lifted high,
but grace thy face with modisty.

598

1766

Beauty And Pride We Often Find
Betrays The Weakness Of The Mind

He Handsom Is And Merit Praise
That Handsom Dos The Proverb Says

PLATE CIII

CAROLINE VAUGHAN'S SAMPLER. 1818
Mary Walden's School
Owned by Mrs. Miles White, Jr.

PLATE CIV

SALLY JOHNSON'S SAMPLER. Newburyport, Mass. 1799
Owned by Mrs. Francis A. Goodhue
Plate presented by Mrs. Arthur Crittenden Smith

599

1770

Trust not to those who love
What God doth disapprove

600

177–

Why Virtue dost thou blame desire,
Which Nature hath imprest

Why Nature dost thou soonest fire,
The mild and Gen'rous breast

601

1771

1. How blest the maid who circling years improve
   Her God the object of her warmest love

2. Whose useful hours successive as they glide
   The book the Needle and the Pen divide

3. Who sees her parents heart exult with joy
   And the fond tear stands sparkling in their eye.

4. Blest with the hope when the lifes cares dismiss
   Of a Kind welcome to the realms of bliss

602

1772

Age does alas disclose the ———— to wise
A thousand troubles hid from youthful eyes

603

1773

Time has Wings and swiftly flies
Youth and Beauty fade away

Virtue is the only prize
Whose sacred joys will ne'er decay

604

1774

O Youth thy Duty Observe
So Ne'er shall thy Pleasures Decay

Twill Prove the Best Honour to Serve
The Glory Twil be to Obey.

605

1774

When Wild Ambition In The Heart We Find
Farewel Content And Quiet Of The Mind
For Glittring Clouds We Leave The Solid Shore
And Wonted Happiness Returns No More

606

1775

1. Let spotless innocence and truth
   All my actions guide
   And guard my unprotected youth
   From vanity and pride.

2. Let truth and virtue guide my feet
   They are angelic charms
   They lead my steps to Jesus seat
   And waft me in his arms

607

1775

Know then this truth enough for man to know,
Virtue alone is happiness below

Alexander Pope. "Essay on Man."

608   **1775**

Seek Virtue and of that Possest   Early your thought to Virtue bend
To Providence resign the rest   Forgive your foe and love your friend.

609   **17—**

(VIRTUE AND HONOR — 1806)

1. Virtue's the chiefest Beauty of the mind
   The noblest Ornament of Human-Kind

2. Virtues our Safe guard and our Leading Star
   That Stirs up reason though the senses err.

610   **1780**

Oh Heavenly Virtue Thine A Sacred Flame
And Still My Soul Pays Homage To Thy Name.

611   **1782**

While idle drones supinely dream of fame
The industrious actually do get the same.

612   **1783**

With early virtues plant your breast
The spacious[1] Arts of Vice detest

*   *   *   *   *   *   *

Learn to contemn all Praise betimes
For flattery's the nurse of crimes.

John Gay.   Dedication of his Fables to William, Duke of Cumberland.

613   **1783**

[THE BULL AND THE MASTIFF]

Seek you to train your Favorite Boy,   Let his Preceptor's Heart be tried
Each caution every care employ.   Weigh well his Manners Life and Scope
And ere you Venture to confide   On these depends thy future hope

John Gay.   Fable IX.

614   **1783**

INDUSTRY

Observe the Ant for she instructs the man
And Preaching Labour gathering all she can
Then brings it to increase her Heap at home
Against the Winter which she knows will come
And when that comes she creeps abroad no more
But lies at home and Feasts upon her store

615   **1784**

In this wide world the scene of woe,   From her clear stream, all comforts flow,
let virtue be thy choice   that can the soul rejoice.

[1] Specious.

616

1784

Stamp virtue's law upon thy youthful heart
Then meek eyed innocence shall never thee desert;
But thou shall imitate the rising sun,
Increase thy virtuous splendor till life's glass hath run.

617

1784

1. Let Virtue be
   a guide to the

2. And Innocence
   Be thy defence

618

1785

d
I blushe   This Morn To See The Sun   When I A Day His Work Is Done
           d   And Min ——————————
So Far Advance   His Stage

619

1785

Excess of wit may often time beguile,
Jests are not always pardoned by a smile—
Men may disguise their malice at the heart,
and seem at ease though pained with inward smart

620

1785

In Virtues ways
I spend my days

621

1785

1. Let me O God my labours so employ   2. I ask no more than my life's wants supply
    That I a competency may enjoy.   And leave their due to others when I die.

622

1785

Beauty Is a Flower That Fadeth Away
But Virtue Is a Jewel That Will Never Decay.

623

1785

Cast off all needless and Distrustful Care
Little is enough and much a Snare

624

1786

Honour and renown
will the ingenious crown

625

1786

The maid who led by wisdom's guiding hand,
Seek's virtue's temple and her law reveres:
She, She alone in honour's dome shall stand,
Crownd with Rewards and rais'd above her peers
Recording annals shall preserve her name,
And give her virtues to immortal fame.

626

1787

Cato doth say to Old and to Young
The first steps to Virtue is bridle the Tongue.

627

1787

1. Beauty soon grows familiar to the eye
Virtue alone has charms that never die

2. For blessings ever wait on virtuous deeds
And tho a late a sure reward succeeds

William Congreve. "The Mourning Bride."

628

1788

O Heaven kind, New form my mind,
And give me views divine.

That my small sum of days to come
With nobler deeds may shine.

629

1788

Whatever different path mankind pursue
Oh happiness 'tis thee we keep in view

'Tis thee in every action we intend
The noblest motive and superior end.

630

1790

Patience will wipe the streaming tear
And hope will paint the pallid cheek of fear

Content will always happiness supply
And Virtue calls a blessing from on high.

631

1790

1. Conscience distasteful truths may tell
But mark her sacred lessons well

2. Whoever lives with her at strife
Loses his better friend for life

632

1790

The Charms of Beauty soon will fade
To Time must yield their power
But Virtues Charms tho' Time invade
Live to the latest hour.
Thy choice Be Virtue then thy Guide her Charms
Listen attentive to her guardian Voice
Her bright example keep in constant view
And all her precepts steadily pursue.
Let Modesty (the females best defence)
Sweetness of temper, Truth, Benevolence
With all the virtues that true bliss impart
Possess thy mind & ever rule thy heart.

633   **1790**

1. Let Youth To Virtue's Shrine Repair,
And Men Their Tribute Bring
Old Age Shall Lose Its Load of Care,
Death Shall Lose Its Sting.

2. Borne Upwards On Seraphic Wing,
Their Happy Souls Shall Soar,
And There Enjoy Eternal Spring,
Nor Fear A Winter More

634   **1791**

Tho Plunged In Ills And Exercised In Care
Yet Never Let The Noble Mind Despair

For Blesings Always Wait On Virtous Deeds
And Tho a late a Sure Reward Succeeds.

634a   **1799**

d

Tho plung in ills and Exercised with [care]
Yet never let the noble mind desp[air]

When prest by dangers and beset ———
The gods their timely succor ———

635   **1792**

To crown both my Age and my Youth
Let me mark where Religion has trod

Since nothing but Virtue & truth
Can reach to the Throne of my God.

636   **1792**

Constraint in all things makes the pleasure less
Sweet is the love that comes with willingness.

637   **1792**

External Pomp and Visible Success
Sometimes contributes to Our Happiness
But that which makes us Genuine and Refined
I A Good Conscience and a Soul Resigned.

638   **1792**

ON HUMAN GRANDEUR

'Tis not in Grandeur peace of mind to give,
Nor are those happiest who in splendor live,
Content alone those blessings can bestow,
Which teach the mind with heart-felt Joy to glow.
Banish vain care and all her dismal train,
And give true pleasure unallay'd by pain.

639   **1793**

'Tis Virtue only makes our bliss below
And all our knowledge is ourselves to know.

Alexander Pope. Essay on Man. Epistle IV.

640   **1793**

The frowns of fortune ne'er regard
But trust Almighty Love

Virtue shall meet her sure reward
In realms of bliss above.

641 **1793**

Be careful your innocence ere to maintain
Be assured it is worthy your care

Since no other distress so deprives us of hope
Or so soon sinks the soul in despair.

642 **1794**

Let Virtue's lamp thy footsteps guide
and shun the dangerous heights of pride,

the peaceful vale the golden mean
the path of life persue serene.

643 **1794**

For age & want save while you may
No morning sun lasts a whole day.

644 **1794**

Our youthful passions soon will take their flight
What flows from virtue gives sincere delight

645 **1794**

1. In all my behaviour, I try to do well
   In all my improvement I'll try to excel

2. May I govern my passions with absolute sway
   And grow wiser and better as life wers away.

Dr. Walter Pope. "The Old Man's Wish."

646 **1794**

"Virtue outshines the stars, outlives the tomb
Climbs up to heaven and finds a peaceful home.
Mr. Pope."

647 **1795**

Count that day lost whose low descending sun
Views from thy hand no worthy action done.

Staniford's Art of Reading. 3rd Edition. Boston. 1803.

648 **1795**

Let virtue inosence and truth
Bring reward to sorry youth
That lerning will direct the mind
The path of happiness to find.

So where celistial virtue wind
Form an incomparable mind
Crowns, scepters, beauties choice and aire
Stand out as shining servents there.

649 **Cir. 1795**

When Virtue's paths do first appear
They lead the mind to be sin[cere]

650   **1796**

Thrice blest is he who through lif's thorny road
Can pass with pleasure and without a sigh
Who views unmov'd this frailty of abode
Who lives in peace, and never fears to die
Who craves but little, and but little wants
Whose aims are noble, and his vices few.

651   **1796**

The Daily Labours of the Bee   And from the most minute and mean
Awake my Soul to Industry   A virtuous mind can morals glean.

652   **1796**

1. Be you to others kind and true   2. Nor neither do nor say to men
   As you would have others be to you   What you are unwilling to take again

                                        Isaac Watts. Divine Songs for Children.

653   **1796**

Sweetly blooms the rose of may   So insideous smiles betray
Glitt'ring with the tears of morn   While they hide the treach'rous thorn

654   **1797**

Improve thy time
Now in thy prime

655   **1797**

1. I envy no other birth nor fame   2. I ask not, wish not to appear
      Their little train or dress   More beauteous, rich or gay
   Nor have my pride erestretch its aim   Lord make me wiser every year
      Beyond what I possess   And better every day

656   **1797**

Sweet the roseate breath of morn   Sweeter far the breath of praise
Sweet the blossom of the thorn   Sweet and useful when it draws
Sweet the incense violets raise   The tender mind to virtues cause

657   **1797**

Remark this truth, enough to know   Seek virtue, and of that possest,
Virtue in youth, is bliss below.   To Providence resign the rest.

658   **1797**

To lead the tender mind to virtue's bower
Pluck out the weed & cultivate the flower

659   **1797**

Reasons whole pleasure all the Joys of sense
Lie in three wo[r]ds health peace and competence
But health consists with temperance alone
And peace oh Virtue peace is all thy own.
                Alexander Pope. "Essay on Man." Epistle IV. Line 79.

659a   **1798**

First Follow nature and you Judgment frame
By her Just standard, which is still the same
Art from that fund a Just suply Provides
Work without Show and without PomP Presides

660   **1798**

1. Would you the bloom of youth should last   2. Time which all things else removes
   Tis virtue that must bind it fast   Still heightens virtue and improves.

661   **1798**

How empty learning And how vain is art
But as it mends the life And guides the heart

662   **1798**

Virtue's sacred lamp alone   Where happiness forever shines
Unerring points the way   With unpolluted ray

663   **1799**

Ye heavens from high the dewy nectar pour,
And in soft silence, shed the kindly shower,
The sick and weak the healing plant shall aid,
From storms a shelter and from heat a shade
All crimes shall cease and ancient fraud shall fail,
Returning justice lift aloft her scale,
Peace o'er the world her olive wand extend,
And white rob'd innocense from heav'n descend.

664   **1799**

——— ——— ——— ——— thy breast   Where every bright virtue alternately glows
That seat of soft passion, that bosom of rest   In a form that is spotless and fair as my
                                                  rose.

665   **1799**

Youth like softened wax with ease will take
Those images that first impressions make
If those are fair their actions will be bright,
If foul, they'll clouded be with shades of night.

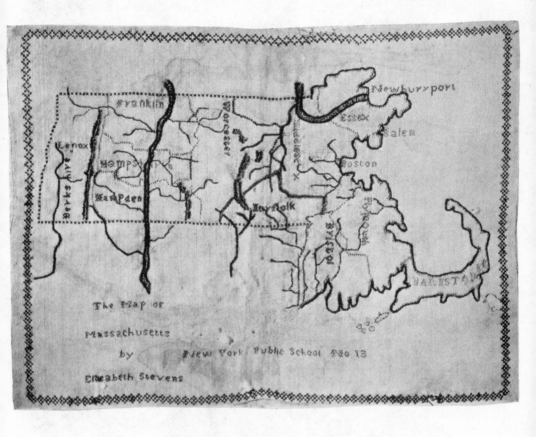

PLATE CV

ELIZABETH STEVENS'S SAMPLER. 1810
New York Public School, No. 13
Owned by Mrs. F. E. Wallace

PLATE CVI

Sukey Makepeace's Sampler. 1750
The Emma B. Hodge Collection

666

Here in this green and shady bower
Delicious fruit and fragrant flowers

667

Youth's a s-t scene[1]
But trust her not

668

Still let bright virtue shine confest
With sweet discretion kind

669

Let Virtue be thy constant guide
And truth in ev'ry word Preside

670

The little ant for one poor grain
Labours & tugs & strives
But we who have a Heaven to obtain
(unfinished)

671

1799

Virtue shall dwell within this seat
Virtue alone can make it sweet

17—

Her minutes fly
More swift than thought.

17—

Let mildness calm the peaceful breast
And wisdom guide the mind.

1800

Whilst knowledge gives to life a zest
And pure religion makes thee blest

1800

1800

O Praise thy language was by Heaven designed—
As manna to the faint bewildered mind,
Beauty and diffidence whose hearts rejoice—
In the kind comfort of thy heavenly voice.
In this wild wood of life wert thou not nigh
Must like the wandering babes lie down and die.
But thy sweet accents wake new vital powers
And make this thorny path a path of flowers

672

1800

ODE TO PEACE

Come peace of mind delightful guest
Return and make thy downy nest
Once more in this sad heart
Nor riches I nor Power Pursue
Nor hold forbidden Joys in view
We therefore need not Part
Where wilt thou dwell if not with me
From avarice and ambition free
And Pleasure's fatal wiles

For whom also dost thou prepare
The sweets that I was wont to share
The banquet of thy smiles
For thee I Panted for thee I Prized
For thee I gladly sacrificed
What ere I loved before
And shall I see thee start away
And helpless hopeless hear thee say
Fareweel we meet no more

[1] Youth is a shadow.

673

1800
THE HERMIT

1. At the close of the day when the hamlet is still
   And mortals the sweet of forgetfulness prove
   When naught but the torrent is heard on the hill
   And nought but the nightingale's song in the grove
   Twas then by the cave of the mountain afar
   The hermit his song of the night thus began
   No more with himself or with nature at war
   He thought as a sage while he felt as a man

2. Oh why thus abandon to darkness and woe
   Why thus to . . . flows thy sad strain
   For spring shall return and a favor bestow
   And no trace of misfortune thy bosom retain.
   See truth, love and mercy in triumph descending
   And nature all glowing in Edens first bloom
   On the cold cheek of death smiles and roses are blending
   And beauty immortal awakes from the tomb.
   (last lines of 6th verse)

Can be found in "The Songster's Companion." Brattleboro, Vt. 1815.
No author given. Another book gives the author as "Beattie."

674

1801

Candour enrobed in spotless white appears
Around her head a fragrant wreath she wears
Indulgence uniformly marks her reign
While information mingles in her train ,
And as the spark of genius brightning glows
The weed of merit gladly she bestows.

675

1801
AN ACROSTIC TO MISS ANNA SANDERS

A virtuous life is surely worth
No small expense or care
Nor is the Ruby so Esteemd
As virtuous persons are

So Anna you should lead your life
And always keep in view
Never from virtue to depart
Delightful is its due
Even in youth be this thy care
Religion always to revere
So that its Blessing you may share

"To Miss Anna Sanders by her very affectionate friend Luther Bayer"

676

1802
THE CONTRAST

1. Virtue alone has that to give
   Which makes it worth our while to live
   For if we live our life in peace
   And if we die our joys increase.

2. Now Vice can only that supply
   Which makes it pain to live or die
   For if we live tis' pain tomorrow
   And if we die tis' endless sorrow.

677

1802

Let virtue guide your mind to rest
The Innocent alone are truly blest

678

1802

Be sovereign grace the guardian of my youth,
May Heaven-born virtue in my breast preside,
While Wisdom, honour, innocence and truth,
Attend my steps, and all my actions guide.

679

1803

Happy the youth who always treads
Fair virtues path which upward leads
To climes beyond the sky,

There seasons no more run their round
But constant verdure clothes the ground
And air breathes love and joy

680

1803

1. Virtue not rolling suns the mind matures

2. Happy the soul that virtue shows
   To fit the place of her repose
   Needless to move for she can dwell
   In her own Grandsire's Hall as well
   Virtue that never loves to roam
   And easy on a native throne
   Of humble turf sits gently down.

681

1804

Peace thou white rob'd child of light
Thine is every softer scene
Young eyed pleasure gay delight

Still attend thy sylvan reign
Whene'er thou deign'st to be the guest

682

1804

PROCRASTINATION

Be wise today 'tis madness to defer
Next day the fatal precedent will plead

Thus on till wisdom is pushed out of life
Procrastination is the thief of Time.

Edward Young. "Night Thoughts." Night I.

683

1804

I choose the path of heav'nly truth
And glory in my choice

Not all the riches of the earth
Could make me so rejoice

684

1804

How Great The Blessing And How Vast The Art
To Live On Little With A Thankful Heart.

685

1804

Be my Ambition only to excell
In the blest art, the art of doing well.

686

1805

She fares the best whose every virtuous deed
With truth is registered in realms above
Eternal happiness shall be her need
Crowned by the blessing of th' Almightys love.

687

1805

Oh innocence protect my youth
And guide me in the paths of truth.

688

1805

Virtue's the friend of life
The soul of health

The poor mans comfort
And the rich man's wealth.

689

1805

Quite equal to our Being's aim
The space to virtue given

And every minute well improved
Secures an age in Heaven.

690

1805

Let us suppose the virtuous mind a rose,
Which nature plants and education blows

691

1805

Let virtue prove your never fading bloom,
For mental beauty will survive the tomb

692

1805

The only amaranthine flower on earth
Is virtue: The only lasting treasure—truth

William Cowper.

693

1805

1. What is the blooming tincture of the skin
   To peace of mind and harmony within
   Or the bright sparkling of the finest eye
   To the soft soothing of a calm reply

2. Can comliness of form or shape or air,
   With comliness of words or deeds compare.
   No. those at first the unwary heart may gain,
   But these, these only can the heart retain.

Nathaniel Low's Almanack. 1804.

694

1806

Oh may our follies like the falling trees
Be stripped ev'ry leaf by autumn's wind
May ev'ry branch of vice embrace the breeze
And nothing leave but virtue's fruit behind

Then when old age life's winter shall appear
In conscious hope all future ills we'll brave
With fortitud our disillusion bear
And sink forgotten in the silent grave.

PLATE CVII

JANE MERRITT'S SAMPLER. 1803
Nine Partners' Boarding School, New York
Owned by Mrs. James Richardson

PLATE CVIII

NANCY BAKER'S SAMPLER. Warren, R. I. 1808
Owned by Thomas W. Aldrich

695

1806

Let virtue heavenly maid your steps attend
Through lifes perplexing scenes your constant friend
While smiling hope will gently point the way
And smooth the path which leads to endless day

696

1806

Ever faithful ever kind,
Firm and gen'rous be thy mind.
Vice a stranger in thine heart

1806

Virtue there a constant guest
Health and friendship crown your days

* * * * * * * *

697

1806

Milder than ——————
May piety my power refine

1806

And like yon rising orb of day
May virtue guide my dubious way.

698

1806

Scarce an ill to human life belongs
But what our follies cause or mutual wrongs
Or if some stripes from providence we feel
He strikes with pitty and but wounds to heal

699

1806

While education cultivates the mind
May sacred virtue lead to joys refined.

700

1807

Virtue is the chiefest beauty of the mind
The noblest ornament of human kind,
Virtue is our safeguard and our guiding star,
That stirs up true reason when our senses err.

701

1807

May virtue o'er our steps preside
[Possession[1]] prove your constant bride

In Heavenly endels [angels] point the way
To blissful realms of perfect day.

702

1807

Merit should be forever plac'd
In Knowledge Judgement Wit and Taste.

703

1807

1. While beauty and pleasure are now in their prime
And folly and fashion expect our whole time
Oh let not those Phantoms our wishes engage
Let us live so in youth that we blush not in age

[1] Illegible.

2. Tho the vain and the gay may attend us a while,
   Yet let not their flattery our prudence beguile;
   Let us covet those charms that will never decay,
   Nor listen to all that deceivers can say.

3. I sigh not for beauty or languish for wealth
   But grant me kind Providence virtue and health
   Then richer than kings, and as happy as they
   My days shall pass sweetly and swiftly away.

704

Thro' Life be this resolve pursued
What'er thy lot may be
To act with perfect rectitude
And keep a conscience free

1807

Hope not thy happiness to find
Abroad, but homeward bend
And always let thy peace of mind
Upon thyself depend.

705

1807

Virtue hath secret charm Which all men love
And those that do not choose her, yet approve.

706

The mind, prepar'd for each event,
In every state maintains content

1808

She hopes the best when storms prevail
Nor trusts too far the prosperous gale.

707

It is neatness points the dart
And virtue guides it to the heart

1808

Let neatness then and virtue strive
To keep a wavering flame alive.

708

1808

Of all the sorrows that attend mankind
With patience bear the lot to thee assign
Nor think it chance, nor murmur at the Load,
that man calls fortune, if [it comes] from God.

709

By Virtue ripened from the bud
The flower[s] angelic odors breathe,

1808

The fragrant charm of being good
Makes gaudy vice to smell like weeds—

710

No worth is so esteemed
  As virtue in the fair
Nor diamond shine so bright
  Celestial pure and clear
Your practice then in youth

1808

Be sure to order so
  always shall ensure
Kindness to friend and foe
Ever respect all virtue laws
Respect it brings and gains applause

711

1809

In family happiness we find
Industry and virtue joined
This early specimen in rhyme
Shows that my hands to work incline

My heart to goodness may it tend
Relieve the poor console the friend
And thus in virtue shine

712

1809

When virtue guides the youthful mind
How pleasing to behold

Beau[ty] and innocence combined
With [   ] more bright than gold

713

1809

May virtue be my only guard.
And heaven at last my sure reward.
Then i shall always happy be

714

1809

Indulge the true Ambition to excel
In that best Art, the Art of living well.

715

1809

All our gaiety is vain
All our laughter is but pain

Only lasting and divine
Is an innocence like thine.

716

1810

May I with innocence and peace
My tranquil moments spend

And when the toils of life shall cease
With calmness meet my end.

717

1810

To feel undeserving of friendly esteem
Is the worst of all evils below
We may suffer from pain but he sings of remorse
Is the heaviest grief one can know

718

1803

Happy the woman who can find
Constant resources in her mind
Thrice happy she whose chief enjoyment
Is placed in regular employment
She for amusement need not roam

Her pleasure centres in her home
And when the spring of life is o'er
She still enjoys the sacred store
Which youth should seek and value most
And when once gain'd can ne'er be lost

720

1810

THE TEAR OF SYMPATHY

No radiant pearl which crested fortune wears
No gem that sparkling hangs from beauties ears
Nor the bright stars which nights blue arch adorn
Nor rising sun that gild the vernal morn,
Shines with such lustre as the tear that breaks,
For others woe down virtues lovely cheeks.

721　　　　　　Cir. 1810

Virtue alone has that to give
Which makes it joy to die or live

But vice can only that supply
Which makes it vain to live or die.
(See also No. 676)

722　　　　　　1810

Virtue and wit, with science join'd
Refine the manners, form the mind

And when with industry they meet
The female character's complete.

723　　　　　　1810
EXTRACT.

Virtue the strength and beauty of the soul
Is the best gift of Heaven; a happiness
That ever above the smiles and frowns of fate,
Exalts great Nature's favorites; it is the only good
Man justly boasts of, or can call his own.

724　　　　　　1811

In youth improve your tender mind
Let virtue be with knowledge join'd

Pursue the paths of truth and love
And you'll arrive to bliss above

725　　　　　　1811

See truth, love and mercy in triumph descending
And nature all glowing in edens first bloom
On the cold cheek of death smiles and roses are blending
And beauty immortal awakes from the tomb.

725a　　　　　　1811

O! lost to virtue, lost to manly thought
Lost to the noble sallies of the Soul
Who think it solitude to be alone.

726　　　　　　1811

I live in a cottage & yonder it stands
And while I can work with these two honest hands
I'm as happy as those that have houses and lands.

727　　　　　　1811

Virtue's a flower which ne'er will fade
It buds in youth and blooms in age.

Make her your friend, seek her in time
Then all true joys of life are thine.

728　　　　　　1811

Loveliness needs no ornament
But is when unadorned, adorned the most

729

1812

Oh that important time could back return
Those mispent hours whose loss I deeply mourn
Accept kind heaven my penitence sincere
My heartfelt sorrow and my fervent prayer.

730

1812

In its true life this transient life regard
A state of trial only not reward;
Though rough the passage peaceful is the port
The bliss is perfect the probation short.

731

1812

Beauties like princes from their very youth
Are perfect strangers to the voice of truth.

732

1812

1. Were innocence our garb alone,
   And natures blooms our only pride.
   The needle still had been unknown
   and worth the want of art supplied.

2. Virtue wit with science join'd
   Refine the manners form the mind.
   And when with industry they meet,
   the female character is complete.
   (See also No. 722)

733

1812

1. Thou canst not steal the roses bloom
   To decorate thy face
   But the sweet blush of modesty
   Will lend an equal grace.

2. Now in the opening spring of Life
   Let every floweret bloom
   The budding virtues in thy breast
   Shall yield the best perfume.

734

1812–14

With Pleasure Let us own our errors past
And make each day a critic on the last.

735

1813

On virtues chains
hangs heavenly gains

736

1813

The flowers the path of life adorn
Yet often will the rugged thorn
Amidst the flowers arise:

Think not then on earth to share
Enjoyment unallied with care
But seek it in the skies.

737

1813

Let no revenge inflame my heart
No anger sieze my mind

But let me have a christian part
Toward God and all mankind.

738

Riches lasting may you share
Innocence and virtue rare

Cir. 1813

Courteous manners void of art
Emblems of the pure in heart

739

The traveler if he chance to stray
May turn uncensored to his way
Polluted streams again are pure,

1813

The deepest wounds admit a cure,
But woman no redemption knows,
The wounds of honor never close.

741

When Nature sheds her beauties rare
Oer tree and shrub, plant and gay parterre
Mark how the bee employs each hour
Extracting sweets from every flower
So gentle maid while youth shall last
Eer the gay morn of life is past
Select each sweet with care and art

1813

To store the head and mend the heart
Happy the woman who can find
Constant amusement in her mind
Thrice happy she whose chief enjoyment
Is placed in regular employment
In works of genius, use or taste
Nor lets one moment run to waste.

742

Oh never let my youthful breast
With angry passions frought

1814

Let malice dark its peace infest
By one revengeful thought

743

Let every rising hour bring
Some useful lesson on its wing

1814

Let every moment as it flies
Record you good as well as wise

744

1814

Hail memory, hail; in thy exhaustless mine,
From age to age unnumber'd treasures shine,
Thought and her shadowy brood thy calls obey,
And Place and time are subject to thy sway.

745

1814

With passions unruffled, untainted with pride
By reason my life let me square
The wants of my nature are cheaply supplied
And the rest are but folly and care

How vainly through infinite trouble and strife
The many their labours employ
Since all that is truly delightful in life
Is what all if they please may enjoy.

746

1814

As yet 'tis mid night, deep, The Weary, clouds
Slow meeting mingle into solid gloom
Now while the drowsy lies lost in sleep
Let me associate with serious night
And contimplate the sedate compeer;
Let me shake off the intrusive cares of day
And lay the meddling senses all aside

PLATE CIX

MARY RUSSELL'S SAMPLER. 1784
The Emma B. Hodge Collection
Plate presented by the Illinois Society of the Colonial Dames

PLATE CX

Ann Robins's Sampler. 1730
Owned by Miss Susan P. Wharton

747

1814

Beauty makes virtue lovelier still appear,
Virtue makes beauty more divinely fair.

748

Let Virtue be your guide
Religion be your friend

749

By care alone we can attain
The Age which slowly here we gain

750

May tenderness thy bosom warm
And sorrow flow at other's harm

751

752

753

O resignation heavenly power
Our warmest thoughts engage
Thou art the safest guide of youth
The sole support of age

754

With Gentle hand your daughters train
The Housewifes various art to gain
Or scenes domestic to preside
The needle wheel and shuttle guide

755

Believe not each aspersing tongue
As most week persons do

756

How blest is she among the fair,
By gentlest stars inclined,
Who cherishes with love sincere,
The virtues of the mind.

1815

Then Mary you shall glide
In safety to life's end.

1815

Then be resolv'd what so much cost
By Indolence shall ne'er be lost

1816

May prudence every act attend
And virtue be thy constant friend.

1816

The Pink will fade the tulip wither
But a virtuous mind will bloom forever

1817

May happy hours, that roll through golden days
Repressing every sad exciting praise
Be thine, 'till that fair hour when all prepared
Angels shall lead thee to a bright abode.

1817

Teach us the hand of love divine
In evils to discern
'Tis the first lesson which we need
The latest which we learn

1817

On Things of use to Fix the Heart
And gild with every graceful art
Teach them with neatest simplest dress
A neat and Lovely Mind to express

1817

But still believe the story wrong
Which ought not to be true.

1818

For these shall live when others die,
And cease the heart to warm,
Prove sweeter than the sweetest eye,
And more than beauty charm.

757   **1818**

My care, my hope, my first request   To follow where the Saints have led
Are all compris'd in this   And then partake their bliss.

758   **1818**

No longer I follow a sound   O happiness now to be found
No longer a dream I pursue   Unattainable treasure Adieu

759   **1818**

Plant in thy breast oh lovely youth
The seed of virtue love and truth
They charm and bloom when beauty fades.

760   **After 1818**

O may their natal morn   And they this life adorn,
Be register'd in Heaven,   With every blessing given.

761   **1819**

In lifes gay morn what vivid hues   No storms with gloomy aspects rise
Adorn the animating views   To cloud the azure of the skies
By flattering fancies drawn   No mists obscure the dawn.

762   **1820**

AN EXTRACT

By love directed and in mercy meant
Are trials suffer'd and afflictions sent
To stem impetuous passions furious tide
To curb the insolence of prosperous pride
To wean from Earth and bid our wishes soar
To that best clime where pain shall be no more.

763   **1821**

Fair virtue, industry, and truth combined
Adorn and elevate the female mind

764   **1821**

Convince the world that you are just and true
Be just in all you say and all you do
What soever be your birth your sure to be
A man of the first Magnitude to me.

765   **1821**

Learn little maid each useful art   Learn to improve thy tender heart
Which may adorn thy youth   In virtue peace and truth

Tho age must show that life's best pursuits are vain,
And few the pleasures to be here enjoyed:
Yet may this work a pleasing proof remain
Of youth's gay period usefully employed

766

1821

If happiness be your pursuit
Plane virtue and contents the fruit.

767

1821

O Modesty! dear friend of truth revive your honoured day
Without you all the charms of youth and beauty lose their sway

768

1821

Ye when forcd wishes do to heaven aspire
Who made those blest abodes their souls desire
If you are wise and hope that bliss to gain
Use well your time spend not an hour in vain
Let not tomorrow your vain thoughts employ
But think this day the last you shall enjoy

769

1822

HAPPINESS

Remember man, the Universal Cause
Acts not by partial, but by general law[s]
And makes what happiness we justly call
Subsist not in the good of one but all,
There's not a blessing individuals find
But some way leans and hearkens to the kind
No bandit fierce, no tyrant mad with pride
No caverned hermit rest all satisfied,
Who most to shun or hate mankind pretend,
Seek an admirer, or would fix a friend,
Each has his share and who would more obtain
Shall find the pleasure pays not half the pain.

Alexander Pope. Essay on Man. Epistle IV.

770

1822

How various her employments whom the world
Calls idle and who justly in return
Esteems that busy world an idler too
Friends, books, her needle and perhaps her pen,
Delightful industry enjoyed at home,
Can she want occupation who has these?

771

1823

Virtue has a thousand Charms
Which vice can seldom see

Till beckoned by the hand of death
Then vice would virtue be.

772

1823

Source of wisdom I implore,
Thy aid to guide me safely o'er,
The slippery path of youth,

O deign to lend a steady ray,
To point the sure the certain way,
To honor and to truth

773

May virtue in your heart preside
May prudence all your actions guide

1823

May peace attend your future hours
May love your pathway strew with flowers.

774

Make an unguarded youth
The object of thy care

1823

Help me to choose the way of truth
And fly from every snare

775

1. We are a garden walled around,
   chosen and made peculiar ground
   A little spot inclosed by grace,
   Out of the worlds wild wilderness,

1823

3. Awake O heavenly wind and come,
   blow on this garden of perfume,
   Spirit divine decend and breathe,
   a gracious gale on plants beneath!

Isaac Watts. Hymns and Spiritual Songs. LXXIV. Verses 1 and 3.

776

The blessings first of Heaven sent
Nor trust your youthful heart

1824

You must Divine assistance have
To act a prudent part.

777

Virtue, soft balm of every woe,
Of every gift the cure,

1824

'Tis thou alone that canst bestow
Pleasures unmix'd and pure.

778

No other care than this I knew
But perseverance brought me through.

1824

779

Life is a gift by Heaven bestowed
And if we rightly use the boon
It is indeed a pleasant road
That leads us to a blissful home

1825

And though some rugged steeps we find
For our refinement doubtless given
Yet resignation gives the mind
A blessed   e'en of Heaven.

780

I will my youthful mind improve
In all that's good admire and love

1825

At Virtue's throne my homage pay
And tread the path to everlasting day

781

We'll therefore relish with content
What'er kind Providence has sent,
Nor aim beyond our Pow'r

1826

For if our stock be very small
'Tis Prudence to enjoy it all
Nor lose the Present hour.

782

Let virtue guide this docile mind
And to my heart its image bind.

1826

783
1826
Virtue is amiable, mild, serene
Without all beauty & all peace within

784
1826
Let meek-eyed innocence her sceptre sway
And teach each wayward passion to obey
Refining every grace her lustre shines
The brightest ornament of female minds.

Thus Mary at ten years will prove
A rich possession of unwed love,
Justly reward her parents anxious care
And the blest fruit herself will doubly share.

785
1826
To temper'd wishes, just desires, is happiness confin'd,
And deaf to folly's call, attends the musics of the mind.

786
1826
While through this fleeting life's short various day
An humble pilgrim here I plod my way
May no ambitious dreams delude my mind
Impatience hence be far & far be pride
Whate'er my lot on Heaven's kind care reclined
Be Piety my comfort Faith my guide.

787
1826
[THE LILY OF THE VALLEY]
'Tis not Beauty that we prize
Like a Summer flower it dies

But humility will last
Fair and Sweet where beauty['s] past.

This can be found in a small collection of "Poems for Children,"
printed and sold by Jesse Cochran. 1815. Windsor, Vt.

788
1827
Tirza I have you near my heart
I have you in my mind

O may you never from grace depart
But be to virtue's sway inclined.

789
1827
Hopes vivid beams the fancy clears
As down the slopes of ills we stray

Smiles through the wilderness of trees
The sunshine of a brighter day

790
1827
When beautys charms decay as soon they must
And all its glories humbled in the dust
The virtuous mind beyond the reach of time
Shall ever blossom in a happier clime

791
1828
Let all my vices be subdued
Replace them Lord with gratitude

792
1828
The morning sun begins the day
And warms all natures face

So virtue doth her beams display
And fill the mind with grace.

793

1828
Virtue should guard the tender fair
From man's deceptive flattering snare

794

1828
Whilst in the morning of your days
Renounce the world and sinful ways
For learning ardently aspire
And may virtue be your first and great desire.

795

1828
Auspicious Hope in thy sweet garden grow
Wreaths for each toil a charm for every woe!

796   Before 1830

Let no one in tears pass my cot   But may I make happy their lot
To whom I can render relief   And dry up the source of their grief.

796a   1829

From purity of heart all pleasure springs
And from an humble spirit all our peace

797

A WISH
Heaven Grant me this The utmost that I crave
Tis to enjoy the good of what I have
Accept my fortune either Good or bad
And be content not say if I had had
With less than this no happiness we know
And more than this the world cannot bestow.

798

The modest snowdrop emblem of fair truth   That unassuming worth will ever find
Convey this lesson to the thoughtless youth   A warm reception in a generous mind.

799

While through lifes various scenes I stray   May wisdom strew my paths with flowers
May virtuous friendship clear my way   And blessings crown my fleeting Hours

800

Yesterdays past tomorrows not thine,   delight virtue vice be sure to shun
today thy life to virtuous arts incline   Shes happy that a virtuous race doth run.

*The accuracy of these verses is due to the great care and
interest of Miss Evelyn M. Coker, who copied and filed them*

SCHOOLS AND SCHOOLMISTRESSES

"One did Commend me to a Wife Fair and Young
Who had French, Spannish and Italian Tongue.
I thank'ed him Kindly and Told him I love'd none such
For I thought one tongue for a Wife too much.
'What love ye not the Larned?' Yes, as my Life
A Learned scholar, but not a Larned Wife!"

THIS Lydia Kneeland laboriously embroidered upon her sampler in 1743, in the Athens of America. She herself did not belong to the unlearned classes, for her brother married the daughter of President Holyoke, of Harvard College, and so she must have echoed the sentiment of the time.

It seems to have been true throughout the Colonial life that the girls were never considered worth educating, except in the "graces." From Massachusetts south, there never seems to be any question during the first century of our country's life that the boy must be educated; so grammar schools, Latin schools, and colleges grew up. In fact, one writer says frankly that, at least in Massachusetts, the break with the past hardly existed, and that the earliest New England schools were best studied in Old England. This is also true in a large measure of the schools in New Jersey after the advent of the Scotch and English. The Swedes had founded a school at Bergen in 1664, but were not very energetic about founding more.

This is not the place to write a history of education in the Colonies, but as no history of the education of girls is available, and as nearly all the samplers which have come down to us were probably made in the schools of the period, it may be interesting to know just how each of the Colonies met the situation.

The records of New Hampshire schools are very meager, and we find that "no public provision for any regular school for the education of females" had been made up to 1815. That date approximately marks the awakening of all the states to the claims of girls for

355

an education such as a boy had received for some time. We are assured that New Hampshire had had good private schools for girls since the Revolution, though the first mentioned is that of Mrs. Montague, in Portsmouth, who had a private school for a year and a half, beginning in 1784. The samplers themselves give us two other Portsmouth schools. In 1802, Mrs. Ward had as her pupil Sarah Catherine Moffat Odiorne, whose ancestors had built the "Manor House" on Odiorne's Point, the first house in New Hampshire. Who Mrs. Ward was we have no means of knowing, nor do we know who Mary E. Hill was who taught a school in Portsmouth, in 1810, when Sarah Fitz-Gerald worked a sampler. (See Plate xcviii.)

Massachusetts, which of course at the time included Maine, is on the other hand very rich in material, but alas! not much better in its treatment of the "female" within its border; for, until the Revolution, a girl's education was considered by most people finished when she could read the New England Primer.

As early as 1642, there was compulsory education in Massachusetts for any town in which there were fifty families. This was frankly said, in 1647, in the Preamble to the Law concerning schools, to be the means of besting the Evil One. "The prince of darkness is shrewd enough to know that where the languages flourish there his power will be so rent and torn that he cannot readily repair it. Few of us perceive the craft and snare of the Devil."

Children of that time were enveloped at home and at school, every day in the week, by an atmosphere saturated with religion. So in many places the Bible and the Catechism were almost the only text-books. The larger towns had English schools, Latin schools, and soon Harvard College was founded. The smaller towns offered little to the boy and less to the girl; for, though the law decreed that every town of fifty families or more should maintain a school, many a town felt that it was cheaper to pay the £20 fine for not doing so.

Often the minister was also the schoolmaster, and often those men in the town who could read and write, taught in rotation. The girls had a very small chance of learning. Dorchester, for instance, left

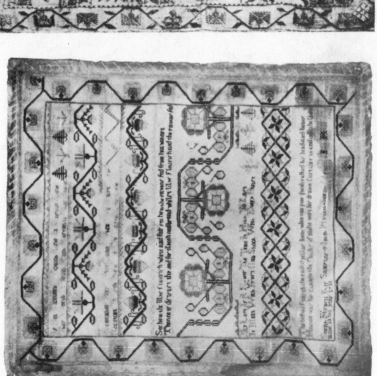

PLATE CXI

ANN TATNALL'S SAMPLER. 1786
Owned by Henry M. Canby, Esq.

SARAH HOWELL'S SAMPLER. Philadelphia. 1731
Owned by Mrs. Clayton McElroy

PLATE CXII

ABIGAIL PINNIGER'S SAMPLER. 1730
Owned by the Rhode Island School of Design

ANN ALMY'S SAMPLER. 1783
Owned by Mrs. John H. Morison

girls' education to the discretion of the selectmen, who decided against co-education. During these first seventy years of supreme indifference to education for girls, the history of the sampler in America is meager also.

As we come to the eighteenth century, there is a distinct change for the worse as regards boys as well as girls. There is less enthusiasm for learning, and the reasons are not far to seek.

"To one familiar with the early history of our state this decadence of the primitive ardor does not seem strange. It would seem more strange had the high level been maintained, for during these seventy years the little bark of state had been tossed on troubled waters. The educational history of Massachusetts is projected on a somber background. Scarcely had the colonists become settled in their new homes along the bay before dissensions among themselves brought the whole enterprise into hazard — dissensions so sharp, differences of opinion so radical, as to reach down to the bed-rock both of their civil and ecclesiastical foundations.

"During this same period heavier calamities had fallen upon them in the terrible struggle known as King Philip's War. Four years of anxious solicitude were followed by fourteen months of continuous and unmitigated horror. As the messengers came in quick succession to the patriarch Job, each telling of a new calamity, until he was stripped and desolate, so from north, east, south, and west, every day, sometimes almost every hour, brought news of villages burned and their inhabitants massacred, or of the troops sent to their rescue ambushed and butchered. From one end of the colony to the other the people in their dreams heard the war-whoop of savages and the crackling of flames, and saw the tomahawk and the scalping-knife doing their bloody work. Happy were they if they were not wakened to the reality.

"When all was over, more than half a million dollars had been spent, thirteen towns had been destroyed, six hundred buildings burned, and six hundred men, the flower of the colony, had been killed. Some towns were so impoverished that their share of the colony tax was remitted, and for three years the smaller towns were relieved from the obligation to support the grammar schools.

"Only six years later, and the gloom of the witchcraft delusion settled like a pall over the province, and swift upon the heels of this calamity came the war with the French, with Sir William Phipps's disastrous expedition against Quebec, and the new Indian atrocities upon the frontier settlements on the north and east.

"Such is the record of these first seventy years, and in them all not one without some danger or some menace of danger. When a French statesman was asked what he did during the Revolution, he replied, 'I lived.' It was much that the schools of Massachusetts lived through the trying vicissitudes of this first period.

"With the close of Queen Anne's War the province entered upon a new epoch, which brought with it changes in the school system whose influence we have not yet outlived. In the early days the fear of Indian invasion had served to hold the settlers somewhat closely together; indeed, in a part of the towns, as in Dedham, the people were forbidden to build beyond a fixed distance of one or two miles from the meeting-house. But now that this danger seemed to be over, the people began to push out into the wilderness.

"Outlying portions of the older towns were occupied, and new settlements made so rapidly that between 1700 and 1760 one hundred and twenty-three towns were incorporated, and during the next ten years forty-five more, chiefly west of the Connecticut."*

Many of these new towns were spread out all over the farming lands, with no nucleus other than the isolated church, which was usually perched on a hill. Thus educational problems were more difficult than before, and led eventually to the town being "districted off" so that each small unit might solve its problems.

There seems to be no doubt that throughout this period girls were entirely dependent on the Dame School and the "finishing school." The Dame School is hard to come at, because no records were preserved of these little schools for very young children, kept in kitchens, or sometimes in little log schoolhouses. Early in the eighteenth cen-

---

* George H. Martin. "Evolution of the Massachusetts Public School System."

tury, in most towns, the horn-book was the only text-book used in these schools. This was a square, flat piece of wood with a handle. Upon the flat part was put a printed sheet containing the alphabet — perhaps the Lord's Prayer or something else, always religious; over this was placed a piece of thin horn bound to the wood by brass strips and nails. These were the first primers, chained to the wall, like the books in a monastery library, and from these every child was taught to read. This was true of boys and girls alike, for boys did not go to public schools until they were seven years old, "having previously received the instruction usual at women's schools." This same scheme of education requires "that the children begin to learn arithmetic at 11 years of age; that at 12 years they be taught to make pens."* This was, of course, after the Revolution, when a slightly more lenient tone towards girls was adopted.

Meantime, the finishing school flourished. It is hard to tell just when it began, but certainly it was "in our midst" as early as 1706. *The Boston News-Letter* for September 9th and 23rd advertised:

> "Mistris Mary Turfrey at the South End of Boston Intends to board Young Gentlewomen: If any Gentlemen desires their Daughters should be under her Education; they may pleas' to agree with her on Terms."

"Mistris Turfrey" does not say that she will teach the "Young Gentlewomen" to make samplers. Perhaps it was because that was the period when samplers were least in favor, and such as were made seem to be the very simple kind, whose form somewhat resembles the horn-book from which girls learned their letters. If sampler art had begun with 1700, one might agree with those who think that the horn-book was the prototype of the sampler. That contention cannot be maintained, but the sampler was a very wonderful adjunct to the horn-book to educate the budding "female" mind. We have records of two quite early eighteenth century samplers made by girls of five, which must have been done at some school-dame's knee.

Apparently Boston, Salem, and Newburyport were the Massachusetts centers for the finishing school, and by 1714, Boston had a real one. *The Boston News-Letter* for April 19th of that year con-

* "System of Education Adopted by the Town of Boston."

tains an advertisement which gives the curriculum of one of these schools.

> "At the House of *Mr. James Ivers* formerly call'd Bowling Green House in Cambridge Street Boston, is now set up a Boarding School, where will be Carefully taught Flourishing,* Embroidery, and all Sorts of Needlework, also Filigree, Painting upon Glass, writing, arithmetick, and singing Psalm Tunes."

This was frivolous, practical, and religious, but furnished not much real education. Perhaps the mixture of a girls' boarding school and the Bowling Green, "where gentlemen, Merchants and others, that have a Mind to Recreate themselves could be accommodated" was not a good one, for Mr. Ivers sold the Bowling Green the next month and so made the boarding school safe for girls.

Mr. Ivers was followed by Mr. Brownell, who apparently wished to out-advertise the school at the Bowling Green House.

> "This is to give Notice, That at the House of *Mr. George Brownell,*† late School Master in Hanover Street Boston, are all sorts of Millinary Works done; making up of Dresses, and flowering of Muslin, making of furbelow'd Scarffs, and Quilting, and cutting of Gentlewomens Hair in the newest fashion; and also young Gentlewomen and Children taught all sorts of fine Works, as Feather-Work, Filagre and Painting on Glass, Embroidering a new way, Turkey-Work for Handkerchiefs two ways, fine new Fashion Purses, flourishing and plain Work, and Dancing cheaper than ever was taught in Boston, Brocaded-Work for Handkerchiefs and short Aprons upon muslin, artificial Flowers work'd with a needle."

These two men were not without their rival in Mrs. Rebecca Lawrence, who had a school in Boston for many years. *The New England Weekly Journal* for Monday, October 4th, 1731, gives a notice of her death.

> "On Saturday last died *Mrs. Rebecca Lawrence,* a noted and useful Schoolmistress in this Town."

From 1741 to 1760, somewhere near Boston, if not in the city itself, some teacher set her children the task of making a semblance of the older type of sampler. There are five of these still in existence, three of which are so alike as to be as nearly identical as the personalities of the makers allow. The cross-borders at the top are alike in sequence, and at the bottom are Adam and Eve, the Tree of Knowledge, and a wonderful fat worm of a serpent.‡

---

* Flourishing thread was a flat linen thread used for darning damask and linen, and also used for netting.
† *News-Letter*, August 27, 1716.
‡ Mary Parker, 1741; Maria Davenport, 1741; Rebekah Owen, 1745; Hannah Tyler, 1753; Ruth Haskell, 1760.

Rebecca Owen made one four years later, but aside from the fact that the serpent has a family resemblance in its obesity, one could not be sure that it was the product of the same school. (See Plates xv and xvi.)

Just at this time Elizabeth Waldron had a boarding school at the foot of the Common. She advertised her removal in *The Boston Weekly News-Letter* for Friday, March 19, 1752.

> "*Elizabeth Waldron* who hath kept a Boarding School at the Bottom of the Common, purposeth next Monday to remove to *Milton*, Within half a mile of the Paper Mills:—Where young Ladies that intend to escape the Distemper may be accommodated as usual."

There had been a universal and often fatal throat distemper in the thirties, and it was perhaps fear engendered by the remembrance that induced this flight.

Salem, in point of time, contributes the next school for finishing young ladies, and it is interesting because it is the first instance that the word Academy is used to designate a girls' school. After 1790, the word became very common, and so it is interesting that in 1748 there was a "Union Academy" in which Mary Crowninshield* embroidered a sampler.

Just at this time the Boston papers were full of advertisements of boarding schools for girls. From February to May, 1748, a very clever person sought pupils, and if she could do well all that she advertised she surely deserved to be a very popular schoolmistress.

> "This may inform young Gentlewomen in Town and Country, That early in the Spring, *Mrs. Hiller* designs to open a Boarding-school at the House where she lives, in *Fifth Street*, at the North End of Boston, next Door to Doctor ——— Wax-Work, Transparent and Filligree, Painting upon glass, Japanning, Quill-Work, Feather-Work and embroidering with Gold and Silver, and several other sorts of Work not here enumerated, and may be supplied with Patterns and all sorts of Drawing and Materials for their work."

Mrs. Sarah Morehead, "at the Head of the Rope Walks, Fort Hill," also taught "Drawing, Japaning, and Painting on Glass."

Certainly by the middle of the century, Boston had become quite prosperous, and was beginning to have most advanced ideas in the handicraft of the time. It is too bad that we cannot tell in which of

* b. 1740 d. John and Anstus (Williams) Crowninshield.

these schools of the period the Boston samplers were made, but the girls certainly had opportunities offered them to learn.

It is impossible to tell now how long each of these schools flourished, since we have only the advertisements to rely upon. A cessation of publicity might mean either that the school had not paid, or had become so popular that it needed no further aid from the press. The next candidate for favor seems to be a shade less ambitious than her predecessors in knowledge, but more so in her stock of goods. The advertisements appear from 1751 to 1753.

> "ELIZABETH MURRAY
> Next door to Deacon Bouteneau's in Cornhill, Boston.
>
> Teaches Dresden, and other kinds of Needle Works, likewise accomodates young Ladies with Board, and half-Board at a reasonable Price; sells flowered and clear Lawns, Cambricks, Muslins, Gauze, newest Fashion Caps, Ruffles, Tippits, Stomachers, Solitairs, Necklaces, Ear Rings, Ivory, Ebony and Bone Stick Fans, Womens Shoes, Stockings, Gloves and Mittens, Canvas, Crewels, Floss, Flowering and Nuns Threads, Needles, Pins and Tapes, with Sundry other Articles." (1751.)

Miss Murray evidently had a deadly rival during her first year, but as the Misses Purcell advertised but once, and Miss Murray kept on advertising, the supposition is that one succeeded and the other did not; but on our former line of argument, the result is a good deal like "the Lady or the Tiger," and one guess is as good as another. Here is the Purcell announcement:

> "Taught by ELINOR and MARY PURCELL opposite the Rev. Mr. Checkley's Meeting House, Summer Street, Boston.
>
> Dresden on Lawn and Muslin, and Work in Imitation of Brussell lace and all other Sorts of Needle Work and Shell Work, and Flower for the Head, in the neatest Manner; Likewise accommodate young Ladies with Board and half Board, at a reasonable Rate.
>
> N.B. Likewise make up all sorts of Millinery Work; after the newest Fashion." (1751.)

Miss Murray continued to call attention to her school:

> "ELIZABETH MURRAY"
>
> "Teaches Dresden and Embroidery on Gauze, tent Stitch, and all sorts of colored Work; takes young Ladies to board or half-board, at a very reasonable Rate; likewise sells Gold and Silver Gymp, Plate, Twist and Thread, Shades of Naples, Floss, and fine Silk, Cambrick and Cotton Thread, and Muslin for Dresden, with a variety of Cambrick and Lawn and Gauze, with other Millinery Goods and white Gauze Shades." (1753.)

PLATE CXIII

APPHA WOODMAN'S SAMPLER. Sanbornton, N. H. 1787
Owned by Miss Anne B. Hamilton

PLATE CXIV

Tryphenia Collins's Sampler. Cir. 1790
Owned by Mrs. B. Osgood Peirce

Miss Murray was followed in 1757 and 1758 by Eleanor McIlvaine, who had a school opposite the Governor's. Her advertisement is modest and short and she does not wish to "board or half-board" her pupils.

The following year a new person steps into the limelight, and thereafter, except for a few vague hints here and there, we hear little of Boston schools for nearly forty years.

> "MRS. JANE DAY opposite the Brazen Head in Cornhill, Boston, Has opened School, and teaches in the neatest and newest manner, Embroidering in Gold and silver, and all sorts of Shaded Work in Colours, Dresden and plain Work, etc. where also Ladies may be boarded or half-boarded as may be most convenient for Town or Country, and can supply her Scholars with Materials for Work.
> N.B. Maker in the newest Fashion all sorts of Millinary Work."

About 1764, Mary Dedman made a most beautiful needlework picture in a Boston school, probably taught by a Mrs. Rawson, but no research has yet brought to light any more knowledge of her school.

Newburyport has been mentioned as another flourishing center for girls' finishing schools, and certainly there were a large number of samplers of a very elaborate kind done in the town. The only specific mention of any school is on a sampler made by Eliza Reed, aged thirteen, "under the tuition of Harriet Ellis." The sampler contains a picture of a large house, which was probably a view of the girl's own home, or the house in which the school was held. The sampler is undated, but is of the type more common after the Revolution; in fact, common as late as samplers were embroidered.

A little later appear three samplers worked by Newburyport girls, Sally Johnson (1799), Mary Little (1800), and Mary Coffin (1801), which bear the trade-mark of some teacher's imagination, stimulated by commerce with the tropics. Each shows one or more negro slaves waiting upon gentlemen and ladies, all have orange trees, and the most elaborate (see Plate civ) contains also banana and date palms. These samplers are not actually alike, but are too nearly so in spirit not to have been done under the same teacher's eye. Perhaps one girl a year was allowed to use this subject as a reward for her deftness with the needle. Joanna Huse of Newburyport in her undated sampler records that she did it in her eleventh year "under the tuition of Maria S. Aiken."

The Revolution slowed down many activities which had to do with the amenities of life; and girls' education of the period might certainly be called one of these. The only girls' school of which we have record during this period is Sarah Stivour's. This school was probably in Salem, since Beverly, Salem, and Lynn girls went there. Four samplers of her teaching have come down to us, and they are all distinguished by a form of very long stitch in crinkly silk to designate the grass in dark green, and in blue and white overhead to indicate the sky. This stitch is often two inches long, and slants in parallel lines from the top, in the case of the sky. The lower edge is in long scallops or waves. The grass below in dark green has the same wavy edge at the top. Upon this precarious perch stand a man, a woman, sheep, and a spotted dog. A floral border surrounds three sides, and sometimes above the alphabets is an arbor.* This school lasted from 1778 to 1786 certainly, and if all the samplers there are could be gathered together we might find that it lasted longer still. (See Plates xc and xci.)

Other Massachusetts schools are recorded before 1800. Miss Southerland had a school in Boston about 1785, where embroidery was taught. No sampler that can be identified has come from this school, but a piece of embroidery done by Hannah G. Gowen, when eleven years old, is still extant, as a proof. This embroidery is in Louis XVI style, a bunch of flowers tied with a bow, embroidered on black satin; and to this is appended a certificate, in French, from her teacher. A rather simple sampler is inscribed, "Salla White her sampler, made by her own hand at Mrs. Horton's School. A.D. 1787." This school was probably either at Springfield or at Longmeadow, where "Salla" lived. It is a little sampler, about eight inches square, done in her ninth year.

The next school that we know of was kept in Salem† by Mrs. Mehitable Higginson, the wife of Mr. John Higginson, Registrar of Deeds for Essex County. Mr. Higginson died just before the Revo-

---

* Betsy Ives, 1778; Nabby Mason Peele, 1778; Mary Gilman Woodbridge, 1779; Sally Witt, 1786.
† "Half Century in Salem." M. C. D. Silsbee.

lution, and his wife and daughter Hetty were very outspoken and loyal supporters of King George. They were so unpopular that they went to Halifax, where they remained until 1782. Dr. Joseph Orne wrote of her to Colonel Timothy Pickering, on her return, "Your old friend, Mrs. Higginson, has returned, but as she is liable to be sent back and is quite as disagreeable to the people as any man would be, there is so great a ferment among them that she is obliged to live with her friends in Beverly."

She and her daughter opened a school in Salem as soon as the war was over. After her mother's death, in 1818, Miss Hetty kept her school for many years, but for younger children, and was much beloved by her pupils. It is said that Miss Hetty could divide a large strawberry among six or eight of her scholars, and that they were more pleased by this atom, given with her praise, than with a saucerful without her approbation. William Bentley, in his Diary, says that this "was the school of fashion for many years, till the infirmities of the mother prevented her better energies."

During this same period, Mr. and Mrs. Nathaniel Rogers also kept a school for "young Ladies" in Salem. In the Holyoke Diaries is a very interesting and formal letter from them to Doctor and Mrs. Holyoke, dated November 6, 1794, in which they "inform them of their determination to relinquish the School which they have heretofore kept for the tuition of young Ladies." The reason was the "injury done to Mrs. ROGERS health by a Sedentary Employment" and "the duties which she owes to her family." The school was reopened in March, 1796.

Salem did not have an entire monopoly of good schools in Essex County, it seems, for in 1802, William Bentley notes with surprise the fact that during a dinner with Captain Gibaut he "assured me that a Mrs. Saunders keeps a school in Gloucester for young ladies, where needlework will bear comparison with any of the work of our Schools not excepting Mrs. Rogers of Salem." Gloucester had another teacher for many years. She finished her earthly career in 1814, and our diarist notes "another among the many Examples of longevity in

School mistresses. Widow Hanna Tucker of Gloucester died Jan. present at Gloucester, æt. 91. For four generations school-mistresses. My school mistress, Madam Jenkins, lived many years over that age. Madam Babbidge of Salem, my next neighbor, lived & taught over 90 years of age. And a tag has been given me by M. Whitford, æt 80, which belonged to Madam Jiggles, marked EI, who was born on the passage to America & lived in the first framed house in Salem & who lived to a very advanced age & was a school mistress."

With the close of the eighteenth century the girl came into her own, and the "Female Academy" multiplied in the land. One of the earliest was at Bridgewater; it was founded in 1799. The building, burned in 1822, was fifty-four feet by twenty-seven, was two stories in height, and had a square tower which rose ten feet above the ridgepole. In 1807, Eliza Wentworth embroidered a sampler at the school, under Miss Martha Pullen, of Abington, who was then Preceptress.

Bradford Academy opened in 1803, and "originated from the sense of want which was felt in relation to education, especially female education." Leicester Academy and many others followed, and education for girls was an established fact. Mr. Littlefield tells us that in Boston, in 1817, there were one hundred and sixty-four private schools, and two thousand two hundred and eighteen girls attending. There were so many girls to educate that the academies would not hold them all; and as many of the conservative, distrusting advanced education, still sent their daughters to the finishing school, the two forms flourished side by side, as they have until this day. We are told that it was a mark of aristocracy in Salem to be admitted to one of these private schools. They were usually kept by some gentlewoman of diminished fortune, who taught the younger children of the better class reading, spelling, sewing, and, most of all, manners. Many a sampler was made in these schools, but the Salem samplers are so varied in their design as to render no grouping sufficiently sure to say that any two were made in the same school.

The result of comparing the descriptions of the samplers sent in is most interesting and intriguing. Many times you feel sure that certain girls must have worked their samplers side by side in school—and yet one can never be certain, because there were vaguely indefinite styles in samplers which pertained over a large part of the country, as there were in clothes. Some years ago there was an exhibition of samplers in an old house in Lowell, Massachusetts; it was not large, and yet two samplers hung side by side which were almost alike. It transpired afterward, when the owners met, that the two as girls had lived in Concord, and that the same teacher had instructed them both. The teacher apparently drew the pattern on the linen in ink, and as there were no ways in those days of transferring patterns, she did them free-hand, and she often set free her imagination at the same time. This would account both for their similarity and for their divergence.

Perhaps the most interesting example of this grouping of descriptions will be found in the samplers worked between 1785 and 1810 in Miss Polly Balch's Seminary in Providence, Rhode Island. It is a unique set of samplers; thirteen it is possible to be sure of, and there are a few more which were quite possibly done there also.

Five of these samplers contain a picture of the Old State House in Providence, or of old University Hall at Brown, and some contain both. The girls were always fairly accurate in the architecture of University Hall, but they were far less sure of the Old State House. The cupola rises and sinks in size, and the clock in the tower sometimes descends into the building itself. Nancy Hall and Sally Alger concentrated on University Hall, and add to the picture of the building the President's House. Above, each has given her idea of the First President's reception at the College. The President stands under curtains, looped back on either side with cords and enormous tassels. Below are pictured the guests on their way to the festivity. The two samplers are not identical, for one incloses hers with an oval, and the other, Sally Alger, uses the pseudo-classic arch, so very common to the samplers made in Miss Balch's School. The arch was echoed by Miss Sarah Stivour's School in Salem, Massachusetts, which was giving us another interesting group of samplers of the same period.

Miss Balch's School was responsible for the wonderful maritime scene done by Nancy Winsor, which is reproduced in color. (See Plates xlv, lxii, xcix, and c.)

Miss Mary Balch, known later variously as "Polly Balch" or "Marm Balch," was the second child of Timothy Balch, a Boston man, who had gone to Newport early in his career, and there married Sarah, daughter of Captain Joseph Rogers, of that city. The daughter Mary was born in Newport, February 9, 1762. Before she was twenty-three she had started a school in Providence, sometime before 1785. At one time the school was in George Street, for a paper of the time says that "A. prominent private-school whose influence lasted many years, was opened on George Street early in 1800 or late in the previous century." The mystery is very puzzling as to just who the teacher was who made the delectable samplers coming from the school. Whoever it was who was responsible, certain it is that she was with Miss Balch from 1785 to 1800. About 1800, the character of those made in Miss Balch's School changes, if, as is probable, the representation of the First Baptist Church by Maria Hopping, and the two of the First Congregational Church, were the work of her pupils. The only other one which we are certain was done in her school, that of Eliza Pearce Jones, is a reversion to the usual type of sampler, hitherto not in the least characteristic of her school.

Strangely, there are two samplers, those of Anna Sanders, 1801, and Nancy Baker, 1808 (see Plate cviii), both made in Warren, which carry on the former tradition of Polly Balch's School. Therefore it seems probable that the sewing teacher was not Miss Balch herself, for Miss Balch's School continued in Providence till her death in 1831; and after that time it was carried on by one of her assistants, Miss Walker, for many years. In 1820, the school was at 427 and 429 North Main Street, in a building which is still standing. Miss Balch's gravestone in the North Burying Ground is still to be seen.

> "Consecrated to the memory
> of Miss Mary Balch
> the 1st to establish a female Academy
> in Providence
> Who departed this life
> Jan. 3rd, 1831, in her 69th year."

Whoever it was who taught needlework at Miss Balch's School, she certainly had by far a finer sense of what the art was capable of than any one who was in a like position. She had a sense of color, form, and design, and she taught her pupils to use their silks so that they not only made harmonious color, but they were applied in such a way as to bring out the luminosity of the silk. The backgrounds in many cases are entirely covered with a whitish silk in split-stitch, which gives a most wonderful sheen to the whole. She had certain mannerisms and certain forms of design, of which each sampler contains one or two, so that they are very easy to identify, even though they are not marked, and they are never commonplace. Aside from the Old State House, usually depicted with five windows on the façade, is a house with nine windows and a fence between the two chimneys. It has two dormer windows in the roof, and a long flight of steps on either side. Polly Turner, of Warren, made an example of this in 1786, at Miss Balch's School, and Anna Sanders made one in Warren in 1801. They are very alike all through, except for the style of dress in the people walking by the house and standing under the trees on either side. Nancy Baker again did it in Warren in 1808. Between these two extremes we find it on Susan Whitmore's sampler, which though undated was certainly made at Miss Balch's School. Again it appears on the funny little sampler of Frances Jones, 1789. Julia Lippit and Eliza Cozzens used the split-stitch background and the arch to frame baskets of fruit in wonderfully harmonious colors, and Susan Whitmore put a basket of fruit under her house and pseudo-classic arch. After 1800, the samplers which come from Miss Balch's School are less elaborate and have a less sure touch. None the less, nowhere else can so interesting a group of samplers be found as those coming from this school, where for many years the girls of the best Rhode Island families were taught.

But Miss Balch's School was the flowering of a rather barren twig. Rhode Island had not paid great heed to education, as far as girls were concerned, but private schools helped there as they did elsewhere. In 1758:

"Sarah Osborne, school mistress in Newport, proposes to keep a boarding school. Any person disirous of sending children may be accomodated and have them instructed in reading, writing, plain work, embroidery, tent stitch, samplers, &c. on reasonable terms."

It is sad to think that no Newport sampler of the date has so far come to hand. About 1770, private schools were few and far between; they were "but little thought of; there were in my neighborhood three small schools, perhaps about 12 scholars each. Their books were the Bible, spelling book and primer."* But in the end, Miss Balch and her numerous rivals changed all this, and gave the Rhode Island girls as good an education as the times considered necessary.

Of Connecticut schools for girls we know but little, and yet there must have been very good ones quite early, if we are to judge by Margaret Calef's wonderful scene which she worked in 1767. (See Plate xxiii.) The perspective and architecture might perhaps be considered odd, for certainly neither the man nor the animals could possibly get inside the house. But sampler land is a very different country from ours, and there the impossible happens every day; so why not enjoy the gorgeousness of a poppy bigger than a poplar tree, and consider it in the light of a perpetual sunset? Samplers come from all the towns which we of later days associate with seats of learning—Middletown, Farmington, New Haven, Hartford.

In 1791, Mrs. Mansfield had a school in New Haven, where Lydia Church embroidered a sampler. One is tempted to think that she made a picture of her school, for that same year Elizabeth Lyon also embroidered a "picture of an old girls school on State Street," and in both ladies and "gentlemen with crooked sticks" walk about, and in each is a flock of sheep.

In Litchfield, Connecticut, "Miss Sarah Pierce opened a School in this town for the instruction of Females in the year 1792, which has very justly merited and acquired a distinguished reputation." The school was opened with one pupil in the dining-room of her house, but it soon grew. The diaries of two girls who went there as day scholars have been printed, and they give the impression of a rather

*Samuel Thurber.

PLATE CXV

PATTY KENDALL STERLING'S SAMPLER. 1806
The Emma B. Hodge Collection

PLATE CXVI

JULIA BOUDINOT'S SAMPLER. 1800
Owned by Mrs. Theodore Weston

casual attendance. During 1797 and 1798, both girls embroidered shawls, so that the work that they did upon their samplers was not wasted. The first building was made in 1798, and in 1827 it was incorporated as the "Litchfield Female Academy." Miss Pierce maintained the school for forty years. In 1802, Nancy Hale, of Glastonbury, who was a pupil in the school, wrote her sisters a letter which gives a far better picture of what a school was in those days than can we, who only imagine.

Litchfield Septr 1802

Dear Sisters

Miss Sophia Hale informs me that she expects her Parents in Litchfield to-morrow who are going directly on to G—y* and she with them & I very soon have retired from my studies to enquire after your health & that of all friends. My Dreams often present me with you enjoying great happiness; but I awake & find it nothing but the visionary fancies of a Dream; not that I am by any means Home-sick tho I wish to hear from their very much indeed. I spend my time very agreeably am very much engaged about my Picture. C Smith began one when she first came here like mine but I have got some ways before her I shall endeavor to be as diligent as possible. I have visited a few times, Miss Pierce gave me an invitation to visit her last Fryday and several others; their was 40 that drank tea in one room at one time; Their was some Gentlemen came in the afternoon and gave us all an invitation to attend a Ball that Evening the greatest part of us attended. Miss P. approves of our dancing very much she says that we set so much that it is very necessary that we should dance sometimes for exercise. Besides Embroidering I study Geography and write Composition I get my lessons in Evening. she does not allow any one to Embroider without they attend to some study for she says she wishes to have them ornament their minds when they are with her.

Parson Morgan of Canaan call'd on me this Afternoon and brought me a Letter from Nancy M. he says that our Friends are all well their & he gave me a very polite invitation to go that way when I go home & make his daughter a visit. He is now on his way to N. Haven— I shall expect a Letter when S. Hale returns, for her Parents are going to leave her here when they return. I hope to finish my Picture before I return home which I hope you will let me stay as long as you possibly are willing Vacation is either 2 or 7 weekes from now their has several left the School since I have been here 2 young Ladies that board in the House with me that are going home tomorrow the school being so much less makes it much better for us that are here. their has been 70 in the School since I have been here but there is two Miss Pierces who assist in the School. If the wether continues as cold as it is now (as very probably it will be) I wish you to bring my Habit when you come after me. Last Sunday we all wore woolen Shawls and several wore cloaks to Meeting and there was several that carried Muffs. Tuesday Morn 9 oClock Coll Hale & Lady have arrived in Town this Morning Colonel Hale I have seen he knew me altho I was with a number of others he says he shall be here either next week or the beginning of week after I shall certainly

* Glastonbury.

expect a Letter then— I have some silk paper in my drawer in the Case of
Drawers I wish you to enclose it in a Letter and send it to me as I am in great
want of some and their is none to be had in town I want it for my Picture I am
with sentiments of esteem your

Affectionate

Sister *Nancy Hale.*

Addressed to

    Miss Hannah Hale

      Glastonbury.*

As we leave New England, we embark on more uncharted seas,
for we leave the familiar English school to encounter those of other
nations. So it gives us quite a shock to find that the Dutch were far
more liberal in their attitude toward educating girls than were our
English ancestors.

Dame Schools were very common in Holland at the time when the
Dutch came to New York, but the records are silent as to whether
they brought their Dame Schools with them or not. An author tells
us that "a continuation of discreet ignorance seems the wisest course"
in discussing them. The school dame was not an early product of
Dutch New Netherlands, except that the summer school, if it con-
sisted of less than twenty children, might be taught by the schoolmaster's wife. The parochial school seems to have taken in both boys
and girls. In 1698, they appear to have had a sort of contest, in which
forty-four boys and twenty-one girls took part, in repeating psalms,
hymns, etc. Dr. Selyns reported that "the girls though fewer in number, had learned and recited more in proportion than the boys." The
girls evidently had their intellects much better attended to in New
York than in New England, but the needle, alas! was neglected, for
almost no Dutch samplers done in New York have come down to us.
The early New York samplers all come from Long Island, where
the English influence was strong. The only exception is the sampler
of Catherine Van Schaick "out 10", worked "Jaer 1763", in Albany.
It is a very plain little sampler, but most interesting, as it stands
almost alone.

New York also had finishing schools, as did all the other large
cities up and down the coast. Before 1800, the Yearly Meeting of the

*Letter owned by George Dudley Seymour, New Haven.

Society of Friends of the State of New York had opened a boarding school. The real name of the school was so long that, like other Quaker schools, it went by a nickname, and was called the "Nine Partners' Boarding School". There the same patterns were used as those at the other Quaker school at West Town, Pennsylvania. The designs are quite simple, and run to scattered flowers and geometric figures. These latter are most often in the form of half hexagons along the edge of the sampler, and have a Dutch or German effect. Another school in New York had the interesting name of "African Free School." Rosena Disery made a sampler at this school in 1820. The sampler was seen in a shop, and unfortunately nothing beyond the name of the girl and the name of the school were reported.

New Jersey offers us the earliest sampler with a teacher's name upon it. Hannah Foster, of Evesham, records in 1743, "Elizabeth Sullivan taught me." The state also had so many schools that one might think that all education in the early nineteenth century centered around Philadelphia and the adjacent coasts of New Jersey. Though the schools were many and all of them enticed the girls on in the art of sampler making, the result as a whole was not thrilling. The samplers are nearly all very simple. In fact, only two of the collection stand out as interesting. In 1808, Eliza F. Budd made an elaborate picture of the Court House at Mount Holly, New Jersey, and crowned the corners and the top of the hip roof with noble urns. Beneath, on the Court House terraces, Ruth gleans the sheaves of Boaz; and on the other side of the approach, King David tends his flocks. And overhead fly birds, quite undisturbed that they are living both in Palestine and New Jersey at the same time.*

The reason for the great numbers of schools in Pennsylvania and New Jersey was that the Society of Friends believed in education; but again, alas! in the early days, not in the education of girls. Female education was limited to the bare understanding of the rudiments. Many have deplored the lack of letters from Colonial women; the lack was not in preserving them, for the absence of letters is the direct

* See also Margaret Kerlin and Sarah Montgomery Blair.

result of insufficient education. It is most amusing, as one reads the educational history of each state, to see how each author in turn calls the period of 1700–1750 one of "gloom and darkness." New Jersey made a struggle in the right direction, but it apparently was a very real struggle. There was a young ladies' seminary in Elizabethstown in 1789, but it soon failed. Two years later a French school was opened to teach the fashionable accomplishments, but no permanent school resulted.

In 1808, Red Bank, a farm belonging to Barnes Smock, was made into a school, whose first teacher was George Morford. In 1825, Mary Ann Burroughs embroidered a sampler at the school and marked it so. The school was made an Academy in 1830, and is or was the most important industrial school in Monmouth County. The Evesham School, which, as we know from the samplers, flourished from 1808 to 1820, at least, furnishes us with a very interesting example of the fact that the schools in Southern New Jersey and Eastern Pennsylvania used common designs. In 1808, Julia Haines, at the Evesham School, used the same flattened oval wreath, a single stitch in width, which the Bristol and Pleasant Hill Boarding Schools employed, and which the North School, Philadelphia, used in even simpler form. Outside this she embroidered a border which is distinctly reminiscent of many which are found on the samplers from the West Town School.

Pennsylvania, very early, thanks to the Moravians, had schools which seem to have taught even the girls some sort of learning. In 1746, the sect founded a school at Lititz, near Bethlehem, in Lancaster County. The school was in the midst of the community, and one suspects was at first only for the children of the Moravians. It had early a national reputation, and was later known as Linden Hall Seminary.

In 1799, Mr. John C. Ogden, "Presbyter in the Protestant Episcopal Church in the United States," printed a book called "An Excursion into Bethlehem of Nazareth, in Pennsylvania." One is led by the title to expect other things, but our learned presbyter certainly

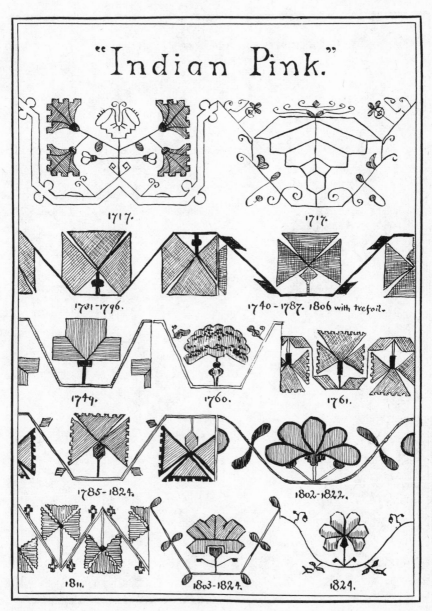

"Indian Pink."

1717.

1717.

1731–1796.

1740–1787. 1806 with trefoil.

1749.

1760.

1761.

1785–1824.

1802–1822.

1811.

1803–1824.

1824.

PLATE CXVII

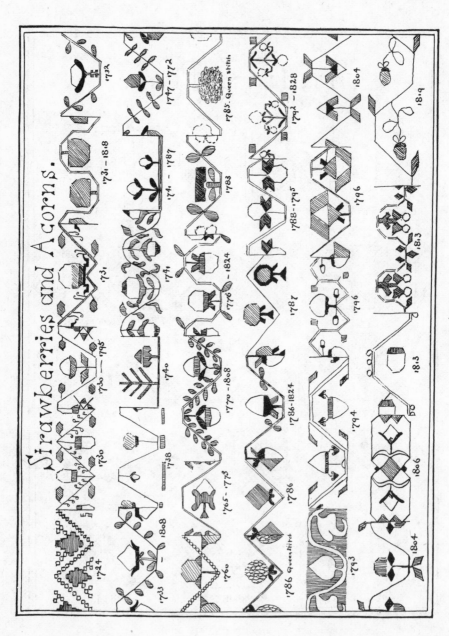

Strawberries and Acorns.

PLATE CXVIII

took his expedition in almost the same spirit in which he might if he had gone to more sacred lands.

He found things much to his taste in this Moravian settlement, and it may have been the seal of his approval which later led good little Episcopalians like our sampler maker to go to this school.

Having gone to the boys' school, our traveler next visited the girls'.

"The hour being convenient for visiting the girls school, so much celebrated, a pleasing groupe appeared in different rooms, under the care of their tutresses, where they learn reading, writing, arithmetic, embroidery, drawing, and music.

Since the application to receive pupils from abroad, have become so frequent and numerous, a new building has been erected for their use, upon a similar model, with the sisters house. A small courtyard, or grass plat, is between these buildings.

In the rear of this, is another small enclosure, which forms a broad grass walk, and is skirted on each side by beds devoted to flowers, which the girls cultivate as their own."

The visitor goes on to explain that the teachers are in no respect like nuns, but nevertheless the "instructresses are treated with due respect. All females are educated by them." Then when he has seen all that there was to see, read their books, and enjoyed their hospitality, he ends enthusiastically with these words:

"The whole system is well calculated to make mankind wiser and better; to ameliorate the conditions of the untutored, and correct the devious: It softens the rugged temper, and expands the benevolent heart."

With this seal of approval from a high dignitary of her church, is it any wonder that some twenty years later Catherine Jones Elder was sent there, so that the good influences of the place might be very strongly felt? Catherine was *seven,* and was sent to Lititz to recover from an unfortunate love affair! A schoolmate had written her a love-letter, and the occasion was felt by her family to demand a separation of the lovers. She made two samplers at the school, one in 1826 and one in 1827. Tradition does not tell whether these very youthful lovers were faithful or not.

Rather earlier than most, the Society of Friends discerned the great lack of education among girls and its consequent retarding force on the growth of the nation. Pennsylvania had had schools perhaps of the same sort that were prevalent farther north, but Philadelphia had no boarding schools until the Revolution. In 1770, Mr. Griscom advertised his private "Academy" at the North End of Philadelphia; but until Mr. Horton started the idea of a separate school for girls in 1795, education for them had been purely ornamental. The same year, Poor's "Academy for young ladies" was at No. 9 Cherry Street.

The Society of Friends carried Mr. Horton's idea out, but in a different form. The "Philadelphia Yearly Meeting" started a school in 1794, to give children "a guarded religious education." The land was purchased at West Town the next year, and in 1796 the school was founded, and the brick building a hundred feet long by fifty-six wide was built. It was three stories high, as Martha Heuling's sampler pictures it for us. In 1799, "5 mo 6", it opened with twenty pupils of both sexes, but by midwinter boasted a hundred of each. From that time on, the school was in continuous session for thirty-seven years, without a single vacation. Scholars entered at any time for a year or more. The sexes were kept strictly apart in the early years. It is somewhat of an indication of the popularity of the school that we have sixteen samplers which were known to have been made there between 1802 and 1820. Of these, ten are distinctly plain, usually showing a vine or conventional border, with a verse—true Quaker plainness. Two show a rather German influence, as they are covered with detached sprays of flowers, like Susanna Cox's (see Plate xciv). Martha Heuling portrayed the first building of the school. Her sampler is, unfortunately, dim with age, and as a consequence the reproduction is quite vague. There were other forms of samplers done in the school. One is in white blocks two inches square,* with the maker's name and the date in black; another is entirely in blue;† while a third has the lettering done with pen and ink.‡ (See Plate cxiii.)

The game of matching descriptions is quite exciting when brought to bear on the Philadelphia collection, though the result is not very definite. From 1796 to 1828, some school in Philadelphia evidently

---

* Hannah E. Deacon, 1816.
† Phebe Ann Speakman, 1820.
‡ Hannah Mendinhall, 1810.

specialized on houses and scenes. Two of the earlier, Susan Lehman's and Hetty Lees', both done in 1799, show half a house on the left, trees, a fence, and half a barn. Thereafter follows a somewhat long line of houses, with weeping willows, poplars, sheep, cattle, men, and women. The sky is sometimes filled with small flowers; one has the sun, one the stars with the sun, and three the American Eagle with outspread wings. They are none of them actually alike, but they give the impression that one mind, having conceived a general type,* used it in varying forms. Another interesting fact develops by this comparison. The Pleasant Hill Boarding School and the Bristol School evidently exchanged patterns; and Mary Hamilton, who went to Mrs. Welchan's School at Maytown, Pennsylvania, in 1812, and Ann E. Kelly, who went to Mrs. Leah Meguire's School, in Harrisburg, in 1825, embroidered samplers whose form is almost identical. The North School, in Philadelphia, echoes in a much simpler form that used by the Pleasant Hill and Bristol Schools.

William Penn provided for education in Delaware, which seemed to his mind most important in order that "all wicked and scandalous living may be prevented and that youth may be successively trained in virtue, and useful knowledge and arts."

It was also agreed that all children of the age of twelve years "shall be taught some useful trade or skill to the [end that] none may be idle, so the poor could may be work to live and the rich if they became poor, may not want."† In his last lines to his wife, William Penn exhorts her to let his "children be husbandmen and housewives; it is industrious, healthy, honest and of good example." In order to gain this result, she is "to spare no cost" for their education.

Penn's high ideals, like those of our Pilgrim and Puritan ancestors, had no long duration in fact; and Delaware fell a prey, as did the other colonies, to the period of "gloom and darkness" which held sway until the middle of the eighteenth century.

The Swedes founded schools early in the eighteenth century

---

* Emily Sharpless, Hetty Lees, Susan Lehman, Eliza Wire, Mary Ann Tawn, Mary Magdalen Wolf, Rebecca Skinner, Margaret Moss, Mary H. Dwier. (See Plates xliv and cii.)
† U. S. Dept. Interior. "Monograph on Education in Delaware."

where they endeavored to educate both boys and girls. In 1717, a school was opened in the house of Johan Gustafsson, in Christiana, Delaware, and the schoolmaster examined the children sent to him. There were eleven scholars, of whom five were girls, whose capabilities were duly recorded by Mr. Gioding:

> Mary Geens, 9 years old, can read Swedish and say the Ten Commandments.
> Mans Gustaf's daughter Anika, 6 years old can spell Swedish tolerably well.
> Anders Gustaf's daughter, Catherina, 12 years old, can read in a book, but must begin to learn to spell right.
> Margaretta, the late Peter Stalcop's daughter, 11 years old, reads Swedish indifferently well, but must learn to spell anew.
> Annika, Anders Gustaf's daughter, 8 years old, can spell a little.

The girls were not so far behind the boys in education, and when the school ended the next year, it was so wonderful a success as to bring tears to the parents' eyes.

The English schools of the same time seem to have been in a much worse way. The Rev. George Ross, in a sketch of the history of his church at New Castle, Delaware, described the condition of education in 1727. "There are some private schools within my reputed district which are put very often into the hands of those who are brought into the country and sold for servants. Some school masters are hired by the year by a knot of families who in their turns entertain him monthly and the poor man lives in their houses like one that begged an alms, more than like a person in credit and authority. When a ship arrives in the river it is a common expression with those who stand in need of an instructor for their children, 'let us go and buy a school master.' The truth is, the office and character of such a person is generally very mean and contemptible here, but it cannot be otherwise 'til the public takes the education of children into their mature consideration."*

This dismal period and dismal education eventually came to an end, and with it the girls' education arose to what was normal throughout the colonies. During the Revolution, John Thelwell had a famous school in Wilmington. His first school was at the foot of Quaker Hill, but he soon moved to the little Senate Chamber over the Market House,† at the corner of King and Third Streets. Most boys

---

* "History of Public School Education in Delaware." Stephen B. Weeks. P. 16.
† "History of Education in Delaware." Lyman Pierson Powell.

and girls were his pupils, at least during part of their school days. The attitude of the times toward girls' education is still quite evident, from the fact that the boys went in the front door, and the girls had to go through a side door up an alley. Miss Debby Thelwell, his eldest daughter, had charge of the girls. Her sister, Miss Polly, was too timid to teach, but after their father's death the two sisters carried on the school for many years.

In 1785, Ann Askew had a school for girls in Wilmington, where Ann Tatnall embroidered a sampler, which resembles in a marked degree those of about 1730. Nineteen years later, her daughter, Eliza Tatnall Sipples, embroidered her sampler at the "Southern Boarding School" in Wilmington. Later the Wilmington Boarding School, which lasted from 1813 to 1824, taught the girls in that city the gentle arts. (See Plate cxi.)

Again, we are disturbed because there is a definite bond of type between samplers. The first pair might easily be put down to family taste. Susannah James, in 1788, and Mary James, in 1798, embroidered their samplers, not entirely alike, but distinctly of the same sort. The other pair is more remarkable. Sarah Bancroft, in 1795 (see Cover), and Sally Brierly, in 1828, thirty-three years apart, each embroidered the same church upon her sampler. That coincidence would not be extremely remarkable except for the fact that the two are almost identical, stitch for stitch. Sally Brierly did not add the scene in front, with the pond, boat, and swans, but she made the groundwork of her sampler more ornate.

On Second Street, Wilmington, from 1790 on, Mrs. Elizabeth Way kept a school. She "was a celebrated teacher of needlework, so important for misses in those times that even the art of shirt-making was strictly attended to; the fitting and cutting were taught here with neatness and care. Most of the older females brought up in this town have been her pupils. Mrs. Way was a very respectable and worthy woman. She had received an education superior to most women of her day and was endowed with a strong mind and strict principles of morality; yet an irritable temper was a drawback to her usefulness and it was annoying to some of her pupils. She was a disciplinarian of the old school and strictly adhered to the wise king's advice. A bunch of switches of cat-o'-nine-tails were freely used to correct the naughty.

"Leather spectacles were worn for slighted work. Much attention was paid to the position, for if the head leaned down Jamestown-weed burs strung on tape were ready for a necklace; or if a person stooped a steel was at hand—this was the length of the waist—and held up the chin by a piece extending around the neck, and a strap confined it down. It was not very comfortable to the wearer, though fitted to make the 'crooked ways straight', but a morocco spider worn on the back confined to the shoulders by a belt was more usual.

"The celebrated painter, Benjamin West, had been a companion of Mrs. Way's childhood and youth. As absent friends they kept up a correspondence and it seemed much pleasure to her to relate anecdotes of his early days."

In 1797, Mr. Crips built the house called the "Old Boarding School." Here, a few years later, Mrs. Capron, who had had a school in Philadelphia, came and taught the young ladies of Wilmington. She was succeeded by Joshua Maule and Eli Hilles. After Mr. Maule died, Samuel Hilles joined his brother, and the school was continued by one or both until about 1832.

Delaware and Maryland children, both boys and girls, we are told, were often sent abroad to English schools, and many must have had private tutors, because plantation life meant that there were, outside the cities, fewer towns than there were in the more northern states. The southern cities, however, furnished the same sort of "finish" to girls that the northern cities did. The following advertisement might as easily have emanated from Boston as from Annapolis:

"MARY SALISBURY proposes keeping school in Annapolis, at the house where Mr. Sparrow lived, near the church, to teach young ladies French and all sorts of fine needlework, tapestry, embroidery with gold and silver, and every other curious work which can be performed with a needle, and all education fit for young ladies except dancing."*

*"History of Education in Maryland." Bernard C. Steiner.

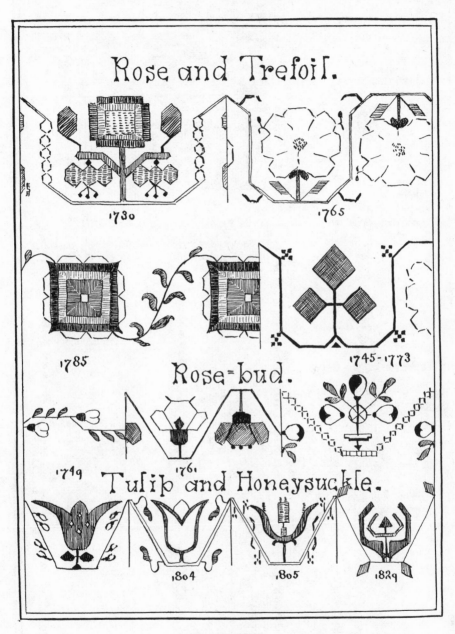

Rose and Trefoil.

1730

1765

1785

1745-1773

Rose-bud.

1749

1761

Tulip and Honeysuckle.

1804

1805

1829

PLATE CXIX

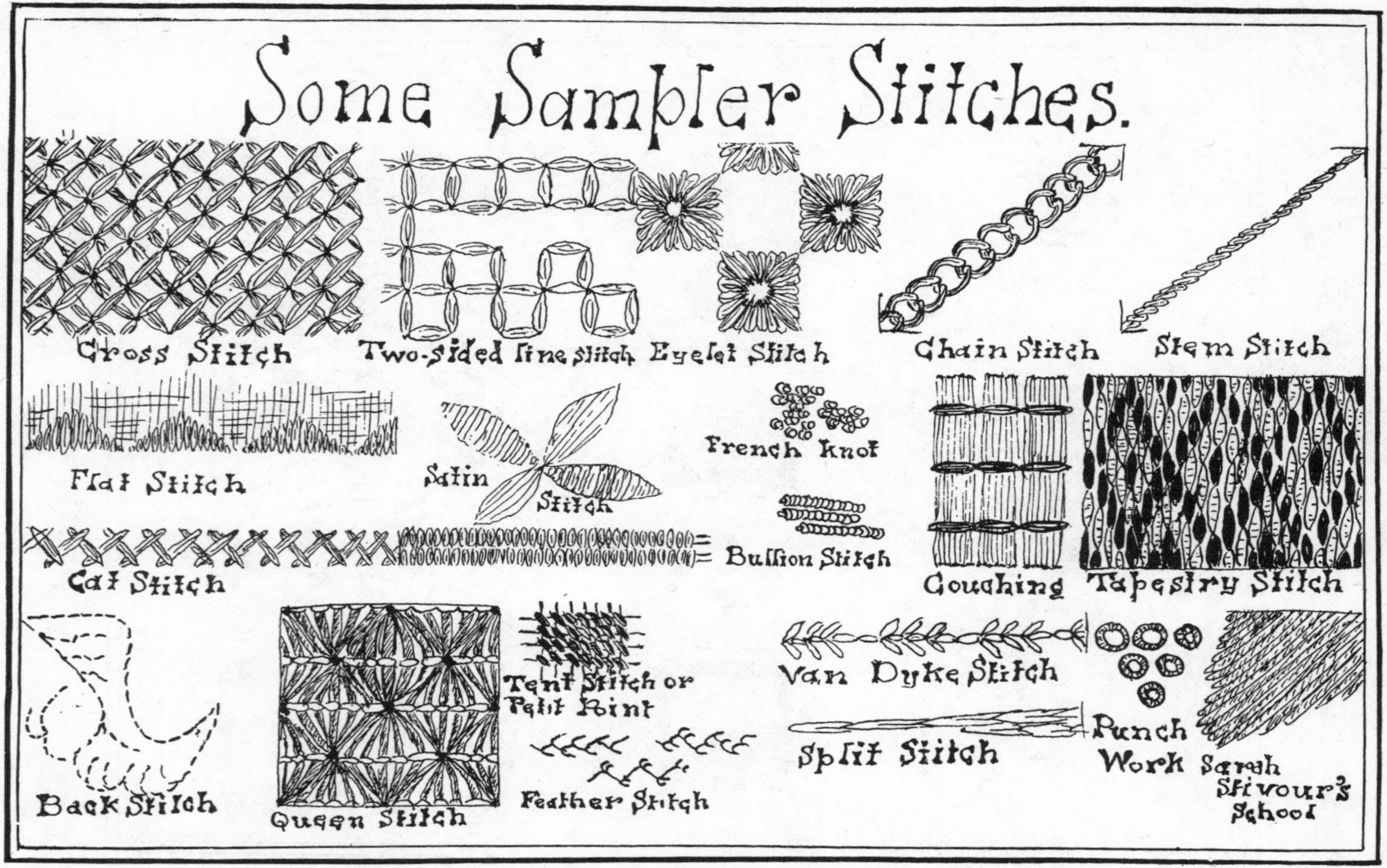

Some Sampler Stitches.

Stem Stitch

Chain Stitch

Tapestry Stitch

Couching

Van Dyke Stitch

Punch Work Sarah Seymour's School

Split Stitch

Two-Sided line Stitch Eyelet Stitch

French Knot

Bullion Stitch

Satin Stitch

Tent Stitch or Petit Point

Feather Stitch

Queen Stitch

Cross Stitch

Flat Stitch

Cat Stitch

Back Stitch

PLATE CXX

The Chesterfield School seems to have existed quite early, for we have samplers marked with the school name from 1795 to 1821.* Teresia Fenwick had a governess, Eleanor Norland, and the sampler done under her care is the only one so far reported which has a Calvary Cross upon it. Mary Robertson may also have been a governess; certainly if the two samplers done under her care are any criterion, she was well beloved, for her pupils gave her their samplers, and she recorded the gift with words of praise and affection. The childish heart is hard to know, and the childish mind is sometimes quite canny in its reading of adult character. Perhaps "the two dear girls" were flatterers, and had gauged Miss Robertson's gullibility. Only one other school in Maryland is known, Mary Walden's, in Baltimore, where, in 1818, Caroline Vaughan embroidered a sampler.

Virginia samplers hardly exist before the nineteenth century, if the records so far gathered are of any value as proof, and there is no school recorded among them. We do know, however, that in 1811 Amelia Hough and Mary Lawrence were the teachers of Amy Ann Phillips, of Waterford, Virginia.

North Carolina boasted a Female Academy at Salem, at least as early as 1805. It was a Moravian school, and, judging the rest of the education by the very elaborate sampler done by Dovey Winslow Wilson while a student, they must have given the girls a very fair knowledge. They allowed her to use not only embroidery, but pen and ink, and oil painting for the face of the mourning woman. And Hillsboro had a school in 1828, where Mary T. Lindsay, of Greensboro, embroidered a simple sampler.

The states to the south give us no inkling at all as to how their girls were educated, for they record neither teachers nor schools upon the rather meager collection of descriptive blanks which have come to hand. Perhaps the Pennsylvania schools received their share of pupils, and governesses and mothers taught the rest. Kentucky seems to have awakened to the academy idea when all the more northern states did, and Ohio had one school at least, at Waynesville, as early as 1807.

* Jane Henderson, Abigail and Margaret Decou.

On the whole, it is quite surprising to find how large a contribution to the history of girls' education these samplers furnish. While the information is meager in itself, it still gives an impetus to the inquiring mind to find out the condition of our forebears; and of course it increases our feeling of smug satisfaction that we of the present day are not as they were, but quite emancipated from the dominating intellect and erudition of man.

ETHEL STANWOOD BOLTON.

A LIST OF EARLY SCHOOLS

MAINE
SAMPLER WORKERS

1799 Temperance P. Jackson, instructress, East Harpswell. — *Eunice Purinton*
1805 Boarding School, Portland. — *Betsy Warren*
1818 Mme. Neil's School, Portland. — *Mary Jane Barker*

NEW HAMPSHIRE

1784–5 Mrs. Montague's School, Portsmouth.
1802 Miss Ward's School, Portsmouth. — *Sarah Catherine Moffat Odiorne*
1810 Mary E. Hills School, Portsmouth. — *Sarah FitzGerald*
Canaan Family (Shakers). Emma Johnson, teacher. — *Hannah Wilson*

VERMONT

MASSACHUSETTS

1706 Mistress Mary Trufrey, South End, Boston.
1714 James Ivers Boarding School, Bowling Green House, Cambridge Street, Boston.
17—–1731 Mrs. Rebecca Lawrence, Boston. Died October 2, 1731.
1739–1741 No school named. — *Anne Wing*
Lydia Kneeland

1742–1747 Mrs. Condy, embroidery school.
1747–1748 Mrs. Hiller, 5th Street, North End, Boston.
1748 Mrs. Morehead, Head of the Rope Walks, Fort Hill, Boston.
1748 Union Academy, Salem. — *Mary Crowninshield*
1750 Susanna Babbidge, Salem. (Cir. æt. 90, 1804, "a superior woman".)
1751 Elinor and Mary Purcell, Summer Street, Boston.
1751–1753 Elizabeth Murray, Cornhill, Boston.
17— Elizabeth Waldron, near the Common, Boston. 1752, removed to Milton.
1757–1758 Eleanor McIlvaine, opposite the Governor's, Boston.
1759 Mrs. Jane Day, opposite the Brazen Head, Cornhill, Boston.

1764 Mrs. Rawson's School (?).

Mary Dedman

1769 Amy and Elizabeth Cumings School, Boston.

1778–1786 Sarah Stivour's School, Salem?

1778 *Betsy Ives*
1778 *Nabby Mason Peele*
1779 *Mary Gilman Woodbridge*
1779 *Sarah Perkins?*
1786 *Sally Witt*

1785 Miss Southerland's School, Boston.

Hannah G. Gowen

1784–1800 Lydia Babbidge, Salem.

    1800 "Died Lydia Babbidge æt. 67 who, with her mother now aged 86, has kept a school for little children. Her mother has been a School Dame above ½ a Century."*

1787 Mrs. Horton's School, Springfield?

Salla White

1788 on Mrs. Higginson's School, later Miss Hetty Higginson's. Miss Higginson died in 1846.*

1790 Priscilla Gill, schoolmistress, Salem.*

1791 Madam Mansfield, Salem. "April 18. Last Saturday died suddenly Madam Mansfield a very aged Matron, who for many years has been a School-Mistress." (d. æt. 82, "the good habits suited to her times & her success."*)

17 to 1794 }
1796 to 18— } Mr. and Mrs. Nathaniel Rogers, Salem.*

1792 Sarah Knight, Schooldame, Ivers Lane, Salem.*

1792 Hannah Mascoll, Schooldame, Salem.*

Lydia Loring

1794 Derby School, Leominster?

Lydia Tyler

1797 Miss Sally Flint's School, Methuen.

1802 Mrs. Saunders, Gloucester.*

Eliza Crocker

1803 Mrs. Dobell's Seminary, Boston.

Pamela Brownell

1803 Westport School, Westport.

Mary Tyler

1803 "A Boston School."

Eliza Wentworth

1807 Bridgewater Academy, Bridgewater.

Roxana Peabody

1808 Bradford Academy, Bradford.

Hannah Loring

1812 Miss Perkins Academy, Boston.

Eliza Pratt (?)
Mary Richardson

1812 Miss Mary Cummings School, Westford.

Mary Ann Barry

1812 Mrs. Rowson's Academy, Boston.

Eliza W. Gale

1813 Mrs. Tufts' School, Charlestown.

—— to 1814 Mrs. Hannah Tucker, Gloucester.*

1818 L. Brigham's School, Marlborough.

Hannah Peters

1818 N. L., "by my superintendency."

Lydia Kimball

1819 L. Johnson's School, Salem?

Lydia Johnson

1825–1828 Groton Female Seminary, Groton.

1825 *Mary Eliza Brannum*
1828 *Almira Bates Brannum*

* William Bentley's Diary.

SAMPLER WORKERS

1825   Mr. Thomas Cole, Salem.

1828   Salem Street Academy, Boston.   *Sarah C. Rendols*

Undated   Harriet Ellis' School, Newburyport.   *Eliza Reed*

Undated   Miss Damon's School, Boston.   *Elizabeth M. Ford*

Undated   Maria S. Aiken's School, Newburyport.   *Joanna Huse*

RHODE ISLAND

1785–1810   Miss Polly Balch's Seminary, Providence.

1785	*Loana Smith*
1786	*Polly Turner*
1786	*Nabby Martin*
1786	*Nancy Winsor*
1788	*Nancy Hall*
1789	*Frances Jones*
1789	*Sally Alger*
1790	*Ann Hamlin?*
1791	*Sophie Packard*
	Judith Paul
1796	*Mary Talbot*
	Phebe Hughes?
1797	*Julia Lippitt*
1798	*Mehitable Hamlin?*
	Eliza Cozzens
[1799]	*Susan Whitmore*
1810	*Eliza Pearce Jones*
Undated	*Maria Hopping?*
Undated	*Unknown. 1st Congregational Church*
After 1814	*Sarah F. Sweet?*

1801   Warren.   *Anna Saunders*
                                                  1809   *Nancy Baker*
1810   West School, Providence?   *Eliza Talbot*

Undated   Jenck's Street School, Providence.   *Abby Mareford*

CONNECTICUT

1791   Mrs. Mansfield's School, State Street, New Haven.   *Lydia Church*
                                                        Elizabeth Lyon?

1792 on   Miss Sarah Pierce's School, Litchfield.   *Jerusha, Mary and Sarah Perry*
                                                    1820   *Marian Lewis*

1816   Miss L. P. Mott's School, Hartford.   *Anna Huntington*

1824   Miss Lucy W. Case, teacher, Canton.   *Clarissa Case*

1825   Sally Hinsdale, New Hartford.   *Sixteen small samplers*

NEW YORK

1800   The School of the Yearly Meeting of the Society of Friends,
       of the State of New York, nicknamed the "Nine Partners   1800   *Eliza Bowne*
       Boarding School", New York City.   1805   *Jane Merritt*

1810   School No. 13.   *Elizabeth Stevens*

1814	Huntington Academy, Long Island.	*Caroline Kelcy*
1820	African Free School, New York City.	*Rosena Disery*

NEW JERSEY

1743	Elizabeth Sullivan, teacher, Salem.		*Hannah Foster*
1797	Sarah Shoemaker, teacher, Pemberton.		*Esther Earl*
1808–1820	Evesham School.	1808	*Jane Haines*
		1820	*Hannah Gardiner*
1810	Westfield School.		*Sarah Lippincott*
1812	Rancocus School.		*Ann Wills*
1813	Haines Neck School.		*Rebecca Peterson*
1816	Greenville School.		*Henrietta Kay*
1817	Great Egg Harbor School. Monthly Meeting of Friends.		*Margaret Lake*
1821	Greenwich School.		*Mary V. Hughes*
1825	Red Bank School.		*Mary Ann Burroughs*
1826	Middletown Academy.		*Leah Conover*
1829	Mrs. Hayward's School, Hackensack.		*Catherine A. Van C. Boyd*
1835	Mrs. Elmendorf's Seminary, Kingston.		*Catherine De Wit Young*

PENNSYLVANIA

1746–1827	Linden Hall Seminary, Lititz, Lancaster County. (1826 and 1827.)		*Catherine Jones Elder*
1796	Mrs. Capron's Boarding School, Philadelphia.		*Peggy Douglas*
1796–1820	The School of the Yearly Meeting of Friends of the City of Philadelphia at West Town, called the "West Town Boarding School." (Quaker.)	1800	*Keziah Mickle*
		1802	*Susanna Cox*
			Mary Lea
			S. W. Miller
		1803	*Eunice Bloomfield*
			Rebecca Black
		1805	*Elizabeth Goodwin*
		1806	*Hannah Ellet*
			Martha Heuling
		1810	*Alice Jarrett*
			Ruth Almy
			Ann Deacon
		1813	*Ann T. Newbold*
		1816	*Hannah E. Deacon*
		1820	*Phebe Ann Speakman*
1808–1827	Bristol School, Bristol. (Quaker.)	1808	*Barbary Eagles*
		1827	*Susanna Magarge*
1808	Pleasant Hill Boarding School.		*Julia Knight*
1808–1813	Mrs. Armstrong's School, Lancaster.	1808	*Fanny Rice*
		1813	*Willamina Rine*

1812	North School, Philadelphia.	*Hannah D. Lambert*
1812	Mrs. Welchan's School, Maytown, near Pottstown.	*Mary Hamilton*
1813–1822	Easton School, Easton.	*Hannah E. Moore*
		Catherine Withcim
1814	Chesterford School, near West Chester.	*Lydia Burroughs*
1818	Ellisburg School, near Philadelphia.	*Mary Coles*
1819	Mrs. Buchanan's School, Wrightsville.	*Mary Fitz*
	Dame School, Philadelphia.	*Mary Magdalen Wolf*
1824	Ruth H. Redman's School, "Strawsburg" [Strasburg].	*Elizabeth Herrher*
1825	Mrs. Leah Meguire's School, Harrisburg.	*Ann E. Kelley*
1827	Northern Liberty School, Philadelphia?	*Jane E. Sharp*
1830	West Chester School.	*Juli Ann Crispin*
1833	Mrs. D. H. Maundel's Seminary, 101 South 5th Street, Philadelphia.	*Victorine Delacroix*

DELAWARE

1775 on	Miss Debby Thelwell, Wilmington. Taught first in her father's school. Later, she and her sister taught many years.	
1785	Ann Askew, teacher, Wilmington.	*Ann Tatnall*
1788	Mme. Abigail Giles, an Englishwoman, Newcastle County.	*Susanna James*
1790 on	Mrs. Elizabeth West, Wilmington.	
1798	"Old Boarding School", Wilmington, taught by	
	1797 Mr. Crips	
	1798–1809 Mrs. Capron of Philadelphia q.v.	
	1809 Joshua Maule and Eli Hilles	
	Later, Eli and Samuel Hilles	
	1828 Samuel Hilles	
1804	Southern Boarding School.	*Eliza Tatnall Sipples*
		Mary Middleton
1809	Frankford School.	*C. Sanderson*
1813–1824	Wilmington Boarding School.	*M. Woodnut*
		Mary Gaw Janvier
1827	Middletown Academy.	
	Girls' School. Miss Isabella Anderson, preceptress.	

MARYLAND

1754	Mary Salisbury, teacher, Annapolis.	
1795–1821	Chesterfield School.	*Jane Henderson*
		Abigail Decou
		Margaret Decou
1798	Easton Academy, Talbot County.	
1802	Eleanor Norland, governess.	*Teresia Fenwick*
1811	Amelia Hough and Mary Lawrence, teachers, Waterford.	*Amy Ann Phillips*

1813 Mary Robertson, teacher.
"Mary Clapham for Mary Robertson. 1813 or 1815 *S.E.Z.* and *M.C.* [Mary Clapham?] through the industry of two dear girls I have been made the proprietor of this very excellent sampler to whom I feel much indebted. M. Robertson, 1816."

1818 Mary Walden's School, Baltimore. *Caroline Vaughan*

VIRGINIA

1809 Piney Grove School, Charles City County. *Tulliania Evans*

NORTH CAROLINA

1805 Salem Female Academy (Moravian School), Salem. *Dovey Winslow Wilson*

1828 Hillsboro School. *Mary T. Lindsay*

KENTUCKY

1808 Domestic Academy, Washington. *Matilda Ward*
Mrs. Keats, principal.

1810 Mrs. Mary Scotts' School, Louisville. *Martha Malvina Miledge Jones*

TENNESSEE

1832 Carthage Female Institute. *Penelope C. Williams*

OHIO

1807 Waynesville School, Waynesville. *Margaret Holloway*

UNIDENTIFIED

1782 Miss Brunton, teacher. *Esther Hoston*

1795 "School of Industry." *Jane Eglow*

1802 Mrs. Woodson's School. *Mary Elizabeth Porthress Doswell*

1814 Laurel Grove School. *Beulah Barton*
Hannah Barton, preceptress.

1816 Polly Huntington, teacher, Lebanon. *Caroline Walton*

1819 Miss Moody's School. *Caroline Carleton*

1819 "Lydia Sata Lee, Instructress." *Mary Chapel*

Samplers probably worked in the same School:

HUNTING SCENE. *Sukey Makepeace*
Grace Welch
Abigail Mears

SCENE WITH BLACK BACKGROUNDS. *Mary Russell*
Patty Coggeshall

MATERIALS, DESIGNS, STITCHES

IN 1738, Sarah Troup embroidered on her sampler, "Let none despise the criss-cross row." It is in this spirit that we would have our readers approach the consideration of the material, design, and stitchery of the sampler. For we are here not considering great works of art, but the spontaneous growth of a handicraft in a very young civilization.

Of the three subjects under discussion, the first is by far the easiest to approach, for we have a very solid foundation in the fact that the greater number of samplers in all periods were worked upon linen. The English writers on samplers tell us that the early hand-looms wove linen but eight or nine inches wide, and adduce from the fact the reason that the early sampler was long and narrow. Perhaps that may have been the case with those very earliest examples, which have so completely disappeared, but a study of the seventeenth century sampler does not bear out the contention. Very many of the samplers of that period have the selvage at the top and bottom. The continental looms were much broader than the English, and the linen for these samplers was evidently imported. Perhaps the truth is that the narrow English loom, and the fact that eight inches was amply wide to accommodate the ordinary repeat pattern, set the style. So the English embroiderer was bound by convention to the narrow form, even though the wide continental linen allowed more freedom in shape and size. Gradually, as the English wove wider linen, the long sampler gave place to the square, and the latter quarter of the eighteenth century saw the final passing of the narrow type. In the latter part of the seventeenth century, the English began to use a mustard colored linen, not very attractive to our modern taste. Toward the middle of the eighteenth century it became quite common. This material was not so much used in America, though there are some examples. The American linen, of the same color, was coarser and rougher than the English,

PLATE CXXI

ARMS OF THE HON. GEORGE BOYD, of Portsmouth, N. H., impaling Brewster
Hatchment embroidered by Submit Boyd, cir. 1795
Owned by Barrett Wendell, Esq.

PLATE CXXII

ARMS OF GOVERNOR THOMAS FITCH, of Connecticut, impaling Hall. Cir. 1773
Owned by Miss Margaret W. Cushing

which was often quite fine enough for the making of lace samplers. We, on the other hand, sometimes used a dark green linen, which is at times mournful and at times artistic. The two Brierly sisters used a light blue.

We have the record of one sampler done on brown linen in different shades of brown and dark green. The result must be rather monotonous and subdued. The linen used was not always the plain homespun which forms the background of the great majority, for once in a while the more elaborately woven "bird's-eye" linen was used. Elizabeth Lea, who lived in Delaware, embroidered on this kind of linen in 1752.

Some of the early samplers were bound with silk tape. Hannah Wiggins did it in 1730; and the habit was never quite abandoned, though the later ribbons were sometimes put on with gathers, and were generally wider than Hannah Wiggins's, which was only half an inch wide. Many put rosettes in the corners, and some children sewed their samplers to paper. Perhaps these were ancient forms of *passe-partout,* and used when parents were too poor or too indifferent to frame the children's work.

Another background was used in England, called "catgut," a kind of canvas, but whether we in America ever used it or not is quite difficult to answer. I fancy that the material is not well known, because in the "Vicar of Wakefield," where a young lady was spoken of as "flourishing upon catgut," most people inferred that she played the violin. One critic, however, discovered that she did no such unmaidenly act. This was merely another way of saying that she did embroidery on canvas, with "flourishing thread," which is a flat, very shiny linen thread. "Flourishing" was advertised to be taught in Boston as early as 1716.

The English began, about 1750, to use tammy cloth and, sad to say, some of our ancestors also used it. This, being of wool, did all the evil things it could: it shrank, it curled, and it furnished food for moths. The stuff itself resembles mohair in its sheen, and was probably chosen because the threads were more even than in linen, and finer in quality. The sampler, when just finished, was probably much more symmetrical and perhaps more attractive than one done on linen. Cotton was sometimes used, but never imparted an elegant appearance. Canary canvas and Penelope canvas were used in the nineteenth century. The finest samplers were embroidered on bolting-cloth, a very transparent woolen gauze, used to bolt flour. This form of sampler was, of course, as useful as food for moths as were those on tammy cloth, and as a result many lovely ones have regrettable holes. Satin was sparingly used for samplers proper, being as a rule reserved for the "mourning pieces," with tombs, willow trees, and mourning shepherdesses. Satin was better for these doleful pictures because usually the tombs and their inscriptions were painted in, and satin was a better medium than anything else for the combination of paint and embroidery. One sampler at least was made on "lute-string" silk. A few of the samplers in Providence, Rhode Island, by a skillful running of blue silk thread from the back, give the effect of a combination of silk and linen that is very charming and quite misleading, if only the right side is seen.

The thread that was used, whatever its nature—silk, linen, wool, or cotton—was always home dyed, and so the resulting color was dependent upon the taste and skill of the dyer. The colors were made from our native herbs, from log-wood, cochineal, and indigo from overseas, from saffron, from the *planta genesta,* which gave its name to a line of Kings, and which now runs wild in Essex County, Massachusetts.

Linen thread was sometimes used, and crewels are known on samplers as early as 1686, but neither of these threads ever really rivalled silk as a medium. Crewels appear somewhat sporadically. Alice Woodwell, of Newburyport, in 1760, used them, and so did Betty Tippit in 1774. This latter sampler is the most remarkable that has come to be recorded. It is about six *feet* long and ten inches wide, and done on rather heavy cotton. The whole is divided into squares, and on each is a crewel-worked flower, fern, or branch. Across the top, running the whole length of the sampler, is embroidered in cross-stitch the verse, "Betty Tippit is my name, and with my needle I wroght the same" etc., with her age, eighteen, and the year, 1774.

Some of the silk thread on our American samplers shows a queer kinkiness, which looks as if it had been twisted in large hanks, and later ravelled to finer thread for use. Some of this silk is on samplers which can be traced back to Essex County, Massachusetts, particularly to the environs of Salem, whence ships went to all parts of the world. The hint has come to us that such silk can be seen in Japan and China, and so we wonder whether these Essex County maidens were not using early spoils from the Orient, brought overseas by Yankee captains. The Dutch of Pennsylvania also used it, and they were traders, too.

The effect of this kinky silk is very attractive, and gives a more interesting surface than the smooth or tightly twisted silks. It is nearly always used in very long stitches,* couched sometimes, and sometimes left free. All the threads they used were wound on cardboard "stars," or on those lovely ivory winders that our merchants brought from China. Most of our great-grandmothers used a gold thimble, which they had inherited, cherished, and handed down till the top was so worn as to let the needle through, instead of pushing it, as its duty was. Some of them had no top at all, like a tailor's thimble. Sometimes chenille was added to make the sampler more elaborate, but this was general only after 1800.

As we turn to design we are already plunged into the midst of a controversy, which depends so much more on tradition than on fact, that it seems in a fair way to continue forever. This is the controversy as to the origin of English design. With a rather grim lack of confidence in English ability to evolve things artistic, the experts seek foreign influence for everything. Some say it is all Italian, and others, looking to broader fields, contend that Holland, Spain, France, Persia, and the other countries may also have contributed. Again some English experts agree that the purely lace sampler antedates those in colored work, while others maintain that those that have the

---

* See Sarah Stivour's School. Sally Witt, Plate xci, and Nabby Mason Peele, Plate xc.

isolated designs in color are the oldest of all. As there are none at all that can be dated with accuracy until about 1610, when Anne Gower, the wife of Governor Endecott, of the Massachusetts Bay Colony, made hers, neither side can prove its claim. So it will be better to say that these three kinds exist, separate often, and oftentimes all upon the same sampler.

The lace sampler certainly was very early, and was the earliest to disappear. Tradition tells us that Catherine of Aragon taught the Bedfordshire women *punto tagliato,* and whether the tradition is true or not, that form appears very early, combined with *punto tirato* and some filet. *Punto tagliato* is lace made on linen, where both the warp and the woof are removed; *punto tirato* is also made on linen, where the threads are drawn, but part of the warp and woof remain to be used as a background. With filet we are all familiar.

The lace sampler, of either kind, was always exquisitely done, particularly about the middle of the seventeenth century, which seems to mark the crest of the wave of all sampler work. These lace samplers contained repeating designs, in almost every case, and so they were worked in bands across the linen. The *punto tagliato* was often enhanced by raised petals of flowers,* and the coats and draperies on small human figures made separately and sewed on. This was not often done in America, but perhaps it is unfair to generalize too much on the few American seventeenth century samplers that remain to us. One always has the feeling that there must have been many more, but that the Indian wars, with their burning houses, and the destruction which comes of careless and indifferent owners through two centuries and more, have diminished them most unfortunately. The lace sampler as developed by the English showed designs that were beautiful and varied, and had real distinction. We in America in the seventeenth century fell rather below the best English level. Our samplers were somewhat shorter, and were not always as elaborate in design.

Turning now to the embroidered design, we find that the seven-

* See Sarah Lord, Plate iii, and the Fleetwood sampler, Plate viii.

teenth and the early eighteenth centuries give us two kinds, one done in white, and one in color. The white embroidery was nearly always done in satin-stitch, in repeating geometric designs. Anne Gower's* sampler is a good example in the seventeenth century, and Grace Tay's† in the eighteenth. This form fell into disuse about the time that the lace sampler did, so that its history in America was nearly over in 1720. We seldom find white thread used in the later samplers, except in darning or stocking stitch. Mary Gill's‡ sampler, done in white cotton, is an illustration of its later use.

In the seventeenth century the designs in color were most complicated and elaborate, and the stitches used were many. The designs were always conventionalized flowers or fruits, partly because the angular cross-stitch and tent-stitch were the most common means of expression, and partly because a repeating motif demanded it. The commonest designs were the rose, "Indian pink," trefoil, strawberry, acorn, and the "Tree of Life." These and others were mixed into most complicated combinations. The designs are sometimes so conventionalized that their origin is lost in obscurity. In addition, there were patterns of a purely geometric character. The popularity of the acorn is supposed to have arisen from King Charles's adventure in the "Boscabelle Oak." Be this as it may, the acorn and strawberry were soon so distorted from their pristine form that it is a bold person who would say with definiteness which is which. Strawberry and acorn became so conventionalized that they resembled each other more than they resembled their original. Two other designs on these early samplers are worth a word, for both so suddenly disappear. The first are the famous "boxers," which can be seen on Elizabeth Robert's§ sampler. Of course, their pose is not the least like a boxer's, though their attitude is always the same. They vary only in what they hold in their upraised hand. They are akin in reality to the Greek Erotes, and the Renaissance Cupids. The second is a design which may be seen in Mary Hudson's‖ sampler near the middle, which resembles an S on

* Plate i.
† Plate x.
‡ Plate lxix.
§ See Plate vi
‖ See Plate ix.

a V-shaped running design. This is called by some the "Stuart S," but another critic, still grudging to England any originality, shows this same design on an Italian towel of an earlier period.

These seventeenth and early eighteenth century samplers are less interesting from a pictorial point of view than many that succeeded them, but from the point of view of design, of use, and of needlework, they make the latter hide their diminished heads.

With the coming of the eighteenth century, many changes came to the American sampler. The original use had passed away, and the new sampler was an exercise for children, and had no longer a place in the maiden's dower chest. So both in England and America the complicated and lovely repeat designs were abandoned, and after a dreary period of alphabets, horn-book style, we emerge again with a new form, with new designs, founded on the old ones, but simplified for childish fingers. In the sampler which contained alphabets only, the cross-border lingered in a debased state, becoming a simple row of cross-stitch or Greek fret, a poor substitute for its former glory. So the sampler, originally made to fix and retain a pattern for later use, was now become a childish exhibition of skill. In England the result was what one writer calls a "thoroughly mixed affair," with isolated bits of pattern strewn across its surface.

About 1725 the border became a frame, and matching the corners tortured the childish mind and fingers. So about this time the old English cross-borders reappear in simple form, and again strawberry, "Indian pink," rose, tulip, and the rest bloom modestly upon our samplers. It would be interesting to know whence these new patterns sprung, for they are entirely lacking in the elaborateness of the earlier century. Yet it seems as if they must, even in earlier days, have lingered somewhere in the background, for the English and American borders of this period resemble each other in their general appearance too closely not to have been developed from a common source. Perhaps after all it was only a combination of nature and the exigencies of an angular stitch which forced both nations to a common result.

Drawings have been made from the many pictures which we have,

PLATE CXXIII

<small>Embroidered Arms of the Gilbert Family</small>
Owned by Mrs. Horatio J. Gilbert

PLATE CXXIV

THE ARMS OF E. DAVIS
Owned by the Rev. Glenn Tilley Morse
Plate presented by Mrs. Perry, Miss Cushing, and Miss Vaughan

and from available samplers, of the strawberry, "Indian pink," rose,*
and other flowers as they appear chronologically upon the samplers.
This was done with the hope that in some way the series would show
development, but the hope was an *ignis fatuus*. No particular evolution is traceable in any of the various forms. Often the same type
persists through a long period, and some are never even approximately
repeated. The Rhode Island School of Design at Providence owns
a sampler made in 1730 by Abigail Pinniger.† It is lovely, though
unfinished, and is an example of the hesitation between the new
eighteenth century and the old seventeenth century types. It has one
cross-border of rose, which was echoed with marvelous exactitude fifty-
three years later, when Ann Almy‡ made her sampler in 1783. Moreover, she copied the earlier type of sampler, containing nothing but
cross-borders throughout, and without the date to guide us it would
inevitably be put in the earlier period. All of which goes to prove
that those who would date samplers which have no date must not be
too sure, but should add that saving clause with which we swear, "to
the best of my knowledge and belief." This same amazing persistence
in type may be seen if one examines the samplers of Sarah Howell, of
Philadelphia, in 1731, and Ann Tatnall, of Wilmington, Delaware,
in 1785. The arrangement is the same; both are framed by "Indian
pink." While the cross-borders are not identical, they differ no more
than would the borders on the samplers of two girls, embroidered under
the same teacher. (See Plate cxi.)

The earlier borders, done in cross-stitch, follow the angular lines
which the stitch demands, but very soon some of the children shook
off the shackles of the stitch, and less stiff vines of a combined satin and
stem-stitch came into favor. The cross-stitch border was, however,
never abandoned. So passion-flowers and forget-me-nots rioted on
the same vine, and blue roses vied with green pinks upon the same
parent stem. We find lovely grapevines and morning glory borders
in the nineteenth century; in fact, there were few flowers which were
sufficiently simple to copy which were not used. The cross-border

* See Plates cxvii, cxviii, cxix.
† See Plate cxii.
‡ See Plate cxii.

of the olden time had entirely passed away in the nineteenth century, or survived only like a thin and tired ghost in the bare cross-stitch division lines between the letters of the alphabet.

Just before the Revolution there was a revival of the lace sampler, this time in "hollie point." Jane Humphreys* (1763) and Mary Clark† (1783) are both good examples of this work. In 1783 we find, too, a drawnwork sampler, and a little later "darned lace"‡ samplers came into vogue. At about this same time there was a tendency, shown best, perhaps, in Sarah Bancroft's sampler (see Cover), to outline the design in black or some dark color. Appha Woodman§ did it, not in cross-stitch, but stem-stitch. Others who copied this method of accentuating the design were Mary J. Condon and Mehitable Foster. The custom never became popular.

The nineteenth century designs echoed those of the century before and added some new ones. In a few instances they elaborated the common forms to almost the same degree that the seventeenth century workers did, but less elegantly.

The stitches that were used throughout the whole period are few; cross-stitch, tent-stitch or petit-point, satin-stitch, and eyelet pretty much comprise the list. Cross-stitch and tent-stitch, with their kindred tapestry stitches learned from the older embroideries, were the foundation. The seventeenth century added back-stitch, which is much like the hand-stitching that our grandmothers did, and rope-stitch, which is done in the opposite direction to stem-stitch, making a more solid line. All through the period the square eyelet-stitch vied in popularity with cross-stitch for making alphabets, and few indeed were the samplers which did not contain one alphabet worked in it. Satin-stitch, originally used mostly in white embroidery, had great vogue in the eighteenth century in making a saw-tooth border-frame for the alphabets, inside the more elaborate floral one. Queen-stitch next came into vogue, and was used, though rather sparingly, until the sampler perished.

* See Plate xxxvi.
† See Plate xxxvii.
‡ See Plate lxix.
§ See Plate cxiii.

During about a decade, at the time of the Revolution, Sarah Stivour, who had a school near or in Salem, used a long-stitch to indicate sky, clouds, and grass.* These stitches were sometimes two or three inches in length, and were always placed diagonally. The outer edge was irregular, and upon this were perched men, women, and sheep. Sometimes the sheep disporting thereon have the aspect of drowning in a dark green sea.

As one contemplates the millions of stitches worked by these young girls, one wonders what their thoughts were as they sewed them. Children are conventional and conservative beings, and so, perhaps, the universality of the employment kept most from boredom. But there must always have been a residuum of the discouraged, and of the rebels "who hated every stitch," and so made their samplers badly or left them unfinished if they could possibly shirk their task. A plodding schoolmistress, whose whole artistic horizon was bordered by alphabets and numerals, must have been torture to an imaginative child, who saw all nature to mimic with her colored threads.

ETHEL STANWOOD BOLTON.

SOME DESIGNS USED

Tree of life   17th century
Fleur-de-lis   17th century
Indian Pink
Pineapple   17th century
Acorns, "Boscabelle oak"
Stuart S   17th century
Strawberry
Rose
Rosebud
Greek fret and geometrical designs
"Wall of Troy"

Trefoil
Greek cross
Tulip
Honeysuckle
Grapevine, after 1800
Morning glory, after 1800
Passion flowers
Forget-me-nots
Fuchsia, 1740
Vine with berries, 1763
Clover

* See Plates xc and xci.

SOME OF THE STITCHES USED

Cross stitch
Tent stitch or petit point
Satin stitch
Rope stitch
Stem stitch
Eyelet stitch
Chain stitch
French knot
Queen stitch
Bullion stitch
Van Dyke stitch
Cat stitch
Hem stitch
Split stitch

Long and short stitch
"Sarah Stivour's" stitch
Tapestry stitch
Darning stitches
Stocking stitch
Punch work
Two-sided line stitch
Flat stitch
Feather stitch   1716
Chenille
"Lazy Daisy" (Mary Train)
                    1795
Knotted stitch (Desire Williams)
                    1754

EMBROIDERED HERALDRY

REVENGEFUL LAERTES, speaking of his father's funeral, said that

"No Trophee, Sword, nor Hatchment o'er his bones
No Noble rite, nor formal ostentation,
Cry to be heard."

When Shakespeare lived, respect for the dead was to be shown in no small measure by display at the funeral. The dramatist had not heard of the modern biographical dictionary which can assuage grief if one is willing to make a liberal expenditure for a memoir and engraved portrait. So it was that the "ordering and marshalling of funerals" had come to be a part of the ostentation of pride as well as of grief. So much so that strife between the two reapers of harvests in these endeavors—the Kings of Arms, on the one side (those who tried to regulate the use of heraldic devices), and funeral undertakers and heraldic painters, on the other—came to blows. Parliament sided with the Kings of Arms in their attempt at a monopoly of the funeral perquisites, but their decision conflicted with the charter of the Painter-stainers Company, and the battle went on. Persons of standing often buried their dead in private, to avoid extortionate fees; while "others again"—to quote Edmondson—"under the notion of their dying seized of estates, had hatchments publicly affixed to the fronts of their houses." In the Netherlands the hatchment, or family coat of arms on a lozenge, was "sett upon theire doores for a yeare following, and the widowe so long kept her house." This custom was observed by Fynes Moryson in his "Itinerary of the Year 1617," and the Dutch of New Netherland may have brought the custom with them. Little, however, has yet been recorded of heraldic embroidery in New York or the South, although much has been written of social life there in Colonial times.

Hatchments were often painted on wood, like those to be seen in English churches. At St. Chad's, in Shrewsbury, for example, there are said to be over one hundred of these memorials of the dead. An excellent example is that brought to this country by William Avery, and now in the rooms of the Dedham Historical Society. More often, no doubt, they were done on canvas stretched over a wooden frame, to be carried in a funeral procession and then hung for a time in the church. The account of the funeral of Colonel Samuel Shrimpton, in 1697/8, mentions heraldic hatchments and death's heads as part of the panoply of grief. The hatchment was in the form of a diamond or lozenge, painted black, with the arms in color upon it in a shield. For a married person it was the custom to divide the lozenge, as well as the shield, by a perpendicular line, and to blacken the half of the lozenge which included the arms of the deceased person. The husband's arms were in the left half of the shield, and the wife's arms in the right half, as seen by the observer. (Heraldry, it should be said, views the coat as on an owner's breast, and the side next his right hand is the dexter side of the shield.)

How far an embroidered hatchment was in actual use at funerals in America cannot be known until specific statements from contemporary Colonial letters and diaries are brought together for study. Perhaps it was the reverential needlework of a gentle lady—an echo merely of an ancient custom, just as the giving of the right hand in greeting is a survival of the ancient sign of trust when one gave over the sword arm into the keeping of another, standing defenseless for the moment.

We may be certain, however, that on both sides of the Atlantic embroidered heraldry was in vogue. In an old English romance, reference is made to the custom of embroidering heraldic devices on the gowns of ladies:

> "A Coronell on hur hedd set,
> Hur Clothys with bestes and byrdes wer bete
> all aboute for pryde."

Hulme, in his "History of Heraldry," writes:

> "In the palmy days of heraldry ladies, if unmarried, wore the paternal arms embroidered on their robes, or if married, the paternal arms and those of their husband, one on either half of their dress, so that in old brasses, stained glass, etc.,

we may see the whole of the dexter half of the figure covered with certain devices, while the sinister half has entirely different forms and tinctures."

In 1773, Rebecca Robins sent to her uncle, John Rowe, the Boston merchant and diarist, an heraldic embroidery which she did at Exeter, in old England. The three little paschal lambs still carry their silver staves and banners, as they did in Rebecca's day. As early as 1715, we find Elizabeth, daughter of Captain John Charnock, of Boston, doing a hatchment of the Charnock arms impaling the arms of King, her mother. One or two examples in the seventeenth century might be named, but the eighteenth century was the period of heraldic embroidery in America. With many of these works of young hands there went stories of romance, if we could but conjure them back from the past. With more, perhaps, were tales of filial sorrow.

It is strange that the custom of embroidering arms seems to have been limited to New England in the New World. So far, none have been found without its bounds, and the period from 1750 to 1770 was by far the most prolific. One advertisement in the *Boston Chronicle* tells us who may have been responsible for the many hatchments and coats of arms which are found in and around Boston:

"Amy & Elizabeth Cumings"
"Hereby inform the public, that they have *This day opened their School* for instructing young ladies in embroidery, Coats of arms, Dresden, Catgut, and all sorts of coloured work, at their house on Corn Hill opposite the Old Brick Meeting, where they have to see, a great variety of Goods suitable for the season. Also blue *China* and yellow ware." (May 1st, 1769.)

Hatchments were most often done on a frame in what is known as ecclesiastical embroidery. They used gold and silver, and wonderful smooth silks. In nearly every case the whole surface was covered with silk, couched or done in long and short stitch, though some— such as Amy Davis's—were entirely worked in cross-stitch. A few combine the two forms. (See Plate cxxiv.)

Captain Nicholas Johnson, of Newburyport, in one of his voyages, in 1773, along the New England coast, came one day upon a deserted ship—perhaps

"As idle as a painted ship
Upon a painted ocean"

or as weird and unhuman as the schooner, with shivering sails, watched by the lad of "Treasure Island" from his unstable coracle. Climbing on board, Johnson took from the cabin an embroidered hatchment, described in heraldic language as "Vert a chevron argent between three leopards' faces of the second. Impaling argent a chevron sable between three columbines azure." Above was a leopard's face pierced by a cruel sword. These three silver leopards' faces proclaim the Fitch family, and the columbine is the symbol of the Hall family. We find that this is probably the hatchment—or, to use the original term, the achievement—of Governor Thomas Fitch, of Connecticut, who married Hannah, daughter of Richard Hall, of New Haven. Was it wrought by the fair Hannah or by a daughter? And where was it bound on its lonely voyage? What a wealth of questioning a mystery like this may call forth! Here and in other examples the mantling or foliage is gracefully and effectively embroidered, showing the color and form with delightful precision. In the case of heraldic pictures (not in a diamond-shaped frame), the decoration is sometimes even more delicate, as in the shields of the Norwood or Gilbert families. (See Plates cxxi, cxxii, cxxiii, cxxv, cxxvi.)

Our ancestors knew little of the rules of heraldry and less about "the right to bear arms," a subject for endless controversy and of little profit. The distinguished Page family, of Virginia, complacently permitted the Pagit arms to adorn a Page family tomb. Thomas Jefferson, the great Democrat, sent to London, in 1771, for his family arms; and ordered his agent, in case none could be found, "to become a purchaser, haveing Sterne's word for it that a coat-of-arms may be purchased as cheap as any other coat." The love of symbolism is inborn, and "the right to bear arms" is only limited in our day by leisure to cultivate a taste for good design along heraldic lines, and a willingness to difference a coat so that it shall not give a false impression as to the ancestry of the user. Even these ideals our Colonial needle worker did not always take to heart. But, such as they are, these examples of heraldic embroidery have a human interest above and beyond that of most Colonial handicraft.

ETHEL STANWOOD BOLTON.

PLATE CXXV

THE IVES ARMS
Embroidered by Rebecca Ives, cir. 1770
Owned by Mrs. Robert Hale Bancroft

PLATE CXXVI

ARMS OF THE HON. HARRISON GRAY, Treasurer of the Province
of Massachusetts, impaling Lewis
Hatchment embroidered by Elizabeth Tracy
Owned by Mrs. John H. Morison

REGISTER OF EMBROIDERED ARMS

BILLINGS

Gules a fleur-de-lis or, a canton argent.

Crest: a buck trippant proper, an arrow in its breast.

"Wrought by Mrs. Eunice (Minot) Glover, mother of John I. Glover, when 15 years old; born Sept. 28, 1781. Her mother's maiden name was Eunice Billings." Cross and Kensington stitches. Framed. C. F. Libbie & Co. auction, Boston, Dec. 6, 1915.

BOYD

Quarterly: 1 and 4, Argent a fess chequy gules and or; 2 and 3, sable a chevron ermine between 3 six pointed estoiles argent (Brewster).

Tapestry hatchment, signed "Submit Boyd", daughter of George Boyd.

Owned by Barrett Wendell, Esq., Portsmouth, N. H. Framed.

Illustrated. Plate cxxi.

CHARNOCK

Argent on a bend sable 3 crosses crosslet of the field.

Impaling: Sable a lion rampant between 3 crosses crosslet or (King).

A hatchment, 1715, by Elizabeth, daughter of Captain John Charnock, of Boston. Mrs. Mary Charnock was daughter of Captain Ralph King, son of Daniel, of Watford, Herts, and Lynn, Mass.

CHEEVER

Per bend dancettée argent and azure, 3 cinquefoils, 2 in chief and 1 in base, counterchanged.

Crest: a stag's head couped.

Embroidered by M[ary] C[heever], 1700. Owned by Mrs. William S. Eaton.

CHESTER

Ermine on a chief sable a griffin passant or.

Miss Sarah Perkins, of Norwich, Conn., sold this embroidered hatchment to W. N. Andrews of that town. It was seen in his shop by Mrs. Coe.

CONEY. See FOXCROFT

CURWEN

Argent a fret gules, on a chief gules a crescent argent.

Impaling: argent a chevron sable between 3 crosses crosslet fitchée (Russell).

Crest: a demi unicorn erased.

Embroidered hatchment, Essex Institute, Salem, Mass.

CUSHING

Quarterly: 1 and 4, [Gules] an eagle displayed [argent] (Cosyn); 2 and 3, [Gules] two dexter hands couped [argent] each bendways, fingers up, one in the 2d quarter, one in the 3d; a canton chequy [or and azure]. (Denvers, of County Norfolk.)

Crest: Two lion's gambs erect erased [sable] supporting a marquis's cor. [or] from which hangs a heart [gules].

An embroidered hatchment 17 inches square, owned by the Misses Newman, Concord, Mass. Deborah Cushing m. Henry Newman, 1781. Cross-stitch and petit point.

The same arms in a hatchment, but embroidered in satin and split-stitch, and with elaborate mantling, is owned by the Misses Vose, of Milton, Mass., and Providence, R. I.

CUTTS?

Argent on a bend engrailed sable, 3 plates.

Crest: a bird rising.

Owned by Mrs. William S. Eaton.

DAVIS

Or a chevron azure between 3 pierced mullets sable.

Crest: a swan rising proper.

Also two supporters in liberty caps, brown coats, and blue boots. Signed Amy Davis, 1753, "being the arms of E Davis And is the Paternal Coat Armour of the Right Honorable Thomas Davis, Kt. Lord Mayar of London Anno 1677." On a stand and used as a fire screen. There was a Sir Thomas Davies, sheriff, 1667.

Owned by Rev. Glenn Tilley Morse, West Newbury, Mass.

Illustrated in color. Plate cxxiv.

DOANE

Azure 2 bars argent [embroidered dark]; on a bend over all gules 3 arrows points downward in bend argent [embroidered] dark.

Impaling: sable [embroidered bluish] a chevron ermine [embroidered or] between 2 lions passant argent [embroidered dark]. (Rich.)

Crest: a sheaf of arrows, points down, or, bound [gules].

Hatchment by Hope Doane, 1750–1830, later wife of Samuel Savage, of Barnstable, Mass. Embroidery, very elaborate.

Henry Savage, Esq., Camden, S. C., from Samuel Savage Shaw, Esq., Boston. Hope Doane was the daughter of Colonel Isaiah and Hope (Rich) Doane, of Cape Cod, Mass.

DUNCAN

Gules a chevron or between in chief two cinquefoils and in base a hunting horn argent [garnished azure].

Crest: a ship with 3 sails spread on foremast, 2 on main and one on mizzen mast.

Motto: Disce pati.

Embroidered hatchment made by Isabella Duncan, daughter of Mrs. Isabella Caldwell Duncan. Owned by Mrs. Richard Morgan, Plymouth, Mass., daughter of Judge Davis. The red has faded.

ELLIS

Per chevron sable and gules a chevron or between 3 fleurs-de-lis argent.

Embroidery by Elizabeth Ellis, born 1732, daughter of Dr. Edward Ellis, of Boston.

Owned by Henry W. Montague, Esq., Boston.

FISK

[   ] three battle axes erect, turned to the sinister, and in chief a crescent.
Crest: an arrow erect, point down.

"The name of Fisk" below. Embroidered hatchment owned by a grandson of General John Fisk, of Salem. Possibly from a painting by John Coles. Gibbs arms (?), but not their crest.
Owned by the Essex Institute, Salem, Mass.

FITCH

Vert (?) a chevron between 3 leopards faces argent.
Impaling: argent a chevron sable between 3 columbines azure (Hall).
Crest: a leopard's face of the field, pierced in the mouth by a sword bend-sinister ways.

Embroidered hatchment found about 1773 at sea, in the cabin of a deserted ship, by Captain Nicholas Johnson, of Newburyport. Owned by his great-granddaughter, Miss Margaret W. Cushing, Newburyport. Arms of Governor Thomas Fitch, who married Hannah, daughter of Richard Hall, of New Haven.
Illustrated. Plate cxxii.

FORBES

Azure a cross pattée argent between 3 bears' heads couped argent muzzled gules.
Crest: a cross of the field.

Hatchment embroidered in silk by Mary Forbes Coffin, in Boston; born 1774, married Henry Phelps, 1795. Owned by Mrs. Charles C. Goodwin, Lexington, Mass.

FOXCROFT

Quarterly per chevron sable and azure a chevron between 3 foxes' heads or.
Crest: A head of the arms.

Embroidered framed arms about 40 by 32 inches. The arms of Coney, Sable, on a fess between 8 conies dormant or, as many escallops of the field, occupy the top of the above shield, the third coney being placed between the two foxes' heads. Elaborate roses and lilies surround the shield. Owned by the Misses Gertrude and Agnes Brooks, Marlborough Street, Boston, daughters of William Gray Brooks.

Francis Foxcroft, of Cambridge, married, 1722, Mehitable Coney. Their daughter married Lieutenant Governor Samuel Phillips, founder of Phillips Academy, Andover, Mass.

GARDNER

[Azure] a chevron [ermine?] between 3 griffins' heads erased [argent?].
Crest: a griffin's head.

For Samuel Gardner (Harvard College, 1732), of Salem.
Embroidered hatchment by Lois Barnard, made before 1769.
Picture in Pickering Genealogy (1897), Volume 1, page 91.
Same arms on a silver teapot owned, 1897, by Colonel Henry Lee, Brookline, Mass.

GERRISH

Argent a dart between 3 escallops sable.

Embroidered hatchment by Elizabeth Gerrish. Owned by the late Mrs. Gordon Prince, Boston.

GILBERT

Azure a chevron ermine between 3 eagles displayed or.

Crest: a lion rampant.

"By the name of Gilbert" and palm branches (?) with pendant chains.
An embroidery, framed, owned by Mrs. Horatio J. Gilbert, Milton, Mass.
Illustrated.   Plate cxxiii.

GRAY

Gules a lion rampant argent within a bordure engrailed of the second.

Impaling: sable a chevron between 3 trefoils slipped argent (Lewis).

Crest: a stag trippant.

Embroidered hatchment by Elizabeth Gray, who married Samuel Alexander Otis, in
1764. Her father, Hon. Harrison Gray, married Elizabeth Lewis, in 1734. Owned by
Mrs. John H. Morison, Boston.
Illustrated.   Plate cxxvi.

IVES

Argent a chevron sable between 3 Moors' heads in profile erased proper.

Embroidered arms of Robert Hale Ives, 22 x 15 inches, worked by his sister, Mrs.
Rebecca Ives Gilman, 1746–1823. Owned by Mrs. Robert H. Bancroft, Boston.
Illustrated.   Plate cxxv.

JONES

Sable a stag statant argent attired or.

No crest.

"By the name of Jones". Embroidered hatchment, framed, arms of Colonel Elisha
Jones, of Weston, Mass., great-grandfather of Henry D. Thoreau, writer. Owned by
Concord (Mass.) Antiquarian Society.

NORWOOD

Ermine a cross engrailed gules.

Crest: a demi lion rampant and erased argent, holding in his gambs a palm branch vert.

"By the name of Norwood" and palm branches [not after Coles]. Framed embroidery by Judith Norwood, of Gloucester, Mass., who died in 1762. Owned by Mrs. J. L.
Stevens, Milton, Mass.

PEIRCE

Argent a fess humettée gules between three ravens rising sable.

Crest: a raven or.

Embroidered hatchment in the Nichols House, Salem, Mass., made by Sarah, daughter
of Jerathmiel Peirce, in 1796. Arms of Peirce, of London.

PICKERING

Ermine a lion rampant [azure] crowned [or].

Embroidered hatchment by [Mrs.] Sarah Pickering [Clarke], 1758.
Picture in Pickering Genealogy, 1897, Volume 1, page 11.

PRESCOTT

Quarterly 1 and 4: Salle a chevron between three owls argent. 2 and 3: Ermine a cross raguly argent [gules?] (Lawrence).

Crest: Out of a mural crown a head (boar's?) erased.

Embroidered hatchment, 24 x 24, framed, given to Groton (Mass.) Historical Society by Rev. F. J. Walton, whose wife is a descendant of the Rev. Daniel Chaplin, who m., 1779, Susanna (b. 1757), daughter of Hon. James and Susanna (Lawrence) Prescott, of Groton.

QUINCY

Gules 7 mascles 3, 3, 1 or.

Impaling: Azure a chevron between 3 crosses crosslet fitchée within a bordure engrailed or (Sturgis).

Crest: A plume of ostrich feathers (?).

Embroidered hatchment owned by Mrs. Josiah Quincy, Boston. An early Josiah Quincy married, 1733, Hannah, daughter of John Sturgis, of Yarmouth.

RIPLEY

Argent a chevron vert between 3 lions rampant or.

Motto: Regard the end.

Embroidered hatchment, 21 x 17 inches, done by Lucy Ripley, at the Hartford Female Seminary, in 1802. Signed L. R. Owned by Laura M. Ripley, of Connecticut.

ROWE

Gules 3 paschal lambs, 2 and 1, staves and banners argent.

Motto: Libera nos Domine.

Embroidered in Exeter, England, the shield surrounded by a wreath of flowers caught at the bottom with a bowknot of blue ribbons. Underneath the ribbon, "17 Rebecca Robins 73." Sent to her uncle, John Rowe, the Boston merchant and diarist, who used the paschal lamb as a crest on silver and seal.

Owned by Mrs. Caleb L. Cunningham, Milton, Mass.

RUSSELL

Argent a chevron between 3 crosses crosslet fitchée sable.

Impaling: Argent a lion rampant gules (Russell?).

Crest: a lion rampant gules.

Hatchment owned by Russell Gray, Esq., Boston. The foliage about the shield was done by Mrs. Horace Gray (born in 1807).

SALTER

[Gules] 10 billets, 4, 3, 2, 1 or, a bordure engrailed argent charged with 8 [hurts and torteaux alternating].

Impaling: Or 3 piles meeting in the base [azure?] (Bryan).

Crest: a unicorn.

Needlework by Mary Salter (Mrs. Henry Quincy, of Boston), 1726–55. For picture, see "Earle's Home Life in Colonial Days," 1898, opposite page 266. Owned by Mrs. Frank Bolles, Cambridge, Mass.

SARGENT

Argent a chevron between 3 dolphins embowed sable.

Impaling: Sable on a chevron between 3 leaves argent as many crosses crosslet of the field (Norwood?).

Crest: an arm erect, grasping a serpent.

An embroidery marked "Nathaniel and Mary Ellery, Anno Dom. 1745." Mary was Nathaniel's daughter by Abigail Norwood. His second wife was Anne, daughter of William and Ann Sargent. *Heraldic Journal*, Volume 4, page 42.

SELBY

Azure a negro head sable, a chief bendy sable and argent.

Sampler, 1678, owned by Mrs. Eugene Hale, Ellsworth, Me.

SHERBURNE

Quarterly: 1 and 4, Vert an eagle displayed argent; 2 and 3, argent a lion rampant or. (Bayley.)

Crest: a unicorn's head argent.

"By the name of Sherburne". Embroidery on silk. Owned by Merrill Spalding, Walnut Street, Brookline, Mass. Colors not as in Burke.

SOUTHWORTH

Sable a chevron between three crosses flory [*i. e.*, crosslet?] argent.

Crest: a bull's head proper.

Embroidered hatchment with elaborate mantling. Mentioned in Governor Bradford's inventory as "a crest". From Major William to David, to Lydia (Mrs. Lebaron), to Priscilla (Mrs. M. A. Hemmett), to Elizabeth (Mrs. Isaac Goodwin), to J. A., to William Bradford Goodwin, of Lowell, present owner. Alice, widow of Edward Southworth, married Governor William Bradford. Fine floss (?) silk on fine mesh canvas.

STEDMAN

Or a cross crosslet vert.

Crest: a demi-virgin, gowned vert, her hair dishevelled, and holding in her dexter hand a cross crosslet fitchée of the same.

Owned by the Historical Society of Old Newbury, Mass.

WILLARD

Argent 3 leopards' heads or.

Crest: Leopard's head.

Made about 1780–90. Miss Susanna Willard, the donor, calls this imaginary.

Embroidered hatchment by Miss Mary Willard, daughter of Joseph, President of Harvard College.

Owned by the Massachusetts Society of the Colonial Dames, Quincy Homestead, Quincy, Mass.

WILLIAMSON

Argent a chevron gules between three trefoils slipped sable.

Crest: out of a ducal coronet gules a dragon's head.

Motto: Constare in sententia.

Embroidered hatchment, 11¾ inches by 9 inches. Owned by Mrs. Henry H. Edes, Cambridge, Mass.

INDEX

INDEX

See also names on pages 29 and 121

See also names on pages 29 and 121

See also names on pages 29 and 121

See also names on pages 29 and 121